Linear Economic Theory

Linear Economic Theory

DANIEL C. VANDERMEULEN
Claremont Graduate School

PRENTICE-HALL, INC., ENGLEWOOD CLIFFS, NEW JERSEY

13-536896-0
Library of Congress Catalog Card Number 76-154540

Current Printing (last digit)
10 9 8 7 6 5 4 3 2 1

PRENTICE-HALL INTERNATIONAL, INC., LONDON
PRENTICE-HALL OF AUSTRALIA, PTY. LTD., SYDNEY
PRENTICE-HALL OF CANADA, LTD., TORONTO
PRENTICE-HALL OF INDIA PRIVATE LIMITED, NEW DELHI
PRENTICE-HALL OF JAPAN, INC., TOKYO

TO ALICE AND DAVID

Preface

I have written an intermediate textbook that uses linear programming to develop the essential core of general equilibrium and welfare theory. Linear programming has distinct advantages in the presentation of economic theory—less formidable mathematical prerequisites, readily applied computational methods, and a well developed concept of duality. By the use of the computational techniques, economic analysis can be carried out in a sequence of simple steps: set up the model as a numerical example; find a specific optimal solution; vary the solution parametrically; plot and draw the resultant piecewise-linear diagrams; extract from the specific example the generic algebraic, geometric, and economic properties. Only the one analytic technique needs to be mastered; it is applied to various models of single plant and multiplant firms, to individual consumers, and to the family as consuming unit. A further advantage is that readers learn to derive for themselves the piecewise-linear analogues to the conventional smooth diagrams.

In Chapter 9 the method of analysis is extended one stage further to include the smoothing of piecewise-linear diagrams. The bridge is the Cobb-Douglas function, which is at one and the same time an infinite collection of linear processes and the simplest member of the class of smooth functions. By a carefully specified limiting process, the results obtained for piecewise-linear functions are carried over to the Cobb-Douglas function and then, with appropriate modifications, to the general case. Thereafter, piecewise-linear and smooth models receive equal attention.

It is the relationship of primal and dual that provides a unifying framework for the entire analysis. The simplex method applied to a typical economic problem, such as the revenue maximizing firm, generates internal or shadow prices for the variables and parameters of the problem. Marginal productivity, marginal cost, marginal utility, and the other important marginal concepts emerge as the dual variables or internal prices for the appropriate optimizing problem. Viewed more broadly, the direct optimizing decisions of an economic unit imply a system of internal or shadow markets. The simplex method applied to the dual problem is a special case of a Walrasian tatonnement process; it successively eliminates excess demand for single commodities and ultimately reduces to zero the value of excess demand in the shadow market system. Primal and dual problems are always solved simultaneously, so an optimum for an economic unit implies equilibrium in the shadow market system, and conversely.

For the industry, for the producing and consuming sectors, and for the economy as a whole, the roles of primal and dual are reversed. When the market system comes into equilibrium it also succeeds in solving some implied or shadow optimizing problem. General equilibrium requires a simultaneous adjustment of all real and shadow markets; it also implies a solution that is in some sense optimal for every economic unit, for every sector, and for the economy as a whole. Thus normative economics, in the Pareto-optimal form, surfaces naturally as a dual to positive economics.

I have dispensed with any mathematical tools that are not strictly necessary, and I believe readers can master the method of analysis without formal mathematics training at the college level. There are rudimentary chapters on linear equations and vectors, and the early portions of the Workbook are designed to clarify any mathematical concepts that may be unfamiliar. I have also tried to make the necessary mathematics intuitively plausible by providing an economic rationale. Thus, the simplex method is developed as an economic decision model or, reversing the customary order, as an economic simulation of a computational process.

A typical Principles course should provide sufficient economic background, particularly since all important economic concepts are derived afresh from linear models. The plan of the book, which is a gradual progression from simpler to more complex models, does not provide optional chapters to omit, but it certainly will permit readers with more advanced training in economics and mathematics to go at a faster pace. For a shortened course, then, it is better to skim than to skip chapters.

The exercises are designed to be an integral part of each chapter, enabling readers to master the method of analysis and to derive all important economic results for themselves. Each set contains some exercises that review the topics covered in the chapter and others that extend the analysis beyond the scope of the chapter. Most exercises have brief titles for quick identification.

Readers familiar with the subject will be able to identify most of the ideas, but the method of presentation is, I believe, largely my own. I owe a particular debt to George Dantzig, whose courses stimulated my thinking along these lines. I have been greatly aided by successive classes of perceptive and forbearing students. Three of my former graduate students have made direct contributions. Kenneth Weiss has ably solved the problems of putting the various models on the computer. Harold Brumm, now assistant professor at the California State College at Los Angeles, has furnished much appreciated assistance in devising exercises. Theodore Tsukahara, Jr., now assistant professor at Pomona College, has made many helpful suggestions.

Claremont, California D.C.V.

Contents

PART III

CONSUMER THEORY

PART IV

MARKETS, INDUSTRIES, AND THE ECONOMY

Linear Economic Theory

I

Introduction

The area of economics we shall be covering—the theory of prices, markets, and the allocation of resources—had attained a high degree of unity by the beginning of World War II. Samuelson, who was himself responsible for much of the unity, explained it in this way:

> An economist of very keen intuition would perhaps have suspected from the beginning that seemingly diverse fields—production economics, consumer's behavior, international trade, public finance, business cycles, income analysis—possess striking formal similarities, and that economy of effort would result from analysing these common elements.
>
> I can make no claim to such initial insight. Only after laborious work in each of these fields did the realization dawn upon me that essentially the same inequalities and theorems appeared again and again, and that I was proving the same theorems a wasteful number of times.[1]

In price and allocation theory, the principal reason for the unity was that economists had constructed basically similar models to predict choice or decisions by both firms and consumers. Both models predicted that each type of economic unit would choose whatever was best or optimal for that unit under the restrictions and limitations it faced. Thus, both firms and consumers were portrayed as striving to optimize subject to constraints, such as limited income or restricted productive capacity. To make the predictive models precise, economists had cast them into mathematical form and converted them into mathematical problems of optimization subject to constraints. To that date mathematicians had developed only one formal

[1]Paul A. Samuelson, *Foundations of Economic Analysis* (Cambridge, Mass.: Harvard University Press, 1948), p. 3.

mathematical method for finding an optimum under constraints, the method introduced by the French mathematician Lagrange around 1800 and later refined. The method was an application of the differential calculus, which was at the time the dominant brand of mathematics. From earlier verbal expositions and diagrammatic presentations, the models of both firm and consumer underwent successive mathematical refinements until they became, by the late 1930's, rigorous applications of the Lagrange method for solving problems of constrained optimization.

The unity that existed at the beginning of World War II was only in the area of traditional price and allocation theory. The 1930's marked the introduction of Keynesian economics or macroeconomics. There was widespread confusion as to how the "new economics," as it has been called, tied in with the traditional economics. Many years passed before the reconciliation came. Surprisingly, the conflict with the new economics had relatively little immediate effect on the bulk of price and allocation theory. The issue was not primarily the formulation of the traditional theory but its relevance to the pressing problems of the 1930's.

Within price and allocation theory, unity was no sooner established than it was disrupted by developments during and immediately after World War II. World wars are such convenient devices for dividing history into periods that one always suspects their use as historical watersheds. But even many years after, it still looks as though World War II marked a significant new phase of development in economic theory, while World War I did not. Perhaps more than anything else, the huge scale of military and civilian governmental operations in World War II revealed an urgent need for systematically planning and coordinating the vast complex of activities. It was primarily a group set up within the U.S. Air Force for this purpose that in 1947 formulated the operations of the Air Force as a linear programming problem and succeeded in finding a method of solution. Contact with economists had directed them to a linear model of the economic system that Leontief had been developing since 1936. Known as the input-output system, it was designed to be a simplified and quantitatively specified model of the entire economy. Research into the input-output system and the collection of data on a vastly enlarged scale were also spurred by governmental assistance during World War II. Both economists and governmental administrators recognized its value in solving allocation problems within a wartime economy and in planning for the reconversion to a peacetime economy after the war.

The input-output model of the economy provided a stimulus and guide to the solution of the similar problems of allocation within the Air Force. But it was the group working within the Air Force who visualized the problem as optimization subject to constraints. The Leontief model was essentially descriptive and predictive and did not contain a criterion for optimization. The Air Force group, notably George B. Dantzig, also devised a computational method for finding an optimal solution: the simplex method. Thus, there became available a second way of formulating and solving problems of constrained optimization. Since the method was computational, its applicability was extended manyfold by the development of electronic computers, a second result of frustrated reaction to the complexity of wartime problems and the inadequacy of existing methods to cope with them.

Having originated in practical problems, linear programming found many applications in industry. Economists also adopted linear programming in the late 1940's and began to reformulate models of firms and the producing sector as a whole. Interestingly, linear programming provided a reinterpretation of the Leontief input-output system which had been the original guide and prototype.[2]

During the same period, another significant development impinged upon consumer theory. In 1944 the mathematician John von Neumann and the economist Oskar Morgenstern published their *Theory of Games and Economic Behavior*. The main topic was the optimal choice of strategies in a situation of rivalry or conflict. As underpinning for their theory, the authors introduced a new concept of utility. Perhaps more important, they explained choice in terms of a preference relation and exposed economists to set theory and axiomatic methods, which had become the distinguishing feature of modern mathematics. Economists then began to reformulate the theory of consumer's choice by employing axiomatic methods, binary relations, and set theory.

These independent developments would have been very significant in themselves but it turned out that, although independent in origin, they were not independent in content. A mathematician who has contributed to both new areas has written: "One of the most striking events in connection with the emergence of modern linear economic model theory was the simultaneous but independent development of linear programming on the one hand and game theory on the other, and the eventual realization of the very close relationship that exists between the two subjects."[3] Neither subject relies on the traditional calculus. Both employ the concepts of linear algebra, set theory, and topology, much of which has since come to be known as the "new mathematics." Thus, since 1930 economists have had to face both the invasion of the "new economics" and the invasion of the "new mathematics." They have succeeded in at least reaching an accommodation with the invaders.

By the early 1950's economists had their choice of two alternative models of the economic system. The traditional or neoclassical model employed the techniques of the calculus, derived smooth curves, and expressed equilibrium by tangency or intersection. Economists could also adopt a model that made

[2]For the origins and early development of linear programming, see the extremely interesting and authoritative account by one of the originators, George B. Dantzig, *Linear Programming and Extensions* (Princeton, N.J.: Princeton University Press, 1963), Chapter 2.

[3]David Gale, *The Theory of Linear Economic Models* (New York: McGraw-Hill Book Co., 1960), p. 216.

no use of the calculus, and had no need for smooth curves, tangency, or intersections. Even before the ink was dry on the new version, the process of reconciliation was under way. Set theory and topology are not just branches of mathematics but a way of unifying mathematics in terms of more basic concepts. It is not surprising, then, that the two versions of the economic system were soon seen to be special cases of a general mathematical formulation. In particular, the development of nonlinear programming filled in the gap between linear programming and optimization by the calculus. Economists have also reexamined traditional concepts and reformulated them in a more general way to fit the broadened mathematical models. By now much of the unity that existed prior to World War II has been restored in price and allocation theory, but with greatly enriched insight and with a broader, much more widely applicable model of the economy. Now that an appreciable amount of unity has been restored we await the next invasion, which, unnoticed, is probably already under way.

Presenting the current expanded version of the economy within the confines of an intermediate textbook raises some knotty problems. The developments of the past 25 years have appreciably elevated the mathematical prerequisites for mastering the theoretical models. Readers who wish to understand economics but not necessarily to practice it cannot be expected to acquire the necessary mathematical background. Although some authors have made notable attempts, it is extremely difficult to provide within the text itself an adequate understanding of the mathematics required for both the traditional and the linear models. Most texts that do not presume a knowledge of mathematics now show, in at least one chapter, how the diagrams for the linear model differ from those of the smooth model. This is not entirely satisfactory since readers without a knowledge of the calculus cannot derive the smooth diagrams for themselves. They are not able to relate either set of diagrams to the mathematical optimization models from which they arise. Further, the reinterpretation of consumer's choice in terms of a preference relation too often receives little attention.

We shall take a different approach. Instead of recapitulating the historical development and giving primary emphasis to the smooth model, we shall begin with the linear model of the economy that has emerged since World War II. There are several advantages. At least in the initial stages, linear models yield more economic output from less mathematical input. As later chapters show, the problem of constrained optimization is easier to set up and easier to understand in linear form. Further, there are relatively simple techniques for deriving the important economic concepts and diagrams. A second advantage is that the smooth model represents a limiting case of the linear model. Where limits exist they are very useful, since properties that hold as the limit is being approached generally remain valid in the limit. The linear model is not the limiting case of the smooth model, and it is more difficult to show convincingly that the properties of the smooth model carry over to the linear model. We shall, then, reverse the pattern of historical development, derive the economic concepts and diagrams first for linear models, and then demonstrate that the results hold over, with appropriate modifications, to the smooth neoclassical version. To get the task under way, we now set up and explain briefly a linear model for the firm.

THE FIRM WITH LINEAR TECHNOLOGY

In the linear programming version of the firm, the technological information is summarized in the form of processes or activities. The simplest possible production process is one that uses a single input and turns out a single output. If the process is also linear, the input required is strictly proportional to the level of output. With the quantity of the input designated by z and the level of output shown by x, the process gives rise to the following linear equation:

$$z = ax.$$

When a process uses two inputs to turn out a single product, two equations, such as the following, describe the process:

$$z_1 = a_1x,$$

$$z_2 = a_2x.$$

Each additional input requires another equation.

The essential characteristic of a process or activity is an emphasis on what goes in and what comes out and not on what goes on inside. This has led some authors to liken a process to a black box into which we see inputs flow and out of which we see outputs emerge. The concept of a process, if it is to be useful, requires that inflows and outflows be uniquely related to each other. The relationship need not be strict proportionality, but when it is, as in the example above, the process or activity is termed linear. A linear process is very much like a favorite recipe treated as sacred by its possessor; for each cake or unit of output precise and invariant amounts of each ingredient or input must be used. The a coefficients in the preceding equations are the precise amounts of each input used for each unit of the product.

Models of the firm may specify many separate inputs that differ widely from each other, such as labor services, purchased power, materials, the services of complicated machinery, and the services of the plant itself. Inputs that the firm can purchase or lease in whatever amounts needed are classified as variable, while those inputs whose supply of services the firm cannot augment or diminish are termed fixed. In simpler versions of the traditional theory of the firm, economists often lump all invariant inputs together as a single fixed factor of production called capital. Under special conditions such a simplification is appropriate. So long as the firm turns out a single product, it must use all inputs on that product or not use them at all. When the firm can produce more than one commodity, it faces a problem of allocating the services of fixed inputs to the various products. The device of a single composite fixed factor is no longer appropriate. Linear programming permits an explicit breakdown of the fixed factor into its separate components and concentrates on the problem of allocating these components optimally over the various products.

The distinction between fixed and variable inputs depends on the length of the time period over which management is making its plans. There is considerable validity to such a distinction since plants cannot be built immediately and orders for machinery must have an appreciable lead time. When there is only a single fixed input, we can define the short run as the time required to augment or contract the services of the fixed input. With many fixed inputs, there may be a whole succession of runs of increasing duration, each merging into the other. The device of a single composite fixed factor creates distortion. The linear programming version of the firm is very flexible in permitting the fixed inputs to become variable either successively or in any pattern that fits the conditions the firm faces.

The traditional smooth version of the firm concentrates on the variable inputs and seeks to determine the optimal amounts to use with the fixed inputs. Linear programming shifts the emphasis to the internal problem of allocating fixed inputs optimally over the set of possible products. No version of the firm can neglect either problem, but there are differences in focus and emphasis. Since linear programming does concentrate on the problem of internal allocation, we shall isolate that problem and assume initially that all inputs are fixed.

The chief contribution of linear programming to the theory of the firm is to provide an explicit model for a multiproduct, multi-input firm. As an illustration, consider a firm with three inputs, all fixed, and five possible products. Each output is produced by a separate linear production process which utilizes the services of all three fixed inputs. Further, one unit of each output requires a fixed amount of every input. The fixed amount is designated by an input coefficient or technological coefficient, for which the symbol a is used. Table 1–1 summarizes the technological conditions. The first subscript refers to the row or input, the second to the column or output. Thus, a_{34} designates the amount of the third input required for one unit of the fourth product. The total amount of each input that a product requires is proportional to the production level. Since the aim of management is to find the optimal output levels, these levels become the unknowns of the problem and are designated by x_1, x_2, x_3, x_4, and x_5. The total amounts of the three inputs that the first product requires are, respectively, $a_{11}x_1$, $a_{21}x_1$, and $a_{31}x_1$. A similar result holds for the remaining products.

TABLE 1–1

Technological Conditions for a Linear Model of the Firm

	Outputs				
Inputs	*One*	*Two*	*Three*	*Four*	*Five*
One	a_{11}	a_{12}	a_{13}	a_{14}	a_{15}
Two	a_{21}	a_{22}	a_{23}	a_{24}	a_{25}
Three	a_{31}	a_{32}	a_{33}	a_{34}	a_{35}

In its search for optimal production levels, management must always stay within the limits imposed by the fixed amounts of the inputs. In any trial-and-error solution management could not use more inputs than available even if it tried. When the decision process is simulated on paper or by a computer, these limits must appear as explicit constraints. The following inequalities express the limitations or constraints to which the firm must conform:

Amount of input required	*Less than or equal*	*Amount available*
$a_{11}x_1+a_{12}x_2+a_{13}x_3+a_{14}x_4+a_{15}x_5$	$\leqq$	b_1
$a_{21}x_1+a_{22}x_2+a_{23}x_3+a_{24}x_4+a_{25}x_5$	$\leqq$	b_2
$a_{31}x_1+a_{32}x_2+a_{33}x_3+a_{34}x_4+a_{35}x_5$	$\leqq$	b_3

The constants b_1, b_2, and b_3 designate the total amount of the services of each fixed input available during the production period. These constants measure machine hours and the like, not number of machines. For each input the total amount required is the sum of the separate amounts required by each product. Only a very special technological assumption justifies the summation of input requirements. Each process operates independently of the others, neither aiding them nor interfering with them. The input requirements for one product are exactly the same when the firm is producing no other products as when it is turning out all other products at high levels. Taken together, constancy of the input requirements and independence of processes imply that there are no economies or diseconomies in production. The traditional version allows for economies and diseconomies in the production of a single commodity as well as for cross-effects between commodities. Later, we shall modify the present extreme assumptions underlying the linear model.

A solution to the system of inequalities is any set of values for the x's such that the left-hand side does not exceed the right-hand side. On economic grounds, we must impose an additional condition; none of the x's can have negative values. Mathematically, changes in sign imply a reversal of direction, so a negative value for one of the x's means running a process backward and converting output into inputs. Before rejecting this possibility we must note that the distinction between output and input is not clear-cut, as the process of growing wheat shows. Also, buildings are demolished and materials sold; and Ulysses' wife stalled off the suitors for 10 years by weaving during the day and pulling out threads by night. However, the preceding examples are instances of different processes, not the same processes run backward, as can be done with a motion picture film. The input coefficients for constructing a building are not the same as those for demolishing a building. Tearing down a building means operating the demolition process at a positive level.

Any set of nonnegative values for the x's that satisfies the inequalities is called a *feasible* solution. Management is not interested in feasible solutions for their own sake but only in finding a feasible solution that will maximize profits. With no variable inputs and no variable cost, maximizing profits is the same as maximizing total revenue. If each product sells in a purely competitive market, management takes the market prices as constant and neglects any effects its sales may have on prices. Hence, total revenue is

$$R = p_1x_1+p_2x_2+p_3x_3+p_4x_4+p_5x_5.$$

Before putting the whole problem together we need to give some attention to the constraints. Inequalities are very difficult to solve; in fact, except for simple special cases, there are no satisfactory methods for solving inequalities directly. By contrast, there exist for linear equations simple general methods of solution applicable in all cases. What is needed, then, is some device for converting inequalities into equations. The condition

Amount required less than or equal to amount available

can be reinterpreted as

Amount required plus amount not used equals amount available.

Hence, if we introduce a specific variable to measure the excess or unused capacity the previous inequalities become equations. The complete problem in equation form is shown below:

$$\begin{aligned}
a_{11}x_1+a_{12}x_2+a_{13}x_3+a_{14}x_4+a_{15}x_5+x_6 \qquad\qquad &= b_1\\
a_{21}x_1+a_{22}x_2+a_{23}x_3+a_{24}x_4+a_{25}x_5 \quad +x_7 \qquad &= b_2\\
a_{31}x_1+a_{32}x_2+a_{33}x_3+a_{34}x_4+a_{35}x_5 \qquad\quad +x_8 &= b_3\\
p_1x_1 \;+p_2x_2 \;+p_3x_3 \;+p_4x_4 \;+p_5x_5 \qquad\qquad &= R(\max).
\end{aligned}$$

The measures of unused capacity, x_6, x_7, and x_8, are called *slack variables*. Since the available capacity cannot be exceeded, slack variables must be positive or zero. The equation at the bottom is called the *objective form* or *objective equation*. The term "objective" is used not as an antonym to subjective but to denote aim or goal. The objective of the firm is to maximize total revenue R. Since minimization may also be the objective in a linear programming problem, the appropriate instruction appears in parentheses after the objective variable R. The slack variables do not appear in the objective form, implying that nonuse of facilities does not add or detract directly from revenue. Of course, nonuse affects revenue indirectly by way of reduced production. If there is any reason to do so, gains or penalties from letting facilities lie idle can be incorporated into the problem.

PLAN OF THE BOOK

The linear programming version of a multiproduct, multi-input firm has been set up and awaits solution. The most generally employed and computationally most efficient means of solving such problems is the *simplex method*, which is explained in detail in Chapter 3. Since the underpinnings of the simplex method rest upon the theory of linear equations, Chapter 2 provides the necessary background. It does, however, emphasize the properties of linear equations and the methods of solution that are most relevant to the simplex method. Readers already adept at solving linear equations may skim Chapter 2 but should check for any special topics they may not have covered.

Chapters 3 and 4 develop the computational methods for solving linear programming problems and give an economic interpretation of these methods. Chapter 4 sets the theme for much of the remainder of the book. Linear programming problems always come in pairs, one problem involving quantities and the other prices. Further, the solution for one problem always provides the solution for the other. The market mechanism of the economic system determines prices and thus solves one of the two problems. In doing so it also solves a problem involving quantities.

Chapter 5 introduces parametric programming techniques in elementary form and uses these techniques to derive marginal cost, marginal revenue productivity, supply, and demand curves for a simple version of a multiproduct firm. The methods are readily adaptable for electronic computers, and computers have been programmed to yield sets of curves for a firm with very many inputs and outputs. Parametric programming methods are the chief means of deriving important economic concepts and are of crucial importance in all subsequent chapters.

To make the transition from algebraic and computational methods to geometric diagrams, some background in vectors and vector spaces is essential. Chapter 6 provides a brief treatment of vectors and Chapter 7 utilizes it for geometric models of a simple multiproduct firm.

The four chapters of Part Two employ the previously developed algebraic and geometric techniques to develop broader models of the firm in both linear and smooth versions. Of key importance is Chapter 9, which demonstrates the method for transferring results from linear to smooth versions of the firm. Part Two introduces into the model of the firm a choice of technological processes, joint products, and the ownership of many plants by a single firm. The multiplant firm is particularly significant since it is the basis for the subsequent analyses of multifirm industries and of the entire producing sector, composed of many industries.

Part Three presents consumer's choice, first by use of a preference relation, then by converting to a linear programming version, and finally by making the transition to the conventional smooth model of utility maximization. Chapter 14 briefly considers the problems of choice and allocation within the family as a prototype for the later treatment of the entire consuming sector.

Part Four puts the pieces together, beginning with a discussion in Chapter 15 of the markets in which the separate economic units confront each other. Chapter 16 develops the purely competitive industry for both single-product and multiproduct firms. For each version of the industry the problems of allocation resemble those analyzed previously for multiplant firms.

Chapter 17 expands the model to the economy as a whole, investigates the existence and stability of general equilibrium, and gives attention to the determination of the price level. The focus and emphasis is upon the interrelationship of separate markets. Chapter 19 also treats general equilibrium for the economy but as the mutual adjustment of the entire producing and consuming sectors. This presentation leads directly to the second member of the pair of linear programming problems, the optimality of the equilibrium that the market mechanism brings about. Chapter 18 bridges the gap between the two treatments by presenting the Leontief input-output system as a special, simplified model of the economy. Chapter 20 briefly takes up the modifications of previous conclusions when markets are not purely competitive but contain elements of monopoly.

Part I

Linear Programming Techniques Applied to the Firm

2

Linear Equations: Elementary Methods of Solution

Linear programming problems are solved by an extension and adaptation of the methods used to solve linear equations. Fortunately, there are simple but powerful algebraic methods that are applicable to any system of equations and are capable of finding solutions, if they exist. The operations are simple, repetitive, and ideally suited to electronic computers, thus assuring solutions for any numerical system that lies within the ever-expanding limits of computer capacity. This chapter explains these algebraic methods of solution and provides some of the underlying rationale. Although the algebraic treatment is self-contained, geometric interpretations are also employed for added insight and understanding. We do not attempt at this time to give a systematic geometric treatment of linear equations, postponing the topic to Chapters 6 and 7.

SOLVING A SINGLE LINEAR EQUATION

The standard linear equation in a single unknown is

$$ax = b.$$

If a does not equal zero ($a \neq 0$), the solution can be written immediately as $x = b/a$. For a single equation in one unknown the algebraic operation of finding the solution is so obvious that little thought is given to the meaning of a solution. For later generalization the following formal definition is needed: a *solution* to a single equation in one unknown x is any number or numerical value assigned to x that makes the equation a true statement.

Specifically, a solution is any number which, multiplied by the number a, yields the number b. If $a \neq 0$, there is a unique number b/a satisfying the condition.

When $a = 0$, division by a is ruled out and two distinct possibilities arise. If b is also zero, the equation is a true statement for any value of x whatsoever. The equation is not binding and is called *vacuous*. Conversely, if $a = 0$ but $b \neq 0$, the left-hand side equals zero regardless of the value chosen for x, and no number can make the equation a true statement. Such an equation is termed *unsolvable*. A vacuous equation is solvable, too readily solvable, in fact, since any number is a solution. Thus single equations in one unknown may be classified as unsolvable ($a = 0$, $b \neq 0$) or solvable, with the two subcategories of vacuous ($a = 0$, $b = 0$), or binding ($a \neq 0$).

As the number of variables increases the concept of a solution has to be broadened correspondingly. For example, a linear equation in two variables,

$$a_1x_1 + a_2x_2 = b \qquad \text{or} \qquad 2x_1 - 3x_2 = 1,$$

needs two numbers to become a true statement. Thus, one solution to the numerical equation is ($x_1 = 2$, $x_2 = 1$). Every solution to the equation is an ordered pair of numbers, one assigned to the first variable or first position and the other to the second.

As the name implies, a linear equation in two unknowns has a geometric representation as a straight line in the coordinate plane. Every ordered pair of numbers that satisfies the equation corresponds to a unique point on the line. Since a straight line is continuous and extends indefinitely in both directions, the number of points is infinite, and the number of solutions must also be infinite. The result can be derived algebraically by converting the linear equation to a more convenient form. If $a_2 \neq 0$, then

$$x_2 = -\frac{a_1}{a_2}x_1 + \frac{b}{a_2}.$$

Each value of x_1 determines a unique value for x_2 and a unique ordered pair satisfying the equation. The number of possible values for x_1 is infinite, and so is the number of ordered pairs.

The linear equation, as shown above, has the *slope-intercept* form. With x_1 equal to zero, $x_2 = b/a_2$ is the value of x_2 where the line crosses the vertical axis, or the vertical *intercept* of the line (see Figure 2–1). The slope is found by letting x_1 change and finding how much x_2 must change in order to satisfy the equation. The symbol Δ is used in mathematics to denote a change in a quantity. Hence, Δx_1 and Δx_2 denote changes of unspecified size in the variables. The slope of a straight line is the rate at which x_2 changes in response to a change in x_1, or the ratio $\Delta x_2/\Delta x_1$. The slope can be found geometrically, as in Figure 2–1, by choosing two points on the line and measuring the changes in x_1 and x_2 between those points. The same procedure can be translated into algebra. Let (x_1^0, x_2^0) and $(x_1^0+\Delta x_1, x_2^0+\Delta x_2)$ be two points on the straight line. Both must satisfy the equation of the line, so

$$a_1(x_1^0+\Delta x_1)+a_2(x_2^0+\Delta x_2) = b$$

and

$$a_1x_1^0+a_2x_2^0 = b.$$

Subtracting the second expression from the first gives

$$a_1\Delta x_1+a_2\Delta x_2 = 0 \qquad \text{or} \qquad \frac{\Delta x_2}{\Delta x_1} = -\frac{a_1}{a_2},$$

which is the coefficient of x_1 in the slope-intercept form.

If $a_1 = 0$ but $a_2 \neq 0$, the slope is zero and x_2 must always equal its vertical intercept, b/a_2, regardless of the value of x_1. Hence, the condition, $a_1 = 0$ but $a_2 \neq 0$, identifies a horizontal line. When $a_2 = 0$, division by a_2 is ruled out, so the equation must be written in the alternative slope-intercept form, $x_1 = -(a_2/a_1)x_2+b/a_1$. The expression b/a_1 is the horizontal intercept and $-a_2/a_1$ is the rate of change of x_1 with respect to x_2. With $a_2 = 0$ but $a_1 \neq 0$, x_1 must be equal to b/a_1 regardless of the value of x_2, so the line is vertical.

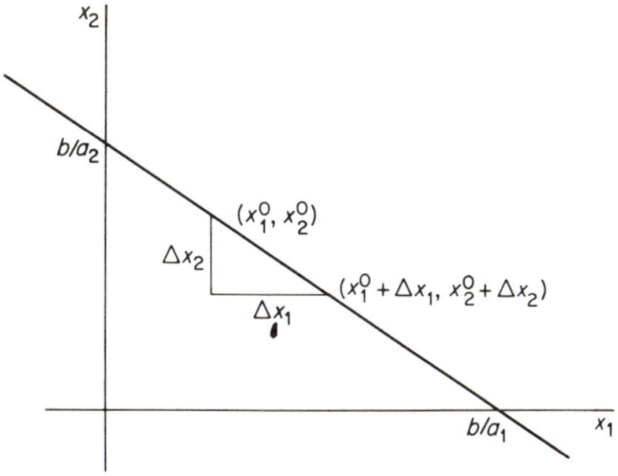

Fig. 2-1 Graph of a Linear Equation

When both a_1 and a_2 are zero, and b also equals zero, the equation is vacuous. Solutions are not confined to the points on any one straight line; any point in the plane represents an ordered pair of numbers satisfying the equation. If both coefficients are zero but b is not zero, the equation is unsolvable and no point in the plane represents a solution.

A linear equation in three unknowns takes the form

$$a_1x_1+a_2x_2+a_3x_3 = b \qquad \text{or} \qquad 2x_1+x_2+4x_3 = 4.$$

Any solution must be an ordered triple of numbers, such as (3, 2, −1). An ordered triple requires three axes for its geometric representation and is a point in three-dimensional space. A linear equation in three unknowns defines a plane in three-dimensional space, and every solution corresponds to a point on that plane. If all coefficients of the unknowns are zero, the equation is again either vacuous or unsolvable, depending on whether b is or is not equal to zero.

As the number of variables increases beyond three, direct geometric representation is not possible, but economic models with more than three variables are commonplace. Fortunately, the algebraic treatment of linear equations generalizes to any number of variables. All that is lost is the ability to draw pictures that correspond to the algebraic conditions. While there is some loss of insight into problems and their solutions, the formal algebraic methods continue to yield valid results. The general linear equation in n unknowns is

$$a_1x_1+a_2x_2+\cdots+a_nx_n = b.$$

A solution requires n numbers, where n designates any positive integer however large. A collection of n numbers, each with a designated position, is called an *ordered n-tuple* and is written as

$$(s_1, s_2, s_3, \ldots, s_n).$$

If at least one of the n variables has a coefficient that is not zero, the equation is solvable but has an infinite number of solutions. When all coefficients are zero, the equation is vacuous or unsolvable, depending on whether b is or is not equal to zero.

SYSTEMS WITH TWO EQUATIONS

Even the simplest system of two equations in a single variable,

$$ax = b \qquad cx = d,$$

adds two more possibilities. If both a and c are not equal to zero, each equation has a unique solution but the solutions need not be identical. For a system of equations a solution is a number or, in general, an ordered n-tuple of numbers that makes *every* equation in the system a true statement. If each of the equations above has a different solution, no such number exists; the system is *inconsistent*, and hence unsolvable, even though every equation is individually solvable. Thus a system of equations may be unsolvable either because it contains an unsolvable equation or because it contains inconsistent equations.

If neither equation is vacuous, the system is solvable only if both equations have the same solution. But then one equation is not needed and is termed *redundant*. If one equation is vacuous, any number will satisfy it, including the number that is the solution to the other equation. Hence, the system is solvable. Clearly a vacuous equation is always redundant.

The most familiar system of equations is the following:

Example 1: A System of Two Equations

$$a_{11}x_1+a_{12}x_2 = b_1 \qquad \text{or} \qquad 2x_1-x_2 = 3$$

$$a_{21}x_1+a_{22}x_2 = b_2 \qquad\qquad 3x_1+2x_2 = 8.$$

Figure 2–2 graphs both equations and their solution. For each equation any ordered pair of numbers corresponding to a point on the line is a solution. The solution to the system is the ordered pair corresponding to the only point the two lines have in common.

To find the solution graphically, draw through the point of intersection the dashed vertical line in Figure 2–2. The distance of this line from the origin along the horizontal axis gives the value of x_1. Similarly, the dashed

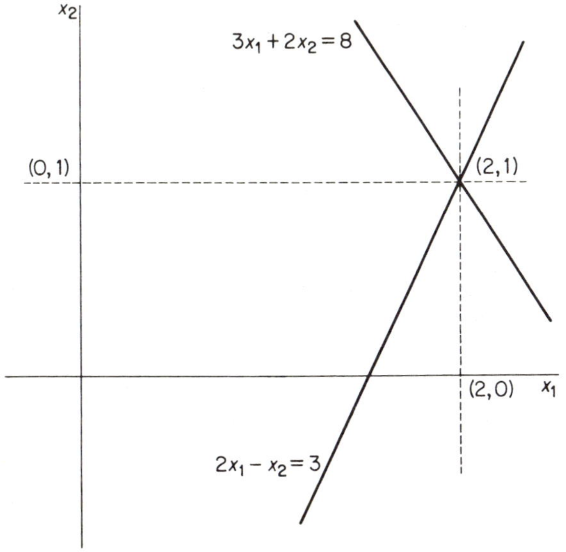

Fig. 2-2 Graphical Solution of Linear Equations

horizontal line through the point of intersection determines the distance on the vertical axis that corresponds to the value of x_2. Solving linear equations by geometric means, although it provides valuable insight, is cumbersome and inexact. Further, beyond three dimensions geometric methods are unavailable. What mathematicians have done is to develop an algebraic method that is, in fact, the algebraic equivalent of drawing horizontal and vertical lines through the point of intersection of the original lines. The algebraic methods generalize readily to systems with any number of variables.

The original system contains the equations of two straight lines intersecting in a point, the coordinates of which are as yet unknown. The unknown point is also the intersection of a unique pair of horizontal and vertical lines. If we knew the equations of the horizontal and vertical lines, we could immediately read off the coordinates of the point as the intercepts of those lines. The problem, then, is to find an algebraic method for transforming the original system of equations into the equations of horizontal and vertical lines having the same point of intersection. The horizontal and vertical lines and the original lines are but two of infinitely many pairs of lines passing through the given point. There are simple general methods for finding the equations of every one of these pairs. We shall present the general method first and then adapt it to the specific problem of finding the horizontal and vertical lines.

What we need are methods of transforming the equations in a system without changing the solution or point of intersection. There are two types of algebraic operations, called *elementary operations*, that have precisely this effect. The first elementary operation, as shown below, is simply to multiply any equation in the system by a constant not equal to zero:

$$h(a_{11}x_1+a_{12}x_2) = ha_{11}x_1+ha_{12}x_2 = hb_1, \qquad h \neq 0.$$

Any ordered pair of numbers that satisfies the original equation obviously continues to be a solution after multiplication of both sides by the same constant. Geometrically the operation has no effect; the straight line in the plane remains unchanged. Since every point on the original line represents a solution to the new equation, each value of h merely determines a different algebraic expression for the same straight line. The aim of the operation is to permit choice of the most convenient algebraic expression in any specific application. An example is the slope-intercept form, shown earlier, where the original equation is multiplied by

$$h = \frac{1}{a_2} \qquad \text{or} \qquad h = \frac{1}{a_1}.$$

To perform the second elementary operation, as shown below, multiply one equation in the system by any constant and add it to another equation:

$$k(a_{11}x_1+a_{12}x_2)+(a_{21}x_1+a_{22}x_2) = kb_1+b_2.$$

Any ordered pair of numbers that is a solution to both original equations must be a solution to the resultant equation. A solution equates the left-hand side of an equation to the constant on the right, so substitution of the ordered pair of numbers into the parentheses creates the obvious equality

$$k(b_1)+(b_2) = kb_1+b_2.$$

Any ordered pair of numbers that satisfies one original equation but not the other cannot reduce both parentheses to the desired constants and cannot make both sides equal. Hence, any point on one original line but not on the other cannot lie on the new line created by the elementary operation. The new line must pass through the point the original lines have in common.

The equation for the new line may be rewritten as

$$(ka_{11}+a_{21})x_1+(ka_{12}+a_{22})x_2 = kb_1+b_2.$$

Straight lines through a given point are distinct only if they have different slopes. As demonstrated earlier, the slope of any line is the negative ratio of the coefficient of x_1 to the coefficient of x_2. Consequently,

$$\frac{\Delta x_2}{\Delta x_1} = -\frac{ka_{11}+a_{21}}{ka_{12}+a_{22}}.$$

Choosing the appropriate value for k yields any specified slope except that of a vertical line. For the equation of the vertical line, the coefficient of x_2 must vanish, so k must be chosen to satisfy the condition

$$ka_{12}+a_{22} = 0 \qquad \text{or} \qquad k = -\frac{a_{22}}{a_{12}}.$$

Similarly, when

$$ka_{11}+a_{21} = 0 \qquad \text{or} \qquad k = -\frac{a_{21}}{a_{11}},$$

the coefficient of x_1 vanishes and determines the equation of the horizontal line through the original point of intersection.

Systematic use of the preceding elementary operations transforms the original system into the equations of horizontal and vertical lines with the same point of intersection. To generate the equation of the horizontal line it is necessary only to multiply the first equation by $k = -a_{21}/a_{11}$ and add it to the second. For reasons that will soon become clear, it is more effective to break the step down into two successive elementary operations, first multiplying equation 1 by $1/a_{11}$ and then adding $-a_{21}$ times the resultant equation to equation 2. After each elementary operation, the resultant equation replaces an equation previously in the system to keep the number constant. Each elementary operation and its effect are shown below for both the general two-equation system and the numerical example:

1. Multiply equation 1 by $1/a_{11}(=\frac{1}{2})$ and replace:

$$x_1-\tfrac{1}{2}x_2 = \tfrac{3}{2} \qquad x_1+\frac{a_{12}}{a_{11}}x_2 = \frac{b_1}{a_{11}}$$

$$3x_1+2x_2 = 8 \qquad a_{21}x_1+a_{22}x_2 = b_2.$$

2. Add $-a_{21}(=-3)$ times equation 1 to equation 2 and insert the resultant equation in place of equation 2:

$$x_1-\tfrac{1}{2}x_2 = \tfrac{3}{2} \qquad x_1+\frac{a_{12}}{a_{11}}x_2 = \frac{b_1}{a_{11}}$$

$$0x_1+\tfrac{7}{2}x_2 = \tfrac{7}{2} \qquad 0x_1+\left(a_{22}-a_{21}\frac{a_{12}}{a_{11}}\right)x_2 = b_2-a_{21}\frac{b_1}{a_{11}}.$$

The second equation now represents the horizontal line. For the equation of the vertical line use the second equation to eliminate x_2 from the first equation. The same sequence of elementary operations is needed:

3. Divide through the second equation by the coefficient of x_2,

$$\left(a_{22}-a_{21}\frac{a_{12}}{a_{11}}\right)=\tfrac{7}{2}.$$

4. Multiply the resultant equation by $-a_{12}/a_{11}$ $(=\frac{1}{2})$ and add it to the first. The final system is

$$x_1+0x_2 = 2 \qquad x_1+0x_2 = \frac{b_1a_{22}-b_2a_{12}}{a_{11}a_{22}-a_{12}a_{21}}$$

$$0x_1+\ x_2 = 1 \qquad 0x_1+\ x_2 = -\frac{b_1a_{21}-b_2a_{11}}{a_{11}a_{22}-a_{12}a_{21}}.$$

Elementary operations can also be applied when there are redundant equations. In a system of two equations in two unknowns, redundancy always means that both equations are merely different algebraic expressions for the same straight line. As shown earlier, by use of the first elementary operation, one equation must be a multiple of the other, so

$$\frac{a_{21}}{a_{11}} = \frac{a_{22}}{a_{12}} \qquad \frac{a_{21}}{a_{11}} = \frac{b_2}{b_1}$$

or

$$a_{22} - a_{12}\frac{a_{21}}{a_{11}} = 0 \quad b_2 - b_1\frac{a_{21}}{a_{11}} = 0.$$

A check of the equation resulting from elementary operations (1) and (2) shows that both the coefficient of x_2 and the right-hand side vanish, creating a vacuous equation. Geometrically, there is only one line, so the two equations cannot be converted into a pair of lines. The appearance of a vacuous equation is an infallible indicator of a redundancy in the original system of equations, a conclusion that generalizes to systems of any size.

If the system is inconsistent, the two lines are parallel, having the same slope but different intercepts. Algebraically,

$$\frac{a_{12}}{a_{11}} = \frac{a_{22}}{a_{21}} \quad \text{but} \quad \frac{b_1}{a_{11}} \neq \frac{b_2}{a_{21}}.$$

After elementary operations (1) and (2) the coefficients of both variables vanish in the second equation, but the constant on the right does not. Thus, in a two-equation system, the elimination of one variable infallibly reveals inconsistency in the form of an unsolvable equation. This conclusion also generalizes appropriately to linear systems of any degree of complexity.

SQUARE SYSTEMS OF EQUATIONS

When equations and unknowns are equal in number, the descriptive term *square system* is often applied. All other systems are classified as *rectangular*.[1] Solving a square system of more than two equations merely requires a longer sequence of the same elementary operations, as the following example demonstrates.

Example 2: A Square System of Three Equations

$$\begin{aligned} 2x_1 + x_2 + 4x_3 &= 4 \\ x_1 + \tfrac{5}{2}x_2 + x_3 &= 5 \\ 4x_1 + 5x_2 + 10x_3 &= 16. \end{aligned}$$

[1]Accurately defined, they are rectangular but not square. We omit the qualification, assuming it to be understood.

As before the aim is to eliminate variables from equations systematically until, ultimately, there is only one variable in each equation. We choose first to eliminate x_1 from equations 2 and 3. The necessary elementary operations are: multiply the first equation by $\frac{1}{2}$; multiply the resultant first equation by -1 and add to the second; multiply the resultant first equation by -4 and add to the third. The system is now in the form

$$\begin{aligned} x_1+\tfrac{1}{2}x_2+2x_3 &= 2 \\ 2x_2-\ x_3 &= 3 \\ 3x_2+2x_3 &= 8. \end{aligned}$$

With x_1 eliminated the second and third equations form a square subsystem that is, except for the indices on the variables, identical with the two-equation system of Example 1. Applying the first three elementary operations to that system but omitting the final elimination of x_3 produces the following result:

$$\begin{aligned} x_1+\tfrac{1}{2}x_2+2x_3 &= 2 \\ x_2-\tfrac{1}{2}x_3 &= \tfrac{3}{2} \\ x_3 &= 1. \end{aligned}$$

The original system has now been reduced to what is aptly called *triangular form*. Each variable has a coefficient of 1 along the diagonal from the upper left corner to the lower right. Below the diagonal all variables are eliminated, creating a triangle. The computational method yielding the triangular form is called *Gaussian*, or *forward*, or *downward elimination*. One minor point needs attention. After elimination of x_1 the coefficient of x_2 may be zero in the second equation but not in the third. There is nothing essential about the order of the equations, so we can interchange them, if we wish, to keep the variables in natural order along the diagonal.

The value of x_3 can be read off from the third equation and substituted into equation 2 to give x_2. Inserting both values in the first equation gives x_1. A more systematic method that requires the same number of computations is *backward* or *upward* elimination of variables. Elementary operations eliminate variables above the diagonal beginning with x_3. The result is the following *diagonal form*:

$$\begin{aligned} x_1 \qquad &= -1 \\ x_2 \quad &= \ \ 2 \\ x_3 &= \ \ 1. \end{aligned}$$

Geometrically, the original system contains the equations of three planes in three-dimensional space. Two planes, if they are not parallel, intersect in a straight line, like the walls of a room. The solution to the system is the point in space where the straight line determined by two planes pierces the third. The elementary operations reducing the system to diagonal form replace the original planes by three planes intersecting in the same point, each of which is perpendicular to one of the axes and parallel to the plane in which the other two axes lie. Hence, each of the derived planes intersects one and only one axis. The distances from the origin to each of these three intersections form the ordered triple of numbers that is the solution to the equation.

If one of the equations is a constant multiple of another, they are merely different algebraic expressions for the same plane. As is true for coincident lines, a unique solution does not exist. As readers can easily verify, whenever one of the two proportional equations is used to eliminate one variable, it also eliminates all other variables and the constant from the other equation. Thus, one of two proportional equations must always become a vacuous equation. With planes, however, there is another way in which redundancy may arise. The line formed by the intersection of two planes may lie wholly in the third plane. Any point on the line corresponds to an ordered triple of numbers satisfying all three equations. The following example, in which no equation is a multiple of another, illustrates the case:

Example 3: A Redundant Square System

$$\begin{aligned} 2x_1 + x_2 + 3x_3 &= 4 \\ x_1 + \tfrac{1}{2}x_2 + \tfrac{7}{2}x_3 &= 4 \\ 4x_1 + 2x_2 + 5x_3 &= 7. \end{aligned}$$

When x_1 is eliminated from the second and third equations, x_2 is eliminated also, and the system becomes

$$\begin{aligned} x_1 + \tfrac{1}{2}x_2 + \tfrac{3}{2}x_3 &= 2 \\ 0x_1 + 0x_2 + 2x_3 &= 2 \\ 0x_1 + 0x_2 - x_3 &= -1. \end{aligned}$$

The elimination of x_3 from the third equation leaves it vacuous. We do not need to know in advance whether a system contains a redundant equation or what geometric form the redundancy may take. The attempt to reduce to triangular form infallibly reveals any redundancy by generating a vacuous equation. Since only two binding equations are left for the three variables, the solution cannot be unique.

When two planes intersect in a straight line that lies wholly within the third plane, there is a simple algebraic explanation. The third equation must consist of a nonzero multiple of the first equation plus a nonzero multiple of the second equation. (In the preceding example the third equation equals $\frac{9}{4}$ times the first equation, minus $\frac{1}{2}$ times the second equation.) As readers may readily verify by substitution, any ordered triple of numbers that satisfies the first two equations must also be a solution to the third equation. When one equation is a multiple of another, we can regard it as the result of multiplying the other equation by a constant and adding to a vacuous equation. The same elementary operation with the sign of the constant reversed cancels the preceding operation and restores the vacuous equation. In a system of many equations, some or all may be multiplied by constants and added to a vacuous equation, creating a redundant equation. Reversing the elementary operations restores the vacuous equation and reveals the redundancy. If all the coefficients in an equation are built up from zero by a set of elementary operations, then reducing any one coefficient to zero requires a reversal of the elementary operations and reduces all coefficients to zero. We can now see why reduction to triangular or diagonal form must infallibly reveal a redundancy in the form of a vacuous equation.

Inconsistency can also arise in either of two ways. When corresponding coefficients in two equations all have the same ratio to each other but the constants have a different ratio, the planes are parallel and no solution exists. Two planes may also intersect in a line that does not meet the third plane. For an illustration we change the constant from 7 to 6 in the third equation of Example 3. This shifts the third plane parallel to itself. The straight line formed by the first two planes, which previously lay within the third plane, now has no point in common with it. With x_1 eliminated from the second and third equations, the system becomes

$$\begin{aligned} x_1+\tfrac{1}{2}x_2+\tfrac{3}{2}x_3 &= 2 \\ 0x_1+0x_2+2x_3 &= 2 \\ 0x_1+0x_2-x_3 &= -2. \end{aligned}$$

Elimination of x_3 from the third equation yields the unsolvable equation

$$0x_1+0x_2+0x_3 = -1.$$

The two geometrically different types of inconsistency also have a unifying algebraic explanation. An inconsistency means that one equation can be formed from an unsolvable equation by elementary operations on one or more of the remaining equations. Reversing the elementary operations restores the unsolvable equation and reveals the inconsistency.

Because redundancy and inconsistency each have a single algebraic explanation there exists a systematic and infallible method for dealing with square systems of three linear equations. We do not need to know in advance anything about the system, not even that it has a solution. The successive elimination of variables ultimately turns up an unsolvable equation if the original system is inconsistent. Otherwise, the system is solvable, although it may not have a unique solution. A redundancy in the original system creates a vacuous equation and prevents a unique solution. When the system is neither inconsistent nor redundant, the coefficients never all vanish in any row, and the process of elimination proceeds smoothly to triangular form, with at most an interchange of equations. Reduction to diagonal form by backward elimination reveals the exact value for each variable in the unique solution.

Since the ultimate goal is the diagonal form, it may seem inefficient to use forward elimination for reaching the triangular form and then to complete the task by a separate process of backward elimination. The diagonal form can be attained directly by eliminating each variable from the equations above the diagonal as well as from those below. Contrary to expectation, direct reduction is computationally less efficient. If, for example, x_2 is eliminated from the first equation as well as the third, the same operation has to be applied to the coefficient of x_3. But these computations are wasted. Ultimately x_3 will be eliminated from the first equation by a single elementary operation, regardless of its coefficient. Rather than recompute coefficients at each stage it is better to let them rest undisturbed until the moment of final extinction. The more variables there are the greater the inefficiency in direct reduction to diagonal form.

Extending the method to square systems of more than three equations is routine. At each stage a given variable must be eliminated from more equations, and there are more variables to eliminate, but the result is simply a greater number of elementary operations. Any redundancy shows up as a vacuous equation, and any inconsistency as an unsolvable equation. In a system with no redundancies the equations are termed *independent*. Hence, every square system containing independent, consistent equations has one and only one solution. Such a system can always be reduced to triangular and then to diagonal form, revealing the unique solution.

RECTANGULAR SYSTEMS OF EQUATIONS

An excess of variables over equations is characteristic of linear programming, so this case merits special attention. A fourth variable added to Example 2 provides the following numerical illustration:

Example 4: A Rectangular System

$$\begin{aligned} 2x_1 + x_2 + 4x_3 + 6x_4 &= 4 \\ x_1 + \tfrac{5}{2}x_2 + x_3 + 3x_4 &= 5 \\ 4x_1 + 5x_2 + 10x_3 - 2x_4 &= 16. \end{aligned}$$

The terms *triangular form* and *diagonal form* are too useful to drop, although they are less apt for rectangular systems. To retain the terms we must choose a subset of variables equal in number to the number of equations, a *square subset*. Note, however, that there can be many square subsets. With four variables and three equations, there are $4\times3\times2/1\times2\times3 = 4$ subsets of three variables. In general the number of square subsets is equal to the combination of n things taken m at a time, where m is the number of equations.[2] Thus, for rectangular systems there is no unique triangular or diagonal form; we must always specify the subset of variables to appear on the diagonal.

Example 4 has the same coefficients for the first three variables as the square system of Example 2 and requires identical operations to reduce to the following triangular form:

$$\begin{aligned} x_1+\tfrac{1}{2}x_2+2x_3+3x_4 &= 2 \\ x_2-\tfrac{1}{2}x_3+0x_4 &= \tfrac{3}{2} \\ x_3-4x_4 &= 1. \end{aligned}$$

The coefficients of x_4 do not determine any of the elementary operations but are transformed by the process. Upward or backward elimination requires the same operations as in the preceding section for the resultant diagonal form:

$$\begin{aligned} x_1 \qquad +12x_4 &= -1 \\ x_2 \quad - 2x_4 &= 2 \\ x_3 - 4x_4 &= 1 \end{aligned} \qquad \text{or} \qquad \begin{aligned} x_1 &= -1-12x_4 \\ x_2 &= 2+2x_4 \\ x_3 &= 1+4x_4. \end{aligned}$$

The equations on the right show more clearly the dependence of solutions on the value of x_4. For each value assigned to x_4, and an infinite number can be assigned, there is a different set of values for the first three variables. In general, when a system of independent, consistent equations has one more variable than equation, there is an infinite number of solutions, one for each of the infinite number of values that can be assigned to the excess variable. As a matter of terminology, the variable assigned a value is called *independent*; the remaining variables are *dependent*. The term "independent" applied to variables does not have the same meaning as when applied to equations. Reduction to diagonal form provides the most convenient set of equations for calculating the values of dependent variables.

Additional variables in the original equations obviously do not affect reduction to diagonal form with respect to the first three variables. They remain in the system along with x_4, their coefficients transformed by the computations. All additional variables not in the square subset are also inde-

[2]The formula for a combination of n things taken m at a time is ${}_nC_m = [n(n-1)(n-2)\cdots(n-m+1)]/(1\cdot2\cdot3\cdots m)$.

pendent variables. For a specific solution each of the independent variables must be assigned a number. In a general system of m equations in n unknowns, where $m < n$, the most that can be done is to solve for m dependent variables in terms of the remaining $n-m$ independent variables. When a specific value is assigned to each of the $n-m$ independent variables, these values can be combined with the constants on the right to give a square system. Each assignment of values alters the numbers on the right and gives different values to the m dependent variables in the diagonal form.

When a rectangular system has many square subsets, some may be reducible to diagonal form, while others may not be. With the remaining variables set at zero, a square subset of variables may form a redundant or inconsistent system. To demonstrate, modify Example 4 by making the coefficients of the first three variables proportional in the second and third equations, as follows:

$$2x_1 + x_2 + 4x_3 + 6x_4 = 4$$

$$x_1 + \tfrac{5}{2}x_2 + x_3 + 3x_4 = 5$$

$$2x_1 + 5x_2 + 2x_3 - 2x_4 = 16.$$

When the time comes to eliminate x_2 from the third equation, x_3 also vanishes. With $x_4 = 0$, the equation is unsolvable. But the coefficient of x_4 is not zero in the third equation, so reduction to triangular form can be completed with x_4 on the diagonal in place of x_3. If the coefficient of x_4 also vanishes but the constant on the right does not, both the third equation and the system are unsolvable. If the constant on the right vanishes as well, one equation is redundant and can be dropped. There are only two independent equations in the four variables.

Once again it does not pay to worry in advance whether a given rectangular system is or is not solvable. The thing to do is to try to solve it, and all necessary information comes to light. If there is at least one variable in each row with a nonzero coefficient, the process of reduction terminates in triangular form and thereby selects an independent and consistent subset. When a vacuous equation appears, the corresponding equation in the original system can be dropped without affecting the solution. The remaining equations can be reduced to triangular form, but there is one more independent variable whose value must be fixed. The appearance of an unsolvable equation indicates that there can be no solution so long as the corresponding equation remains in the original system.

BASES AND PIVOT OPERATIONS

A square subset of variables that can be reduced to triangular and, hence, to diagonal form has special significance in linear programming and is called a *basis*. Thus, in the rectangular system of Example 4, the first three variables or, alternatively, the first three columns constitute a basis. A vital step in searching for an optimal solution is shifting from one basis to another. To illustrate by Example 4, we might wish to insert x_4 on the diagonal in place of x_2. The basis becomes (x_1, x_4, x_3) instead of (x_1, x_2, x_3). Fortunately we do not have to go back to the original system and repeat the whole process of reduction with respect to the new set of variables. We can begin with the system in diagonal form relative to the first three variables, as shown in the preceding section. If x_4 is to enter in the second row, its coefficient in that row cannot be zero. Otherwise, x_4 cannot replace x_2 in the basis. The condition is satisfied in the example. All we need to do is convert the coefficient of x_4 to unity in the second equation and eliminate x_4 from the first and third equations. The following elementary operations do the job: multiply the second equation by $-\frac{1}{2}$; multiply the resultant second equation by -12 and add to the first equation; multiply the resultant second equation by 4 and add to the third equation. Relative to the new basis the equations become

$$
\begin{aligned}
x_1 \qquad + 6x_2 &= 11 \\
x_4 \quad - \tfrac{1}{2}x_2 &= -1 \\
x_3 - 2x_2 &= -3.
\end{aligned}
$$

Shifting from one basis to another is the crucial step in solving linear programming problems. The sequence of operations that shifts a system from one basis to another is called a *pivot operation* or *pivoting*. The *pivot* is the nonzero coefficient of the new variable in the row in which it enters the basis. Since pivot operations eliminate variables both above and below the diagonal, a succession of pivot operations reduces a system of equations directly to diagonal form. As explained earlier, direct reduction to diagonal form is computationally less efficient than successive forward and backward elimination. However, in solving linear programming problems, the rationale of the method emerges more clearly when pivot operations are used exclusively, both for reduction to diagonal form and for shifting bases. We shall follow this practice in subsequent chapters.

SYSTEMS WITH MORE EQUATIONS THAN VARIABLES

Although we shall not encounter systems with an excess of equations over variables, we can outline briefly the requirements for a solution. Unless one equation is a multiple of another, three equations in two unknowns represent three distinct lines in the plane. If one equation is a multiple of another, both equations generate the same straight line and one equation is redundant. The lines may be distinct but two may be parallel to each other, denoting an unsolvable system. If no pair of lines is parallel, each pair intersects in a point, and the third line either passes through that point or does not. The first possibility means a redundant system, the second an unsolvable system. Algebraically, two equations can always be used to eliminate both variables from a third equation, making it either a vacuous or an unsolvable equation. Putting the geometric and algebraic results together we can conclude that a vacuous equation appears when two lines are not distinct or when all three lines pass through a point, and that an unsolvable equation turns up when the three lines do not have a point in common. Hence, for a solution to exist the excess equation must be redundant. Obviously, any additional equations must also be redundant. The result generalizes to systems of any size. Thus a system of m equations in n variables, where m exceeds n, can have a solution only if at least $m-n$ equations are redundant. When more than $m-n$ equations are redundant, the system has fewer independent equations than variables and cannot have a unique solution.

SUMMARY

For any system of linear equations there is a simple repetitive or iterative process that terminates within a finite number of operations. The process reveals whether the system is unsolvable and, for solvable systems, goes on to generate the solutions in the clearest and most usable form. Only if there are as many independent, consistent equations as there are variables, will the solution be a unique ordered n-tuple of numbers. When there is an excess of variables over independent, consistent equations, the number of solutions becomes infinite. When equations exceed variables there is no solution unless the excess equations are redundant.

EXERCISES

1. Apply elementary operations to the following systems of equations and classify each system as solvable, solvable but redundant, or unsolvable. If a system is solvable, find all solutions. Verify the results by graphing the equations for each system.

(a) $$\begin{aligned} 4x_1+5x_2 &= 7 \\ 2x_1+3x_2 &= 4. \end{aligned}$$

(b) $$\begin{aligned} 3x_1+2x_2 &= 3 \\ 8x_1+4x_2 &= 8. \end{aligned}$$

(c) $$\begin{aligned} 3x_1-\ x_2 &= 6 \\ 2x_1-\tfrac{2}{3}x_2 &= -4. \end{aligned}$$

(d) $$\begin{aligned} -\tfrac{3}{4}x_1+1x_2 &= 6 \\ 3x_1-4x_2 &= -24. \end{aligned}$$

2. Apply elementary operations to the following systems of equations and classify each system as solvable, solvable but redundant, or unsolvable. If a system is solvable, find all solutions.

(a) $$\begin{aligned} 3x_1+2x_2+2x_3 &= 84 \\ 4x_1+3x_2+1x_3 &= 119 \\ 2x_1+4x_2+2x_3 &= 140. \end{aligned}$$

(b) $$\begin{aligned} 2x_1+4x_2+6x_3 &= 8 \\ 3x_1-2x_2+1x_3 &= 4 \\ 1x_1+2x_2+3x_3 &= 6. \end{aligned}$$

(c) $$\begin{aligned} 3x_1+2x_2+1x_3 &= 2 \\ 6x_1+5x_2+4x_3 &= 10 \\ 9x_1+8x_2+7x_3 &= 18. \end{aligned}$$

(d) $$\begin{aligned} 3x_1+2x_2+1x_3 &= 6 \\ 9x_1+4x_2+5x_3 &= 12 \\ x_1-2x_2+3x_3 &= 0. \end{aligned}$$

3. Test the following systems for solvability. If solvable, check for uniqueness of solution. Verify your conclusions by graphing each system of equations.

(a) $$\begin{aligned} 2x_1+4x_2 &= 11 \\ -5x_1+3x_2 &= 5 \\ x_1-x_2 &= -2. \end{aligned}$$

(b) $$\begin{aligned} 2x_1-3x_2 &= 6 \\ 5x_1-\tfrac{15}{2}x_2 &= 15 \\ \tfrac{4}{3}x_1-2x_2 &= 4. \end{aligned}$$

(c) $$\begin{aligned} 3x_1+2x_2 &= 9 \\ 4x_1+3x_2 &= 10 \\ 7x_1+\tfrac{14}{3}x_2 &= 20. \end{aligned}$$

(d) $$\begin{aligned} 4x_1-x_2 &= 8 \\ 2x_1+5x_2 &= 4 \\ 3x_1+x_2 &= 3. \end{aligned}$$

What are the requirements for solvability? For uniqueness of solution?

4. (a) For two equations in two unknowns, construct a numerical system that is redundant and one that is unsolvable.

(b) For three equations in two unknowns, construct two numerical systems that are redundant for geometrically different reasons and two numerical systems that are unsolvable for geometrically different reasons. In each case demonstrate that the system is redundant or unsolvable. State specifically what changes are required to make the unsolvable systems solvable.

(c) Carry out the instructions of (b) for three equations in three unknowns.

5. Are the following systems solvable? If so, show all possible solutions.

(a) $$\begin{aligned} 2x_1+7x_2+4x_3 &= 10 \\ \tfrac{1}{3}x_1+\tfrac{7}{6}x_2+\tfrac{7}{3}x_3 &= 5. \end{aligned}$$

(b) $$\begin{aligned} x_1+2x_2-3x_3-4x_4 &= 6 \\ x_1+3x_2+3x_3-2x_4 &= 4 \\ 2x_1+5x_2-2x_3-5x_4 &= 10. \end{aligned}$$

(c) $$\begin{aligned} 2x_1+3x_2+4x_3+4x_4 &= 12 \\ x_1+2x_2+3x_3+3x_4 &= 0 \\ x_1 \qquad -x_3-x_4 &= 16. \end{aligned}$$

6. Find all possible bases with respect to which the following system can be reduced to diagonal form:

$$\begin{aligned} 3x_1+x_2+2x_3+4x_4 &= 6 \\ 2x_1+2x_2+x_3+4x_4 &= 12 \\ 4x_1+4x_2+5x_3+8x_4 &= 12. \end{aligned}$$

Determine how the following changes in the coefficients of x_4 affect the number of bases for the system:

(a) Change from 8 to 4 in equation 3;

(b) Restore the original coefficient in equation 3 and change from 4 to 2 in equation 1.

7. (a) Reduce the following system to diagonal form by forward then backward elimination, keeping a count of the number of separate multiplications and additions that have to be performed:

$$\begin{aligned} 2x_1 + 4x_2 + 6x_3 &= 8 \\ 3x_1 + 1x_2 + 7x_3 &= 7 \\ 4x_1 + 10x_2 + 13x_3 &= 20. \end{aligned}$$

(b) Reduce to diagonal form directly by pivot operations and keep a count of the number of separate arithmetical operations. Which method is computationally more efficient?

(c) How many arithmetical operations are required to eliminate the second variable from the first equation by a pivot operation? Generalize the result to a system with n variables. In backward elimination, how many separate operations are needed to eliminate any *one* coefficient from above the diagonal? Does the number of variables affect the result? State a general conclusion about the efficiency of forward and backward elimination over pivot operations as the number of variables increases.

8. A firm has three fixed inputs and is technologically capable of producing three outputs. The following table summarizes the technological conditions as the amounts of each input needed to produce one unit of each output:

	Output		
Input	*One*	*Two*	*Three*
One	2	3	1
Two	1	2	2
Three	3	2	4

The available amounts of the three inputs are $b_1 = 30$, $b_2 = 20$, $b_3 = 40$. Denote the unknown output levels by (x_1, x_2, x_3). Determine whether technological conditions permit the firm to produce all three outputs and also to utilize fully in their production the available supplies of all three inputs. Investigate what happens when each of the following changes occurs separately: b_1 is increased to 35, then to 40; b_3 is reduced to 20. Give an economic interpretation.

3

Solving Linear Programs: The Simplex Method

The solution of linear equations provides the basis for methods of solving linear programming problems, but more is required. To solve a linear program we must ferret out from the totality of solutions a specific solution that is in some sense optimal, as, for example, the amounts to produce for maximum profits. Chapter 2 has established one unfortunate fact of life about a system of linear equations; if solvable, it has either a unique solution or an infinite number of solutions and nothing in between. If there is a unique solution it is both maximum and minimum. There is no choice and no economic problem. Thus, linear programming is applicable only when the number of solutions is infinite, as will always be true when variables exceed equations in a consistent system.

In most linear programming problems, such as the multiproduct firm, solutions are acceptable only if none of the variables has a negative value. Reflecting the origin of linear programming in practical problems, a solution is termed *feasible* if all variables have nonnegative values. It might seem that the restriction of variables to the nonnegative range would facilitate the search for an optimal solution by reducing the number of solutions to be considered. The restriction to feasible solutions turns out to be helpful, but it does not reduce the solutions to a finite number. A system of equations, if feasible, has either one nonnegative solution or an infinite number.

The way out of the difficulty, as discovered by George Dantzig and incorporated in the simplex method, is to work with square subsets. We can select a subset of variables equal in number to the equations, set the remaining variables at zero, and in effect create a square system of equations. The number of square subsets is finite. For the system of three equations in eight variables in Table 3–1, the number of distinct subsets of three variables is the combination of eight things taken three at a time, or $\frac{8 \times 7 \times 6}{1 \times 2 \times 3} = 56$. Thus, by confining our attention to square subsets we have at most 56 systems of equations to solve, a formidable task by hand but manageable given the aid of computers. We can then substitute the values of the variables for each solution into the objective form and identify a solution that yields the largest net revenue.

Trying to solve all 56 square systems is very inefficient. Some systems may be inconsistent and need not be considered at all; others may contain redundant equations and not have a unique solution;[1] and still others may yield solutions with a negative value for some variable. The simplex method achieves much of its computational efficiency because it screens out and passes over all inconsistent, redundant, and infeasible subsets, thus eliminating much needless computation.

As defined in Chapter 2, a square subset of variables, which can be reduced to diagonal form, is called a *basis*. The variables in the square subset are termed *basic variables*, and the rest are *nonbasic variables*. To obtain a *basic solution* set all nonbasic variables equal to zero and solve for the values of the basic variables. A *basic feasible* solution is a solution in which none of the basic variables has a negative value. In a basic feasible solution, the number of variables with strictly positive values cannot exceed the number of equations but may fall short of it, since variables in the basis can also equal zero. In terms of the definitions just introduced, the simplex method selects and compares only those square subsets that yield basic feasible solutions.

We have postponed perhaps too long the answer to a vital question. To be sure, restricting attention solely to basic feasible solutions must simplify the computations, but how can we be sure that it will not also restrict us from finding the best possible solution? The answer is given by a fundamental theorem of linear programming, which is most clearly stated in two parts: If a linear programming problem has a unique optimal feasible solution, that solution *must* be a basic feasible solution; if a linear programming problem has more than one optimal feasible solution, at least one of these optimal solutions must be a basic feasible solution. Thus, we may utilize the computational shortcut of considering only basic feasible solutions secure in the knowledge that there can be no better solution than the best of the basic feasible solutions.

The simplex method also satisfies another criterion of computational efficiency. Once we have found a basic feasible solution that yields, say, a total revenue of $100, we have no further interest in solutions that yield a smaller amount of revenue. The simplex method has a built-in ratchet that

[1]As demonstrated in Chapter 2, even though the system itself contains only independent and consistent equations, a square subset of variables with all other variables ignored may be either inconsistent or redundant.

prevents any slipping back to solutions that are inferior to the one just attained. Subsequent solutions will generally be better than the present solution but in special circumstances they may be merely just as good.

Enough has been written to establish the general rationale of the simplex method. The time has come to describe the computations in detail. The model to be used is that of the purely competitive firm with three fixed inputs and five possible products. In addition to the general model with symbolic coefficients, a specific numerical example will be used to illustrate the necessary computations. Both appear in Table 3–1.

As explained in Chapter 1, the first five variables represent the unknown output levels that are to be chosen in such a way as to maximize total revenue R. For the present, variable inputs are assumed not to be needed, so there is no variable cost. Hence, the same combination of outputs that maximizes revenue also maximizes net revenue, which is the excess of total revenue over total cost. With no variable cost, the r coefficients in the revenue equation or objective form are simply the market prices of the commodities, which management assumes are not affected by its own production levels. The a coefficients represent the amount of each input required for one unit of the respective output. The total amount of each input required or demanded by any production plan is the expression on the left-hand side involving the first five variables. The slack variables measure for each input the excess, if any, of the fixed total supply over the amount required. The constants on the right designate the total available supply of services from each type of fixed input, machine hours rather than number of machines. A fixed input can also represent a plant whose services are measured in terms of the percentage of available capacity allotted to each output. The three equations are a detailed and precise specification of the vague term, fixed factor of production, so commonly used in the traditional theory of the firm. Management's task is to choose a set of production levels that maximizes revenue within the ceilings imposed by the fixed inputs.

In recent years it has been fashionable to develop computer simulations of economic processes. We shall reverse the procedure and present an economic simulation of a computational process. Each algebraic operation will be rationalized and interpreted as a decision taken by management. This should provide intuitive insight into why the simplex method works and also establish a foundation for the subsequent economic interpretation of a firm with linear technology.

THE SIMPLEX METHOD

The first step in the simplex method is to find some basic feasible solution, however far from optimal it may be. For systems of equations in general there is no way of knowing in advance of actual computation whether a particular square subset will yield a nonnegative solution or, indeed, whether any square subset will. To meet this problem, a formal procedure has been devised to test whether a system of equations is feasible and, if so, to generate a basic feasible solution. Since the procedure is, in essence, a special application of the simplex method, it will be explained at the end of the chapter. For the example in Table 3–1, no difficulty arises.

TABLE 3–1

A Linear Model of a Multiproduct Firm

$$
\begin{array}{lllll}
a_{11}x_1+a_{12}x_2+a_{13}x_3+a_{14}x_4+a_{15}x_5+x_6 & & & = b_1 \\
a_{21}x_1+a_{22}x_2+a_{23}x_3+a_{24}x_4+a_{25}x_5 & +x_7 & & = b_2 \\
a_{31}x_1+a_{32}x_2+a_{33}x_3+a_{34}x_4+a_{35}x_5 & & +x_8 & = b_3 \\
r_1x_1 \;+r_2x_2 \;+r_3x_3 \;+r_4x_4 \;+r_5x_5 & & & = R(\max) \\
 & & & \\
3x_1+\;\; 2x_2+\;\; 2x_3+\;\; \tfrac{3}{2}x_4+\;\; 4x_5+x_6 & & & = 84 \\
4x_1+\;\; 3x_2+\;\; 1x_3+\;\; 1x_4+\;\; 6x_5 & +x_7 & & = 119 \\
2x_1+\;\; 4x_2+\;\; 2x_3+\;\; 1x_4+\;\; 1x_5 & & +x_8 & = 140 \\
6x_1+\;\; 5x_2+\;\; 4x_3+\;\; 2x_4+\;\; 5x_5 & & & = R(\max)
\end{array}
$$

The set of three slack variables provides an initial basic feasible solution, and this favorable result always occurs when the original constraints are of the $\leqq$ form and the constants on the right are nonnegative. Thus the special method for generating an initial basic feasible solution is needed only when the original constraints include equations or inequalities of the $\geqq$ form.

The initial solution is

$$\{x_6 = b_1(84);\; x_7 = b_2(119);\; x_8 = b_3(140);\; x_1 = x_2 = x_3 = x_4 = x_5 = 0\}.$$

It contains only slack variables at positive levels and has the economic meaning of producing nothing and letting the services of all fixed inputs go costlessly to waste.[2] In the present case, the solution cannot be optimal since the coefficients in the revenue function are market prices and must be positive for every product.[3] Management can increase revenue by producing any of the products, but there is a good prima facie case for selecting the output with the highest selling price. Hence the new entrant into the basis is the variable with the largest positive coefficient in the objective function.

[2]We could introduce a penalty for waste by giving the slack variables negative coefficients in the objective form. There is no justification for doing so unless idleness incurs some special costs, such as extra maintenance, which can be avoided by use. It was this possibility that Keynes incorporated into his concept of user cost. If idleness does not have specific costs, the revenue foregone represents the correct penalty for idleness and induces optimal economic decisions.

[3]The solution would be optimal if each output required variable inputs and the value of the variable inputs per unit of output exceeded the selling price.

The rule of largest positive coefficient chooses the first output. The next decision is how much to produce. Since selling prices are assumed independent of the firm's sales, each unit of product one adds to revenue at a rate of \$6 per unit, a greater rate than that of any other output. Hence the desired level of production is the maximum permitted by the input capacities. To find the production limit imposed by each input, set all other variables equal to zero and solve the following equations:

$$a_{11}x_1 = b_1 \qquad a_{21}x_1 = b_2 \qquad a_{31}x_1 = b_3$$

$$3x_1 = 84 \qquad 4x_1 = 119 \qquad 2x_1 = 140.$$

The production ceilings imposed by the inputs are $b_1/a_{11} = 28$, $b_2/a_{21} = 29\frac{3}{4}$, and $b_3/a_{31} = 70$. The first input limits the production of x_1 to 28 units, which is the lowest ceiling and the effective limit.

As noted in the preliminary discussion, the simplex method is restricted to basic feasible solutions. Hence, when x_1 enters, one variable in the previous solution must drop out. As x_1 increases to the limit imposed by the first input, the excess capacity of that input, x_6, is driven to zero, but the excess capacities of the other inputs, though reduced, remain positive. Thus x_6, the variable first driven to zero by the increase in x_1, is eliminated from the basis.

In constructing the numerical example, we have assumed that the first product requires the services of all three inputs, as shown by positive *a* coefficients. There is no reason why an *a* coefficient cannot be zero, but then the input imposes no barrier at all to production and can be ignored in calculating limits.

Algebraically, at least, an *a* coefficient, say a_{21}, can be negative. The economic interpretation is that the second input is actually an output of the first productive process, a joint product with x_1. Shifted to the right-hand side of the constraints $(-a_{21}x_1)$ becomes positive, showing that increases in x_1 augment rather than deplete the supply of the second input. In detailed and complex models of the firm, there are many possibilities for joint production as well as for feeder processes that provide inputs for subsequent production. Thus, in broader economic models and in other problems to which linear programming is applied, allowance must be made for negative coefficients. With a_{21} negative and the first productive process turning out quantities of the second input, the initial amount obviously cannot be a barrier to the production of x_1. The algebraic reason for ignoring negative coefficients is that the equation $a_{21}x_1 = b_2$, where $a_{21} < 0$, cannot have a solution with a positive value for x_1. But it will have a negative solution. Hence, if x_1 is introduced in a row in which it has a negative coefficient the new solution will not be feasible.

When a new variable enters, an old variable must exit. To find the variable to drop, ignore negative and zero coefficients in the column of the entering variable. For each positive coefficient in the column, form the ratio of the constant on the right to the coefficient in the same row. Drop the variable in a row where the ratio is smallest, since it is driven to zero first. When two or more variables tie for lowest ratio, we can drop any one and get a new basic feasible solution. To break the tie, choose randomly or follow some other simple rule that ensures a unique selection.[4] By rejecting zero and negative *a* coefficients and by dropping variables in accordance with the smallest ratio, the simplex method guarantees that the new solution will be feasible if the present solution is.

There is the intriguing algebraic possibility that all *a* coefficients may be negative or zero. For the present economic model, this would imply a production process that turned out products without the use of inputs. Both output and revenue could be expanded without limit, and no finite maximum would exist. In any linear programming problem, the absence of a positive coefficient in the column of the entering variable is like a flashing red light. All computations stop, and a check must be made for errors in the data or in the formulation of the problem. It is interesting to note, however, that the classic long-run model of the purely competitive firm under constant returns to scale is precisely of this type. Within the model as formulated, if it pays to produce at all, it pays to expand without limit; but then other barriers not contained explicitly in the model of the firm come into operation.

Applied to the present example the general rule determines that x_6 is to leave the basis and x_1 is to enter. The next step is to convert the system to the new basis. What is required is a pivot operation with a_{11} as the pivot, converting the coefficient of x_1 to unity in the first row and reducing it to zero elsewhere. The required elementary operations are: (1) multiply the first equation by $1/a_{11}(=\frac{1}{3})$; (2), (3), and (4) to the second and third equations and the objective form add, respectively, $-a_{21}(=-4)$, $-a_{31}(=-2)$, and $-r_1(=-6)$ times the new first equation. These computations affect all constants and coefficients in the system except those of x_7 and x_8, the other variables in the basis. The results appear in Table 3–2.

When the objective form is included, there are four equations but only three basic variables to appear on the diagonal. Hence, the term *diagonal form* is appropriate for the constraints but not for the problem as a whole. Sometimes R is transferred to the left-hand side as $+1(-R)$ to complete the diagonal, but this remedy has no advantages at present. The term generally applied to a linear programming problem as displayed in Table 3–2 is *canonical form.* A canonical form in mathematics denotes a standard form to which all members of a given class can be reduced by mathematical opera-

[4]In the theory of linear programming and occasionally in numerical problems, the method of breaking ties makes a difference, and some methods, such as choosing the lowest subscript, may prevent an optimum from being attained. The difficulty, which reveals a minor but correctible defect in the simplex method, is not worth worrying about at this stage. We shall discuss it more fully near the end of the chapter.

tions. To display any linear programming problem in its canonical form carry out the following operations:

1. Express all constraints as equations rather than inequalities.
2. Reduce the constraints to diagonal form with respect to a subset of variables that forms a basis.
3. Eliminate the basic variables from the objective form.

All linear programming problems with at least one basis permit the preceding operations to be performed and are reducible to the same format. Hereafter, we shall use the more appropriate term, *canonical form*, in place of diagonal form except when referring to the constraints alone.

TABLE 3–2

The Second Basic Feasible Solution

$$
\begin{array}{lllllllll}
x_1 & +\bar{a}_{12}x_2 & +\bar{a}_{13}x_3 & +\bar{a}_{14}x_4 & +\bar{a}_{15}x_5 & +\bar{a}_{16}x_6 & & & = \bar{b}_1 \\
 & +\bar{a}_{22}x_2 & +\bar{a}_{23}x_3 & +\bar{a}_{24}x_4 & +\bar{a}_{25}x_5 & +\bar{a}_{26}x_6 & +x_7 & & = \bar{b}_2 \\
 & +\bar{a}_{32}x_2 & +\bar{a}_{33}x_3 & +\bar{a}_{34}x_4 & +\bar{a}_{35}x_5 & +\bar{a}_{36}x_6 & & +x_8 & = \bar{b}_3 \\
 & +\ \bar{r}_2x_2 & +\ \bar{r}_3x_3 & +\ \bar{r}_4x_4 & +\ \bar{r}_5x_5 & +\ \bar{r}_6x_6 & & & = R-\bar{R} \\
* & & & & & & * & * &
\end{array}
$$

$$
\begin{array}{lllllllll}
x_1 & +\ \frac{2}{3}x_2 & +\ \frac{2}{3}x_3 & +\ \frac{1}{2}x_4 & +\ \frac{4}{3}x_5 & +\ \frac{1}{3}x_6 & & & = 28 \\
 & +\ \frac{1}{3}x_2 & -\ \frac{5}{3}x_3 & -\ 1x_4 & +\ \frac{2}{3}x_5 & -\ \frac{4}{3}x_6 & +x_7 & & = \ \ 7 \\
 & +\ \frac{8}{3}x_2 & +\ \frac{2}{3}x_3 & +\ 0x_4 & -\ \frac{5}{3}x_5 & -\ \frac{2}{3}x_6 & & +x_8 & = 84 \\
 & +\ 1x_2 & +\ 0x_3 & -\ 1x_4 & -\ 3x_5 & -\ 2x_6 & & & = R-168 \\
* & & & & & & * & * &
\end{array}
$$

When the variables in a basis are separated an asterisk under each column is a convenient way of identifying them. Since it is both uneconomical and confusing, particularly in large algebraic systems, to display all computations on coefficients, the standard practice is to indicate such computations symbolically by placing a bar over a coefficient. Thus, $\bar{a}_{25}$ indicates that the original coefficient, a_{25}, has been transformed by whatever computations are needed to reduce to canonical form with respect to the given basis. With another basis the same symbols would be used, but the sequence of computations would be different. To get at the economic meaning of the barred coefficients it is, however, necessary to go behind the symbols and examine the actual computations.

With nonbasic variables omitted, the new solution is

$$x_1 = \bar{b}_1 = \frac{b_1}{a_{11}} = 28$$

$$x_7 = \bar{b}_2 = b_2 - a_{21}\left(\frac{b_1}{a_{11}}\right) = 119 - 112$$

$$x_8 = \bar{b}_3 = b_3 - a_{31}\left(\frac{b_1}{a_{11}}\right) = 140 - 56.$$

Since $\bar{b}_1 = b_1/a_{11}$ is the level of production for the first output and $a_{21}(b_1/a_{11})$ is the total amount of the second input required by that level of production, $\bar{b}_2 = b_2 - a_{21}(b_1/a_{11})$ is the unused capacity. A similar conclusion holds for $\bar{b}_3$.

An astute management, noting the excess capacities, will undoubtedly investigate whether another product can profitably be introduced to absorb the unused resources. If a product is available that does not require the services of the first input, it can be produced without cutting back on the first product, augmenting revenue. Otherwise, a second product causes a cutback of the first, and the gain in revenue from the new product must be balanced against the loss in revenue from the old. Since market prices are assumed constant, the crucial piece of information is the rate at which the first output must change in response to the production of the new product. That rate of change depends on the relative size of the requirements for the first input. If the second product is produced and the first input continues to be fully utilized, the following condition must be met:

$$a_{11}\Delta x_1 + a_{12}\Delta x_2 = 0.$$

As a reminder, the symbol Δ is the standard mathematical way of designating a change in a variable. The equation states that the increased use of the input by the second product, $a_{12}\Delta x_2$, must be offset by a decrease in use by the first product, $a_{11}\,\Delta x_1$, leaving total utilization constant. The rate of change of x_1 with respect to x_2 is

$$\frac{\Delta x_1}{\Delta x_2} = -\frac{a_{12}}{a_{11}}.$$

Hence, for each unit increase in x_2, the production of x_1 must be cut back by a_{12}/a_{11} units, and the loss of revenue is $r_1(a_{12}/a_{11})$. The net change in revenue from a unit of x_2 is $r_2 - r_1(a_{12}/a_{11})$. Only if the expression is positive does it pay to introduce the second product.

In eliminating r_1 from the objective form the pivot operation requires that the first equation be multiplied first by $1/a_{11}$, then by $-r_1$, and added to the objective function. As readers may verify, these operations are precisely those needed to convert the coefficient of x_2 into the expression for the net change in revenue shown above. The foregoing example illustrates an important general property of the simplex method, which may be stated formally as follows: when a system has been reduced to canonical form with respect to a given basis, each $\bar{r}$ coefficient in the objective form measures the net change in revenue from increasing the corresponding variable by one unit and making the necessary adjustments of the variables in the basis.

The elimination of x_1 from the objective function adds the term $-[r_1(b_1/a_{11})]$ to the right-hand side. The brackets represent the revenue obtained from producing x_1 to the limit of the input capacity. Since x_1 is the only product in the basis, the brackets represent the total revenue yielded by the particular solution, denoted symbolically by $\bar{R}$. In any basic feasible solution, the nonbasic variables are zero and the basic variables have zero coefficients in the objective form, so the left-hand side is zero. Hence, $0 = R-\bar{R}$, or $R = \bar{R}$, the amount of revenue yielded by the particular basic feasible solution. For the numerical example, $\bar{R} = 168$.

A glance at Table 3–2 shows that the solution is not optimal since $\bar{r}_2 = 1$. Had all $\bar{r}$ coefficients been negative or zero, no improvement would have been possible. Thus, the general criterion for an optimal solution is that all $\bar{r}$ coefficients be negative or zero.[5] When slack variables form the basic feasible solution, no computations are necessary, and the criterion applies to the original r coefficients.

The choice of entering variable is determined by the largest $\bar{r}$ coefficient. Ties may exist but they can be broken by random choice or some other simple rule. The second output is the sole candidate in the present example. Since x_2 adds to revenue at a net rate of \$1 per unit, it pays to make the largest possible increase. We have the data on excess capacities:

$$\bar{b}_2 = b_2 - a_{21}\left(\frac{b_1}{a_{11}}\right) = 7; \qquad \bar{b}_3 = b_3 - a_{31}\left(\frac{b_1}{a_{11}}\right) = 84.$$

We also know the requirements of the second output for both inputs, $a_{22} = 3$ and $a_{32} = 4$. The first impulse is to match input requirements to excess capacities, as follows:

$$a_{22}x_2 = \bar{b}_2 \quad \text{or} \quad 3x_2 = 7; \qquad a_{32}x_2 = \bar{b}_3 \quad \text{or} \quad 4x_2 = 84.$$

The lower of the ceilings, imposed by the second input, is $x_2 = \frac{7}{3}$.

Unfortunately, this simple and direct method is not correct so long as

[5]For variables in the basis, the $\bar{r}$ coefficients are zero, indicating formally that a unit increase in production must be balanced by a unit decrease in order to satisfy the constraints.

the second product requires the services of the first input ($a_{12} > 0$). Every increase in product two withdraws amounts of the first input from product one, cutting back its output. But a cutback in product one, if $a_{21} > 0$, frees some previously used capacity of the second input, permitting an expansion of product two. The increase in the second product then induces a second round of effects by further reducing the level of the first product. The repercussions go on endlessly, though fortunately with diminishing magnitude.[6]

The way out of the difficulty is to allow for the reduction in x_1 and calculate the *net* requirement of product two for the second input. As derived earlier, the rate of change of x_1 with respect to x_2 is

$$\frac{\Delta x_1}{\Delta x_2} = -\frac{a_{12}}{a_{11}}.$$

Hence, each unit of x_2 causes a cutback of a_{12}/a_{11} units in x_1, and this frees $a_{21}(a_{12}/a_{11})$ units of the second input. The net amount of the second input required by one unit of x_2 is

$$a_{22}-a_{21}\left(\frac{a_{12}}{a_{11}}\right) \quad \text{or} \quad 3-4\left(\frac{2}{3}\right) = \frac{1}{3}.$$

The correct production ceiling is not $\frac{7}{3}$ but $7/\frac{1}{3} = 21$. As readers can easily verify, the pivot operation applied to a_{11} converts a_{22} into

$$\bar{a}_{22} = a_{22}-a_{21}\left(\frac{a_{12}}{a_{11}}\right),$$

which is the desired net input requirement. A similar conclusion holds for $\bar{a}_{32}$. The correct output limits are, therefore,

$$\frac{\bar{b}_2}{\bar{a}_{22}} = \frac{7}{\frac{1}{3}} = 21; \qquad \frac{\bar{b}_3}{\bar{a}_{32}} = \frac{84}{\frac{8}{3}} = 31\tfrac{1}{2}.$$

The smaller of the two ratios determines both the limit to production and the variable in the present basis that is the first to reach zero.

In the numerical example both $\bar{a}_{22}$ and $\bar{a}_{32}$ are positive, but this will not always occur. Even though none of the original a coefficients are negative, the barred coefficients may have negative values, implying that the induced reduction in existing products frees more of an input than the new product requires. An example is $\bar{a}_{35} = -\frac{5}{3}$ in Table 3–2. When an $\bar{a}$ coefficient is negative or zero, the corresponding input is no barrier to the production of

[6]Readers with sufficient mathematical background may suspect and be able to confirm that the successive increases in x_2 form a convergent geometric series.

the entering product and can be disregarded. We may now restate the general rule for selecting the variable to drop from any nonoptimal basic feasible solution. From the $\bar{a}$ coefficients of the entering variable select those that are positive. Form ratios of each barred constant on the right to each positive $\bar{a}$ coefficient in the same row. The smallest such ratio determines the variable to be dropped and the row in which the pivot lies for the next operation. Ties may be broken by random choice or any other simple rule. In the special case where the basic feasible solution consists of slack variables only, the $\bar{a}$ coefficients are simply the original coefficients. We have supplied an economic rationale to give a plausible basis for the general rule, but the rule as stated above is valid for any application of the simplex method.

Applying the general rule we introduce x_2, drop x_7, and perform the indicated pivot operation, with the result shown in Table 3–3. The solution is not optimal, so x_3, having the largest $\bar{r}$ coefficient, is introduced. By the rule of minimal positive ratio, x_8 is dropped, and another pivot operation yields the optimal solution of Table 3–4.

TABLE 3–3

The Third Basic Feasible Solution

$$
\begin{array}{lllllllll}
x_1 & & +\ 4x_3 & +\frac{5}{2}x_4 & +0x_5 & +\ 3x_6 & -2x_7 & & = 14 \\
 & x_2 & -\ 5x_3 & -3x_4 & +2x_5 & -\ 4x_6 & +3x_7 & & = 21 \\
 & & +14x_3 & +8x_4 & -7x_5 & +10x_6 & -8x_7 & +x_8 & = 28 \\
 & & +\ 5x_3 & +2x_4 & -5x_5 & +\ 2x_6 & -3x_7 & & = R-189 \\
* & * & & & & & & * &
\end{array}
$$

When the basic feasible solution consists of output levels only, as in Table 3–4, a subtle change occurs in the interpretation of capacity. Originally, capacity was defined in terms of available amounts of fixed inputs, machine hours, and the like. In the solution of Table 3–4, $\{x_1 = \bar{b}_1 = 6; x_2 = \bar{b}_2 = 31; x_3 = \bar{b}_3 = 2\}$, the $\bar{b}$ constants become output levels, and capacity is rede-

TABLE 3–4

The Optimal Solution

$$
\begin{array}{lllllllll}
x_1 & & & +\bar{a}_{14}x_4 & +\bar{a}_{15}x_5 & +\bar{a}_{16}x_6 & +\bar{a}_{17}x_7 & +\bar{a}_{18}x_8 & = \bar{b}_1 \\
 & x_2 & & +\bar{a}_{24}x_4 & +\bar{a}_{25}x_5 & +\bar{a}_{26}x_6 & +\bar{a}_{27}x_7 & +\bar{a}_{28}x_8 & = \bar{b}_2 \\
 & & x_3 & +\bar{a}_{34}x_4 & +\bar{a}_{35}x_5 & +\bar{a}_{36}x_6 & +\bar{a}_{37}x_7 & +\bar{a}_{38}x_8 & = \bar{b}_3 \\
 & & & +\ \bar{r}_4x_4 & +\ \bar{r}_5x_5 & +\ \bar{r}_6x_6 & +\ \bar{r}_7x_7 & +\ \bar{r}_8x_8 & = R-\bar{R}
\end{array}
$$

$$
\begin{array}{lllllllll}
x_1 & & & +\ \frac{3}{14}x_4 & +\ 2x_5 & +\ \frac{1}{7}x_6 & +\ \frac{2}{7}x_7 & -\ \frac{2}{7}x_8 & = 6 \\
 & x_2 & & -\ \frac{1}{7}x_4 & -\ \frac{1}{2}x_5 & -\ \frac{3}{7}x_6 & +\ \frac{1}{7}x_7 & +\ \frac{5}{14}x_8 & = 31 \\
 & & x_3 & +\ \frac{4}{7}x_4 & -\ \frac{1}{2}x_5 & +\ \frac{5}{7}x_6 & -\ \frac{4}{7}x_7 & +\ \frac{1}{14}x_8 & = 2 \\
 & & & -\ \frac{6}{7}x_4 & -\ \frac{5}{2}x_5 & -\ \frac{11}{7}x_6 & -\ \frac{1}{7}x_7 & -\ \frac{5}{14}x_8 & = R-199
\end{array}
$$

fined as a set of production levels that fully utilizes the fixed inputs. This is a frequent practice in industry where, for example, the capacities of steel or paper mills are stated in terms of tons of output. When there is a single homogeneous product, it is economically more meaningful to measure capacity in terms of output. However, as even the present simple linear model shows, a multiproduct firm poses difficulties, since each basic feasible solution gives a measure of capacity in terms of three distinct products, and there may be many basic feasible solutions. At times a weighted index is devised to get a single figure, but, as always, difficult questions arise over the proper choice of weights.

The measurement of capacity in terms of output levels, despite its ambiguity, does not affect the application of the simplex method to the multiproduct firm but does alter the economic interpretation. For a numerical illustration go back to Table 3–1 and change r_4 from 2 to 3. At each stage $\bar{r}_4$ will be one unit higher than shown.[7] Since $\bar{r}_4 = -\frac{6}{7}$ in Table 3–4, a unit increase raises it to $\frac{1}{7}$, and the solution is no longer optimal. Each unit of product four now makes a net addition to revenue, so it pays to produce at the highest possible level. That level is no longer dictated by the excess capacities of the inputs. The inputs for the fourth product must be diverted from the three products currently being turned out. The ceiling for x_4 occurs when the diversion of inputs forces one of the current outputs to zero.

When products are introduced to take up the excess capacity of inputs, the $\bar{a}$ coefficients measure the net input requirements per unit of output. With three outputs in the basis the $\bar{a}$ coefficients cannot have the same meaning, but they do contain precisely the information needed to calculate which output reaches zero first. Each $\bar{a}$ coefficient for x_4 measures the rate at which one of the basic variables changes with respect to x_4, as we now show.

As x_4 increases, the total use of each input must remain constant. Hence, all four outputs must vary in such a way that there are mutually offsetting changes in the utilization of each input. The appropriate equations for expressing this requirement are

$$\begin{aligned}
a_{11}\,\Delta x_1 + a_{12}\,\Delta x_2 + a_{13}\,\Delta x_3 + a_{14}\,\Delta x_4 &= 0\\
a_{21}\,\Delta x_1 + a_{22}\,\Delta x_2 + a_{23}\,\Delta x_3 + a_{24}\,\Delta x_4 &= 0\\
a_{31}\,\Delta x_1 + a_{32}\,\Delta x_2 + a_{33}\,\Delta x_3 + a_{34}\,\Delta x_4 &= 0
\end{aligned}$$

$$\begin{aligned}
3\,\Delta x_1 + \quad 2\,\Delta x_2 + \quad 2\,\Delta x_3 + \quad \tfrac{3}{2}\,\Delta x_4 &= 0\\
4\,\Delta x_1 + \quad 3\,\Delta x_2 + \quad 1\,\Delta x_3 + \quad 1\,\Delta x_4 &= 0\\
2\,\Delta x_1 + \quad 4\,\Delta x_2 + \quad 2\Delta x_3 + \quad 1\,\Delta x_4 &= 0.
\end{aligned}$$

[7]As readers can check, a one-unit increase in $\bar{r}_4$ does not affect the choice of entering variable in Tables 3-1–3-3. There is no change in the order in which the simplex method chooses basic feasible solutions.

The term $a_{11}\,\Delta x_1$, which may be positive or negative, measures the change in the first product's use of the first input, and similar explanations hold for the other terms.

Since we wish to find the changes in the first three products induced by a change in the fourth, the standard procedure is to reduce to diagonal form with respect to the first three variables in the equations. But the work has already been done. The coefficients of all four variables are the same as those in the original constraints, so reduction to diagonal form requires the same operations and has the same effect on the coefficients of the fourth variable as did the corresponding reduction of the original system. The result is

$$\begin{aligned} \Delta x_1 \qquad\qquad &+ \bar{a}_{14}\,\Delta x_4 = 0 \\ \Delta x_2 \qquad &+ \bar{a}_{24}\,\Delta x_4 = 0 \\ \Delta x_3 &+ \bar{a}_{34}\,\Delta x_4 = 0; \end{aligned} \qquad \begin{aligned} \Delta x_1 \qquad\qquad &+ \tfrac{3}{14}\,\Delta x_4 = 0 \\ \Delta x_2 \qquad &- \tfrac{1}{7}\,\Delta x_4 = 0 \\ \Delta x_3 &+ \tfrac{4}{7}\,\Delta x_4 = 0. \end{aligned}$$

The rates of change are

$$\frac{\Delta x_1}{\Delta x_4} = -\bar{a}_{14} = -\frac{3}{14}; \qquad \frac{\Delta x_2}{\Delta x_4} = -\bar{a}_{24} = \frac{1}{7};$$

$$\frac{\Delta x_3}{\Delta x_4} = -\bar{a}_{34} = -\frac{4}{7}.$$

A perhaps surprising result is that the rate of change of x_2 with respect to x_4 is positive, implying that increases in the fourth product expand rather than cut back production of the second. There is no escape from the algebraic result; the only way that the exact amounts of inputs can be provided for x_4 is by cutting back two products and expanding the third. To see why this result occurs we can compare the input requirements of x_4, $(\frac{3}{2}, 1, 1)$, with those of x_2, (2, 3, 4). The input requirements of x_4 and x_2 are almost in inverse order of size. Thus, x_4 and x_2 mesh together well or complement each other in the use of inputs. When an $\bar{a}$ coefficient is negative and the rate of change positive, the two products are termed *complementary* in the use of inputs or *complements.* Similarly, a positive $\bar{a}$ coefficient implies that the products are *competitive* for inputs or *substitutes* for each other. A zero value denotes independence.

Since $\bar{a}$ coefficients vary with the basis, the relationship of complementarity or substitution between two products is not immutable and may change when a new variable comes into the basis. Thus, products are substitutes or complements only relative to a specific basis, so the more accurate terms *relative complement* and *relative substitute* will be used whenever confusion might otherwise arise.

When a new product comes into the basis, only the relative substitutes impose a barrier to its increase. To show this precisely, we can rewrite the equations in Table 3–4 as follows:

$$\begin{aligned} x_1 &= \bar{b}_1 - \bar{a}_{14}x_4 = 6 - \tfrac{3}{14}x_4 \\ x_2 &= \bar{b}_2 - \bar{a}_{24}x_4 = 31 + \tfrac{1}{7}x_4 \\ x_3 &= \bar{b}_3 - \bar{a}_{34}x_4 = 2 - \tfrac{4}{7}x_4. \end{aligned}$$

The other nonbasic variables remain at zero and can be ignored. To find the limit for x_4, ignore the second equation, set the remaining equations equal to zero, and solve. The solutions are

$$x_4 = \frac{\bar{b}_1}{\bar{a}_{14}} = \frac{6}{3/14} = 28; \qquad x_4 = \frac{\bar{b}_3}{\bar{a}_{34}} = \frac{2}{4/7} = \frac{7}{2}.$$

Since x_3 reaches zero first, it is dropped from the basis and x_4 is brought in at the level of $\frac{7}{2}$. In algebraic terms, the variable to drop and the pivot, $\bar{a}_{34}$, lie in the row with minimum ratio of $\bar{b}$ constant to positive $\bar{a}$ coefficient.

There is also an interesting economic reinterpretation of the $\bar{r}$ coefficients. To demonstrate, assume that the three constraints have been reduced to diagonal form but that no variables have been eliminated as yet from the objective form. With unneeded variables dropped, the equations are

$$\begin{aligned} x_1 \qquad\qquad &+ \bar{a}_{14}x_4 = \bar{b}_1 \\ x_2 \qquad &+ \bar{a}_{24}x_4 = \bar{b}_2 \\ x_3 &+ \bar{a}_{34}x_4 = \bar{b}_3 \\ r_1x_1 + r_2x_2 + r_3x_3 &+ r_4x_4 = R. \end{aligned}$$

Elimination of the first three variables from the objective form yields

$$(r_4 - r_1\bar{a}_{14} - r_2\bar{a}_{24} - r_3\bar{a}_{34})x_4 = R - (r_1\bar{b}_1 + r_2\bar{b}_2 + r_3\bar{b}_3)$$

or

$$\bar{r}_4x_4 = R - \bar{R}.$$

The parentheses on the right contain the products of market prices and output levels, clearly the total revenue yielded by the basic feasible solution.

If the simplex method is to work, $\bar{r}_4$ must be the net rate at which total revenue changes in response to variations in x_4, due allowance being made for necessary adjustments in the basic variables. The diversion of sufficient resources to produce one unit of the fourth product adds directly to revenue r_4 dollars. Balanced against this is the loss of revenue from the products in the current basis. From the previously derived equations, when x_4 increases by one unit or $\Delta x_4 = 1$, the basic variables respond as follows:

$$\Delta x_1 = -\bar{a}_{14}\,\Delta x_4 = -\bar{a}_{14}; \qquad \Delta x_2 = -\bar{a}_{24}; \qquad \Delta x_3 = -\bar{a}_{34}.$$

Multiplication of each change in output by the revenue per unit gives the following change in revenue from currently produced products:

$$r_1\,\Delta x_1 + r_2\,\Delta x_2 + r_3\,\Delta x_3 = -r_1\bar{a}_{14} - r_2\bar{a}_{24} - r_3\bar{a}_{34}.$$

When x_4 increases by one unit, the algebraic sum of the direct and indirect changes in revenue is

$$r_4 + r_1\,\Delta x_1 + r_2\,\Delta x_2 + r_3\,\Delta x_3 = r_4 - r_1\bar{a}_{14} - r_2\bar{a}_{24} - r_3\bar{a}_{34}.$$

The expression on the right is the previously derived formula for $\bar{r}_4$.

In the present simplified version of the firm, no variable inputs are needed, and there is no variable cost. Further, nothing has to be paid for the services of fixed inputs, since these inputs have already been acquired and go costlessly to waste if not used. Yet for each product there is a cost, its opportunity cost. For the fourth product the management has two choices: produce a unit of x_4 or continue to use the same resources to produce the first three products. The opportunity cost for product four is the revenue foregone from the most lucrative alternative, which is producing the first three products. If inputs are diverted from producing one unit of x_4 to producing the first three products, $\Delta x_4 = -1$, and the gain in revenue is $r_1\bar{a}_{14} + r_2\bar{a}_{24} + r_3\bar{a}_{34}$. This is also the amount the firm foregoes by producing a unit of x_4 or the unit opportunity cost of x_4. It pays to produce a product only if its revenue per unit exceeds its opportunity cost per unit. But this is precisely the information given by

$$\bar{r}_4 = r_4 - (r_1\bar{a}_{14} + r_2\bar{a}_{24} + r_3\bar{a}_{34}).$$

We may, then, interpret $\bar{r}_4$ either as the net rate of change of revenue with respect to x_4, which is $\Delta R/\Delta x_4$, or as the excess of revenue per unit over opportunity cost per unit.

When a product not produced has an $\bar{r}$ coefficient of zero, there is no gain and no loss in introducing it. To provide a numerical example, change r_4 to $2\frac{6}{7}$ in Table 3–1 and $\bar{r}_4$ will be zero in Table 3–4. When x_4 is introduced, displacing x_3, a second basic feasible solution results that is also optimal. But there is no longer any reason why x_4 should be expanded until it displaces x_3. Additional units of x_4 have no effect on revenue. For every intermediate value of x_4 between 0 and $\frac{7}{2}$ there is an optimal production plan with four outputs at positive levels. Equations on page 45, that relate basic variables to values of x_4 permit the calculation of each production plan. Thus, zero coefficients in the objective form for an optimal solution always imply additional basic feasible solutions that are also optimal and, even more, an infinite number of feasible, but not basic, solutions that are equally good. When the simplex method finds one optimal solution, it also reveals whether there are others and provides all the information needed to derive them.

In the introduction to this chapter we gave some general reasons for the efficiency of the simplex method. Each has now received specific verification. The rule for dropping variables screens out inconsistent, redundant, and infeasible subsets. It guarantees that, if the present solution is basic and feasible, the new solution will also be. Bringing in the variable with the largest $\bar{r}$ coefficient prevents any slipping back to inferior solutions and also, in most cases, permits a jump over intermediate solutions that are better than the present solution but not so good as the one chosen. The fundamental reason for the success of the method is that reduction to canonical form builds into the barred coefficients exactly the information needed to test for optimality and to generate a better solution. We have so far distinguished two clearly recognized outcomes of the process: no $\bar{r}$ coefficients are positive and an optimum has been reached; no $\bar{a}$ coefficients are positive in the column of the entering variable and no finite maximum exists. The simplex method is a repetitive or iterative process. Its usefulness depends on its reaching one of the outcomes in a finite number of iterations and, preferably, in a small number. Since the number of basic feasible solutions is finite, it is tempting to conclude that the number of iterations must also be finite, but there is one rather tricky possibility that must be examined.

DEGENERATE SOLUTIONS AND CIRCLING

A problem previously mentioned but not yet discussed is a tie for the variable to be dropped. To provide a numerical example, change b_2 from 119 to 112 in Table 3–1. The production ceilings for x_1 become

$$\frac{b_1}{a_{11}} = \frac{84}{3} = 28; \qquad \frac{b_2}{a_{21}} = \frac{112}{4} = 28; \qquad \frac{b_3}{a_{31}} = \frac{140}{2} = 70.$$

Since product one uses fully both the first and second inputs, x_6 and x_7 go to zero simultaneously and either can be dropped. However, whichever variable is dropped, the other remains in the basic feasible solution, but at a level of zero. For conformity with Table 3–2, x_6 will be dropped. At the next iteration, when x_2 is to be brought in, the relevant information lies in the two columns shown below:

$$\cdots + \tfrac{2}{3}x_2 + \cdots = 28$$

$$\cdots + \tfrac{1}{3}x_2 + \cdots = \ \ 0$$

$$\cdots + \tfrac{8}{3}x_2 + \cdots = 84.$$

By the rule of minimum ratio of constant to positive $\bar{a}$ coefficient, a new variable always enters in a row where the constant is zero, provided that the $\bar{a}$ coefficient is positive. But to ensure a feasible solution the new variable enters at a level of zero. Since $\bar{r}_2 = 1$, the rules of the simplex method call for product two to be brought into the basis even though none of it is produced and there is no increase in revenue.

For the successful application of the simplex method a variable must be introduced even though its level remains at zero and there is no change in the objective variable. A continuation of the present example shows why. Except for the differences on the right-hand side the pivot operation introducing x_2 has the same results as in Table 3–3, so the solution becomes

$$\begin{aligned} x_1 \quad + 4x_3 + \cdots &= 28 \\ x_2 - 5x_3 + \cdots &= 0 \\ +14x_3 + \cdots &= 84 \\ + 5x_3 + \cdots &= R - 168. \end{aligned}$$

Since the $\bar{r}$ coefficients are not changed from Table 3–3, x_3 is the variable to enter and the other nonbasic variables can be ignored. The coefficient of x_3 is negative in the row of the zero, so x_3 is introduced, as before, in row 3. As readers may verify, the pivot operation introducing x_3 raises x_2 to 30 and also gives the optimal solution.[8]

When at least one of the basic variables in a basic feasible solution equals zero, the solution is termed *degenerate*, and the general condition is called *degeneracy*.[9] In the model of the multiproduct firm degeneracy may arise when two or more inputs are available in just the right ratio for one of the products. It may also occur when fewer than three products—in general fewer than m products—can fully utilize the available inputs. In economic terms, the general characteristic of degeneracy is that fewer products have to be produced, simplifying the problem. For example, if we change b_3 to 56 as well as b_2 to 112 in Table 3–1, the first product utilizes fully all resources and yields maximum revenue. The rules of the simplex method do, however, require that x_2 and x_3 be brought into the solution because of positive $\bar{r}$ coefficients, and the resultant optimal solution is doubly degenerate.

[8]In the present numerical example the change in b_2 did not alter the sequence in which variables enter the basis nor the set of variables comprising the optimal solution. In general there will be changes in both, since altering the constants may make previously feasible solutions infeasible. The topic is covered in detail in Chapter 5.

[9]Readers may wonder about the use of the term *degeneracy*. A flip answer can be given that, whenever a problem or its solution becomes simpler, mathematicians label it degenerate. There is, however, a core of truth in the answer. The term *degeneracy* is applied, among other uses, to a reduction in the dimension of a space; planes degenerate into lines and lines into points. In the present example, $x_3 = 0$, so the solution lies in the coordinate plane of the other two variables. Since there is a reduction in the dimension from three to two, the solution is degenerate. Further clarification will be given in Chapter 6.

A degenerate optimal solution is economically simpler and presents no mathematical difficulties. Also, an isolated degenerate solution on the way to the optimum is no problem. What may cause difficulty is a sequence of nonoptimal degenerate solutions. There is a remote possibility that *circling* or *cycling* may occur. Suppose that there are, say, six degenerate solutions with the same value of R. The rules for selecting entering and departing variables may choose, successively, degenerate solutions 1–6. When solution 6 is reached the simplex method may then choose degenerate solution 1, after which the sequence is repeated again and again. Circling can never arise when R increases from one solution to the next, since the simplex method never slips back to inferior solutions. However, when R stays constant from iteration to iteration because variables are entering at zero levels, there is nothing to prevent a return to an equally good solution.

Circling is like a rare side effect of an otherwise completely effective drug. In an overwhelmingly high percentage of problems, an $\bar{a}$ coefficient that is negative or zero will show up in the row of the zero, nudging the system up from its degenerate plateau. For the extremely rare problem in which circling may occur another ingredient is added. The core of the difficulty is a rigid rule for breaking ties among departing variables. If, say, the variable of lowest subscript is always chosen, previous circles will be indefinitely repeated. Computer codes can forestall the appearance of circling by relying on more sophisticated methods of breaking ties.[10] With the remote possibility of circling removed, the simplex method, once set in operation, requires only a finite number of iterations to find an optimal solution or to discover that no finite optimum exists.

FINDING AN INITIAL BASIC FEASIBLE SOLUTION

The only remaining defect of the simplex method is that in some cases it can't get started. If the constraints are equations or inequalities of the $\geqq$ form, there is no obvious initial basic feasible solution. Even in small systems and most certainly in larger systems of, say, ten equations in twenty variables, there is no way of spotting a basis that is likely to yield a nonnegative solution. To solve this difficulty, a systematic method has been devised, called *Phase I* of the simplex method, which will find a basic feasible solution if one exists. What we have described as the simplex method so far in the chapter is termed *Phase II* of the simplex method, the sequence of operations that leads from any basic feasible solution to an optimal solution, if one exists.

[10] Dantzig, *op. cit.*, p. 231, reported in 1963 that circling had never occurred in any application of the simplex method to an actual problem but only in two numerical examples specially constructed to demonstrate the possibility of circling. This being the case, many computer codes do not incorporate any special antidote for circling but instead utilize the core memory for more generally needed subroutines.

For an illustration of Phase I, the following numerical example, which occurs in Chapter 10, suffices:

$$\begin{aligned} 4z_1+12z_2+\ 8z_3+5z_4 &\geqq 72 \\ 4z_1+\ 9z_2+12z_3+3z_4 &\geqq 60 \\ 8z_1+20z_2+22z_3+8z_4 &= C\ (\text{min}). \end{aligned}$$

Since the left-hand side can exceed the right-hand side, an equality can be created only by subtracting positive quantities on the left. When slack variables or, as they are often called, *surplus variables* are inserted, they must have coefficients of -1, as shown below:

$$\begin{aligned} 4z_1+12z_2+\ 8z_3+5z_4-z_5 \qquad &= 72 \\ 4z_1+\ 9z_2+12z_3+3z_4 \qquad -z_6 &= 60. \end{aligned}$$

The basic solution consisting of surplus variables ($z_5 = -72$; $z_6 = -60$) is not feasible. To get the process started, we simply create artificially an initial basic feasible solution by inserting into each constraint an additional variable with a coefficient of $+1$. The artificial variables resemble the slack variables of the earlier numerical example but, unlike slack variables, they do not have any meaning at all in terms of the original problem. The simplex method now has an initial basis and will shift from basis to basis if given an objective form and proper instructions about minimizing or maximizing. So long as any artificial variable remains at a positive level, we do not have a set of true or admissible variables that forms a basic feasible solution to the original constraints. Thus, the objective has to be minimizing the value of the artificial variables and, if possible, reducing their value to zero. With artificial variables and a new objective form added the Phase I problem is

$$\begin{aligned} 4z_1+12z_2+\ 8z_3+5z_4-z_5 \qquad +z_7 \qquad &= 72 \\ 4z_1+\ 9z_2+12z_3+3z_4 \qquad -z_6 \qquad +z_8 &= 60 \\ z_7+z_8 &= W(\text{min}). \end{aligned}$$

The variables z_7 and z_8 are purely artificial and have no significance whatsoever in terms of the original problem. They will, however, permit the simplex method to be initiated. The new objective form—the original form can be set aside for the present—is called the *infeasibility form* and contains only the artificial variables. By the rules of the simplex method, the artificial variables cannot become negative, so the infeasibility form has a lower limit of zero. If we direct the simplex method to minimize W, it will shift obediently from basis to basis until no further reduction is possible. If the original problem has a basic feasible solution, the minimizing process can never terminate in a value of W greater than zero, since it is not the true minimum. There is always an attainable basic feasible solution in which the artificial variables are all dropped from the basis, become nonbasic variables with zero values, and force W to zero. Since the simplex method always finds an optimal solution whenever one exists, Phase I cannot terminate with $W > 0$ if the original problem has a basic feasible solution.

We can now interpret the possible outcomes. *Phase I terminates with* $W > 0$. Two different conditions may account for the result. The system of equations may be inconsistent and have no solution whatsoever in terms of the true variables. Or the equations may have a solution only if at least one variable is negative. *Phase I terminates with* $W = 0$. Again there are two possibilities. If no artificial variables appear in the basis, the constraints are independent, consistent, and feasible. With redundant but consistent and feasible constraints, there is no square subset capable of being reduced to diagonal form. Phase I terminates in a basis that contains one artificial variable for each redundant equation, but the artificial variables in the basis all have values of zero since the pivot operations in a redundant system reduce the appropriate constants on the right to zero.

When Phase I terminates in a basis containing only admissible variables, the artificial variables can be dropped. The basic variables are eliminated from the true objective form, and Phase II proceeds just as if Phase I had not been necessary. Artificial variables at zero levels in the final basis cannot be dropped. Instead, the rule is to drop every variable, artificial or admissible, whose barred coefficient is positive in the infeasibility form. The reason is that any later increase in these variables above the level of zero would create an infeasible solution. The artificial variables that are retained never rise above zero in Phase II and merely permit the simplex method to be applied to redundant systems of constraints.[11] An alternative possibility is to drop redundant constraints, but there are often compelling practical reasons for not doing so. In fact, several important applications of linear programming, such as transportation and blending problems, typically contain a redundancy in the form of a balancing equation that shows the total to be equal to the sum of its parts. Balancing equations may be conceptually important ingredients of models as well as a check on the accuracy of computations.

For experience readers should carry out the Phase I operation for the numerical example. The first step is to reduce to full canonical form with respect to the artificial variables. In a minimizing problem it is also necessary to remember that the negative coefficient of largest numerical value determines the entering variable.

[11]If a consistent system of equations is not redundant, but does contain square subsets that are redundant, Phase I of the simplex method may terminate at such a basis with artificial variables included at zero levels. However, there will be multiple optima. Inspection of the objective form will show an admissible variable with a zero coefficient that can be introduced. Similarly, Phase I may terminate in a degenerate solution with artificial variables included at zero levels. Again there will be an alternative basis with artificial variables excluded. Although alternative optima exist it may not be worthwhile to instruct a computer to find them. The computer can be programmed instead to follow the general rule of dropping all variables with positive barred coefficients in the infeasibility form.

EXERCISES

1. For a firm with two fixed inputs and four potential outputs, the following table summarizes the technological conditions as the amount of each input required for one unit of each output:

	Output			
Input	*One*	*Two*	*Three*	*Four*
One	3	1	1	3
Two	2	1	2	1

The revenue coefficients for the outputs are $r_1 = 10$, $r_2 = 4$, $r_3 = 5$, and $r_4 = 6$. The available amounts of the inputs are $b_1 = 90$ and $b_2 = 80$. Set up as a linear programming problem and find the optimal solution.

(a) In the optimal solution classify the outputs not produced as relative complements or relative substitutes of the outputs in the basis. Explain the meaning of the distinction.

(b) For each output not produced compute the opportunity cost per unit and compare with its unit revenue. Change the net revenue coefficient of x_3 to $r_3 = 6$. What are the implications of this change?

(c) After restoring r_3 to its original value, change the amount of the second input to $b_2 = 90$. How does this change affect the optimal solution? Explain the economic meaning of the result.

2. For a firm with three fixed inputs and five potential outputs, the following table summarizes the technological conditions as the amount of each input required for one unit of each output:

	Output				
Input	*One*	*Two*	*Three*	*Four*	*Five*
One	3	2	2	6	8
Two	2	2	1	4	4
Three	3	4	3	6	4

The revenue coefficients are $r_1 = 8$, $r_2 = 8$, $r_3 = 6$, $r_4 = 12$, and $r_5 = 8$. The available supplies of the inputs are $b_1 = 60$, $b_2 = 40$, and $b_3 = 80$. Set up as a linear programming problem and find the optimal solution.

(a) In the optimal solution, classify the outputs not produced as relative substitutes, or as relative complements, or as independent, of the outputs in the basis. Explain the meaning of the distinctions.

(b) For each output not produced compute the unit opportunity cost and compare with its unit revenue. Change the revenue coefficient of x_4 to $r_4 = 16$. What are the implications of this change?

3. *The Computational Efficiency of the Simplex Method.*
   (a) In the numerical example of the text treat the first four variables in the constraints and the right-hand side as a system of equations. Show that there can be a solution in which all four variables are positive. How many such solutions are there? What value must the original r_4 coefficient have to make these feasible but nonbasic solutions optimal? How can we always detect the presence of nonbasic optimal solutions?
   (b) Chapter 2 established that the attempt to reduce to diagonal form infallibly reveals redundancy or inconsistency. What is the signal that one or the other is present? Check the third row of Table 3–3 to determine whether any nonbasic variable, together with x_1 and x_2, forms an inconsistent or redundant square subsystem of equations. Explain why the simplex method always passes over such subsets of variables no matter how large their revenue coefficients happen to be.
   (c) Is there any variable in row 3 of Table 3–3 that forms, together with x_1 and x_2, an infeasible square subsystem of equations? State the rule that directs the simplex method past such subsets.
   (d) In Table 3–4 introduce x_4 into the solution and increase it to the maximum permissible level. Calculate the change in total revenue. State the rule that prevents the simplex method from slipping back to a less satisfactory solution than the one just attained.
   (e) Use the evidence of the preceding parts to write an explanation for the computational efficiency of the simplex method.

4. *Special Types of Optimal Solutions*
   (a) By changing only one of the original revenue coefficients make the solution in Table 3–2 optimal. Describe in economic terms the decision that the firm is making. Explain why the change causes it to be optimal.

   By changing only *two* of the original revenue coefficients make the solution in Table 3–3 optimal. Use the preceding economic rationale as a guide.
   (b) By changing the amounts of two inputs make x_1 the only output produced in the optimal solution. Similarly, by changing the amount of one input make x_1 and x_2 the only outputs produced. In each case apply the simplex method to find the optimal solution. What term describes this type of solution.

   Compare the solutions in (a) and (b). What differences are there in the reasons for not producing additional outputs?
   (c) Change the original input coefficients of the second output to $a_{22} = \frac{8}{3}$, $a_{32} = 3$. Find the new optimal solution and compare the successive iterations with the tables in the text. In what two important ways is the new sequence of iterations different from the original sequence? Examine carefully the rules of the simplex method to determine why it may not always make the best choice of variable and may have to correct the choice later. With the input coefficients unaltered what other changes could cause the same set of variables to appear in the optimal solution at the same levels?

5. *Multiple Optima and Degenerate Solutions.*
   (a) For a two-input model of the firm, construct two separate basic feasible solutions that yield the same value of R. Put together into a four-output model of the firm and solve by the simplex method. How many pairs of outputs are there? From the canonical form of the optimal solution determine which pairs constitute feasible optimal solutions, and which

do not. What is the maximum number of outputs that can appear at positive levels in an optimal solution to this problem?

(b) Select one of the basic feasible solutions constructed in (a). Choose another set of four input coefficients to form a redundant square system. Assign revenue coefficients so that the maximum total revenue from either product alone in the redundant system is the same as the total revenue for both products in the selected basic feasible solution. Combine into one model and solve by the simplex method. Write down all basic feasible solutions that are optimal. How many pairs of outputs appear in these optimal solutions? Increase by the same percentage the revenue coefficients for the products in the redundant subsystem. Which of the solutions remain optimal, and what special common property do they possess?

(c) To the *basic feasible solution* chosen for (b) add a product that uses both inputs in the ratio in which they are available. Assign the revenue coefficient that equates the total revenue for this product alone to the total revenue from the remaining two products. Solve by the simplex method and determine all possible basic optimal solutions. What enables you to infer from the optimal solutions that one output has input requirements proportional to the available amounts? What solutions remain optimal when the revenue coefficient of that output increases?

6. Apply *Phase I* of the simplex method to the following numerical examples and find a basic feasible solution if one exists. If you find a basic feasible solution, express the original problem in canonical form with respect to that basis.

(a) The illustrative example in the text. Before beginning, be sure to reduce to full canonical form with respect to the artificial variables.

(b)

$$\begin{aligned} 4z_1 + z_2 + z_3 + 2z_4 &= 8 \\ 4z_1 + 2z_2 + 4z_3 + 4z_4 &= 4 \\ 1z_1 + 3z_2 + 2z_3 + 1z_4 &= C \text{ (min)}. \end{aligned}$$

Convert to the correct initial form and apply Phase I of the simplex method. Write as a square subsystem each of the six pairs formed from the first four variables. Are any of the pairs basic solutions? Basic feasible solutions? Compare with the results of Phase I.

(c) In the preceding example, change the constant in the second row to 8. Apply Phase I and interpret the result.

7. *A Firm with More Inputs than Outputs.*

In the following version of the firm there are four inputs but only two outputs. Introduce slack variables and solve by the simplex method.

$$\begin{aligned} x_1 + x_2 &\leqq 6 \qquad & x_1 + 2x_2 &\leqq 10 \\ 4x_1 + 3x_2 &\leqq 21 \qquad & 5x_1 + 4x_2 &= R(\text{max}). \\ 2x_1 + x_2 &\leqq 10 \end{aligned}$$

In what essential way does this optimal solution differ from the one in the text.

4

Input Prices and the Dual Linear Programming Problem

The optimal solution provides a set of output levels that maximizes revenue. It also determines the precise amount of each input to allocate to each of the products. For the example of Chapter 3 the following table shows the optimal input quotas:

	Output		
Input	*One*	*Two*	*Three*
One	$a_{11}\bar{b}_1(18)$	$a_{12}\bar{b}_2(\ 62)$	$a_{13}\bar{b}_3(4)$
Two	$a_{21}\bar{b}_1(24)$	$a_{22}\bar{b}_2(\ 93)$	$a_{23}\bar{b}_3(2)$
Three	$a_{31}\bar{b}_1(12)$	$a_{32}\bar{b}_2(124)$	$a_{33}\bar{b}_3(4)$

Summing by rows gives the total supply of each input. If the original technological data are correct, and if no errors or chance variations occur in production processes, the foregoing allocation of inputs should permit optimal production levels to be attained.

The preceding solution to the allocation of resources resembles the method followed in wartime or in centrally controlled economies. By one means or another priorities are assigned to industries and scarce resources are allocated to them in accordance with the priorities. The allotment of quotas contrasts with the peacetime method in a free economy, where prices and markets perform the major role in allocating resources. One justification for a price system is that it permits decentralized decision making and does not require a fully worked-out central plan.

A multiproduct, multi-input firm is in many respects a small-scale version of the economy and has to solve a similar problem of allocating resources. In fact, when an economy consists mainly of such firms, the short-run allocation of resources occurs to a large extent within firms, and the guidance of market prices is considerably reduced. In the simplest version of a purely competitive economy, each firm is assumed to produce only one product and not to be able to shift to another. In the short run, when one factor of production is taken as fixed, the problem for the firm is simply *how intensively* to use the fixed input and not *how* to use it in the sense of selecting the products to which it should be allocated. The market price of the single product and the market prices of the variable inputs together determine how much to produce. By contrast, when fixed inputs are trapped within a multiproduct firm in the short run, there are alternative uses for the fixed inputs but no market prices to guide their allocation within the firm. The present chapter explores the possibility of devising a system of internal prices and thus simulating the decentralized decision making of a free economy.

The general role of prices in allocating resources within a free economy should be well known and will be summarized only briefly. For the economy as a whole both input and output prices are free to vary, and determinate levels are established by a balance of economic forces. An excess of the quantity demanded over the quantity offered at a given price raises the price, and a deficiency causes it to fall. With given technology a set of both input and output prices determines what products can be produced at a profit and which incur losses. Products incurring losses are contracted and, if the situation remains unfavorable, are finally dropped from production. Profitable commodities are expanded and take up the resources freed.

In the model of the multiproduct firm under purely competitive conditions, the prices of the outputs are assumed to be constant. What is needed, then, is a set of internal prices for the services of the fixed inputs that will guide management to the most profitable set of products. The word "services" cannot be emphasized too strongly. A firm must decide what it is worth to the firm to have the use of a machine for a specified period of time, not what the machine itself is worth to the firm. Thus, the prices sought are akin to rental prices or leasing prices rather than to purchase prices. The two types of prices are, of course, related by the process of capitalization, but it is the price of the services that is required at present.

The services of the fixed inputs may have market prices, but such prices are not relevant to the decisions of the firm unless it can augment the supply of inputs by either purchase or rental or diminish the supply by sale or lease. However, as will be demonstrated in Chapter 5, the difference between the internal price of an input and the market price is an accurate guide in deciding whether to expand or contract the supply of input services.

THE USE OF PRICES IN THE SIMPLEX METHOD

We shall first introduce internal prices as a convenient practical method for determining whether the present basis is optimal. Later, the broader economic significance will be explored. A simple, direct way of testing for optimality is to choose a set of input prices such that the products currently produced just break even. Management can then use the same prices to calculate unit costs for the products not being produced. If any of these shows an excess of selling price over unit cost, the solution is not optimal.

To find the set of internal prices, we need only translate into equations the foregoing verbal conditions. Since the input requirements are constant it is a simple matter to calculate unit cost once the input prices are given. Let y_1, y_2, and y_3 designate the, as yet unknown, internal prices of the three inputs. Then, $a_{11}y_1$, $a_{21}y_2$, $a_{31}y_3$ designate, respectively, the cost of each input per unit of the first product, and their sum, $a_{11}y_1+a_{21}y_2+a_{31}y_3$, is the unit cost of the first product. With the first three outputs as the basis, the following equations express the equality of unit cost and market price:

$$
\begin{aligned}
a_{11}y_1+a_{21}y_2+a_{31}y_3 &= r_1 \\
a_{12}y_1+a_{22}y_2+a_{32}y_3 &= r_2 \\
a_{13}y_1+a_{23}y_2+a_{33}y_3 &= r_3;
\end{aligned}
$$

$$
\begin{aligned}
3y_1+\ 4y_2+\ 2y_3 &= 6 \\
2y_1+\ 3y_2+\ 4y_3 &= 5 \\
2y_1+\ 1y_2+\ 2y_3 &= 4.
\end{aligned}
$$

When compared with the original problem in Table 3–1, the preceding system consists of what we shall call the vertical equations, since each equation utilizes the coefficients in a column of the original system. If we can reduce the vertical equations to diagonal form, we shall obtain a unique solution and, hence, a unique set of input prices equating market price and unit cost for products in the basis. So long as the original square subset is reducible to diagonal form, the new square subset with rows and columns interchanged will also be reducible to diagonal form.[1] Thus, each basic feasible solution in terms of outputs implies a unique set of input prices.

[1] A square subset can always be reduced to diagonal form if no row is a linear combination of the remaining rows and if no column is a linear combination of the remaining columns. Reduction to diagonal form with respect to x_1, x_2, and x_3 proves that neither of these linear combinations is present. When rows become columns and columns become rows for the input price equations, neither type of linear combination can be present.

The solution to the vertical or price equations is ($y_1 = \frac{11}{7}$; $y_2 = \frac{1}{7}$; $y_3 = \frac{5}{14}$). The total value of input services is

$$V = y_1 b_1 + y_2 b_2 + y_3 b_3 = (\tfrac{11}{7})84 + (\tfrac{1}{7})119 + (\tfrac{5}{14})140 = 199.$$

Unit cost having been equated to price for products in the basis, the only ones that yield revenue, total revenue R and the total value of input services V must be equal. When the focus is upon decision making by the firm, the term *internal price* is descriptive and appropriate. The broader economic term is *imputed input price*. The demand for inputs is derived from the demand for outputs, and the total value of inputs to the firm is measured by the total value of the products they produce. The total value of the outputs is transferred or imputed to the inputs, and the value assigned to a unit of an input is called the imputed input price. In the present model only the three fixed inputs contribute productive services, so it is in accord with economic theory that the total value of the products be imputed to these three inputs. For each product, produced or not, the unit cost based on the imputed input prices will be called the *imputed unit cost*.

The internal or imputed input prices provide a test for profitability of products not being produced. For the fourth and fifth outputs the differences between selling price and imputed unit cost are

$$r_4 - [a_{14}y_1 + a_{24}y_2 + a_{34}y_3]$$
$$2 - [\tfrac{3}{2}(\tfrac{11}{7}) + 1(\tfrac{1}{7}) + 1(\tfrac{5}{14})] = 2 - \tfrac{20}{7} = -\tfrac{6}{7}$$

and

$$r_5 - [a_{15}y_1 + a_{25}y_2 + a_{35}y_3]$$
$$5 - [4(\tfrac{11}{7}) + 6(\tfrac{1}{7}) + 1(\tfrac{5}{14})] = 5 - \tfrac{105}{14} = -\tfrac{5}{2}.$$

These are precisely the values for $\bar{r}_4$ and $\bar{r}_5$ in Table 3–4. In Chapter 3 the $\bar{r}$ coefficients were interpreted as the excess of selling price over unit opportunity cost. It is intuitively plausible that the opportunity cost per unit and the imputed unit cost be equal, and a simple algebraic proof buttresses intuition.

To find the opportunity cost in Chapter 3, we first solved, on page 43, the following equations for output changes.

$$a_{11}\,\Delta x_1 + a_{12}\,\Delta x_2 + a_{13}\,\Delta x_3 = -a_{14}\,\Delta x_4$$
$$a_{21}\,\Delta x_1 + a_{22}\,\Delta x_2 + a_{23}\,\Delta x_3 = -a_{24}\,\Delta x_4$$
$$a_{31}\,\Delta x_1 + a_{32}\,\Delta x_2 + a_{33}\,\Delta x_3 = -a_{34}\,\Delta x_4.$$

The solution shows how each basic variable responds to a change in the non-basic variable x_4, specifically:

$$\Delta x_1 = -\bar{a}_{14}\,\Delta x_4; \qquad \Delta x_2 = -\bar{a}_{24}\,\Delta x_4; \qquad \Delta x_3 = -\bar{a}_{34}\,\Delta x_4.$$

We now multiply both sides of each equation by y_1, y_2, and y_3, respectively, and then add the equations. The left-hand side becomes:

$$(y_1a_{11}+y_2a_{21}+y_3a_{31})\ \Delta x_1+(y_1a_{12}+y_2a_{22}+y_3a_{32})\ \Delta x_2+(y_1a_{13}+y_2a_{23}+y_3a_{33})\ \Delta x_3.$$

But the expressions in parentheses are the imputed unit costs of the products in the basis and are, by the vertical equations, equal to r_1, r_2, and r_3, respectively. Hence, multiplying the equations for output changes by the y's and then adding yields the following single equation:

$$r_1\ \Delta x_1+r_2\ \Delta x_2+r_3\ \Delta x_3 = -(a_{14}y_1+a_{24}y_2+a_{34}y_3)\ \Delta x_4.$$

Finally, we may eliminate Δx_1, Δx_2, and Δx_3 by using the previously obtained solutions. The result is

$$-r_1\bar{a}_{14}\ \Delta x_4-r_2\bar{a}_{24}\ \Delta x_4-r_3\bar{a}_{34}\ \Delta x_4 = -(a_{14}y_1+a_{24}y_2+a_{34}y_3)\ \Delta x_4.$$

Cancelling Δx_4 from both sides and changing signs gives the desired equality of unit opportunity cost and unit imputed cost:

$$r_1\bar{a}_{14}+r_2\bar{a}_{24}+r_3\bar{a}_{34} = a_{14}y_1+a_{24}y_2+a_{34}y_3.$$

There are, thus, two equivalent ways of testing the profitability of nonbasic products, each algebraically valid and economically sound.

Solving the vertical equations for a new set of variables is an algebraic method applicable to any linear programming problem. Nonetheless, the economic example provides such an apt interpretation of the y's that their designation as "prices" has become almost standard in linear programming and is used even when the relevance is remote. The other general term for the y's is *multipliers.*

The two methods of calculating $\bar{r}$ coefficients have been given plausible economic interpretations for products, but the same computations must also be applied to the slack variables as well as to all variables in problems with no economic interpretation. For any variable x_j, $\bar{r}_j$ may be calculated in either of the following equivalent ways:

$$\bar{r}_j = r_j-(r_1\bar{a}_{1j}+r_2\bar{a}_{2j}+r_3\bar{a}_{3j}) = r_j-(a_{1j}y_1+a_{2j}y_2+a_{3j}y_3),$$

where the basis is (x_1, x_2, x_3) and (y_1, y_2, y_3) are the solutions to the vertical equations for the basis.

When a slack variable appears in the basic feasible solution—as, for example, x_8 in Table 3–3—its $\bar{r}$ coefficient in terms of prices is

$$\bar{r}_8 = r_8-(a_{18}y_1+a_{28}y_2+a_{38}y_3) = 0-0y_1-0y_2-1y_3 = 0,$$

or

$$y_3 = 0.$$

If a solution contains a slack variable, an input is not being fully utilized. Since the amount of each input is a constant, the supply curve is a vertical line. With the amount demanded falling short of the amount supplied at every positive price, it is consistent with economic theory that the price fall to zero.

For a slack variable not in the basis, such as x_6 in Table 3–4, the $\bar{r}$ coefficient in terms of prices is

$$\begin{aligned}\bar{r}_6 &= r_6 - (a_{16}y_1 + a_{26}y_2 + a_{36}y_3) \\ &= 0 - (\ 1y_1 + \ 0y_2 + \ 0y_3) = -y_1 = -\tfrac{11}{7}.\end{aligned}$$

Similarly, $\bar{r}_7 = -y_2 = -\frac{1}{7}$ and $\bar{r}_8 = -y_3 = -\frac{5}{14}$, as can be verified by checking the previously derived solutions to the vertical equations against the $\bar{r}$ coefficients in Table 3–4. The result is a computational bonanza. The elementary operations that reduce the system to canonical form, when applied to the slack variables, also yield the correct set of input prices. To take advantage of this windfall, a second version of the simplex method has been devised, called the *revised simplex method* or the *simplex method with multipliers*.

With the introduction of input prices, we can give a somewhat different economic rationale for the application of the simplex method to the multiproduct firm. The management first selects a set of outputs satisfying the constraints. The revenue from these products is imputed to the inputs by choosing input prices such that the total value of input services V equals total revenue R. Products not currently produced are tested for profitability by comparing the market price with the unit cost based on the imputed input prices. The product with the largest excess of market price over imputed unit cost is brought into production, raising R and generating a new set of input prices that cause V to increase by the same amount as R. The objective of management can be restated as seeking to maximize the value of the input services and, hence, of the inputs themselves. In any economic model of the firm, inputs have their greatest value when employed in the most profitable way, so the search for the most profitable set of products raises the value of inputs, but not necessarily by the same amount as total revenue. It is a special feature of linear models and of all other models with constant returns to scale that the total value of input services always equals the total value of outputs.

The computational process simulates partially the competitive process in the economy. With fixed supplies of inputs and constant prices in output markets, a group of competitive firms would tend to bid up input prices until all excess of selling price over unit cost is squeezed out. Suppose that there are firms outside the group, perhaps newly formed, that can use the same inputs to produce different products. If these firms have products that are profitable at the prevailing level of input prices, they will expand, bid away inputs, and cause a generally higher level of input prices. There are, however, various special and artificial aspects of the computational process. The number of outputs produced is restricted to no more than the number of fixed inputs. Unit cost does not vary with the level of output. Both special features are a direct consequence of the linear technology. A further difficulty shows up in Table 3–3, where $\bar{r}_6 = -y_1 = 2$, or $y_1 = -2$. An imputed input price, unlike a market price, can be negative in a nonoptimal solution. For an optimal solution no $\bar{r}$ coefficients can be positive and no input price negative, so long as slack variables are present. In the absence of slack, when the original constraint is an equation and the entire supply of an input must be used, the imputed price may become negative in an optimal solution. Chapter 5 provides the economic interpretation.

THE DUAL LINEAR PROGRAMMING PROBLEM

We have now found a useful but secondary role for input prices in allocating fixed resources within a firm. To obtain prices for inputs the management must first find a basic feasible set of outputs. It can then calculate the imputed unit cost for products not being produced and determine whether any are worth producing. For prices to play a major role in the allocative process, they must be the sole guide in determining how much of each output to produce and how much of each input to devote to each of the outputs. There must also be some criterion for evaluating different sets of input prices and determining whether the present set of prices can be replaced by a better set. The dual linear programming problem for the multiproduct firm fits these general requirements.

To any linear programming problem there corresponds a second problem, its dual, which is constructed from the latent symmetries in the original problem. The most important symmetry has already been used; the coefficients in the columns of any linear program can be combined with a new set of variables to form a system of vertical equations or inequalities, which constitute the constraints of the dual. In contrast to the dual, the original problem is called the *primal linear programming problem* or *primal*, for short. The preceding discussion on input prices for the primal provides economic insight into the constraints of the dual. Each basic feasible solution of the primal generates a set of input prices, but the set is not optimal if any product has a market price in excess of its imputed unit cost. In allocating inputs by the use of internal prices there is no point in considering a set of prices that leads to a nonoptimal production plan. A set of prices is acceptable, then, only if unit cost equals or exceeds price for every product. For product one the requisite condition is

$$r_1-(a_{11}y_1+a_{21}y_2+a_{31}y_3) \leqq 0$$

or

$$r_1 \leqq a_{11}y_1+a_{21}y_2+a_{31}y_3.$$

A similar inequality holds for every other product. With sides interchanged these inequalities are the constraints of the dual shown in Table 4–1.

The objective form for the dual is found by symmetry. The coefficients in the objective form of the primal become the constants on the right in the constraints of the dual. Hence, the constants on the right in the primal become the coefficients in the objective form of the dual. For the model of the multiproduct firm the objective variable in the dual is the value of inputs. What is hard to explain on economic grounds is why any firm would wish to minimize the value of the inputs it owns. Further consideration will be given later to the economic meaning of this requirement. Mathematically, minimizing the objective form is unavoidable, or the dual would be unbounded. Any solution that satisfies the constraints would still satisfy the constraints after multiplication by any positive constant, however large. Since the constants on the right in the primal are, by convention, nonnegative, the objective form of the dual, having nonnegative coefficients, would increase without limit.

TABLE 4–1

The Dual of the Multiproduct Firm

$$\begin{aligned}
a_{11}y_1+a_{21}y_2+a_{31}y_3 &\geqq r_1\\
a_{12}y_1+a_{22}y_2+a_{32}y_3 &\geqq r_2\\
a_{13}y_1+a_{23}y_2+a_{33}y_3 &\geqq r_3\\
a_{14}y_1+a_{24}y_2+a_{34}y_3 &\geqq r_4\\
a_{15}y_1+a_{25}y_2+a_{35}y_3 &\geqq r_5\\
b_1y_1+b_2y_2+b_3y_3 &= V(\min)
\end{aligned}$$

Primal and dual linear programming problems are related to each other by the following operations: (1) interchange rows and columns of coefficients in the constraints; (2) reverse the direction of inequalities in the constraints; (3) interchange the constants on the right and the coefficients in the objective form; and (4) reverse the direction of optimization. Apply these operations to the dual in Table 4–1 and the result is the primal in inequality form.[2]

[2]The relationships between primal and dual stand out most clearly when both sets of constraints are inequalities. Note that the vertical inequalities for the slack variables of the primal do not need to appear explicitly as constraints in the dual. The inequalities

$$\bar{r}_6 = -y_1 \leqq 0; \qquad \bar{r}_7 = -y_2 \leqq 0; \qquad \bar{r}_8 = -y_3 \leqq 0$$

simply state that the dual variables must be nonnegative.

Thus, linear programming problems always come in pairs. The coefficients and constants of any one problem, when symmetrically rearranged, form the other member of the pair. If one problem is called the primal, the other is its dual. There is no rule for determining which problem is to be the primal.[3] In particular fields of application, the primal is likely to be the problem that was formulated first or the problem that bears a more direct and natural relation to the subject matter.

The dual to the numerical example of Chapter 3 is shown in Table 4–2. Slack, or better, surplus variables are appended to convert the inequalities to equations. Since the left-hand side can exceed the constant on the right, equality can be guaranteed only by subtracting a positive quantity. In economic terms, the surplus variables can, perhaps, be best defined as subsidies. If the unit cost on the left exceeds the market price on the right, the surplus variables represents the amount of the subsidy required for the product to break even. We may add it to the market price or, as is done in the dual, subtract it from the unit cost.

TABLE 4–2

The Dual to the Numerical Example

$$
\begin{array}{llllll}
3y_1+4y_2+2y_3-y_4 & & & & & = 6 \\
2y_1+3y_2+4y_3 & -y_5 & & & & = 5 \\
2y_1+1y_2+2y_3 & & -y_6 & & & = 4 \\
\tfrac{3}{2}y_1+1y_2+1y_3 & & & -y_7 & & = 2 \\
4y_1+6y_2+1y_3 & & & & -y_8 & = 5 \\
84y_1+119y_2+140y_3 & & & & & = V(\min)
\end{array}
$$

The main consequence of negative coefficients for the surplus variables is the absence of an obvious initial basic feasible solution. For practice, readers may add artificial variables and initiate Phase I of the simplex method. An easier way out is to exploit a special feature of the present problem, namely, the presence of at least one column with positive coefficients only. The variable corresponding to such a column and the requisite number of surplus variables always form a basic feasible solution. For simplicity choose y_1 and raise it to a level such that unit cost equals market price for at least one output. Since unit cost can exceed market price in each constraint but not fall short of it, the highest rather than the lowest value must be found for y_1. Setting all other variables at zero and solving each equation

[3]In the early development of linear programming, the primal was identified as a minimizing problem with $\geqq$ constraints and the dual as a maximizing problem with $\leqq$ constraints. Some authors still retain this convention, but there is no longer any consensus, and the likelihood of consensus diminishes as the number of applications increases.

for y_1 shows that $y_1 = \frac{5}{2}$ in the second equation is the largest value. A pivot operation on y_1 in the second row gives the basic feasible solution in Table 4–3. As readers may verify, the pivot operation turns all constants negative except in the second row. Changing all signs in these constraints brings the four surplus variables into the basis at positive levels. The system can be rearranged to show the basic variables in natural order along the diagonal, but there is no need to do so.

TABLE 4–3

The Initial Basic Feasible Solution to the Dual

$$
\begin{array}{cccccccccc}
 & +\frac{1}{2}y_2 & +\ 4y_3 & +y_4 & -\ \frac{3}{2}y_5 & & & & = & \frac{3}{2} \\
y_1 & +\frac{3}{2}y_2 & +\ 2y_3 & & -\ \frac{1}{2}y_5 & & & & = & \frac{5}{2} \\
 & +2y_2 & +\ 2y_3 & & -\ 1y_5 & +y_6 & & & = & 1 \\
 & +\frac{5}{4}y_2 & +\ 2y_3 & & -\ \frac{3}{4}y_5 & & +y_7 & & = & \frac{7}{4} \\
 & +0y_2 & +\ 7y_3 & & -\ 2y_5 & & & +y_8 & = & 5 \\
 & -7y_2 & -28y_3 & & +42y_5 & & & & = & V-210 \\
* & & & * & & * & * & * & &
\end{array}
$$

Once any linear programming problem has been displayed in canonical form, the repetitive computational process, or *simplex algorithm*, takes over. Since the aim is minimization, the entering variable must have a negative coefficient of largest numerical size in the objective form. Anyone who prefers a single rule for selecting the new variable may simply change all signs in the original objective form and maximize. The next step is to bring in y_3, select the positive coefficients in its column, and determine the pivot by the rule of minimum ratio. The use of the maximum ratio in Table 4–2 was an improvised device for getting an initial basic feasible solution. Once it is found, the standard rule applies. Readers should carry out the remaining iterations to the optimum to be shown in Table 4–4.

The economic implications of the solution in Table 4–3 deserve some comment. The first input has a price of $\frac{5}{2}$ but the other two input prices, being nonbasic variables, are zero. Each row and each surplus variable corresponds to a product. Since $y_5 = 0$, the second product breaks even but all others require subsidies of the indicated amounts. For further insight into the economic meaning of the solution we need the vertical equations for the columns in the basis. The existence of such vertical equations depends on the mathematical structure of the problem and not on its being a primal or dual. In fact, each problem is the dual of the other, so the distinction cannot be crucial. Any basis has as many columns as rows and generates two square systems of equations. If one is uniquely solvable, so is the other. The columns in the basis are (1, 4, 6, 7, 8), and the original coefficients of Table 4–2 yield the following vertical equations:

$$
\begin{aligned}
3x_1+2x_2+2x_3+\tfrac{3}{2}x_4+4x_5 &= 84 \\
-x_1 &= 0 \\
-x_3 &= 0 \\
-x_4 &= 0 \\
-x_5 &= 0.
\end{aligned}
$$

The first equation in symbolic form is

$$a_{11}x_1+a_{12}x_2+a_{13}x_3+a_{14}x_4+a_{15}x_5 = b_1.$$

The meaning of the equation is that the first constraint in the primal must be satisfied with equality. Each dual variable, if it is not a surplus variable, corresponds to a row or constraint in the primal. When a variable appears in a basic feasible solution for the dual, the corresponding constraint in the primal is satisfied with equality. For the multiproduct firm the implication is that output levels have been chosen in such a way as to use fully the available supply of the designated input. Each surplus variable corresponds to a row in the dual and, hence, to a column or variable in the primal. Since surplus variables have zero coefficients in the dual objective form, the appearance of a surplus variable in a basic feasible solution implies a zero value for the corresponding variable of the primal. For the multiproduct firm dual variables are subsidies, so the economic implication is that the corresponding product incurs a loss, requires a subsidy, and is not produced.

By way of the vertical equations, the preceding basic feasible solution for the dual implies the following set of output levels: ($x_2 = 42$; $x_1 = x_3 = x_4 = x_5 = 0$). Four of the outputs require subsidies and are not produced. The second product is produced to the limit of the available supply of the first input, without regard for the supplies of the other inputs. To produce 42 units of x_2 requires 126 and 168 units, respectively, of the second and third inputs, but the available supplies are only 119 and 140 units. Except for sign the excess demand for the inputs is equal to the barred coefficients of y_1 and y_2 in the objective form of Table 4–3. The result must always hold, as we shall now prove.

For the primal there are two equivalent ways of deriving the barred coefficients in the objective function: reduction to canonical form and the use of multipliers determined by the vertical equations. The equivalence of the two methods depends on the mathematical structure of the problem, not its economic content, and holds for any linear programming problem. By symmetry, the second barred coefficient, expressed in terms of multipliers, must be

$$\begin{aligned}\bar{b}_2 &= b_2-(a_{21}x_1+a_{22}x_2+a_{23}x_3+a_{24}x_4+a_{25}x_5)\\ &= 119-(\ 0\ +3(42)+\ 0\ +\ 0\ +\ 0\ ) = -7.\end{aligned}$$

For $\bar{b}_3$ a similar formula holds.[4] Since the expression in parentheses is the amount required by the production plan, $\bar{b}_2$ measures the excess of supply over demand for the second input. The negative sign means that excess supply is negative or that demand exceeds supply.

Figure 4–1 shows the situation in graphical form. Pending the derivation of the actual demand curves in Chapter 5, we are using downward-sloping straight lines to portray the demand for inputs. It is the intersections that matter and not the shapes of the curves. Fixed amounts of the inputs imply the vertical supply curves in the graphs. The demand curve for the first input intersects the supply curve at $y_1 = \frac{5}{2}$, determining $y_1 b_1 = V = 210$. The remaining inputs, whose prices are zero, have the indicated amounts of excess demand or negative excess supply.

When the formula for a barred objective coefficient is applied to any surplus variable, such as y_4, the result is

$$\bar{b}_4 = 0-(-1x_1+0x_2+0x_3+0x_4+0x_5) = x_1.$$

For every surplus variable, whether in the basis or not, the barred objective coefficient equals the implied production level of the corresponding output. In the numerical example, $\bar{b}_5 = x_2 = 42$. When a surplus variable appears in the basic feasible solution, the barred coefficient and the corresponding output level must be zero. If the surplus variable is positive, we can say that the product requires a subsidy and is not produced. However, the solution may be degenerate with the surplus variable equal to zero. Products are not necessarily produced if they do not require a subsidy.[5]

A nonoptimal solution of the dual can occur in two ways. The coefficient of an input price may be negative, indicating that the production plan requires more of the input than is available. Or the coefficient of a surplus variable may be negative, implying a negative output level. In either case the proposed production plan cannot be a feasible solution to the primal. The conclusion applies to all linear programming problems: a solution to the dual that is not optimal implies a solution to the primal that is not feasible, and vice versa.

[4]Clearly $\bar{b}_2$ and $\bar{b}_3$ in the dual, which measure excess supplies of inputs, are not the same as $\bar{b}_2$ and $\bar{b}_3$ in the primal, which represent output levels. In both cases the bars simply indicate the effects of the particular computations needed to reduce the system to canonical form for a given basis.

[5]A degenerate optimal solution to the dual implies multiple optima in the primal. There are at least two equally good production plans, but the dual happens to settle on one of them.

Briefly summarized, the solution in Table 4–3 has the following economic implications. One input price is set at a positive level and the rest at zero. Demand equals supply for the input at the positive price and exceeds it for the others. Only one product breaks even and the rest require subsidies. Higher input prices are needed to eliminate excess demand, but at the same time unit cost must be lowered to permit more products to break even. Both of these seemingly irreconcilable objectives are attained by the next iteration of the simplex method. The variable chosen for entry into the basis, y_3, has the largest excess of demand over supply or the negative coefficient of greatest numerical value in the objective form. Bringing y_3 into the basis means raising the price of the third input above its zero level. As readers may verify, the rule of minimum ratio brings y_3 into the basis in the first row at a level of $\frac{3}{8}$. The subsequent pivot operation reduces y_1 from $\frac{5}{2}$ to $\frac{7}{4}$. The new value of V is $\frac{7}{4}(84)+\frac{3}{8}(140) = 199.5$, a reduction from the previous level of 210. Raising y_3 lowers the value of inputs because it causes a large decline in y_1. In Figure 4–1, the rise in y_3 to $\frac{3}{8}$ to eliminate excess demand causes a downward shift in the demand curve for y_1. The price of the first input adjusts sufficiently to keep excess demand at zero ($\bar{b}_1$ remains at zero). The decline in y_1 more than offsets the rise in y_3, so V is smaller.

The unit cost of x_1 declines from $3(\frac{5}{2})+4(0)+2(0) = 7.5$ to $3(\frac{7}{4})+4(0)$

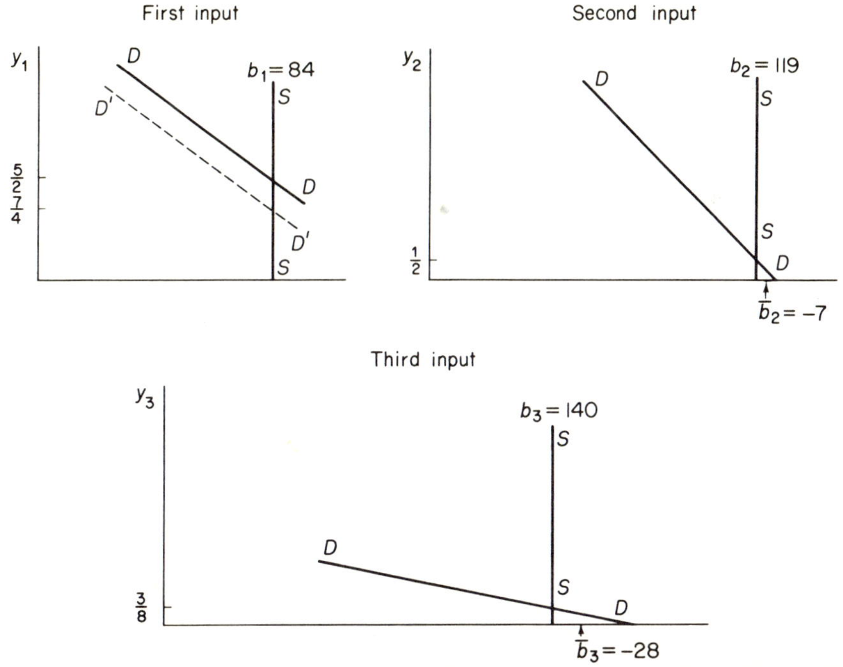

Fig. 4-1 Demand and Supply Curves for Inputs in the Dual

$+2(\frac{3}{8}) = 6$, which equals the revenue coefficient for x_1. Alternatively, y_3 enters in the first row, displacing y_4, which is the subsidy for x_1. Since the first product now breaks even, it can be produced. Because of the constraints of the dual no product can ever do better than break even. The levels of x_1 and x_2 are adjusted to utilize fully the available supplies of both the first and third inputs.

By symmetry with the primal, $\bar{b}_3$ must measure the net rate at which V changes with respect to y_3. The value of $\bar{b}_3$ is (-28) and y_3 is raised to the level of $\frac{3}{8}$, implying the correct reduction of 10.5 in V. Exercise 7 at the end of the chapter confirms this result and provides economic and mathematical insight into why it must hold.

After y_3 enters the basis, the demand for the second input is still excessive. The final step of introducing y_2 gives the optimal solution of Table 4–4. Since there are no negative coefficients in the dual objective form, there are no excess demands for inputs or negative output levels. The optimal solution to the dual provides a production plan that is a feasible solution to the primal.

TABLE 4–4

The Optimal Solution to the Dual[a]

$$
\begin{array}{lllllllll}
y_1 & & & -\frac{1}{7}y_4 & +\frac{3}{7}y_5 & -\frac{5}{7}y_6 & & & = \frac{11}{7} \\
& y_2 & & -\frac{2}{7}y_4 & -\frac{1}{7}y_5 & +\frac{4}{7}y_6 & & & = \frac{1}{7} \\
& & y_3 & +\frac{2}{7}y_4 & -\frac{5}{14}y_5 & -\frac{1}{14}y_6 & & & = \frac{5}{14} \\
& & & -\frac{3}{14}y_4 & +\frac{1}{7}y_5 & -\frac{4}{7}y_6 & +y_7 & & = \frac{6}{7} \\
& & & -2y_4 & +\frac{1}{2}y_5 & +\frac{1}{2}y_6 & & +y_8 & = \frac{5}{2} \\
& & & 6y_4 & +31y_5 & +2y_6 & & & = V-199
\end{array}
$$

[a]For a clearer presentation the first three rows have been reshuffled to put y_1, y_2, and y_3 in order on the diagonal. This can be done without destroying any correspondences between primal and dual.

Not only does the optimal solution to the dual provide a feasible solution to the primal but, as Table 4–4 shows, it provides the optimal solution. The coefficients of the surplus variables in the objective form are identical with the optimal production levels found in Chapter 3. The constraints of the dual admit a set of input prices only if the resultant unit cost equals or exceeds price for every product. A feasible but nonoptimal solution to the primal is characterized by an excess of market price over imputed unit cost for at least one product. Hence, no set of prices corresponding to a feasible but nonoptimal solution of the primal could ever show up as a basic feasible solution to the dual. Two possibilities remain: (1) sets of prices corresponding to infeasible solutions of the primal, in which either input constraints are violated or output levels are negative; and (2) the set of prices determined by the optimal solution to the primal. By disposing of negative coefficients in the objective form, the simplex method systematically eliminates all sets of prices implying infeasible solutions of the primal. Hence, if the dual reaches an optimal solution, the corresponding output levels must be the optimal solution to the primal. The only alternative to the existence of an optimal solution is that, at some iteration, there are no positive $\bar{a}$ coefficients in the column of the entering variable and V takes off toward $-\infty$. Since only the optimal solution to the dual satisfies the constraints of the primal, an unbounded solution to the dual is clear proof that the primal has no feasible solution. Conversely, the existence of any feasible solution to the primal, even an all-slack solution, proves that the dual cannot be unbounded.

The relationships between the primal and dual are vitally important in the theory of linear programming. Both the statement and the proof of the fundamental theorems rely on simultaneous consideration of the two problems. The discussion in the preceding paragraph relating optimality of the dual to feasibility of the primal can be restated formally as one of the most important theorems of linear programming: If both the primal and dual linear programming problems have feasible solutions, both have optimal solutions, and the optimal values of the two objective variables will be equal.

A simple diagram can be used to clarify the theorem and the method of proof. For each basic feasible solution of the primal there is a set of input prices such that the value of inputs equals total revenue, $V_p = R_p$. The subscripts denote primal. Similarly, each basic feasible solution of the dual implies a set of outputs such that total revenue equals value of inputs, $R_d = V_d$. The reason is that the only products produced are those for which unit cost equals market price. In the primal both R_p and V_p rise toward a maximum and in the dual both V_d and R_d decline toward a minimum, as shown below:

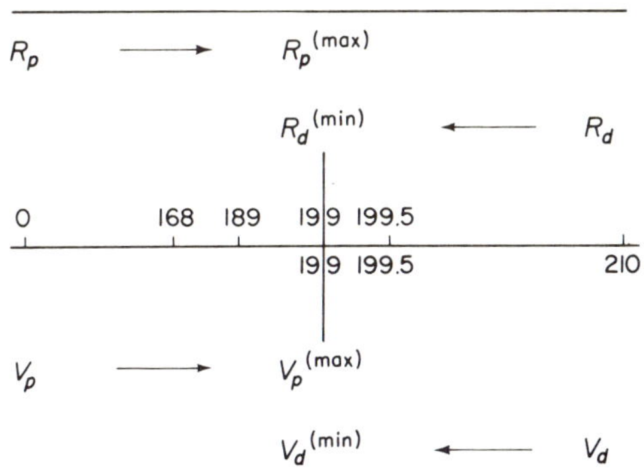

The distances indicate relative size but not exact size of the solutions to the primal and dual. For each solution of the primal and the dual there is a set of outputs and a set of input prices. The primal converges on the optimum from below and the dual from above. The minimum value of V_d cannot be less than the maximum value of V_p, and the maximum value of

R_p cannot be greater than the minimum value of R_d, so all four must be equal.[6] Since any feasible but nonoptimal solution of the primal has a V_p less than the maximum V_p and the minimum V_d, its very existence proves that V_d cannot decrease without limit and must have an optimal solution, provided that a basic feasible solution to the dual can be found that will get the simplex method started. Since feasibility for one problem prevents unboundedness in the other problem, the feasibility of both problems insures that the simplex method can get started and must terminate in an optimal solution.

Certain symmetries exist between the optimal solutions to the primal and the dual that have a plausible economic meaning. When a surplus variable appears in the dual at a positive level, the corresponding product incurs a loss and is not produced. In Table 4–4, for example, $y_7 = \frac{6}{7}$, $y_8 = \frac{5}{2}$, and $x_4 = x_5 = 0$. Although the present example does not show it, a symmetrical result holds for slack variables in the primal. If a slack variable appears in the primal at a positive level, the corresponding input is in excess supply and has a zero price in the solution to the dual. The preceding relations have plausible economic interpretations but they are also of fundamental importance to the theory of linear programming, since they hold if and only if the primal and dual solutions are optimal. Thus, necessary and sufficient conditions for a pair of solutions to be optimal are as follows: Whenever a surplus variable appears at a positive level in the dual, the corresponding primal variable must be zero; whenever a slack variable appears at a positive level in the primal, the corresponding dual variable must be zero.

THE PRIMAL AND DUAL AS MARKET PROCESSES

In economics the equilibrium of a market is portrayed by the intersection of a supply curve and a demand curve. At the equilibrium price the quantity sellers wish to supply equals the amount buyers wish to purchase. The equality of supply and demand does not, however, explain how the equilibrium price came to be established nor how it will vary when conditions change. What is needed is some dynamic process that shows how price and quantity change over time when not in equilibrium. The two most widely used market processes trace back to two famous economists, who were contemporaries in the latter half of the nineteenth century. The Walrasian

[6]The reason why minimum V_d cannot be less than maximum V_p is the ability of the simplex method to find an optimum if one exists. The optimal solution of the dual satisfies the constraints of the primal and yields negative or zero $\bar{r}$ coefficients for all products—imputed unit cost equals or exceeds price. But so does the optimal solution to the primal. If the minimum V_d of the optimal solution to the dual is less than the maximum V_p, the simplex method applied to the primal could terminate at the first of these solutions with no way of getting to the true maximum. This is impossible. A similar argument rejects a maximum of R_p greater than a minimum of R_d, so equality is the only possibility.

process, named after Léon Walras, attributes changes in price to differences between the quantity sellers wish to supply and the quantity buyers wish to purchase. At a price below the equilibrium level, as shown by the dotted line in Figure 4–2, the quantity demanded exceeds the quantity supplied and exerts an upward pressure on the price. Conversely, above the equilibrium level there is excess supply, exerting a downward pressure. The upward or downward pressure continues, but with diminishing magnitude, until the equilibrium is reached.

In his alternative process Alfred Marshall emphasized the vertical rather than the horizontal difference between supply and demand curves. The supply curve shows the minimum price at which sellers will offer the given quantity, and the demand curve indicates the maximum price buyers are willing to pay. In the Marshallian process output expands whenever the demand price exceeds the supply price, as along the dashed line in Figure 4–2, and output contracts whenever the supply price is greater. As the amount supplied approaches the intersection of the curves the pressure diminishes and finally ceases.

For the multiproduct firm the dual resembles a Walrasian process in the markets for inputs. So long as excess demand exists, the simplex method continues to select an input price and raise it to the level that eliminates excess demand. As each new input price is raised above zero, the prices remaining in the basis are adjusted to keep demand equal to supply; the $\bar{b}$ coefficients remain at zero. The process continues until it finds a set of prices that eliminates positive excess demand for all inputs. Where there is negative excess demand, or excess supply, the input receives a zero price.

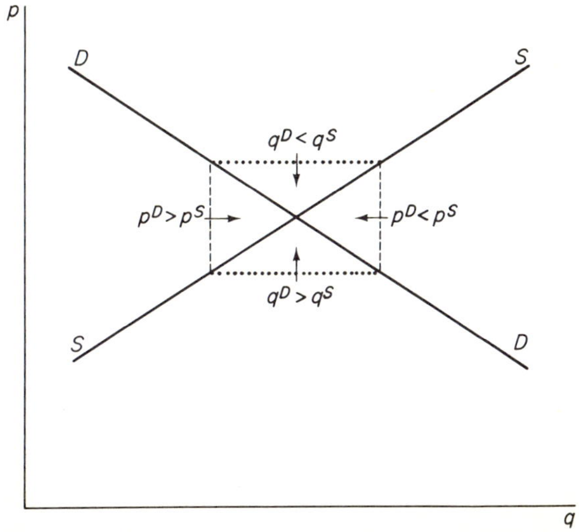

Fig. 4-2 Walrasian and Marshallian Market Processes

Thus, the dual terminates in a set of prices that reduces to zero the value of excess demand for every input. A Walrasian process operating in a set of markets produces the same result. Prices continue to change so long as any excess demand or excess supply is present, except when excess supply exists at a zero price. Being a computational process, the dual has special features that are not likely to be present in market processes. But both the dual linear programming problem and the market mechanism are similar in principle and achieve the same result, reducing to zero the value of excess demand for every input.

The primal linear programming problem for a multiproduct firm resembles a Marshallian process in the market for outputs. The opportunity cost per unit or its equivalent, the unit imputed cost, is the minimum price at which the firm is willing to supply a product. If the market or demand price exceeds the supply price, the firm expands output until the limit of capacity is reached and the unit imputed cost rises into equality with the market price. There are again special features attributable to the linear technology and the computational requirements, but the primal operates on essentially the same principle as a Marshallian process and attains the same result.

In the present version of a multiproduct firm, output prices and input quantities are fixed. For the economic system as a whole all quantities and all prices are, in general, free to vary. Thus, the multiproduct firm operates under simplified conditions and has to solve only part of the allocative problem. For this reason it provides an excellent starting point in analyzing the allocative mechanism for the economy as a whole. The chief analytic devices for explaining allocation within the economy are supply and demand curves. In Chapter 5 we shall apply linear programming techniques to the derivation of the firm's supply curves for outputs and demand curves for inputs.

For the present we have assumed only a general familiarity with the market mechanism and have demonstrated that the primal and dual linear programming problems are solved by analogous processes. But this is only half of the story. The theory of linear programming proves that the final solution to the dual implies an optimal solution to the primal. For the multiproduct firm we know what the primal problem is, the maximization of revenue. Also, the primal can be solved independently of the dual, so the final solution to the dual simply provides alternative conditions for an optimal solution to the primal. Consider, instead, the economic system under pure competition. There is no agency like the management of a multiproduct firm that seeks to allocate resources directly by solving the primal problem. There are only individual consuming and producing units linked together by the market mechanism. Further, it isn't even clear what the primal problem is. Is there any objective function that the economic system succeeds in maximizing, not by conscious direction but by the independent decisions of many individuals? What we have in the market system is a dual process that converges toward a solution in which the value of excess demand is zero in every market. Thus, the market mechanism solves the dual problem and is, in effect, a dual in search of a primal. In later chapters we shall use an expanded version of a multiproduct firm to show by analogy what primal optimizing problem the dual market process succeeds in solving.

THE DUAL AND DECENTRALIZED DECISION MAKING

For the purpose of relating allocation within the firm to allocation within the economy, or vice versa, the dual is of fundamental importance. Earlier in the chapter we raised another possibility, the use of internal prices as a practical method of decentralized decision making within the firm. The top management chooses a set of prices for the services of fixed inputs. The manager of each producing division can use whatever amount he wishes but must charge the amount used into costs at the internal price. Products are not produced if they show imputed unit cost in excess of selling price. Internal prices must be varied if the amount demanded does not equal the fixed supply.

When we view the dual as a process or a trial-and-error method of finding the optimal set of prices, serious difficulties arise. Despite the mathematical symmetries between the primal and the dual, many of which can be interpreted plausibly for the multiproduct firm, a basic economic difference remains. The constraints of the primal are fundamental and cannot be violated in practice, even unknowingly. The constraints of the dual, that unit cost never fall below market price, are artificial and can be disregarded merely by sacrificing revenue. The iterations of the primal resemble an idealized trial-and-error process that an astute management might hit upon. The simplex method as applied to the dual must be carried out on paper.[7] Since a nonoptimal solution of the dual requires the use of more inputs than are available or a negative production level, it could never be attained by the firm.

For the present simplified model of a multiproduct firm, the simulation of market processes as a device for decentralized management is not feasible, even when carried out solely on paper. When the top management announces a set of internal prices for the inputs, the divisional product managers will find that the unit cost exceeds the market price, falls below it, or equals it. In the first case they produce nothing and report no demand for inputs. In the second case they wish to produce without limit, and in the third they are indifferent about the level of output. There is simply no way of getting a meaningful figure for the quantities of the inputs demanded at the posted

[7]As we shall show in Chapter 15, the Walrasian market process, strictly interpreted, is also a paper process, so the property is not peculiar to the dual linear programming problem.

prices. The difficulty stems from the constant returns to scale for each product, which is inherent in the linear technology. If the market price is constant and unit cost does not rise with output, either zero output is optimal, or any level is as good as any other, or there is no finite optimum. When firms or divisions of firms are subject to constant returns, it is the fixity of inputs that determines production levels. If each product has fixed inputs of its own but also shares other fixed inputs with the remaining products, the top management can use a simulated market process for the prices of the shared inputs. Later models of multiplant firms will confirm this conclusion.

The most frequently used term for the dual variables is *shadow prices.* We can go further and state that, for the present model of a multiproduct firm, the dual is a shadow process. Remove the primal and understanding of the dual vanishes. Without the primal, we would be hard put to explain why unit cost is constrained to equal or exceed unit revenue, or why a firm would ever seek to minimize the value of its inputs. These peculiarities become acceptable only when we realize that a dual so formulated converges to the optimal solution of the primal. Also, minimizing the value of inputs becomes significant when, with the aid of the primal, we are able to show that it is a device for reducing to zero the value of excess demand. The dual is significant not as a practical decision-making process within the firm but rather because it defines alternative optimal conditions for the primal and provides a link to market processes.

EXERCISES

1. *The Implicit Multipliers in the Primal and Dual*

(a) Chapter 3 displays four basic feasible solutions to the numerical example. For each solution solve the corresponding vertical equations for the internal prices and compare these prices with the objective coefficients of the slack variables. Use these internal prices to calculate the barred objective coefficients for all nonbasic variables.

(b) For each iteration of the primal, draw a set of supply and demand curves for the three inputs, similar to those in the present chapter. Identify the price of each input and the amount of excess demand or supply. Explain what is happening to the demand for inputs on the way to the optimal solution. In what fundamental way does the pattern of changes differ from that for the dual?

(c) In solving the dual problem of the present chapter, the simplex method turns up three basic feasible solutions. Solve the vertical equations for columns in the basis to find the implied output levels and compare with the objective coefficients of the surplus variables. Use the implied output levels to calculate the barred objective coefficients for all nonbasic variables. Show that the implied output levels determined by feasible, nonoptimal solutions to the dual do not satisfy the constraints of the primal. State and demonstrate a similar conclusion regarding the prices in feasible but nonoptimal solutions to the primal.

2. *Additional Examples of Implicit Multipliers*

For Exercise 1, 2, or 7 of Chapter 3, carry out the instructions in (a) and (b) only of the preceding exercise. Either use previous results or apply the simplex method. Make the appropriate modifications in the instructions for number of solutions and number of inputs.

3. *The Dual Problem for a Multiproduct Firm*

Select the numerical example from Exercise 1, 2, or 7 of Chapter 3. Carry out the following steps:

(a) Set up and solve the dual. At each iteration determine the implicit output levels and use them to calculate the barred objective coefficients of the dual. Check the feasibility of the implied output levels as solutions to the primal.

(b) For each iteration of the dual, draw a set of supply and demand curves for the inputs similar to those in the text of the present chapter.

4. *The Relationships between Primal and Dual*

(a) A basic feasible solution to the primal maximizing problem for the multiproduct firm has the following barred coefficients in the objective form: a negative coefficient for an output, a positive coefficient for an output, a negative coefficient for a slack variable, and a positive coefficient for a slack variable. Interpret each coefficient in terms of the corresponding dual. Identify the coefficients that prevent a feasible solution to the dual and explain why.

(b) A basic feasible solution to the dual minimizing problem for the multiproduct firm has the following barred coefficients in the objective form: a negative coefficient for an input price, a positive coefficient for an input price, a negative coefficient for a surplus variable, a positive coefficient for a surplus variable. Interpret each coefficient in terms of the corresponding primal. Identify the coefficients that prevent a feasible solution to the primal and explain why.

5. *Special Solutions of the Primal and Dual*

(a) The following special types of optimal solution to the primal may arise: an optimal solution containing a slack variable, a degenerate optimal solution, or multiple optima. What does each of these special solutions imply about the optimal solution to the dual? For convenient illustrations of each case, modify the numerical example of Chapter 3 in the ways suggested in the text or in Exercise 4 of Chapter 3.

(b) Explain the economic meaning of the following special optimal solutions to the dual of the multiproduct firm: an optimal solution containing a surplus variable, a degenerate optimal solution, and multiple optima. Show what each implies about the optimal solution to the primal. For specific illustrations use or modify the numerical example in Chapter 4.

6. *Reduction of the Vertical Equations to Diagonal Form*

(a) Show that interchanging equations in any system cannot affect the solution. From the foregoing result demonstrate that any square system of equations with a unique solution can be reduced to diagonal form with the variables in natural order along the diagonal.

(b) Write symbolically a 3×3 system of equations and construct the corresponding vertical equations. Show that both systems have identical coefficients along the diagonal. Choose corresponding pivots on the diagonals for both systems. Demonstrate that the two pivot operations leave all diagonal coefficients equal in both the horizontal and vertical systems. Does this mean that if one system of equations is uniquely solvable the other must also be?

(c) Choose some 3×3 system that cannot be reduced to diagonal form, such as Example 3 of Chapter 2. Show that the corresponding vertical equations also cannot be reduced to diagonal form.

7. *Complementarity and Substitution in the Dual*

For the primal we gave an economic analysis of the $\bar{a}$ coefficients and presented an alternative interpretation of the $\bar{r}$ coefficients as the excess of market price over opportunity cost. This exercise provides an analogous treatment for the dual.

(a) Write in symbolic form the primal revenue-maximizing problem for a firm with *three* outputs and *five* inputs. Write, also in symbolic form, the corresponding dual minimizing problem. For a numerical example rewrite Table 3–1 as a dual problem, replacing x's with y's and using the same numbers in each row with the following changes: raise b_4 from 2 to 4 and b_5 from 5 to 10 in the objective function.

Reduce to canonical form with respect to (y_1, y_2, y_3) by first expressing the constraints alone in diagonal form and then eliminating the basic variables from the objective equation. Show the resultant solution in both numerical and symbolic form as is done in the text. How do the barred numerical coefficients of (y_6, y_7, y_8) differ from those of (x_6, x_7, x_8) in Table 3–4?

Write the expression for a barred objective coefficient in terms of the $\bar{a}$ coefficients. Calculate each barred objective coefficient both by the preceding formula and by the use of output multipliers. After checking the two sets of results, verify that the solution is optimal.

(b) *Follow the method used in Chapter* 3 *for the primal* to show that the $\bar{a}$ coefficients of the dual measure the rate of change of the basic variable in the row with respect to the nonbasic variable. Express the $\bar{a}$ coefficients for one nonbasic variable as *rates of change*. What is the economic meaning of the $\bar{a}$ coefficients when both basic and nonbasic variables are input prices; when a surplus variable appears in the basis?

(c) (Optional) Follow the steps in Chapter 4 to demonstrate that both methods of calculating barred objective coefficients for the dual must yield identical results.

(d) Two commodities are classified as substitutes if an increase in the price of one raises the quantity demanded of the other, as complements if a rise in the price of one reduces the quantity demanded of the other. If the quantity of a substitute or complement is fixed, how will the change in demand affect its price? Use your answer to redefine substitutes and complements in terms of changes in both prices. (To reconcile the results with Chapter 3 note that commodities are substitutes *on the supply side* if a rise in the price of one *reduces* the quantity supplied of the other. Since a rise in supply price normally causes an increase in quantity supplied, redefine substitutes and complements on the supply side in terms of ratios of quantity changes and check with the definition of Chapter 3.)

Use the sign of the $\bar{a}$ coefficients in the dual to determine from the price changes whether a nonbasic input is a substitute or a complement of a basic input—that is, an input whose price is in the basis. For one of the nonbasic input prices, express the barred objective coefficient symbolically in terms of the $\bar{a}$ coefficients. When an input price not in the basis increases by one unit, what is the direct effect on the total value of the inputs, the indirect effect? Relate the indirect effect to complementarity and substitution. How must the direct and indirect effects be related to each other in an optimal solution?

(e) For the optimal solution to the numerical example draw supply and demand curves similar to those in the text for the three inputs whose prices are in the basis and for one other. Identify on the diagram the total value of each input.

For the nonbasic input price, find the value of the *original* objective coefficient that creates a second basic optimal solution and then choose some convenient value that makes the previous solution nonoptimal. Illustrate each of these changes on the diagram for that input. Show specifically what happens on the supply and demand diagrams for the basic inputs when the nonbasic input price is raised by one unit. Explain in terms of the diagrams how raising a nonbasic input price can lower the total value of all inputs.

(f) State the rule by which the simplex method determines the variable to drop from the basis. Does a complement or a substitute leave the basis? Use the preceding diagrams to give an economic justification for the rule on selecting the variable to drop. Identify on the diagrams the variable that drops out.

5

Parametric Linear Programming: Supply and Demand Curves

Preceding chapters have developed computational techniques for finding an optimal production plan under given conditions. But conditions do change, and much of economic theory deals with the reactions of firms and consumers to changing conditions. Demand and supply curves, for example, show how buyers and sellers react to variations in prices. Linear programming provides methods for computing the response of an optimal solution to changes in quantities that were originally assumed to be constant. Various special names have been given these techniques, but they can best be subsumed under the general designation of *parametric linear programming*. The present chapter applies these techniques to the multiproduct firm, deriving supply and marginal cost curves for outputs, marginal revenue productivity and demand curves for inputs.

THE SUPPLY CURVE FOR AN OUTPUT

A supply curve graphs the amount supplied at each level of price when all other conditions remain unchanged. For the multiproduct, purely competitive firm the conditions that must be held constant are the technology, the prices of all variable inputs, and the prices of all other products. There may or may not be fixed inputs but, if there are, we need to specify the precise combination, since different combinations of fixed inputs generate different supply curves. We can imagine a controlled experiment with the multiproduct firm as subject. One output price alone is varied systematically, and at each level the firm decides how much to produce and supply. We observe the quantity supplied and plot it against the price of the product. Statistical techniques applied to the set of price-quantity points yield an empirical supply curve.

Economic theory replaces the firm of reality with a mathematical model that, hopefully, incorporates all salient features of the firm but only the salient features, not the vast detail. From the mathematical model, we then predict how the firm is likely to respond to changing prices.[1] When the mathematical model is highly specific, the supply curve can be derived as a simple function and graphed. When the model is formulated merely in general terms, only general properties of the supply curve, such as the direction of its slope, can be inferred.

Economic models of the firm generally assume that the management seeks maximum net revenue. Hence, economic models predict that at each level of price the firm will supply the amount that maximizes net revenue. For the linear model, then, we must find at each level of the output price a solution that is optimal. Deriving a supply curve by repeated applications of the simplex method would be excessively tedious but is, fortunately, unnecessary. Once an optimal solution has been found for any one set of output prices, relatively few operations are needed to obtain all possible optimal solutions as one of the output prices varies continuously.

Shown below is a model of a multiproduct firm with four possible products, two fixed inputs, and one variable input:

$$\begin{aligned}
a_{11}x_1+a_{12}x_2+a_{13}x_3+a_{14}x_4+x_5 \qquad\qquad &= b_1\\
a_{21}x_1+a_{22}x_2+a_{23}x_3+a_{24}x_4 \qquad +x_6 \qquad &= b_2\\
a_{31}x_1+a_{32}x_2+a_{33}x_3+a_{34}x_4 \qquad\qquad -z_3 &= 0\\
p_1x_1+\ p_2x_2+\ p_3x_3+\ p_4x_4 \qquad\qquad -c_3z_3 &= R(\max).
\end{aligned}$$

We shall follow the practice of using the symbol b when inputs are fixed and the symbol z when inputs are variable. For the variable input the total amount purchased, z_3, is shown on the left. Thus, the third equation states that excess demand is zero, which is equivalent to demand equaling supply. The market price for the variable input is c_3. Net revenue R measures the excess of the revenue from outputs over the cost of the variable input.

Reduction to canonical form with respect to (x_5, x_6, z_3) yields

$$\begin{aligned}
a_{11}x_1+a_{12}x_2+a_{13}x_3+a_{14}x_4+x_5 \qquad\qquad &= b_1\\
a_{21}x_1+a_{22}x_2+a_{23}x_3+a_{24}x_4 \qquad +x_6 \qquad &= b_2\\
-a_{31}x_1-a_{32}x_2-a_{33}x_3-a_{34}x_4 \qquad\qquad +z_3 &= 0\\
(p_1-c_3a_{31})x_1+(p_2-c_3a_{32})x_2 \qquad\qquad &\\
+(p_3-c_3a_{33})x_3+(p_4-c_3a_{34})x_4 &= R-0.
\end{aligned}$$

[1]Ideally, the supply curve predicted by the mathematical model should be tested by a controlled experiment, but economists can rarely do this. At best, they must use data generated by actual production decisions, where other conditions were unfortunately not held constant. The technique of multiple regression applied to such historical data yields valuable results but is inferior to controlled experimentation.

The coefficients in the objective form measure the excess of the selling price over unit variable cost, the net revenue per unit, for which the familiar r coefficients will be used. Having converted the objective coefficients to net revenue we can drop the variable input equation, since it in no way restricts the choice of output levels. The resultant model appears below with numerical coefficients that permit the exact derivation of supply curves:

$$\begin{aligned} 3x_1 + x_2 + x_3 + 3x_4 + x_5 \qquad &= 90 \\ 2x_1 + x_2 + 2x_3 + x_4 \qquad + x_6 &= 80 \\ 10x_1 + 4x_2 + 5x_3 + 6x_4 \qquad &= R(\max). \end{aligned}$$

The net revenue coefficients are the result of combining the following equations:

$$\begin{aligned} 6x_1 + 3x_2 + 5x_3 + 4x_4 - z_3 &= 0 \\ 16x_1 + 7x_2 + 10x_3 + 10x_4 - 1z_3 &= R(\max). \end{aligned}$$

For experience, readers should apply the simplex method to the numerical illustration. The optimal solution in both symbolic and numerical form is

$$\begin{aligned} x_1 \quad + \bar{a}_{13}x_3 + \bar{a}_{14}x_4 + \bar{a}_{15}x_5 + \bar{a}_{16}x_6 &= \bar{b}_1 \\ x_2 + \bar{a}_{23}x_3 + \bar{a}_{24}x_4 + \bar{a}_{25}x_5 + \bar{a}_{26}x_6 &= \bar{b}_2 \\ \bar{r}_3x_3 + \bar{r}_4x_4 + \bar{r}_5x_5 + \bar{r}_6x_6 &= R - \bar{R}; \end{aligned}$$

$$\begin{aligned} x_1 \quad - \quad x_3 + 2x_4 + x_5 - x_6 &= 10 \\ x_2 + 4x_3 - 3x_4 - 2x_5 + 3x_6 &= 60 \\ - \quad x_3 - 2x_4 - 2x_5 - 2x_6 &= R - 340. \end{aligned}$$

At prevailing market prices for outputs and the variable input, product three is not produced even though its selling price greatly exceeds the unit variable cost. Obviously other products can use more profitably the limited services of the fixed inputs. The rise in net revenue that will bring the third output into production can readily be calculated, and from it the rise in market price. The formula derived in Chapter 3 yields

$$\bar{r}_3 = r_3 - [\bar{a}_{13}r_1 + \bar{a}_{23}r_2] = 5 - [-1(10) + 4(4)] = -1.$$

The expression in parentheses is the unit opportunity cost of the third product in terms of the first two. When net revenue equals opportunity cost, x_3 is at the threshold of production. The critical value of r_3 is determined by the following equation:

$$\bar{r}_3 = r_3 - [-1(10) + 4(4)] = r_3 - 6 = 0.$$

When $r_3 = 6$, two optimal solutions exist; x_3 can enter the basis without increasing or reducing net revenue. Any further rise in r_3 tips the balance in favor of product three.

Since $\bar{a}_{13} = -1$, x_2 must be the variable dropped. Thus, product three displaces a product with which it is competitive in the use of resources, not one with which it is complementary. It is a special feature of the present example that one of the products in the basis is a complement and the other a substitute. Both could have been substitutes. Producing x_3 increases the output of its complement, x_1. The constraints for the basic optimal solution (x_1, x_3) are

$$\begin{aligned} x_1 + \tfrac{1}{4}x_2 \qquad\quad + \tfrac{5}{4}x_4 + \tfrac{1}{2}x_5 - \tfrac{1}{4}x_6 &= 25 \\ + \tfrac{1}{4}x_2 + x_3 - \tfrac{3}{4}x_4 - \tfrac{1}{2}x_5 + \tfrac{3}{4}x_6 &= 15. \\ * \qquad\qquad * \qquad\qquad\qquad\qquad & \end{aligned}$$

To find the next optimal solution as r_3 continues to rise, we shall use the following formulas, in which r_3 appears explicitly:[2]

$$\begin{aligned} \bar{r}_2 &= r_2 - [\bar{a}_{12}r_1 + \bar{a}_{22}r_3] = 4 - [\tfrac{1}{4}(10) + \tfrac{1}{4}r_3] = \tfrac{3}{2} - \tfrac{1}{4}r_3 \\ \bar{r}_4 &= r_4 - [\bar{a}_{14}r_1 + \bar{a}_{24}r_3] = 6 - [\tfrac{5}{4}(10) - \tfrac{3}{4}r_3] = -\tfrac{13}{2} + \tfrac{3}{4}r_3 \\ \bar{r}_5 &= r_5 - [\bar{a}_{15}r_1 + \bar{a}_{25}r_3] = 0 - [\tfrac{1}{2}(10) - \tfrac{1}{2}r_3] = -5 + \tfrac{1}{2}r_3 \\ \bar{r}_6 &= r_6 - [\bar{a}_{16}r_1 + \bar{a}_{26}r_3] = 0 - [-\tfrac{1}{4}(10) + \tfrac{3}{4}r_3] = \tfrac{5}{2} - \tfrac{3}{4}r_3 \\ R &= r_1\bar{b}_1 + r_3\bar{b}_2 = 10(25) + r_3(15) = 250 + 15r_3. \end{aligned}$$

When r_3 has the critical value 6 the coefficients are $\bar{r}_2 = 0$, $\bar{r}_4 = -2$, $\bar{r}_5 = -2$, $\bar{r}_6 = -2$, and $R = 340$. There is no change as yet from the original optimal solution.

As r_3 continues to rise, x_3 obviously remains in the basis but its level cannot increase so long as x_1 shares the basis. It will be profitable to retain x_1 in the basis unless an $\bar{r}$ coefficient goes positive. The only coefficients that increase as r_3 rises are $\bar{r}_4$ and $\bar{r}_5$. To determine the next critical value for r_3, set both of these coefficients equal to zero and solve, as shown below:

$$\begin{aligned} \bar{r}_4 &= -\tfrac{13}{2} + \tfrac{3}{4}r_3 = 0 \qquad \text{or} \qquad r_3 = 8\tfrac{2}{3}, \\ \bar{r}_5 &= -5 + \tfrac{1}{2}r_3 = 0 \qquad \text{or} \qquad r_3 = 10. \end{aligned}$$

When the net revenue of the third product passes $8\frac{2}{3}$, it pays to introduce product four.

[2] A minor ambiguity arises with respect to the meaning of the $\bar{a}$ coefficients. So long as x_2 appears in the second row in the basis, there is no conflict between the variable with subscript 2 and the variable appearing in row 2. Earlier, $-\bar{a}_{24}$ was shown to be the rate of change of x_2 with respect to x_4, but there was no need to decide whether the first subscript referred to the variable or the row in the basis. When x_3 replaces x_2 in the second row of the basis, $-\bar{a}_{24}$ must become the rate of change with respect to x_4 of the variable appearing in row 2 of the basis, regardless of its subscript.

The reason that $\bar{r}_4$ increases with r_3 can be found in the original formula,

$$\bar{r}_4 = r_4 - \bar{a}_{14} r_1 - \bar{a}_{24} r_3.$$

Only if $\bar{a}_{24}$ is negative will $\bar{r}_4$ increase with r_3. But a negative $\bar{a}_{24}$ means that the two products are relative complements and that the introduction of x_4 will free resources for expanded production of x_3. Further, a negative $\bar{a}_{24}$ means that x_4 must enter in the first row, displacing x_1. The constraints for the next optimal solution are

$$\begin{aligned} \tfrac{4}{5}x_1 + \tfrac{1}{5}x_2 \qquad + x_4 + \tfrac{2}{5}x_5 - \tfrac{1}{5}x_6 &= 20 \\ \tfrac{3}{5}x_1 + \tfrac{2}{5}x_2 + x_3 \qquad - \tfrac{1}{5}x_5 + \tfrac{3}{5}x_6 &= 30. \end{aligned}$$

The $\bar{r}$ coefficients relative to the new basis are

$$\begin{aligned} \bar{r}_1 &= 10 - \quad [\tfrac{4}{5}(6) + \tfrac{3}{5}r_3] = \quad \tfrac{26}{5} - \tfrac{3}{5}r_3 \\ \bar{r}_2 &= \ 4 - \quad [\tfrac{1}{5}(6) + \tfrac{2}{5}r_3] = \quad \tfrac{14}{5} - \tfrac{2}{5}r_3 \\ \bar{r}_5 &= \ 0 - \quad [\tfrac{2}{5}(6) - \tfrac{1}{5}r_3] = -\ \tfrac{12}{5} + \tfrac{1}{5}r_3 \\ \bar{r}_6 &= \ 0 - [-\tfrac{1}{5}(6) + \tfrac{3}{5}r_3] = \quad \tfrac{6}{5} - \tfrac{3}{5}r_3 \\ R &= \quad 6(20) + r_3(30) \ = 120 + (30)r_3. \end{aligned}$$

Since the only coefficient that increases with r_3 is $\bar{r}_5$, the next critical value is $r_3 = 12$. When r_3 passes 12, the slack variable x_5 replaces x_4, and the constraints for the final solution are

$$\begin{aligned} 2x_1 + \tfrac{1}{2}x_2 \qquad + \tfrac{5}{2}x_4 + x_5 - \tfrac{1}{2}x_6 &= 50 \\ 1x_1 + \tfrac{1}{2}x_2 + x_3 + \tfrac{1}{2}x_4 \qquad + \tfrac{1}{2}x_6 &= 40. \end{aligned}$$

All $\bar{a}$ coefficients are positive in the second row, so further increases in r_3 reduce the $\bar{r}$ coefficients of all nonbasic variables. Net revenue rises in accordance with the expression $R = 40r_3$.

Table 5–1 summarizes the preceding results. Figure 5–1 graphs the first two columns as the supply schedule or supply curve of the third product.[3] As shown on pages 79 and 80, market price is $p_3 = v_3 + c_3 a_{33} = r_3 + 5$. The four vertical line segments, including the first segment on the vertical axis, form the supply curve. They show the unique quantity supplied at each level

[3]The traditional economic model of the firm generates smooth curves, and the supply curve has become the standard economic term for expressing the response of quantity to price. To emphasize the unity of economic theory we shall continue to use the term even though Figure 5–1 is not a curve in either the strict mathematical or the popular definition.

TABLE 5–1

The Effects of a Rising Price for Product three

r_3	x_3	x_1	x_2	x_4	R	$y_1 = (-\bar{r}_5)$	$y_2 = (-\bar{r}_6)$
0 to 6	0	10	60	0	340	2	2
6 to $8\frac{2}{3}$	15	25	0	0	$250+15r_3$	$5-\frac{1}{2}r_3$	$-\frac{5}{2}+\frac{3}{4}r_3$
$8\frac{2}{3}$ to 12	30	0	0	20	$120+30r_3$	$\frac{12}{5}-\frac{1}{5}r_3$	$-\frac{6}{5}+\frac{3}{5}r_3$
12 and above	40	0	0	0	$0+40r_3$	0	$0+\frac{1}{2}r_3$

of price except those levels that correspond to the dotted horizontal segments. At each critical value of r_3, a variable outside the basis has an $\bar{r}$ coefficient of zero, implying a second basic optimal solution. Total net revenue remains the same when the third product is produced in the amount shown by either solution or at any level in between. When the optimum is unique we can predict that the firm will choose it. With a whole set or range of optimal solutions all we can do is predict that the firm will make its choice within the range and not outside it. Some other criterion besides maximum net revenue is needed to narrow the range further. One possibility is that the firm adheres to the present production plan until there is some positive advantage to changing. Production would then take place at the lower end of the range when the price had risen to the critical level and at the upper end when it had fallen.

With maximum net revenue the only criterion, the supply curve consists solely of the vertical line segments, minus their end points. As the dotted lines

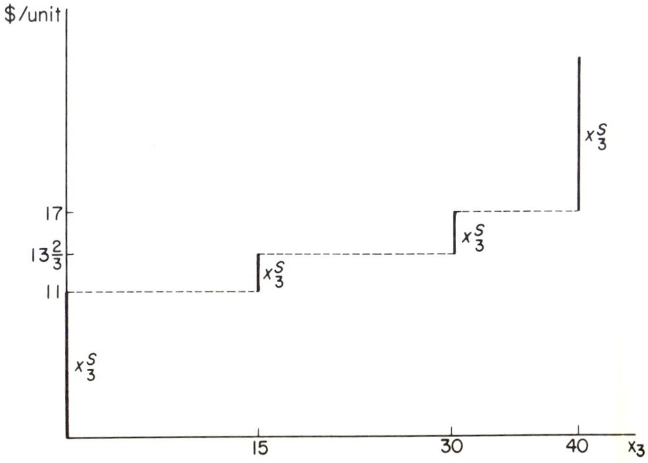

Fig. 5-1 The Supply Curve for a Product

indicate, the supply curve is not defined, or does not exist, at prices corresponding to multiple optima. The limitation has little practical significance. Even if numbers are rounded off to two or three decimal places, the critical values are a tiny fraction of the total of all possible prices. What is overwhelmingly probable is that the market price will lie inside the ranges of the vertical segments and determine a unique output level.

For larger models of a multiproduct firm, the same general method generates a supply curve, but computers can best carry out the calculations. There are likely to be many more shifts of basis and many more vertical segments. The underlying rationale is the same: searching for products that free resources for the product that is becoming increasingly more valuable.

A supply curve for a product emerges from the conceptual experiment of varying a single price and observing the reactions of the firm. Economic theory predicts that the firm will supply the unique quantity that maximizes net revenue, if one exists. Linear programming is a mathematical method of optimization applicable to the firm under certain technological conditions. It provides techniques for calculating the changes in an optimal solution as a coefficient in the objective form varies. The market price of a product appears as a coefficient in the objective function either directly or as an important component of the net revenue coefficient. Hence, parametric linear programming applied to the objective function yields directly all data needed to construct the supply curve for a product. The more familiar method is first to derive a marginal cost curve and then to show that it can serve as a supply curve under certain conditions. It is important to realize that a firm's supply curve for a product can be constructed without reference to marginal cost, but the marginal cost curve does provide some of the underlying economic rationale. Total and marginal cost emerge from a different conceptual experiment and require another type of parametric programming. Once we have developed the new technique in the following section we shall derive cost curves and relate them to the supply of an output.

MARGINAL REVENUE PRODUCTIVITY CURVES FOR INPUTS

In deriving the supply curve for a product, the conceptual experiment is to vary the price of one product and observe the reactions of the firm. We now wish to determine the results of varying the amount of one fixed input with all other conditions unchanged. The experimental approach would be to assign to the firm different amounts of the input and observe its decisions. The result would be a set of points associating net revenue with the amount of the input. Economic theory predicts that at each level of the input the associated net revenue will be the maximum attainable.

Varying a fixed input sounds like a contradiction in terms. To show that it is not we must make some subtle distinctions between a constant, a parameter, and an independent variable. A parameter is often defined paradoxically as a variable constant, but temporary constant would be a better designation. A parameter is constant for any one experiment or decision but varies from one experiment to another. For example, to determine its effects on the volume of a gas, temperature is held constant for a single experiment but varied systematically over a series of experiments. Market price in the preceding section provides an economic example. An important ingredient in the theory of a purely competitive firm is the hypothesis that the management treats a market price as a parameter. At each level of prices the management takes these prices as given and makes a decision without trying to anticipate changes in prices and without making any allowance for possible effects of its own decisions on the level of prices. When a price does change the same decision process is simply repeated, treating the new level as given.

When the decisions of a firm are viewed as a succession of controlled experiments, the market price of a product plays the role of a parameter. But the object of a set of experiments is to find some general law or functional relationship. For the firm we want to know how the quantity supplied varies with the market price. The emphasis shifts from the details of the process that produced the results to the nature of the results. The most important property is that the quantity supplied depends on price and tends to change when the price changes. In the final generalization the market price becomes an independent variable in the supply function or supply curve. Thus, to the management as subject of the experiment market price is a parameter, but to the economist as observer or experimenter market price is an independent variable.

In the present section it is an input that undergoes the same metamorphosis. The amount is fixed for any one decision but varies systematically from decision to decision. The results show how total net revenue varies with changes in an input, and the input has progressed to the stage of being an independent variable. What we need for calculating the net revenue function is its value in all possible optimal solutions as one input varies with all other conditions constant. Repeated applications of the simplex method are again unnecessary; once we have found a single optimal solution, parametric linear programming requires only a few operations to generate all possible optimal solutions as one input varies. To facilitate the process we shall first make some minor modifications in the format of an optimal solution.

A Modified Canonical Form

As developed in Chapter 3 the simplex method applies elementary operations to the fixed inputs and converts them to output levels. In the course of the computations all traces of the original input levels are lost.

To retain the input levels in the optimal solution we assign each input a separate column and rewrite the two-input model in the following revised form:

$$\begin{aligned}
a_{11}x_1+a_{12}x_2+a_{13}x_3+a_{14}x_4+\ x_5+0x_6 &= b_1+0b_2\\
a_{21}x_1+a_{22}x_2+a_{23}x_3+a_{24}x_4+0x_5+\ x_6 &= 0b_1+b_2\\
r_1x_1\ +r_2x_2\ +r_3x_3\ +r_4x_4\ +0x_5+0x_6 &= 0b_1+0b_2+R(\max).
\end{aligned}$$

Pivot operations no longer alter b_1 and b_2 but merely transform their coefficients. The revised form shows explicitly that b_1 and b_2 have the same coefficients as the slack variables x_5 and x_6. Each elementary operation is applied to an entire row or equation, so coefficients that are originally identical remain identical throughout all operations in the reduction to canonical form. The result is another computational windfall of the simplex method. We can simply borrow the coefficients from the slack variables, affix them to the inputs, and express the optimal output levels as explicit linear functions of b_1 and b_2. For the numerical example of the first section, the revised canonical form is

$$\begin{aligned}
x_1\quad - x_3+2x_4+\ x_5-\ x_6 &= \quad b_1-\ b_2\\
x_2+4x_3-3x_4-2x_5+3x_6 &= -2b_1+3b_2\\
-\ x_3-2x_4-2x_5-2x_6 &= -2b_1-2b_2+R.
\end{aligned}$$

With $b_1 = 90$ and $b_2 = 80$ the optimal output levels are

$$x_1 = 90-80 = 10; \qquad x_2 = -2(90)+3(80) = 60.$$

The coefficients of the inputs have an important role to play, so we assign them distinct symbols, called $\bar{e}$ coefficients. Also, a slight rearrangement of variables simplifies the subsequent analysis. For the general two-input model, the optimal solution becomes

$$\begin{aligned}
x_1 &= \bar{e}_{11}b_1+\bar{e}_{12}b_2\\
x_2 &= \bar{e}_{21}b_1+\bar{e}_{22}b_2-\\
-R &= -y_1b_1-y_2b_2
\end{aligned}
\begin{bmatrix}
\bar{a}_{13}x_3+\bar{a}_{14}x_4+\bar{a}_{15}x_5+\bar{a}_{16}x_6\\
\bar{a}_{23}x_3+\bar{a}_{24}x_4+\bar{a}_{25}x_5+\bar{a}_{26}x_6\\
\bar{r}_3x_3\ +\bar{r}_4x_4\ +\bar{r}_5x_5\ +\bar{r}_6x_6
\end{bmatrix}.$$

All nonbasic variables appear on the right-hand side in brackets, preceded by a negative sign. The coefficients within the brackets have the same sign as when they appear on the left, so the criterion for optimality remains unchanged. Also, as readers may verify, performing a pivot operation on variables within the brackets has precisely the same effect as performing the pivot operation on the left-hand side and transferring the results directly into the brackets. The modified form focuses attention on the important relationship between inputs and the outputs they are producing. When we consider only the first input and the corresponding slack variable x_5, the first equation becomes $x_1 = \bar{e}_{11}b_1 - \bar{a}_{15}x_5$. Since $\bar{e}_{11} = \bar{a}_{15}$, increasing the first input by one unit and letting that unit stand idle has no effect on output. Output depends on the amount of the input actually used, not the total amount available.

The Economic Interpretation of the ē Coefficients

To determine the economic meaning of the $\bar{e}$ coefficients, let b_1 change with b_2 constant. The new levels for the outputs are

$$x_1 + \Delta x_1 = \bar{e}_{11}(b_1 + \Delta b_1) + \bar{e}_{12}b_2$$

$$x_2 + \Delta x_2 = \bar{e}_{21}(b_1 + \Delta b_1) + \bar{e}_{22}b_2.$$

Subtraction of the original levels gives

$$\Delta x_1 = \bar{e}_{11}\Delta b_1 \qquad \bar{e}_{11} = \frac{\Delta x_1}{\Delta b_1}$$

or

$$\Delta x_2 = \bar{e}_{21}\Delta b_1 \qquad \bar{e}_{21} = \frac{\Delta x_2}{\Delta b_1}.$$

The $\bar{e}$ coefficients measure the rate of change of an output with respect to an input and will be called *productivity coefficients*. The relationship between an output and an input is not an invariant technological datum but depends on the other products in the basis. Each new product entering the basis requires a different pivot operation and generates a different set of $\bar{e}$ coefficients. The more accurate term is *relative* productivity coefficients, relative to a given basis, but we shall omit the adjective whenever the meaning is clear.

A glance at the numerical example shows that productivity coefficients can be negative. In fact, if all a coefficients are positive in the original formulation, and if all inputs are fully utilized, some $\bar{e}$ coefficients have to be negative. The reason is the inflexible input requirements. Neither product can increase unless greater amounts of both inputs become available. When an input is constant, one product must be cut back to free resources for the expansion of the other. In the numerical example, the $\bar{e}$ coefficients are positive along the principal diagonal, the diagonal that runs downward from left to right. The explanation lies in the process of reducing to diagonal form. Since the variable x_1 is introduced in the first row, the first input represents the barrier to expanded production. The limit to the production of x_2 is the amount of the second input remaining after x_1 is produced to the full amount permitted by b_1. A greater amount of the first input allows greater production of x_1, but at the same time reduces the residual amount of the second input that is available for x_2. Similarly, with b_1 constant an increase in the available amount of b_2 permits greater production of x_2 but only at the cost of withdrawing larger amounts of b_1 from the production of x_1. The row in which an output enters the basis identifies the input that is the bottleneck. Hence, in the numerical example $\bar{e}_{11}$ and $\bar{e}_{22}$ must be positive, and the remaining coefficients must be negative.

In larger models it remains true that an output must have a positive $\bar{e}$ coefficient relative to the input in whose row it enters. Also, there must be at least one negative coefficient in each row and each column. Otherwise one input could not increase without violating the constraints on the other inputs. Beyond these requirements, there can be great variety in the patterns of positive and negative $\bar{e}$ coefficients.

An $\bar{e}$ coefficient, like the marginal physical productivity of an input, measures the rate of change of an output with respect to an input, but the two rates of change are defined in different ways. The marginal physical productivity of an input has come to be identified with the mathematical concept of a partial derivative, the rate of change of one variable with respect to another, *all* remaining variables being held constant. In defining the $\bar{e}$ coefficients, all inputs save one are held constant, but more than one output must be free to vary, or the constraints do not remain binding. Chapter 8 derives genuine marginal physical productivities for the linear model, and Chapter 9 relates them to the analogous concept for the conventional smooth model.

A Reinterpretation of the Dual Variables

With the inputs in separate columns reduction of the constraints to diagonal form generates the $\bar{e}$ coefficients, which can then be used in the final step of eliminating the basic variables from the objective form. The result of multiplying the first constraint by $-r_1$, the second by $-r_2$, and adding both to the objective form is

$$\text{coeff. of } b_1 = 0-(r_1\bar{e}_{11}+r_2\bar{e}_{21}) = -\left(\frac{r_1\,\Delta x_1}{\Delta b_1}+\frac{r_2\,\Delta x_2}{\Delta b_1}\right) = -\frac{\Delta R}{\Delta b_1}$$

$$\text{coeff. of } b_2 = 0-(r_1\bar{e}_{12}+r_2\bar{e}_{22}) = -\left(\frac{r_1\,\Delta x_1}{\Delta b_2}+\frac{r_2\,\Delta x_2}{\Delta b_2}\right) = -\frac{\Delta R}{\Delta b_2}.$$

The $\bar{e}$ coefficients show how the basic outputs respond to changes in inputs. Multiplying each change in output by its r coefficient converts to the change in revenue. The resultant rate of change in revenue with respect to an input is the *marginal revenue productivity* of that input. In the linear model of the firm we can interpret R as either revenue or net revenue, the excess of revenue over the cost of variable inputs. When the unit variable cost is subtracted from the selling price of each output, the coefficients of the fixed inputs become their marginal *net* revenue productivities. The concept most widely used in economics is the marginal revenue productivity. For consistency with the customary presentation, we shall, for the present, take r_1 and r_2 to be market prices.

There is a second method for deriving coefficients in the objective form: Multiply the original constraints by y_1 and y_2 and subtract both constraints from the original objective function. The result is

$$\text{coeff. of } b_1 = 0 - 1y_1 - 0y_2 = -y_1$$

$$\text{coeff. of } b_2 = 0 - 0y_1 - 1y_2 = -y_2.$$

Since both methods must yield the same answer, the dual variables have to be the marginal revenue productivities of the corresponding inputs.

Previously we interpreted the dual variables as imputed or internal prices for the inputs. There is no conflict at all in dual variables being both prices and marginal revenue productivities. Every price in economics is a rate of change. The converse is not necessarily true, but surprisingly many rates of change in economics do have meaningful interpretations as prices. A market price, or rate of exchange, is also a rate of change between quantities, one of which is usually money. As the prefix emphasizes, a rate of exchange denotes a rate of change when the quantities that vary belong to different economic units. An internal price is a rate of change of one quantity with respect to another within an economic unit. Thus, an internal price for an input is the rate at which the value of output responds to changes in the input. If the value of output is to be realized in dollars, there must be a separate and subsequent exchange of output for dollars in the market.

Prior to any actual exchange, market prices place values on outputs, which a purely competitive firm accepts. The internal monetary price of an input is the rate at which the production process converts units of the input into value of output. To give internal prices a more concrete meaning, economists often simulate a market mechanism by assuming fictitious markets and fictitious exchanges within an economic unit. Thus, dual variables are sometimes interpreted as the prices at which top management leases the services of fixed inputs to production managers. All prices then become rates of exchange. Though often useful, the device is not necessary for defining and understanding internal prices.

As noted previously, we cannot interpret the $\bar{e}$ coefficients as marginal physical productivities because all remaining variables do not remain constant. There is no similar problem in identifying the dual variables as marginal revenue productivities. Marginal revenue productivity is the rate of change of revenue with respect to one input, all other *inputs* being constant. There is no requirement that all but one output remain fixed. In fact, all outputs must be free to vary so management can choose the optimal amount of each output and the maximum attainable revenue from each combination of inputs. Marginal physical productivities depend solely on technological data whereas marginal revenue productivities require economic data as well, plus the decision to maximize revenue.

The original problem shows revenue as a linear function of output levels. Reduction to canonical form converts revenue to a linear function of the inputs, with the dual variables as their coefficients. The same general result holds for all linear programming problems. Reduction to canonical form always converts the objective variable to a linear function of the quantities in the constraints, the dual variables serving as the coefficients. There is no way to overemphasize the importance of this general result. Much of economic theory consists of optimization subject to constraints. By setting up economic problems initially in linear form, we can derive in a simple and direct way many important economic concepts. We shall make repeated use of this method in subsequent chapters.

An Alternative Method for Calculating $\bar{a}$ Coefficients

The $\bar{e}$ coefficients are highly useful repositories of the technological data. As already shown, they can be applied to the original b coefficients to yield output levels and to the original r coefficients to generate marginal revenue productivities of the inputs. Finally, when affixed to the original input requirements the $\bar{e}$ coefficients produce the $\bar{a}$ coefficients or rates of substitution between outputs. For verification, assume that the inputs are available in amounts just sufficient to turn out one unit of an output not in the basis and write these inputs in separate columns, as shown below:

$$a_{11}x_1 + a_{12}x_2 = 1a_{13} + 0a_{23} = a_{13}$$

$$a_{21}x_1 + a_{22}x_2 = 0a_{13} + 1a_{23} = a_{23}.$$

Solving these equations by reduction to diagonal form generates the $\bar{e}$ coefficients for the middle columns and, as demonstrated earlier, gives the $\bar{a}$ coefficients on the extreme right. Hence,

$$x_1 = \bar{e}_{11}a_{13} + \bar{e}_{12}a_{23} = \bar{a}_{13}$$

$$x_2 = \bar{e}_{21}a_{13} + \bar{e}_{22}a_{23} = \bar{a}_{23}.$$

If both $\bar{a}$ coefficients are positive, both x_1 and x_2 can be produced at positive levels when inputs are in the proportion required for the third output. Hence, when the level of x_3 increases and inputs are withdrawn, both x_1 and x_2 must decrease, implying that x_3 is competitive with both products in the basis. If one of the $\bar{a}$ coefficients is negative, inputs can be freed in the correct proportion for x_3 only if one output in the present basis is increased and the other decreased. Thus, a negative $\bar{a}$ coefficient implies complementarity with the output in its row.

Further insight into the underlying conditions for complementarity can be gained from the $\bar{e}$ coefficients. From the numerical example,

$$\bar{a}_{13} = 1(1)-1(2) = -1$$
$$\bar{a}_{23} = -2(1)+3(2) = 4.$$

Thus, x_3 is complementary with x_1 and competitive with x_2. As explained earlier, the first input is the bottleneck for x_1 and the second input for x_2. Since product three has relatively greater requirements for the second input than for the first ($a_{13} = 1$, $a_{23} = 2$), it competes with product two and is complementary with product one.

Deriving a Marginal Revenue Productivity Curve

We are now ready to construct the marginal revenue productivity curve for the first input. Since the first input finally becomes an independent variable, we shall anticipate and use throughout the symbol for a variable input, z_1. In revised canonical form the solution to the numerical example becomes

$$\begin{aligned} x_1 &= 1z_1 - 1b_2 \\ x_2 &= -2z_1 + 3b_2 - \\ -R &= -2z_1 - 2b_2 \end{aligned} \begin{bmatrix} -\ x_3 + 2x_4 + \ x_5 - \ x_6 \\ +4x_3 - 3x_4 - 2x_5 + 3x_6 \\ -\ x_3 - 2x_4 - 2x_5 - 2x_6 \end{bmatrix}.$$

As z_1 continues to increase, x_2 declines to zero and ultimately passes into the negative or infeasible range. Similarly, since b_2 is a positive constant, decreases in z_1 ultimately force x_1 into the infeasible range. With $b_2 = 80$, the permissible limits for z_1 are

$$\text{upper limit:} \quad x_2 = -2z_1 + 240 = 0 \quad \text{or} \quad z_1 = 120$$
$$\text{lower limit:} \quad x_1 = 1z_1 - 80 = 0 \quad \text{or} \quad z_1 = 80.$$

So long as z_1 does not pass beyond these limits, the present solution remains feasible. But does it also continue to be optimal? It must, since changes in the fixed inputs have no effect on the $\bar{r}$ coefficients. These depend solely on the choice of basis and the pivot operations required for reduction to canonical form. An optimal solution to a linear programming problem must be feasible and must satisfy the criterion of optimality, that all $\bar{r}$

coefficients be zero or negative. The preceding discussion illustrates an important theorem in linear programming: As the constants in the constraints change, a solution remains optimal so long as it continues to be feasible.

Since the dual variables are the solutions of the vertical equations, they depend solely on the columns in the basis and not on the quantities in the constraints. Hence, for the range over which the present solution remains feasible, we can write R as the following function of z_1:

$$R = 2z_1 + 160 \qquad 80 \leqq z_1 \leqq 120.$$

The equation is linear and graphs as a straight line segment.

As z_1 increases beyond the upper limit, the basis must change. We could choose a value of z_1 above the upper limit and apply the simplex method once more from the beginning. This is inefficient and unnecessary. A single pivot operation, appropriately chosen, generates the new optimal solution. The entering variable must appear in the same row as the output variable just forced to zero. Further, when introduced, the new variable must have a positive $\bar{e}$ coefficient with respect to z_1. Otherwise, the slightest increase in z_1 simply generates another infeasible solution. When a new variable enters the basis in a given row, all coefficients in that row are divided by the $\bar{a}$ coefficient of the new variable. To convert the $\bar{e}$ coefficient from negative to positive the entering variable must have a negative $\bar{a}$ coefficient.

If only one variable has a negative $\bar{a}$ coefficient in the critical row, it must be introduced; otherwise a criterion of optimality is needed to insure that the new solution is optimal as well as feasible. The $\bar{r}$ coefficients must remain negative or zero after the new variable comes in. Consider two possible candidates, x_s and x_t, to be introduced in the second row:

$$\begin{aligned} &\bar{a}_{1s}x_s + \bar{a}_{1t}x_t \\ &\bar{a}_{2s}x_s + \bar{a}_{2t}x_t \\ &\bar{r}_s x_s \;\; + \bar{r}_t x_t. \end{aligned}$$

If x_s is chosen, the appropriate pivot operation generates the following new $\bar{r}$ coefficient for x_t:

$$\bar{r}_t - \bar{r}_s \frac{\bar{a}_{2t}}{\bar{a}_{2s}} = \bar{a}_{2t}\left(\frac{\bar{r}_t}{\bar{a}_{2t}} - \frac{\bar{r}_s}{\bar{a}_{2s}}\right).$$

Since $\bar{a}_{2t} < 0$, the new $\bar{r}$ coefficient will be negative or zero only if the parenthesis is positive or zero, that is, if

$$\frac{\bar{r}_t}{\bar{a}_{2t}} - \frac{\bar{r}_s}{\bar{a}_{2s}} \geqq 0 \qquad \text{or} \qquad \frac{\bar{r}_t}{\bar{a}_{2t}} \geqq \frac{\bar{r}_s}{\bar{a}_{2s}}.$$

To ensure that the new solution will be optimal, the entering variable x_s must have the smallest ratio of $\bar{r}$ coefficient to $\bar{a}$ coefficient in the row where it will appear. If two variables have the same ratio, either can be introduced and the other will have a new $\bar{r}$ coefficient equal to zero. Readers may show that, if $\bar{a}_{2t}$ is positive, the pivot operation introducing x_s converts the $\bar{r}$ coefficient of x_t to a numerically larger negative number, preserving optimality.

In the numerical example the candidates for admission in the second row are x_4 and x_5. The ratios that determine the entering variable are

$$\frac{\bar{r}_4}{\bar{a}_{24}} = \frac{-2}{-3} = \frac{2}{3} \qquad \text{and} \qquad \frac{\bar{r}_5}{\bar{a}_{25}} = \frac{-2}{-2} = 1.$$

Thus x_4 must be chosen and, after a pivot operation, the new optimal solution is[4]

$$\begin{aligned} x_1 \quad &= -\tfrac{1}{3}z_1 + b_2 \\ x_4 \quad &= \tfrac{2}{3}z_1 - b_2 - \\ -R &= -\tfrac{2}{3}z_1 - 4b_2 \end{aligned} \begin{bmatrix} \tfrac{2}{3}x_2 + \tfrac{5}{3}x_3 - \tfrac{1}{3}x_5 + x_6 \\ -\tfrac{1}{3}x_2 - \tfrac{4}{3}x_3 + \tfrac{2}{3}x_5 - x_6 \\ -\tfrac{2}{3}x_2 - \tfrac{11}{3}x_3 - \tfrac{2}{3}x_5 - 4x_6 \end{bmatrix}.$$

The solution remains optimal over the range of z_1 for which it is feasible. The upper limit, as determined now by x_1 reaching zero, is

$$-\tfrac{1}{3}z_1 + 80 = 0 \qquad \text{or} \qquad z_1 = 240.$$

The corresponding function for net revenue is

$$R = \tfrac{2}{3}z_1 + 320 \qquad 120 \leqq z_1 \leqq 240.$$

At the lower limit for z_1, $R = 400$, the same value reached at the upper limit of the previous line segment. Thus, as will be shown in Figure 5–2, the net revenue function consists of line segments joined together. The vertex where they meet corresponds to a degenerate solution. When z_1 reaches 120, the amounts of the two inputs, (120, 80), are exactly proportioned to the requirements of the first output, (3, 2). The first output alone is produced and total revenue is $R = r_1 x_1 = 10 \times 40$. Either x_2 or x_4 can be in the basis with x_1 but only at zero level. As z_1 increases from 80 to 120, the solution (x_1, x_2) remains optimal over the entire range including the endpoints. As z_1 increases from 120 to 240, the solution (x_1, x_4) remains optimal over the

[4]Rather than interchange rows we have shown the variables on the upward-sloping diagonal. The positive $\bar{e}$ coefficient for b_2 in the first row indicates that z_1 has now increased to such an extent that b_2 is the bottleneck for x_1. In reducing to canonical form along the principal diagonal, x_4 would have to be introduced in the first row and x_1 in the second.

entire range including the endpoints. When $z_1 = 120$, there are two optimal bases and two different sets of values for the dual variables.[5]

A further increase in z_1 can only bring in the slack variable x_5 with the resultant optimal solution:

$$\begin{aligned} x_5 &= z_1 - 3b_2 \\ x_4 &= 0z_1 + b_2 - \\ -R &= 0z_1 - 6b_2 \end{aligned} \begin{bmatrix} -3x_1 - 2x_2 - 5x_3 - 3x_6 \\ +2x_1 + x_2 + 2x_3 + x_6 \\ -2x_1 - 2x_2 - 7x_3 - 6x_6 \end{bmatrix}.$$

Since neither $\bar{e}$ coefficient is negative, further increases in z_1 simply pile up as slack with no effect on production and revenue. The marginal revenue productivity of the first input drops to zero and remains there. The next and final segment of the revenue function is

$$R = 480 \qquad 240 \leqq z_1.$$

As z_1 increases, its marginal revenue productivity falls from 2 to $\frac{2}{3}$ to 0. At the same time, the marginal revenue productivity of b_2 rises from 2 to 4 to 6. To show that these results are not peculiar to the specific numerical example, we make use of the symbolic formulation on page 92. The variable x_s is introduced into the second row, and the requisite pivot operation is performed. The new value of marginal revenue productivity for the first input, y_1^1, is related to the original value, y_1^0, by the following expression:

$$-y_1^1 = -y_1^0 - \bar{r}_s \frac{\bar{e}_{21}}{\bar{a}_{2s}} \qquad \text{or} \qquad y_1^1 = y_1^0 + \bar{e}_{21} \frac{\bar{r}_s}{\bar{a}_{2s}}.$$

Unless $\bar{r}_s = 0$, indicating multiple optima, or x_s is a slack variable, y_1 must decline, since all three barred coefficients in the second term are negative. But x_s is chosen because $\bar{r}_s/\bar{a}_{2s}$ is the smallest such ratio, so y_1 declines by the smallest possible amount. When x_s is a slack variable, $\bar{e}_{21} = \bar{a}_{2s}$ and $\bar{r}_s = -y_1^0$. Hence $y^1 = y_1^0 - y_1^0 = 0$. As expected an input's marginal revenue productivity falls to zero when it simply piles up as slack.

For the second input the new marginal revenue productivity is

$$y_2^1 = y_2^0 + \bar{e}_{22} \frac{\bar{r}_s}{\bar{a}_{2s}}.$$

[5] There are not multiple optimal solutions to the primal, strictly defined, with at least one nonbasic variable having a zero barred objective coefficient. As readers may verify by setting up the original problem with $b_1 = 120$ and applying the simplex method, a tie occurs for the variable to drop from the basis. One choice leads to the optimal solution (x_1, x_2) with all barred objective coefficients negative for nonbasic variables, and the other choice leads to a similar result with (x_1, x_4) in the basis. The dual, however, does display multiple optimal solutions.

Since $\bar{e}_{22}$ is positive, y_2 increases but by the smallest possible amount. Both inputs are required for every output, so the inputs are, as expected, complementary. An increase in one input creates added demand for the other and raises its price. That the rise in price is minimal is consistent with the objective of economizing. The increasingly scarce input must be used in such a way as to hold down the rise in price.

Two inputs are complementary in the production of a particular product if their $\bar{e}$ coefficients are of opposite sign in the row of that product. To demonstrate we hold the output constant and let the inputs vary. In the first row the changes in inputs must satisfy the following requirement:

$$\bar{e}_{11}\,\Delta z_1 + \bar{e}_{12}\,\Delta z_2 = 0 \qquad \text{or} \qquad \frac{\Delta z_2}{\Delta z_1} = -\frac{\bar{e}_{11}}{\bar{e}_{12}}.$$

With $\bar{e}$ coefficients of different sign, an increase in one input must accompany an increase in the other. When there are only two inputs and each is required for every output, the inputs must be complements in the production of both outputs in the basis. With many inputs there may be pairs with $\bar{e}$ coefficients of the same sign in some but not all rows. They are substitutes for each other in the production of the corresponding products. So long as every output requires positive amounts of every input, pairs of inputs cannot be substitutes in the production of all outputs in the basis, but they can be complements.

To complete the total revenue function, the first input must decline from its original level. For the initial optimum, as shown on page 91, the lower limit for z_1 depends on

$$x_1 = 1z_1 - 1b_2 = z_1 - 80 = 0.$$

When z_1 passes below 80, x_1 must be replaced by a variable that converts $\bar{e}_{11}$ from positive to negative. With several candidates available, the *rule of minimum ratio* again determines the choice, since no $\bar{r}$ coefficient can be positive after the pivot operation.

In the numerical example, the candidates for replacement of x_1 are x_3 and x_6, with ratios

$$\frac{\bar{r}_3}{\bar{a}_{13}} = \frac{-1}{-1} = 1 \qquad \text{and} \qquad \frac{\bar{r}_6}{\bar{a}_{16}} = \frac{-2}{-1} = 2.$$

When x_3 is introduced by a pivot operation the resultant solution is

$$\begin{aligned} x_3 &= -z_1 + b_2 \\ x_2 &= 2z_1 - b_2 - \\ -R &= -3z_1 - b_2 \end{aligned} \begin{bmatrix} -x_1 - 2x_4 - x_5 + x_6 \\ +4x_1 + 5x_4 + 2x_5 - x_6 \\ -x_1 - 4x_4 - 3x_5 - x_6 \end{bmatrix}.$$

The range for the solution to remain feasible is

$$x_3 = -z_1 + 80 = 0 \quad \text{or} \quad z_1 = 80;$$

$$x_2 = 2z_1 - 80 = 0 \quad \text{or} \quad z_1 = 40.$$

The segment of the revenue function is

$$R = 3z_1 + 80 \qquad 40 \leqq z_1 \leqq 80.$$

As expected, a decline in z_1 raises its marginal revenue productivity. A decreasing input has a positive rather than a negative $\bar{e}$ coefficient in the row of the departing variable, reversing the effect of the pivot operation.

Further decreases in z_1 can only bring the slack variable x_6 into the second row. Readers can carry out the necessary computations and verify that the remaining line segment of the revenue function is

$$R = 5z_1 + 0b_2 \qquad 0 \leqq z_1 \leqq 40.$$

The preceding calculations are summarized in Table 5–2 and graphed in Figure 5–2.

TABLE 5–2

Total Revenue and Marginal Revenue Productivities

z_1	R	y_1	y_2
0 to 40	$5z_1 + 0$	5	0
40 to 80	$3z_1 + 80$	3	1
80 to 120	$2z_1 + 160$	2	2
120 to 240	$\frac{2}{3}z_1 + 320$	$\frac{2}{3}$	4
240 and over	$0z_1 + 480$	0	6

The graph of total revenue consists of line segments meeting in vertices. The mathematical term for such a graph is *piecewise-linear function*; the function is linear over each interval but changes constants between intervals. The vertices of the graph correspond to degenerate optimal solutions of the revenue maximization problem. Both inputs are exactly proportioned to the needs of one product, which is produced at the maximum attainable level. Any other variable could be included in the basis at zero level but would not necessarily fulfill the criterion of optimality. There are two variables, either of which can be introduced to provide a degenerate optimal solution. One of these solutions remains feasible as well as optimal for increases in z_1, the other for decreases.

The slope or rate of change of total revenue is constant over each interval, so the graph of marginal revenue productivity must consist of

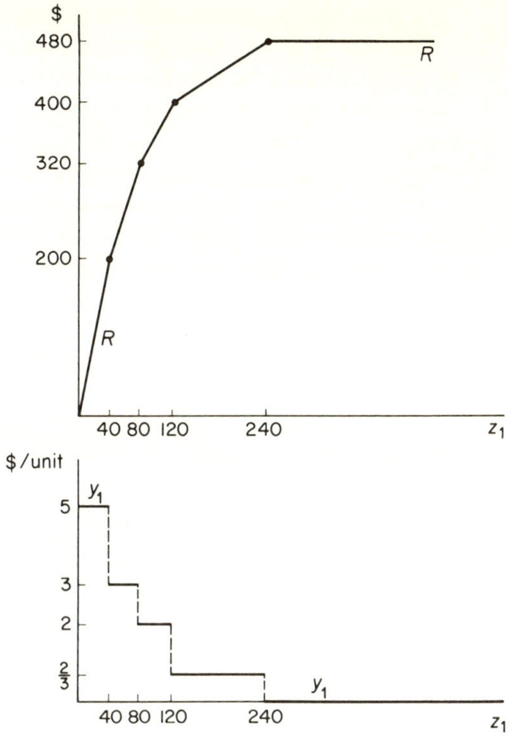

Fig. 5-2 Total Revenue and Marginal Revenue Productivity

horizontal line segments. The mathematical term for such a graph is *step function*. At each step there are two distinct values for marginal revenue productivity, one holding for an increase in z_1, the other for a decrease.[6] There is no way of eliminating the ambiguity and, fortunately, no need to do so. When the amount of the first input falls in a vertical gap, the firm simply uses both inputs in the production of one product and produces no other. A change in z_1 brings a second product into production, but the choice is not the same for an increase as for a decrease. Despite constancy over intervals there is a general pattern of declining marginal revenue productivity as an input increases.

As z_1 increases, total revenue ultimately reaches a plateau and marginal revenue productivity falls to zero. The results follow directly from the assumption that excess amounts of an input go costlessly to waste. In the numerical example, the firm simply ran out of products and had no choice

[6]Since there are two values for y_1 at each step, the graph does not satisfy the strict mathematical definition of a function. Either the upper or the lower endpoint needs to be omitted. However, *step function* is too descriptive a term to drop, so we shall continue to use it even though marginal revenue productivity is not strictly a function.

to make. There could be additional products that use relatively large amounts of z_1 but turn out relatively little revenue. As Exercise 10 at the end of the chapter shows, such products may actually lower revenue by taking resources away from more profitable products. So long as the firm has the option of letting z_1 go costlessly to waste, it will never choose an output that adds a downward-sloping segment to total revenue. But if idle capacity has a cost, such as extra maintenance, the loss of revenue from inefficient production may be less than the cost of idleness. In such a case, total revenue slopes downward and marginal revenue productivity becomes negative. The same result could also occur if, for some reason, the firm is required to use all available inputs.

In Figure 5–2 the graph of total revenue begins at the origin. For this to occur, the second input must go costlessly to waste, and all products must use the first input. A product that does not require the first input continues to yield revenue when z_1 reaches zero and the total revenue curve intersects the vertical axis. At the other end of the graph a product that does not require the second input permits revenue to rise indefinitely at a constant rate. If the second input does not go costlessly to waste, there will be an initial segment intersecting the horizontal axis to the right of the origin. Exercise 10 provides confirmation for the foregoing statements.

MARGINAL COST CURVES FOR OUTPUTS

In the simplest model of the firm with a single product, one variable and one fixed input, the marginal cost of the product consists solely of the increased outlay on the variable input. When a firm has several potential outputs, an increase in one deprives the firm of revenue from the others. There is an opportunity cost in addition to the variable cost. We shall first derive both total and marginal opportunity cost and then combine them with the cost of the variable input.

With a net revenue coefficient of zero, a product has no direct effect on net revenue. If produced it does, however, use resources and deny to the firm the net revenue obtainable from other products. To find the indirect effect that one output has on net revenue, we set its net revenue coefficient equal to zero and transfer the variable to the right-hand side of the equations. The following modified version of the multiproduct firm shows x_3 shifted to the right-hand side and combined with b_1 and b_2 to denote the amounts of the inputs available for the remaining products:

$$
\begin{aligned}
a_{11}x_1 + a_{12}x_2 + a_{14}x_4 + x_5 \qquad\quad &= 1(b_1 - a_{13}x_3) + 0(b_2 - a_{23}x_3) \\
a_{21}x_1 + a_{22}x_2 + a_{24}x_4 \qquad + x_6 &= 0(b_1 - a_{13}x_3) + 1(b_2 - a_{23}x_3) \\
r_1x_1 \;\; + r_2x_2 \;\; + r_4x_4 \qquad\qquad &= -0(b_1 - a_{13}x_3) - 0(b_2 - a_{23}x_3) + R(\max).
\end{aligned}
$$

Reduction to canonical form with respect to an optimal basis, say (x_1, x_2), generates $\bar{e}$ coefficients before the parentheses or, alternatively, transforms the constants and coefficients into their barred representations. The right-hand side appears in either of the following equivalent formats:

$$\begin{aligned} &= \bar{e}_{11}(b_1 - a_{13}x_3) + \bar{e}_{12}(b_2 - a_{23}x_3) &&= \bar{b}_1 - \bar{a}_{13}x_3 \\ &= \bar{e}_{21}(b_1 - a_{13}x_3) + \bar{e}_{22}(b_2 - a_{23}x_3) &&= \bar{b}_2 - \bar{a}_{23}x_3 \\ &= -y_1(b_1 - a_{13}x_3) - y_2(b_2 - a_{23}x_3) + R &&= -\bar{R} + (r_1\bar{a}_{13} + r_2\bar{a}_{23})x_3 + R. \end{aligned}$$

When written out, the two versions of the objective function become

$$R = y_1 b_1 + y_2 b_2 - (y_1 a_{13} + y_2 a_{23})x_3 = \bar{R} - (r_1\bar{a}_{13} + r_2\bar{a}_{23})x_3.$$

As x_3 increases it causes net revenue to decline at a rate that is equal to the imputed unit cost or the unit opportunity cost.

The numerical example of the present chapter takes the following form:

$$\begin{aligned} x_1 \quad + 2x_4 + x_5 - x_6 &= 10 + x_3 \\ x_2 - 3x_4 - 2x_5 + 3x_6 &= 60 - 4x_3 \\ -2x_4 - 2x_5 - 2x_6 &= -340 + 6x_3 + R. \end{aligned}$$

Whenever we need the $\bar{e}$ coefficients or the internal input prices we can borrow them from the slack variables. The next step is to vary x_3 parametrically and find net revenue as a function of x_3. We know from previous results, and can readily verify, that the preceding solution is optimal when $x_3 = 0$. It remains optimal and feasible so long as x_3 does not go beyond 15 and force x_2 into the negative range. Thus, the first linear segment of the net revenue function is $R = 340 - 6x_3$, where $0 \leqq x_3 \leqq 15$. Readers should apply the method of the preceding section to complete the parametric variation of x_3 and verify the results summarized in columns 1 and 2 of Table 5–3.

TABLE 5–3

The Total Cost of an Output

(1) Range x_3	(2) Net revenue R	(3) Opportunity $340 - R$	(4) Cost variable input $c_3 a_{33} x_3$	(5) Total C_3
0 to 15	$340 - 6x_3$	$6x_3$	$5x_3$	$11x_3$
15 to 30	$380 - \frac{26}{3}x_3$	$\frac{26}{3}x_3 - 40$	$5x_3$	$\frac{41}{3}x_3 - 40$
30 to 40	$480 - 12x_3$	$12x_3 - 140$	$5x_3$	$17x_3 - 140$

Figure 5–3a graphs the net revenue from other products as a function of x_3. At each level of x_3 its internal or opportunity cost is the decline in net revenue from the maximum attainable when x_3 is not produced, or $340 - R$. These downward vertical deviations are calculated in column 3 and plotted in Figure 5–3b. When x_3 reaches 40 units it is using all 80 units of the second input. No further increase is possible and the opportunity cost curve ends in a point. For the variable input cost we use the data on page 80, $c_3 = \$1$ and $a_{33} = 5$. Column 5 shows the sum of both costs, the total cost C_3 of product three.

We now introduce the price of x_3 and determine in two equivalent ways whether the third product is worth producing and, if so, what the optimal level is. Figure 5–3d graphs total cost C_3 against the total revenue from x_3, $R_3 = p_3x_3$. As p_3 increases from zero, the revenue line rotates upward, but x_3 does not break even until $p_3 = 11$ and the revenue line coincides with the first segment of total cost. Since net revenue $(R_3 - C_3)$ is zero, it is a matter of indifference to the firm whether x_3 is produced at all or at any level along the

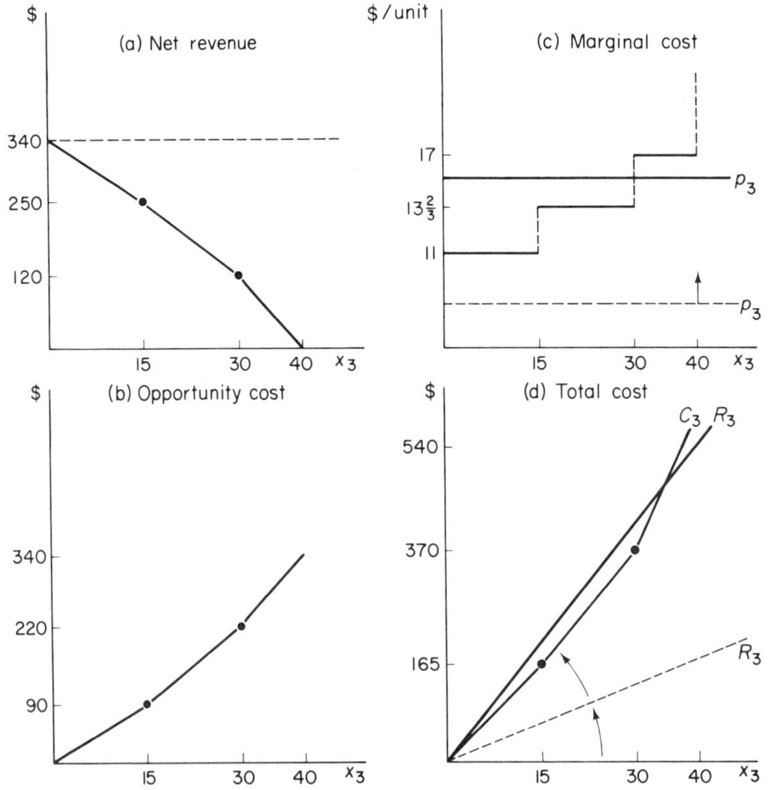

Fig. 5-3 Cost and Revenue Curves

segment. After any further increase in price, however slight, revenue increases more rapidly than cost up to the first vertex, and $x_3 = 15$ gives the maximum vertical difference between revenue and cost. The unique optimum remains at the first vertex until $p_3 = 13\frac{2}{3}$, the slope of the next cost segment. Then, R_3 and C_3 become parallel, and all outputs on the next segment yield the same net revenue. As p_3 rises, the second vertex becomes and remains the unique optimum until p_3 reaches 17. Further rises in price cause the firm to produce x_3 to the limit of the available capacity.

The slope of the total cost function or the rate of change of total cost with respect to output, $\Delta C_3/\Delta x_3$, is the *marginal cost* of x_3, for which the symbol w_3 will be used. Marginal cost is the coefficient of x_3 in the total cost function and can be written in either of the following equivalent forms:

$$w_3 = (y_1 a_{13} + y_2 a_{23} + c_3 a_{33}) = (r_1 \bar{a}_{13} + r_2 \bar{a}_{23} + c_3 a_{33}).$$

Thus, marginal cost equals imputed or opportunity cost per unit plus the variable unit cost. At a vertex there are two slopes of the total cost function and two values of marginal cost, one holding over the left-hand segment and the other over the right-hand segment. Hence, Figure 5–3c plots the marginal cost curve as horizontal line segments with vertical gaps corresponding to the vertices. When the horizontal price line coincides with a segment of the marginal cost curve, total revenue and total cost are parallel and there is no unique optimum. A price line passing through a vertical gap corresponds to a vertex and determines a unique optimal output.

We can now explain the quantity supplied in terms of marginal cost. If p_3 lies in a vertical gap, marginal cost exceeds price for higher outputs and falls short of it for lower outputs. Above the gap total cost increases with output at a greater rate than total revenue. Below the gap, $w_3 < p_3$, and total revenue decreases with output at a greater rate than total cost. Since increases or decreases in output are unprofitable, the firm chooses to supply the quantity corresponding to the vertical gap and continues to do so for any price lying between the successive marginal cost segments. As the price varies within the gap, it traces out a vertical segment of the supply curve as derived in the first section. Readers may verify that the horizontal segments of the marginal cost curve do in fact coincide with the horizontal gaps in the supply curve, and that the open vertical segments of the supply curve fill the vertical gaps of the marginal cost curve. Compare Figures 5–3c and 5–1.

For the linear model of the firm the horizontal segments represent marginal cost, and the supply curve is undefined. The vertical segments minus the endpoints form the supply curve, but marginal cost is undefined. By contrast, in the traditional version of the firm, the supply curve is identified as the marginal cost curve everywhere above the point of minimum average variable cost. The two versions of the firm can easily be reconciled as special applications of the same general principle. The marginal cost curve, as customarily drawn, is continuous and upward sloping. A continuous curve, by definition, has no vertical gaps and must be drawn without lifting pen from paper. Being continuous, the marginal cost curve must intersect a horizontal price line in a point. The upward slope insures that marginal cost exceeds price after the intersection and is less than price before the intersection. Thus, the intersection, like the vertical gap, identifies the optimal output. If marginal cost is continuous but downward sloping, the intersection is not the optimum. The firm would be better off either expanding or contracting.

A continuous upward-sloping marginal cost curve has no vertical gaps and no horizontal line segments and is the locus of all optimal output levels. Since the firm chooses the output at which price equals marginal cost, the marginal cost curve shows the amount supplied for each price on the vertical axis. When we draw a marginal cost curve we are showing how cost varies with output, or we are expressing marginal cost as a function of output. By contrast, the supply curve shows how output varies in response to price, or defines output as a function of price. When we use the marginal cost curve as a supply curve, we implicitly interchange independent and dependent variables. Price, which equals marginal cost in an optimal solution, becomes the independent variable on the vertical axis in place of output on the horizontal axis. So long as the marginal cost curve is continuous and upward-sloping, we do not have to draw a new diagram for the supply curve but can simply reinterpret the marginal cost curve as the supply curve.[7] Whenever the marginal cost curve slopes upward but is not continuous and has vertical gaps, we must draw the supply curve as a vertical line segment within each gap. At the absolute limit of productive capacity, the marginal cost curve ends in a point but the supply curve continues vertically upward.

DEMAND CURVES FOR INPUTS

The graph of marginal revenue productivity emerges from the conceptual experiment of assigning to a firm, or to a set of otherwise identical firms, different amounts of one input, all other inputs being constant. The management accepts each assigned quantity as fixed and chooses a revenue maximizing combination of outputs. The sequence of optimizing decisions determines total revenue and its slope, marginal revenue productivity, as functions of the input that is being varied. Under appropriate technological and economic conditions, a linear programming model predicts the decisions of the firm for all possible levels of the input.

A demand curve for an input requires a different conceptual experiment.

[7]Mathematically, marginal cost is a function of output, $w = f(x)$. By the first-order condition for maximum net revenue, marginal cost equals market price, $w = p = f(x)$. The supply curve is the inverse function $x = f^{-1}(p)$. For example, if $w = cx = p$, then $x = (1/c)p$. An inverse function must exist whenever the original function is continuous and has a nonzero slope of the same sign at every point.

The firm is able to buy whatever amount it needs of one input, but the price is systematically varied. The management accepts each assigned price as fixed and searches for the output combination that is optimal under the given conditions. The given conditions have to be precisely specified since they affect the optimal solution and the amount of the input demanded at each price. Generally, output prices are held constant as well as technological conditions. For the remaining inputs there are two possibilities; either the quantity or the price may remain fixed. When there are many inputs, some may have fixed prices, others fixed quantities. Each specific combination will, in general, determine a different demand curve. We take up first the case in which the only remaining input is fixed in amount.

The linear model must be modified, as follows, to include the variable input in the objective form:

$$\begin{aligned} 3x_1 + x_2 + x_3 + 3x_4 - z_1 &= 0 \\ 2x_1 + x_2 + 2x_3 + x_4 \qquad + x_6 &= 80 \\ 10x_1 + 4x_2 + 5x_3 + 6x_4 - c_1 z_1 &= R(\max). \end{aligned}$$

The revised problem implies that management can buy or lease at a price c_1 the desired amount z_1 of the first input. With the cost of the first input subtracted, R becomes net revenue.

The simplest initial basic feasible solution is (z_1, x_6), with canonical form:

$$\begin{aligned} -3x_1 - x_2 - x_3 - 3x_4 + z_1 &= 0 \\ 2x_1 + x_2 + 2x_3 + x_4 \qquad + x_6 &= 80 \\ (10-3c_1)x_1 + (4-c_1)x_2 + (5-c_1)x_3 + (6-3c_1)x_4 &= R - 0c_1. \end{aligned}$$

If the price of the variable input is very high, all products are unprofitable, and the initial solution is optimal. Inspection of the objective form shows that product three is the first to reach the margin of profitability, when the input price declines to $c_1 = 5$. With x_3 replacing x_6, the optimal solution becomes

$$\begin{aligned} x_1 + \tfrac{1}{2}x_2 + x_3 + \tfrac{1}{2}x_4 + \tfrac{1}{2}x_6 &= 40 \\ (5-2c_1)x_1 + \tfrac{1}{2}(3-c_1)x_2 \quad + \tfrac{1}{2}(7-5c_1)x_4 - \tfrac{1}{2}(5-c_1)x_6 &= R - 40(5-c_1). \end{aligned}$$

The first equation, which is always satisfied, has been dropped. The remaining constraint is multiplied by $-(5-c_1)$ and added to the previous objective form, thus retaining c_1 in the $\bar{r}$ coefficients. With $c_1 = 5$, all $\bar{r}$ coefficients are negative for nonbasic products in the second solution. As c_1 declines, product two is the first to reach the verge of profitability when $\frac{1}{2}(3-c_1) = 0$ or $c_1 = 3$. Thus, so long as the price of the first input remains in the range $3 < c_1 < 5$, the unique optimal solution is $x_3 = 40$, and the amount of the first input required is $1x_3 = 40$ units. Readers may continue the process and verify the results as shown in Table 5–4.

TABLE 5–4

A Demand Schedule for an Input

Variable input		*Variable in basis*	*Price of fixed input* $(= -\bar{r}_6)$
Price (c_1)	*Quantity* (z_1)		
$c_1 > 5$	0	$x_6 = 80$	$y_2 = 0$
$5 > c_1 > 3$	40	$x_3 = 40$	$0 < y_2 < 1$
$3 > c_1 > 2$	80	$x_2 = 80$	$1 < y_2 < 2$
$2 > c_1 > \frac{2}{3}$	120	$x_1 = 40$	$2 < y_2 < 4$
$\frac{2}{3} > c_1 > 0$	240	$x_4 = 80$	$4 < y_2 < 6$

The first two columns are graphed in Figure 5–4 as the demand curve for the first input. The horizontal line segments are dotted to show that the quantity demanded is indeterminate at these prices. Since there is only one effective constraint, basic feasible solutions consist of one variable only. The horizontal line segments represent multiple optima or feasible but not basic solutions, which are weighted averages of the basic solutions at the endpoints. The management can utilize any amount of the first input along a horizontal segment by choosing the appropriate combination of two products. But all combinations are equally profitable. Once again, when there are ties, optimization can narrow the range of choice but cannot predict a unique choice. The demand curve is not defined along horizontal line segments.

Each vertical segment of the input demand curve corresponds to the

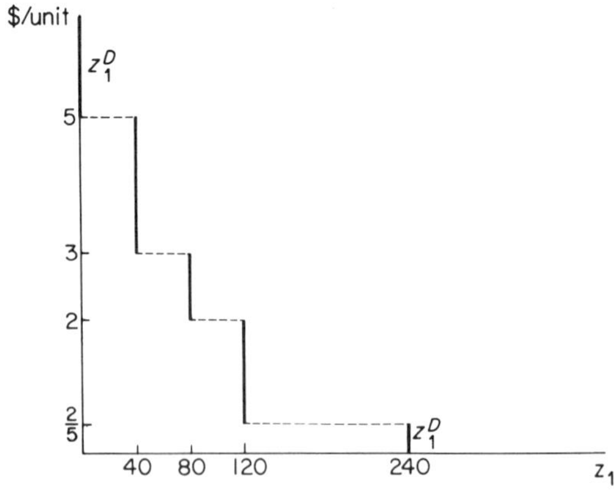

Fig. 5-4 The Demand Curve for an Input

sole production of a different product. The decline in c_1 does reduce the unit variable cost of the products at different rates, but this is only part of the explanation. A product comes into production only when its price exceeds the sum of the variable and imputed cost per unit. As Table 5–4 confirms, the decline in price of the variable input raises the internal price of the fixed input. Consequently, the marginal or unit cost curve of an output may be shifting upward even though the unit variable cost is declining. For example, when $c_1 = 5$ and $y_2 = 0$, the unit cost of x_3 is $1(5)+2(0) = 5$; but when $c_1 = 2$ and $y_2 = 2$, the unit cost is $1(2)+2(2) = 6$. Conversely, the unit cost of x_4, which uses relatively less of the fixed input, declines. As the variable input becomes cheaper, economy in the use of the fixed input becomes an ever more important criterion in choosing products.

We can derive an input demand curve simply by setting up the problem in correct form and varying the appropriate parameter. But we can also predict the amount of the input the firm will wish to purchase by comparing the separate effects that use of the input has on revenue and cost. Readers may go back to Figure 5–2 and draw in a total cost line, $C_1 = c_1 z_1$, to go with the total revenue function. As c_1 declines from an initially high level, the cost line rotates downward. For a few values of c_1 at which the cost line is parallel to a revenue segment, there is indeterminacy; otherwise the unique optimal quantity of z_1 occurs at a vertex. Alternatively, the horizontal segments of the marginal revenue productivity curve correspond to horizontal gaps on the input demand curve. When the input price line passes through a vertical gap in the marginal revenue productivity curve, increases in z_1 cause revenue to rise at a slower rate than cost, and decreases in z_1 cause revenue to decline at a greater rate than cost. As c_1 varies within a vertical gap it causes no change in the optimal quantity of z_1 and traces out a vertical segment of the input demand curve.

In the customary economic version of the firm, marginal revenue productivity curves are continuous and downward sloping. Continuity eliminates vertical gaps and insures intersection with any horizontal price line within the range of the curve. A downward slope through the point of intersection guarantees that both larger or smaller amounts of the input reduce net revenue. As the price line shifts, the points of intersection with the marginal revenue productivity curve reveal the optimal amounts of the input. By switching the independent variable from quantity on the horizontal axis to input price on the vertical axis, we can reinterpret a continuous, downward-sloping marginal revenue productivity curve as an input demand curve.[8] If the MRP curve is upward sloping, intersections with the price line do not represent maximum net revenue. When the MRP curve is downward sloping but not continuous, there are vertical gaps through which the

[8]There is also a requirement that total revenue exceed total variable cost. Otherwise, the firm chooses the option of producing nothing, and the input demand curve coincides with the vertical axis.

price line may pass. These vertical gaps form parts of the input demand curve but not of the MRP curve. Ranges of constant slope imply that the optimum is not unique and that the demand curve does not exist.

With more than one fixed input, the same methods generate a demand curve for a variable input. Regardless of the number of inputs, the variation of one input with all others constant traces out an MRP graph, whose open vertical segments form the demand curve. Alternatively, we can derive a demand curve directly from the effects of the input price on the objective coefficients. With additional variable inputs, their market prices can also be incorporated into the net revenue coefficients. The demand curve for one variable input requires that the prices, not the quantities, of all remaining variable inputs remain constant. All we need to do is let one input price vary in the objective coefficients and compute the effects on the optimal solutions. Alternatively, we may leave one of the input prices out of the objective coefficients and let the quantity of the input vary. Since the prices of the other variable inputs remain, the objective variable is net revenue. Varying one input traces out the graph of marginal net revenue productivity, whose vertical gaps represent the input demand curve. No matter how many variable and fixed inputs there are, the demand curve for any one input consists of the vertical gaps in its marginal net revenue productivity graph. When it is the only variable input, we can drop the adjective "net."

Taxation of Outputs and Demand Curves for Inputs

A wide variety of taxes has been imposed on business firms, but only a few general types will be considered here. A lump-sum tax, of which the general property tax is an example, does not vary with the levels of production or the profits earned by the firm. Such a tax appears as a constant subtracted from R in the objective function. It does not affect the choice of products or production levels, since the combination that maximizes net revenue before the subtraction of a constant also maximizes net revenue after subtraction. Further, the marginal revenue productivities or internal prices of the fixed inputs are not altered, being the solutions of the vertical equations for outputs in the basis. The imputed value of the fixed inputs will, however, exceed net revenue by the amount of the tax. A lump-sum tax cannot affect the internal allocation process of the firm since it applies uniformly to all decisions. Within the linear model, a lump-sum tax can only influence the decision whether to operate or shut down. When the tax exceeds maximum net revenue firms shut down.

Although net revenue is not identical with taxable business income, it can be used to illustrate the effects of a tax on corporate income. When net revenue is taxed at a constant rate t, management seeks to maximize net revenue after taxes, $R - tR = (1-t)R$. Again, within the simple linear model there is no effect on the choice of products and production rates, since

$(1-t)R$ is maximized whenever R is. However, the objective form will not be consistent unless both sides are multiplied by $(1-t)$, as follows:

$$r_1(1-t)x_1+r_2(1-t)x_2+r_3(1-t)x_3+r_4(1-t)x_4 = (1-t)R.$$

There is no change in the relative profitability of the various products, which is the determinant of the optimal solution. The marginal revenue productivities of the inputs are reduced, but in the same proportion, so the process of internal allocation is unaffected.

A proportional tax on net revenue is equivalent to taxing every product at a fixed percentage of its net revenue per unit. If there is no variable cost, the tax becomes a fixed percentage of the selling price, an example of which is a general sales tax. When unit variable cost is positive for at least some products, a tax that is a percentage of selling prices will not have a proportional effect on all net revenue coefficients. As a consequence, the internal process of allocation and the optimal solution may be altered. Of course, if the same percentage tax is levied also on the prices of the variable inputs, the net revenue coefficients will change proportionately.

The final example is a tax on a single commodity, which may be either a fixed amount per unit or a fixed percentage of the selling price. In either case there is a reduction in the net price received by the seller, which affects the optimizing decision. The imposition of a tax or the variation in a tax already imposed is equivalent to a change in the selling price, which was analyzed earlier in the chapter. However, we are now in a position to show how a tax on a single commodity, or a change in its price, affects the graph of marginal revenue productivity and the demand for an input.

For a product not in the basis, a change in price or a change in the rate at which it is taxed affects its eligibility for entering the optimal solution by directly affecting its own $\bar{r}$ coefficient. Of more interest is a tax on a product already in an optimal solution. To illustrate by use of the numerical example, product one only is assumed subject to a tax. Product one appears in two optimal solutions (x_1, x_2) over the range $80 \leqq z_1 \leqq 120$, and (x_1, x_4) over the range $120 \leqq z_1 \leqq 240$. With (x_1, x_2) the solution, the marginal revenue productivities are defined by

$$y_1 = \bar{e}_{11}r_1+\bar{e}_{21}r_2 = 1(10)-2(4)$$

$$y_2 = \bar{e}_{12}r_1+\bar{e}_{22}r_2 = -1(10)+3(4).$$

When a tax of a fixed amount per unit is imposed on x_1, the net revenue coefficient becomes (r_1-t). The marginal revenue productivities must change by the following amounts:

$$\Delta y_1 = -\bar{e}_{11}t = -1t \qquad \Delta y_2 = -\bar{e}_{12}t = -(-1)t = t.$$

With only two inputs the tax must have opposite effects on their marginal revenue productivities. For the solution (x_1, x_4), the effects of the tax on x_1 are

$$\Delta y_1 = \tfrac{1}{3}t \qquad \Delta y_2 = -\tfrac{2}{3}t.$$

The effect on each marginal revenue productivity is reversed.

For the first input, a tax increase on product one lowers its marginal revenue productivity in the range 80–120 and raises it in the range 120–140. Both effects shorten the vertical segment of the demand curve at $z_1 = 120$. The horizontal price line may continue to pass through the shortened vertical segment but it may also end up either above or below the segment. The result depends on the position of c_1 in the original segment and the relative size of $\bar{e}_{11}$ in the two solutions. Thus, a tax on product one may increase the demand for the first input, reduce it, or leave it the same.

The various curves employed in the theory of the firm result from a continuous variation of one parameter, all others being constant. When a second parameter varies, it causes a shift in the previously derived curve. A proportional change in the net revenue coefficients for all products causes the demand curve for an input to shift vertically without changing shape. A change in one output price, like a tax on one product, changes the shape of the graph by shifting some connecting horizontal segments but not others. A symmetrical problem arises when we vary the quantity of an input and examine its effect on the supply curve for an output. The supply curve shifts to the left or to the right depending on whether the appropriate $\bar{e}$ coefficient is negative or positive.

SUMMARY AND SYNTHESIS

We have now virtually completed the application of computational methods to the current model of a multiproduct firm and can profitably review the results. The simplex method searches out a solution that is optimal under given conditions. The internal process of reaching an optimal solution may be given an interpretation in terms of supply and demand analysis: The management expands an output so long as its demand price exceeds the supply price and raises an input price whenever demand exceeds supply. The resultant optimal solution gives levels for those quantities that are free to vary and internal prices for those quantities that are fixed. The use of supply and demand analysis within the firm links decision making by the firm to the equilibrating mechanism of the economy as a whole.

The economic theory of the firm focuses not primarily upon the process of attaining an optimum but upon the adaptation of the firm to changes in underlying conditions. The adjustment of the firm to a continuously varying parameter traces out the locus of all possible optimal solutions. Thus, the total revenue curve for an input represents an upper boundary of revenue;

each amount of the input could be used nonoptimally to yield less revenue but there is no way of obtaining greater revenue. Similarly, the total cost curve for an output is a lower boundary.

Parametric linear programming is a computational method for finding all optimal solutions as one or more parameters vary. The familiar demand and supply curves show the effects of varying a single parameter. When a second parameter changes, the curves shift. The application of parametric programming corresponds to a conceptual experiment in which the conditions facing the firm are systematically varied. As the firm adjusts optimally to each set of conditions, the resultant decisions are observed and tabulated or graphed.

Economic theory posits as a broad generalization that firms seek maximum net revenue, the largest possible value of $R-C$. The variation of a parameter influences decisions by changing the difference between R and C. When an input or an output varies in quantity it generally affects both revenue and cost. Further, the effects may be both direct and indirect. Producing an extra unit of a product at a positive price adds directly to revenue and directly to cost if the inputs used have positive prices. But an extra unit of one product may also affect both the revenue and the cost of other products. When we wish to isolate separate effects we can do it by setting up a parametric programming problem in the appropriate form. If all inputs are fixed and their use is costless to the firm, changes in output levels affect revenue only. Setting the price of a product equal to zero and varying it parametrically yields the negative change in revenue from other products. Since a decline in R has the same effect on net revenue as an increase in C, we often find it convenient to interpret the loss in revenue from other products as a cost to the firm, the opportunity or internal cost of the product being varied. When the other products use inputs with positive prices, the opportunity cost consists of the decline in net revenue, not in revenue alone.

A single application of parametric programming yields demand and supply curves directly. But it may be more instructive, particularly for graphical representation, to derive the same result by two successive parametric variations. Letting an output vary with a zero net revenue coefficient permits us to find opportunity cost and then total cost as a function of output. We next introduce the output price and let it vary, causing the total revenue line to rotate. The maximum difference between total revenue and cost identifies at each price either a unique optimal output, which the firm supplies, or a range of optimal outputs for which the quantity supplied is indeterminate. The end result must be the same as when we vary output price in the objective function and obtain directly the solutions that are optimal at all levels of the price. Both methods yield the supply curve of an output.

EXERCISES

1. *The Supply Curve for an Output*

$$\begin{aligned} 3x_1 + 6x_2 + 3x_3 + 6x_4 + x_5 \quad &= 150 \\ 2x_1 + 8x_2 + 12x_3 + 1x_4 \quad + x_6 &= 180 \\ 4x_1 + 12x_2 + 8x_3 + 4x_4 \quad &= R(\max). \end{aligned}$$

(a) Reduce the preceding model of a multiproduct firm to canonical form with respect to the first basis on the left. Verify that it is the optimal solution.

(b) Treat all r coefficients as market prices. Let the price of some nonbasic output vary from zero upward and find the solutions that are optimal at all levels of the price. Present the results in the form of Table 5–1, omitting the input prices, and graph the supply curve. Explain the relationship of the supply curve to the marginal opportunity cost curve for the product.

(c) After the product whose price is rising has entered the basis, express marginal opportunity cost for each nonbasic product as a linear function of the increasing price. For each of these products determine whether the marginal opportunity cost curve shifts upward or downward. What economic relationship determines the direction of change? Give an economic interpretation of the selection of new variables for the basis as the price of a basic product continues to rise. Draw the graphs.

(d) Add a variable input, choosing input coefficients and a market price that leave the net revenue coefficients unchanged. How does the presence of a variable input, or of several variable inputs, affect the marginal cost curve and the supply curve of (b)?

2. *Marginal Revenue Productivity and the Input Demand Curve*

(a) If you have not already done so, reduce the numerical example of Exercise 1 to canonical form with respect to the first basis on the left and verify that it is the optimal solution.

(b) Let one of the inputs vary parametrically and find the solutions that are optimal at all levels of the input. Determine the total revenue function and the marginal revenue productivities and present in the form of Table 5–2. Plot both total revenue and the marginal revenue productivity of the input that is varying. Show how the demand curve for the input can be derived from its marginal revenue productivity graph.

(c) Assume that the input chosen in (b) can be purchased in any amount needed at the going market price. Find the firm's demand curve for the input by the direct method of varying the market price parametrically over the entire range of nonnegative values. Present the results in the form of Table 5–4.

3. *Total and Marginal Cost for an Output*

(a) In the numerical example for Exercise 1, set the net revenue coefficient for a nonbasic product equal to zero and transfer the variable to the right-hand side. (If you have done Exercise 1, choose the same nonbasic product.) Apply parametric programming to find net revenue as a function of the nonbasic output. Choose an input coefficient and a market price for a variable input. Present the results in the form of Table 5–3 and draw graphs similar to those in Figure 5–3.

(b) Explain the distinction between opportunity cost and internal or imputed cost. Show algebraically why they must be equal in the linear model of a multiproduct firm.

4, 5, and **6.** *An Alternative Numerical Example*

Apply the instructions for Exercises 1, 2, and 3 to the following alternative model:

$$\begin{aligned} x_1+2x_2+2x_3+6x_4+4x_5+x_6 \quad &= 120 \\ x_1+4x_2+8x_3+3x_4+1x_5 \quad +x_7 &= 180 \\ 2x_1+6x_2+8x_3+8x_4+3x_5 \quad &= R(\max). \end{aligned}$$

7, 8, and **9.** *A Second Alternative Example*

Apply the instructions for Exercises 1, 2, and 3 to the numerical example in Table 3–1.

10. *Parametric Programming When Inputs Exceed Outputs*

(a) If you have not already done so, reduce the numerical example of Exercise 7 in Chapter 3 to canonical form with respect to (x_1, x_2, x_5, x_6). Verify that it is the optimal solution.

(b) Treat the r coefficients as market prices. Let the price of one product vary over the entire nonnegative range. Present the results in tabular form and graph the supply curve. When both outputs are being produced, how does a rise in one price make the solution nonoptimal and force a change of basis? Give an economic interpretation.

(c) In the original optimal solution assign each input a separate column on the right-hand side and find the barred coefficients for both the constraints and the objective form. Let one of the inputs vary over the entire nonnegative range and present the results in tabular form. Graph the total revenue and marginal revenue productivity curve for the input. In what two economically different ways can a solution become infeasible?

11. *Parametric Programming in the Dual*

(a) Set up the dual to the numerical example of the text and reduce to canonical form with respect to what you know to be the optimal solution. Let the original coefficient of y_1 in the objective form vary parametrically and find the critical values at which the solution is about to change. Give an economic interpretation of what occurs at each change of solution. Graph the results and identify the curve.

(b) Assign each constant a separate column on the right-hand side and find the barred coefficients for both the constraints and the objective function in the original optimal solution. Give an economic interpretation of one column of barred coefficients in the constraints. Write the coefficients of the objective function in symbolic form and interpret. Let r_3 vary parametrically over the entire nonnegative range and present the results in a table showing how V and the objective coefficient of r_3 vary. Plot r_3 and its objective coefficient and identify the resultant curve. In economic terms, what happens when the solution to the dual is allowed to become infeasible?

(c) What general conclusions can you draw about the relationships between parametric programming in the dual and in the primal?

12. *Full Utilization and Negative Marginal Revenue Productivity*

(a) In the numerical example of the text omit the slack variables and reduce r_4 from 6 to 4 and r_3 from 5 to 3. With slack omitted the available amounts of both inputs must always be utilized fully. Let z_1 vary parametrically over the entire permissible range. Find the total revenue as a function of z_1 and graph. Note that the curve must end in a point when there are no further products to introduce.

What effects do the reductions in r_3 and r_4 have on the marginal revenue productivities or internal prices of both inputs? Would either product ever be produced if the inputs did not have to be used fully and could go costlessly to waste?

(b) For every unused unit of the first input the firm incurs a cost of \$2 for extra maintenance. Thus, the slack process for the first input has an objective coefficient $r_5 = -2$. Show algebraically that the barred objective coefficient for the slack process no longer equals $-y_1$ but differs from it by a constant amount. Similarly, the second input has an extra maintenance cost of \$2 a unit so $r_6 = -2$.

Carry out the parametric variation of z_1 with a *cost for slack included*. From the computations carried out in (a) you already have all data needed to calculate all barred coefficients for the slack processes in all prior solutions. Find the remaining segments of the revenue function and complete the graph. What is the effect of extra maintenance costs on the marginal revenue productivities or internal prices of both inputs?

13. *A Tax on a Single Product: Two Different Results*

(a) In the numerical example of the text, introduce a tax per unit on the second product, making the net revenue coefficient $(r_2 - t_2) = (4 - t_2)$. Let the value of t_2 vary from zero upward. Over what range of t_2 does the current solution remain optimal? What happens to total revenue and the internal prices of the inputs over this range?

Let the tax go beyond the range of the current solution. Which product comes in and which product does it replace? What is the economic relation of the entering product to x_2? Express total tax revenue as a function of t_2 and find the maximum tax revenue that can be raised.

(b) Add to the numerical example a new product x_7 with coefficients $(a_{17} = 8,\ a_{27} = 7,\ r_7 = 29)$. Present the model in canonical form with respect to (x_1, x_2) and verify that it is still the optimal solution. Again let a tax on the second product vary from zero upward and find the range of optimality for the initial solution.

Let the tax go beyond the range of the initial solution. Which product comes in and which product does it replace? Express total tax revenue as a function of t_2 and find the maximum amount of tax revenue that can be raised by taxing x_2. In economic terms what is the reason for the difference between (a) and (b)?

14. *Equiproportional Taxes on Products*

(a) In the numerical example of the text, assume initially no variable inputs and use the revenue function $R = 16x_1 + 7x_2 + 6x_3 + 10x_4$. Note the change in p_3 from 10 to 6. Present in canonical form and verify that (x_1, x_2) remains the optimal solution. All products are taxed at the same percentage rate t of their market prices. Write the expression for the barred objective coefficient of a nonbasic product and show that t may increase to any level short of 100% taxation without affecting the optimal basis. How do total revenue and the internal prices of the inputs change as the tax rate increases?

(b) Add a variable input using the coefficients and input market price in the equation on page 80 of the chapter but making the following change: reduce a_{33} from 5 to 1. Express each net revenue coefficient in terms of the output market price, the tax rate t, and the unit variable cost of the product. For some nonbasic product find the barred objective coefficient. Show that it can be separated into two expressions, one based on output prices less taxes and the other constructed similarly from the unit variable cost of the products. Write in symbolic form.

Let the tax rate t vary from zero upward. Find the value of t for which the optimal basis is about to change. Since all prices after tax change proportionately, what explains the introduction of a new product? Introduce the new product and at the critical level of t calculate the following quantities for each solution: total revenue, total variable cost, total tax paid, and total net revenue. How does the shift in products affect the tax paid and the net revenue received? Graph total tax paid as a function of the tax rate over the range of both solutions. How do you explain the effect on net revenue and the taxes paid?

15. *Finding Tax Rates That Maximize Tax Revenue*

Base your answers on the numerical example and optimal solution of the first section in the present chapter.

(a) What is the maximum amount of tax that can be imposed on a unit of the first product without causing a change in output levels? What is the maximum amount of subsidy that can be granted to a unit of the first product without causing a change in output levels?

(b) Find the maximum unit tax and subsidy for the second product which will leave output levels unchanged.

(c) Suppose that a tax is levied on each unit produced of both commodities. Find all possible combinations of taxes on both commodities which will not cause a change in output levels. (Hint: Express the critical conditions as linear functions of the two taxes and then plot.)

(d) Find the maximum amount of tax revenue which can be raised without causing output levels to change. (Hint: Set up the problem as a linear programming maximizing problem, with output levels constant and taxes as the variables.)

16. *The Effect of Input Levels on Output Supply Curves*

In the numerical example as set up on page 91, treat the net revenue coefficients as market prices and demonstrate that changes in market prices do not affect the feasibility of the solution. What is the analogous conclusion regarding the variation of fixed inputs?

Find the range of $r_1(= p_1)$ over which the solution remains optimal and graph as one segment of the supply curve for x_1. Let z_1 vary within the feasible range and determine the effect on the segment of the supply curve for x_1. Find the corresponding segments when z_1 is at the lower limit of the feasible range and when it is at the upper limit. Show both graphically and algebraically how the variation in z_1 affects the quantity supplied of x_1.

Let z_1 increase into the next feasible range and find the new optimal solution. Calculate and graph the segment of the supply curve for x_1 when z_1 is at the lower limit of the new feasible range and when it is at the upper limit. Show both graphically and algebraically how the variation in z_1 affects the quantity supplied of x_1. What do the two cases together show about the effect of an input on the quantity supplied of an output? Which input is the bottleneck for x_1 in each range? Incorporate this information in a fuller explanation of how an input affects the supply of an output.

Compare the preceding result with the example in the text showing how a change in an output price affects the marginal revenue productivity of an input. Write symbolically in terms of the $\bar{e}$ coefficients the expressions for x_1 in terms of the inputs and for y_1 in terms of the output prices. Show that the following statement must hold in general: If an increase in the amount of a previously fixed input raises or lowers the amount supplied of an output in the basis, then an increase in the price of that output must raise or lower the internal price of the input. That is, the price and the quantity variations go in the same direction.

6

Vectors and Vector Spaces

Chapter 5 portrayed the linear version of the firm by diagrams that are the counterparts of those used in the conventional theory: marginal cost and supply curves for outputs, marginal revenue productivity and demand curves for inputs. These diagrams show the response of the firm to changes in important parameters but do not display in one graph the optimizing problem that the firm is seeking to solve. For this some knowledge of vectors and vector spaces is needed. The present chapter provides the necessary background and uses it to give a graphical interpretation of linear programming problems and the simplex method of solving them.

VECTORS

Though usually unrecognized, vectors are a frequent phenomenon in everyone's daily experience. In a course in which several examinations are given, the set of scores by a student on these examinations forms a vector. Similarly, the set of prices for all commodities is a vector, as is the set of all quantities produced during a period. A vector, then, is an ordered set of numbers, but as will be seen shortly some restrictions must be placed on the choice of number. The qualification "ordered" simply means that places are distinguished and it makes a difference which number occupies each place. For example, if antimacassars are the first commodity and automobiles are the second, it makes no economic sense to interchange the numbers representing the production of each. Thus, production levels are appropriately regarded as a vector in which each commodity is assigned a fixed place.

In the definition of a vector, the key words are "ordered set" and "numbers." Both are essential. There can be ordered sets of entities other than numbers; for example, words, where the place a letter occupies obviously makes a difference. Or there can be sets of numbers that are not ordered. The set of odd positive integers whose square is less than 100 consists of five numbers, but the order in which they are written is inessential. Hence, it is not a vector.

There is another reason why a set of five integers does not form a vector. The numbers from which vectors are formed must constitute a *field.* In mathematics a field is a set of numbers for which the operations of addition, subtraction, multiplication, and division are universally possible, except for division by zero. Integers alone will not do, since division of an integer by an integer does not always yield another integer. If division is to be universally possible, it is necessary to go outside the set of integers and use fractions to designate the result of division. The set of all integers and all fractions, which is the set of *rational* numbers, does constitute a field and can be used to form vectors. However, it is more convenient to use the more inclusive field of real numbers.[1] Vectors also can be given a more abstract definition without any requirement that they be ordered sets of numbers, but such an abstraction has no relevance for the economic application to be made in this book. Thus, the term vector will be used without qualification to designate what is from a broader point of view only a subspecies of vectors, ordered sets of *real* numbers. Ordered sets of real numbers possess all the properties of vectors, but other entities possess them as well.

In mathematics a set is designated by enclosing the members or components within curly braces, as follows: $\{a, b, c, \ldots\}$, where the letters may denote any objects whatsoever. When sets are ordered, and particularly when the components are numbers, it is customary to indicate the added requirement of order by using parentheses or square brackets in place of curly braces. Thus, vectors are usually written as ordered pairs, ordered triples, or their generalization, ordered n-tuples, in the following way:

$$\mathbf{a} = (a_1, a_2); \qquad \mathbf{b} = (b_1, b_2, b_3); \qquad \mathbf{c} = (c_1, c_2, \ldots, c_n).$$

Since a shorthand symbol for vectors is needed, they will be designated, as above, by boldface lowercase letters. Ordinary lowercase letters with subscripts will represent the real numbers that are the components or elements.

Vectors, being ordered n-tuples of real numbers, can be regarded as a generalization of the concept of number. Alternatively, we may proceed in the opposite direction and regard a real number as a special case of a vector with but a single component. As yet, however, there is an important differ-

[1]Besides integers and fractions the field of real numbers contains the irrational numbers, such as $\sqrt{2}$ and π. Unlike rational numbers there is no simple criterion for distinguishing irrational numbers. Their salient property is the result obtained by including them, a one-to-one correspondence between numbers and points on a line. If only rational numbers are used, there are gaps, points to which no number corresponds.

ence; we have some idea of the properties of real numbers and the algebraic operations to which they may be subjected, but operations on vectors remain undefined. The next task is to devise algebraic concepts and operations for the manipulation of vectors. Naturally, the algebra of real numbers furnishes a guide and model.

Equality of Vectors

The first requirement is a definition of equality. For sets in general, two sets are equal if they contain identical members; for vectors there is the added condition that the same members appear in the same positions. Thus, for two vectors we can write

$$(a_1, a_2, a_3) = (b_1, b_2, b_3) \qquad \text{or} \qquad \mathbf{a} = \mathbf{b},$$

if and only if $a_1 = b_1$, $a_2 = b_2$, $a_3 = b_3$. The definition can readily be extended to vectors with any number of components. If any two comparable components are not equal to each other, the vectors are not equal: $\mathbf{a} \neq \mathbf{b}$.

Addition of Vectors

The addition of two vectors can also be defined in straightforward fashion as the addition of components in matching positions. Thus,

$$\mathbf{a}+\mathbf{b} = (a_1, a_2, a_3)+(b_1, b_2, b_3) = (a_1+b_1, a_2+b_2, a_3+b_3),$$

or

$$(5, 3, -2)+(1, 4, 3) = (6, 7, 1).$$

Clearly, addition is possible only if both vectors have the same number of components. Further, the addition of two vectors must always yield a third vector, since adding pairs of real numbers always provides real numbers to form the components of the third vector.

The addition of real numbers possesses certain general properties that we often use without conscious thought. These same properties hold for the addition of vectors. First of all, the order in which two vectors are added does not affect the result, since the order in which the components are added makes no difference. Thus, the addition of vectors, like the addition of real numbers, is *commutatative*. Symbolically, $a+b = b+a$ for real numbers and $\mathbf{a}+\mathbf{b} = \mathbf{b}+\mathbf{a}$ for vectors.

The addition of three or more vectors requires simply the addition of all matching components. Further, it makes no difference to the result if we group or associate together some of the vectors to get a subtotal before adding the remaining vectors. Thus, the addition of vectors, like the addition of real numbers, is *associative*, as is shown symbolically by

$$\mathbf{a}+(\mathbf{b}+\mathbf{c}) = (\mathbf{a}+\mathbf{b})+\mathbf{c}.$$

It is immaterial whether we first associate **b** and **c** together before adding **a** to their sum, or whether we first combine **a** and **b**.

Zero or Null Vectors

An important characteristic of the real number system is the existence of the number zero, which has the following unique property: $a+0 = a$, for any real number a. For vectors, a vector with all components zero plays the same role. Thus, if $\mathbf{0} = (0, 0, 0)$, then for any three-component vector,

$$\mathbf{a}+\mathbf{0} = (a_1, a_2, a_3)+(0, 0, 0) = (a_1, a_2, a_3) = \mathbf{a}.$$

A vector with all components zero is called a *zero vector* or *null vector* and will be designated by a boldface zero. Since vectors can be added only if they contain the same number of components, there is a whole collection of null vectors each with a different number of zero components.

Scalar Multiplication

Since any vector can be added to itself, we are tempted to write $\mathbf{a}+\mathbf{a}=2\mathbf{a}$. But as yet no meaning has been assigned to the product of a real number and a vector. The operation will now be defined in such a way as to give validity to the foregoing equation. For any vector $\mathbf{a} = (a_1, a_2, a_3)$ and any real number r we give the following definition:

$$r\mathbf{a} = r(a_1, a_2, a_3) = (ra_1, ra_2, ra_3).$$

Thus, multiplication of a vector by a real number r yields a new vector whose components are the original components, each multiplied by r. For example, if $r = 2$, all components are doubled. Since multiplication by a real number has the effect of changing all components in the same ratio or scale, the operation is called *scalar multiplication*, and r is called a *scalar*. When working with vectors, it is customary to apply the term scalar to any real number, whether it is used in multiplication or is simply one of the components.

Linear Combinations of Vectors

Scalar multiplication and vector addition can be combined, as follows:

$$\begin{aligned} r\mathbf{a}+s\mathbf{b} &= r(a_1, a_2, a_3)+s(b_1, b_2, b_3) = (ra_1, ra_2, ra_3)+(sb_1, sb_2, sb_3) \\ &= (ra_1+sb_1, ra_2+sb_2, ra_3+sb_3). \end{aligned}$$

The result is an ordered triple of real numbers and, hence, another three-component vector. An expression such as $r\mathbf{a}+s\mathbf{b}$, in which vectors are multiplied by scalars and added, is called *a linear combination of vectors.* Linear combinations of vectors are the key concept in defining vector spaces.

Scalar multiplication also provides a convenient way to define the subtraction of vectors. Thus,

$$\mathbf{a}-\mathbf{b} = \mathbf{a}+(-1)\mathbf{b} = (a_1-b_1, a_2-b_2, a_3-b_3).$$

Subtraction of vectors is equivalent to multiplying by the scalar -1 and adding. There is also the important result

$$\mathbf{a}-\mathbf{a} = \mathbf{a}+(-1)\mathbf{a} = (a_1-a_1, a_2-a_2, a_3-a_3) = (0, 0, 0) = \mathbf{0}.$$

Subtraction of any vector from itself always yields the null vector.

Row and Column Vectors

In systems of linear equations the coefficients in any one equation or row are an ordered set of numbers, called a *row vector.* Similarly, the coefficients of any one variable are an ordered set of numbers and form a *column vector.* To emphasize the distinction we shall enclose row vectors in parentheses, as in preceding pages, and column vectors in square brackets. A linear combination of column vectors takes the form

$$r\mathbf{a}+s\mathbf{b} = r\begin{bmatrix} a_1 \\ a_2 \end{bmatrix} + s\begin{bmatrix} b_1 \\ b_2 \end{bmatrix} = \begin{bmatrix} ra_1+sb_1 \\ ra_2+sb_2 \end{bmatrix}.$$

For systems of linear equations superscripts and subscripts will denote row and column vectors, respectively. Thus, for two equations in two unknowns,

$$\mathbf{a}_1 = \begin{bmatrix} a_{11} \\ a_{21} \end{bmatrix}; \qquad \mathbf{a}^1 = (a_{11}, a_{12}); \qquad \mathbf{a}_2 = \begin{bmatrix} a_{12} \\ a_{22} \end{bmatrix}; \qquad \mathbf{a}^2 = (a_{21}, a_{22}).$$

Later sections of this chapter deal primarily with columns of coefficients in linear equations. To smooth the transition we shall shift over to the column notation for vectors. But columns of numbers do waste space, so we shall, when convenient, write the components in a row but enclose them in a square bracket to denote a column vector. Thus, $\mathbf{c} = [c_1, c_2, \dots, c_n]$ is a column vector, and readers may mentally restore it to the proper position. The preceding algebraic properties of vectors are independent of the form in which they are written.

In setting up a problem we may first choose one form for vectors and later wish to convert to the other form. For example, in linear programming the coefficients of a variable or a column in the primal become the coefficients of an equation or row in the dual. Shifting a vector from column to row form, or vice versa, is a mathematical operation called *transposition*, which is shown symbolically by affixing the superscript ^{T} to a vector. If $\mathbf{a}_1$ is the first column vector of the primal, then

$$\mathbf{a}_1^T = \begin{bmatrix} a_{11} \\ a_{21} \end{bmatrix}^T = (a_{11}, a_{21}),$$

which is the first row vector in the dual. Thus, $\mathbf{a}_1^T$ denotes a row vector, called the *transpose* of $\mathbf{a}_1$. The transpose of a row vector is a column vector. Two successive transpositions merely restore the original vector, which explains why the dual of the dual is the primal.

Multiplication of Vectors

The precedent established by vector addition suggests that we simply multiply corresponding elements and enter the results as components in a new vector. While consistent with vector addition, such a procedure does not give the most useful mathematical results and has not been adopted. Instead, the product of two vectors is formed by first multiplying corresponding elements and then adding the results, as follows:

$$\mathbf{a}^T\mathbf{b} = (a_1, a_2)\begin{bmatrix} b_1 \\ b_2 \end{bmatrix} = a_1b_1 + a_2b_2.$$

Although not essential, it is customary to write the first vector in row form, the second in column form. When two vectors are multiplied, the result is not another vector but a single real number or scalar. Hence, $\mathbf{a}^T\mathbf{b}$ is called the *scalar product* of the two vectors. We must be careful not to confuse scalar multiplication and scalar product. Scalar multiplication is multiplication of a vector by a real number or scalar, which yields another vector. The scalar product is the multiplication of a vector by a vector, which yields a real number or scalar.

Scalar products provide a succinct notation for linear equations. If $\mathbf{a}^1 = (a_{11}, a_{12})$ is some row vector of coefficients and $\mathbf{x} = [x_1, x_2]$ is an unknown vector, we can write a linear equation equivalently as

$$\mathbf{a}^1\mathbf{x} = b_1 \qquad (a_{11}, a_{12})\begin{bmatrix} x_1 \\ x_2 \end{bmatrix} = b_1 \qquad a_{11}x_1 + a_{12}x_2 = b_1.$$

The vector notation is especially efficient when there are many variables. Also, if $\mathbf{p}$ is a vector of prices and $\mathbf{q}$ is a vector of the corresponding quantities, $\mathbf{p}^T\mathbf{q} = p_1q_1 + p_2q_2 = R$. Thus, the scalar product is a convenient way of writing the total revenue from a set of products.

We shall not have occasion to use the scalar product of vectors in later chapters and shall not develop the topic further. It is presented here to round out the algebra of vectors. Unlike real numbers there is no operation of division for vectors. Division reverses the results of multiplication and is termed the inverse operation to multiplication. The minimum requirement for division to be possible is that multiplication of two entities yield a third entity like themselves. For example, the multiplication of two real numbers yields a third real number. Vectors do not pass this minimal test since the product of two vectors is not another vector. The operation can not be reversed to give back one of the original vectors.

VECTOR SPACES

The foregoing algebraic relations can be displayed geometrically. The basic link between algebra and geometry, for which we give no proof, is a one-to-one correspondence between the set of all real numbers and all points on a line. If we choose an interval on a line and arbitrarily associate any two real numbers with the endpoints, then each number between the two chosen corresponds to one and only one point lying in the interval, and all other real numbers have geometric counterparts in points lying outside the interval. For simplicity the numbers customarily chosen are 0 and 1. We assign 0 to the left endpoint of the interval as we face it, and 1 to the right endpoint. This being done, we may speak of numbers or points interchangeably, since to every point there corresponds one and only one number, and with every number there is associated one and only one point.

To represent a pair of numbers we need a pair of lines. These lines can intersect at any angle and at any point, but for simplest results we choose perpendicular lines and have the point of intersection correspond to 0 on both lines. It also helps to choose a unit interval of the same length on each line. Otherwise certain useful geometric properties are lost; an algebraic square becomes a geometric rectangle, and distance does not have a clear interpretation.

Once axes and unit intervals are selected, every ordered pair of numbers determines a unique point in space. To plot a vector, we must first associate members of the ordered pair with the straight lines chosen as axes. Customarily, the first number is assigned to the horizontal axis, and the second number to the vertical. At every point along the horizontal axis, the second number in the pair is zero, and at every point on the vertical axis, the first number is zero. To locate the point associated with the vector $\mathbf{a} = [a_1, a_2]$, we first note that $\mathbf{a}$ can be written as the sum of two vectors,

$$\mathbf{a} = [a_1, a_2] = [a_1, 0] + [0, a_2].$$

In plotting a vector we first find the point on the horizontal axis corresponding to $[a_1, 0]$. We then treat this point temporarily as a new origin and locate $[0, a_2]$ with respect to it. The resultant point relative to the permanent origin is the geometric representation of the vector.

Vector Addition

The preceding geometric portrayal of vector addition carries over to vectors that do not lie on axes. By the method of the previous paragraph each vector can be located relative to perpendicular axes. One vector is then chosen as a temporary origin, and the second vector is plotted relative to this origin, as shown in Figure 6–1. The resultant point relative to the permanent origin is the geometric representation of the sum $\mathbf{a}+\mathbf{b} = [a_1+b_1, a_2+b_2]$. By virtue of the commutativity of vector addition, it makes no difference which vector serves as the temporary origin for the other.

In the geometric interpretation the addition of distances along horizontal and vertical axes replaces the addition of numbers. What is the meaning, then, of a negative component for the second vector? Since distance itself cannot be negative, a negative sign implies a reversal of direction. For example, the point $[1, 0]$ is the same distance to the right of the origin as the point $[-1, 0]$ is to the left. Hence, if $a_1 = 2$ and $b_1 = -3$, the result of moving two units to the right and three units to the left is a net movement of

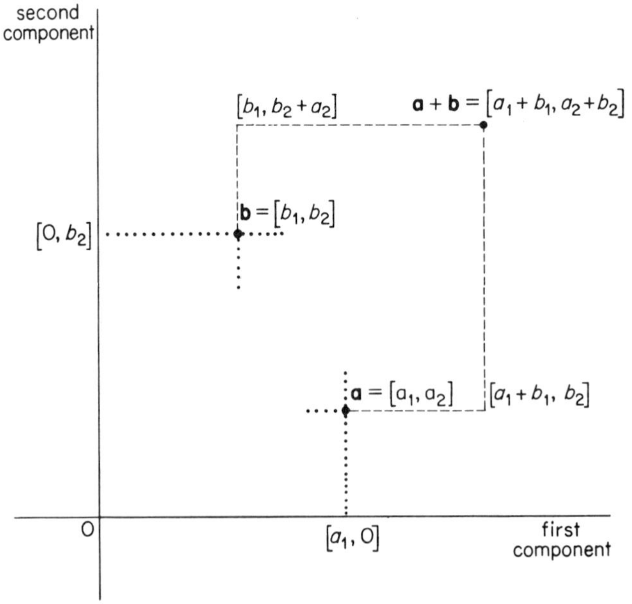

Fig. 6-1 Vector Addition

one unit to the left with respect to the permanent origin. The difference of two vectors, $\mathbf{a}-\mathbf{b}$, can be plotted easily as $\mathbf{a}+(-1)\mathbf{b}$, which means measuring b_1 leftward and b_2 downward. A further useful result is

$$\mathbf{a}-\mathbf{a} = [a_1-a_1, a_2-a_2] = [0, 0] = \mathbf{0}.$$

Thus, the null vector is identified as the origin.

Scalar Multiplication

Scalar multiplication has a particularly simple geometric representation for vectors on the axes. If the vector $[a_1, 0]$ is multiplied by 2, the resultant vector $[2a_1, 0]$ is a point on the horizontal axis twice as far from the origin. The result shows up most clearly for the unit vector, $\mathbf{u}_1 = [1, 0]$. Any point on the horizontal axis is represented by

$$x_1\mathbf{u}_1 = x_1[1, 0] = [x_1, 0]$$

for some specified value of x_1, and the distance from the origin varies proportionately with the magnitude of x_1. The horizontal axis may thus be defined as the set of all scalar multiples of the unit vector $\mathbf{u}_1 = [1, 0]$ by a real number. If the scalar x_1 is confined to the nonnegative range, the set of all scalar multiples is the nonnegative semiaxis or halfline.[2] Similar results follow for the vertical axis by taking all scalar multiples of the second unit vector $\mathbf{u}_2 = [0, 1]$. Unit vectors are important also in spaces of higher dimension. The convention followed in two dimensions is generalized; the symbol $\mathbf{u}$ is reserved for unit vectors and the subscript denotes the place occupied by unity. Thus, in three dimensions

$$\mathbf{u}_1 = [1, 0, 0]; \qquad \mathbf{u}_2 = [0, 1, 0]; \qquad \mathbf{u}_3 = [0, 0, 1].$$

If a vector $\mathbf{a}$, not on an axis, is multiplied by a scalar, the resultant vector is a point lying on the same straight line through the origin. A straight line through the origin passing through the point $\mathbf{a} = [a_1, a_2]$ has a slope equal to a_2/a_1. The straight line from the origin through the point $r\mathbf{a} = [ra_1, ra_2]$ has the slope $ra_2/ra_1 = a_2/a_1$ and is the same line. Scalar multiplication leaves the slope unchanged, so the set of all scalar multiples of a fixed vector $\mathbf{a}$ defines a straight line through the origin. If only nonnegative multiples are permitted, the result is a *half-line* from the origin or *ray*. Each vector generates one and only one ray from the origin containing itself, but many vectors generate the same ray.

The fact that every vector lies on a unique half-line through the origin

[2]The nonpositive semiaxis can be defined by letting x_1 take on values of zero or less, but it is often simpler to use all nonnegative multiples of the vector $[-1, 0]$.

suggests another way of locating vectors, by moving a specified distance from the origin in the given direction. When vectors are used in physics, the salient properties are distance and direction. In fact, vectors are customarily represented not as points in space but as arrows of given length and direction. The reason is that many important physical concepts, such as force, are best described by two quantities, the magnitude of the force and the direction in which it is exerted. If two forces with different magnitudes and different directions are acting simultaneously on a body, the result can be portrayed correctly by adding vectors. As Figure 6–2 shows, the tip of one arrow becomes the temporary origin for drawing another arrow, shown as a dashed line for clarity. A single arrow from the origin to the tip of their sum represents the single force and direction that produces the same effect as the two separate forces acting in different directions. Since vector addition is commutative, either the tip of **a** or the tip of **b** can serve as temporary origin. If both are used, the result is a parallelogram with the desired point as the vertex opposite the origin.

Neither force nor direction nor analogues of these concepts have much relevance in most economic interpretations. Economists generally use vectors to represent collections of quantities that are measured in different units and cannot be added to get a single number. The distance between vectors

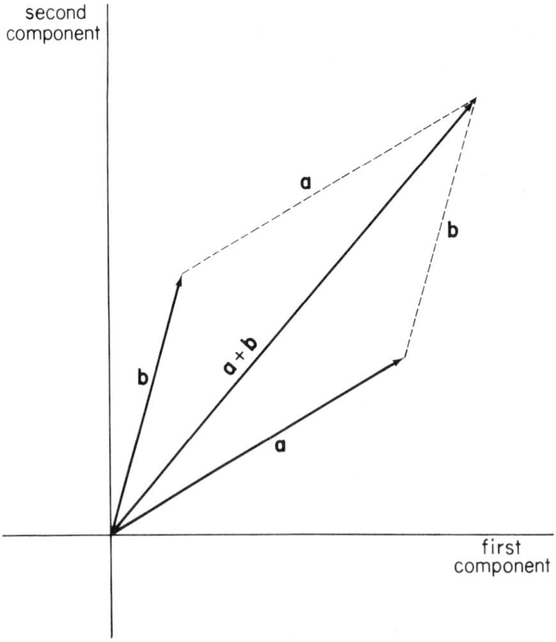

Fig. 6-2 Vectors as Directed Line Segments: Addition of Vectors

corresponds to the hypotenuse of a right-angled triangle. For example, the length of the vector **a**, its distance from the origin, is the hypotenuse of the triangle whose sides are formed by a_1 and a_2. The length of the hypotenuse and, hence, the distance between vectors, requires that the components be squared and then added. But quantities measured in different units cannot be meaningfully added before or after squaring. Since length or distance is a geometric property, it is there for the using. Physicists can use it, but economists generally cannot, just as they cannot in general use the negative numbers. Directed line segments are, however, a very convenient way to portray the addition of vectors and can be used so long as we do not attribute general economic significance to the length of vectors or the distance between them. There is one special case where distance does have economic meaning, when all vectors lie on the same half-line. It is easy to show both geometrically and algebraically that multiplication of a vector by a nonnegative scalar causes distance from the origin to be multiplied by the same scalar. Thus, an equiproportional change in economic quantities corresponds to the same proportional change in distance along a ray. What we cannot do when quantities are measured in different units is to compare distances from the origin along two distinct rays.

Linear Combinations of Vectors

The unit vectors illustrate most clearly the sweeping results that emerge from the combination of scalar multiplication and vector addition. Multiplication of $\mathbf{u}_1$ by any real number x_1 means that any point on the horizontal axis can be chosen as temporary origin for the addition of another vector. If $\mathbf{u}_2$ is multiplied by any real number x_2, any vector on the vertical axis can be chosen for addition. It is intuitively obvious that the combined operations can locate any point in the space. Thus, the linear combination

$$x_1\mathbf{u}_1+x_2\mathbf{u}_2 = x_1[1, 0]+x_2[0, 1] = [x_1, x_2]$$

determines the unique point lying x_1 units from the origin along the horizontal axis and x_2 units in the vertical direction. The numbers used in the linear combination are called the *coordinates* of the point relative to the unit vectors, or the *rectangular coordinates* of the point.

Even if the vectors do not lie on the axes, similar results follow. Multiplying the vector **a** by any real number r permits any point on a line through the origin to be chosen as temporary origin for vector addition. If **b** does not lie on the same line through the origin as **a**, then multiplying the vector **b** by any real number s permits any point on the second line to be chosen for addition. As the temporary origin traverses the infinitely extensive first line, the infinitely extensive second line sweeps through the entire space. Any ordered pair of real numbers (r, s), used in the linear combination $r\mathbf{a}+s\mathbf{b}$, locates a unique point in space. The numbers (r, s) are the coordinates of the point *relative* to the axes determined by **a** and **b**, or the *oblique coordinates.*

Depending upon the axes chosen, a given ordered pair of real numbers locates a different point in space. For example, with respect to the rectangular axes the ordered pair (1, 1) corresponds to the point

$$1\mathbf{u}_1+1\mathbf{u}_2 = 1[1, 0]+1[0, 1] = [1, 1].$$

Relative to **a** and **b**, the same pair of coordinates locates the point

$$1\mathbf{a}+1\mathbf{b} = 1[a_1, a_2]+1[b_1, b_2] = [a_1+b_1, a_2+b_2].$$

The final bracket shows the coordinates relative to rectangular axes; that is,

$$1\mathbf{a}+1\mathbf{b} = (a_1+b_1)\mathbf{u}_1+(a_2+b_2)\mathbf{u}_2.$$

Thus, the coordinates (1, 1) relative to **a** and **b** locate the same point as the coordinates (a_1+b_1, a_2+b_2) relative to $\mathbf{u}_1$ and $\mathbf{u}_2$. The same pair of coordinates locates a different point, depending on the axes chosen. Or, alternatively, the same point acquires different coordinates when the axes are changed.

If **a** and **b** lie on the same line through the origin, it is still true that every ordered pair of numbers determines one and only one point, but every such point must lie on the same line. For example, if $\mathbf{b} = 2\mathbf{a}$, then

$$r\mathbf{a}+s\mathbf{b} = r\mathbf{a}+s(2\mathbf{a}) = (r+2s)\mathbf{a} = t\mathbf{a}.$$

Every linear combination of **a** and **b** can be expressed as some scalar multiple of **a**. Since the equation $r+2s = t$ can be satisfied by infinitely many pairs of values for r and s, the same point $t\mathbf{a}$ may be expressed as infinitely many linear combinations of **a** and **b**. Hence, when **a** and **b** lie on the same line through the origin, points off the line have no coordinates and each point on the line has infinitely many. Three vectors not lying on the same line through the origin can also be used to locate points in the plane, but not very efficiently. Three numbers are required for coordinates, and the coordinates are not unique.

Finding the Oblique Coordinates of a Point

Given two fixed vectors, each ordered pair of numbers determines a unique point in the space. The numbers used in the linear combination of the given vectors are the coordinates of the point relative to these vectors or to the axes they generate. Suppose that we reverse the procedure, choose a point **b** in space, and then ask for the coordinates of the point relative to the given axes. If $\mathbf{a}_1$ and $\mathbf{a}_2$ are the fixed vectors generating the axes, the problem is to find the unknown pair of numbers (x_1, x_2) such that

$$x_1\mathbf{a}_1 + x_2\mathbf{a}_2 = \mathbf{b}.$$

The answer can be found geometrically in two dimensions, as shown in Figure 6–3. Draw a line through $\mathbf{b}$ parallel to the axis generated by $\mathbf{a}_2$. The distance along this line to the point of intersection with the axis generated by $\mathbf{a}_1$ measures $x_2\mathbf{a}_2$, and the distance from the point of intersection to the origin measures $x_1\mathbf{a}_1$. The numerical value assigned x_1 depends on the distance of $x_1\mathbf{a}_1$ from the origin relative to the distance of $\mathbf{a}_1$. For example, if $\mathbf{a}_1$ is 3 in. distant and $x_1\mathbf{a}_1$ is 5 in. distant, the value of x_1 is $\frac{5}{3}$. A similar procedure determines the value of x_2. Although correct in concept, such a geometric solution is necessarily somewhat inexact in two or three dimensions and totally inapplicable in more than three dimensions.

To find a more general and more exact method, we first rewrite the equation, as follows:

$$x_1\begin{bmatrix} a_{11} \\ a_{21} \end{bmatrix} + x_2\begin{bmatrix} a_{12} \\ a_{22} \end{bmatrix} = \begin{bmatrix} b_1 \\ b_2 \end{bmatrix} \quad \text{or} \quad \begin{bmatrix} x_1a_{11} + x_2a_{12} \\ x_1a_{21} + x_2a_{22} \end{bmatrix} = \begin{bmatrix} b_1 \\ b_2 \end{bmatrix}.$$

Since corresponding components must be equal, we can drop the brackets

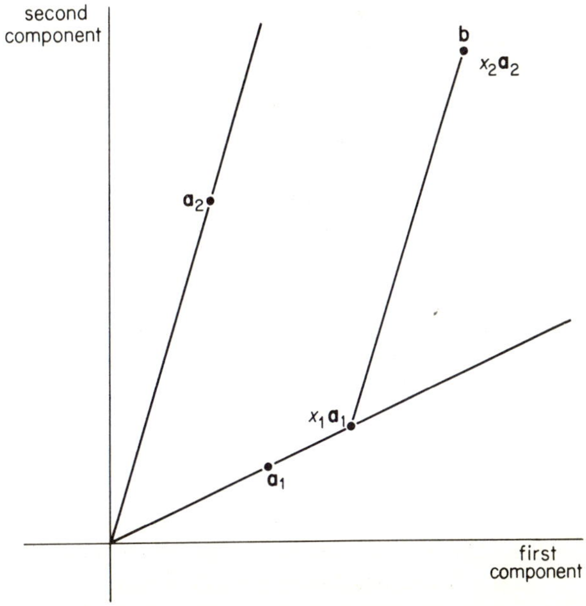

Fig. 6-3 Finding the Oblique Coordinates of a Point

and write the equality of vectors as the familiar pair of two linear equations in two unknowns. Thus, one geometric analogue of solving two linear equations in two unknowns is finding the unknown coordinates of a point with respect to two fixed vectors. There are two other geometric analogues as well, a familiar one being the intersection of two straight lines, as displayed in Chapter 2.

Chapter 2 demonstrated that elementary operations applied to a system of linear equations do not affect the solution values and can be used to solve any system that has a solution. Elementary operations, when combined into pivot operations, reduce the original system to diagonal form, expressed below by vectors:

$$x_1\begin{bmatrix}1\\0\end{bmatrix}+x_2\begin{bmatrix}0\\1\end{bmatrix}=\begin{bmatrix}\bar{b}_1\\\bar{b}_2\end{bmatrix} \qquad \text{or} \qquad x_1\mathbf{u}_1+x_2\mathbf{u}_2=\bar{\mathbf{b}}.$$

Relative to the unit vectors, the vector $\bar{\mathbf{b}}$ has rectangular coordinates $(x_1 = \bar{b}_1, x_2 = \bar{b}_2)$. But x_1 and x_2 are unchanged by the elementary operations, so the original point $\mathbf{b}$ has oblique coordinates $(\bar{b}_1, \bar{b}_2)$ relative to $\mathbf{a}_1$ and $\mathbf{a}_2$.

Elementary operations are examples of *linear transformations*, which relocate all points in a space in a systematic and consistent way. Any linear combination of vectors before the transformation persists after the transformation as the same linear combination of the relocated vectors. Thus, all linear transformations preserve linear combinations. In addition, the transformations performed in sequence to obtain the diagonal form have a very special effect; they rotate the oblique axes into a perpendicular position and stretch or compress the axes until $\mathbf{a}_1$ and $\mathbf{a}_2$ become unit vectors.

The original problem was to find the unknown coordinates of $\mathbf{b}$ relative to $\mathbf{a}_1$ and $\mathbf{a}_2$. This problem is not easy to solve directly so we replace it by the problem: Find a point $\bar{\mathbf{b}}$ that has the same coordinates relative to $\mathbf{u}_1$ and $\mathbf{u}_2$ as the original point $\mathbf{b}$ has with respect to $\mathbf{a}_1$ and $\mathbf{a}_2$. Elementary operations on vectors provide a simple but infallible method for transforming $\mathbf{a}_1$ and $\mathbf{a}_2$ into the unit vectors, without changing the coordinates of any point. Once this is done, we have the answer, since the components of $\bar{\mathbf{b}}$, or of any other vector, serve as its coordinates relative to $\mathbf{u}_1$ and $\mathbf{u}_2$.

In the foregoing exposition, $\mathbf{a}_1$ and $\mathbf{a}_2$ were assumed not to lie on the same line through the origin. If they are collinear, we must next ask whether $\mathbf{b}$ does or does not lie on the same line. If it does not, the point $\mathbf{b}$ cannot be reached by any linear combination of $\mathbf{a}_1$ and $\mathbf{a}_2$. Coordinates for $\mathbf{b}$ do not exist; the system of equations is unsolvable. When $\mathbf{b}$ does lie on the same line, it can be expressed in infinitely many ways as a linear combination of $\mathbf{a}_1$ and $\mathbf{a}_2$. One vector must be dropped for a unique answer; one equation is redundant. Thus, unsolvability and redundancy both have simple geometric interpretations. Points in the plane can also be located relative to any collection of vectors, however large, provided that at least two are not collinear with the origin. But neither the coordinates nor the solutions to the corresponding equations can be unique.

Linear Independence, Spanning Sets, and Dimension

Any system of linear equations, however large, has a unique solution only when the vector **b** has unique coordinates relative to the column vectors of coefficients in the equations. In the plane too few vectors, too many vectors, and collinear vectors all cause trouble. To find the conditions under which all points in any vector space have unique coordinates, we shall use the plane as a guide and restate the requirements in a form that generalizes to spaces of any finite dimension. Relative to any two vectors in the plane, the origin or null vector has the following equation:

$$x_1\mathbf{a}_1+x_2\mathbf{a}_2 = \mathbf{0}.$$

The equation always holds for $(x_1 = 0,\ x_2 = 0)$, supplying one pair of coordinates for the origin. If $\mathbf{a}_1$ and $\mathbf{a}_2$ are not collinear through the origin, it is the only solution, and the coordinates are unique. When $\mathbf{a}_1$ and $\mathbf{a}_2$ are collinear, $\mathbf{a}_1 = r\mathbf{a}_2$. There are always nonzero solutions, specifically, $(x_1 = 1,\ x_2 = -r)$ and any multiple of these values. When the preceding vector equation has the unique solution $x_1 = x_2 = 0$, the vectors are termed *linearly independent*. If there are also nonzero solutions, the vectors are *linearly dependent*.

Linearly independent vectors always assign unique coordinates to the origin; linearly dependent vectors never do. Further, the coordinates of all other points can be unique if and only if the coordinates of the origin are unique. Suppose that the point **b** has the following two distinct sets of coordinates:

$$x_1^1\mathbf{a}_1+x_2^1\mathbf{a}_2 = \mathbf{b}$$
$$x_1^2\mathbf{a}_1+x_2^2\mathbf{a}_2 = \mathbf{b}.$$

Subtracting the second row from the first gives

$$(x_1^1-x_1^2)\mathbf{a}_1+(x_2^1-x_2^2)\mathbf{a}_2 = \mathbf{b}-\mathbf{b} = \mathbf{0}.$$

The parentheses contain nonzero coordinates for the origin, so $\mathbf{a}_1$ and $\mathbf{a}_2$ are linearly dependent. Conversely, if they are linearly independent, the parentheses must vanish, and **b** cannot have more than one set of cordinates. Unique coordinates for the origin imply unique coordinates for every point in the space.

Unit vectors assign unique coordinates to the origin and are, therefore, linearly independent. Further, any set of vectors that can be reduced to diagonal form must be linearly independent. Since elementary operations do not alter solutions, the same set of values, $x_1 = x_2 = 0$, must satisfy both the following original and transformed equations:

$$x_1\begin{bmatrix}a_{11}\\a_{21}\end{bmatrix}+x_2\begin{bmatrix}a_{12}\\a_{22}\end{bmatrix} = \begin{bmatrix}0\\0\end{bmatrix} \qquad x_1\begin{bmatrix}1\\0\end{bmatrix}+x_2\begin{bmatrix}0\\1\end{bmatrix} = \begin{bmatrix}0\\0\end{bmatrix}.$$

The number of unit vectors equals the number of components in the vectors that constitute the space. A large number of components prolongs the elementary operations but does not otherwise affect the process of reducing the diagonal form. Hence, in any vector space reduction to diagonal form proves linear independence.

What prevents reduction to diagonal form is the appearance of a row of zeros. When the equations are expressed in terms of column vectors, a row of zeros means that one unit vector is missing and has been replaced by a multiple of another unit vector, which represents a point on that unit vector's axis. The origin cannot have unique coordinates since the unit vector and its multiple can always be given offsetting nonzero coefficients in a linear combination. With two-component vectors the set of the one unit vector [1, 0] and its multiple k [1, 0] generates only the axis of the unit vector and provides coordinates, but not unique coordinates, only for points on that axis. Since elementary operations preserve coordinates of points after relocation, the original pair of vectors must have been collinear. When we attempt to reduce three-component vectors to diagonal form and get a row of zeros, the resultant set consists of two unit vectors and a multiple of one of them. It generates only the coordinate plane of the two unit vectors. Hence, the original set must also consist of three vectors lying in the same plane.

Three or more two-component vectors cannot be linearly independent even when one pair of vectors can be transformed into the unit vectors. The third column provides the following nonzero coordinates for the origin:

$$\bar{a}_{13}[1, 0]+\bar{a}_{23}[0, 1]-1[\bar{a}_{13}, \bar{a}_{23}] = [0, 0].$$

If no pair of two-component vectors reduces to diagonal form, all must lie on the same line through the origin and are necessarily dependent.

A collection of vectors generates or *spans* a space, or forms a *spanning set*, if every vector in the space can be expressed as some linear combination of the vectors in the collection. The unit vectors constitute a spanning set for the space in which they lie. But if one unit vector is missing, the remaining unit vectors cannot provide coordinates for any column vector with a nonzero component in the row where the missing unit vector has a one. Any other collection with fewer vectors than components cannot be transformed into the full set of unit vectors and cannot be a spanning set. Some mathematicians define the dimension of a space as the minimum number of vectors required to span the space. The number cannot be less than the number of unit vectors, so we now see why the dimension of a space can be identified by the number of components in the vectors. The unit vectors are also linearly independent and, hence, provide unique coordinates. Any set in which the number of vectors exceeds the number of components cannot be linearly independent. A collection of vectors that both spans a space and is linearly independent is termed a *basis* for the space. Thus, a basis contains both the maximum number of linearly independent vectors in a space and the minimum number necessary to span it. The maximum number of linearly independent vectors and the number of vectors in a basis are alternative definitions for the dimension of a space. There are infinitely many bases for any vector space, but a collection of vectors can be a basis if and only if it can be transformed by pivot operations into the full set of unit vectors, with no unit vectors missing and no other vectors present.

We have now succeeded in showing that the term basis as used in linear programming is a special application of a broad general concept that is essential to the theory of vector spaces. A basis for a linear programming problem is, in fact, a basis for the space in which the vectors of coefficients are points. Each square subset of vectors is a basis for the space if and only if it can be reduced to diagonal form and thus transformed into the set of unit vectors for the space. At each iteration the simplex method shifts from one basis to another by inserting a new column vector in place of one of the original column vectors. Only a single pivot operation is needed to transform the new vector into one of the unit vectors and make the substitution. Since the full set of unit vectors must be maintained, the new vector cannot have a zero in the row where the unit vector it is replacing has a one. Hence, the pivot must be a nonzero component of the entering vector.

Subspaces

If some unit vectors are missing, the remaining vectors are linearly independent but do not span the entire space in which they lie. They do span a proper subspace[3] with dimension equal to the number of remaining unit vectors. A single unit vector in any space generates a one-dimensional subspace or line through the origin. In three-dimensional space, two unit vectors generate a two-dimensional subspace or plane through the origin, as shown below:

$$x_1[1, 0, 0]+x_2[0, 1, 0] = [x_1, x_2, 0].$$

The set of all vectors with third component zero is one of the three coordinate planes. Any other collection of vectors that reduces through pivot operations to a proper subset of the unit vectors also spans a subspace with dimension equal to the number of unit vectors.

[3]Since every space is contained within itself, it is one of its own subspaces but not a proper subspace, which has lesser dimension than the space itself.

For maximum generality, mathematicians define a space or subspace as the set of all linear combinations of a collection of vectors. Every collection generates a space but many collections generate the same space. The smallest number of vectors in any spanning set determines the dimension. We can apply pivot operations to any collection of vectors, count the number of distinct unit vectors that emerge, and thus determine the dimension of the space or subspace the original vectors span.

Any set of three equations in three unknowns always has a unique solution when the vectors of coefficients are a basis for the space. However, a variable may have a value of zero in the solution, say ($x_1 = \bar{b}_1$, $x_2 = \bar{b}_2$, $x_3 = 0$). The set of all linear combinations of $\mathbf{a}_1$, $\mathbf{a}_2$, and $\mathbf{a}_3$ in which x_3 is always zero also defines a two-dimensional subspace, since $\mathbf{a}_3$ might as well be missing. Thus, the preceding degenerate solution implies that **b** lies in the plane generated by $\mathbf{a}_1$ and $\mathbf{a}_2$, but $\mathbf{a}_3$ does not. A doubly degenerate solution means that **b** lies on the line formed by only one of the coefficient vectors. When only two of the three coefficient vectors are linearly independent, all three lie in the same plane through the origin. Only when **b** lies in the same plane is there a solution, but it is not unique.

Spaces of Higher Dimension

All preceding results can be generalized algebraically to vectors of more than three components, but no explicit geometric representation is possible. The situation is not unlike flying a plane. At low speeds and in favorable weather it is possible to fly either by sight or by instruments, but when the visibility is poor enough or the speed high enough, instruments must take over. Similarly, in two and three dimensions, vectors can be presented either geometrically or algebraically, but beyond three dimensions algebra must take over. In higher dimensions, vectors have more components and linear combinations require more multiplications and additions, but the basic meaning remains the same. Also, elementary transformations require longer chains of the same kind of computations, but they remain the best way of determining the dimension of a space and of finding the unknown coordinates of a point.

It is interesting to note that many of the geometric terms are retained even though they have no explicit representation. The set of all n-tuples is called an n-dimensional space and each n-tuple is designated as a point. In three-dimensional space any two linearly independent vectors—one less than the dimension of the space—determine a plane through the origin. In n dimensions, $n-1$ linearly independent vectors determine a subspace that is called a *hyperplane*. Regardless of dimension, the solvability of linear equations depends upon the vector **b** lying in the space generated by the vectors of coefficients. Uniqueness of the solution requires that the vectors be linearly independent.

NONNEGATIVE SOLUTIONS OF LINEAR EQUATIONS

Linear programming admits only nonnegative solutions and, hence, only nonnegative linear combinations of vectors. If x_1 and x_2 cannot be negative, the linear combination of unit vectors

$$x_1[1, 0]+x_2[0, 1] = [x_1, x_2]$$

locates only those points bounded by the nonnegative semiaxes, which form the nonnegative or northeast *quadrant* in the coordinate plane. With oblique axes the nonnegative linear combination $x_1\mathbf{a}_1+x_2\mathbf{a}_2$ similarly locates only those points lying between the halflines generated by $\mathbf{a}_1$ and $\mathbf{a}_2$, as is shown in Figure 6–4.

The simplest example in three dimensions is a nonnegative combination of three linearly independent vectors. Each vector determines a ray and nonnegative linear combinations of each pair of vectors generate the flat face or facet lying between the rays. The set of all nonnegative linear combinations of the three vectors is a solid pyramidal figure bounded by the three facets, as drawn in Figure 6–5. As both drawings suggest, a nonnegative linear combination of vectors generates a *cone*, but a special type of cone. A cone generated by a finite number of vectors has flat sides or *facets*. The more

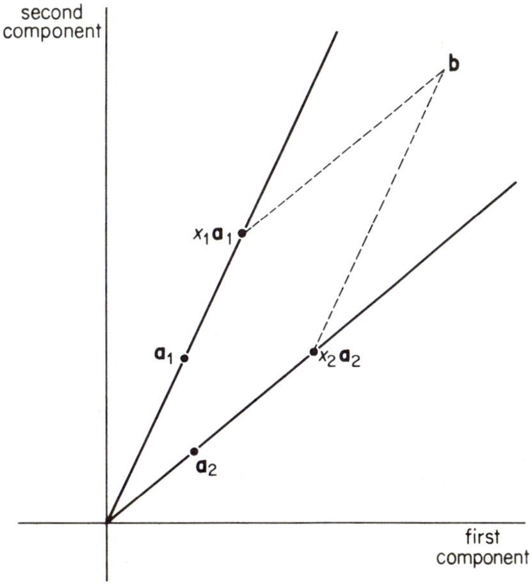

Fig. 6-4 A Nonnegative Linear Combination of Vectors

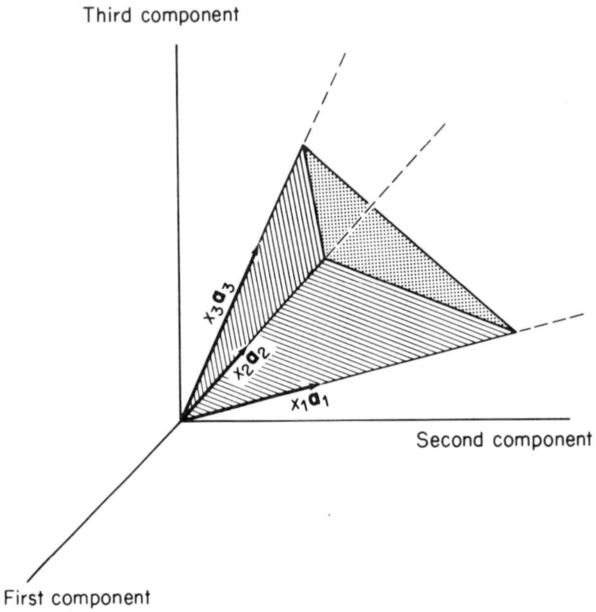

Fig. 6-5 A Cone in Three Dimensions

familiar type of cone, which serves as a receptacle for ice cream, has no facets. It is called a circular cone and is generated by an infinite number of rays, causing the facets to shrink to zero width and disappear. To emphasize the distinction, a cone generated by a finite number of vectors or rays is called *polyhedral*, meaning many sided. Its cross section is a polyhedron rather than a circle or other smooth figure.

The set of all nonnegative linear combinations of vectors also has the property of being *convex*, which means that any two points in the set can be joined by a line segment that also lies entirely within the set. More will be said later about the important property of convexity. For the present we merely note that, precisely defined, the set of all nonnegative linear combinations of a finite collection of vectors is a *convex polyhedral cone.*

In two-dimensional space the clearest example of a convex polyhedral cone is one generated by two linearly independent vectors, $\mathbf{a}_1$ and $\mathbf{a}_2$. As shown in Figure 6–4, we can locate any point in the cone by vector addition, using only the half-lines generated by $\mathbf{a}_1$ and $\mathbf{a}_2$. Relative to $\mathbf{a}_1$ and $\mathbf{a}_2$ all points in the cone have nonnegative coordinates. Hence, the vector equation

$$x_1\mathbf{a}_1 + x_2\mathbf{a}_2 = \mathbf{b}$$

has a nonnegative solution if and only if the vector $\mathbf{b}$ lies in the cone generated by $\mathbf{a}_1$ and $\mathbf{a}_2$.

A cone generated by a basis for a space has the simplest geometric representation. But a convex polyhedral cone is defined as the set of all nonnegative linear combinations of any collection of vectors, regardless of number or linear independence. We must not let the geometric image that is the origin of the term limit its mathematical meaning. Another example of a cone is the following nonnegative linear combination of the unit vectors and their negatives:

$$x_1[1, 0]+x_2[0, 1]+x_3[-1, 0]+x_4[0, -1].$$

Since each quadrant is present as a subcone formed by a pair of vectors, every point in the plane also lies in the cone. Thus, paradoxically, a space is a special type of cone.

Any other pair of linearly independent vectors and their negatives also generate the entire two-dimensional space as the cone:

$$x_1\mathbf{a}_1+x_2\mathbf{a}_2+x_3(-\mathbf{a}_1)+x_4(-\mathbf{a}_2).$$

Further, any point in the plane can be written as a nonnegative linear combination of only two vectors, by assigning zeros to the other x's. In Figure 6–6, the subcones generated by $(\mathbf{a}_1, \mathbf{a}_2)$, $(-\mathbf{a}_1, \mathbf{a}_2)$, $(-\mathbf{a}_1, -\mathbf{a}_2)$, and $(\mathbf{a}_1, -\mathbf{a}_2)$ cover the whole plane. The result has an important application in linear programming. In some problems, we wish to let variables be either positive

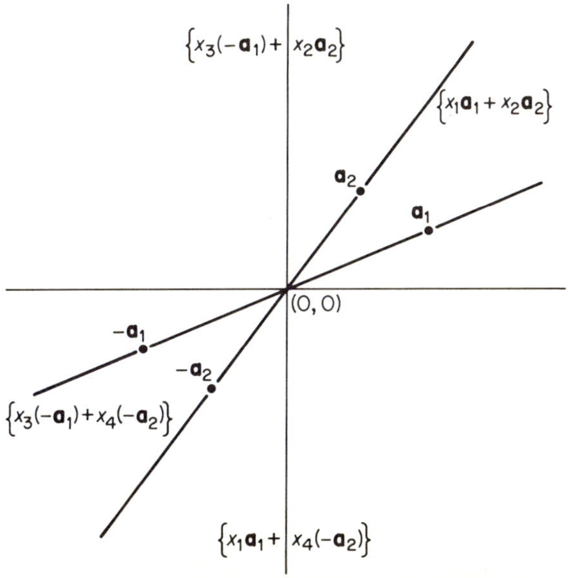

Fig. 6-6 The Plane as a Cone

or negative, but the rationale of the simplex method requires all solutions to be feasible. To permit negative solutions we include the column vectors a second time with signs reversed, converting the problem to the following form:

$$x_1'\mathbf{a}_1+x_1''(-\mathbf{a}_1)+x_2'\mathbf{a}_2+x_2''(-\mathbf{a}_2) = \mathbf{b}.$$

No matter where the vector **b** lies in the plane, it is within a cone generated by a pair of linearly independent vectors. Since $\mathbf{a}_1$ and $-\mathbf{a}_1$ are linearly dependent, as are $\mathbf{a}_2$ and $-\mathbf{a}_2$, neither pair can be reduced to diagonal form, and the corresponding variables can never appear together in a basic feasible solution. Since $x_1\mathbf{a}_1 = (x_1-x_1'')\mathbf{a}_1$, x_1 is positive when x_1' appears in a solution and negative when x_1'' is present.

THE GEOMETRY OF THE SIMPLEX METHOD

The simplex method solves linear programming problems by separating feasible from infeasible solutions and then choosing from the feasible solutions one that is optimal. We present a geometric analysis of feasibility here but postpone optimality to Chapter 7. The multiproduct firm of Chapter 5, with both inputs one-tenth as large, provides the following example:

$$x_1\begin{bmatrix}a_{11}\\a_{21}\end{bmatrix}+x_2\begin{bmatrix}a_{12}\\a_{22}\end{bmatrix}+x_3\begin{bmatrix}a_{13}\\a_{23}\end{bmatrix}+x_4\begin{bmatrix}a_{14}\\a_{24}\end{bmatrix}+x_5\begin{bmatrix}1\\0\end{bmatrix}+x_6\begin{bmatrix}0\\1\end{bmatrix} = \begin{bmatrix}b_1\\b_2\end{bmatrix}$$

$$x_1\begin{bmatrix}3\\2\end{bmatrix}+x_2\begin{bmatrix}1\\1\end{bmatrix}+x_3\begin{bmatrix}1\\2\end{bmatrix}+x_4\begin{bmatrix}3\\1\end{bmatrix}+x_5\begin{bmatrix}1\\0\end{bmatrix}+x_6\begin{bmatrix}0\\1\end{bmatrix} = \begin{bmatrix}9\\8\end{bmatrix}.$$

The numerical version appears in Figure 6–7.

Feasible solutions exist if **b** lies in the cone generated by the vectors of coefficients on the left. It is geometrically evident that, if **b** lies in the cone generated by all vectors, it must lie in the cone generated by at least one pair of vectors. There is much to be gained by choosing subsets of vectors that are a basis for the space. When **b** lies in the cone of a basis for the space, it has unique coordinates that can be efficiently determined by reduction to diagonal form.

In the example of the multiproduct firm all constraints are of the $\leqq$ form and all constants on the right are nonnegative, implying that **b** lies in the nonnegative quadrant or orthant.[4] Slack variables bring in the unit vectors, whose cone is the nonnegative orthant and guarantee at least one feasible

[4]The two axes divide the plane into four regions or quadrants and are also mutually perpendicular or orthogonal. The term *orthant*, derived from orthogonal, is synonymous with quadrant in two dimensions and can be used in spaces of higher dimension, where quadrant does not apply.

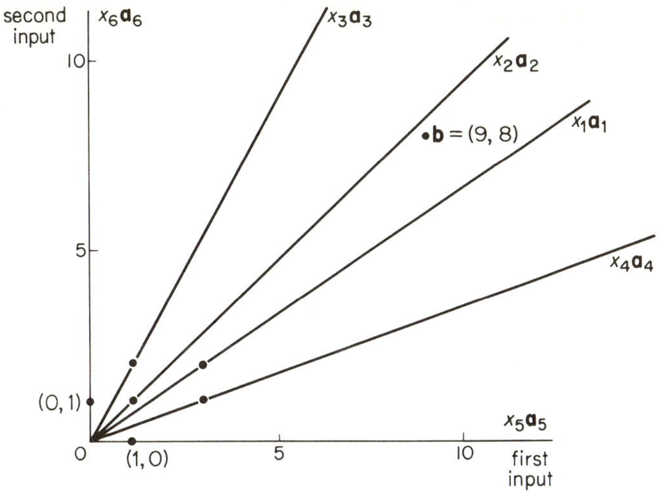

Fig. 6-7 Graph of Numerical Problem

solution. Inequalities of the $\geqq$ form bring in surplus variables and the negatives of the unit vectors, whose cone is the nonpositive orthant. Since **b** lies in the nonnegative orthant, surplus variables do not provide an initial basic feasible solution. The conclusion holds whenever all components of **b** are positive and there is at least one constraint of the $\geqq$ form.

In the numerical example, the total number of basic solutions is $(6 \times 5)/(1 \times 2) = 15$. As readers may verify, nine of these basic solutions are also feasible. With the net revenue coefficients used on page 80, the simplex method chooses in succession (x_5, x_6), (x_1, x_6), (x_1, x_3), and finally (x_1, x_2). At each iteration the system of constraints is reduced to diagonal form with respect to the vectors in the basis. Geometrically, the vectors in the basis are transformed into the unit vectors and all other vectors are relocated in space in such a way as to retain their coordinates relative to the basic vectors. The next-to-last iteration is

$$x_1\begin{bmatrix}1\\0\end{bmatrix}+x_2\begin{bmatrix}\frac{1}{4}\\\frac{1}{4}\end{bmatrix}+x_3\begin{bmatrix}0\\1\end{bmatrix}+x_4\begin{bmatrix}\frac{5}{4}\\-\frac{3}{4}\end{bmatrix}+x_5\begin{bmatrix}\frac{1}{2}\\-\frac{1}{2}\end{bmatrix}+x_6\begin{bmatrix}-\frac{1}{4}\\\frac{3}{4}\end{bmatrix}=\begin{bmatrix}\frac{5}{2}\\\frac{3}{2}\end{bmatrix}.$$

Figure 6–8 shows the graph.

The rays of the basic vectors have been rotated into a perpendicular relation to each other, and all other rays have been rotated in such a way as to preserve the original relation to the basic vectors. All rays that were originally inside the cone generated by $\mathbf{a}_1$ and $\mathbf{a}_3$ are to be found in the nonnegative orthant, and all rays that were outside originally are outside the nonnegative orthant. The $\bar{a}$ coefficients, which are the components of a

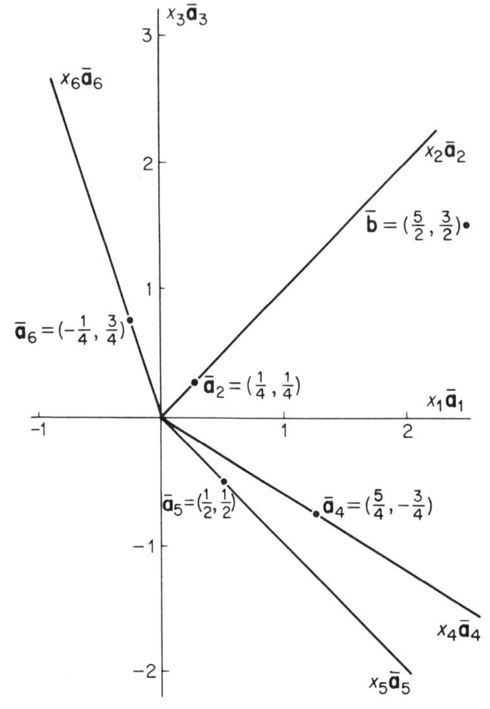

Fig. 6-8 Graph of the Third Iteration

nonbasic vector, are rectangular coordinates after the basis is transformed into unit vectors and also oblique coordinates when the basic vectors are in their original position. For the second vector, the following relations hold:

$$\bar{\mathbf{a}}_2 = \bar{a}_{12}\mathbf{u}_1 + \bar{a}_{22}\mathbf{u}_2 \qquad \mathbf{a}_2 = \bar{a}_{12}\mathbf{a}_1 + \bar{a}_{22}\mathbf{a}_3$$

$$[\tfrac{1}{4}, \tfrac{1}{4}] = \tfrac{1}{4}[1, 0] + \tfrac{1}{4}[0, 1] \qquad [1, 1] = \tfrac{1}{4}[3, 2] + \tfrac{1}{4}[1, 2].$$

The signs of the $\bar{a}$ coefficients show the location of the corresponding vector with respect to the original cone generated by the basic vectors. If both $\bar{a}$ coefficients are positive, as is true for $\mathbf{a}_2$, the vector lies inside the cone of $\mathbf{a}_1$ and $\mathbf{a}_3$. A vector outside the original cone, such as $\mathbf{a}_4$, has a positive coefficient relative to the nearer of the two rays $x_1\mathbf{a}_1$, and a negative coefficient relative to the farther, $x_3\mathbf{a}_3$.

In earlier chapters, we explained the sign of an $\bar{a}$ coefficient in economic terms as measuring competitive or complementary relations between products. In an absolute sense, all outputs are competitive for inputs, but outputs are more highly competitive with each other the more alike their input requirements. If a product has input requirements that lie between those of the outputs in the basis, it is relatively competitive with both. A product outside the cone of the basic outputs is a relative complement of the output with the more distant input requirements and a relative substitute of the product with input requirements more like its own. Both $\bar{a}$ coefficients can be negative only if the vector lies originally in the negative cone, $x_1(-\mathbf{a}_1)+x_3(-\mathbf{a}_3)$. Such a process yields inputs instead of using them. Unless there is a cost attached, the firm is getting something for nothing and will expand without limit.

The choice of variable to drop in the simplex method has a simple geometric rationale. If x_4 is to come in at the next iteration, x_3 cannot be dropped, since $\mathbf{b}$ does not lie in the cone of $\mathbf{a}_1$ and $\mathbf{a}_4$. But x_4 has a negative coefficient in the row of x_3, and x_3 will not be dropped. Thus, the rule of disregarding negative $\bar{a}$ coefficients guarantees that the more distant vector, lying on the opposite side of $\mathbf{b}$, will never be dropped. An entering vector, such as $\mathbf{a}_2$, may lie in the cone of the present basis. It is geometrically evident that the vector dropped must be relatively nearer to $\mathbf{a}_2$ than to $\mathbf{b}$. In the transformed locations of Figure 6–8, ratios of coordinates show the relative distances of $\bar{\mathbf{b}}$ and $\bar{\mathbf{a}}_2$ from the axes. For example, if $\bar{b}_2/\bar{b}_1 < \bar{a}_{22}/\bar{a}_{12}$, the ray on which $\bar{\mathbf{b}}$ lies has the smaller slope. The vector $\bar{\mathbf{a}}_2$ is nearer the vertical axis, which corresponds to $\mathbf{a}_3$, but $\bar{b}_2/\bar{b}_1 < \bar{a}_{22}/\bar{a}_{12}$ implies $\bar{b}_2/\bar{a}_{22} < \bar{b}_1/\bar{a}_{12}$. By the rule of minimal ratio, the simplex method drops the vector in the second row, which is also the vector $\bar{\mathbf{a}}_3$ on the vertical axis. Thus, the rule of minimal ratio always inserts the new vector between $\bar{\mathbf{b}}$ and the vector being dropped, assuring continued feasibility. Readers may use the numerical example as a verification. Whenever the vector $\mathbf{b}$ lies on the ray generated by any one vector, it can be expressed as a unique multiple of that vector alone. The simplex method requires that another vector appear in the solution but the corresponding value of x must be zero, indicating a degenerate solution. In higher dimensions there is wider choice of a vector to drop, but the rules of the simplex method guarantee that $\mathbf{b}$ will lie within the cone of the new basis.

EXERCISES

1. Add the following pairs of vectors and show the results graphically: [2, 4], [3, 2]; [2, −4], [−3, 2]; [−6, 3], [9, 5]. Find the scalar product of each pair.

2. Find the following linear combinations of vectors and show graphically how the linear combinations are formed: (a) 2[2, 4] + 3[3, 2]; (b) 2[2, −4] − 3[−3, 2]; (c) $\frac{1}{3}$[−6, 3] + 1[9, 5].

3. (a) Find the *points* which have coordinates (12, 20) with respect to each of the following pairs of vectors: [2, 5], [3, 4]; [4, 2], [3, 10]; [1, 1], [12, 20].

(b) Find the *coordinates* of the point [12, 20] with respect to each of the preceding pairs of vectors.

4. (a) Determine whether the following points [b_1, b_2] do or do not have coordinates (x_1, x_2) with respect to the corresponding set of vectors

$\mathbf{a}_1$ and $\mathbf{a}_2$. If coordinates exist, determine whether they are or are not unique.

	$\mathbf{b}$		$\mathbf{a}_1$		$\mathbf{a}_2$
(1)	[11, 5]	with respect to	[2, −5]	and	[4, 3].
(2)	[24, 3]	with respect to	[1, −2]	and	[1, 1].
(3)	[4, −6]	with respect to	[3, 3]	and	[−1, −1].
(4)	[6, −24]	with respect to	[$-\frac{3}{4}$, 3]	and	[1, −4].

(b) Plot each point [b_1, b_2] relative to the corresponding vectors and explain the results in terms of linear independence of vectors.

5. Does each of the following points **b** have coordinates **x** with respect to the corresponding set of vectors, and, if so, are the coordinates unique? In each case give the reason for the result.

(a) [11, 5, −2] with respect to [2, −5, 1] and [4, 3, −1].
(b) [8, 18, 16] with respect to [2, 6, 4] and [−3, −9, −6].
(c) [6, 4, 10] with respect to [1, 1, 2], [2, 3, 5], and [−4, −2, −5].
(d) [12, 0, 16] with respect to [2, 1, 1], [3, 2, 0], and [4, 3, −1].

6. (a) Determine whether the origin does or does not have unique coordinates in terms of each of the following sets of vectors:

(1) [1, 2], [2, 1].
(2) [1, 2], [3, 6].
(3) [1, 2, 4], [−2, 3, −2], [3, 4, 10].
(4) [1, 2, 4], [2, 4, 8], [3, 4, 10].

(b) On what property of the vectors does the uniqueness of a solution depend? Show that any point in the space, other than the origin, has unique coordinates if the origin does.

7. (a) Graph the vectors for the following two-equation system:

$$6x_1+3x_2+1x_3+0x_4 = 12$$
$$3x_1+6x_2+0x_3+1x_4 = 9.$$

(b) Apply elementary operations to reduce the system to diagonal form with respect to $\mathbf{a}_1$ and $\mathbf{a}_2$. After each operation plot the resulting vectors, and summarize the effect on the vectors.

8. The present exercise repeats Exercise 6 of Chapter 2 with a different interpretation. From the following collection of vectors determine how many distinct bases can be chosen for the space in which all vectors lie: [3, 2, 4]; [1, 2, 4]; [2, 1, 5]; [4, 4, 8].

It is only necessary to perform on all vectors the pivot operations required to reduce three of them to diagonal form.

Explain how the following changes in the fourth vector affect the number of bases that the collection yields: (a) Change the third component from 8 to 4, (b) *restore* the original third component and change the first component from 4 to 2. Give a geometric interpretation of the effect that each change has on the number of bases for the space.

9. For each of the following collections of vectors determine the dimension of the space (or subspace) they generate. In each case state whether the addition of another vector to the collection could raise the dimension of the space (or subspace):

(a) [4, 2], [5, 3], [1, 1];
(b) [2, $\frac{1}{3}$], [7, $\frac{7}{6}$], [4, $\frac{7}{3}$].

(c) [2, 3, 1], [4, −2, 2], [6, 1, 3];
(d) [3, 4, 2], [2, 3, 4], [2, 1, 2];
(e) [3, 9, 1], [2, 4, −2], [1, 5, 3], [1, 1, 1].

10. Interpret geometrically the solution of the following system:

$$x_1\begin{bmatrix}2\\1\\2\end{bmatrix}+x_2\begin{bmatrix}4\\3\\5\end{bmatrix}+x_3\begin{bmatrix}-6\\3\\-2\end{bmatrix}=\begin{bmatrix}12\\4\\10\end{bmatrix}.$$

11. (a) For each of the following five vectors determine graphically whether it is or is not a nonnegative linear combination of the pair of vectors [−3, 3], [4, 2].
(1) [−2, 8]. (2) [2, 10]. (3) [6, 12].
(4) [−12, −6]. (5) [1, 5].
(b) Find algebraically the coefficients, that is, the scalars x_1 and x_2, for each linear combination.
(c) What do the sign and relative size of the coefficients tell about the location of each vector relative to the members of the pair?

12. *A Geometric Interpretation of the Simplex Method*

For the constraints only in the numerical example of Exercise 1 of Chapter 5, carry out the following instructions:
(a) Graph the constraints and determine which of the basic solutions are feasible and which are not.
(b) Reduce to diagonal form with respect to the first and third vectors. Graph the results. Relate the quadrant in which each of the transformed vectors lies to its original position relative to $\mathbf{a}_1$ and $\mathbf{a}_3$. Interpret the result in terms of relative substitutes and complements.
(c) Determine graphically which vectors will preserve feasibility when x_1 leaves the basis and which will not. Make a similar determination when it is x_3 that leaves the basis. Explain how the simplex method distinguishes between the two classes of vectors and always chooses an entering vector that preserves feasibility.

7

Geometric Versions of the Multiproduct Firm

From the background material on vector spaces we can construct two geometric interpretations of the multiproduct firm and of linear programming problems in general. Each version explains best some of the decisions the management must make, and together they provide a unified model for the firm.

THE MULTIPRODUCT FIRM IN INPUT SPACE

Net revenue adds another component to the column vectors and another dimension to the vector space. For the multiproduct firm with two inputs the vector equation is

$$x_1\begin{bmatrix} a_{11} \\ a_{21} \\ r_1 \end{bmatrix} + x_2\begin{bmatrix} a_{12} \\ a_{22} \\ r_2 \end{bmatrix} + x_3\begin{bmatrix} a_{13} \\ a_{23} \\ r_3 \end{bmatrix} + x_4\begin{bmatrix} a_{14} \\ a_{24} \\ r_4 \end{bmatrix} + x_5\begin{bmatrix} 1 \\ 0 \\ 0 \end{bmatrix} + x_6\begin{bmatrix} 0 \\ 1 \\ 0 \end{bmatrix} = \begin{bmatrix} b_1 \\ b_2 \\ R \end{bmatrix}.$$

Above each of the rays in the two-dimensional space, net revenue increases at the constant rate shown by the net revenue coefficient. There are four rays from the origin in three-dimensional space plus the two rays generated by the slack variables. These rays have zero value for R everywhere and are simply the axes measuring the amounts of the respective inputs. The set of all non-negative linear combinations of the six vectors forms a cone in three-dimensional space, as depicted in Figure 7–1. The problem is to find the vector or combination of vectors that attains the highest point, or the largest value of R, without exceeding the input limitations.

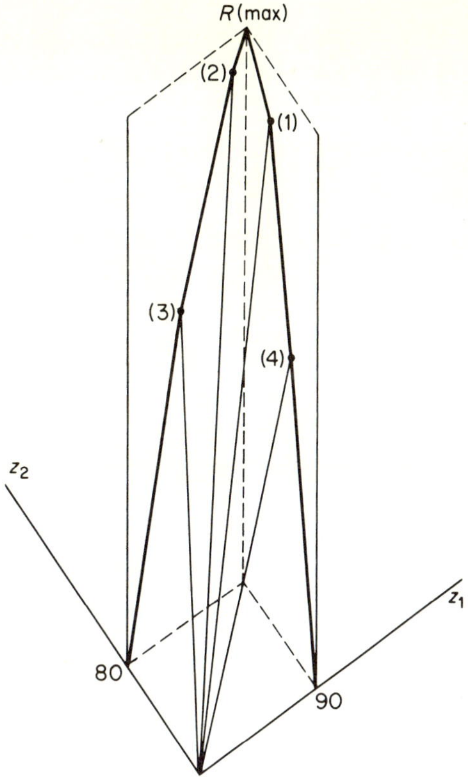

Fig. 7-1 The Revenue Maximization Problem in Three Dimensions

Three-dimensional diagrams are valuable in visualizing the general nature of a problem, but they are often cumbersome when trying to find the specific solution. Fortunately, all essential information can usually be summarized in two-dimensional graphs. To this end we first convert the unit in which each product is measured to the amount that returns \$1 of net revenue at current prices. If, say, the net revenue is \$2 per unit of output when measured in conventional units, we change to half-units. When the size of the unit is cut in half, so are the input requirements per unit. The *a* coefficients must be divided by 2, the magnitude of the net revenue coefficient. In general, to convert every output to the unit that yields \$1 of net revenue, we divide all components in each column vector by the net revenue coefficient. When the input requirements are scaled to half-units of output, it takes twice as many half-units of output to use the same amount of one input. Hence, in the optimal solution the number of new units of each output equals the number of original units times the net revenue coefficient. To restore the solution to the original units we merely divide the output levels by the respective net revenue coefficients.

In numerical form the multiproduct firm becomes

$$x_1\begin{bmatrix}\frac{3}{10}\\ \frac{1}{5}\\ 1\end{bmatrix}+x_2\begin{bmatrix}\frac{1}{4}\\ \frac{1}{4}\\ 1\end{bmatrix}+x_3\begin{bmatrix}\frac{1}{5}\\ \frac{2}{5}\\ 1\end{bmatrix}+x_4\begin{bmatrix}\frac{1}{2}\\ \frac{1}{6}\\ 1\end{bmatrix}+x_5\begin{bmatrix}1\\ 0\\ 0\end{bmatrix}+x_6\begin{bmatrix}0\\ 1\\ 0\end{bmatrix}=\begin{bmatrix}90\\ 80\\ R\end{bmatrix}.$$

The first two components in each of the first four vectors represent combinations of inputs that yield \$1 of net revenue. What we need is not just four combinations but all possible combinations of inputs yielding \$1 of net revenue. The first two components in each vector determine points in a subspace, called the input subspace or, for short, the input space. It is customary in economics to identify spaces or subspaces by the quantities measured along the axes. For any two products, the cone formed by the input vectors contains all input combinations capable of turning out the two products. If s and t are nonnegative real numbers, the cone for products 1 and 2 is

$$s\begin{bmatrix}a_{11}\\ a_{21}\\ 1\end{bmatrix}+t\begin{bmatrix}a_{12}\\ a_{22}\\ 1\end{bmatrix}=\begin{bmatrix}sa_{11}+ta_{12}\\ sa_{21}+ta_{22}\\ s+t\end{bmatrix}.$$

To find all combinations of inputs that yield \$1 of net revenue, we merely require that $s+t=1$. Hence, if any two vectors each yield \$1 of net revenue, so does any weighted average of the two vectors. A nonnegative linear combination whose coefficients add to 1 is called a *convex linear combination.* It may be written more simply as

$$(1-t)\mathbf{a}_1+t\mathbf{a}_2 \qquad \text{or} \qquad \mathbf{a}_1+t(\mathbf{a}_2-\mathbf{a}_1) \qquad 0 \leqq t \leqq 1.$$

A convex linear combination of vectors has an important geometric representation. Let $\mathbf{v}=[v_1, v_2]$ be some unknown vector that is a convex linear combination of the fixed vectors $\mathbf{a}_1$ and $\mathbf{a}_2$. Ignoring for the moment the net revenue component, we can write the combination $\mathbf{v}$ in the following ways:

$$\mathbf{v} = \mathbf{a}_1 + t(\mathbf{a}_2-\mathbf{a}_1) \qquad \mathbf{v}-\mathbf{a}_1 = t(\mathbf{a}_2-\mathbf{a}_1)$$

$$\begin{bmatrix}v_1\\ v_2\end{bmatrix}=\begin{bmatrix}a_{11}\\ a_{21}\end{bmatrix}+t\begin{bmatrix}(a_{12}-a_{11})\\ (a_{22}-a_{21})\end{bmatrix} \qquad \begin{bmatrix}v_1-a_{11}\\ v_2-a_{21}\end{bmatrix}=\begin{bmatrix}t(a_{12}-a_{11})\\ t(a_{22}-a_{21})\end{bmatrix}.$$

When $t=0$, $\mathbf{v}$ coincides with $\mathbf{a}_1$, and when $t=1$, $\mathbf{v}$ coincides with $\mathbf{a}_2$. Whenever t has any intermediate value, the line joining $\mathbf{v}$ and $\mathbf{a}_1$ has the same slope as the line passing through $\mathbf{a}_1$ and $\mathbf{a}_2$, as the following demonstration shows:

$$\frac{v_2-a_{21}}{v_1-a_{11}}=\frac{t(a_{22}-a_{21})}{t(a_{12}-a_{11})}=\frac{a_{22}-a_{21}}{a_{12}-a_{11}}.$$

There is only one line through $\mathbf{a}_1$ with a specified slope, so $\mathbf{v}$ must lie on the line that passes through $\mathbf{a}_1$ and $\mathbf{a}_2$. Further, the vertical and horizontal distances from $\mathbf{a}_1$ to $\mathbf{v}$ are a proper fraction t of the corresponding distances from $\mathbf{a}_1$ to $\mathbf{a}_2$, so $\mathbf{v}$ must lie between $\mathbf{a}_1$ and $\mathbf{a}_2$. As t increases continuously from zero to one, it traces out the line segment from $\mathbf{a}_1$ to $\mathbf{a}_2$. Thus, every convex linear combination or weighted average of any two fixed vectors determines a point on the line segment that joins them.

When t takes on negative values or positive values greater than 1, $\mathbf{v}$ continues to be a point on the line joining $\mathbf{a}_1$ and $\mathbf{a}_2$, but it no longer lies between them. As t assumes all possible positive and negative values, $\mathbf{v}$ traces out the entire line. The segment of the line between the two fixed vectors corresponds to the range of t between zero and one. In three dimensions, the line segment joining two points also consists of all convex linear combinations of the two vectors. With the revenue components included the resultant line in three dimensions lies directly above the line segment in the input plane and is horizontal at a level of \$1.

Isorevenue Contours

For each pair of products in the numerical example, convex linear combinations of the vectors give amounts of inputs that return \$1 of net revenue. From the first four vectors there are $(4\times 3)/(1\times 2) = 6$ possible pairs. Geometrically, we simply join by line segments all pairs of points, representing \$1 of net revenue, as is done in Figure 7–2. The combinations

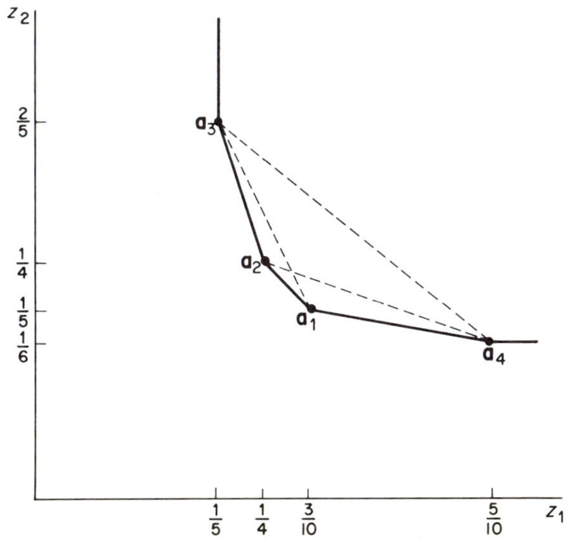

Fig. 7-2 An Isorevenue Contour

shown by dashed line segments are clearly inefficient. For example, the line segment joining $\mathbf{a}_3$ and $\mathbf{a}_4$ lies farthest from the origin and requires more inputs per dollar of revenue than any other combination. All inefficient combinations can be eliminated, leaving the solid piecewise-linear contour.

We are not quite finished, since the possibility of slack remains. Division by zero is impossible, so slack vectors cannot be converted to unit revenue form. A slack vector can, however, be added to any other vector, as is done below:

$$\mathbf{a}_1 + x_5\mathbf{a}_5 = \begin{bmatrix} a_{11} \\ a_{21} \\ 1 \end{bmatrix} + x_5 \begin{bmatrix} 1 \\ 0 \\ 0 \end{bmatrix} = \begin{bmatrix} a_{11} + x_5 \\ a_{21} \\ 1 \end{bmatrix}.$$

As x_5 increases from zero it traces out a line segment extending horizontally from the point $\mathbf{a}_1$. The increased amounts of the first input go costlessly to waste so revenue remains constant. Similarly, the addition of $x_6\mathbf{a}_6$ to $\mathbf{a}_1$ generates a vertical line segment of constant revenue. Both of these line segments are inferior to combinations of $\mathbf{a}_1$ with other vectors and are not included in the isorevenue contour. The vertical line segment from $\mathbf{a}_3$ and the horizontal line segment from $\mathbf{a}_4$ do, however, become indefinitely long extensions of the isorevenue contour in Figure 7–2.

In the present example all vectors contribute line segments to the isorevenue contour, but this need not always occur. Some products with heavy input requirements relative to their selling prices may have points of unit revenue that lie beyond the minimal isorevenue contour. In terminology borrowed from game theory such vectors are dominated by the remaining vectors and may be eliminated from consideration.

Once we have constructed the isorevenue contour for \$1 of net revenue, we can easily draw the contour for any other level. Along each ray both inputs increase proportionately, and net revenue keeps pace with them. The unit revenue point on each ray establishes a unit distance corresponding to \$1 of net revenue. Just as we do on the axes we can use the unit distance to locate on each ray the point that corresponds to any amount of net revenue. Joining points of equal revenue on each ray gives a piecewise-linear contour parallel to the unit revenue contour. When dominated vectors or combinations of vectors have been eliminated, every point in input space lies on one and only one isorevenue contour. Further, that contour represents the maximum net revenue the input combination can yield under given prices and technological conditions. The totality of all nonintersecting isorevenue contours is called the *isorevenue map*.

The firm can use any combination of inputs that does not exceed the amounts available. It is confined to the rectangle in input space whose outer vertex is $\mathbf{b} = (b_1, b_2)$. The problem is to choose a point in the rectangle that has the highest attainable net revenue. Geometrically, the problem is to find the isorevenue contour that has the greatest distance from the origin but still maintains at least one point of contact with the rectangle. For the numerical example, as depicted in Figure 7–3, the isorevenue contour through the vertex satisfies the conditions. When one of the inputs is in short supply, as when $b_2 = 20$ or $b_1 = 30$, the most distant contour may have a vertical or a horizontal segment that is coincident with a side of the rectangle. Slack appears in the optimal solution. Thus, net revenue will always be maximized on the outer boundary of the input rectangle, but there may not be a unique optimum at the vertex.

On the isorevenue map the optimal solution always lies in the cone of two adjacent vectors. So long as the input vector **b** remains within a cone its location does not affect the choice of products, but the location does affect the level at which each is produced. In the numerical example, all inputs are devoted to the production of x_2 when **b** lies on the ray generated by $\mathbf{a}_2$, and all inputs are devoted to x_1 when **b** lies on the opposite ray. Further, as **b** moves along a line segment from the second ray to the first, x_2 declines continuously and x_1 rises continuously. The location of **b** relative to the two rays determines the relative size of the two output levels. To demonstrate we assume that **b** happens to lie on the unit revenue line between $\mathbf{a}_1$ and $\mathbf{a}_2$. The vector **b** is a convex linear combination of $\mathbf{a}_1$ and $\mathbf{a}_2$ as well as a non-negative linear combination with x_1 and x_2 as coefficients. Hence:

$$(1-t)\mathbf{a}_1 + t\mathbf{a}_2 = \mathbf{b} \qquad \text{and} \qquad x_1\mathbf{a}_1 + x_2\mathbf{a}_2 = \mathbf{b}.$$

As t varies from 0 to 1, **b** moves linearly from $\mathbf{a}_1$ to $\mathbf{a}_2$. At every point $x_2 = t$ and $x_1 = 1-t$. Larger values for **b** merely increase x_1 and x_2 proportionately

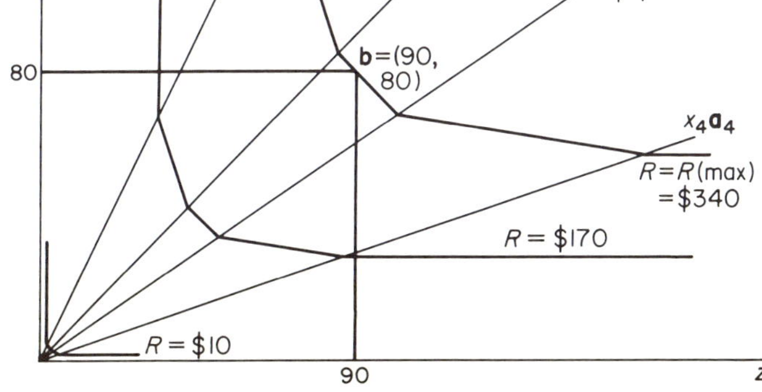

Fig. 7-3 Geometrical Solution to Revenue Maximization Problem

but do not change their ratio: $x_2/x_1 = t/1-t$. Solving for t in terms of x_1 and x_2, we get

$$x_1 t = x_2 - t x_2 \qquad \text{or} \qquad t = \frac{x_2}{x_1+x_2} \qquad \text{and} \qquad 1-t = \frac{x_1}{x_1+x_2}$$

Thus, the position of **b** relative to the two optimal rays determines the relative size of x_1 and x_2 in the optimal solution.

The Net Revenue Function

When the second input remains constant and the first takes on all values from zero upward, the locus of all optimal solutions is the horizontal line at $z_2 = 80$. See Figure 7–4. With z_1 very small, the second input cannot be fully employed and the optimal solution lies in the cone formed by $\mathbf{a}_3$ and the slack vector $\mathbf{a}_6 = [0, 1]$. When z_1 reaches the ray generated by $\mathbf{a}_3$, both inputs are in the exact proportion required for the third product, which uses the entire supply. Since x_6 has fallen to zero, a continued increase in z_1 must bring x_2 into the solution. Chapter 5 established that the entering variable must have a negative $\bar{a}$ coefficient in the row in which it enters. The geometric meaning is that the entering vector and the departing vector must lie on opposite sides of the vector that remains, thus insuring continued feasibility.

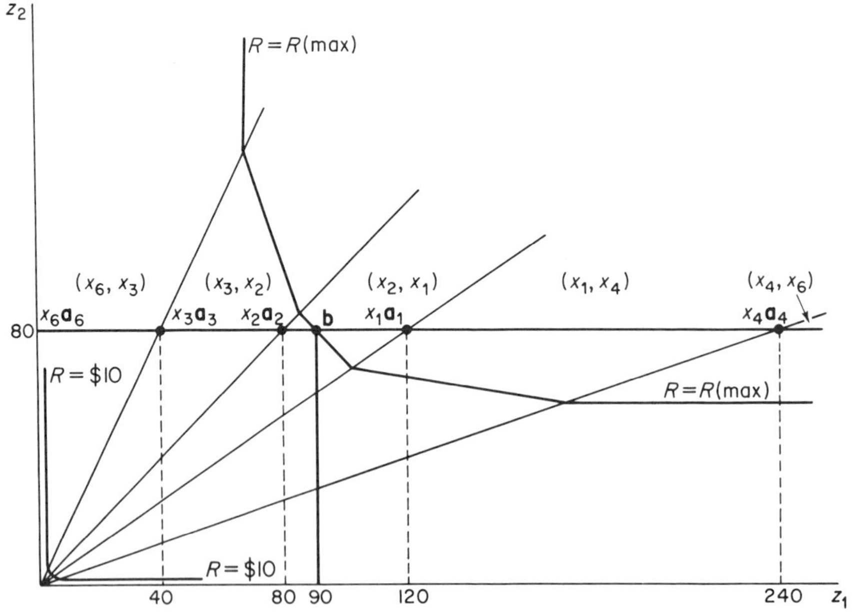

Fig. 7-4 Parametric Variation of z_1

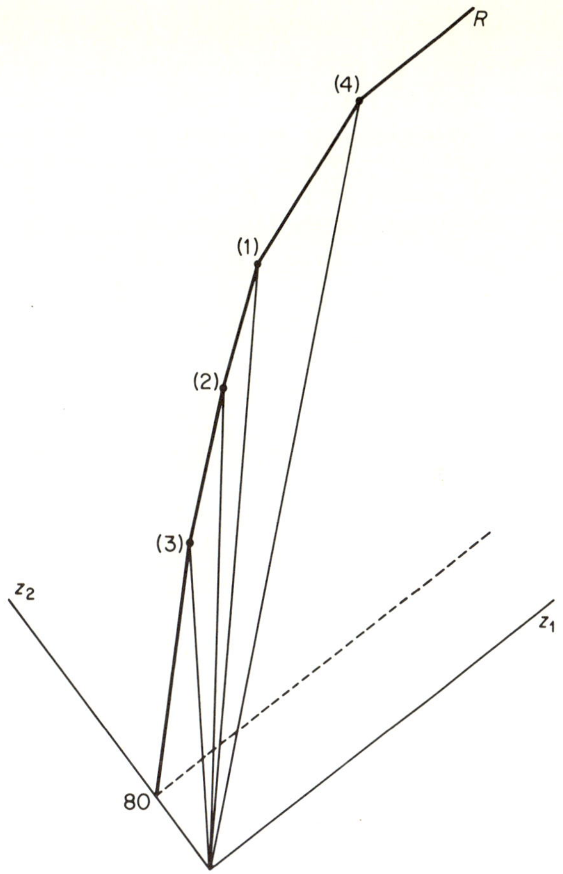

Fig. 7-5 Parametric Variation of z_1 in Three Dimensions

There are two other choices for entering vector, but the isorevenue map shows clearly that only $\mathbf{a}_2$ keeps the solution optimal. As z_1 continues to increase, the pattern repeats itself. Within each cone one solution remains both optimal and feasible. When z_1 reaches a ray, the solution becomes degenerate and compels a change of basis.

In the third dimension above the horizontal line, net revenue is responding to increases in the first input with the second constant. As depicted in Figure 7–5, a slice through the three-dimensional surface perpendicular to the input plane gives a piecewise-linear contour. When graphed in two dimensions, the contour is the total revenue function derived in Chapter 5 and drawn in Figure 5–2 on page 97.

The parametric methods of Chapter 5 generate explicit linear equations for each segment of the net revenue function. Reduction to canonical form converts the objective function into a linear equation of the following type:

$R = y_1 z_1 + y_2 b_2$. The coefficients of the inputs are marginal revenue productivities, which remain constant so long as the solution is feasible. The geometric formulation of the present chapter extends the applicability of the net revenue function. So long as the vector **b** lies anywhere within a cone the same two vectors or outputs constitute the only solution that is both optimal and feasible, and the basis is unchanged. But the values of the dual variables or marginal revenue productivities depend solely on the basis and not at all on the right-hand side. Hence, the same linear segment of the revenue function, $R = y_1 z_1 + y_2 z_2$, holds for all values of z_1 and z_2 within the given cone. The ratios of inputs along the boundary rays determine the range of feasibility. Each linear revenue function holds over a range of input ratios, and the entire function can be rewritten in the more general form of Table 7–1.

TABLE 7–1

The Complete Net Revenue Function

Ratio of inputs z_1/z_2	*Net revenue* R
0 to $\frac{1}{2}$	$5z_1 + 0z_2$
$\frac{1}{2}$ to 1	$3z_1 + 1z_2$
1 to $\frac{3}{2}$	$2z_1 + 2z_2$
$\frac{3}{2}$ to 3	$\frac{2}{3}z_1 + 4z_2$
3 and over	$0z_1 + 6z_2$

The net revenue function results from the conceptual experiment of assigning to the firm all possible input combinations and observing the net revenue associated with each choice of production plan. Economic theory posits that the firm will choose the production plan that maximizes net revenue. When technology is linear and competition is pure, a linear programming model can be used to predict choice. Parametric programming derives explicit linear revenue functions, one of which holds for every point in the input plane. When net revenue is held constant at any value, say $R = \bar{R}$, each of the five linear equations provides a segment on the isorevenue contour. Except when $y_2 = 0$, the equations have the general form

$$z_2 = -\frac{y_1}{y_2} z_1 + \frac{\bar{R}}{y_2}.$$

The slope of each line segment is the negative ratio of the marginal revenue productivities.

With only two inputs and relatively few products, we can always find the unit revenue contour graphically by joining all pairs of isorevenue points and eliminating the methods that waste inputs. In the linear model one isorevenue contour determines the entire map. As the number of processes increases, geometric methods become tedious, and with more than three inputs they are inapplicable. So long as there are specific numerical data, computers can provide piecewise-linear functions up to the limits of their capacities. But economic theory is not concerned primarily with specific problems but rather with the general properties that an entire class of problems must possess if they are to have solutions. Both the graphical presentation and the parametric programming methods give insight into these general properties. The chapters in Part Two generalize the computational and geometric results and apply them to more complex models of the firm.

THE MULTIPRODUCT FIRM IN OUTPUT SPACE

Linear combinations of vectors in input space provide one very instructive geometric interpretation of the multiproduct firm, but there is another, equally useful version in output space, where quantities of the outputs are measured along the axes. The second version is based upon the graphical solution of linear equations as the intersection of straight lines or planes. As demonstrated on page 120, a straight line can be expressed as the product of two vectors. Thus the second geometric interpretation rests upon the multiplication of vectors rather than their addition, which is the essential operation in forming linear combinations. The scalar product provides the link between a straight line and the algebra of vectors, but in the treatment that follows such a linkage is unnecessary and is omitted. We do need, however, a geometric interpretation for linear inequalities and their intersections.

Half-spaces and Convex Sets

A constraint such as $a_{11}x_1+a_{12}x_2 \leqq b_1$ consists of an equality or equation and a strict inequality. Any set of values for x_1 and x_2 that satisfy the equation represent a point on the corresponding straight line. A pair of values that satisfies the strict inequality must also lie on some straight line, say, $a_{11}x_1+a_{12}x_2 = b_1^*$, where b_1^* is a number smaller than b_1. In slope-intercept form, the equation becomes

$$x_2 = -\frac{a_{11}}{a_{12}}x_1+\frac{b_1^*}{a_{12}}.$$

The constant in an equation affects only the intercept of the line and not its slope. If a_{12} is positive, the strict inequality is satisfied by all points on all parallel lines whose intercept is less than b_1/a_{12}. Thus, the original constraint defines a region consisting of all points on or below a given straight line. The region is called a *closed half-space*. If a_{12} is negative, the region consists of all points on or above the given line, but it is also a closed half-space.

The rest of the space consists of all points satisfying the inequality

$$a_{11}x_1 + a_{12}x_2 > b_1.$$

A strong or strict inequality, such as the one above, does not include equality. Hence, the corresponding half-space does not include the straight line that forms a boundary and is called an *open* half-space. The distinction is standard in point-set theory; a set is closed if it contains all its boundary points, open if it contains none of them. A two-dimensional space may be partitioned into either a closed half-space and an open half-space, or into two open half-spaces and a straight line separating them. The straight line may be adjoined as boundary to either half-space by including equality with either the greater than or less than inequality. Any change in the size or sign of the coefficients gives a different straight line and a different partition into half-spaces.

In three dimensions, the equation

$$a_{11}x_1 + a_{12}x_2 + a_{13}x_3 = b_1$$

defines a plane. The set of points satisfying

$$a_{11}x_1 + a_{12}x_2 + a_{13}x_3 < b_1$$

consists of all points on parallel planes with smaller intercepts. Thus, in three dimensions an equation and two strict inequalities also partition the entire space into two open half-spaces and the separating plane, or into one closed and one open half-space. In higher dimensions direct geometric representation is impossible but the terminology is retained. The equation

$$a_{11}x_1 + a_{12}x_2 + \cdots + a_{1n}x_n = b_1$$

defines a *hyperplane*, and each of the corresponding strict inequalities defines an open half-space.

Of special importance are the half-spaces formed by the axes. Written out in full the equations for the horizontal and vertical axes are

$$0x_1 + x_2 = 0 \qquad x_1 + 0x_2 = 0.$$

The first equation is satisfied when $x_2 = 0$ and x_1 has any value whatsoever. For the second equation, the variables are interchanged. The first equation, or horizontal axis, creates the upper- and lower-coordinate open half-spaces, defined by $x_2 > 0$ and $x_2 < 0$. The second equation is the dividing line between the right and left open coordinate half-spaces, defined by $x_1 > 0$ and $x_1 < 0$.

Like linear equations, linear inequalities can be solved simultaneously, and the solution consists of all points that satisfy both conditions. For example, the solution to the pair of inequalities $x_2 \geqq 0$, $x_1 \geqq 0$ is the intersection of the upper-coordinate closed half-space with the right-coordinate closed half-space. It is the upper right, or nonnegative quadrant. Two closed half-spaces, like two straight lines, need not intersect, as is shown by the half-spaces $x_1 \geqq 5$, $x_1 \leqq 4$. Parallel boundaries are a necessary condition for failure to intersect but not a sufficient condition, as can be demonstrated merely by interchanging the numbers on the right.

The results carry over to closed half-spaces not determined by the axes, such as the following:

$$(1) \qquad a_{11}x_1 + a_{12}x_2 \leqq b_1 \qquad \text{or} \qquad 3x_1 + 2x_2 \leqq 18$$

$$(2) \qquad a_{21}x_1 + a_{22}x_2 \leqq b_2 \qquad \qquad x_1 + 2x_2 \leqq 10.$$

With all constants and coefficients positive, the half-spaces extend below two downward-sloping lines, as depicted in Figure 7–6. A convenient way to identify the relevant closed half-space is to draw short perpendicular lines into the space. The set of points satisfying both inequalities consists of all points lying on or below both straight lines. In linear programming we are interested only in those points with nonnegative coordinates. Hence, two more inequalities must be added, those defining the upper- and the right-coordinate closed half-spaces: $x_1 \geqq 0$ and $x_2 \geqq 0$. The resultant intersection

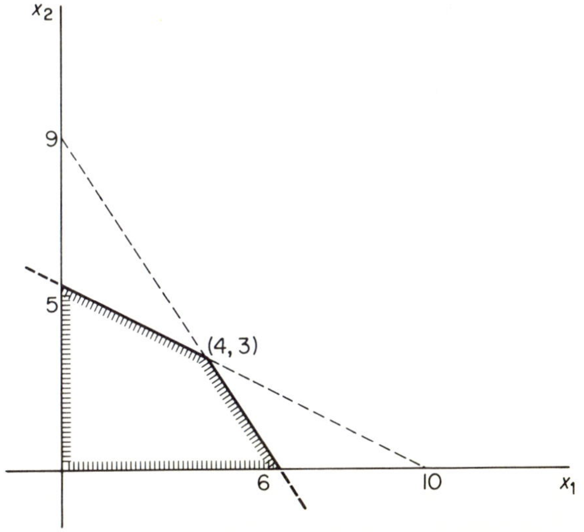

Fig. 7-6 The Intersection of Half-Spaces

of all four closed half-spaces is the set bounded by the two line segments and the two axes. It is called the *feasible set* or the *constraint set* in linear programming.

The feasible set, which consists of all solutions to the inequalities of a linear programming problem, has very useful properties. First of all, the set contains all its boundary points and is, therefore, a closed set. It is closed because it is the intersection of closed half-spaces, which are themselves closed sets. Second, as can be verified visually, we can choose any two points in the feasible set, draw the line segment joining them, and all points on the line segment also lie in the set.

As shown on page 144, the straight line segment joining two points consists of all convex linear combinations, or weighted averages, of the two vectors. Mathematicians call a set *convex* if every pair of points in the set has all its convex linear combinations also within the set. Readers can readily visualize sets that are not convex, such as a star, a doughnut, or an artist's palette. A convex set cannot have any holes in it or any indentations in its boundaries, since both will be filled in by line segments joining members of the set. For linear programming the most useful property of closed convex sets is their affinity for optimization, as subsequent examples will show.

GRAPHICAL METHODS OF SOLUTION

To the numerical constraints graphed in Figure 7–6, we add the following net revenue function:

$$R = x_1 + x_2 \qquad \text{or} \qquad x_2 = -x_1 + R.$$

Maximizing R means choosing the straight line with slope -1 that has the largest vertical intercept. The revenue line is moved parallel to itself upward and to the right as far as it can go without losing contact with the feasible set. In its maximal position the revenue line passes through a boundary point and has the entire feasible set contained in its closed lower half-space, $R \leqq R(\max)$. Readers may draw in the revenue line and verify that the optimum occurs at the vertex where both constraints are satisfied with equality. The optimum can also occur at a vertex on either axis, where one product is not produced and one constraint goes slack. It is possible but highly improbable for the revenue line to coincide with a boundary segment, indicating multiple optima. All points on the line segment or all weighted averages of the terminal solutions yield the same net revenue. The constraint set in output space shows all possible pairs of output levels that the firm can produce from the given amounts of the inputs, but only the outer boundary represents efficient use of the inputs. It is called the *efficiency frontier* or *product transformation contour*.

With more than two products we can display the optimal solution in two-dimensional output space only if we know beforehand the optimal pair of outputs. When there are only two inputs, the optimal solution can be shown graphically in input space regardless of the number of products. Conversely, with many inputs but only two products, output space is the obvious choice. In the following numerical example the firm has four fixed inputs and only two outputs:

$$\begin{array}{lll}
(1) & 5x_1 + x_2 \leqq 57 & x_2 \leqq -5x_1 + 57 \\
(2) & 2x_1 + x_2 \leqq 24 & x_2 \leqq -2x_1 + 24 \\
(3) & x_1 + 2x_2 \leqq 21 & x_2 \leqq -\frac{1}{2}x_1 + \frac{21}{2} \\
(4) & x_1 + 4x_2 \leqq 38 & x_2 \leqq -\frac{1}{4}x_1 + \frac{19}{2} \\
 & 3x_1 + 3x_2 = R(\max) & x_2 = -1x_1 + \frac{R}{3}.
\end{array}$$

The inequalities are written in slope-intercept form on the right to facilitate graphing.

The problem for the firm is to choose which inputs to use fully and which to use partially. To acquire additional experience with the simplex method, readers should find the optimal solution and check with the graphical result. The feasible set shown in Figure 7–7 is the intersection of six closed half-spaces. Since the revenue line has a slope of -1, the optimal solution lies at the intersection of the second and third constraints, whose slopes are -2 and $-\frac{1}{2}$, respectively. Whenever the slope of the revenue line lies between the slopes of two constraints, the optimal solution occurs where the constraints meet in a vertex. If the slope of the revenue line lies beyond the range of the slopes for all constraints, the optimum lies on an axis. The final possibility is coincidence of the revenue line with a constraint, giving multiple optima.

At the optimum the second and third inputs are used fully to yield ($x_1 = 9, x_2 = 6$). To complete the solution we need to calculate the amounts of unused inputs or value of slack variables for the remaining two constraints. The results are ($x_3 = 6, x_6 = 5$). When a slack variable appears, a constraint is satisfied by a strict inequality only, indicating that the solution lies in the interior of the closed half-space formed by the constraint.

With the optimum at a vertex, a net revenue coefficient must change by a discrete amount to generate a new optimum. For example, the solution in Figure 7–7 remains the unique optimum so long as the slope of the objective function stays inside the range from $-\frac{1}{2}$ to -2. With r_2 constant at 3, r_1 may lie between $\frac{3}{2}$ and 6. When $r_1 = \frac{3}{2}$ the revenue line coincides with the line segment determined by the third constraint. The two vertices are optimal

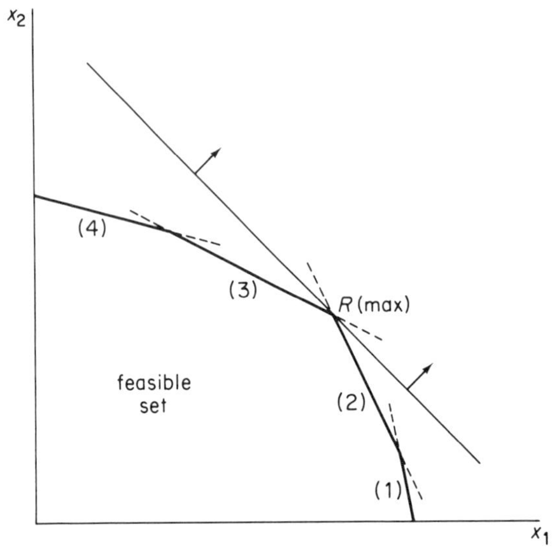

Fig. 7-7 A Product Transformation Contour

basic solutions, but every point on the line segment or every weighted average of the vertices is also an optimal solution. As r_1 varies upward from zero, the optimal solution traverses the entire outer boundary of the feasible set. Readers may calculate the range of r_1 over which each vertex remains optimal and the values of r_1 for which multiple optima or flat-faced solutions occur. Variations in r_1 also change the imputed values of the inputs, as may be determined by parametric programming techniques.

A constraint that is binding contributes to the outer boundary of the feasible set. As the supply of, say, the second input rises, the second constraint shifts to the right, reducing the line segment it contributes to the boundary. An increase in b_2 from 24 to 26 reduces the contribution to a point, since the second constraint then passes through the intersection of the first and third. With any further augmentation the third input ceases to affect production decisions. Conversely, reductions in the second input make the constraint more binding and lengthen the segment it contributes to the outer boundary. Continued reductions of b_2 shrink and finally eliminate the segments formed by other constraints until ultimately the second input alone governs all production decisions.

A MINIMIZATION PROBLEM

The mathematical dual to the revenue maximization problem of earlier chapters has only two variables and can be displayed graphically in two dimensions. The dual is

(1)	$3y_1 + 2y_2 \geqq 10$	$y_2 \geqq -\frac{3}{2}y_1 + 5$
(2)	$y_1 + y_2 \geqq 4$	$y_2 \geqq -y_1 + 4$
(3)	$y_1 + 2y_2 \geqq 5$	$y_2 \geqq -\frac{1}{2}y_1 + \frac{5}{2}$
(4)	$3y_1 + y_2 \geqq 6$	$y_2 \geqq -3y_1 + 6$
	$90y_1 + 80y_2 = V(\text{min})$	$y_2 = -\frac{9}{8}y_1 + \frac{V}{80}$

The variables in the problem are the imputed prices of inputs, so the constraints must be graphed in input-price space, as is done in Figure 7–8.

All coefficients and constants are positive, but the inequalities are reversed, so the closed upper half-spaces become relevant. The feasible set consists of all points in the first quadrant on or beyond the boundaries of the closed half-spaces. Since the variables can exceed in value any number, however large, the set is not bounded from above, and V has no maximum value. The feasible set is bounded from below, so a finite minimum is attainable. As readers may check, the feasible set satisfies the condition for convexity. With the upper half-spaces representing the inequalities, convexity

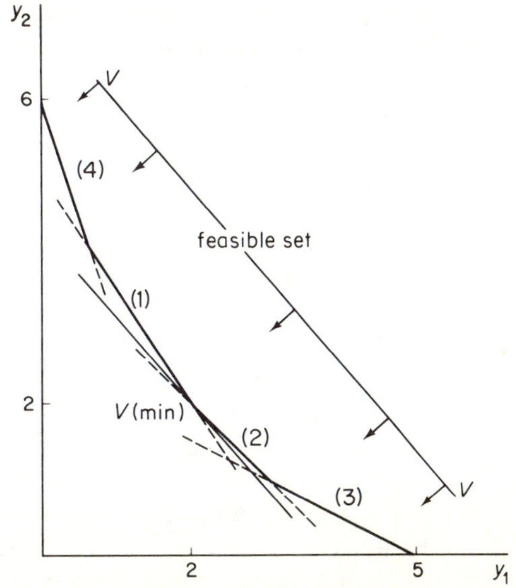

Fig. 7-8 Graph of Dual for Multiproduct Firm

of the set requires that the boundary bulge toward the origin, if it is not a single line segment.

The slope of the objective function, $-\frac{9}{8}$, lies between the slopes of the first two constraints, identifying their vertex as the optimal solution. Since the first two constraints are satisfied with equality, the first two products have imputed unit cost equal to net revenue and are produced. The remaining products have imputed unit cost in excess of net revenue. The results of the dual check with the previously determined optimal solution of the primal. Changes in the coefficients of the objective form, which are the amounts of the inputs, cause the optimal solution to traverse the lower boundary of the feasible set. Readers may calculate the significant ranges and interpret the results. A change in a net revenue coefficient causes a constraint to shift.

METHODS OF CONSTRAINED OPTIMIZATION

Much of economic theory results from optimization subject to constraints. The three principal methods for finding a constrained optimum are linear programming, nonlinear programming, and the differential calculus. It has been shown, at a high level of mathematical abstraction and generality, that the three methods are special cases of a broad, general theory of constrained optimization. We can also convey by two-dimensional diagrams the basic similarities and specific differences among the three methods. The important criteria are the type of constraint or constraint set and the mathematical form of the objective function. We shall first summarize in a formal way the properties of linear programming, beginning with the constraint set or the feasible set.

A set is bounded if all members of the set lie within some finite distance from the origin. In two-dimensional space, a set is bounded from below if the entire set lies above and to the right of some point in the space. Similarly, a set is bounded from above if it lies entirely within the lower-left quadrant with respect to some point in the space. When both conditions hold, the set is bounded. Closed, bounded, convex sets have properties that are extremely useful in optimization.

When the objective function is linear, each value of the objective variable partitions the space into a closed half-space and an open half-space. For the linear objective function $R = r_1x_1 + r_2x_2$, with both coefficients positive, a specific value of R, say $\bar{R}$, creates a closed lower half-space, $R \leqq \bar{R}$, and an open upper half-space, $R > \bar{R}$. The revenue line cannot be in maximal position if any point in the constraint set lies in the upper open half-space. Hence, the revenue line cannot pass through the interior of the set. The solution cannot be feasible unless at least one member of the constraint set lies on the revenue line; the revenue line cannot lie entirely outside the set.

For a maximum the revenue line must pass through a boundary point and have the entire set contained in the lower closed half-space. In general, to include minimization as well as negative coefficients in the objective function, an optimum requires that the entire feasible set lie in *one* of the closed half-spaces formed by the objective function.

A set that is closed, bounded, and convex has the following important property: Through every point on its boundary there passes at least one straight line one of whose closed half-spaces contains the entire set. Such a line is called a *supporting line* or, in general, a *supporting hyperplane*. The conclusion is that every boundary point of such a set must be an optimum for some choice of linear objective function. Further, no matter what linear objective function is chosen, it will have an optimum somewhere on the boundary. In Figure 7–7, the objective function traverses the entire boundary of the feasible set including the axes, if the coefficients of the objective function take on all values, negative and zero as well as positive, but are not both zero at the same time.

A constraint set that is bounded only from one direction but not the other restricts the direction of optimization. If the constraint set is bounded only from above and the objective function has positive coefficients, maximization is possible but not minimization. Similarly, a set that is bounded only from below, as in Figure 7–8, permits a positive weighted objective function to be minimized but not maximized. When all coefficients are negative in an objective function, we merely change all signs and reverse the direction of optimization. Objective coefficients of different signs create difficulties. For example, in Figure 7–8, V cannot be minimized if the coefficient of y_1 is negative. Both b_1y_1 and V itself decrease without limit as y_1 increases within the constraint set. For a finite minimum to exist, y_1 must have an upper limit even though y_2 does not. A similar conclusion holds when the objective function is to be maximized on a constraint set that is not bounded from below. Variables with negative coefficients must have lower limits. In most linear programming problems, where the variables are restricted to non-negative values, the constraint set is bounded from below but not necessarily from above.

When a set is open and the objective function is linear, there cannot be a maximum or minimum on that set, even though the objective variable stays within a finite range. For a simple example, consider the function $f(x) = 5x$, on the open interval $0 < x < 1$. By the very definition of real numbers, no maximum or minimum value exists.

When the constraint set is not convex, a maximum or minimum may exist, but the optimal solution is harder to identify and much more difficult to compute. Like the simplex method, most computational methods identify a point as optimal if there is no feasible path leading away from it along which the solution improves. Such methods are incapable of distinguishing between the top of a molehill and the peak of a mountain. The earth is

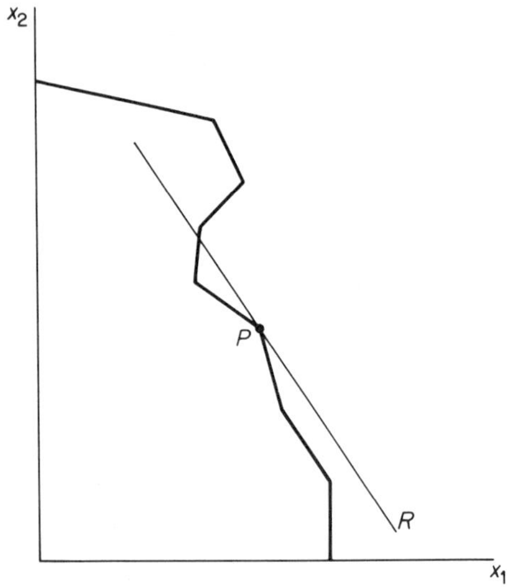

Fig. 7-9 A Constraint Set that is not Convex

obviously not a convex set. As we move away from the optimum in linear programming, the solution never gets better and it usually gets steadily worse. When the constraint set is not convex, as in Figure 7–9, the boundary may curl back and cross the objective line again. As we move along the boundary away from the vertex P, the situation gets worse before it gets better, but it does eventually get better. Convexity eliminates the distinction between mountains and molehills; it assures us that there is only one summit, although it may be a plateau, and finding it locates the optimum. To identify a boundary point as an optimum we need only look at the points in its immediate neighborhood. If none of these is a better solution, no point in the constraint set is. When the constraint set is not convex, there may be local optima, such as molehills, that are not global optima.

So long as the constraints are linear, a linear objective function in its optimal position either passes through a single vertex or coincides with a line segment joining two vertices. In the first case, many supporting lines pass through the same boundary point, and the coefficients may change in the objective function without affecting the optimal solution. In the second case, there are many optimal solutions for one objective function; the objective variable lies on an optimal plateau. We can rule out the possibility of multiple optima by making the constraints nonlinear or curvilinear, as in Figure 7–10. Any supporting line passes through one and only one boundary point. There may still be more than one supporting line through some boundary points. The boundary consists of arcs of curves that meet in a vertex like a Gothic arch. Such a boundary is *piecewise curvilinear*.

When only one supporting line can be drawn through a boundary point, it is called the tangent line at that point. With a piecewise-linear boundary, any tangent line must coincide with a whole line segment of the boundary. With a piecewise-curvilinear boundary, a tangent line, if one exists, passes through only one point of the boundary. But there is no unique supporting line and, hence, no tangent line at the vertices. When we rule out vertices and make the boundary a smooth curve, every point on the boundary has a tangent line different from the tangent line at any other point, as is true for a circle. Every point on the boundary is the unique optimum for some linear objective function, and every linear objective function has a unique optimum somewhere along the boundary of the constraint set.

The objective function need not be linear but may be a curve, such as $R = x_1x_2$, that we are trying to push as far from the origin as possible. The existence of an optimum thus depends on the properties of the objective function as well as those of the constraint set. We shall omit any statement of the general properties that objective functions must possess in order to yield maxima or minima on various types of constraint sets.

Until fairly recently the differential calculus provided the standard technique, and virtually the only technique, for optimization subject to constraints. The differential calculus identifies an optimum by tangency of the objective function to the boundary of the constraint set. The boundary of the constraint set must be smooth, assuring that tangency is possible. The constraint set need not be convex, but, if it is not, there may be many points of tangency to the same line.

In linear programming, the objective function is linear, and the constraint set is closed, bounded in at least one direction, and piecewise linear along its boundary. Nonlinear programming fills in the whole area between linear programming and the calculus. The simplest example retains the constraint set of linear programming but changes the objective function to

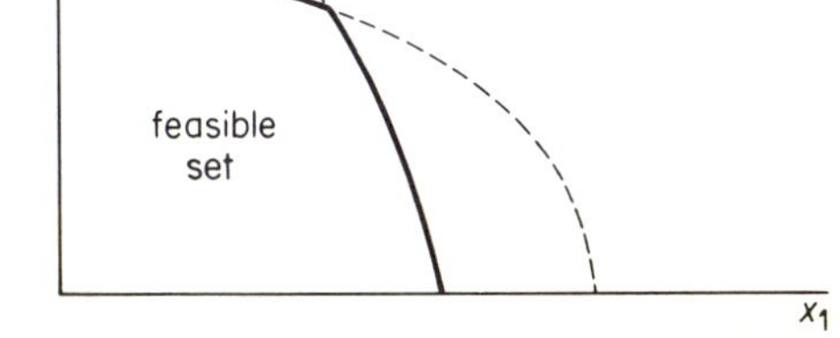

Fig. 7-10 A Piecewise-Curvilinear Constraint Set

nonlinear, such as a hyperbola. A slightly more complex case of nonlinear programming combines a linear objective function with a piecewise-curvilinear boundary for the constraint set. Finally the objective function may become nonlinear while the constraint set retains the piecewise-curvilinear boundary. The constraint set of nonlinear programming is usually assumed to be convex. Otherwise, general conclusions are very hard to come by.

EXERCISES

1. *Finding Maximum Revenue Graphically*

(a) The following vectors represent input and revenue coefficients for a set of vectors: [15, 9, 3], [6, 9, 2], [1, 4, $\frac{1}{2}$], [2, $\frac{1}{2}$, $\frac{1}{4}$], [24, 21, 3]. Convert each vector to the unit revenue form; assign symbols; and plot. Find the complete isorevenue contour graphically.

(b) If $\mathbf{b} = [6, 6]$, show the optimal solution and estimate the maximum revenue from the graph. Check the graphical results by reducing to canonical form with respect to the optimal basis.

2. *Deriving a Revenue Function*

For the numerical example in Exercise 1 of Chapter 5 graph the isorevenue contour for some convenient level of R. Let z_1 vary with b_2 constant. For each of the ranges over which a given solution remains optimal and feasible, identify the optimal basis. Ignoring all nonbasic variables, reduce the left- and right-hand sides to canonical form with respect to each basis and find the appropriate segment of the total revenue function. Present in the form of Table 7–1. Check against earlier results if you did the exercise.

3. *An Alternative Numerical Example*

Apply the instructions of the preceding exercise to the numerical example of Exercise 4 of Chapter 5.

4. *Extra Maintenance Costs for Idle Inputs* (A graphical analysis of Exercise 12 of Chapter 5.)

(a) In the numerical example of Chapter 5, which is also used in the text of the present chapter, reduce r_3 from 5 to 3 and r_4 from 6 to 4. Recompute the input coefficients required for \$1 of net revenue. Adjust all processes to some convenient level of revenue and graph. Assume that both inputs must be fully used and omit the slack processes. Find the new total revenue function and present in the form of Table 7–1. Graph total revenue and the marginal revenue productivity as z_1 varies with $z_2 = 80$.

To be realistic, the requirement that the firm use fully whatever amounts it has of both inputs must be reinterpreted as: either use fully or not at all. Slack processes are available but cannot be combined with production processes. Show that total revenue drops abruptly to zero everywhere outside the cone of the production processes. What happens to the isorevenue map and the total revenue graph if the firm can combine slack and production processes and let inputs go partially idle at no cost?

(b) Introduce a cost for extra maintenance of \$2 for each unit of an input not used. For the slack processes $r_5 = -2$ and $r_6 = -2$. When slack is costless the isorevenue contour for zero revenue consists of both axes. Now the firm can obtain zero revenue only by using some units of an input productively to offset the cost of letting the rest stand idle. Find the convex linear combinations of $\mathbf{a}_4$ and $\mathbf{a}_5$ and of $\mathbf{a}_3$ and $\mathbf{a}_6$ that have zero revenue coefficients. Plot each vector so found. How does R vary along the rays generated by these vectors? Draw the isorevenue contour for $R = 0$. Derive the following result: When any vector with a zero revenue coefficient is added to a point on any isorevenue contour it adds to that contour a line segment parallel to its own ray (e.g., the slack vectors in Figure 7–2). Use this result to complete the isorevenue contour on your graph. By reducing to canonical form with respect to (x_4, x_5) and (x_3, x_6), find the remaining segments of the total revenue function and the range over which each remains feasible.

Show that straight lines from points on the axes parallel to the nearer of the isorevenue rays are isorevenue contours with negative values of R. Find the marginal revenue productivities of the inputs along these lines. Complete the isorevenue map. Hold z_2 constant at 80 and let z_1 increase from zero upward. Graph R with respect to z_1. On both the isorevenue map and the total revenue graph, identify the ranges where R is negative, where the marginal revenue productivity or internal price of b_2 is negative, and where the marginal revenue productivity of z_1 is negative. Explain why a high market price for a variable input may cause a negative internal price for a fixed input.

Suppose that both inputs are fixed and the amounts lie in the cone of negative total revenue. Within the problem as formulated has the firm any choice except to keep producing? What other options might be added to the problem to make it more realistic?

5. *The Parametric Variation of a Net Revenue Coefficient*

In the first section of Chapter 5 we allowed r_3 to vary from zero upward and determined the successive optimal solutions. Explain how the upward variation of r_3 affects the isorevenue map of the present chapter. Show graphically all critical levels at which changes in r_3 are about to force a change in the optimal solution. After each change of basis redraw the isorevenue contour and explain what has happened. Identify the entering and departing variables and check against Table 5–1.

During the increase in r_3, what is happening to the internal prices of the inputs relative to each other?

6. *A Graphical Presentation of Exercise* 13, *Chapter* 5

(a) A tax on a product reduces net revenue per unit and shifts the isorevenue point on the ray. When x_2 alone is taxed at the rate of t_2 dollars per unit, show graphically the upper limit to the taxation of x_2. Express the condition algebraically and solve for the corresponding tax rate. Show graphically what occurs when the tax rate goes beyond the level. What is the economic explanation?

(b) Add the product x_7 to the graph with vector [8, 7, 29]. Show graphically why an increase in t_2 produces different results from (a). What is the economic explanation?

7. *A Graphical Presentation of Exercise* 14, *Chapter* 5

(a) All products are taxed at the same proportion t of their market prices. Show geometrically the effects on the isorevenue map and the optimal solution of increases in such a tax when there are no variable inputs.

(b) Add a variable input with the coefficients and market price specified in Exercise 146 on page 113. Show on a graph how a doubling of the tax rate affects an isorevenue contour and give an algebraic explanation. Let the tax rate increase from zero upward and identify the level of the tax at which the optimal solution changes. Illustrate graphically how the change to a new solution affects the amount of the tax paid and the level of net revenue.

8. *Convex Linear Combinations and Isorevenue Contours*

(a) To determine whether a vector $\mathbf{v}$ lies on the line through $\mathbf{a}_1$ and $\mathbf{a}_2$, first write the vector equation $\mathbf{v} = \mathbf{a}_1 + t(\mathbf{a}_2 - \mathbf{a}_1)$ as two linear equations in the single unknown t. Verify the following statements: (1) If $\mathbf{v}$ does not lie on the line, the system is inconsistent. (2) If $\mathbf{v}$ lies on the line, the system is redundant. (3) If $\mathbf{v}$ lies on the line segment joining $\mathbf{a}_1$ and $\mathbf{a}_2$, t lies in the range $0 \leqq t \leqq 1$.

(b) Use the preceding results to determine which of the following vectors lie on the line through $\mathbf{a}_1 = [2, 3]$ and $\mathbf{a}_2 = [3, 1]$ and which are convex linear combinations: $[7, -7]$; $[\frac{5}{2}, 2]$; $[1, 1]$; $[-4, 1]$; $[\frac{7}{3}, \frac{7}{3}]$; [0,7;] $[5, 4]$; $[\frac{1}{3}, \frac{1}{2}]$; $[4, 5]$. Check the results graphically.

(c) A vector may not lie on the line through $\mathbf{a}_1$ and $\mathbf{a}_2$ but some point on its ray, $s\mathbf{v}$, where $s \geqq 0$, may do so. To find the value of s corresponding to the point, set up the vector equation $s\mathbf{v} = \mathbf{a}_1 + t(\mathbf{a}_2 - \mathbf{a}_1)$ as a system of linear equations and solve for s and t. For those vectors in (b) that do not lie on the line find the value of s, if any, at which the ray intersects the line. Under what conditions does the ray fail to intersect the line? Which vectors generate rays that intersect the line in a convex linear combination? Show the required condition graphically. Verify the following statement: If $x_1\mathbf{a}_1 + x_2\mathbf{a}_2$ is a nonnegative linear combination, then

$$\frac{x_1}{x_1+x_2}\mathbf{a}_1 + \frac{x_2}{x_1+x_2}\mathbf{a}_2$$

is a convex linear combination.

(d) What happens to the isorevenue point for an output when its net revenue coefficient doubles or is cut in half? Show generally that, when the net revenue coefficient varies over the entire nonnegative range, the isorevenue point traces out the entire ray, except for the origin. That is, $s\mathbf{a}_2 = 1/r_2\mathbf{a}_2$ for the second output. Use this result to find the values of r_2 at which the second output yields the same revenue as a weighted average of the first and third outputs, and the third and fourth outputs in the numerical example of the text.

Show graphically the optimal solution to the numerical example when the first three outputs lie on the same isorevenue line segment. How many of the basic solutions are both feasible and optimal? Explain precisely how the simplex method gives the same answer.

(e) Suppose that r_3 varies in the numerical example of the text. Use the results of (c) to find the values of r_3 at which the following conditions exist: a weighted average of $\mathbf{a}_1$ and $\mathbf{a}_3$ yields the same revenue as $\mathbf{a}_2$; a weighted average of $\mathbf{a}_3$ and $\mathbf{a}_4$ yields the same revenue as $\mathbf{a}_1$.

9. *Closed Half-Spaces and Feasible Sets*

Carry out the instructions below for each of the following five sets of inequalities:

(1)
$$\begin{aligned} 15x_1 + 5x_2 &\leqq 60 \\ 7x_1 + 12x_2 &\leqq 84 \\ 4x_1 + 3x_2 &\leqq 24 \\ x_1 \geqq 0,\ x_2 &\geqq 0 \end{aligned}$$

(2)
$$\begin{aligned} 9x_1 + 3x_2 &\geqq 54 \\ 16x_1 + 8x_2 &\leqq 80 \\ 8x_1 + 8x_2 &\geqq 32 \\ x_1 \geqq 0,\ x_2 &\geqq 0 \end{aligned}$$

(3)
$$\begin{aligned} 6x_1 + 3x_2 &\geqq 120 \\ 2x_1 + 2x_2 &\geqq 60 \\ x_1 + 4x_2 &\geqq 40 \\ x_1 \geqq 0,\ x_2 &\geqq 0 \end{aligned}$$

(4)
$$\begin{aligned} x_1 - x_2 &\leqq 1 \\ \tfrac{1}{3}x_1 + \tfrac{1}{3}x_2 &\geqq 1 \\ 5x_1 + 6x_2 &\geqq 15 \\ x_1 \geqq 0,\ x_2 &\geqq 0 \end{aligned}$$

(5)
$$\begin{aligned} 40x_1 + 50x_2 &\leqq 200 \\ 1x_1 + 4x_2 &\leqq 80 \\ -5x_1 + 10x_2 &\leqq 100 \\ x_1 \geqq 0,\ x_2 &\geqq 0. \end{aligned}$$

(a) Graph each system of inequalities and determine whether or not a feasible set exists.

(b) For each feasible set state whether it is bounded from above only, from below only, or whether it is bounded. Give justifications for your answers.

(c) For the systems yielding feasible sets determine which ones yield optima under each of the following conditions:

(1) An objective function with positive coefficients is to be maximized.
(2) An objective function with one negative coefficient is to be maximized.
(3) An objective function with positive coefficients is to be minimized.
(4) An objective function with one negative coefficient is to be minimized.

10. *A Graphical Solution When Constraints Exceed Variables*

(a) Graph the following problem and find the optimal solution graphically:

$$\begin{aligned} x_1 \qquad &\leqq 4 \\ x_2 &\leqq 6 \\ 3x_1 + 2x_2 &\leqq 18 \\ 11x_1 + 5x_2 &\leqq 55 \\ 3x_1 + 5x_2 &= R(\max) \\ x_1 \geqq 0,\ x_2 &\geqq 0. \end{aligned}$$

(b) Verify the result by reducing to canonical form with respect to the variables in the graphical solution.

(c) Describe what happens on the graph when a coefficient in the revenue function varies over the entire nonnegative range. Also explain what occurs when the constant in the third constraint varies over its maximum range.

11. *A Minimizing Problem with an Excess of Constraints*

(a), (b) Carry out the instructions (a) and (b) of Exercise 10 with respect to the following dual minimizing problem for a multiproduct firm:

$$\begin{aligned}
\left(\frac{25}{4}\right)y_1 + 2y_2 &\geqq 1250 \\
4y_1 + 2y_2 &\geqq 1200 \\
y_1 + \ y_2 &\geqq 500 \\
y_1 + 2y_2 &\geqq 700 \\
2y_1 + 3y_2 &= V(\min) \\
y_1 \geqq 0,\ y_2 &\geqq 0.
\end{aligned}$$

(c) Describe what happens when a coefficient in the objective function varies over the entire nonnegative range. Also explain what occurs when the constant r_3 in the third constraint varies over its maximum range.

12. *The Feasible Set for Nonlinear Constraints*

(a) Graph the following nonlinear constraints, and indicate what is the feasible set:

$$\frac{x_1^2}{16} + \frac{x_2^2}{4} \leqq 1$$

$$x_1^2 + \frac{x_2^2}{16} \leqq 1$$

where $x_1 \geqq 0$, $x_2 \geqq 0$.

(b) Graph the following nonlinear constraints, and indicate what is the feasible set:

$$x_1 + x_2 + \sqrt{2x_1x_2} \geqq 6$$

$$(x_1+2)(x_2+1) \geqq 10$$

where $x_1 \geqq 0$, $x_2 \geqq 0$.

SUPPLEMENTARY READINGS FOR PART ONE

For an authoritative and comprehensive treatment of linear programming, which does not require a knowledge of matrices, the best book is:

Dantzig, George B. *Linear Programming and Extensions*, Princeton, N.J.: Princeton University Press, 1963.

Readers will find a systematic, detailed, and rigorous exposition of the computational techniques employed in Part One, as well as of many additional methods applicable to various special problems. The first three chapters are a particularly valuable and interesting account of the development of linear programming by one of the foremost pioneers.

For further grounding in vectors and the solution of linear equations, the best relatively brief book for students of economics and business is:

Hadley, G., *Linear Algebra*, Reading, Mass.: Addison-Wesley Publishing Co., 1961.

The book also contains an introduction to matrices.

Among the books on linear programming that use matrix algebra, readers are likely to find the following two particularly useful:

Gass, Saul I., *Linear Programming: Methods and Applications*, 3rd ed., New York: McGraw-Hill Book Company, 1969.

Llewelyn, Robert W., *Linear Programming*, New York: Holt, Rinehart and Winston, 1964.

The second book has a notably clear, simple, and extensive treatment of parametric programming methods.

Also highly recommended is:

Baumol, William J., *Economic Theory and Operations Analysis*, 2nd ed., Englewood Cliffs, N.J.: Prentice-Hall, Inc., 1965.

Chapters 5–8 cover linear programming at somewhat the same level as in Part One of this book, but add brief treatments of nonlinear and integer programming.

Part II

Economic Models of the Firm

8

A Multiprocess, Single-Product Firm

To explain the techniques of linear programming and their application to economics we chose as an illustrative example a multiproduct firm. While a multiproduct firm is both more general and more realistic than a single-product firm, the example selected suffers from limitations that will now be successively removed. The most severe limitation is the restriction of each output to a single production process. Each product requires inputs in a single fixed ratio and simply cannot use excess amounts of any input. Economic theory has traditionally placed great stress on substitutability between inputs, even to the point of assuming continuous substitutability. Within the confines of a linear technology, it is the presence of additional processes that permits substitution between inputs.

A second limitation, though somewhat less serious, is that each process in our model turns out only a single product. We need to allow for joint products and their effects on optimizing decisions. Finally, relatively few firms in our present-day economy confine their activities to a single plant. A multiplant firm has internal problems of allocation that differ in significant ways from those of a single-plant firm. Also, in looking ahead, we note that the problems of allocation for a multiplant firm are basically similar to those of a multifirm industry, although they are solved by different means. To prepare the way for the later analysis of both industry and economy we shall give attention to the allocative problem within multiplant firms.

The standard model of the firm in economic theory employs smooth curves and not the piecewise-linear contours or step functions of the linear version. As processes increase in number, the line segments shrink in length and piecewise-linear contours approach the smooth contours customarily presented. Further, the conditions of optimality derived for the linear model carry over to the smooth version. We shall continue to employ a linear model to derive the conditions for optimality, but shall hereafter generalize the results by the conceptual process of letting the number of processes increase without limit.

The present chapter introduces multiple processes in the simple case of a single-product firm and also explores the problem of allocation within a single-product, multiplant firm. Chapter 9 makes the transition to the conventional smooth version of a single-product firm. Chapter 10 brings in joint products in the course of developing an alternative, cost-minimizing model of the firm. Finally, Chapter 11 puts the previous results together into a multiprocess, multiproduct model, first for a single plant and then for a multiplant firm. In all cases we first apply the previously developed techniques to the linear model and then generalize the results.

THE TECHNOLOGICAL OPTIMIZING PROBLEM

A choice of processes inevitably brings with it the problem of optimal choice and the selection of a criterion to determine optimality. We could introduce economic data in the form of market prices and require that the maximization of net revenue determine the choice of processes. This criterion must determine the final solution, but we can get more insight into the decision making of the firm by breaking the decision down into three separate problems to be solved in stages. First there is the technological optimizing problem which does not require economic data in the form of market prices. The next problem, cost minimization, builds upon the results of the first problem and introduces prices for inputs but not for outputs. Having determined the least costly way of producing each output level, the firm then uses output prices to select the output level that maximizes net revenue.

The Technological Maximizing Problem

In solving the technological optimizing problem firms are assumed to use a criterion of technological efficiency, which takes a particularly simple form when there is only one product. For each combination of inputs, output is maximized. The technological maximizing problem shown below introduces in both symbolic and numerical form four different processes for a single product, denoted by x.

$$v_1\begin{bmatrix} a_{11} \\ a_{21} \\ 1 \end{bmatrix} + v_2\begin{bmatrix} a_{12} \\ a_{22} \\ 1 \end{bmatrix} + v_3\begin{bmatrix} a_{13} \\ a_{23} \\ 1 \end{bmatrix} + v_4\begin{bmatrix} a_{14} \\ a_{24} \\ 1 \end{bmatrix} \leqq \begin{bmatrix} b_1 \\ b_2 \\ x \end{bmatrix};$$

$$\tfrac{3}{10}v_1+\tfrac{1}{4}v_2+\tfrac{1}{5}v_3+\tfrac{1}{2}v_4 \leqq 9$$
$$\tfrac{1}{5}v_1+\tfrac{1}{4}v_2+\tfrac{2}{5}v_3+\tfrac{1}{6}v_4 \leqq 8$$
$$1v_1+1v_2+1v_3+1v_4 = x(\max).$$

The symbol v denotes the level of the processes. When operated at a higher level a process uses proportionately more of both inputs and turns out proportionately more product. In some specific cases the level of a process can be identified with, say, the speed of an assembly line or with some other measurable variable that is neither an output nor an input. Since the processes are soon eliminated from the problem, we shall not pause to discuss them in detail. For ease of graphing, each process is scaled to one unit of output. Except for the different objective variable, the model is essentially the same as the revenue maximization problem of earlier chapters. To permit easier graphing, both fixed inputs have been cut to one-tenth their previous size.

The optimal solution for one specific input combination gives one point on one isoproduct contour. We need a systematic method for finding all points on all isoproduct contours. In simple problems like the present numerical example, geometric methods provide an answer. Just as we did in finding an isorevenue contour, we can plot the unit output point on each ray and join by a line segment every pair of points. Processes or combinations of processes that require more inputs for a given output are eliminated, leaving a piecewise-linear contour as near the origin as possible.

To derive the equation of the contour we employ the same algebraic methods that yielded the net revenue function of Chapter 7. When the first two processes are optimal, we can ignore the remaining processes, apply pivot operations to the constraints only, and express the problem in the following way:

$$\begin{aligned} v_1 \qquad &= \bar{e}_{11}z_1+\bar{e}_{12}z_2 \\ v_2 &= \bar{e}_{21}z_1+\bar{e}_{22}z_2 \\ 1v_1+1v_2 &= \quad 0z_1+\quad 0z_2+x(\max). \end{aligned}$$

The $\bar{e}$ coefficients are not quite the same as those found in Chapter 5; they measure the effect of inputs on process levels and not directly on output. Since the original a coefficients are all positive, one $\bar{e}$ coefficient must be negative in each row and each column. When an input increases, it raises the single output by way of one process and lowers it by way of the other process. For the net effect of each input on the product, we eliminate process levels from the objective function, getting

$$0 = -(\bar{e}_{11}+\bar{e}_{21})z_1-(\bar{e}_{12}+\bar{e}_{22})z_2+x.$$

As in all preceding problems, the coefficients for z_1 and z_2 are the dual variables and must be positive. Using a single symbol to denote each set of parentheses, we rewrite the equation as

$$x = \bar{e}_1 z_1 + \bar{e}_2 z_2.$$

With the second input held constant, a change in the first input produces the following effect on output:

$$\Delta x = \bar{e}_1 \, \Delta z_1 \qquad \text{or} \qquad \bar{e}_1 = \frac{\Delta x}{\Delta z_1}.$$

Thus, $\bar{e}_1$ and also $\bar{e}_2$ are revealed to be the rates of change of output with respect to each input, or the marginal productivities of the inputs. As in all prior examples, reduction to canonical form converts the objective variable to a linear function of the quantities in the constraints with the dual variables as the coefficients. Hence, the marginal productivities of the inputs are the dual variables of the technological maximizing problem.

Readers have undoubtedly learned from their study of economics that, if a concept is important, it is likely to be a marginal something-or-other. There is a second lesson to be learned; if a concept is important in economics, it is also likely to be the dual variable to some optimizing problem. The reason is clear. The term marginal denotes a rate of change, and a dual variable always measures the rate of change of the objective variable with respect to the quantity in a constraint. Both the objective variable and a quantity in a constraint are highly significant in any problem, so their rate of change becomes an important economic concept.

Dual variables are also interpreted as internal or shadow prices, but it may not be immediately obvious that a marginal productivity is also a price. Not all prices in economics are rates of change or exchange between money and a commodity. Rates of exchange between two commodities are also regarded as prices, real or barter prices as they are often called. For a single-product firm, the sole product provides a unique measure of real value, and the value of an input to the firm is the rate at which it can be exchanged for output through the process of production. Thus, marginal productivities represent internal barter prices for inputs in terms of the sole output.

Reduction to canonical form with respect to an optimal basis eliminates the process levels and generates a linear output function that remains valid so long as the solution remains feasible. The same pair of vectors yields feasible solutions for all points lying in their cone, and the same linear output function also applies everywhere in the cone. To extend the output function to all points in the input space, we apply the techniques of parametric programming developed in Chapter 5. Except for the replacement of net revenue by output, the present numerical example is the same as the one used earlier and has the piecewise-linear output function shown in Table 8–1.

TABLE 8-1

A Piecewise-Linear Output Function

Range of ratios		Output function
z_2/z_1	x/z_1	$x = \bar{e}_1 z_1 + \bar{e}_2 z_2$
2 and over	5	$5z_1 + 0z_2$
1 to 2	4 to 5	$3z_1 + 1z_2$
$\frac{2}{3}$ to 1	$\frac{10}{3}$ to 4	$2z_1 + 2z_2$
$\frac{1}{3}$ to $\frac{2}{3}$	2 to $\frac{10}{3}$	$\frac{2}{3}z_1 + 4z_2$
0 to $\frac{1}{3}$	0 to 2	$0z_1 + 6z_2$

If x is assigned any positive value, the five equations provide the line segments for a single isoproduct contour, as drawn in Figure 8–1. Because output varies proportionately with the use of inputs, all contours are parallel to any one, and distance from the origin along any ray measures output.

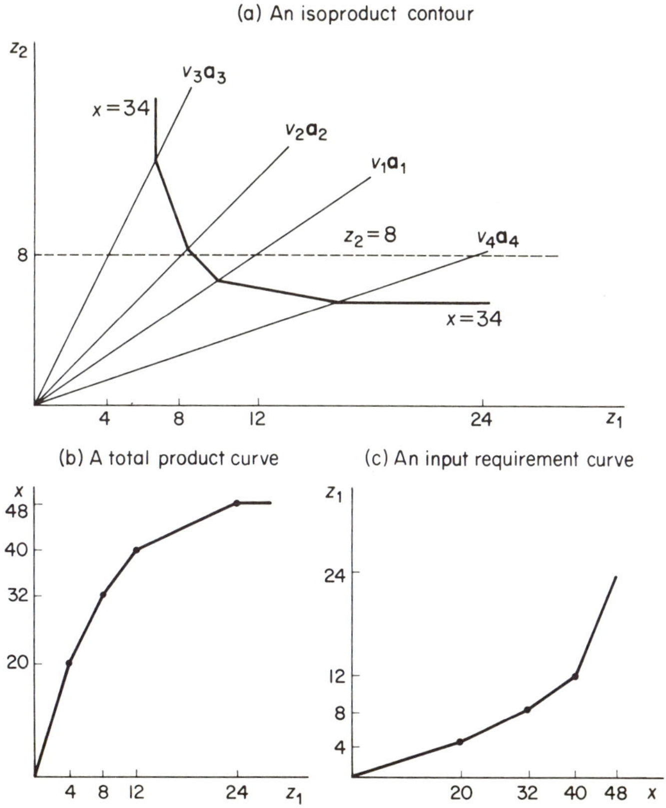

Fig. 8-1 Graphs for a Piecewise-Linear Output Function

For any one segment of an isoproduct contour, the equation can be written symbolically as

$$z_2 = -\frac{\bar{e}_1}{\bar{e}_2} z_1 + \frac{x}{\bar{e}_2}.$$

The slope of the line segment is $-\bar{e}_1/\bar{e}_2$, the negative ratio of the marginal productivities. From segment to segment, the combination of processes and the ratio of marginal productivities both change.

With one input constant, the piecewise-linear output function shows the variation of output in response to change in the variable input. Each portion of the output function contributes a linear segment to the total product curve, whose slope is the marginal productivity of the variable input. Figure 8–1 also shows the result of holding the second input constant at eight units and restricting the input combinations to a horizontal line in input space. Over each cone one segment of the output function holds. When the second input is held constant at a higher level, proportionately more of the variable input is used and proportionately more output is turned out. On the total product curve each segment, except the final horizontal segment, is lengthened in proportion to the increase in the fixed input.

The Technological Minimizing Problem

There is also a technological minimizing problem, shown below, in which one input is minimized for constant levels of output and the remaining input:

$$\begin{aligned}
1v_1 + \quad 1v_2 + \quad 1v_3 + \quad 1v_4 &\geqq q \\
-a_{11}v_1 - a_{12}v_2 - a_{13}v_3 - a_{14}v_4 &\geqq \quad -b_1 \\
a_{21}v_1 + a_{22}v_2 + a_{23}v_3 + a_{24}v_4 &= 0q - 0b_1 + z_2(\text{min}).
\end{aligned}$$

For uniformity, all signs are changed and the direction of the inequality is reversed in the second constraint. Once again, reduction to canonical form converts the objective variable to a linear function of the quantities in the constraints. With both inputs and output treated as variables, the resultant function can be written as

$$z_2 = \bar{a}_2 x - \bar{s} z_1.$$

With z_1 held constant, $\Delta z_2 = \bar{a}_2 \, \Delta x$, so $\bar{a}_2$ is the rate of change of the second input with respect to the output, or the *marginal input requirement* for the second input. When x is constant, $\Delta z_2 = -\bar{s}\,\Delta z_1$ or $\bar{s} = -\Delta z_2/\Delta z_1$. Hence, $\bar{s}$ is the negative of the rate of change of z_2 with respect to z_1 along an isoproduct contour. It is called the *rate of technical substitution*, to which some authors add the qualification, marginal.

Except in one situation, the technological maximizing problem and the technological minimizing problem must give the same answer. If the firm is using minimal amounts of inputs for a given output level, it cannot increase output while holding inputs constant. When x is held constant and z_1 varies parametrically, the input function traces out an isoproduct contour that coincides through all of its length with the major part of the isoproduct contour arising from the maximization problem. What is missing is the vertical line segment generated by the slack process for the second input. When z_2 is variable a firm seeking to minimize the amount used would never let it go idle. But if the firm happens to have a large amount of z_2 the best solution may be to let some of it lie idle rather than use it in processes where its marginal productivity becomes negative.

With slack ruled out, the marginal productivity of the second input, $\bar{e}_2$, never becomes zero. We can divide through the output function by $\bar{e}_2$ and compare it with the input function as is done below:

$$z_2 = -\frac{\bar{e}_1}{\bar{e}_2}z_1 + \frac{x}{\bar{e}_2} \qquad z_2 = -\bar{s}z_1 + \bar{a}_2 x.$$

Equating the coefficients of z_1 gives

$$\bar{s} = \frac{\bar{e}_1}{\bar{e}_2} = -\frac{\Delta z_2}{\Delta z_1}.$$

The rate of technical substitution between z_2 and z_1 along an isoproduct contour is the ratio of the marginal productivity of z_1 to the marginal productivity of z_2. The coefficients of x are $\bar{a}_2 = 1/\bar{e}_2$, showing that the marginal requirement for the second input is the reciprocal of its marginal productivity. If z_1 is chosen for minimization instead of z_2, the resultant input function is

$$z_1 = \bar{a}_1 x - \frac{1}{\bar{s}} z_2.$$

With the horizontal rather than the vertical isoproduct segment ruled out, the output function can be divided by $\bar{e}_1$, and similar comparisons can be made.

By setting up the problem of minimizing z_1 and applying parametric programming we can compute from the numerical example the input function for z_1, as shown in Table 8–2. With x constant the input function graphs as the isoproduct contour, except for the missing horizontal segment. When the amount of the second input is fixed, the input function graphs as the input requirement contour of Figure 8–1c. The slope of each segment is the marginal

TABLE 8-2

A Piecewise-Linear Input Function

Range of ratios		Input function
z_2/z_1	z_1/x	$z_1 = \bar{a}_1 x - (1/\bar{s})z_2$
2 and over	$\frac{1}{5}$	$\frac{1}{5}x - 0z_2$
1 to 2	$\frac{1}{4}$ to $\frac{1}{5}$	$\frac{1}{3}x - \frac{1}{3}z_2$
$\frac{2}{3}$ to 1	$\frac{3}{10}$ to $\frac{1}{4}$	$\frac{1}{2}x - 1z_2$
$\frac{1}{3}$ to $\frac{2}{3}$	$\frac{1}{2}$ to $\frac{3}{10}$	$\frac{3}{2}x - 6z_2$

input requirement, which is the reciprocal of the marginal productivity, the slope for the corresponding segment on the total product contour. Because z_1 is being minimized, the input requirement contour ends in a point and does not continue vertically upward.

The economic theory of the firm customarily begins at this point, after the technological optimizing problem has somehow been solved. The management is assumed to possess all required technological data in the form of an output function or an input function. The reason for omitting the technological optimizing problem is not that it is believed to be unimportant or routine. There is full recognition that the problem may be very difficult to solve and that its successful solution is of the utmost importance. The reason for excluding the problem is that its solution does not require specific economic data in the form of prices. So long as output has a positive price, the firm always wishes to maximize output from given inputs regardless of the specific value the output price may take. Similarly, so long as input prices are positive, their level does not affect the firm's decision to minimize one input for a constant level of the other. Thus, the technological optimizing problem requires only the very minimal economic assumption that prices are greater than zero.

What is involved in this distinction is the proper boundary between economics and engineering or technology. It may be arbitrary and unduly restrictive to confine economic decision making to those problems in which specific prices are required. The consequence, particularly for multiproduct, multiprocess, multiplant firms, is to classify a substantial portion of the internal allocative process as technological or noneconomic. Later chapters will supply specific examples and will give readers a basis for evaluating the distinction customarily made in the formulation of economic models.

THE COST MINIMIZING PROBLEM

The output function shows for each combination of inputs the technologically most efficient use. Though each input combination can be employed efficiently in one and only one way, each output level can be efficiently produced by the many combinations of inputs lying on an isoproduct contour. The cost-minimizing problem introduces prices for inputs and seeks the least costly way of producing each level of output. In linear programming format, the problem is

$$
\begin{aligned}
&(1) \qquad & 5z_1 + 0z_2 &\geqq q \\
&(2) \qquad & 3z_1 + 1z_2 &\geqq q \\
&(3) \qquad & 2z_1 + 2z_2 &\geqq q \\
&(4) \qquad & \tfrac{2}{3}z_1 + 4z_2 &\geqq q \\
&(5) \qquad & 0z_1 + 6z_2 &\geqq q \\
& & c_1z_1 + c_2z_2 &= 0q + C(\text{min}).
\end{aligned}
$$

The constraints can be written as equations but it is more convenient to use inequalities. Each constraint defines a closed half-space, and cost is to be minimized on the intersection of the upper closed half-spaces. The lower boundary of the feasible set is the isoproduct contour. Figure 8–2 displays the graphical solution for $c_1 = 6$, $c_2 = 4$, and $q = 20$. The objective function or cost equation can be written as

$$z_2 = -\frac{c_1}{c_2}z_1 + \frac{C}{c_2} \qquad \text{or} \qquad z_2 = -\frac{3}{2}z_1 + \frac{C}{4}.$$

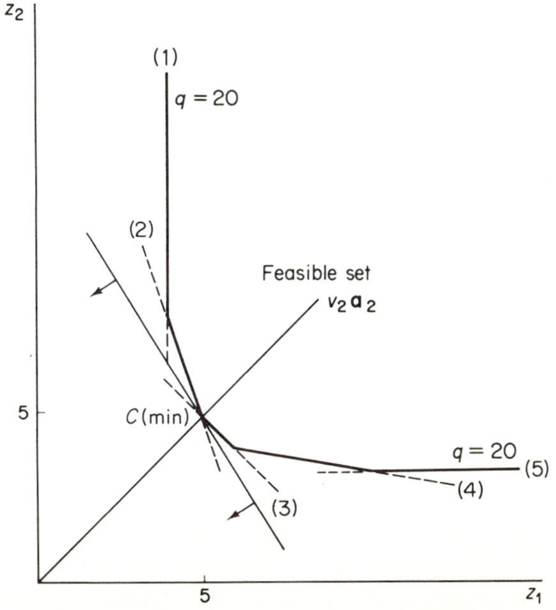

Fig. 8-2 Minimization of Cost on the Isoproduct Map

When the optimal solution is at a vertex, the slope of the cost line must lie between the slopes of the two line segments forming the vertex. Hence, the optimum is at the intersection of the constraints (2) and (3), whose slopes are -3 and -1.

In minimal position the cost line can also coincide with one of the line segments in the isoproduct contour. In linear programming parlance there are multiple optima; the vertex at each end of the segment is an optimal solution, and so are all weighted averages of the two basic solutions. What is more important for future use is that a flat-faced solution represents a position of tangency. The slope of the cost line, $-c_1/c_2$, which is the negative ratio of input prices, equals the slope of the isoproduct contour, $-\bar{e}_1/\bar{e}_2$, which is the negative ratio of the marginal productivities. It is this same condition of tangency or equality that defines minimal cost for the customary version of the firm with a smooth production function. For a unique optimum at a vertex the ratio of input prices is less than the ratio of marginal productivities on one segment and greater on the other.

We now have minimal cost for one level of output, but what is needed is minimal cost for all levels of output, or cost as a function of output. So long as input prices do not change, it is geometrically evident that minimal cost is attained at corresponding vertices or along corresponding segments on every isoproduct contour. But corresponding points on isoproduct contours lie on rays through the origin and along rays output, inputs, and total cost all vary proportionately. From the geometric method of deriving isoproduct contours, each vertex must lie on a ray generated by one of the production processes. Thus, as output varies the optimal process is operated at different levels. When the cost line coincides with a segment, the firm can choose any weighted average of the processes at the vertices. Minimal cost is determined, but the choice of an input combination is not.

In Figure 8–2, the second process is optimal and the cost of a unit of output is $c_1a_{12}+c_2a_{22} = 6(\frac{1}{4})+4(\frac{1}{4}) = \frac{5}{2}$. The total cost function is

$$C = (c_1a_{12}+c_2a_{22})x = \tfrac{5}{2}x,$$

which graphs as a straight line from the origin. The coefficient of x represents marginal cost, which is constant and graphs as a horizontal line. We can obtain the same results more rigorously by reducing the cost minimizing problem to canonical form and thus expressing cost as function of output.

With the original technological data available we can go back and solve simultaneously both the technological optimizing problem and the cost minimizing problem. The input prices determine the cost of each process and the problem is to minimize cost subject to a single output constraint. The optimal solution is likely to contain only the single process with lowest unit cost, but there may also be multiple optima.

Short-Run Cost

Economists apply the terms *long run* or *planning period* to the situation in which all inputs are variable. During the planning period before a plant is built, management is free to choose any combination of inputs. Once a plant is built, it may take considerable time to change the amounts of some inputs such as plant or heavy equipment, and it may not be economically expedient to make the change until the equipment is ready for replacement. Thus, there is a contrast between shorter periods over which some inputs remain fixed and longer periods over which adjustments can be made. Unless there are only two inputs there is no clear-cut distinction between a short run and a long run. Management faces a sequence of successively longer decision periods over which the number of fixed inputs progressively decreases. In a linear programming problem with many inputs, successively longer runs are shown by converting constants on the right to variables.

The present example has only two inputs so the customary distinction between short-run and long-run cost can be made. With the second input constant we can obtain the cost of the variable input, or the *total variable cost*, simply by multiplying the input function by the price of the variable input, as is done below:

$$\text{TVC} = c_1 z_1 = c_1 \bar{a}_1 x_1 - \frac{c_1}{\bar{s}} b_2.$$

With $c_1 = 6$ and $z_2 = 8$, readers can easily convert the input function of Table 8–2 to a total variable cost function. The graph of total variable cost differs only in vertical scale from the input requirement curve of Figure 8–1c.

In the short run there is also the cost of the fixed input or the *fixed cost*. Since the services of the fixed input appear in the constraints, the appropriate price is the rental or leasing price, although many firms follow an elaborate procedure of allocating the original cost of a fixed facility over its service life. In either case the result is to add a constant component to cost that is independent of output levels, and total short-run cost becomes

$$C = c_1 \bar{a}_1 x - \frac{c_1}{\bar{s}} b_2 + c_2 b_2 = c_1 \bar{a}_1 x + \left(c_2 - \frac{c_1}{\bar{s}} \right) b_2.$$

Table 8–3 shows total, marginal, and average short-run cost when $c_1 = 6$, $c_2 = 4$, and $z_2 = 8$. The various short-run cost curves are graphed in Figure 8–3, together with the comparable long-run cost curves.

Short-run total cost lies everywhere above long-run total cost except for one output. The point of equality can be identified easily from the isoproduct map of Figure 8–4. As x increases with $z_2 = 8$, the amount of z_1 required traces out a horizontal line. Each cone contributes a line segment to the

TABLE 8–3

Short-Run Cost

Range x	*Total cost* $C = c_1\bar{a}_1x+[c_2-(c_1/\bar{s})]b_2$	*Marginal cost* $c_1\bar{a}_1$	*Average cost* $C/x = c_1\bar{a}_1+[c_2-(c_1/\bar{s})](b_2/x)$
0 to 20	$(6/5)x+\ 32$	6/5	$(6/5)+(32/x)$
20 to 32	$2x+\ 16$	2	$2+(16/x)$
32 to 40	$3x-\ 16$	3	$3-(16/x)$
40 to 48	$9x-256$	9	$9-(256/x)$

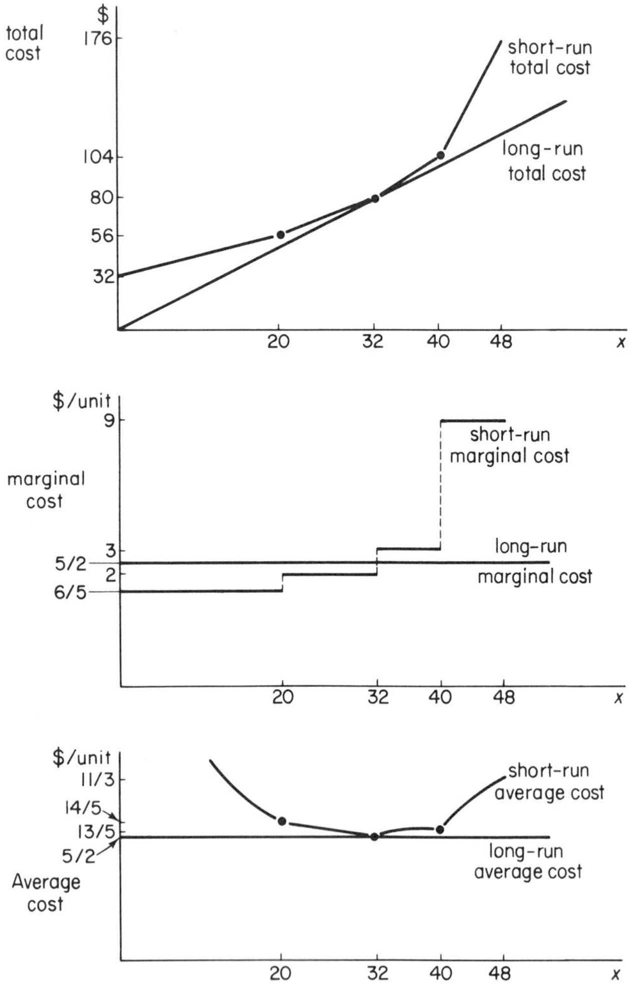

Fig. 8-3 Long-Run and Short-Run Cost Curves

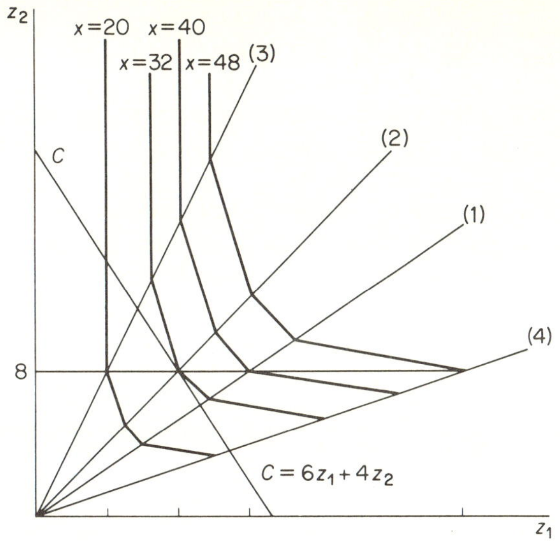

Fig. 8-4 Short-Run Cost on the Isoproduct Map

short-run total cost curve and each ray a vertex. At the given input prices the second process or ray represents the most economical way of producing any level of output when both inputs are variable. When the horizontal line intersects the second ray the corresponding output is produced at the lowest possible cost. The short-run solution coincides with the long-run optimal solution, so both costs must be the same. For every other output level the firm is forced in the short run to employ input combinations that it would not choose in the long run, so the cost must be higher.

The foregoing example illustrates an important principle in economics and, more generally, in mathematics. An optimum subject to more constraints or to more stringent constraints cannot be better than an optimum subject to fewer constraints or to less stringent constraints. The reason is clear: More constraints, if binding, or more stringent constraints cut down the feasible set. The previous optimum may remain in the feasible set but better points cannot possibly be introduced.

Each value at which z_2 is held constant determines a different set of short-run cost curves. If, say, z_2 is doubled, two effects occur. Total fixed cost, which is the vertical intercept, also doubles. Further, in passing through each cone on the isoproduct map, both z_1 and x increase to twice their previous levels. All segments in the short-run total cost curve double in length, and the vertex on the long-run curve occurs at a level of output that is twice as large. There is, thus, an infinite family of short-run total cost curves, one for each value of z_2, each member of which has a single vertex on the long-run curve. Because fixed cost is present, division by output converts a piecewise-linear total cost curve into a piecewise-curvilinear average cost curve. There is also an infinite family of short-run average cost curves, each with a vertex on the horizontal long-run average cost curve.

An important special case for future consideration occurs when long-run total cost is minimized everywhere along a line segment of an isoproduct contour. For a numerical example let $c_1 = c_2 = 4$. As readers may verify, the cost line coincides with the third segment in an isoproduct contour, and the long-run cost function becomes $C = 2x$. The third segment of the input function enables us to make the following recalculation of the corresponding segment in short-run total variable cost:

$$z_1 = \tfrac{1}{2}x - 1z_2 \qquad c_1 z_1 = 2x - 32.$$

With the addition of fixed cost, short-run total cost becomes

$$C = c_1 z_1 + c_2 b_2 = (2x - 32) + 32 = 2x.$$

As the horizontal line $z_2 = 8$ cuts across the appropriate cone, every input combination on the line minimizes long-run total cost for some level of output. Hence, short-run total cost must equal long-run total cost over an entire interval for z_1 and for x. It follows that short-run and long-run marginal cost coincide over an interval, as must both average cost curves. An important general relationship emerges that will be useful later: When a constant input line passes through a point of tangency between the cost line and an isoproduct contour, the short- and long-run total cost curves are also tangent at that output, and marginal cost is the same in both short and long run.

When the original technological data are available, we can always go back and solve simultaneously the technological minimizing problem and the cost minimizing problem. With only a single variable input, it is only necessary to multiply the objective function by the price of that input. In canonical form the objective function becomes

$$c_1 z_1 = c_1 \bar{a}_1 x - \frac{c_1}{\bar{s}} b_2.$$

The coefficients are the dual variables of the combined cost and technological minimizing problems. The coefficient of output is obviously its marginal cost, but the coefficient of the fixed input is not so easily recognized. With x constant, a larger amount of b_2 reduces the amount of z_1 needed and its cost. Thus, the coefficient is the rate of change of variable cost with respect to the fixed input. Net revenue is the difference between total revenue and total cost, but with output constant net revenue increases only when cost decreases. Hence, the coefficient of b_2 is its marginal net revenue productivity, or $y_2 = c_1/\bar{s}$. The second term in the short-run total cost function is

$(c_2 \times c_1/\bar{s})b_2$. When output is low and little z_1 is used, relatively large amounts of the fixed input are employed, and its marginal net revenue productivity is lower than the market price. The situation is reversed at higher levels of output beyond the point of equality between long- and short-run costs. When short-run and long-run total cost coincide over an entire line segment, $c_2 = c_1/\bar{s} = y_2$.

THE OPTIMUM FOR THE FIRM

Once a firm has determined the minimal cost for all levels of output, it can easily select an output level that maximizes net revenue. The maximum vertical difference between the total revenue line, $R = px$, and the short-run total cost curve identifies an optimal output level in Figure 8–5a. When

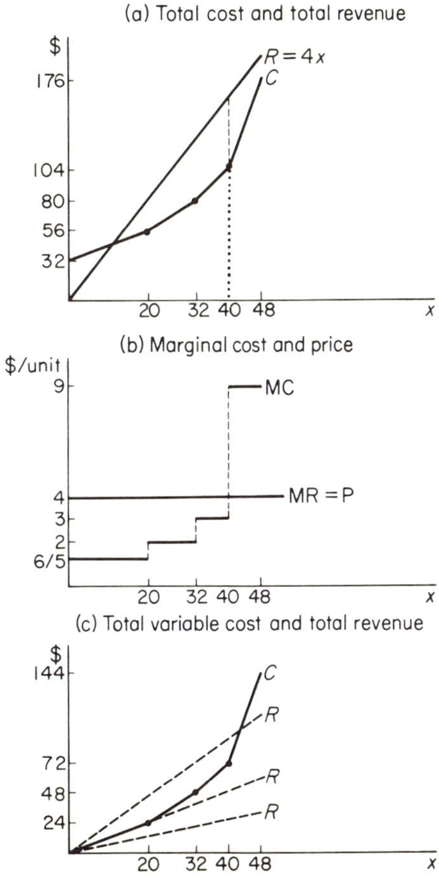

Fig. 8-5 The Short-Run Optimal Output

there is a unique optimum, total cost increases more rapidly than total revenue after the vertex and less rapidly before. Hence, the optimum can also be identified in Figure 8–5b by the output price line passing through a vertical gap in the marginal cost curve. When a segment of total cost is parallel to the total revenue line, the price line coincides with a segment of the marginal cost curve. There is no unique optimum and no supply curve. Once again, the open vertical segments in the marginal cost function constitute the supply curve.

Because of the constant returns to scale inherent in the linear technology, long-run total cost is a straight line through the origin. Since total revenue is also a straight line through the origin, the only options open to the firm are to expand the plant without limit, choose indifferently any scale of operation, or not to produce at all. As a long-run model for the firm, the linear version is obviously an unsatisfactory first approximation, and we shall have to modify it in later chapters. Except when a firm is planning a new installation, some inputs will be constant, and we shall continue for the present to examine the firm under these conditions.

When the total revenue line lies everywhere below short-run total cost, the firm has no incentive to continue operations indefinitely. Before we can predict what the firm will do in the short run, we need to specify carefully the options open to it. One possibility is that the fixed input can be leased to others at the going price c_2. Leasing to others is profitable if the internal price or marginal revenue productivity is less than the going price. As shown in the preceding section, the internal price of the input equals its market price along the long-run total cost line. If leasing to others is possible it is preferable to production when the total revenue line drops below long-run total cost and, hence, short-run total cost.

If leasing is not possible and the firm wishes to retain ownership of the facilities, it must choose between continuing to produce and shutting down wholly or partially. A shutdown, complete or partial, means that the slack process for the fixed input enters the optimal solution. When the slack process has no cost attached to it, we can easily identify the conditions under which a shutdown becomes optimal. With leasing ruled out, the going rental or leasing price is irrelevant to any decision, as is the fixed cost, c_2b_2. Figure 8–5c compares total variable cost and total revenue. The initial segment of total variable cost corresponds to the first cone on the isoproduct map, in which the slack process for the second input appears. When the total revenue line coincides with the initial segment of total variable cost, there are multiple optima. Production at full capacity, a complete shutdown, or anything in between yields the same net revenue. When total revenue and total variable cost are equal, average revenue, which is the output price, must equal average variable cost, an alternative condition that is often used. Along total cost lines through the origin, average and marginal cost are equal. The firm shuts down when the output price falls below the lowest segment of the marginal cost curve, which is also the lowest horizontal segment of average variable cost.

Unused inputs need not always go costlessly to waste, as the familiar example of an automobile battery attests. Letting a battery go idle reduces its service life, which can be translated into a cost of idleness. For a battery the slack process has a negative coefficient in the objective form. Similarly, when a plant is shut down, special maintenance may be necessary to keep it in operating condition or to prevent it from becoming a public nuisance. When a slack process has a cost, total variable cost does not fall to zero when output does and has a positive vertical intercept. The first segment becomes flatter and the total revenue line can decline further before a shutdown becomes the preferred alternative. The initial segment of the marginal cost curve lies at a lower level, but average variable cost becomes the arc of a curve and has only the right endpoint in common with the marginal cost segment. Exercise 7 confirms the preceding assertions.

The Revenue Maximizing Problem

The optimum for the firm can also be found by first solving the revenue maximizing problem either directly or by use of the previously derived output function. With only one output, multiplication by the output price converts the objective function from output maximization to revenue maximization. When reduced to canonical form, the revenue function becomes

$$px = p\bar{e}_1 z_1 + p\bar{e}_2 z_2.$$

The coefficients are the marginal revenue productivities or internal prices for the inputs. By choosing $p = 3$ and $z_2 = 8$, readers may convert the output function of Table 8–1 into the piecewise-linear total revenue function of Figure 8–6. The total cost equation, using the previously selected input prices, is

$$C = c_1 z_1 + c_2 z_2 = 6z_1 + 4(8) = 6z_1 + 32.$$

The maximum vertical difference between total revenue and short-run total cost identifies an optimal amount of the first input. Alternatively, we can plot the respective slopes as the marginal revenue productivity and the price of the first input. For the present set of numerical values, the input price line coincides with a horizontal segment of the marginal revenue productivity curve. By referring back to Table 8–3, readers may verify that the output price, $p = 3$, also coincides with a segment of the marginal cost curve. The result must always hold, since

$$c_1 \bar{a}_1 = p \quad \text{implies} \quad c_1 = \frac{1}{\bar{a}_1} p \quad \text{or} \quad c_1 = \bar{e}_1 p.$$

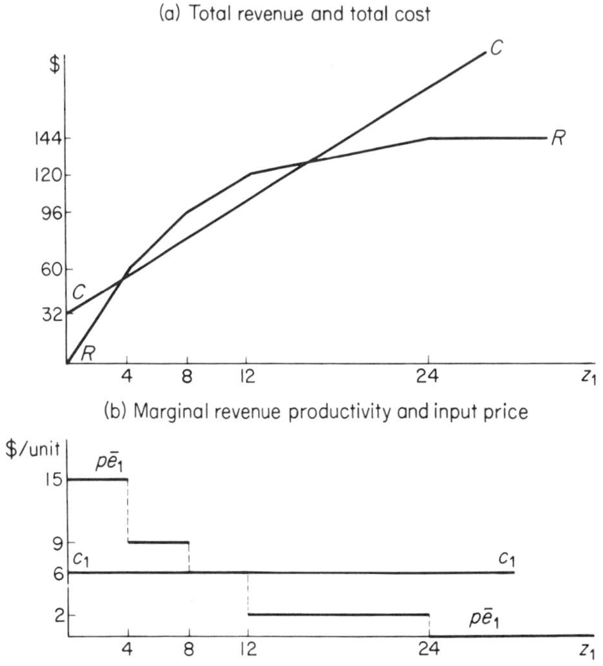

Fig. 8-6 The Optimal Amount of the Variable Input

Because the marginal productivity is the reciprocal of the marginal input requirement, the equality of marginal cost and output price requires the equality of MRP and input price. With a slight rise in the output price, the optimal solution lies in a vertical gap of the marginal cost curve, and the MRP curve shifts upward, permitting c_1 to pass through a vertical gap. The optimum of the firm can be expressed equivalently in terms of marginal cost and output price or in terms of marginal revenue productivity and input price.

A SINGLE-PRODUCT MULTIPLANT FIRM

There are few firms with a single plant, so the model of a multiplant firm is of interest in its own right as well as being a precursor to the study of a multifirm industry. If the plants are completely independent of each other, optimizing decisions can be made for each plant separately, and the results are no different from what they would be under separate ownership. We assume then that the plants share at least one input, which may be merely the services of the top management. In the two-plant model shown below, there is a fixed input for each plant (b_1, b_2), and a third input b_3 that is fixed for the firm but shared by the plants in a proportion that is to be determined.

$$
\begin{array}{llllllll}
a_{11}v_1+a_{12}v_2+a_{13}v_3 & & & \leqq b_1 \\
& a_{24}v_4+a_{25}v_5+a_{26}v_6 & \leqq & \quad b_2 \\
a_{31}v_1+a_{32}v_2+a_{33}v_3+a_{34}v_4+a_{35}v_5+a_{36}v_6 & & \leqq & \quad\quad b_3 \\
1v_1+\ 1v_2+\ 1v_3+\ 1v_4+\ 1v_5+\ 1v_6 & & = & 0b_1+0b_2+0b_3+x(\max).
\end{array}
$$

The plants produce the same product, and each has three processes from which to choose. Each plant could use variable inputs whose prices would then be incorporated in net revenue coefficients, but to concentrate on the main issue we omit such inputs. Each process is scaled to one unit of output, but the conversion to revenue simply requires multiplication by the market price.

The optimal solution to the technological maximizing problem contains three processes, one of which may be a slack process for either of the first two inputs. On the grounds of technological efficiency alone, the corresponding plant is not operated fully or is completely shut down. A plant could also be operated below full capacity for economic reasons if its processes had heavy requirements for variable inputs. Conceivably, the third input could be in such short supply that neither plant could operate at capacity. Or the third input could be so plentiful it could not be used fully. We shall, however, concentrate on the case where no slack processes appear.

When the optimal solution is reduced to canonical form, the objective function becomes

$$x = \bar{e}_1 b_1 + \bar{e}_2 b_2 + \bar{e}_3 b_3.$$

The equation forms one segment of an output function for the firm as a whole, which remains valid within specific ratios for the inputs. In any numerical problem parametric programming will generate the entire output function for the firm. The coefficients are the internal real prices for the inputs or their marginal productivities. Since the marginal productivities are the dual variables, a process appearing in the optimal solution, say the first, must satisfy the following condition:

$$1-a_{11}\bar{e}_1-0\bar{e}_2-a_{31}\bar{e}_3 = 0 \qquad \text{or} \qquad a_{11}\bar{e}_1+a_{31}\bar{e}_3 = 1.$$

The marginal productivities of the inputs, or their real prices within the firm, are set at such a level that only the most efficient processes break even. For a process not in the optimal basis, say the third, the following condition holds:

$$1-a_{31}\bar{e}_1-0\bar{e}_2-a_{33}\bar{e}_3 < 0 \qquad \text{or} \qquad a_{31}\bar{e}_1+a_{33}\bar{e}_3 > 1.$$

The opportunity cost of the inputs, or what they can yield in the optimal processes, exceeds the unit output of the nonoptimal process.

The optimal solution determines each plant's share of the third input, but we need to examine the underlying economic rationale. We can perform the conceptual experiment of assigning to one plant all possible amounts of the third input from zero to the total amount available. For each assigned quantity, the maximum output is found for the plant and plotted against the amount of the third input. The result is a total product curve for the shared input in one plant, from which we can derive a marginal productivity curve. The experiment can be repeated for the other plant. If we denote by z_{31} the amount of the shared input allotted to the first plant, and by z_{32} the amount going to the second plant, then $z_{31}+z_{32} = b_3$. By measuring z_{31} and z_{32} in opposite directions, we can display both marginal productivity curves on one graph, as in Figure 8–7.

The optimal division of the shared input occurs when a horizontal segment of one marginal productivity function passes through a vertical gap in the other function. Both to the right and to the left of this division, the plant losing input has a higher marginal productivity than the plant gaining it. From previous results we know that the horizontal segment corresponds to two processes and the vertical gap to one. In the optimal solution, the marginal productivity of the third input within the firm will be at the level of the horizontal segment. If top management sets an internal price at that level, the manager of the plant using one process knows exactly how much of the third input he wants. The manager of the plant using two processes is not able to determine the quantity to demand, but he will have no incentive to change if he is allotted the remainder.

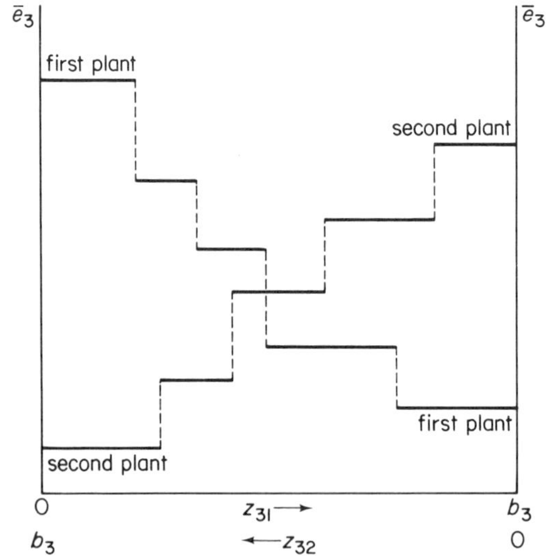

Fig. 8-7 The Optimal Allocation of a Fixed Input

Other, much less likely, outcomes could occur. Horizontal segments on the two curves could coincide, implying multiple optima and an indeterminate allocation of the third input. Or vertical gaps could coincide, implying only one process in each plant and a degenerate optimal solution. The allocation is determined but the marginal productivity is not. Each of these solutions requires that all coefficients and constants take on one special set of values. They are, therefore, much less likely to occur. With many plants the details of the solution become more complex, but the same general result must hold; for any pair of plants there must be no possibility of increasing output by shifting the shared input.

If each plant produces a different product, the marginal productivities of the shared input cannot be compared, since they are measured in different units. The firm cannot solve the problem of allocating the shared input using technological data alone. However, market prices for outputs permit the calculation of the marginal revenue productivity in each plant. A diagram like Figure 8–7 shows the optimal allocation.

EXERCISES

Unless otherwise specified, the exercises are based on the following numerical example of a single-product, multiprocess firm:

$$\begin{aligned} 6v_1 + 4v_2 + 3v_3 + 12v_4 + 9v_5 &\leqq b_1 \\ 4v_1 + 6v_2 + 12v_3 + 2v_4 + 3v_5 &\leqq b_2 \\ 10v_1 + 10v_2 + 10v_3 + 10v_4 + 10v_5 &= 0b_1 + 0b_2 + x(\max). \end{aligned}$$

Exercises 1, 3, and 4, the latter two based on the first, provide a full numerical model for the firm.

1. *The Technological Optimizing Problem*

(a) Plot the technological data for the numerical example and draw an isoproduct contour for some convenient level of output. On the basis of the graph make and justify a simplification in the numerical example. Use the geometrical diagram as a guide in deriving algebraically the output function. Present the function in the format of Table 8–1, adding a column for the rate of technical substitution $\bar{s}$. Hold z_2 fixed at the level of 6. Derive and plot the corresponding total product curve for z_1. Double the level at which z_2 is held fixed and plot the new total product curve on the same diagram. Give a general explanation of how the total product curve for z_1 changes as z_2 varies parametrically.

(b) Set up the technological minimizing problem for the numerical example with z_1 in the objective function. Explain how to derive an input function for z_1. To what extent does the input function for z_1 coincide with the output function? Use the results of (a) to present the input function for z_1 in the format of Table 8–2. For the two previously chosen fixed levels of z_2, derive and plot on one diagram the input requirement curve for x and z_1. Explain how to draw the input requirement curve corresponding to any specified level of z_2.

2. The numerical example is the same as that in Exercise 1 of Chapter 5, with a process added and the objective coefficients equalized. For review and synthesis apply parametric programming or use previously obtained results to derive the output function.

3. *The Cost Minimizing Problem* (A Continuation of Exercise 1)

(a) *Long-Run Cost*

For each of the following sets of input prices, ($c_1 = 2$, $c_2 = 1$) and ($c_1 = 2$, $c_2 = 2$), write long-run total cost as a function of the inputs and show graphically in input space the minimization of total cost for a given level of output. In each case how does the ratio of input prices compare with the ratio of the marginal productivities derived in Exercise 1? Generalize the results by letting c_1/c_2 vary from zero upward. By comparing the ratio of input prices with the ratio of marginal productivities identify the crucial ratios. State precisely how the optimum varies as c_1/c_2 traverses its entire range.

To find the long-run total cost curve let x vary parametrically. Identify in input space the locus of all optimal solutions as x varies with $c_1 = 2$, $c_2 = 1$. On a single diagram plot against x the total cost of each process as x varies. Show that the long-run total cost curve is the lower boundary of cost defined by the cost of the least expensive process. Identify long-run marginal cost.

Find the locus of optimal solutions in input space as x varies with $c_1 = 2$, $c_2 = 2$. Is there a unique long-run total cost curve?

(b) *Short-Run Cost*

Let $z_2 = 6$ and draw in the locus of all possible short-run solutions on the isoproduct map of Exercise 1. Find the values of z_1 and x at which a change of basis occurs. Explain the significance of the intersection between the short-run locus of solutions and the long-run locus.

Convert the input function of Exercise 1 to a total variable cost function when $c_1 = 2$ and $z_2 = 6$. Add the fixed cost when $c_2 = 1$ and find total, marginal, and average short-run cost. Present in the format of Table 8–3. Graph the short-run cost curves together with the corresponding long-run curves as in Figure 8–3.

What is the effect on the locus of short-run solutions and on the short-run total cost curve when z_2 varies parametrically? What happens when z_2 remains at the original level but the price of the fixed input becomes $c_2 = 2$? Sketch the graph of short-run and long-run total cost in this case.

(c) *The Short-Run Optimum*

Draw diagrams similar to Figure 8–5 and find the short-run optimal output for $p = \frac{3}{2}$, $c_2 = 1$. As a check convert the original numerical example to the maximization of net revenue subject to a single input constraint. Find by inspection the process that yields maximum net revenue. Let the output price change to $p = 2$ and explain what occurs on the diagrams and in the net revenue maximizing model. Explain how to obtain the supply curve for the output by explicit use of parametric programming. Alternatively, derive the supply curve from the diagrams.

4. *The Revenue Maximizing Problem* (A Continuation of Exercise 1)

(a) *Long-Run Total Revenue*

Explain how to convert from an isoproduct map in input space to an isorevenue map. When is total cost minimized for a given level of total revenue? From the output function of Exercise 1 construct the total revenue function when $p = \frac{3}{2}$. As both inputs increase proportionately, what happens to total revenue and to the marginal revenue productivities? Identify the optimal process when both inputs can be purchased at the prices $c_1 = 2$, $c_2 = 1$. Using the vector for the optimal ray express total revenue and total cost as function of z_1 alone. Determine whether there is an optimal solution.

(b) *Short-Run Total Revenue*

Using the results of (a), present in tabular form the short-run total revenue function for z_1 when $z_2 = 6$. Graph as functions of z_1 both short-run total revenue and the long-run total revenue found in (a). How are they related to each other? Add short-run total cost when $c_1 = 2, c_2 = 1$ and find the optimal amount of z_1 in the short run.

As a check convert the original numerical example directly to the maximization of *net* revenue subject to a single fixed input constraint. Explain how to derive the demand curve for z_1 by explicit use of parametric programming. Use the previously obtained revenue data to construct the demand curve geometrically.

5. *Internal and External Real Prices for Inputs and Outputs*

In each of the following parts treat the marginal productivities of the inputs as dual variables or internal real prices.

(a) Use the internal real prices of the inputs to draw an economic distinction between a process that appears in the optimal solution and one that does not.

(b) Show that an input in excess supply has an internal real price of zero.

(c) Show that when the firm pays the inputs their internal real prices the inputs receive the total amount of the output they produce.

(d) From the external monetary prices of an input and an output derive in symbolic form the corresponding real price of the input, that is, the number of units of the output for which one unit of the input can be exchanged. What is the real price of the output in terms of the input?

(e) If one input is variable and its external or market real price is constant, show diagrammatically the optimal amount for the firm to purchase. Derive a demand curve for the input as its real market price varies. Convert to a demand curve in terms of the monetary price.

(f) Treat $\bar{a}_1$ as the internal real price of the output in terms of the variable input z_1. Show diagrammatically the optimal output when the external real price of the output is constant. Derive a supply curve as the real market price varies and convert to a supply curve in terms of the monetary price. How are the demand curves of (e) related to the supply curves of (f)?

6. *Neutral Technological Change*

Technological change is an important and pervasive influence on economic models. It enters through the technological optimizing problem; the technological data change, altering the solution to the problem and modifying the isoproduct map. Technology may change in many ways but, particularly in the study of growth, economists stress what has been termed *neutral* technological change. There are several types, each identified by the name of the economist who introduced it. This exercise relates each type of neutral technological change to the technological optimizing problem for the linear model of the firm.

(a) *Hicks Neutral Technological Change*

The increase in efficiency affects all inputs proportionately. In the numerical example of the *text* reduce all input coefficients in the same proportion, multiplying all by some proper fraction $1/k$. Reduce to canonical form with respect to some basis and determine which barred coefficients are affected by the presence of k. State precisely the effects of Hicks neutral technological change on the isoproduct map, the output function, the marginal productivities of the inputs, and the total product curve for z_1 with z_2 constant. In what sense is this type of technological change neutral?

(b) *Harrod Neutral Technological Change*

Only labor increases in efficiency in a two-input model where the second input is capital. In the numerical example of the *text* multiply all coefficients in the first row only by some proper fraction $1/k$.

(1) Let $k = 2$ and plot an isoproduct contour similar to that in Figure 8–1a. Summarize the effect of Harrod neutral technological change on the position and slope of the segments in the contour. With z_2 constant, what is the effect on the range of z_1 over which a given solution remains optimal? With z_1 constant, what is the effect on the range of z_2?

(2) Reduce either the symbolic or the numerical problem to canonical form and determine which barred coefficients are affected by the presence of $1/k$. Derive one segment of the output function and write in symbolic form. How does the presence of $1/k$ affect the ranges of z_1 and z_2 over which a given segment remains optimal? Rewrite Table 8–1, inserting k wherever it belongs. Let $k = 2$ and check the table with the geometric results.

(3) Hold z_2 constant at 8. Recompute and redraw the total product curve of Figure 8–1b when $k = 2$. Hold z_1 constant at 3 and plot on one diagram both the original total product curve for z_2 and the revised curve when $k = 2$. Plot on another diagram both marginal productivity curves for capital. Assume there is no technological change but z_1 is held constant at 6 units. Compare the effects on the total product and marginal productivity curves of capital.

(4) When labor increases in efficiency a smaller amount can do the same job. A second way of incorporating Harrod neutral technological change into the model is to measure labor in units of constant efficiency, the size of the unit decreasing as efficiency increases. Check previous calculations to show that k may be combined either with $\bar{e}_1$ or with b_1 in the output function. Assume labor is originally measured in man-hours. Give a specific reinterpretation of the labor coefficients and the available supply of labor when $k = 2$.

(5) In growth models the significance of Harrod neutral technological change is that it allows both labor and capital to grow at the same steady rate. The key requirement is that the marginal productivity of capital must not change so long as the ratio of output to capital x/z_2 does not change. To both the original and the revised version of Table 8–1 add a column showing the range of x/z_2 over which each segment remains optimal. Show that the key requirement is met.

(c) Technological change is *Solow neutral* when capital alone rather than labor alone becomes more efficient. When both Harrod neutral and Solow neutral technological change occur together, is the result necessarily Hicks neutral?

7. *The Cost of Idle Capacity and Its Effect*

When an idle plant requires extra maintenance, the slack process for the plant has a positive labor coefficient. Taking the first input to be labor services, change the slack process for the plant to $\mathbf{a}_6 = [\frac{1}{10}, 1, 0]$ in the numerical example of the *text*. Redraw an isoproduct contour and recalculate the appropriate segment of the output function and of the input function for z_1. What significant difference appears?

Using the same input prices as in the text find the new total variable cost function and redraw Figure 8–5c. Also redraw the marginal cost curve. Show on both diagrams the level of the output price at which the firm becomes indifferent between operating and shutting down. How does it compare with the analogous price when idleness has no cost?

Calculate and draw on the marginal cost diagram the average variable cost corresponding to the first segment of the total variable cost. Does the usual rule hold that a firm shuts down when the output price falls below the minimum average variable cost? Give an explanation.

8. *Allocation within a Multiplant Firm*

Take the numerical example of the *text* as the first plant and the numerical example of the *exercises* as the second plant in a two-plant firm. The plants share the first input, and the firm possesses a total amount $b_1 = 24$. Within the first plant the second input is fixed at the level $b_2 = 8$. Within the second plant the remaining input, now relabeled, is fixed at the level $b_3 = 6$. From previously derived results put together a table showing for each plant the range of z_1 and the marginal productivity over that range.

(a) Plot the marginal productivity of z_1 within each plant on a single diagram similar to Figure 8–7. Determine both the firm-wide level of the marginal productivity and the optimal division between plants.

(b) The solution in (a) identifies a set of processes within each plant that is presumably optimal for the firm. Set up the technological maximizing problem for the firm and reduce to canonical form with respect to these processes. Verify that the geometrically derived solution is optimal. Write down one segment of the output function for the firm.

(c) Make the following reductions in the shared input: $b_1 = 21, 14, 4$. Shift the second plant's marginal productivity curve to the left by the appropriate number of units and determine what the optimal solution will be in each case. Point out the distinctive features of each case and discuss the implication for the allocation of the input between plants.

(d) Increase the shared input to 40 and then to 64. Discuss the implications. How do decreases and increases of the shared input affect its marginal productivity?

9

The Smooth Version of a Single-Product Firm

A technological process represents a proportional relationship between all inputs and the output or outputs they produce. With a single process a combination of inputs can be utilized fully only if it lies on the appropriate ray through the origin. When there are several processes, inputs can be used in a variety of ways, and a criterion of optimality must be invoked. The solution to the technological optimizing problem eliminates inefficient processes or combinations of processes and establishes that any vector of inputs is most efficiently employed by a convex linear combination of adjacent processes. When slack processes are included, the entire nonnegative orthant consists of cones formed by adjacent rays. The cones overlap only along the boundary rays. In the special case of multiple optima, all input combinations within a cone of adjacent vectors may also be employed with equal efficiency by processes that are not adjacent. The results previously derived and graphed for two inputs hold in general when there are more than two inputs.

Within each cone formed by adjacent processes, the marginal productivities of all inputs remain constant, and the maximum attainable output becomes a linear function of the inputs. To each assigned level of output there is a corresponding line segment in two-dimensional input space or a segment of a plane or hyperplane in spaces of higher dimension. Since output increases proportionately with the use of all inputs, the line segments or the plane segments are parallel within cones formed by adjacent rays. We can join together the segments denoting the same level of output in all cones and form a piecewise-linear isoproduct contour. Hence, the entire nonnegative orthant of input space is partitioned into a set of isoproduct contours or an isoproduct map, which shows for each input combination the maximum output it can produce.

For each cone the input ratios vary within limits but the marginal revenue productivities are constant. Along the boundary rays, where two cones overlap, the input ratios are constant but each marginal productivity may have the value appropriate to either cone or any value in between. In the two-dimensional case, the marginal productivities and their ratio, the rate of technical substitution, remain constant along each line segment but change abruptly from one segment to the next. The economic theory of the firm, as customarily presented, shows the isoproduct contours as smooth curves without linear segments or vertices. But this version of the firm also bypasses the technological optimizing problem and assumes simply that the technological data are available to the firm in the form of a smooth output function. To unify the two versions of the firm, we shall go through the conceptual process of converting a piecewise-linear output function into a smooth output function.

THE TRANSITION TO A SMOOTH OUTPUT FUNCTION

Between a pair of adjacent processes we may introduce a third process that uses less of each input than their linear combination. In two dimensions, the cone of adjacent vectors is divided into two smaller cones, and the corresponding line segment in each isoproduct contour is replaced by two shorter line segments lying nearer the origin. The process introduced must not, however, be so highly superior that it replaces one or both of the adjacent processes in the isoproduct contour and fails to reduce the number of segments. The intermediate process must be superior to the linear combination of adjacent processes but only to that linear combination. We can repeat the procedure, inserting a superior process into each of the newly formed cones and further shortening the line segments. The insertion of new processes can continue indefinitely. Between any two rays, however close, there is always a third ray. Realistically, it is impossible to continue the procedure forever but we can make a mental leap and state the conditions that are being approached. As the number of processes increases without limit, line segments shrink toward zero length and cones shrink toward zero width. A line segment of zero length is a point and a cone of zero width is a ray. Hence, in the limit there is an infinite set of processes or rays each contributing one point to an isoproduct contour.

Increasing the number of processes without limit eliminates line segments from the contours but does not necessarily remove vertices. To see why this is so, choose any vector, say [1, 1]. Letting the number of vectors increase without limit may transform the contour below the point and the contour above the point into arcs of smooth curves. But arcs of smooth curves may meet in a vertex, and each isoproduct contour may be piecewise curvilinear.

When the firm seeks to minimize cost for some prescribed level of output, the boundary of the constraint set is piecewise curvilinear, and optimization requires nonlinear programming. There are two types of optimal solution, a cost line passing through a vertex and a cost line tangent to one of the smooth arcs. In linear programming both types of solutions also occur, but we can always ignore tangency and concentrate on solutions at the vertices. Tangency in the linear model occurs for only a few price ratios and is overwhelmingly improbable. Besides, solutions within line segments are no better than solutions at either terminal vertex. In nonlinear programming there is no reason for either type of solution to be more likely, and solutions at vertices are either better or worse but not equally good. Because both types of optimal solution may occur, the conditions for optimality become more complex.

The traditional theory of the firm is at the opposite end of the spectrum from the linear version; it rules out vertices and states the conditions for optimality in terms of tangency alone. That the smooth version of the firm was the first to be developed is attributable, in part, to historical accident. The differential calculus, to which vertices are an anathema, was devised to solve problems in physical science. It had reached a relatively high stage of development early in the nineteenth century and was applied to the firm around the middle of that century. By contrast, linear and nonlinear programming were devised to solve problems that were essentially economic in nature, but their development did not take place until World War II and shortly thereafter. Even if it had not been historically the first version, the smooth model of the firm would undoubtedly have assumed an important role in economics. We shall not give further explicit attention to nonlinear programming but shall proceed directly to a geometric presentation of the traditional version of the firm.

To eliminate vertices we must require that each isoproduct contour have a tangent line at every point. It is not enough to insert a superior process between every two processes; the isoproduct points on all rays must be so chosen as to lie on a curve, every point of which has a tangent line. An alternative explanation provides further insight. With a finite number of processes, there are two types of rays: boundary rays, which represent actual processes, and interior rays within cones, which are positive linear combinations of the boundary rays. Along boundary rays the marginal productivities are not unique but lie only within ranges. Along an interior ray the marginal productivities have unique constant values, but the ray itself does not represent a technological process. We now let the number of technological processes increase and focus attention on an interior ray. As processes are inserted on both sides of the ray, the cone in which it lies shrinks in width. But no matter how close the boundary rays are, an interior ray is still a positive linear combination of those rays and retains the property of having unique constant marginal productivities. As the number of rays increases without limit the boundary rays approach each other and also approach the position of some interior ray. At every stage the interior ray has unique marginal productivities, and it retains this property in the limit as the cone shrinks to zero width. Thus, as the number of rays increases without limit each ray becomes both an interior and a boundary ray; each ray represents a single technological process that can be used alone but also has unique constant marginal productivities.

When a point on a contour has a tangent line, the corresponding ray has the properties of both an interior and a boundary ray. A vertex corresponds to a ray that is a boundary ray only. When every point on any one contour has a tangent line, every ray has a unique linear output function that can be written as

$$x = \bar{e}_1 z_1 + \bar{e}_2 z_2.$$

The marginal productivities, which are the coefficients of the inputs, remain constant along any one ray but change from ray to ray. For any specified level of output the tangent line to the isoproduct contour is

$$\bar{e}_1 z_1 + \bar{e}_2 z_2 = q \qquad \text{or} \qquad z_2 = -\frac{\bar{e}_1}{\bar{e}_2} z_1 + \frac{1}{\bar{e}_2} q \qquad \text{or} \qquad z_2 = -\bar{s} z_1 + \bar{a}_2 q.$$

As in Chapter 8, $\bar{s}$ denotes the rate of technical substitution of z_2 for z_1 along a contour, and $\bar{a}_2$ is the marginal requirement of the output for the second input.

So long as the second input does not go slack, the given output function can be converted to an input function for z_2, as is done above. The nonnegative orthant of input space is now partitioned into an infinite number of cones, each of which has shrunk to zero width. Alternatively, the nonnegative orthant of input space is partitioned into an infinite set of isoproduct contours, each of which has a tangent line at every point. Each tangent line also generates an upper closed half-space. A given isoproduct contour is the lower boundary for the intersection of all upper closed half-spaces generated by its tangent lines. The intersection of the closed half-spaces is a convex set containing all input combinations capable of turning out at least as much output as that specified by the isoproduct contour.

From the isoproduct map we can now derive a marginal productivity curve for z_1. With the second input constant, z_1 traverses a horizontal line in input space and crosses all rays. For each ray or process there is a single value for the marginal productivity that differs from those of neighboring rays. Contrary to the piecewise-linear model, each amount of z_1 must have one and only one marginal productivity. There also cannot be horizontal line segments over which the marginal productivity remains constant as z_1 changes. What guarantees these results is the elimination of both corners and line segments from the isoproduct contours.

We are tempted to draw marginal productivity as the familiar continuous and smooth curve, but we do not yet have any justification for doing so. All we know is that each amount of z_1 has a unique marginal productivity, and that the marginal productivity must change when z_1 changes. There is as yet nothing to guarantee that the marginal productivity changes continuously. The graph of marginal productivity may contain vertical gaps or discontinuities, as in Figure 9–1. Discontinuous functions are hard to handle mathematically. Besides, as we saw in Chapter 5, vertical gaps in a marginal productivity curve become part of the input demand curve and destroy the correspondence between the two curves. For both economic and mathematical reasons, the traditional theory of the firm makes the additional assumption that all marginal productivity curves are continuous. On the isoproduct map, not only must a tangent exist at every point but the slope of the tangent line must change continuously along every contour.

For purely mathematical reasons, to permit a standard application of the differential calculus, the traditional theory of the firm goes still further and assumes that each marginal productivity curve has a tangent line at every point and that the slope of this tangent line changes continuously. The marginal productivity curve no longer has vertices and becomes a smooth curve. As a reminder, continuity merely implies the absence of vertical gaps but permits corners. The presence of a tangent line at every point eliminates corners and a continuous change in the slope of the tangent imposes a higher degree of smoothness. Hereafter, we shall use the terms *smooth output function*

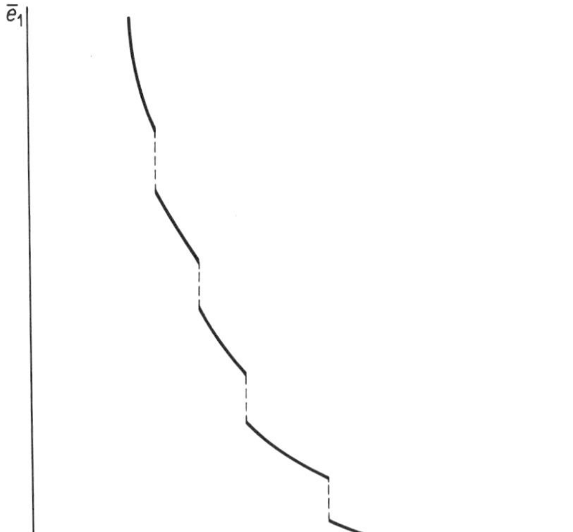

Fig. 9-1 A Discontinuous Marginal Productivity Curve

and *smooth version of the firm* with the precise meaning that all marginal productivity curves have a tangent line at every point and that the slope of the tangent line changes continuously. The effect of this assumption on the isoproduct contours is greater smoothness, but the effect is hard to describe precisely in nonmathematical terms. Smooth curves are easier to visualize and to draw. There is great advantage in using them when the aim is merely to display general tendencies or relationships.

The assumption of a smooth output function places very specific restrictions on technological conditions and on the scientific relationships that underlie technology. Readers may well ask: What assurance is there that actual technological conditions conform to the assumptions of continuity and smoothness? There is no assurance and no way of finding out whether the assumptions are satisfied, but hardly anyone would expect the mathematical requirements of continuity and smoothness to be fulfilled exactly. The most that can be expected is that actual technological conditions do not differ greatly from smooth isoproduct contours.

What is the point, then, of making these restrictive assumptions about technological conditions? The reason is that, if the assumptions are made, the very powerful mathematical tool of the differential calculus becomes available. An idealized version, or mathematical model, of the firm can be set up, and the conditions for an optimum can be clearly stated. It is standard procedure in modern science not to spend time verifying assumptions directly but rather to set up a mathematical model, draw inferences, and check inferences against actual conditions by experiment or in other ways. The mathematical model of the firm based on the calculus is in this scientific tradition, but the empirical testing of the model has been neither so extensive nor so exacting as in physical science.

The linear version of the firm is also a mathematical model with restrictive assumptions and is thus a simplification or idealization of actual conditions. There is little point in arguing that either is in general the better model, since the applicability of the models varies from industry to industry and has to be determined by empirical test in each case. Economic theory is, however, greatly enriched by the availability of both versions of the firm, since they are highly complementary to each other. The strong point of the smooth model is that the differential calculus may be used to express, at a high level of generality, necessary and sufficient conditions for an optimum. The weakness of the smooth model is the difficulty or impossibility of finding solutions when the number of inputs goes beyond three. Approximate solutions have to be found by methods that often use piecewise-linear functions. The strength of the linear model lies in the availability of methods for finding exact optimal solutions. Since it is possible conceptually to derive one version from the other, we can avail ourselves of the complementary advantages of both versions and obtain an enriched, unified, and more broadly applicable theory of the firm.

LINEARLY HOMOGENEOUS OUTPUT FUNCTIONS

We have now demonstrated what is required to go from a finite set of production processes to a smooth output function of a type used frequently in economic theory. The number of processes must, conceptually, increase without limit and in such a way that each new process is superior to one and only one linear combination of existing processes. Further, the isoproduct points on all rays must be chosen in such a way that the resultant isoproduct contour has a smoothly turning tangent line. The isoproduct map represents the function and shows its two salient characteristics. Each isoproduct contour is labeled with a number showing the output that can be produced by every combination of inputs on the contour. Each ray can be labeled with a pair of numbers representing the constant marginal physical productivities for every combination of inputs on the ray. Since output changes proportionately with inputs, the output function derived from production processes is a special type of function whose characteristics will now be examined.

A function, $x = f(z_1, z_2)$, is termed *homogeneous of the first degree* when proportional changes in both independent variables, z_1 and z_2, are accompanied by the same proportional change in the dependent variable x. Since first degree and linear are often used interchangeably, such a function is also called *linear and homogeneous* or *linearly homogeneous.* When the independent variables are inputs with nonnegative values, a linearly homogeneous output function has the economic property of constant returns to scale. We can easily visualize the properties of a linearly homogeneous function of two nonnegative variables. Imagine the nonnegative orthant of two-dimensional space to be covered by a pile of wet sand or some other plastic material that can readily be shaped. The shaping is to be done by a thin rigid rod anchored at the origin. Across the input plane the rod must move continuously like the hand of a clock from twelve to three, never backtracking. However, unlike the hand of a clock, the rod may trace out any vertical pattern whatsoever. On economic grounds we must rule out dipping below the input plane, which means negative output, but otherwise any vertical pattern the rod may follow is consistent with constant returns to scale. The reason is that a still photograph taken at any instant will show a ray through the origin in three-dimensional space. Along any such ray the two inputs and the output they produce change in the same proportion. Any function that is generated by rays, whatever their number, falls into the class of linearly homogeneous. Conversely, any function that is homogeneous of the first degree can be decomposed into rays.

While any conceivable vertical path is consistent with linear homogeneity, only a few general patterns have attained wide applicability in economics. One is the piecewise-linear output function derived earlier. With slack vectors included, the rod that shapes the production surface coincides with each input axis. It travels along one plane for some positive distance and then shifts abruptly to another plane. As displayed in Figure 9–2a, the general pattern is a rise to a peak at diminishing rates followed by a decline to an input axis at increasing rates. When smoothed by the method described earlier in the chapter, the piecewise-linear production surface takes the form shown in Figure 9–2b. The vertical pattern is a smooth rise, at a steadily decreasing rate, from an axis to a maximum, followed by a smooth decline to an axis at a continuously increasing rate.

The Cobb–Douglas function, which is often used in economics, has a smooth production surface of the type shown in Figure 9–2b. It represents the simplest and most direct generalization from a piecewise-linear to a smooth output function. We shall employ the Cobb–Douglas function to make the transition from the linear model of the firm to a smooth model,

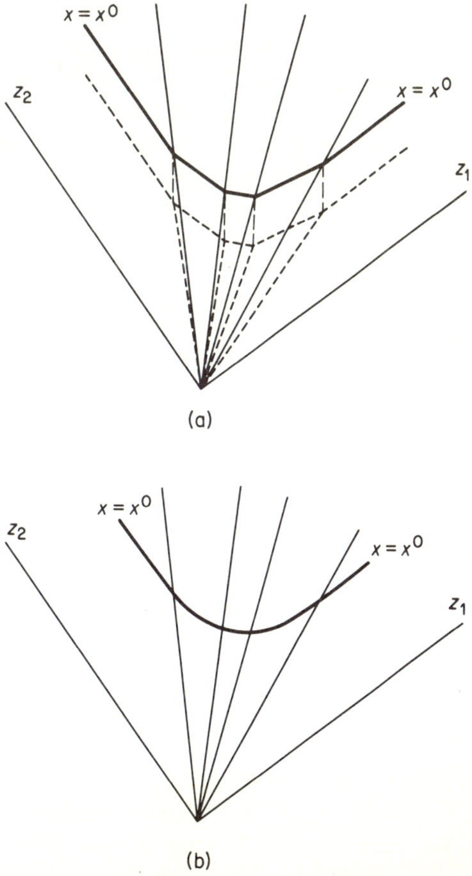

Fig. 9-2 Production Surfaces for Linearly Homogeneous Functions

showing how previously derived results carry over. Subsequently, we shall use the Cobb–Douglas function as a base for exploring in greater generality the properties that smooth output functions may possess.

THE COBB–DOUGLAS FUNCTION

The Cobb–Douglas function has the following mathematical form:

$$x = kz_1^a z_2^b \qquad k,\, a,\, b > 0 \qquad a+b = 1.$$

To verify that the function does display constant returns to scale we multiply both inputs by some positive number t, as follows:

$$x = k(tz_1)^a(tz_2)^b = t^{a+b}kz_1^a z_2^b = t^1(kz_1^a z_2^b).$$

Output does change in the same proportion (t) as both inputs. We note for future use that output is multiplied by the factor t^{a+b} when each input is multiplied by the factor t. Output increases less than proportionately when $a+b < 1$, more than proportionately when $a+b > 1$.

Derivation of the marginal productivities requires use of the calculus, so we merely state the results:

$$\bar{e}_1 = ka\left(\frac{z_2}{z_1}\right)^{1-a} \qquad \bar{e}_2 = kb\left(\frac{z_1}{z_2}\right)^{a}.$$

Along any ray the ratio of inputs and, hence, their marginal productivities must remain constant. The Cobb–Douglas function can be expressed equivalently as a linear function of the inputs with the marginal productivities as coefficients. As we now show, both the linear form and the original form are equal to each other:

$$\begin{aligned} x = \bar{e}_1 z_1 + \bar{e}_2 z_2 &= ka\left(\frac{z_2}{z_1}\right)^{1-a} z_1 + kb\left(\frac{z_1}{z_2}\right)^{a} z_2 \\ &= kaz_2^{1-a}z_1^{a-1}z_1 + kbz_1^a z_2^{-a} z_2 \\ &= kaz_1^a z_2^{1-a} + kbz_1^a z_2^{1-a} \\ &= k(a+b)z_1^a z_2^{1-a} = kz_1^a z_2^b. \end{aligned}$$

In the piecewise-linear model, a single linear output function holds within each cone. The Cobb–Douglas function yields a different linear output function for each ray.

Along either axis, where one input is zero, the Cobb–Douglas function records zero output. Hence, contours for positive levels of output cannot have points on the axes. For any ratio of inputs, however small, there is always a productive process. Slack processes can never enter the solution of the technological optimizing problem, and the isoproduct contours never become horizontal or vertical. As drawn in Figure 9–3, the isoproduct contours approach but do not touch the axes as either input increases without limit. In so doing, the contours become steadily flatter or steeper but never actually attain horizontal or vertical slopes.

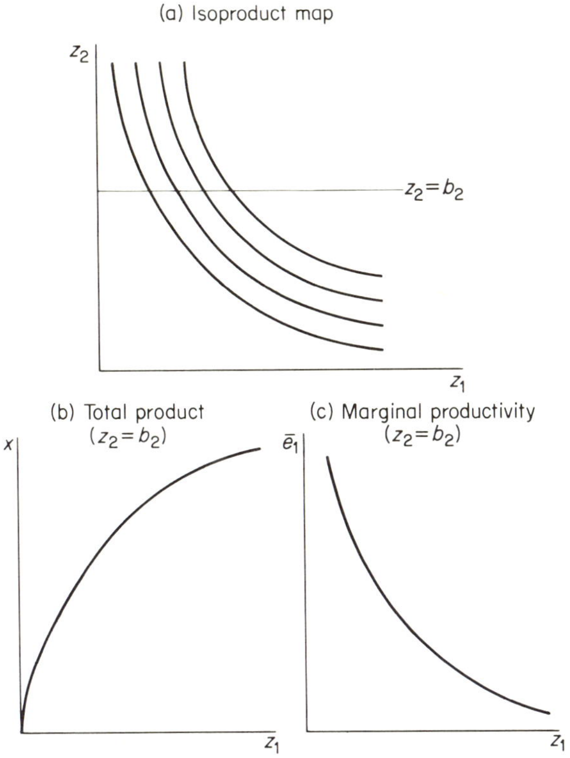

Fig. 9-3 The Cobb–Douglas Function

With the second input held constant, z_1 traverses a horizontal line in input space and crosses successively all rays. Output increases at a rate equal to the marginal productivity of the first input, which was earlier shown to be $\bar{e}_1 = ka(z_2/z_1)^{1-a}$. As z_1 increases with z_2 constant, its marginal productivity steadily declines but never reaches zero, since slack never appears. Total product increases in Figure 9–3 at a steadily declining rate, and marginal productivity approaches, but does not reach, the horizontal axis.

ECONOMIC OPTIMIZATION WITH A COBB–DOUGLAS FUNCTION

Solving the cost minimization problem combines technological data and input prices into the various cost curves for the product. Alternatively, revenue maximization utilizes the output price and the technological information to derive the various revenue product curves. The final optimum for the firm requires either a confrontation of cost of production with revenue from the sale of the product or a confrontation of revenue produced with the cost of buying inputs.

To find the total cost curve when both inputs are variable, we first choose some level of output and minimize cost on the set of all input combinations that can produce outputs equaling or exceeding the chosen level. In the piecewise-linear version, the feasible set is the intersection of a finite number of closed half-spaces. For a smooth output function, the feasible set becomes the intersection of the infinite number of closed upper half-spaces determined by the tangent lines, with a smooth curve as lower boundary. Both input prices being positive, the cost minimizing solution must be tangency at a point on the isoproduct contour that bounds the feasible set.

The equation for an isoproduct contour is $q = \bar{e}_1 z_1 + \bar{e}_2 z_2$. The slope equals the negative ratio of the marginal productivities, which vary from point to point. The linear total cost function, $C = c_1 z_1 + c_2 z_2$, has a constant slope, $-c_1/c_2$. Tangency implies the following equality of slopes:

$$-\frac{\bar{e}_1}{\bar{e}_2} = -\frac{c_1}{c_2} \quad \text{or} \quad \frac{c_1}{\bar{e}_1} = \frac{c_2}{\bar{e}_2} = w.$$

The symbol w, which equals the common ratio between the price of each input and its marginal productivity, has a familiar economic meaning. Substitution for c_1 and c_2 in the cost equation gives

$$C = c_1 z_1 + c_2 z_2 = w\bar{e}_1 z_1 + w\bar{e}_2 z_2 = w(\bar{e}_1 z_1 + \bar{e}_2 z_2) = wq.$$

When output is varied parametrically with input prices constant, all points of tangency identifying minimal cost must lie on the same ray in input space. Consequently, $\bar{e}_1$, $\bar{e}_2$, and w all remain constant, and the long-run cost function is $C = wx$. The coefficient of x is the rate of change of cost with respect to output, which is the marginal cost or internal price of the output.

In the smooth version of the firm optimization also determines internal prices for the quantities originally held constant, but they are called *Lagrange multipliers* rather than dual variables. A Lagrange multiplier is also the rate of change of the objective variable with respect to a quantity in a constraint. The main difference is that Lagrange multipliers change continuously and smoothly when the constrained quantity varies, whereas dual variables stay constant over ranges and then change abruptly. What is most important for the economic theory of the firm is that constrained optimization generates internal prices in both versions.

The condition of tangency identifies a ray along which the input requirements remain fixed. We can, then, rewrite total cost in terms of the input requirements for this ray or process, calling it the first. If a_{11} and a_{21} denote the input requirements, the unit cost of the process is $c_1a_{11}+c_2a_{21}$, and long-run cost is $C = (c_1a_{11}+c_2a_{21})x = wx$. Every other point on any iso-product contour also lies on a ray along which the input requirements are fixed, but unit cost must be higher for any input combination at which the cost line intersects the contour. For each process there is a total cost line through the origin on the cost-output diagram. The lowest of these lines becomes the long-run cost curve.

With the second input constant, combinations of inputs must be chosen from a horizontal line in input space. To find total variable cost we repeat the procedure of Chapter 8 and first convert the linear output function into the following explicit input function:

$$z_1 = \frac{1}{\bar{e}_1}x - \frac{\bar{e}_2}{\bar{e}_1}b_2 = \bar{a}_1x - \frac{1}{\bar{s}}b_2.$$

Total variable cost becomes

$$c_1z_1 = \frac{c_1}{\bar{e}_1}x - \frac{c_2\bar{e}_2}{\bar{e}_1}b_2 = c_1\bar{a}_1 - \frac{c_1}{\bar{s}}b_2.$$

With the addition of fixed cost, short-run total cost is

$$C = c_1z_1 + c_2b_2 = \frac{c_1}{\bar{e}_1}x + \left(c_2 - \frac{c_1\bar{e}_2}{\bar{e}_1}\right)b_2.$$

The coefficient of x, which is marginal cost, may also be written as $c_1\bar{a}_1$. Figure 9–4a shows short-run total cost (SRTC) in relation to long-run total cost (LRTC).

The point of tangency between the long-run and short-run cost curves corresponds to the intersection in input space of the horizontal line and the optimal ray. At all points on the optimal ray $c_1 = \bar{e}_1w$ and $c_2 = \bar{e}_2w$, so the terms in parentheses before b_2 in the short-run equation become

$$c_2 - \frac{c_1\bar{e}_2}{\bar{e}_1} = \bar{e}_2w - \frac{\bar{e}_1w\bar{e}_2}{\bar{e}_1} = \bar{e}_2w - \bar{e}_2w = 0.$$

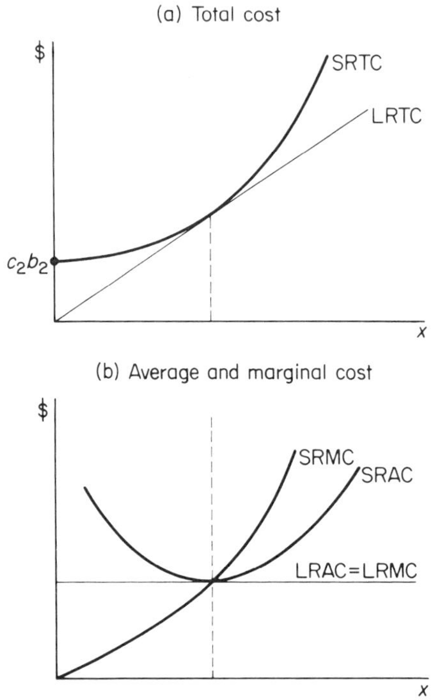

Fig. 9-4 Cost Curves for the Cobb–Douglas Function

Hence, in both the short and long run, total cost has the same value, $C = (c_1/\bar{e}_1)x = c_1\bar{a}_1 x = wx$. At any other level of output the management is not free in the short run to choose the process that minimizes the cost of both inputs at the going prices. Except at one output the short-run total cost curve must lie above the lower boundary of cost represented by the long-run cost curve. As z_1 increases relative to z_2, the marginal productivity steadily falls and the short-run curve becomes progressively steeper. For each level at which the second input is held constant, there is a different short-run curve. A higher level of b_2 means that its horizontal line intersects the optimal ray at a proportionately higher level of output. The short-run total cost curve touches the long-run curve at a proportionately greater distance from the origin. There is, then, an infinite family of short-run curves, one for each value of the second input.

Figure 9–4b shows how marginal and average cost are related in both the short and long run. Division of long-run total cost by output shows that long-run average cost (LRAC) is constant and equal to long-run marginal cost (LRMC). Short-run marginal cost (SRMC) is the coefficient of x, or $c_1/\bar{e}_1 = c_1\bar{a}_1$. It rises steadily as the marginal productivity falls, crossing the long-run marginal cost curve when the horizontal input line crosses the optimal ray. Short-run average cost (SRAC) is subject to two conflicting influences, the rise in marginal cost and the decline in fixed cost per unit of output. Initially the decline in unit fixed cost predominates; later the rise in marginal cost predominates, resulting in a U-shaped curve. For the one output that is optimal in both short and long run, all comparable measures of cost are equal, and short-run marginal cost also passes through the minimum point of the short-run average cost curve. The reason for the second result is that the internal price of the fixed input, $c_1(\bar{e}_2/\bar{e}_1)$, equals the market price c_2, causing the terms in parentheses before b_2 to vanish.

As demonstrated for the piecewise-linear case, there is no long-run optimal solution when the output function is homogeneous of the first degree. Depending upon the relationship of output price to long-run marginal cost, the possibilities are indefinite expansion, zero output, or indifferent selection from among all nonnegative output levels. To find the optimal output in the short run we plot total variable cost only against total revenue in Figure 9–5a. Fixed cost merely causes a parallel upward shift of the total cost curve and does not affect the optimal output. Provided that the slope of the cost curve is increasing, the vertical gap between revenue and cost narrows on both sides of the output at which both slopes are equal. The slopes plot in Figure 9–5a as price and marginal cost, so marginal cost must be rising at the optimum and must intersect the price line from below.

When a single-product firm maximizes output for each combination of inputs, it also maximizes revenue. Multiplication of each level of output by

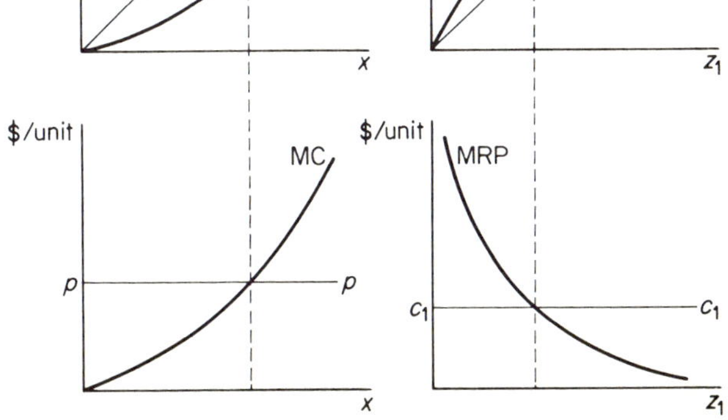

Fig. 9-5 The Short-Run Optimum

the constant output price converts the isoproduct map into an isorevenue map. With the second input constant total revenue is $px = p\bar{e}_1z_1 + p\bar{e}_2b_2$. In Figure 9–5b the firm also seeks the maximum difference between the total revenue produced by the variable input and the total amount paid to it, c_1z_1. Equal slopes again identify the maximum vertical difference but the curvature is now in the revenue function, which must have a decreasing slope. When the slopes are plotted, the marginal revenue productivity curve slopes downward and intersects the horizontal input price line from above. The two sets of diagrams are equivalent ways of identifying the short-run optimum for the firm. Equality of marginal revenue productivity and input price, $p\bar{e}_1 = c_1$, implies $p = c_1/\bar{e}_1 = c_1\bar{a}_1$, which is the equality of output price and marginal cost. This simple inverse relationship between the two sets of diagrams holds only when there is a single product and a single variable input. What remains generally true is that the technological data may be combined either with input prices or with output prices to provide alternative ways of identifying the optimum of the firm.

Finding the optimal solution under given conditions is only the first step toward the ultimate goal of predicting how the firm will respond to changes in input and output prices. As the output price varies and the horizontal price line shifts up and down, the intersection with the marginal cost curve is the locus of all optimal solutions. Economic theory predicts that the firm will supply at each price the quantity that maximizes net revenue. Hence, with price on the vertical axis becoming the independent variable in place of quantity on the horizontal axis, the marginal cost curve can be reinterpreted as a supply curve. A similar switch of dependent and independent variables converts the continuous, downward-sloping marginal revenue productivity curve into the demand curve for the variable input.

ECONOMIC OPTIMIZATION WITH OTHER LINEARLY HOMOGENEOUS FUNCTIONS

The Cobb–Douglas function belongs to a class, known in growth theory as *well-behaved functions*, whose total product curves rise steadily at a diminishing rate and whose marginal productivity curves approach but do not touch either axis. What makes the Cobb–Douglas function well behaved is its smooth, convex isoproduct contours that also approach but do not touch the axes. Any other linearly homogeneous function with such contours has similar curves for product, revenue, and cost, but linear homogeneity also permits great variety in the isoproduct map. Contours that approach the axes imply that any ratio of inputs, however small, can be used productively. A more plausible assumption, at least in some cases, is that there are minimal positive ratios of the inputs at which output falls to zero and below which production is impossible.

Figure 9–6 provides an illustration. The two boundary rays, beyond which production is impossible, form the contour for zero output. Within their cone all combinations are productive, but processes near the boundary rays are less productive and have more distant isoproduct points. Instead of approaching the axes, the isoproduct contours approach the boundary rays and ultimately slope upward. The slope of an isoproduct contour is the negative ratio of the marginal productivities and can become positive only when one of the marginal productivities goes negative. Near the lower boundary, it is z_1 that is available in relatively large amounts and becomes unproductive. Near the upper boundary, it is z_2.

When z_2 is held constant and z_1 traverses a horizontal line, output does not rise above zero until z_1 passes the first boundary ray, and output reaches zero again on the second boundary ray. The resultant total product and marginal productivity curves of z_1 are also drawn in Figure 9–6. When the horizontal input line crosses an isoproduct contour at the point where it

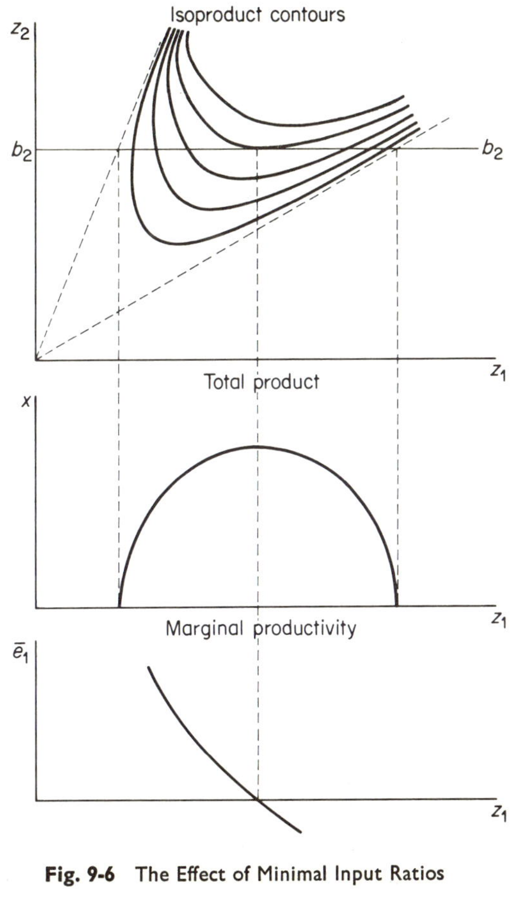

Fig. 9-6 The Effect of Minimal Input Ratios

becomes horizontal, the marginal productivity of z_1 falls to zero and the total product reaches its peak.

If both inputs have to be used fully, upward-sloping isoproduct contours can be the correct answer to the technological maximizing problem. They do show the maximum output each input combination can produce. But upward-sloping contours and the resultant downward-sloping total product curve can never pass the technological minimizing test. For any level of output the firm always chooses the rising portion of the total product curve where z_1 is smaller. Similarly, costless slack processes also eliminate all rays along which either input has a negative marginal productivity, replacing the upward-sloping portions of the contours with vertical and horizontal line segments. As z_1 increases from zero along the horizontal input line the firm lets enough of the second input remain idle to permit productive use of the remaining amount. Just as in the linear model, the slack process on the vertical axis forms a cone with the nearest of the productive processes. With the upward-sloping portions of the contours ruled out, the nearest productive process or ray is the one along which z_2 has zero marginal productivity. As Figure 9–7a shows, there is an initial linear segment from the origin to the

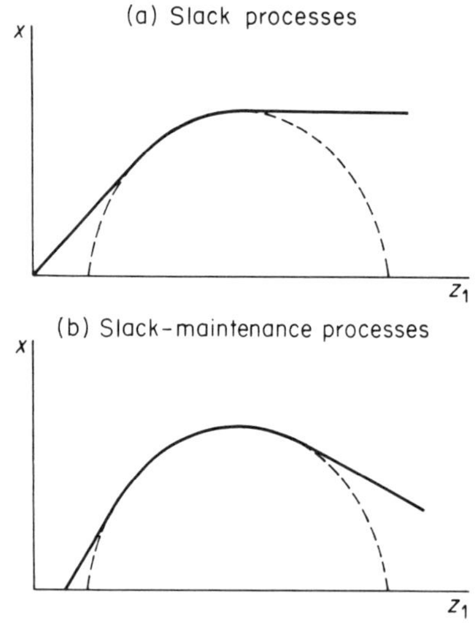

Fig. 9-7 Slack and Slack-Maintenance Processes

point of tangency on the total product curve, the segment reflecting only partial use of the total available amount of z_2. Similarly, if z_1 can go partially unused, the downward-sloping portion gives way to an indefinite horizontal extension.

Inputs cannot always go costlessly to waste, as the previously cited example of an automobile battery attests. Letting a battery remain idle reduces its service life, which may be interpreted as a decline in the output it can produce. For a battery the slack process has a negative rather than a zero coefficient in the objective function. Alternatively, by recharging, other inputs may be used to offset the decline in output through disuse of the battery. The term *slack-maintenance process* will be used to designate this possibility. As a simplification, we assume that all decline in service life through disuse can be exactly offset, so a slack-maintenance process has an output coefficient of zero.

A slack-maintenance process uses positive quantities of both inputs, one in idleness and the other to offset the effects of idleness. It is represented in input space by an upward-sloping ray, along which output is zero. As readers may verify, when any vector with zero output is added to another vector, it contributes to the isoproduct contour a line segment parallel to its own ray. Isoproduct contours then terminate in upward-sloping line segments parallel to the slack-maintenance processes rather than in horizontal and vertical line segments parallel to the slack processes. The economic meaning is that it pays to use an input in the early ranges of negative marginal productivity rather than incur the input cost of idleness. Figure 9–7b shows how the total product curve is modified when both inputs have slack-maintenance processes.

Smooth, convex isoproduct contours that approach either the axes or other rays in the input plane have the same general type of production surface. The rod that shapes it rises smoothly from one ray at a diminishing rate and descends to the other ray at an increasing rate. Economists also make frequent use of a different type of linearly homogeneous production surface that is generally bell shaped. Instead of continuing to descend toward the input plane at an increasing rate, the rod that shapes the surface tapers off toward the axes or, possibly, other rays. The change in curvature produces an indentation in the surface, which is no longer the boundary of a convex set in three dimensions. Similarly, as in Figure 9–8, the isoproduct contours also display a change in curvature and are no longer the lower boundaries of convex sets in two dimensions. The total product curve takes on the shape of the production surface and is generally bell shaped.

When the curvature changes and the contours bulge outward from the origin, each point on such a portion represents a process that is inferior to linear combinations of other processes. It would not survive the technological maximizing test. The portions of contours that bend outward from the origin are dominated and would be replaced by linear combinations even if slack processes did not exist.[1] With costless slack processes, all rising portions of the contours, along which one input has a negative marginal productivity, give way to horizontal and vertical line segments. The initial phase of the total product curve, along which output rises at an increasing

[1]The conclusion does not necessarily hold when the output function is not linearly homogeneous and cannot be decomposed into linear processes or rays.

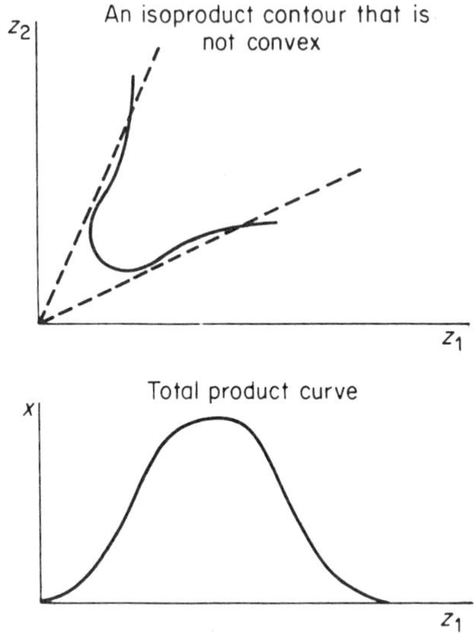

Fig. 9-8 An Isoproduct Contour that is not Convex

rate, is replaced by a straight line segment from the origin to a point of tangency on the curve, which readers may draw in. Also, the total product curve never decreases as z_1 increases but remains constant at its maximum value. Readers may make the appropriate modifications when slack is not costless.

As noted earlier, the conventional theory of the firm bypasses the technological optimizing problem and begins with an output function. The dominated portions of the isoproduct contours and total product curve are retained in the technological possibilities even though they cannot pass the technological optimizing test. In the course of solving the economic optimizing problem, the theory rejects the dominated portions as economically irrelevant, since they imply a negative marginal productivity for one input and could never be optimal at any set of positive prices. Since the end results are the same little harm is done, but it is preferable on methodological grounds to exclude from the output function technologically inferior methods of production.

OPTIMIZATION UNDER INCREASING AND DECREASING RETURNS TO SCALE

If all inputs are variable, linearly homogeneous output functions leave scale of plant or firm indeterminate. They can be used satisfactorily only if one or more inputs are fixed or if scale is either independently determined or not relevant to the problem under study. Modern technology provides many instances where returns to scale are not constant for either plants or firms, and output functions must reflect these technological conditions.

When output does not expand along rays at the same rate as inputs, the marginal productivities of the inputs cannot remain constant, but their ratio can. Homogeneous functions, of which linearly homogeneous functions are a special case, possess marginal productivities whose ratio remains constant so long as the ratio of inputs does not change. The simplest homogeneous functions are the Cobb–Douglas type:

$$x = kz_1^a z_2^b \qquad k, a, b > 0.$$

As shown earlier in the chapter, output increases more rapidly than input if $a+b > 1$, less rapidly if $a+b < 1$. Above any ray in input space, output either increases at an increasing rate and its curve bends upward, or output increases at a decreasing rate and its curve bends downward but does not actually decline. For both technological and economic reasons, steadily increasing returns or steadily decreasing returns from zero upward are even less plausible than constant returns. They indicate either that efficiency increases indefinitely with scale of plant or that the smaller the plant the more efficient it will be. Far more acceptable is the combination of an initial phase of increasing returns followed ultimately by decreasing returns. Functions that display such a pattern are more complex mathematically but we can discuss their general properties and portray them geometrically.

Along each ray in input space the marginal productivities of both inputs initially increase, reach peak values, and then decline as diminishing returns set in. The decline need not set in at the same output on each ray, but we can simplify the discussion without appreciably sacrificing generality by assuming that it does. There is, then, a single isoproduct contour that marks the

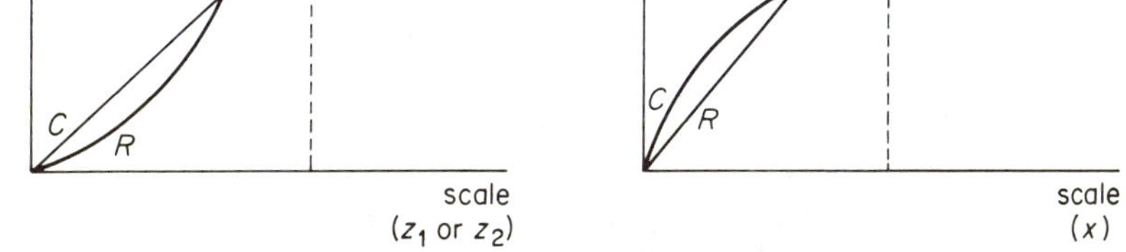

Fig. 9-9 Increasing Followed by Decreasing Returns to Scale

boundary between the initial phase of increasing returns and the subsequent phase of diminishing returns. Above any selected ray both output and total revenue increase at an increasing rate up to a point of inflection and then continue to increase but at a decreasing rate, tracing out the general pattern of Figure 9–9a. Above each ray total cost increases linearly so long as input prices are constant. There are now two levels of output at which total revenue and total cost have the same slope. It is only when the revenue curve is bending downward that equality of slopes marks the largest vertical difference and the most profitable scale of operations. When total revenue is still rising at an increasing rate, equality of slopes identifies the minimum of net revenue.

Alternatively, in Figure 9–9b, input prices and the technological data are combined into a cost function by solving the cost minimization problem. For given input prices and a constant ratio of marginal productivities, total cost is minimized along one ray for all levels of output. The following condition holds:

$$\frac{c_1}{c_2} = \frac{\bar{e}_1}{\bar{e}_2} \quad \text{or} \quad \frac{c_1}{\bar{e}_1} = \frac{c_2}{\bar{e}_2} = w.$$

By contrast with constant returns to scale, marginal cost (w) is no longer constant. In the phase of increasing returns, $\bar{e}_1$ increases and w decreases, and the relationship is reversed when diminishing returns set in. At first the total cost curve rises at a decreasing rate, or bends downward, up to a point of inflection. Thereafter it rises at an increasing rate, or bends upward. Total revenue (px) is linear, but it is parallel to the total cost curve at two outputs. Net revenue is maximized at the higher level of output, where the cost curve is bending upward, but is minimized at the lower output.

As output expands along a ray, long-run marginal cost declines to a minimum on the boundary contour *between increasing and decreasing returns*, and rises thereafter. Short-run marginal cost is subject to an additional influence, the change in the marginal productivity of z_1 as its ratio to the constant z_2 varies. When the horizontal input line crosses the optimal ray, marginal cost is equal in both the short and long run. At any lower level of output, marginal cost is smaller in the short run. At any point on one isoproduct contour the effect of scale is the same, but the short-run ratio of z_1 to z_2 is lower and the marginal productivity of z_1 is higher. Beyond the optimal ray the short-run ratio is less favourable and the marginal productivity of z_1 is lower. Hence, the short-run marginal cost curve must intersect the long-run curve from below.

When the cost of the fixed input is taken into account, short-run total cost lies everywhere above long-run total cost except when the horizontal input line crosses the optimal ray. Before the point of tangency, short-run marginal cost is the smaller and short-run total cost increases at a lower rate. Beyond the point of tangency short-run cost rises more rapidly. Division by output converts both total cost curves into U-shaped average cost curves, with the short-run curve everywhere higher except at one point. Figure 9–10 summarizes the relationships among the various cost curves. Each level at which z_2 is held constant generates another short-run marginal cost curve passing through a different point on the long-run curve and a new pair of short-run total and average cost curves tangent at different points to their long-run counterparts. Thus, the long-run average cost curve becomes the boundary of an infinite family of short-run curves, each member of which is tangent to it. The mathematical term for such a boundary curve is *envelope*, and the term has also been adopted in economics.

If total revenue does not exceed total variable cost in the short run, the firm is paying out to the variable input more than it is taking in and will exercise the option of shutting down unless shutting down incurs costs that can be avoided by continued operation. In either case, the short-run marginal cost curve above the minimum of average variable cost is the locus of optimal levels of output and can be converted to a supply curve.

In the long run, the optimal output or optimal scale of operations is also shown by the intersection of the horizontal price line and the marginal cost curve. It is doubtful, though, that the marginal cost curve represents a

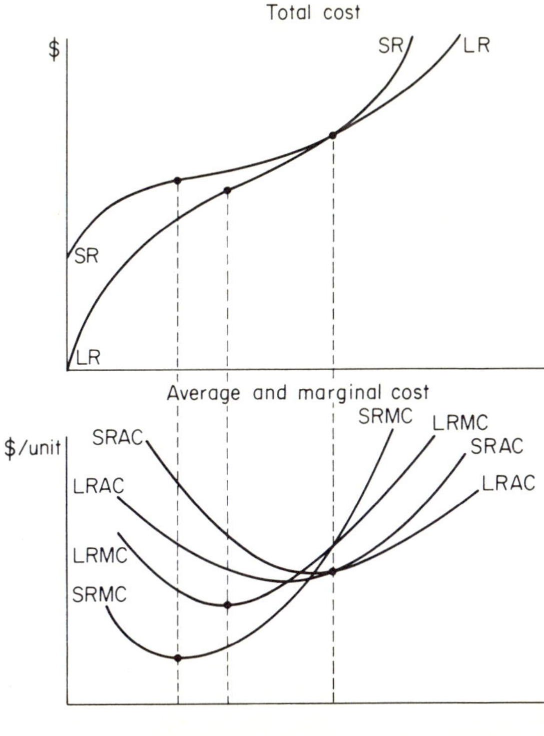

Fig. 9-10 Long- and Short-Run Cost Curves

meaningful long-run supply curve. For given input prices and a given output price, the intersection of the price line with the marginal cost curve determines the most profitable scale of operations. It will not be the most profitable scale if prices change either before or after construction. Suppose, for example, that the output price is high relative to input prices and the most profitable scale is well beyond the optimal scale, at which average cost is a minimum. The high output price and high profits are likely to attract other firms into the field, driving the output price down. A firm that chooses the most profitable scale under present prices will be saddled with overlarge, inefficient capacity in the future. Maximum profitability under present conditions is but one of the factors entering into long-run decisions. We cannot assume it is the only factor and identify the locus of most profitable levels of output as the long-run supply curve.

A FINAL GENERALIZATION AND SUMMARY

In Chapters 8 and 9 we have been engaged in broadening and generalizing the technological conditions open to a firm. Looking back we can see that there are two key questions, the answers to which largely determine what the technology is. The first question is: How do the marginal productivities of the inputs vary along a contour when output is constant but the ratio of the inputs varies continuously? The second question is: How do the marginal productivities of the inputs vary along a ray where the ratio of inputs is constant but output and both inputs vary continuously?

The simplest possible technological condition expressed by a contour is that the marginal productivities are constant and independent of the ratio of inputs. Such is the case when there are two linear processes, each capable of producing the output with the use of one input alone. The cone is the entire nonnegative orthant and the isoproduct contours are parallel straight line segments from axis to axis. The marginal productivities also do not vary along rays and are independent of both input levels and input ratios.

All linearly homogeneous output functions retain the property that input levels have no effect on the marginal productivities but they permit great variety in the response to changing input ratios. With a finite number of linear processes, the marginal productivities vary only from cone to cone. Smooth isoproduct contours that approach both axes guarantee that the marginal productivities will respond continuously and smoothly to variations in input ratios and that they will take on all possible positive values. If the contours meet the axes but are not tangent to them, the marginal productivities remain positive but both very large and very small positive values are cut off. When smooth contours approach rays inside the nonnegative orthant, the contours slope upward and the marginal productivities extend into the negative range as well as taking on all possible positive values.

There can also be great variety in the way marginal productivities respond to input levels with the ratio constant. In the special cases previously examined, the input levels either have no effect on the marginal productivities or have a symmetrical effect. In both cases the rate of technical substitution or ratio of marginal productivities remains constant along rays and the contours are parallel.

There is no reason why the ratio of marginal productivities must always be constant along rays; some inputs may well be better adapted to large-scale production than others. To illustrate this possibility first in the simplest possible way, we shall assume that the rate of technical substitution, $\bar{s} = \bar{e}_1/\bar{e}_2$, steadily declines as both inputs increase along rays, at least after some level is passed. For each level of output there is still a cost minimizing input combination where the cost line is tangent to the isoproduct contour. As output varies parametrically with input prices constant, the locus of all cost minimizing combinations is a curve in input space known as the *expansion path.* In all previous cases the expansion path has been a ray. With the isoproduct contours flattening out along rays, the cost line with constant slope must have its point of tangency progressively higher up on the contours. The expansion path bends continuously upward across the rays. The result is economically plausible. It is the second input that is becoming relatively more efficient and the second input that is being used in ever larger ratios to the first.

The more rapidly the isoproduct contours flatten out along rays the more sharply will the expansion path bend upward. The expansion path may become vertical or even bend backward toward the vertical axis, indicating that the amount of z_1 actually declines even as output is increasing. Such an input is termed *inferior* by analogy with *inferior commodities* in the theory of consumer choice. We shall examine the phenomenon of inferiority at some length in Chapter 13.

There is no reason why we must limit the technology to simple general patterns of changes in the rate of technological substitution along all rays. The direction of change in the ratio of marginal productivities may reverse itself repeatedly along any one ray and the pattern need not be the same on all rays. The expansion path need not show any persistent tendency and need not display any simple general pattern. Since the contours are smooth, it will be a smooth curve. One input can decrease as output increases but obviously not both, so the expansion path cannot bend back downward and intersect itself. Also, since the path is the solution to a cost minimizing problem it must terminate if output reaches a peak and begins to decline. Otherwise, there need not be any limitations on the expansion path.

Above the expansion path, whatever it may be, output and revenue vary in essentially the same pattern as shown in Figure 9–9. Also, the solution of the cost minimizing problem generates cost as a basically similar function of output. The requirements for an optimum remain the same: cost minimization, $c_1/c_2 = \bar{e}_1/\bar{e}_2$ or $c_1/\bar{e}_1 = c_2/\bar{e}_2 = w$; net revenue maximization, $w = p$; or in combined form, $p\bar{e}_1 = c_1$, $p\bar{e}_2 = c_2$. The marginal revenue productivity must equal the market price for every variable input.

Have we now gone as far as we can go in relaxing technological requirements within the traditional version of a purely competitive firm? The answer is yes. The economic theory of the firm seeks results of the greatest generality that are applicable under the broadest possible technological conditions. Insofar as possible it avoids being tied down to simple, specialized output functions, although it eagerly accepts such functions as special cases whenever they are reasonably accurate summaries of the technology in specific industries. The economic model does, however, rest on optimization and assumes that the underlying technological conditions permit optimization. For cost minimization, the isoproduct contours must be the lower boundaries of convex sets and must be smooth curves to permit use of the calculus. For a unique long-run optimum, output must increase along rays as more of both inputs are used, at least up to some level, and output must ultimately rise at a decreasing rate. Technological conditions may vary widely, but, so long as they can be summarized in a smooth output function with the foregoing properties, the firm can attain an optimum, and the traditional model of the firm applies.

We have now completed our treatment of the single-product, purely competitive firm in both the piecewise-linear and the smooth versions. Both versions are basically similar in using optimization to predict choice. Both models are also alike in generating rates of change or internal prices for the quantities under constraint, marginal revenue productivities for inputs and marginal cost for output. In other respects, there are differences of detail arising from the difference in underlying conditions. In the smooth version, minimal cost is identified by tangency of the cost line to the smooth boundary of the constraint set. With piecewise-linear contours, the typical solution is a supporting line through a vertex. Both are special cases of optimization on convex sets, of which nonlinear programming with piecewise-curvilinear contours represents an intermediate case.

In the smooth version, intersection of the horizontal price line with a smooth upward-sloping marginal cost curve identifies the optimal output. Marginal cost is a rising step function in the linear model, and the optimum typically occurs when the horizontal price line passes through a vertical gap in the marginal cost function. Both satisfy the general requirement for an optimal output; cost must increase more rapidly than revenue when output increases, and cost must decrease less rapidly than revenue when output declines. With an appropriate reinterpretation of variables, the smooth marginal cost curve represents the supply curve, but the open vertical gaps in marginal cost form the supply curve in the linear model. Similar differences appear when the optimal amount of an input is identified by the use of marginal revenue productivity curves.

The linear version includes a solution of the technological optimizing problem and an explicit derivation of an output function from raw technological data in the form of input requirements. The traditional version assumes that the technological optimizing problem has somehow been solved and simply begins with an output function that has the requisite mathematical properties for optimization by the firm. The limitation of the linear model, particularly in the long run, is the constant return to scale, which the traditional model may replace with more general functions.

In other ways the smooth model also gives a better portrayal of long-run conditions, the linear model of short-run conditions. Economists have typically distinguished between long and short run by the fixity of an input, but this is only part of the distinction and probably not the most important part. In the long run, or better, in the planning period before a plant is built, the firm has the maximum choice of technological possibilities. The decision to build a plant involves the selection of particular processes and specific types of equipment. Once the plant is built, the full range of technological possibilities is no longer available to the firm. Both the choice of processes and the substitutability of inputs are greatly reduced. In growth theory, the distinction is often made very specific by assuming that the planning is done with a Cobb–Douglas function, which is essentially an infinite set of processes. Once the long-run decision is made, the technological possibilities shrink to one or several linear processes. The two versions are highly complementary in that the linear model reflects the inevitable restriction of technology in the short run whereas the smooth version contains the broad spectrum of methods potentially available before construction occurs.

EXERCISES

1. *Increasing the Number of Processes*

Using the numerical example in the *text* of Chapter 8 adjust the coefficients to an output level of 60 units. Add the following processes, each of which also yields 60 units: [11, 30]; [13, 20]; [16, 13]; [22, 11]; [40, 9]. Plot the new isoproduct contour. By selecting two adjacent processes from the original example, identify the triangular region within which a new isoproduct point must lie if the new process is to dominate the linear combination of adjacent processes but not replace either process. Calculate the new output function and present in a table. Plot the total product curve for z_1 when $z_2 = 8$. Summarize the effects of introducing the new processes.

2. *Isoproduct Contours and Production Surfaces*

(Where possible support the discussion by two- and three-dimensional sketches.)

(a) What happens to a piecewise-linear production surface when the isoproduct point on one ray moves nearer the origin? Farther from the origin? Describe the effect on the production surface of introducing a new process that dominates a linear combination of two processes but does not replace either process.

(b) Assume that the procedure of inserting new processes continues until an entire line segment is replaced by an arc of a curve that is convex to the origin and nearer to it. Describe the corresponding effect on the production surface. What happens to the production surface when a line segment on an isoproduct contour gives way to an arc of a curve that is concave to the origin and farther from it? State a general relationship between the vertical pattern of the forming ray for the surface and the shape of isoproduct contours. Succinctly, how do bulges in the contours relate to bulges on the surface?

(c) Describe the smooth production surface when no slack processes are present and there are minimal ratios of inputs below which production is impossible. How does the presence of slack processes affect the surface?

(d) Suppose that there are production processes capable of turning out the product using either input alone. Describe the isoproduct contours and the production surface for both the piecewise-linear and smooth cases.

(e) Assume that the isoproduct contours of (d) are concave rather than convex to the origin. What does the production surface look like? Draw a smooth isoproduct contour that changes from convex to concave and describe the production surface.

3. *The Cobb–Douglas Function and the Optimum for the Firm*
Use the specific output function $x = 64z_1^{1/2}z_2^{1/2}$.

(a) Plot several points and draw an isoproduct contour. Verify algebraically that output is proportional to distance from the original along any ray, except the axes. Describe the production surface.

(b) From the formulas of the text find specific expressions for the marginal productivities and show that they are constant along rays. With $z_2 = 16$, find expressions for the total product and the marginal productivity of z_1. Plot both.

(c) Find the optimal ray for each of the following pairs of input prices: $(c_1, c_2) = (1, 1)$; $(2, 1)$; $(1, 3)$. Derive marginal cost and the long-run total cost function along each ray.

(d) With $z_2 = 16$ and $c_1 = c_2 = 1$, find short-run total, marginal, and average cost. Graph in relation to long-run cost as in Figure 9–4. Explain the point of tangency. How is the point of tangency affected by increasing the level of z_2 to 64, or reducing it to 4?

(e) Choose some suitable price for the output and display the optimum of the firm as in Figure 9–5a.

(f) Write the equations for the total revenue and the marginal revenue productivity of z_1 when $z_2 = 16$. Give an alternative graphical presentation of the short-run optimum for the firm and show algebraically that the two versions are equivalent.

4. *Technological Conditions in the Long and Short Run*
In the planning period the technological possibilities open to the firm are summarized by the Cobb–Douglas function of the preceding exercise: $x = 64z_1^{1/2}z_2^{1/2}$. After the plant is built there are only four production processes available, which have the following isoproduct points on the contour $x = 64$: $[16, \frac{1}{16}]$; $[1, 1]$; $[\frac{1}{4}, 4]$; $[\frac{1}{64}, 64]$. Derive the total product curve, including costless slack processes. Present on the same diagram both the smooth and the piecewise-linear total product curve for z_1 when $z_2 = 16$. Also show on one graph the two marginal productivity curves for z_1.

5. *Minimal Ratios for Inputs*

(a) Take z_2 to represent the services of the plant, z_1 to be the services of labor. Technological conditions do not permit production to take place unless the ratio of labor services to plant services exceeds some minimal ratio, say, $z_1/z_2 > 4/11$ or $z_2/z_1 < 11/4$. Assume initially that the plant must be fully utilized. To the numerical example in the *text* of Chapter 8 add the following processes: $\mathbf{a}_5 = [\frac{1}{4}, \frac{3}{5}, 1]$; $\mathbf{a}_6 = [\frac{3}{10}, \frac{3}{4}, 1]$. Plot the new isoproduct contour and compute the new segments of the total product curve.

(b) Introduce an additional process and an additional upward-sloping segment on the isoproduct map after first verifying the following requirements: the new process cannot lie in the cone of existing processes; the new process cannot lie above the boundary ray for zero output; each successive upward-sloping segment of the isoproduct contour must be flatter than the preceding. Show that as additional processes are introduced the slope of the contour must approach that of the boundary ray.

(c) Assume that the plant can go unused but not costlessly. Labor must be used for extra maintenance. What is the separate effect on the isoproduct contour of each of the following slack-maintenance processes: [4, 11, 0]; [2, 7, 0]? Show on the same graph the total product curves for z_1 in the two cases.

(d) Verify that the following smooth output function is linearly homogeneous: $x = (3z_1 - z_2)^{1/2}(2z_2 - z_1)^{1/2}$. Find the ratios of the inputs below which production cannot take place.

6. *A Firm with Two Plants*

Chapter 8 presented a piecewise-linear version of a two-plant firm with one input fixed in each plant and one shared input fixed for the firm. Convert to the analogous smooth version on the assumption that both plants have linearly homogeneous output functions. Draw separate isoproduct maps for each plant and explain how to derive from them the total product and marginal productivity curves of each plant for the shared input. Display the optimal allocations in a graph. Suppose that top management sets an internal price for the shared input. By use of supply and demand curves show how the management could find the price that would guide each plant to the optimal solution for the firm.

7. *Increasing Followed by Decreasing Returns*

For an example of increasing followed by decreasing returns assume that the output function has the following simple properties discussed in the chapter: The marginal productivities of both inputs first increase at the same proportional rate along every ray up to the same contour and thereafter decrease at the same proportional rate along every ray.

(a) Draw a smooth isoproduct map portraying the technological conditions. Explain how to convert to an isorevenue map at a constant output price. Write the expression for the slope of an isorevenue contour. How does total revenue vary above any ray as the scale of operation increases? Explain why either z_1 or z_2 can be used to measure scale of plant along any ray.

Introduce input prices. Show graphically and then write down the conditions for minimizing cost subject to a constant level of revenue. With constant input prices what is the expansion path? Draw total revenue and total cost as functions of scale and determine the optimal output. How are the marginal revenue productivities of both inputs related to their respective prices before the optimum, after the optimum, at the optimum?

(b) Show graphically and then write down the conditions for minimizing cost at a given level of output. Derive the expression for marginal cost. Explain how total cost varies with output along the expansion path and illustrate by graphing total cost against output. Draw in the revenue function and identify the optimal output. Show algebraically that the requirements for an optimum imply the conditions derived in (a).

(c) Hold the second input constant. Compare the short-run and long-run marginal productivity of z_1 for the same level of output before, at, and after the intersection of the horizontal line with the expansion path. Consider only the region of diminishing returns. Use this information to draw the short-run marginal cost curve in proper relation to the long-run curve. What happens when the level of the fixed input is raised or lowered?

(d) Assume input prices are the same in both short and long run. Compare short- and long-run total cost for the same level of output before, at, and after the intersection of the horizontal line with the expansion path. Utilize this information as well as that derived in (c) to draw the short- and long-run total cost curves in proper relation to each other. Consider only the region of diminishing returns. Draw also the pair of average cost curves. What happens on both diagrams when the level of the fixed input is raised or lowered?

(e) A straight line from the origin to a point on the total cost curve has slope C/x, which equals average cost. Show that as x increases average cost declines up to the output at which the ray through the origin is tangent to the total cost curve, whose slope is marginal cost. Use this information to draw the long-run average and marginal cost curves in proper relation to each other. Do the same for the short-run curves.

10

Joint Products and Cost Minimization: An Alternative Version of the Firm

Because of the ease with which they illustrate economic principles, single-product firms have received the bulk of the attention in economics, particularly in textbooks. In reality, a firm whose actual or potential output is restricted to a single product is almost impossible to find. Even in the industry that is the prototype for the purely competitive model, agriculture, there are few single-product firms. In the industries where monopolistic competition, oligopoly, and monopoly prevail, firms are notoriously multiproduct.

Earlier chapters developed a linear model of a multiproduct firm in which each product had a single process. We are now in a position to include as well a choice of processes for each product. So long as each process has but one output, the products are technologically independent of each other. With unlimited inputs the production of one output would have no effect on the production of any other. What ties outputs together are their competing claims on the scarce inputs. A model of the multiproduct firm in which each product has a separate set of processes does not differ significantly from the earlier version in which each product had only a single process. The objective of the firm remains the choice of those processes that maximize net revenue, and the output the process happens to turn out is irrelevant to the choice. The only new feature is that the optimal solution may contain several processes turning out the same product.

A COST MINIMIZATION MODEL WITH JOINT PRODUCTS

A process that turns out a single product represents a prevalent but nonetheless special case. Joint products have a long history in economics, as the old standby of wool and mutton attests, and modern technology also furnishes examples in oil refining, nuclear fission, and many other areas. The simplest case of joint production is a process that turns out two products with the use of one input. It is the closest analogue to the processes in preceding chapters, which used two inputs to produce a single output. The corresponding linear programming problem is the following:

$$\begin{aligned} e_{11}z_1+e_{12}z_2+e_{13}z_3+e_{14}z_4 &\geqq q_1 \\ e_{21}z_1+e_{22}z_2+e_{23}z_3+e_{24}z_4 &\geqq q_2 \\ c_1z_1 \;+c_2z_2 \;+c_3z_3 \;+c_4z_4 &= C(\text{min}). \end{aligned}$$

There are four input-using processes, each of which turns out two products in fixed ratio to each other. The e coefficients are analogous to the a coefficients, or input coefficients, in the revenue maximizing model. They measure the number of units of output produced for each unit of input employed and are called *output coefficients.* The symbol q, for quantity or quota, is used for constant levels of output, just as the symbol b has been employed in place of z when inputs are fixed. The presence of inequalities in the constraints gives management some leeway; production quotas may be exceeded if it is more economical to do so. The inequalities have to be of the $\geqq$ form or cost would always be minimized at zero. The presence of fixed output quotas is a departure from the usual economic model of the firm but it has a counterpart in the business world. Firms often do produce under contract or to order rather than for sale in an open market.

Strictly interpreted, a process that uses only one input to produce two outputs is not very plausible, but the interpretation can be broadened. Each process may use additional inputs, say z_7 and z_8, which can be purchased in the market. If the amounts required vary proportionately with the level of each process, the following additions can be made to the problem:

$$\begin{aligned} a_{71}z_1+a_{72}z_2+a_{73}z_3+a_{74}z_4-z_7 \qquad\qquad &= 0 \\ a_{81}z_1+a_{82}z_2+a_{83}z_3+a_{84}z_4 \qquad\qquad -z_8 &= 0 \\ c_1z_1 \;+c_2z_2 \;+c_3z_3 \;+c_4z_4 \;+c_7z_7+c_8z_8 &= C(\text{min}). \end{aligned}$$

Since the additional constraints are not binding, they can be used to eliminate z_7 and z_8 from the objective form and then dropped. The result is to add to the market price of each principal input the cost of using additional inputs. Hence, the coefficients for each process can be reinterpreted to include the cost of all inputs required by the process.

The following numerical example will be used:

$$\begin{aligned} 4z_1+12z_2+\ 8z_3+5z_4-z_5 \qquad &= 72 \\ 4z_1+\ 9z_2+12z_3+3z_4 \qquad -z_6 &= 60 \\ 8z_1+20z_2+22z_3+8z_4 \qquad &= C(\min). \end{aligned}$$

Slack or, better, surplus variables z_5 and z_6 have been inserted to convert the constraints to equations. Each surplus variable represents the amount by which the respective output quota is exceeded. Since z_5 and z_6 have zero objective coefficients, no penalty is incurred in the form of storage or other costs for the overfulfillment of quotas. Nor is there any gain from excess production.

The surplus variables, having coefficients of -1, do not form an initial basic feasible solution. Readers can find an initial basic feasible solution by applying Phase I of the simplex method, as demonstrated at the end of Chapter 3, or by the shortcut method applied to the dual in Chapter 4. As may be verified, the simplex algorithm, once launched, yields (z_1, z_2) as optimal solution. The results are displayed below, both numerically and symbolically, in the revised canonical form of Chapter 5.

$$\begin{aligned} z_1 &= -\tfrac{3}{4}q_1 + 1q_2 \\ z_2 &= \tfrac{1}{3}q_1 - \tfrac{1}{3}q_2 - \\ -C &= -\tfrac{2}{3}q_1 - \tfrac{4}{3}q_2 \end{aligned} \begin{bmatrix} 6z_3 - \tfrac{3}{4}z_4 + \tfrac{3}{4}z_5 - 1z_6 \\ -\tfrac{4}{3}z_3 + \tfrac{2}{3}z_4 - \tfrac{1}{3}z_5 + \tfrac{1}{3}z_6 \\ \tfrac{2}{3}z_3 + \tfrac{2}{3}z_4 + \tfrac{2}{3}z_5 + \tfrac{4}{3}z_6 \end{bmatrix};$$

$$\begin{aligned} z_1 &= \bar{a}_{11}q_1 + \bar{a}_{12}q_2 \\ z_2 &= \bar{a}_{21}q_1 + \bar{a}_{22}q_2 - \\ -C &= -w_1q_1 - w_2q_2 \end{aligned} \begin{bmatrix} \bar{e}_{13}z_3 + \bar{e}_{14}z_4 + \bar{e}_{15}z_5 + \bar{e}_{16}z_6 \\ \bar{e}_{23}z_3 + \bar{e}_{24}z_4 + \bar{e}_{25}z_5 + \bar{e}_{26}z_6 \\ \bar{c}_3z_3 + \bar{c}_4z_4 + \bar{c}_5z_5 + \bar{c}_6z_6 \end{bmatrix}.$$

Since the objective is to minimize cost rather than maximize revenue, the optimal solution is attained when the $\bar{c}$ coefficients for nonbasic variables are all positive or zero. The introduction of any new variable will then either raise cost or leave it unchanged.

In the revenue maximization model, reduction of the constraints to diagonal form gives the outputs in the basis as linear functions of the inputs and the remaining nonbasic variables. Similarly, when cost is minimized subject to output quotas, reduction to diagonal form expresses each input in the basis as a linear function of the output levels and the remaining nonbasic variables. If, say, q_1 changes with q_2 and the nonbasic variables remain constant, the corresponding changes in the inputs required are

$$\Delta z_1 = \bar{a}_{11}\,\Delta q_1 \qquad \Delta z_2 = \bar{a}_{21}\,\Delta q_1.$$

Hence,

$$\bar{a}_{11} = \frac{\Delta z_1}{\Delta q_1} \quad \text{and} \quad \bar{a}_{21} = \frac{\Delta z_2}{\Delta q_1}.$$

These are the rates of change of the first and second inputs with respect to the level of the first output. Because of the resemblance to input coefficients, the symbol a is used. However, since the results hold only for a single basic feasible solution, bars are placed above the coefficients to warn that they are *relative input coefficients.*

If each of the input-using processes yields positive amounts of both products, as in the numerical example, then one $\bar{a}$ coefficient must be negative and one positive in each column.[1] The only way that one product can increase while the other remains constant is by expanding the use of one input and cutting back on the other. The coefficients $\bar{a}_{11}$ and $\bar{a}_{21}$ are the rates of change of the two inputs as the first product varies and the second is unchanged. Hence, the coefficients must differ in sign, as must $\bar{a}_{12}$ and $\bar{a}_{22}$. An important implication of negative $\bar{a}$ coefficients is that the equations can hold only for finite ranges of the output quotas.

Except for sign the coefficients of q_1 and q_2 are the same as those of the surplus variables z_5 and z_6. The difference in sign is explained algebraically by the negative coefficients for z_5 and z_6 in the original equations. On economic grounds it is clear that the use of inputs must remain constant if a quota is reduced by one unit and its overfulfillment is increased by one unit.

If z_3 changes with all other variables in the bracket constant, the results are

$$\begin{aligned} \Delta z_1 &= -\bar{e}_{13}\,\Delta z_3 \\ \Delta z_2 &= -\bar{e}_{23}\,\Delta z_3 \end{aligned} \quad \text{or} \quad \begin{aligned} \frac{\Delta z_1}{\Delta z_3} &= -\bar{e}_{13} \\ \frac{\Delta z_2}{\Delta z_3} &= -\bar{e}_{23}. \end{aligned}$$

Like the $\bar{a}$ coefficients in the revenue maximization model, the $\bar{e}$ coefficients with negative signs affixed measure rates of substitution, but in this case between inputs. If $\bar{e}_{13}$ is positive, the third input tends to displace the first and is competitive with it. By contrast, when $\bar{e}_{13}$ is negative, an increase in the third input stimulates the use of the first, so the two are complementary.

Since the $\bar{e}$ symbol has been used previously with a somewhat different meaning, we need to clarify the use of symbols and head off possible confusion. Basically, the symbol e denotes the rate of change of an output with

[1]In contrast to the revenue maximization model, the negative rather than the positive coefficients lie along the diagonal corresponding to the variables. This is a general result whenever the coefficients are all positive and the inequalities are of the $\geqq$ form. In reducing to diagonal form with respect to any basis, the highest production quota rather than the lowest input ceiling determines the row in which a variable is introduced.

respect to an input, just as the symbol a shows how an input changes in response to an output. Except in the present context, the symbol e, with or without bars, always has the same basic meaning. As explained in Chapter 3, it is standard practice in linear programming to indicate the effect of pivot operations on a coefficient by placing a bar over it. Thus, $\bar{e}_{13}$ indicates that the original coefficient e_{13} has been transformed by the algebraic operations reducing the constraints to diagonal form. Unfortunately, $\bar{e}_{13}$ denotes a rate of change between inputs and violates our general convention, just as $\bar{a}_{ij}$ in Chapter 3 measures the rate of change between outputs rather than between an input and an output. Instead of increasing the number of symbols we have chosen to let the inconsistency remain and call attention to it. Except when they are the barred coefficients of nonbasic variables, the symbol e always denotes the response of an output to a change in an input, and the symbol a always denotes the response of an input to a change in an output.

In the revenue maximization model, the $\bar{r}$ coefficients were obtained by two methods, elementary operations and the solution of the vertical equations for columns in the basis. Since the basic mathematical structure is identical, the same two methods must be available for the present model, but the economic interpretations differ. With the constraints in diagonal form, the requisite elementary operations yield for z_3

$$\bar{c}_3 = c_3 - (c_1\bar{e}_{13} + c_2\bar{e}_{23}).$$

For revenue maximization the analogous result is

$$\bar{r}_3 = r_3 - (r_1\bar{a}_{13} + r_2\bar{a}_{23}).$$

As has been shown, the expression in the immediately preceding parentheses is the unit opportunity cost of the third product, the revenue lost from the first two products as a result of producing one unit of x_3. The first term in parentheses, $(c_1\bar{e}_{13} + c_2\bar{e}_{23})$, has an analogous interpretation. If one unit of the third input is not used, the expression in parentheses is the cost of replacing it by the appropriate combination of changes in the first two inputs.[2]

When revenue is maximized for fixed input levels, the choice of one product deprives the firm of the revenue from other products. When cost is minimized for given output levels, the choice of one input saves the firm the amount that would otherwise have to be spent for the next most efficient combination of inputs. By analogy we may call the amount saved, $c_1\bar{e}_{13} + c_2\bar{e}_{23}$, the *opportunity value* of the input. Just as opportunity cost is value or revenue foregone, so is opportunity value cost avoided. An input whose

[2]If one unit of z_3 is replaced, $\Delta z_3 = -1$. Hence, $\Delta z_1 = -\bar{e}_{13}\ \Delta z_3 = \bar{e}_{13}$, and $\Delta z_2 = -\bar{e}_{23}\ \Delta z_3 = \bar{e}_{23}$. The indicated changes in the first two inputs will keep both output levels constant when a unit of the third input is withdrawn.

opportunity value exceeds its market price has a negative $\bar{c}$ coefficient. Its use causes a net reduction in cost.

In any linear programming problem there always exist multipliers, or dual variables, that are the solutions of the vertical equations for columns in the basis. For the present model and the solution (z_1, z_2) the equations are

$$e_{11}w_1+e_{21}w_2 = c_1 \qquad 4w_1+4w_2 = 8$$
$$e_{12}w_1+e_{22}w_2 = c_2 \qquad 12w_1+9w_2 = 20.$$

The values of w_1 and w_2 found from these equations can be used to calculate all barred coefficients in the objective form. The procedure is to multiply the first constraint, in its original form, by w_1, the second similarly by w_2, and subtract the results from the objective form. For a nonbasic variable, such as z_3, the barred coefficient is

$$\bar{c}_3 = c_3-(w_1e_{13}+w_2e_{23}).$$

The barred coefficients for the surplus variables become

$$\bar{c}_5 = 0-(-1w_1+0w_2) = w_1 = \tfrac{2}{3}$$
$$\bar{c}_6 = 0-\quad(0w_1-1w_2) = w_2 = \tfrac{4}{3}.$$

Once again reduction to canonical form yields the multipliers as a computational windfall.[3] For the production quotas, the coefficients in the objective form differ only in sign from those of the surplus variables.

To find the economic meaning of w_1 and w_2, we examine the objective function:

$$C = w_1q_1+w_2q_2+\bar{c}_3z_3+\bar{c}_4z_4+\bar{c}_5z_5+\bar{c}_6z_6.$$

If q_1 changes with all other variables constant, the effect is

$$\Delta C = w_1\,\Delta q_1 \qquad \text{or} \qquad w_1 = \frac{\Delta C}{\Delta q_1}.$$

Thus, w_1 is the rate of change of total cost with respect to q_1, or the marginal cost of the first output. Similarly, w_2 is the marginal cost of the second output. On algebraic as well as economic grounds, the coefficients of the surplus variables are also the respective marginal costs; overfulfilling adds to cost at the same rate as producing for a larger quota. In the revenue maximization model, reduction to canonical form converts revenue from a function of outputs to a function of inputs. Similarly, in the cost minimization model, reduction to canonical form converts cost from a function of inputs to a

[3]With slack variables the barred coefficients are the negatives of the multipliers; with surplus variables the barred coefficients are the multipliers themselves.

function of outputs. If the respective solutions are optimal, the results are the upper boundary of revenue and the lower boundary of cost.

The revenue maximizing problem determines marginal revenue productivities, which are also internal or imputed prices for the inputs. Cost minimization generates for each product its marginal cost, which also serves as an internal or imputed price. From the solution to the vertical equations we see that the entire cost of the inputs in the basis is allocated or imputed to the outputs at the prices w_1 and w_2. In revenue maximization we can calculate for each output not in the basis its imputed unit cost or imputed marginal cost. The decision to produce rests upon a comparison of the selling price or the net revenue per unit with the imputed marginal cost. In the cost minimization problem we can calculate for an input not in the basis the value of output one unit can turn out. With products valued at their internal or imputed prices, one unit of the third input yields the amount $(w_1e_{13}+w_2e_{23})$ which is the internal or imputed marginal revenue productivity of the third input. It pays the firm to use the third input when its imputed marginal revenue productivity exceeds the market price, or when $\bar{c}_3 = c_3-(w_1e_{13}+w_2e_{23}) < 0$.

THE GRAPH OF THE COST MINIMIZATION MODEL

The cost minimization model can be graphed as a linear combination of vectors in the two-dimensional output space. For ease in graphing, each process or vector is adjusted, as shown below, to a uniform cost of \$220:

$$\begin{matrix} \mathbf{e}_1 & \mathbf{e}_2 & \mathbf{e}_3 & \mathbf{e}_4 \\ \begin{bmatrix} 110 \\ 110 \\ 220 \end{bmatrix} & \begin{bmatrix} 132 \\ 99 \\ 220 \end{bmatrix} & \begin{bmatrix} 80 \\ 120 \\ 220 \end{bmatrix} & \begin{bmatrix} 137\frac{1}{2} \\ 82\frac{1}{2} \\ 220 \end{bmatrix}. \end{matrix}$$

The vectors are plotted in Figure 10–1. For this model, a process is dominated if it yields smaller amounts of the products for a given cost of inputs. Thus, all processes or combinations of processes that lie nearer the origin are eliminated. The result is an *isocost contour* in output space, analogous to the isorevenue contour in input space. It shows for each ratio of products the maximum amounts that can be produced at a given input cost.

The surplus variables add horizontal and vertical segments but in a position opposite to those contributed by slack variables. The line segments joining isocost points for the four genuine processes contain all combinations of output quotas that can be exactly met at given cost. Outside the cone determined by the genuine processes, the stated quotas can be reached only by overproducing one product and costlessly disposing of the surplus. For a cost of \$220 process 3 yields 80 units of product 1, and no other process

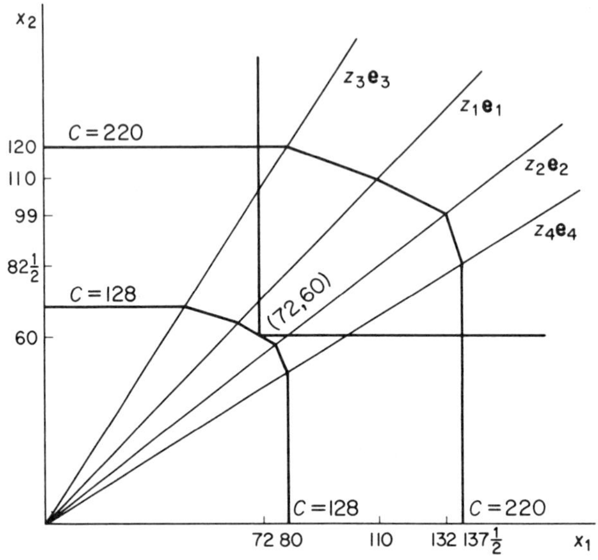

Fig. 10-1 Graph of the Cost Minimization Model

yields fewer units at the same cost. Along the horizontal segment from the third ray to the axis, the same amounts of both products are being turned out, so the cost is constant. At each point on the segment a different amount of x_1 is being disposed of costlessly to reach a quota. Algebraically, the horizontal line segment is the following nonnegative linear combination of vectors:

$$1\begin{bmatrix}80\\120\\220\end{bmatrix}+z_5\begin{bmatrix}-1\\0\\0\end{bmatrix}=\begin{bmatrix}80-z_5\\120\\220\end{bmatrix}.$$

As z_5 varies from 0 to 80, it traces out the horizontal segment back to the vertical axis. The vertical segment is found in a similar way.

The lowest attainable cost occurs on the contour that lies nearest the origin and has at least one point in common with the feasible set $\{x_1 \geqq 72, x_2 \geqq 60\}$. The cone that contains the point $(x_1 = 72, x_2 = 60)$ identifies the optimal processes. The nearer the quota point is to one of the rays, the higher will be the level at which the process is operated.

COST AS A FUNCTION OF THE OUTPUTS

An isocost contour, like an isorevenue contour, is a piecewise-linear function. Once dominated processes have been eliminated, the equations of the line segments can be found by reducing to canonical form with respect to adjacent pairs of processes. Earlier in the chapter the numerical problem is shown in canonical form relative to the first two processes. The linear cost function generated by that solution is

$$C = \frac{2}{3}x_1 + \frac{4}{3}x_2 \qquad 1 \leqq \frac{x_1}{x_2} \leqq \frac{4}{3}.$$

Since cost varies proportionately, the isocost contours are parallel, and the same linear cost function holds everywhere within the cone formed by the adjacent rays. Hence, as shown in the equation, outputs can be treated as variables rather than as fixed quotas.

The technique of parametric programming, as developed in Chapter 5, determines the limits within which a given solution remains optimal and generates the new optimal solution when the ratio of outputs passes beyond these limits. What parametric programming does is to eliminate algebraically all dominated processes or combinations of processes. In higher dimensions it is indispensable, but in two dimensions we can use the simpler geometric method to identify all optimal solutions. For review and for a useful synthesis of the geometric and computational approaches, readers may derive the cost function by parametric programming in Exercise 3. The cost function presented in Table 10–1 has been derived by reducing to canonical form with respect to adjacent, undominated vectors.

TABLE 10–1

A Piecewise-Linear Cost Function

Range of x_2/x_1	$C = w_1x_1 + w_2x_2$
$\frac{3}{2}$ and over	$0x_1 + \frac{11}{6}x_2$
$\frac{3}{2}$ to 1	$\frac{1}{2}x_1 + \frac{3}{2}x_2$
1 to $\frac{3}{4}$	$\frac{2}{3}x_1 + \frac{4}{3}x_2$
$\frac{3}{4}$ to $\frac{3}{5}$	$\frac{4}{3}x_1 + \frac{4}{9}x_2$
$\frac{3}{5}$ to 0	$\frac{8}{5}x_1 + 0x_2$

Any desired isocost contour can be obtained by assigning a value to C. Since the coefficients of x_1 and x_2 are their respective marginal costs, w_1 and w_2, the slope of any contour is $-w_1/w_2$, the negative ratio of the marginal costs. For isorevenue contours, the slope is the negative ratio of the marginal revenue productivities. When production quotas are fixed, two adjacent, undominated processes are optimal if their cone contains the quota point. If the second output is subject to a quota, but the first output is not, the firm is free to produce any combination along a horizontal line. Within each cone the same combination of processes remains optimal, and the minimal cost can be calculated from the appropriate segment of the cost function in

Table 10–1. Figure 10–2a shows the total cost as a piecewise-linear function of x_1 with q_2 fixed at 60 units. Since the slope increases from segment to segment, marginal cost plots as the rising step function of Figure 10–2b.

The unusual features of the graphs that need further clarification are the initial horizontal segment, over which marginal cost is zero, and the final phase in which marginal cost is constant despite an indefinitely large increase in x_1. In both cases quotas are overfulfilled and a surplus variable enters the solution. With q_2 fixed at 60, there is no technological process or combination of technological processes that will produce fewer than 40 units of the first output. If cost is interpreted strictly as cost of production, the cost function is not defined for $x_1 < 40$ and simply ends in a point at $x_1 = 40$. A broader interpretation as cost of supplying specified amounts of outputs permits a decision to overproduce and dispose of the surplus. If disposal incurs no penalty, the total cost of supplying less than 40 units is the same as the total cost of supplying 40 units, so the marginal cost of supplying x_1 is zero. At the other end of the range, when x_1 exceeds 100 units, every technological process turns out more than 60 units of q_2. Producing exactly 60 units of q_2 and more than 100 units of x_1 is technologically impossible, so the cost of production is not defined. By combining production and disposal, however, 60 units of q_2 can always be supplied, so any amount of x_1 above 100 units can be supplied at constant marginal cost.

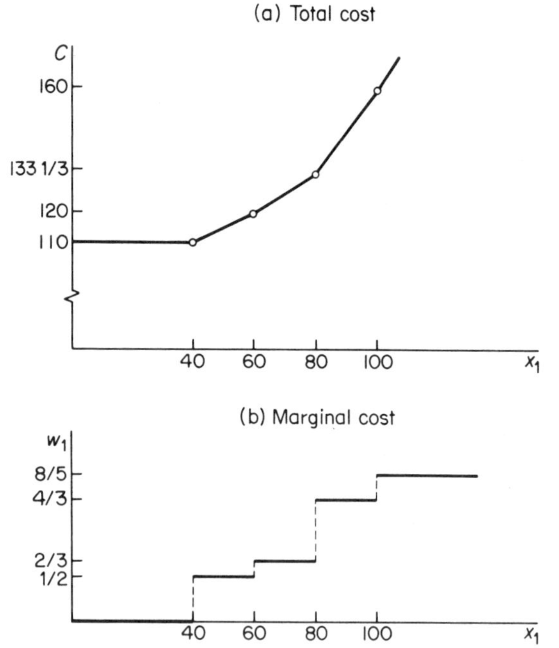

Fig. 10-2 Cost Curves for a Joint Product ($q_2 = 60$)

In the present example, overfulfillment merely extends the range over which total cost is defined. Overfulfillment can also be less costly than exact fulfillment. As an illustration, readers may introduce in Figure 10–1 inefficient processes that lie in the cone of the horizontal and vertical segments but nearer the origin. With these points included, the isocost contour bends backward toward the origin. Not only is the cost of meeting quotas higher, but the marginal cost of one output becomes negative. Below $x_1 = 40$, the total cost curve has a downward-sloping segment, and above $x_1 = 100$ there is a steeper segment than with overfulfillment. Of course, if disposal is not costless, the surplus variables must have positive coefficients in the objective form and must also contribute upward-sloping rather than horizontal and vertical segments to the isocost contours.

The graphs of total and marginal cost emerge from the experiment of assigning to the firm successive quotas for one product with the other product constant. The firm determines for each quota the optimal combination of processes, and the resultant minimal cost is plotted against the quantity of the product. The supply curve arises from a different experiment in which the selling price of a product is systematically varied. At each assigned price the firm determines the optimal amount to produce and sell, which is then plotted against the selling price. When the price of the first product is explicitly introduced, the model becomes

$$\begin{aligned} e_{11}z_1+e_{12}z_2+e_{13}z_3+e_{14}z_4-x_1 \quad &= 0 \\ e_{21}z_1+e_{22}z_2+e_{23}z_3+e_{24}z_4 \quad -z_6 &= q_2 \\ c_1z_1+c_2z_2+c_3z_3+c_4z_4-p_1x_1 \quad &= (C-R)(\text{min}); \end{aligned}$$

$$\begin{aligned} 4z_1+12z_2+8z_3+5z_4-x_1 \quad &= 0 \\ 4z_1+9z_2+12z_3+3z_4 \quad -z_6 &= 60 \\ 8z_1+20z_2+22z_3+8z_4-p_1x_1 \quad &= (C-R)(\text{min}). \end{aligned}$$

The first constraint may be dropped after it has been used, with the following results, to eliminate x_1 from the objective form:

$$\begin{aligned} (c_1-e_{11}p_1)z_1+(c_2-e_{12}p_1)z_2+(c_3-e_{13}p_1)z_3 & \\ +(c_4-e_{14}p_1)z_4 &= (C-R)(\text{min}); \\ (8-4p_1)z_1+(20-12p_1)z_2+(22-8p_1)z_3 & \\ +(8-5p_1)z_4 &= (C-R)(\text{min}). \end{aligned}$$

By finding the successive optimal solutions as p_1 varies upward from zero, readers may verify that the supply curve consists of the open vertical line segments that join the horizontal segments cf the marginal cost curve. As shown by Figure 10–2b, when the price rises above $\frac{8}{5}$, the firm has an incentive to produce the first product without limit and to dispose of ever-increasing quantities of the second commodity. Obviously other constraints, omitted from the problem, must begin to operate at some stage. Either disposal will cease to be costless or the market price will fall after production passes some upper limit.

The objective function for $C-R$, shown above, reveals that unit cost exceeds unit revenue for every process until p_1 reaches $\frac{8}{5}$ and the fourth process just breaks even. Seemingly, it does not pay the firm to operate when the first product sells for less than $\frac{8}{5}$, and it pays to expand without limit as soon as the price goes above that level. The first part of the conclusion does not hold when the second product is produced under contract or sold to order. Total revenue is $R = p_1x_1+p_2q_2$, where p_2 is the contract price and p_2q_2 is fixed revenue, analogous to fixed cost. Readers may draw several total revenue lines in Figure 10–2 with different vertical intercepts p_2q_2. If total revenue nowhere equals or exceeds total cost, the firm shuts down and fulfills its contract by purchasing the second product in the market, if it can. Otherwise the firm may incur a penalty for nonfulfillment of contract, which is analogous to incurring otherwise avoidable maintenance cost by shutting down a plant. When the total revenue intercept lies below the total cost intercept of Figure 10–2, the firm has an incentive to produce only if the profits from x_1 offset the excess of cost over revenue for q_2. The price of x_1 relative to its marginal cost determines the optimal amount of x_1 to produce. When the contract price covers the full cost of producing q_2, the revenue line shifts upward. Net revenue is larger but the optimal amount of x_1 remains the same.

A SINGLE-INPUT, MULTIPROCESS FIRM

So far each process has represented the use of a different input. We may instead follow the procedure of Chapter 8 and interpret each process as a different way of using the same input. The constraints remain the same as in the preceding example, but process levels replace the inputs and the objective form becomes

$$v_1+v_2+v_3+v_4 = z(\text{min}).$$

For simplicity each process is scaled to one unit of the single input z, but the actual coefficients of the numerical example can also be used.

If the first two processes are optimal, reduction of the constraints to diagonal form gives

$$\begin{aligned} v_1 \qquad &= \bar{a}_{11}q_1+\bar{a}_{12}q_2 \\ v_2 &= \bar{a}_{21}q_1+\bar{a}_{22}q_2 \\ v_1+v_2 &= \quad 0q_1+ \quad 0q_2+z. \end{aligned}$$

The $\bar{a}$ coefficients are input coefficients relative to each process. When reduction to canonical form is completed, the objective function becomes

$$0 = -(\bar{a}_{11}+\bar{a}_{21})q_1-(\bar{a}_{12}+\bar{a}_{22})q_2+z = -\bar{a}_1q_1-\bar{a}_2q_2+z.$$

Since the equation holds everywhere within the same cone, we may treat the outputs as variables and write the linear input function as follows:

$$z = \bar{a}_1x_1+\bar{a}_2x_2.$$

If x_2 is held constant while x_1 varies, $\Delta z = \bar{a}_1 \Delta x_1$ or $\bar{a}_1 = \Delta z/\Delta x_1$. Hence, $\bar{a}_1$ and $\bar{a}_2$ are the *marginal input requirements* of the respective products. Each output is being turned out by a combination of two input-using processes, so a change in one output quota alters both process levels. The marginal input requirement for a product is the sum of the changes in the input used by each process.

The complete piecewise-linear input function can be derived by parametric programming or by reducing to canonical form with respect to adjacent, undominated processes. We can use the earlier numerical example simply by reinterpreting the objective coefficients as amounts of z rather than as prices of the various inputs. Hence, z replaces C, and Table 10–1 shows a piecewise-linear input function. The isocost contours of Figure 10–1 become iso-input contours. The more familiar terms for such contours in output space are *product transformation curve* or *efficiency frontier.*

Readers may question the inclusion of horizontal and vertical segments in the efficiency frontier. Both segments require overproduction and disposal of excess quantities, actions that are not easy to reconcile with the usual concept of efficiency. As we have formulated the problem, overproduction and costless disposal are technological possibilities open to the firm. Suppose that there is a production process with an iso-input point inside the cone of the horizontal segment but below it. If used to produce a combination of outputs on the horizontal segment, such a process will require more of the input than does costless disposal. The process cannot pass the technological minimizing test. It is technologically possible for the firm to obtain the quantities on the horizontal segment, but there is no more efficient way than overproduction and costless disposal. When z is minimized for given levels of x_1 and x_2, both disposal processes appear in the solution. However, when x_1 is being maximized for given levels of z and x_2, the solution always occurs at the right endpoint and the horizontal segment never appears. Similarly, the maximization of x_2 never generates the vertical segment. The results are analogous to those derived for the slack processes in Chapter 8 on page 177. In this case it is the technological minimizing problem that generates the entire contour.

If disposal is not costless—that is, if the input has to be used in the disposal process—the corresponding segments are no longer horizontal and vertical but intersect the axes at lower levels of output than in Figure 10–1. There may be productive processes, not shown in Figure 10–1, that turn out relatively small amounts of x_1 but are less efficient than costless disposal. When disposal incurs an input cost, these processes may become more efficient than disposal and may contribute line segments to the transformation curve.

With the input held constant the equation for a specific transformation curve is

$$x_2 = -\frac{\bar{a}_1}{\bar{a}_2}x_1 + \frac{b}{\bar{a}_2} = -\bar{t}x_1 + \bar{e}_2 b.$$

The slope of the transformation curve is the negative ratio of the marginal input requirements, which remain constant within each cone. The ratio of the marginal input requirements is the *rate of product transformation*, for which the symbol $\bar{t}$ will be used. With the input constant, the rate of product transformation measures the rate at which one product can be exchanged for the other by means of production. It is analogous to the rate of input substitution or rate of technical substitution, which measures the rate at which one input can be substituted for the other in producing a given level of output. Along the vertical segment $\bar{a}_2 = 0$ and the equation for the transformation curve has to be written in the alternative form:

$$x_1 = -\frac{\bar{a}_2}{\bar{a}_1}x_2 + \frac{b}{\bar{a}_1} = \frac{1}{\bar{t}}x_2 + \bar{e}_1 b.$$

As always, the marginal productivities $\bar{e}_1$ and $\bar{e}_2$ are the reciprocals of the corresponding marginal input requirements $\bar{a}_1$ and $\bar{a}_2$.

With the second product constant the input function is $z = \bar{a}_1 x_1 + \bar{a}_2 q_2$, and Figure 10–2a shows how the total amount of the input required varies with x_1. Figure 10–2b displays the marginal input requirement of the first product rather than its marginal cost. When there is only one input, $C = cz$. Both total cost and the total amount of the input used have similar graphs and differ only with respect to the units of measurement on the vertical axis. Also, $C = c\bar{a}_1 x_1 + c\bar{a}_2 x_2 = w_1 x_1 + w_2 x_2$. The marginal cost of a product is simply the marginal input requirement multiplied by the input price.

THE TRANSITION TO A SMOOTH INPUT FUNCTION

A piecewise-linear input function is the solution of the technological optimizing problem for a finite number of processes. Each process turns out the two products in a fixed ratio, and intermediate combinations of outputs require two processes. Following the example of Chapter 9 we can smooth the input function by the device of inserting between any two processes a third process that dominates their linear combination and only their linear combination. The intermediate processes must yield more output from the given amount of input, so the smooth contour must lie beyond each line segment. As explained in Chapter 9, the insertion of superior intermediate processes eliminates line segments but not necessarily corners formed by arcs of curves. To meet the requirements of optimization by the differential calculus the points must be so chosen that each contour has a smoothly turning tangent line at every point.

The intersections with the axes require some explanation. If two products are truly joint, neither can be produced alone, and points on an axis can be attained only by disposing of the other product. So long as there is a production process for any positive ratio of outputs, however small, disposal processes merely contribute horizontal and vertical tangents at the axes. When there are ratios of products too small to be produced, horizontal and vertical line segments form part of the contours, if disposal is costless.[4]

When the iso-input contours are smoothed, cones shrink to rays and line segments to points. Since the marginal input requirements are constant within cones, they remain constant along the rays that replace the cones. Thus, along each ray the input required is a specific linear function of the output levels, $z = \bar{a}_1 x_1 + \bar{a}_2 x_2$. With z assigned a value, the equation gives the tangent line to the corresponding contour at its point of intersection with the ray. The slope of the tangent line is the negative ratio of the marginal input requirements, $-\bar{a}_1/\bar{a}_2 = -\bar{t}$, where $\bar{t}$ is the rate of product transformation. The technological optimizing test eliminates dominated processes and insures that the transformation curve must be concave to the origin, as drawn in Figure 10–3. As x_1 increases relative to x_2 the transformation curve becomes steeper. There are two related economic interpretations. The more of x_1 the firm produces the larger are its marginal input requirements relative to those of x_2. Secondly, for successive equal increases in x_1 the firm must give up ever larger amounts of x_2.

ECONOMIC OPTIMIZATION WITH A SMOOTH INPUT FUNCTION

Once again there are two equivalent ways of displaying the optimum for the firm. Solving the cost minimizing problem combines technological data and input prices to derive cost as a function of the output levels. With

[4]There will be vertices unless the curved portion of the contour approaches horizontal and vertical slopes. For a horizontal slope, $\bar{a}_1/\bar{a}_2 = \bar{e}_2/\bar{e}_1$ must approach zero as x_2/x_1 increases. As the technological limits are approached, the second product requires ever larger amounts of the input per unit of output. Or, what is equivalent, the marginal productivity approaches zero in the production of x_2.

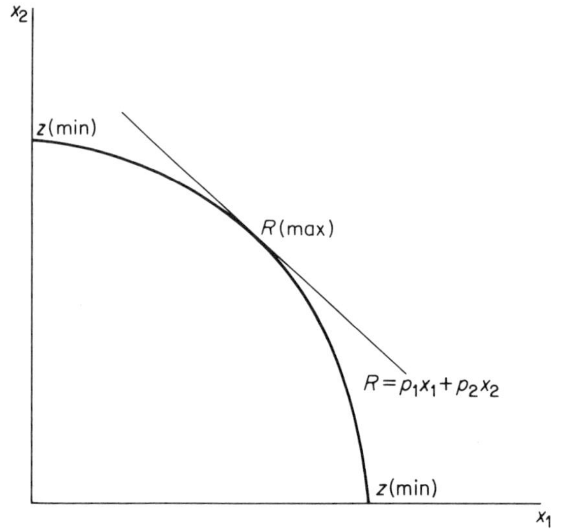

Fig. 10-3 A Smooth Product Transformation Curve (Iso-input Contour)

only a single input, minimizing the use of the input also minimizes its cost and yields directly the total cost function, $C = c\bar{a}_1x_1 + c\bar{a}_2x_2 = w_1x_1 + w_2x_2$. The transformation curves become isocost contours and total cost varies proportionately with the output levels along rays.

When both outputs sell at constant prices, total revenue is $R = p_1x_1 + p_2x_2$. For a specified amount of z, the revenue maximizing condition is tangency of the revenue line to the transformation curve. Tangency, or equality of slopes, implies

$$-\frac{p_1}{p_2} = -\frac{\bar{a}_1}{\bar{a}_2} \quad \text{or} \quad \frac{p_1}{\bar{a}_1} = \frac{p_2}{\bar{a}_2} \quad \text{or} \quad p_1\bar{e}_1 = p_2\bar{e}_2 = y.$$

As always, optimization imparts to the quantity under constraint an internal price, in this case the marginal revenue productivity y which must have the same value in the production of both outputs. When rearranged the tangency conditions also imply the equality of selling price and imputed marginal cost for both products:

$$p_1 = y\bar{a}_1 \qquad p_2 = y\bar{a}_2.$$

Substitution into the total revenue function gives

$$R = p_1x_1 + p_2x_2 = y\bar{a}_1x_1 + y\bar{a}_2x_2 = y(\bar{a}_1x_1 + \bar{a}_2x_2) = yz.$$

The maximization of revenue for a given level of the input converts total revenue into a linear function of the input with the marginal revenue productivity as the coefficient. With a smooth input function, each ratio of output prices determines a different optimal ray and a different value for y. As z varies parametrically with the output prices constant, all optimal solutions lie on the same ray in output space, and R varies proportionately with z, as in Figure 10–4.

With the second output held constant, say by previous contract, the firm is constrained to a horizontal line in output space. The input function can be converted to the following short-run revenue function for x_1:

$$p_1x_1 = \frac{p_1}{\bar{a}_1}z - \frac{p_1\bar{a}_2}{\bar{a}_1}q_2 = p_1\bar{e}_1z - \frac{p_1\bar{a}_2}{\bar{a}_1}q_2.$$

When the fixed revenue from the contract, p_2q_2, is included, short-run total revenue becomes

$$R = p_1\bar{e}_1z + \left(p_2 - \frac{p_1\bar{a}_2}{\bar{a}_1}\right)q_2.$$

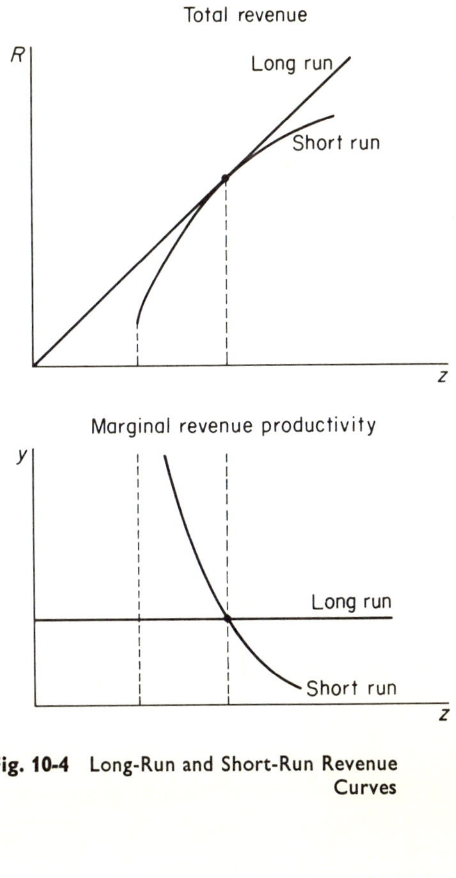

Fig. 10-4 Long-Run and Short-Run Revenue Curves

The amount of the input cannot go to zero even when x_1 is zero, since a sufficient amount must be used to supply the quota q_2. Thus, as drawn in Figure 10–4, the short-run total revenue curve begins at positive levels for both R and z. As x_1 increases, its marginal input requirements rise steadily, and the marginal revenue productivity of z in the first output declines steadily. The short-run total revenue curve rises at a steadily declining rate. At the point of intersection of the horizontal output line with optimal ray, $p_1/p_2 = \bar{a}_1/\bar{a}_2$, the terms in parentheses before q_2 vanish, and total revenue is equal in both the short and long run. At all other levels of the input, the firm receives less revenue in the short run because it is committed to supplying a fixed amount of the second product and cannot attain the optimal ratio of outputs. The short-run marginal revenue productivity curve slopes downward and intersects the long-run curve when the horizontal output line is crossing the optimal ray.

Readers may introduce an input price c and determine in either diagram of Figure 10–4 the optimal amount of the input to use in the short run. If the firm merely loses the fixed revenue for failing to deliver, it never produces when short-run total cost exceeds short-run total revenue. Hence, the short-run marginal productivity curve serves as a demand curve only below the intersection with the long-run curve. There may also be a contractual penalty for failure to deliver, or the firm may place a value on the damage to its reputation. It then continues to produce so long as the short-run loss does not exceed the penalty. The short-run demand curve extends upward by an amount that depends on the size of the penalty.

Whenever all inputs and all outputs are variable, either input functions or output functions that are homogeneous of the first degree give unsatisfactory results for a purely competitive firm. Depending on the relative levels of input and output prices, the courses of action open to the firm are to expand without limit, shut down, or choose indifferently among all possible output or input levels. For more plausible results we relax the assumption that the input requirements are constant along rays. With their ratio constant both marginal input requirements may initially decrease along rays up to some iso-input contour and increase thereafter. As z increases the long run total revenue curve initially bends upward to a point of inflection and then bends downward. The maximum difference between the total revenue curve and the total cost line, or the point of equal slopes, determines the optimal amount of the input to use when both outputs are free to vary at constant prices. To encompass still broader technological possibilities we may allow the ratio of marginal input requirements or rate of product transformation to vary along rays. As noted in Chapter 9, the economic theory of the firm seeks the greatest possible generality and avoids being tied to specific technological conditions. But the theory does rest on optimization and must assume that the technology permits the firm to optimize. Hence, the input required must rise along rays and ultimately at an increasing rate. For revenue to be maximized at each level of the input, the product transformation curves must be the upper boundaries of convex sets. Such contours are concave rather than convex with respect to the origin.

JOINT PRODUCTS AND MULTIPLANT FIRMS

There is a direct cost minimizing analogue to the earlier revenue maximizing version of a firm with two plants. In the analogous case each plant turns out a different primary product but both plants turn out jointly the same third product. The objective of the firm is to allocate optimally between plants the common output rather than the shared input. Exercise 10 at the end of the chapter covers this problem.

We wish to investigate more fully a different type of jointness between products that depends heavily on the cost minimizing version of the firm. The output of one process or plant often serves as an input to other processes or other plants. Modern industry furnishes many examples. Aluminum ingots, the output of the reduction process, become an input for later rolling or extrusion processes, which in turn feed their outputs into various fabricating processes. It is hard to think of an industry where such relationships are absent, and the producing sector as a whole utilizes an incredible number of such intermediate outputs or feeder processes.

To allow for the greatest generality, we assume that the output of each plant, besides being sold in the market, also serves as one of the inputs for the processes of other plants. Not all outputs fit this general pattern. Some outputs may be pure intermediate goods that are never sold but only directed into other processes within the firm. Also some outputs may be sold only in the market and never used within the firm. When either of these conditions hold, some coefficients become zero and the model simplifies. To derive the most general results, we assume that all outputs of every plant are both sold in the market and used within the firm.

To begin most simply, each of the two plants has only a single process and no fixed inputs. The process turns out one product and uses as inputs the output of the other plant and labor services. The firm has final output quotas to meet for both products either because of prior contracts or prior management decisions. The objective is to satisfy these quotas at minimal cost, where cost can be measured either in terms of the amount of labor used or the total amount of wages paid to labor. The model is

$$\begin{aligned} e_{11}x_1 - a_{12}x_2 &\geqq q_1 \\ -a_{21}x_1 + e_{22}x_2 &\geqq \qquad q_2 \\ a_{01}x_1 + a_{02}x_2 &= 0q_1 + 0q_2 + z(\min) \end{aligned}$$

or

$$ca_{01}x_1+ca_{02}x_2 = 0q_1+0q_2+C(\text{min}).$$

We could simplify the model by setting e_{11} and e_{22} equal to one, but for later use of the model there are good reasons for not doing so. Part of the output of an industry may also be used as an input in that same industry, and we are extending the same possibility to plants. If a_{11} denotes the amount of the first output used for each unit of its own production, then $e_{11} = (1-a_{11})$ measures the net output of the first process. Obviously, e_{11} must be positive and normally will be not much different from one. Since $a_{12}x_2$ is the amount of the first product used in the production of the second, the first constraint can be rewritten as

$$x_1 \geqq a_{11}x_1+a_{12}x_2+q_1.$$

Total output equals or exceeds the amount used within the firm plus the market quota.

Reduction to canonical form again converts the objective variable to a linear function of the quantities in the constraints, as shown below:

$$z = \bar{a}_1q_1+\bar{a}_2q_2 \qquad \text{or} \qquad C = cz = w_1q_1+w_2q_2.$$

An increase in q_1 creates both a direct and an indirect demand for more labor. Labor is directly required in the production of x_1, and labor is indirectly required because x_1 uses x_2 and x_2 uses labor. Since x_2 in turn uses x_1, any change in the final quota for the first product gives rise to a whole sequence of successively smaller adjustments. The marginal input requirements in the input function summarize the result of these successive adjustments and show in a single coefficient the total direct and indirect labor requirements per unit of a final quota.

With only two processes there is no choice, but we can state for subsequent use the condition for a process to be included in the optimal solution. In terms of the dual variables, the barred objective coefficient for the first process is zero when

$$ca_{01}-(w_1e_{11}-w_2a_{21}) = 0 \qquad \text{or} \qquad w_1e_{11} = ca_{01}+w_2a_{21}.$$

With each product valued at its internal price or marginal cost, the value of the output the process turns out must equal the value of the inputs employed.

We next consider the more realistic case, shown below, where each plant has a choice of processes and a fixed input:

$$\begin{aligned}
v_1 + v_2 + v_3 - a_{14}v_4 - a_{15}v_5 - a_{16}v_6 &\geqq q_1 \\
-a_{21}v_1 - a_{22}v_2 - a_{23}v_3 + v_4 + v_5 + v_6 &\geqq q_2 \\
-a_{31}v_1 - a_{32}v_2 - a_{33}v_3 &\geqq -b_3 \\
-a_{44}v_4 - a_{45}v_5 - a_{46}v_6 &\geqq -b_4 \\
a_{01}v_1 + a_{02}v_2 + a_{03}v_3 + a_{04}v_4 + a_{05}v_5 + a_{06}v_6 &= z(\text{min}).
\end{aligned}$$

The first three processes and b_3 belong to the first plant, the next three processes and b_4 belong to the second plant. Each process is scaled to yield one unit of net output. Multiplication by the price of labor converts the objective function to the minimization of cost, $C = cz$. Reducing the optimal solution to canonical form converts the objective variable to the following linear function of the constrained quantities:

$$C = w_1q_1 + w_2q_2 - y_3b_3 - y_4b_4.$$

The condition for a process, say the first, to appear in the optimal solution is

$$ca_{01} - (w_1 - w_2a_{21} - y_3a_{31}) = 0$$

or

$$w_1 = ca_{01} + w_2a_{21} + y_3a_{31}.$$

Based on the market price for labor and internal prices for the other quantities, an optimal process must have a value of output equal to the cost of its inputs. When the cost of the inputs exceeds the value of the output, a process is never used.

The optimal solution determines firm-wide prices for the output of each plant. Further, the conditions for an optimal solution require that a product have the same price as output and as input. Suppose, then, that the firm adopts the policy of setting internal prices at which each plant sells to the other. The plant buying the intermediate input treats it like a purchase in an external market. The decision model for the first plant becomes

$$\begin{aligned}
v_1 + v_2 + v_3 &\geqq x_1 \\
-a_{31}v_1 - a_{32}v_2 - a_{33}v_3 &\geqq -b_3 \\
c_1v_1 + c_2v_2 + c_3v_3 &= C(\text{min}).
\end{aligned}$$

For each process, such as the first, the cost coefficients have the form $c_1 = ca_{01} + w_2a_{21}$, where w_2 is the price set by the firm. The plant bases its decisions on its own total output x_1 rather than the firm's quota q_1. As x_1 varies parametrically it traces out the marginal cost curve shown in Figure 10–5.

From the second plant the firm needs a demand curve for x_1 and gets it by varying w_1 parametrically with other conditions unchanged. Readers may set up the model for the second plant, holding the fixed input b_4 and total output x_2 constant. The total demand for x_1, shown on Figure 10–5, is the sum of the final quota q_1 and the demand by the second plant. As in previous examples, the demand curve for an input consists of the open vertical segments in a marginal revenue productivity curve. The intersection of the marginal cost curve and the demand curve determines the price that clears the internal market for x_1. Only at that price is the first plant willing to supply the quantity demanded. Assume that the firm chooses the market clearing price for w_1 and makes a similar, interrelated choice for w_2. In Chapter 4 we established that the simultaneous solution of the primal and dual generates internal prices that select the optimal processes in the primal and reduce to zero the value of excess demand in the internal markets for inputs. Exercise 5 extends the results to the internal markets for outputs. By choosing the internal market clearing prices, the firm is, in effect, solving the dual and insuring an optimal solution to the primal. When each plant accepts the firm – wide prices and optimizes independently, it will choose the processes that appear in the optimal solution for the firm as a whole. There are, of course, other possible relationships between the curves in Figure 10–5, which readers may investigate.

As just shown, the solution of the internal problem of allocation for the firm with two plants resembles the adjustment of two interrelated markets. To pursue the implications in the simplest form we shall first assume that the number of processes is unlimited and shift over to a smooth version. Within the firm an optimal solution requires that the marginal cost curve for the

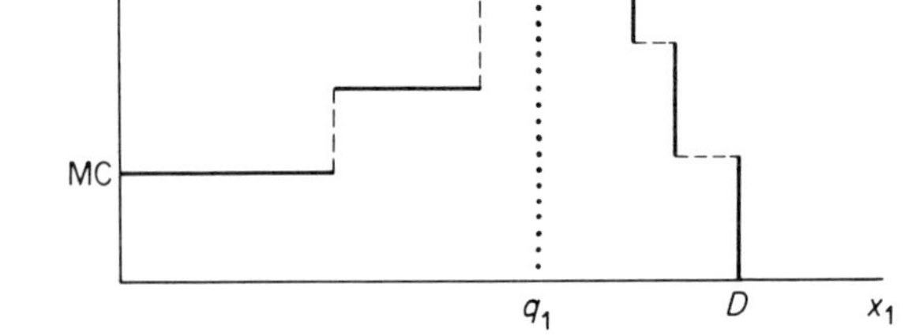

Fig. 10-5 Optimum for Intermediate Input

plant producing a product intersect the marginal revenue productivity curve of the plant that uses it as input. Suppose that the two plants were separate firms selling and buying in the market at given prices. The firm selling x_1 would produce up to the point where the marginal cost equaled the market price. The firm buying x_1 would expand its use up to the level at which the marginal revenue productivity equaled the same market price. Thus, the result would be the same as intersection of the curves within the firm, equality of marginal cost and marginal revenue productivity.

Allocation within the firm can thus be shown to resemble a market process. What is even more significant is that the market process can be shown to solve an optimizing problem even though there is no central direction. The problem for the management of the firm is to minimize the cost of labor or its use subject to fixed output levels and capacity limitations within each plant. Solving the primal problem in linear programming form selects the optimal combination of processes. It also generates internal prices for the quantities under constraint that can be used to express the conditions for optimality. Independent firms buying and selling in the market also succeed in satisfying these conditions for optimality. Hence, we conclude that they have unintentionally solved the primal problem and have minimized the cost or use of labor for whatever levels of output they may produce. If both firms were to be combined into one and the output levels were retained as quotas, the management of the combined firm would choose the same solution and would generate the previous market prices as internal prices.

EXERCISES

Unless otherwise specified the exercises utilize the following alternative numerical example:

$$
\begin{matrix} e_1 & e_2 & e_3 & e_4 & q \\ \begin{bmatrix} 8 \\ 1 \\ 10 \end{bmatrix} & \begin{bmatrix} 15 \\ 5 \\ 20 \end{bmatrix} & \begin{bmatrix} 2 \\ 2 \\ 4 \end{bmatrix} & \begin{bmatrix} 1 \\ 3 \\ 5 \end{bmatrix} & \begin{bmatrix} 40 \\ 80 \\ C \end{bmatrix} \end{matrix}.
$$

1. *Solving a Cost Minimizing Problem*

(a) Set up the numerical example as a cost minimizing version of a multi-input firm. For practice in solving a minimizing problem find an initial basic feasible solution and then apply the simplex method to obtain the optimal solution. Check the results by graphing.

(b) Classify the nonbasic inputs as competitive or complementary with the inputs in the basis. Use the graph to verify the results. What happens to an input in the basis when a complement enters the basis?

(c) Identify the dual variables and explain the economic meaning. For one of the nonbasic inputs calculate the $\bar{c}$ coefficient by two equivalent methods and give an economic interpretation of each method.

2. *The Derivation of Cost as a Function of the Outputs*

(a) In the numerical example change the cost coefficients in each process to a uniform level of 20 and make the appropriate adjustments in the other coefficients. Graph the isocost contour. Also show on the graph the feasible set and the optimal contour.

(b) Using the graph as a guide, derive algebraically total cost as a function of the outputs and present in the form of Table 10–1.

(c) With x_2 constant at 60, find total cost as a function of x_1. Graph both total and marginal cost. Explain the initial and terminal segments.

(d) If $p_1 = \frac{2}{3}$, will the firm produce at all and, if so, at what level of x_1? The decision to produce generally requires further data. Assume initially that the firm merely loses the revenue from x_2 if it fails to fulfill the contract. Determine graphically or otherwise what the firm's decision will be at each of the following contract prices: $p_2 = 1, \frac{4}{3}, \frac{3}{2}, 2$. What is the effect of a lump-sum penalty for nondelivery equal to one-half the revenue from the contract?

(e) (Optional) Compare the effect of fixed cost on the decisions of a single-product firm with the effect of fixed revenue on the decisions of a single-input firm. Would the effect be analogous if, unrealistically, the single-input firm had received payment in advance and did not have to make a refund for failure to deliver? Compare also leasing of fixed inputs with buying output in the market to fulfill the contract.

3. *Obtaining the Cost Function by Parametric Programming*

For the *numerical example in the text* derive the total cost function by the parametric programming methods of Chapter 5. The rules are the same for a minimizing problem. In fact, the problem may be converted to the maximization of $(-C)$ by changing all signs in the objective function.

4. *Deriving the Opportunity Value of an Input*

In Chapter 5 we found the opportunity cost for an output by assigning it a zero objective coefficient and transferring it to the right-hand side of the equation. We then let the output vary parametrically and derived by parametric programming the total revenue from other products as a function of the output being varied. Since a decline in revenue has the same effect on net revenue $(R-C)$ as an increase in cost, we chose to interpret the decline in revenue from other products as the opportunity cost of the output being varied.

In the numerical example used in the text, assign z_3 a zero objective coefficient and shift it to the right-hand side. Apply parametric programming to find the cost of other inputs as a function of z_3. Show the graph. Interpret the decline in cost of other inputs as an increase in revenue and graph as the opportunity value of z_3.

Show that the marginal opportunity value of z_3 can be expressed as $(c_1\bar{e}_{13}+c_2\bar{e}_{23})$ and is equal to the imputed marginal productivity $(w_1e_{13}+w_2e_{23})$. Graph the marginal revenue productivity of z_3 and derive a demand curve from it. Describe how you could obtain a demand curve for z_3 directly from the numerical example by varying its price.

5. *The Dual to the Cost Minimizing Model of the Firm*

Set up and solve the dual to the *numerical problem in the text*. What is the economic meaning of the dual? In Chapter 4 we interpreted the iterations in the dual as eliminating excess demand for the inputs. Can you give a similar interpretation for the present dual as eliminating excess demand or supply for the outputs? Treat the quotas as vertical demand curves for the outputs.

6. *Cost of Disposal and Noxious By-Products*

To the cost minimizing *example of the text* add the following two input-using processes: $e_5 = [4, 2, 8]$, $e_6 = [4, 10, 22]$. Also include a cost for storing or disposing of excess production by revising the disposal processes as follows: $e_7 = [-1, 0, 2]$, $e_8 = [0, -1, 8]$.

(a) Revise the graph in Figure 10–1 to include the changes made and find the new isocost contour for some appropriate level of cost. Now that they no longer have zero objective coefficients the disposal processes can be treated like any other process in obtaining the isocost contour.

Recompute the affected segments of the total cost function and present the function in tabular form. Graph total cost and marginal cost as functions of x_1 with x_2 constant. How much does it cost the firm to supply exactly zero units of x_1? How much would it cost if the sixth process were not available? Try different combinations of contract prices for x_2 and market prices for x_1. Explain how the changes in technological and disposal conditions affect the decisions of the firm.

(b) In an alternative interpretation of the example treat x_1 as a noxious by-product such as gallons of waste dumped in a river. The sixth process now becomes a method of production that cuts down x_1 but reduces x_2 as well. The disposal process z_7e_7 is a method of eliminating the undesirable by-product, but at a cost. Dumping in the river can be regarded as a disposal process that is costless to the firm but not to the community.

Assume that the government makes an assessment of the damage done by dumping in the river and passes it on to the firm in the form of a tax per unit of x_1. How great must the damage be per unit of x_1 to justify a partial elimination by change of productive methods; to justify complete elimination?

7. *The Technological Optimizing Problems*

(a) Treat the *numerical example of the text* as a single-input, multiprocess model of the firm. The technological minimizing problem is to minimize z for each pair of output levels. Set up one technological minimizing problem and explain how to derive the input function. Present a table showing the input function. Include in separate columns the marginal input requirements for each product and the rate of product transformation.

(b) The technological maximizing problem is to maximize one output for constant levels of the other output and the input. Set up the technological maximizing problem and show symbolically the equation that results from its solution. In what essential way do the solutions to the two types of technological optimizing problems differ?

8. *The Revenue Maximizing Version of a Single-Input Firm*

The optimum for the single-product firm is most frequently shown by first calculating cost as a function of output. For the single input firm, the analogous procedure is to calculate revenue as a function of the input. The text presented the solution for the smooth version of the firm. The present exercise provides the piecewise-linear equivalent. For a guide readers may refer back to Chapter 8, where cost is derived as a linear function of output.

(a) *The Long-Run Total Revenue Function*

With $p_1 = 2$ and $p_2 = 2$, set up the *numerical example of the chapter* as maximization of revenue for a constant level of z. Find the optimal solution and derive long-run total revenue as a function of z. Check with Figure 10–1 and identify the expansion path in output space.

(b) *The Short-Run Variable Revenue Function*
Set up the *example of the text* as the maximization of p_1x_1 with q_2 and z constant. Holding q_2 constant at 60 let z vary parametrically and calculate total *variable* revenue as a function of z. In lieu of repeating computations you may use previously obtained results in the text or exercises, specifically the output function of Exercise 7b.

(c) Add fixed revenue, p_2q_2, to get short-run total revenue. Plot short-run total revenue and long-run total revenue as functions of z. Show that the two are equal only when the horizontal output line crosses the optimal ray. Explain geometrically what happens to short-run total revenue at very low levels of x_1, specifically why R and z cannot go to zero. Also draw on one diagram the long-run and short-run marginal revenue productivity curves.

(d) Choose three convenient values for the input price and show graphically the short-run optimum for the firm on both diagrams. Determine the short-run demand curve for the input under each of the following contractual conditions: the firm merely loses the fixed revenue for failure to deliver; the firm pays an additional lump-sum penalty equal to 50% of the fixed revenue; a penalty of 100%.

9. *Economic Optimization with a Smooth Input Function*

(a) Use the specific function $z = (x_1^2+x_2^2)^{1/2}$. Verify that it is a linearly homogeneous input function. The marginal input requirements are, respectively,

$$\bar{a}_1 = \frac{x_1}{(x_1^2+x_2^2)^{1/2}} \qquad \bar{a}_2 = \frac{x_2}{(x_1^2+x_2^2)^{1/2}}.$$

Verify that the marginal input requirements are constant along rays, that is when $x_2 = hx_1$ for $h>0$. Write the input function in the form $z = \bar{a}_1x_1+\bar{a}_2x_2$ and show that it can be reduced to the original form of the function.

(b) Draw an iso-input contour for some convenient value of z. How does z vary with output along the axes? Describe the input surface, that is, the vertical path that a forming rod anchored at the origin must take. Write the algebraic expression for the rate of product transformation $\bar{t}$. Describe how $\bar{t}$ changes along the contour as x_1 increases from zero.

(c) Find algebraically the revenue maximizing solution and the optimal ray for each of the following sets of prices: $(p_1, p_2) = (1, 1)$, $(3, 4)$, $(8, 6)$. By the method developed on page 240 calculate the marginal revenue productivity of the input and write total revenue as a function of the input along each ray. How does total cost vary along each ray if the input price is $c = 5$? What are the implications for a long-run optimum?

(d) With $c = 5$ and the second output constant at $x_2 = 8$, find short-run total cost as a function of the variable output x_1. Check total and marginal cost for a few selected values such as $x_1 = 0, 4, 6, 8$ and draw a sketch of the curve. Let $p_1 = 3$ and $p_2 = 4$. What is the fixed revenue of x_2? How does it compare with the fixed cost? Check $x_1 = 6$ as the optimal solution and draw in the total revenue line. What happens if the price of the fixed output rises or falls?

(e) With x_2 constant at 8, $p_1 = 3$, and $p_2 = 4$, locate on the iso-input map the output combination that is optimal in both the short and long run. Explain how short-run and long-run total revenue are related to each other before and after the optimal value of x_1. What amount of z is used and what is the total revenue when $x_1 = 0$?

Express x_1 symbolically as an explicit linear function of z and x_2. Convert to a variable revenue function and add fixed revenue to get short-run total revenue. Use the earlier expressions for $\bar{a}_1$ and $\bar{a}_2$ and the data given above to find the numerical function for short-run total revenue. Check the marginal revenue productivity of z for the selected values $x_1 = 4, 6, 8$. Sketch short-run total revenue as a function of z together with long-run total revenue. At what values of z and R does the curve begin and at what values is revenue the same in the long and short run?

10. *The Optimal Allocation of a Product Between Plants*

Chapter 8 took up the allocation of a shared input among plants. The analogous problem for the present chapter is allocating an output quota optimally among plants. A firm has two plants, each of which is the sole producer of one product. Each plant produces another product jointly, and that product is the same in both plants. There are quotas for the outputs produced exclusively in one plant and a firm-wide quota for the output both plants can produce. Both plants use the same input and each has several joint production processes.

Take the numerical example of the *text* to be the first plant and the numerical example of the *exercises* to be the second plant. The first product can be turned out by both plants and has a firm-wide quota $q_1 = 200$. The remaining product in the first plant has a quota $q_2 = 60$. The product produced exclusively by the second plant, now relabeled x_3, has the same quota $q_3 = 60$. There is only one input z.

Set up the linear programming model of the firm. Use the results derived in the text and in Exercise 2 to show graphically the optimal distribution of the first product between plants. Determine what processes form the optimal solution. Verify that the solution is optimal for the firm by reducing to canonical form with respect to these processes. Identify the dual variables and write one segment of the input function for the firm.

Let the quota for the shared product vary and describe in terms of the graph other types of solutions that might arise. Suppose that the top management sets an internal price for the first product and offers to buy from the plant managers whatever amounts they choose to produce. What general principle must the top management follow in searching for an internal price that will assure the fulfillment of a firm-wide quota? Check the possible graphical solutions to determine what conditions create difficulties for this plan of decentralized decision making.

Show the corresponding graphical solution under smooth technological conditions and examine the possibility of decentralized decision making.

11

The Theory of the Multiproduct Firm: Synthesis and Generalization

We are now ready to put together into a single model the results of all preceding chapters. In the most general formulation, the firm uses jointly more than one input, produces jointly more than one output, and has a choice of processes. In addition, the firm may also have several plants, each of which either specializes in a single product or produces a variety of products. We shall develop a general model of the firm first in the linear version and then transfer the results to a smooth version.

With the possible exception of some types of services, all outputs require more than one input, and many processes turn out more than one product. The simplest example of jointness with respect to both inputs and outputs is a technological process that utilizes two inputs and yields two products. A slight difficulty with such a process is that there is no unique and obvious measure for its level. In practice, the problem is likely to be solved by settling upon whichever input or output is most important or most easily measured. An example is furnished by petroleum refining, which utilizes a multiplicity of inputs and turns out a wide variety of products. The commonly used measure for the level of the activity is an input, barrels of crude oil, or throughput, as it is called. Initially, we shall avoid any such commitment to any one input or output and assume that the level of the process can be measured independently. The speed of a paper machine or of an assembly line provides such a measure.

To include the results of preceding chapters we begin with a firm that has four technological processes, each of which jointly requires two inputs and jointly yields two outputs. In vector form the technological conditions are

$$v_1\begin{bmatrix}e_{11}\\e_{21}\\a_{11}\\a_{21}\end{bmatrix}+v_2\begin{bmatrix}e_{12}\\e_{22}\\a_{12}\\a_{22}\end{bmatrix}+v_3\begin{bmatrix}e_{13}\\e_{23}\\a_{13}\\a_{23}\end{bmatrix}+v_4\begin{bmatrix}e_{14}\\e_{24}\\a_{14}\\a_{24}\end{bmatrix}=\begin{bmatrix}x_1\\x_2\\z_1\\z_2\end{bmatrix}.$$

The level of each process determines the amount of each output produced or supplied and the amount of each input required or demanded. The total amounts supplied or demanded, which form the vector on the right, depend on the levels of all four processes. The vectors can be expanded into a system of four linear equations, of which only the first appears below:

$$e_{11}v_1+e_{12}v_2+e_{13}v_3+e_{14}v_4 = x_1.$$

By setting all coefficients equal to zero in any one row, we revert to earlier single-product or single-input versions.

Introducing input prices and output quotas sets the model up as the following cost minimization problem:

$$\begin{aligned}
&e_{11}v_1+e_{12}v_2+e_{13}v_3+e_{14}v_4 &&\geqq q_1\\
&e_{21}v_1+e_{22}v_2+e_{23}v_3+e_{24}v_4 &&\geqq \quad q_2\\
&a_{11}v_1+a_{12}v_2+a_{13}v_3+a_{14}v_4-z_1 &&= 0\\
&a_{21}v_1+a_{22}v_2+a_{23}v_3+a_{24}v_4 \qquad -z_2 &&= 0\\
&\qquad\qquad\qquad c_1z_1+c_2z_2 &&= 0q_1+0q_2+C(\text{min}).
\end{aligned}$$

The input equations can be dropped after being used to eliminate z_1 and z_2 from the objective form. As readers may verify, the cost coefficient of the first process becomes $c_1a_{11}+c_2a_{21}$, and the other coefficients take on similar form. So long as the input prices and input coefficients are constant, the unit cost of each process is unchanged, and the problem is formally similar to the cost minimization model of the preceding chapter. Reduction to canonical form generates cost as the linear function of the outputs,

$$C = w_1x_1+w_2x_2,$$

which holds so long as the particular solution remains feasible. The treatment can be completed by finding the remaining segments of the piecewise-linear cost function, drawing isocost contours, and deriving the total and marginal cost of supplying one output with the other constant.

When both inputs are constant and both outputs can be sold at constant prices, the problem becomes revenue maximization with objective form, $R = p_1x_1+p_2x_2$. The first two constraints, which are not binding, can be used to eliminate the outputs from the objective form and generate revenue coefficients for the processes, such as $r_1 = p_1e_{11}+p_2e_{21}$. Reduction to canonical form converts revenue to a linear function of the inputs, $R = y_1z_1 +y_2z_2$. We can then find the remaining segments of the revenue function by parametric programming, plot the isorevenue contours, and derive both total and marginal revenue product curves. Except in one respect, the problem is identical to the revenue maximization model of earlier chapters. When the price of a product changes it affects the revenue coefficients of all processes and not just one. Finding the supply curve of a product is a slightly more difficult problem of parametric programming, but one that is readily solved.

Other situations may also arise, creating different optimizing problems. For example, there is the interesting hybrid case, in which one input is fixed and one product is sold under contract. Also, only a single input or output may be fixed, or there may be three binding constraints. With constant prices available for the variable quantities, each problem fits the linear programming format and yields results that are essentially similar to those of earlier chapters. One important task remains: to make the transition to smooth input and output functions for a firm with jointly required inputs and jointly produced outputs. These results will also turn out to be highly useful in later analyses of industries and the entire economy. The first step is to solve explicitly the technological optimizing problem for the linear model.

THE TECHNOLOGICAL OPTIMIZING PROBLEM

A single-product firm can solve the technological optimizing problem by the simple criterion that more output is preferable to less. A multiproduct firm has to cope with the added complication that more of one product generally means less of another. The firm cannot tell whether it is better off unless it can weigh the gain in one product against the loss in the other. But this requires that the firm assign relative weights or relative valuations to the products. On purely technological grounds there is no basis for valuing one product more highly than another. Market prices determine the values of products to a purely competitive firm, but their introduction converts the problem to economic optimization. The firm must settle for a weaker criterion: other things being equal, more of any one product is preferable to less of that same product. The technological maximizing problem consists of maximizing one output subject to constant levels for the other output and all inputs.

For the model of the preceding section, one technological maximizing problem is

$$\begin{aligned}
a_{11}v_1+a_{12}v_2+a_{13}v_3+a_{14}v_4 &\leqq b_1 \\
a_{21}v_1+a_{22}v_2+a_{23}v_3+a_{24}v_4 &\leqq \qquad b_2 \\
-e_{11}v_1-e_{12}v_2-e_{13}v_3-e_{14}v_4 &\leqq \qquad\qquad -q_1 \\
e_{21}v_1+e_{22}v_2+e_{23}v_3+e_{24}v_4 &= 0b_1+0b_2-0q_1+x_2(\max).
\end{aligned}$$

Reduction to canonical form with respect to the optimal set of processes generates the following linear output function:

$$x_2 = \bar{e}_{21}z_1 + \bar{e}_{22}z_2 - \bar{t}x_1.$$

As usual, the coefficients, which are the dual variables, remain constant so long as the solution remains feasible. In any specific problem parametric linear programming will determine appropriate ratios for z_1, z_2, and x_1, within which an optimal solution remains feasible. Parametric techniques will also generate the complete piecewise-linear output function. With the other variables held constant, $\bar{e}_{21}$ is the rate of change of x_2 with respect to z_1 and $\bar{e}_{22}$ is the rate of change of x_2 with respect to z_2. Thus, $\bar{e}_{21}$ and $\bar{e}_{22}$ are the marginal productivities of the first and second inputs, respectively, in the production of the second output.[1]

With both inputs fixed the output function becomes

$$x_2 = -\bar{t}x_1 + (\bar{e}_{21}b_1 + \bar{e}_{22}b_2).$$

The equation plots as a downward-sloping straight line in output space and determines one segment of the product transformation curve or efficiency frontier, whose slope is $-\bar{t}$. As in previous cases, $\bar{t}$ is the rate of product transformation, the amount of x_2 that must be given up to permit a unit increase in x_1. The piecewise-linear transformation curve of Figure 11–1a is concave with respect to the origin, and the segments become steeper as x_1 increases. Thus, from segment to segment unit increases in x_1 require successively larger reductions in x_2. The piecewise-linear transformation curve must be concave to the origin; any convex portion would be dominated and would be replaced by a linear combination of extreme vectors.

There is an alternative criterion of technological efficiency, minimizing the use of one input subject to constant levels for the remaining input and both outputs. Readers may set up the appropriate problem with greater than or equal constraints for q_1, q_2, and $-b_1$, and with z_2 as the variable to be minimized. Reduction to canonical form with respect to an optimal solution yields the following function:

$$z_2 = \bar{a}_{21}x_1 + \bar{a}_{22}x_2 - \bar{s}z_1.$$

The coefficients of x_1 and x_2 are the marginal requirements of those products

[1]We have been following the general practice of using the symbol e for the rate of change of an output with respect to an input and the symbol a for the rate of change of an input with respect to an output. A bar above a symbol indicates that it is not an original datum but the result of the computations reducing the problem to canonical form. In Chapter 5, $\bar{e}_{21}$ and $\bar{e}_{22}$ appeared as productivity coefficients in the constraints. Now they are marginal productivities in the objective form. To avoid an excessive proliferation of symbols we are counting on the context to make the meaning clear.

for the second input. With x_1 and x_2 held constant, the input function becomes the following equation of a straight line in input space:

$$z_2 = -\bar{s}z_1 + (\bar{a}_{21}q_1 + \bar{a}_{22}q_2).$$

The line is one segment of the input substitution curve, whose slope is $-\bar{s}$. As before, $\bar{s}$ is the rate of input substitution or the rate of technical substitution. When z_1 increases by one unit, $\bar{s}$ measures the amount by which z_2 can be reduced without affecting the level of either product. The piecewise-linear input substitution contour of Figure 11–1b is convex to the origin, becoming flatter as z_1 increases. Thus, from segment to segment substitution of z_1 for z_2 becomes increasingly more difficult as z_2 declines; successive unit increases in z_1 replace smaller amounts of z_2. Piecewise-linear substitution contours must be convex to the origin, since concave portions would be dominated by linear combinations of extreme vectors.

The input and output functions cannot contain conflicting information, and they must always contain precisely the same information except when inputs go slack or outputs become surplus. When slack does not appear in the solution, an input obviously cannot be producing the maximum output

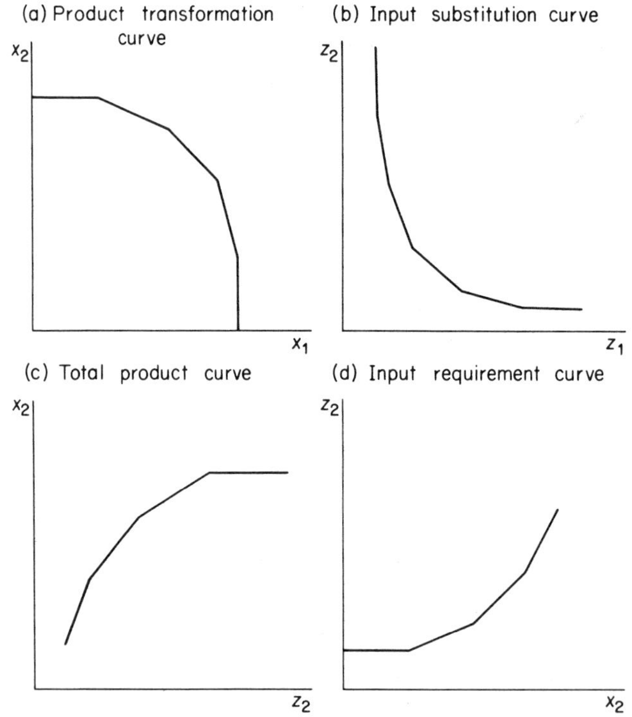

Fig. 11-1 The Linear Version of a Multiproduct Firm

if the amount of the input can be reduced without affecting the output level. For a given combination of inputs, the technological maximizing problem yields optimal output levels. We may then choose the pair of optimal output levels and solve the technological minimizing problem. The original input combination must be one solution to this technological minimizing problem, provided that slack or surplus variables do not appear in the solutions to the respective problems. So long as the second input does not go slack, its marginal productivity $\bar{e}_{22}$ will not be zero. We can divide the output function by $\bar{e}_{22}$ and rewrite it in the following way as an input function:

$$z_2 = -\frac{\bar{e}_{21}}{\bar{e}_{22}}z_1 + \frac{1}{\bar{e}_{22}}x_2 + \frac{\bar{t}}{\bar{e}_{22}}x_1.$$

Since the two forms of the input function must contain identical information, the coefficients of each variable must be equal. Hence,

$$-\bar{s} = -\frac{\bar{e}_{21}}{\bar{e}_{22}} \qquad \bar{a}_{22} = \frac{1}{\bar{e}_{22}}.$$

The rate of input substitution equals the ratio of the marginal productivities of the two inputs in producing the second output. Also, as expected, the marginal requirement of the second product for the second input is the reciprocal of the corresponding marginal productivity.

So long as the second product is not being overproduced ($\bar{a}_{22} \neq 0$), the original input function can be converted to the following explicit output function:

$$x_2 = -\frac{\bar{a}_{21}}{\bar{a}_{22}}x_1 + \frac{1}{\bar{a}_{22}}z_2 + \frac{\bar{s}}{\bar{a}_{22}}z_1.$$

Equating corresponding coefficients gives

$$-\bar{t} = -\frac{\bar{a}_{21}}{\bar{a}_{22}}.$$

The rate of product transformation is the ratio of the marginal requirements of the first and second products for the second input.

The original decisions to maximize x_2 rather than x_1 and to minimize z_2 rather than z_1 are arbitrary. We can reformulate the technological optimizing problems to maximize x_1 or to minimize z_1. Solving the alternative problems yields the following output and input functions:

$$x_1 = \bar{e}_{11}z_1 + \bar{e}_{12}z_2 - \frac{1}{\bar{t}}x_2$$

$$z_1 = \bar{a}_{11}x_1 + \bar{a}_{12}x_2 - \frac{1}{\bar{s}}z_2.$$

Both output functions and both input functions must contain the same information when neither input goes slack and neither output becomes surplus. Graphically, a point on the transformation curve represents both the maximum vertical distance and the maximum horizontal distance from the axes, except when the point lies on a horizontal or vertical segment. If x_1 is not maximized, a whole sloping segment can be moved to the right. But in moving to the right, it also moves upward. When either x_1 or x_2 is maximized, both are, and the segment cannot be shifted. A similar argument holds for inputs except that the distances are minimal. If the first input does not go slack and the first output does not become surplus, we can divide the output function by $\bar{e}_{11}$, the input function by $\bar{a}_{11}$, and equate the matching coefficients as follows:

$$\frac{1}{\bar{s}} = \frac{\bar{e}_{12}}{\bar{e}_{11}} \qquad \bar{a}_{11} = \frac{1}{\bar{e}_{11}} \qquad \frac{1}{\bar{t}} = \frac{\bar{a}_{12}}{\bar{a}_{11}}.$$

The full conditions for technological efficiency can be summarized in either of the following equivalent ways:

$$\bar{s} = \frac{\bar{e}_{21}}{\bar{e}_{22}} = \frac{\bar{e}_{11}}{\bar{e}_{12}} \qquad \text{or} \qquad \bar{t} = \frac{\bar{a}_{21}}{\bar{a}_{22}} = \frac{\bar{a}_{11}}{\bar{a}_{12}}.$$

Technological efficiency requires that marginal productivities of the inputs have the same ratio in the production of both outputs. Alternatively, both products must have marginal requirements for the two inputs that form the same ratio. Each condition implies the other:

$$\frac{\bar{e}_{21}}{\bar{e}_{22}} = \frac{\bar{e}_{11}}{\bar{e}_{12}} \qquad \text{implies} \qquad \frac{\bar{e}_{21}}{\bar{e}_{11}} = \frac{\bar{e}_{22}}{\bar{e}_{12}} \qquad \text{or} \qquad \frac{\bar{a}_{11}}{\bar{a}_{12}} = \frac{\bar{a}_{21}}{\bar{a}_{22}}.$$

Readers need to keep in mind that the second subscript on an $\bar{e}$ coefficient refers to an input but the second subscript on an $\bar{a}$ coefficient refers to an output. Hence,

$$\bar{e}_{21} = \frac{1}{\bar{a}_{12}} \qquad \text{and} \qquad \bar{e}_{12} = \frac{1}{\bar{a}_{21}}.$$

The conditions for technological efficiency have a highly plausible explanation. When the marginal input requirements have the same ratio for both products, the inputs freed by a reduction in one product can be fully absorbed by the other product. If the ratios are not equal, one of the inputs can only be partially reabsorbed and goes slack. Similarly, with equal ratios of marginal productivities, an increase in one input can fully restore the reduction in both output levels caused by a decrease in the other input. Hence, along an input substitution contour both output levels can be maintained merely by interchanging units of inputs. When the two inputs do not have the same ratio of marginal productivities, the firm can obtain constant levels of both products only by overproducing one product and disposing of the surplus.

Maximizing x_2 for a given level of x_1 can never yield the vertical segment on the transformation curve. The only way to generate the vertical segment is to set low levels for x_2, maximize x_1, and dispose of the excess amounts of x_2. Similarly, the vertical segment of the substitution curve requires that z_1 be minimized for high levels of z_2, part of which is not used. The essential portion of the technological information relates output quotas exactly met to input levels fully utilized. There are four alternative technological optimizing problems. For the central or essential portions of either the product transformation curve or the input substitution contour the firm can solve any one of the four problems. The solutions to each remaining problem merely fill in a missing horizontal or vertical segment.

Readers may question whether slack and surplus processes really belong among the technological processes. For an answer, consider the technological maximizing problem in which specified amounts of the inputs are available and the firm seeks from these inputs the largest amount of one output for a constant amount of the other. If it is technologically possible to use less than the full amount of an input, choosing a slack process is one of the options open to the firm. The only productive process that can use fully the available inputs may be highly inefficient, or there simply may not be any such process. The firm may well be better off letting part of the input go idle and using the rest very efficiently. Alternatively, the management may find that it gets the maximum amount of x_2 by using the inputs fully, overproducing x_1, and costlessly disposing of the surplus. To make these decisions the firm needs only technological information and not economic data.

The preceding paragraph introduces a possibility that we shall consider briefly and then drop. As the prescribed level for x_1 decreases, very low quotas must ultimately be met by disposing of the surplus costlessly and adding a horizontal segment to the product transformation curve. But before the horizontal segment appears the firm may meet low quotas for x_1 by letting one of the inputs go partially idle. Hence, a slack process for an input may appear in the optimal solution and contribute a sloping segment to the product transformation curve. Similarly, overproducing may be the better way of using an excess input, and a disposal process may contribute a downward-sloping segment to an input substitution contour. As the number of processes increases, these possibilities are much less important and the introduction of economic data makes a further substantial reduction in their significance. We can, then, with little loss of generality assume that the downward-sloping segments of both curves correspond to exact fulfillment of output quotas and full utilization of both inputs.

The output and input functions also provide two additional diagrams. When x_1 and z_1 are the quantities held constant, the output function for x_2 becomes

$$x_2 = \bar{e}_{22}z_2+(\bar{e}_{21}b_1-\bar{t}q_1).$$

The equation plots as the piecewise-linear total product curve of Figure 11–1c. With q_1 fixed, z_2 cannot be reduced to zero. The output function results from the maximization of x_2, so a disposal process for x_2 cannot appear in the optimal solution, and the graph begins at positive levels for both z_2 and x_2. Since b_1 is fixed, large amounts of z_2 go partially unused and the final segment is horizontal. Alternatively, we may use the input function,

$$z_2 = \bar{a}_{22}x_2+(\bar{a}_{21}q_1-\bar{s}b_1),$$

which plots as the piecewise-linear input requirement curve of Figure 11–1d. The fixity of b_1 sets an upper limit to the production of x_2. Since z_2 is being minimized, the curve ends in a point rather than continuing vertically upward.

SMOOTHING THE OUTPUT AND INPUT FUNCTIONS

With a single product and two inputs, the isoproduct contours lie in two-dimensional space and consist of the pieces or segments cut from lines by the cones of adjacent, undominated rays or processes. When one output depends on the level of the other output as well as upon the amounts of the two inputs, the isoproduct contours for one output lie in three-dimensional space. They are formed in a strictly analogous way from the triangular pieces cut from planes by the cones that are generated by *three* adjacent, undominated rays or processes. The technique of smoothing the piecewise-linear surface is essentially the same; into every cone formed by three adjacent rays we insert an intermediate process that dominates their linear combination and only their linear combination. If we imagine a balloon stretched tightly over a surface composed of triangular pieces, the procedure is to inflate the balloon into a smooth surface while keeping it fixed at the vertices. Smoothness requires first that there be a tangent plane at every point, that is, that there be no corners or cusps. Second, the tangent plane must turn smoothly, without lurches, along any curve on the surface.

The resultant smooth output function can be expressed in general functional notation as

$$x_2 = f_2(x_1, z_1, z_2).$$

Having been derived from linear processes, the function retains the property of linear homogeneity. If x_1, z_1, and z_2 all change proportionately, then x_2

changes in the same proportion. The same method of smoothing also yields input functions, such as

$$z_2 = g_2(z_1, x_1, x_2).$$

When the output and input functions are smoothed, so are all the two-dimensional diagrams derived from the functions. Figure 11–2 shows the results of smoothing each of the four piecewise-linear contours.

As in the piecewise-linear case, each of the four possible output or input functions must contain all essential information on productive processes. At the very most, the functions can differ only with respect to slack or disposal processes. We are assuming that any positive ratio of outputs, however small, can be produced and that any positive ratio of inputs, however small, can be fully utilized. If the products are truly joint, neither can be produced alone. The smooth version of the product transformation curve, as drawn, becomes horizontal and vertical as it reaches the axes. If there are efficient processes that turn out each product separately, the contour will have a negative slope as it reaches the axes. Also, whenever the products must be jointly produced and there is a lower limit to their ratio, horizontal and

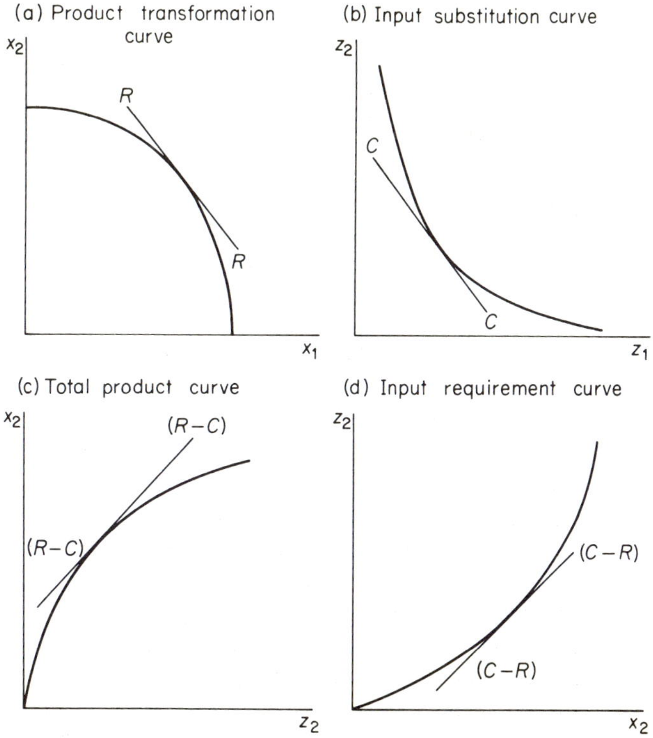

Fig. 11-2 The Smooth Version of a Multiproduct Firm

vertical segments representing disposal fill out the contour. A transformation contour could also slope upward at the axes if disposal is not costless.

When inputs are jointly required and any positive ratio, however small, can be fully employed, the input substitution contours approach but do not touch the axes. Readers may work out the conditions under which these contours either intersect the axes or have terminal linear segments. Under the assumptions we have made, slack and disposal processes have negligible effects. Except at the axes, any one of the four functions contains all essential information and can be used to derive all diagrams.

In the process of smoothing, cones shrink to rays, and the rays retain all essential properties. The most important result is that there is a linear output function for each ray in the three-dimensional space. Whenever x_1, z_1, and z_2 change proportionately, the second product has the following linear function:

$$x_2 = \bar{e}_{21}z_1 + \bar{e}_{22}z_2 - \bar{t}x_1.$$

The coefficients remain constant so long as z_1, z_2, and x_1 stay on the same ray in three-dimensional space, but they vary from ray to ray. A smooth function that is homogeneous of the first degree is essentially an infinite collection of linear functions, each one of which is valid for a specified ratio of the independent variables.

With only a single product, there is an input substitution curve for every level at which it is held constant. When there are two products both must be held constant to generate an input substitution contour. As both outputs vary proportionately, the input substitution contour shifts but retains the same slope along every ray. Linear homogeneity accounts for this result. Thus, as outputs vary along a ray in output space, they generate an entire map of parallel input substitution contours. The difficulty is that every ratio of outputs, or ray in output space, generates a different map of input substitution contours. The input substitution contours for one ratio of outputs interesect those drawn for different ratios. There is a whole infinite collection of isoproduct maps superimposed on each other in input space.

To demonstrate how the different maps are related, we choose a point in input space. The given combination of inputs generates an entire product transformation curve in output space. In turn, every point on the transformation curve, or pair of output levels, generates an entire input substitution contour. Thus, the initial point in input space gives rise to a curve or infinite set of points in output space, which in turn generate a whole infinite family of input substitution contours. Every contour in the infinite family must pass through the initially chosen point in input space. If an output pair is a solution to the technological maximizing problem, the corresponding input combination must be a solution to the technological minimizing problem. The conclusion holds so long as slack or disposal processes do not appear in the solutions. The pattern is now clear. Through every point in input space there passes a whole infinite family of input substitution contours. Each contour corresponds to one point on the unique product transformation curve that the input combination generates. A symmetrical conclusion holds for points in output space.

Adding a single output or a single input to earlier models complicates the geometric exposition. The solution to the technological optimizing problem no longer partitions output space or input space into a single set of nonintersecting curves. The technological possibilities are too varied to be displayed adequately by two-dimensional diagrams. For reasonably simple diagrams we must also use economic data to derive isocost contours in output space or isorevenue contours in input space.

ISOCOST AND ISOREVENUE CONTOURS

With both inputs fixed, there is a single product transformation curve enclosing the set of feasible outputs. The objective of the firm, to maximize revenue on the feasible set, is achieved at the point of tangency of the revenue line $R = p_1 x_1 + p_2 x_2$ with the transformation curve, as depicted in Figure 11–2a. Tangency implies that

$$\frac{\bar{a}_{21}}{\bar{a}_{22}} = \frac{p_1}{p_2} = \frac{\bar{a}_{11}}{\bar{a}_{12}}.$$

The two equalities can be rewritten as

$$\frac{p_2}{\bar{a}_{22}} = \frac{p_1}{\bar{a}_{21}}, \quad \frac{p_2}{\bar{a}_{12}} = \frac{p_1}{\bar{a}_{11}} \qquad \text{or} \qquad p_2 \bar{e}_{22} = p_1 \bar{e}_{12}, \quad p_2 \bar{e}_{21} = p_1 \bar{e}_{11}.$$

Thus, maximum revenue implies that the second input has the same marginal revenue productivity in the production of both products, and a similar condition holds for the first input. Shifting an input increases one output and decreases the other, changing their ratio. The product mix is optimal when, as above, the rate at which revenue increases for one product exactly matches the rate at which it decreases for the other.

With inputs variable, the previously chosen optimal pair of outputs can be produced by any combination of inputs on an entire input substitution contour. Cost is minimized, as shown in Figure 11–2b, at the point of tangency of the cost line $C = c_1 z_1 + c_2 z_2$ with the input substitution contour. Equality of slopes implies that

$$\frac{\bar{e}_{21}}{\bar{e}_{22}} = \frac{c_1}{c_2} = \frac{\bar{e}_{11}}{\bar{e}_{12}}.$$

The two equalities can be rewritten as

$$\frac{c_2}{\bar{e}_{22}} = \frac{c_1}{\bar{e}_{21}}, \quad \frac{c_2}{\bar{e}_{12}} = \frac{c_1}{\bar{e}_{11}} \qquad \text{or} \qquad c_2\bar{a}_{22} = c_1\bar{a}_{12}, \quad c_2\bar{a}_{21} = c_1\bar{a}_{11}.$$

Thus, minimal cost implies that each product has the same marginal input cost in terms of both inputs. The firm cannot reduce cost by altering the input mix. The rate at which cost declines upon withdrawal of one input matches exactly the rate at which it rises with increasing use of the other input.

With inputs and outputs both variable, the two conditions for optimality must hold simultaneously. The originally chosen input combination must be the cost minimizing combination for the revenue maximizing output pair. We can show both conditions on one diagram by first deriving the isorevenue map in input space or the isocost map in output space.

With output prices constant but outputs variable, the firm can solve a revenue maximization problem. In its linear form the model of the present chapter contains four revenue yielding processes subject to two input constraints. It does not differ in any essential way from the model of Chapter 8. Maximizing revenue and letting the inputs vary parametrically generates an entire piecewise-linear isorevenue map in input space, which can then be smoothed. Reduction to canonical form yields the revenue function $R = y_1z_1+y_2z_2$. The coefficients of the inputs, their marginal revenue productivities, remain constant within cones in input space, or along rays after smoothing. Similarly, with input prices given the present model sets up as a cost minimizing problem in the form of Chapter 10. The resultant cost function $C = w_1x_1+w_2x_2$ plots as an isocost map in output space. The coefficients of the outputs, their marginal costs, remain constant within cones or along rays after smoothing.

Before proceeding, we need to clarify the relationship between product transformation curves, which intersect, and isocost contours, which do not. When input prices are constant all input combinations that can be purchased at a given cost lie on a cost line in input space. Each input combination on that line can be used with a different selection of processes to produce a variety of output pairs. Some of these output pairs will be inferior to other output pairs in that one product can be increased with the other constant. Maximizing one output with the other constant eliminates inefficient output pairs and generates the product transformation curve as the outer boundary of the outputs producible by a given input combination.

Every point on the cost line in input space generates its own product transformation curve. Further, every output pair on every one of these curves uses inputs that have the same cost. Some of these output pairs will be inferior to others in that one output can be increased with the other constant. To eliminate inefficient uses of a given *value* of inputs we can maximize one output subject to a constant level of the other and to a constant input cost.

Letting the remaining output vary parametrically generates the outer boundary of the set of outputs producible at given cost. Previously we have found the cost function and isocost contours by minimizing cost for prescribed output levels. The results must coincide. Minimizing cost for given output levels and maximizing output for a given cost level both require the choice of the most efficient processes.

When a firm is not restricted to a single input combination but can choose any point on an entire line segment, it cannot be worse off and is very likely to be better off. As Exercise 1 at the end of the chapter confirms for the linear model, product transformation curves must be inside the isocost contour and generally have only a single point or vertex lying on the contour. In general, each output pair on the isocost contour requires a different input combination to produce it with least cost.

In the smooth version there is a single process for each combination of inputs. Linear combinations of other processes can also use the same amounts of the inputs but will yield different output pairs. The totality of such linear combinations generates the smooth version of a product transformation curve. When the firm can vary input combinations along the cost line, it chooses for each combination the single most efficient process and not a linear combination of processes. Thus, as Figure 11–3 shows, each product transformation curve is tangent to the isocost contour at the point that corresponds to the use of the single most efficient process. The isocost contour is an envelope curve similar to the long-run total cost curve. It furnishes another illustration of the principle that an optimum subject to more con-

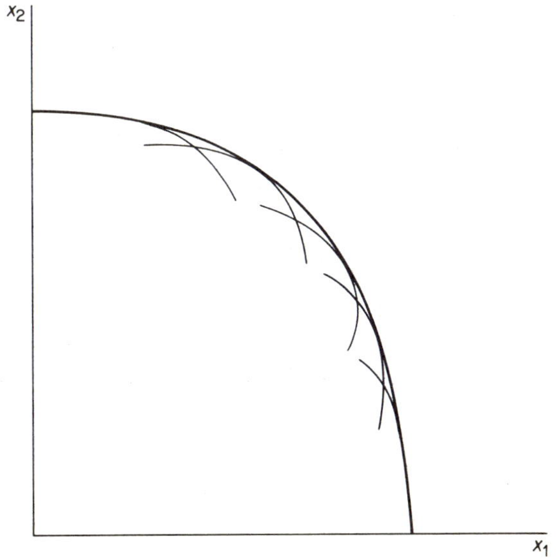

Fig. 11-3 The Isocost Contour as an Envelope Curve

straints or more stringent constraints cannot be better than an optimum subject to fewer or less stringent constraints. A strictly analogous relationship exists between input substitution curves and an isorevenue contour.

As cost varies with input prices constant, each cost line in input space generates a different isocost contour in output space. Under linear homogeneity these contours must be parallel. As inputs vary along a ray in input space their marginal productivities remain constant and they generate a family of parallel product transformation curves. When a cost line intersects a ray in input space, the corresponding isocost contour is tangent to the corresponding product transformation curve. With both input prices and marginal productivities constant, the marginal cost of the outputs does not vary and the slope of the isocost contours does not change. Hence, the family of parallel cost lines in input space gives rise to a family of parallel isocost contours in output space. Analogously, the family of parallel revenue lines in output space gives rise to a family of parallel isorevenue contours in input space.

THE ECONOMIC OPTIMIZING PROBLEM

Figure 11–4a shows the double requirement for optimality. Cost must be minimized on the set of all input combinations that yield revenue equaling or exceeding some specified amount. Hence, the cost line $C = c_1 z_1 + c_2 z_2$ must be tangent to an isorevenue contour. Since the slope of a contour is the negative ratio of the marginal revenue productivities, equality of slopes implies

$$\frac{c_1}{c_2} = \frac{y_1}{y_2} = \frac{p_2 \bar{e}_{21}}{p_2 \bar{e}_{22}} = \frac{p_1 \bar{e}_{11}}{p_1 \bar{e}_{12}}.$$

Input prices and marginal revenue productivities must form the same ratio. Also, by canceling prices in the final two ratios, we can show that the same condition holds for the marginal productivities. Hence, the cost line is tangent to an input substitution contour, as required.

Alternatively, we may first minimize cost for given output levels and generate the isocost map in output space. Revenue must then be maximized on the set of all output pairs whose cost does not exceed a specified amount (Figure 11–4b). Tangency of the revenue line $R = p_1 x_1 + p_2 x_2$ to an isocost contour implies

$$\frac{p_1}{p_2} = \frac{w_1}{w_2} = \frac{c_2 \bar{a}_{21}}{c_2 \bar{a}_{22}} = \frac{c_1 \bar{a}_{11}}{c_1 \bar{a}_{12}}.$$

Readers may show that the two sets of optimizing conditions are equivalent, that each can be derived from the other. Since the conditions are equivalent, the solution of either problem identifies both an optimal ray in output space and an optimal ray in input space. The firm has determined the optimal ratio in which outputs are to be produced and the optimal ratio in which inputs are to be employed in their production. What the firm has not yet determined is the optimal point on either ray, or the most profitable scale of operation.

We turn now to the question of the most profitable scale of operation. Since the output function is linearly homogeneous, maximization converts revenue to a linear function of the inputs, $R = p_2\bar{e}_{21}z_1 + p_2\bar{e}_{22}z_2$, which holds along a ray. With input prices constant, total cost also increases linearly along rays. The difference between revenue and cost, if positive, grows without limit. The difficulty, which we encountered earlier, is inherent in linearly homogeneous functions. To circumvent it we again assume that the marginal productivities first increase then decrease along rays but always maintain the same ratio to each other. As the scale of operations increases along the optimal input ray, total revenue first rises at an increasing rate, and the curve bends upward. After a point of inflection revenue continues to rise but at a decreasing rate, and the curve bends downward (Figure 11–4c). Along the optimal ray the ratio of the marginal revenue productivities remains constant and equal to the ratio of the input prices. Hence, if one input is adding more to revenue than it costs, so is the other. The largest vertical difference between revenue and cost, or the most profitable scale of operation occurs

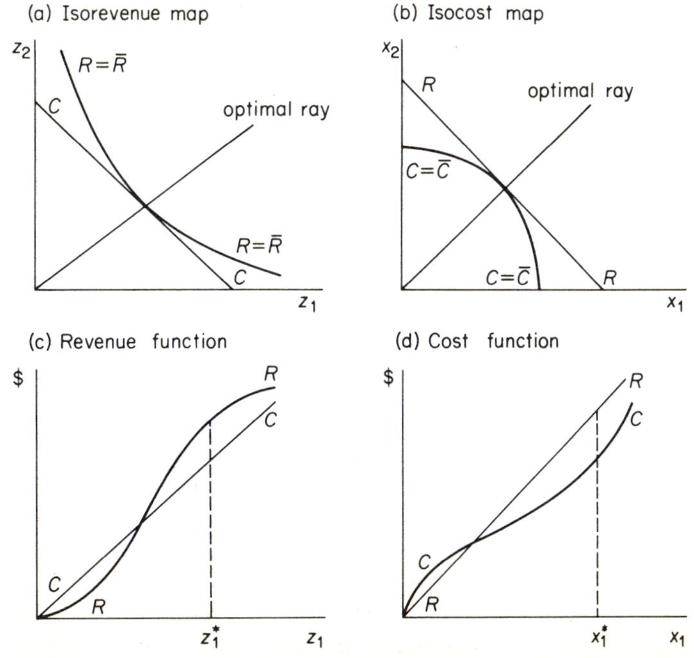

Fig. 11-4 The Full Conditions for Optimality

when the marginal revenue productivity of each input falls into equality with its constant market price.

We may use instead the isocost map in output space. The solution to the cost minimizing problem generates the following cost function:

$$C = w_1 x_1 + w_2 x_2 = c_2 \bar{a}_{21} x_1 + c_2 \bar{a}_{22} x_2.$$

Along the optimal ray both marginal input requirements first decrease and then increase, but always maintain a constant ratio. The total cost curve first rises at a decreasing rate, bending downward, and then at an increasing rate, bending upward (Figure 11–4d). The largest vertical difference between revenue and cost, or the most profitable scale of operation, occurs when the marginal cost of each output rises into equality with its market price. But, $p_2 = c_2 \bar{a}_{22}$ implies $p_2/\bar{a}_{22} = p_2 \bar{e}_{22} = c_2$. Equality between marginal cost and output price implies equality between marginal revenue productivity and input price, and conversely. Since similar relations hold between all inputs and all outputs, the two sets of conditions for optimal scale are equivalent.

The full requirements for a maximum of net revenue take a familiar form: marginal revenue productivity must equal market price for each input or marginal cost must equal market price for each output. Either set of equalities implies all the subsidiary conditions for optimality derived earlier in the chapter. But these subsidiary conditions, taken together, are also sufficient to determine the most profitable scale of operation. Equality of marginal revenue productivities and input prices obviously implies tangency of the cost line to an isorevenue contour, but tangency in turn combines two separate conditions of optimality. The revenue line must be tangent to a product transformation curve, as in Figure 11–2a, selecting the optimal output mix. At the same time the input combination (z_1^*, z_2^*) that generates the transformation curve must also be the cost minimizing combination. Hence, the input substitution contour for the optimal output pair (x_1^*, x_2^*) must be tangent to the cost line at (z_1^*, z_2^*).

With optimal ratios determined for both inputs and outputs, the firm needs only to find the optimal amount of one input or one output. The total product curve for z_2 in terms of x_2 (Figure 11–2c) provides a solution. With $x_1 = x_1^*$ and $z_1 = z_1^*$, the firm seeks the maximum difference between the revenue from x_2 and the cost of z_2. Net revenue, $NR = p_2 x_2 - c_2 z_2$, attains its maximum at the point of tangency with the total product curve, whose slope is $\bar{e}_{22}$. The slope of the net revenue line is c_2/p_2, so tangency implies $\bar{e}_{22} = c_2/p_2$ or $p_2 \bar{e}_{22} = c_2$. The firm has attained the most profitable scale of operations if the marginal revenue productivity equals the input price when $z_2 = z_2^*$, which is its value on the optimal ray. The input requirement curve (Figure 11–2d) provides an alternative condition for optimality.

When one input is constant, say z_2, the firm is confined to a horizontal line on the isorevenue map. Only when the horizontal input line crosses the optimal ray is the firm able to employ the optimal input mix. The short-run total revenue curve lies everywhere below the long-run curve except at one point. For every assigned value of z_2 there is a different short-run curve, but only when $z_2 = z_2^*$ is the firm able in the short run to attain the full long-run equilibrium. Similar relationships exist between the long-run and short-run total cost curves.

The ultimate goal in formulating any economic model of the firm is to predict how the firm will respond to changing conditions, especially variations in market prices. To obtain this information and summarize it in demand and supply curves we must first find the optimum under the specified conditions and then let the selected market price vary parametrically. When a model contains many variables, there will be a variety of demand curves for each input and of supply curves for each output, depending on the specific combination of variables held constant. For example, in deriving the long-run demand curve for z_2, we let the quantities of all inputs and outputs vary but hold their prices constant. In the short run, the quantity of z_1 is held constant rather than its price, but we also have to decide whether the quantity of each output is constant or its price. Demand and supply curves result from the conceptual experiment of varying a single price to the firm and observing the results under carefully specified conditions. In mathematical models of the firm we use the technique of constrained optimization followed by parametric variation. The technique of deriving demand and supply curves remains constant from model to model but the specific results do not.

Under still more general technological possibilities, not even the ratio of marginal productivities need be constant along rays. The firm cannot avail itself of the simplifications and guidelines developed earlier in the chapter. It cannot first select the optimal output and input mixes and then identify the optimal point on either ray. Management has to consider simultaneously all combinations of outputs and inputs as possible candidates for the optimal solution. Fortunately, the conditions for maximum net revenue remain the same, equality between marginal revenue productivity and price for each input or equality between marginal cost and price for each output. The requirements for optimality can also be displayed geometrically by simultaneous tangency between: a cost line and an input substitution contour; a revenue line and a product transformation curve; a net revenue line and a total product curve. Although the requirements for an optimal solution remain the same, the possibility of finding a solution diminishes greatly as generality increases. Computational methods are available only under very specific conditions.

The economic theory of the firm strives for the greatest possible generality. It avoids being tied down to specific technological conditions or to particular computational methods. As noted earlier, the theory does rest on optimization and must assume that the technological conditions do permit the firm to attain an optimum. The technology must be such that revenue increases along rays in input space and ultimately at a decreasing rate. All curves between pairs of variables must display the same general pattern of convexity and concavity as the four diagrams of Figure 11–2.

A MULTIPLANT, MULTIPRODUCT FIRM

Chapter 8 investigated a single-product firm with two plants, each of which had a separate fixed input. There was, in addition, a third input, fixed in amount for the firm but shared by the plants. The optimal allocation between plants occurred when the marginal productivity of the input in one plant passed through a vertical gap in the marginal productivity curve for the other plant. When both curves are smoothed, intersection, or equal levels of the marginal productivity determine the optimal division between plants. The decision rests on technological grounds alone; prices are not needed. If each plant produces a different product, then output prices are needed to allocate the shared input between plants.

We shall consider briefly a firm with two plants, each of which turns out the same two products jointly. There are two inputs, fixed for the firm but shared by the plants. To concentrate on the main issue we assume initially that these are the only two inputs. Each plant has its own set of productive processes, but the objective of the firm is to allocate the available inputs optimally to the productive processes, regardless of the plant in which they operate. The model does not differ essentially from the single-plant version developed earlier in the chapter.

In the production of any one output, an input must have the same marginal productivity in each plant. Otherwise the firm could shift the input between plants and obtain more of that one output without sacrificing any units of the other output. When a plant receives an allotment of inputs, it must employ those inputs in such a way that the ratio of the marginal productivities is the same in both products. Only under this condition is one output maximized for a given level of the other. The two conditions together imply that both inputs must have the same ratio of marginal productivities in both products everywhere throughout the firm. Any distribution of inputs among plants that satisfies both conditions determines one point on the product transformation curve for the firm. There are many such points, so technological conditions alone are not sufficient to determine the allocation of inputs among plants. Output prices are needed to determine optimal output levels and fix the allocation of inputs among plants.

To see why technological optimization does not determine allocation uniquely, we can use the device of assigning the shared inputs to one plant in all possible ways. A plant no longer has a unique marginal productivity curve for an input but a different curve for each assigned amount of the other input. There are many points of intersection between many pairs of curves for the two plants. When each plant has its own fixed input, diminishing returns set in as larger amounts of the shared inputs are assigned to one plant. The shape of the product transformation curve for the firm changes, but the general results remain the same. At each point on the curve nothing can be gained by shifting the shared inputs between plants.

SUMMARY AND GENERALIZATION

We have at long last developed a general model of the multiproduct, multi-input firm, so it is a convenient point to review the basic assumptions and the analytic techniques on which the model rests. Readers are by now well aware that essentially the same analytical or mathematical technique has been applied in every situation. An optimum is found by initially holding some quantity or quantities constant. The quantity or quantities are then varied parametrically, which is equivalent to the conceptual experiment of assigning different amounts successively to the firm and observing the optimal solutions. Virtually every curve in the linear or conventional version of the firm is derived by this technique. For linear models the simplex method can be used to find an initial optimum, and parametric programming techniques can be employed to generate the appropriate piecewise-linear or step functions that portray the successive optimal solutions as parameters vary. Within the calculus there is a similar technique for locating the initial optimal solution and tracing the response of the optimal quantities to changes in parameters. The smooth curves customarily drawn for the firm are all based on this technique of parametric variation.

In every linear programming problem, optimization converts the objective form to a linear function of the quantities held constant, with the dual variables serving as the coefficients. The dual variables are thus the rates of change of the quantity being optimized with respect to the quantities held constant initially. When the quantity optimized is money, as in the maximization of revenue, the dual variables have the dimensions of dollars over physical units and are often interpreted as prices. All prices, even market prices, are rates of change. The special feature about market prices or rates of exchange is that they are rates of change of a quantity possessed by one economic unit with respect to a quantity possessed by another unit external to the first. It is often convenient to treat changes within an economic unit as if they were fictitious exchanges between distinct units. Hence, the term internal price or shadow price is often used to designate rates of change within a unit.

Exchange between distinct economic units need not involve money but may be simply the trading of one commodity for another at a given rate of exchange or real price. Hence, the coefficients of the inputs in the output function, which we have called marginal physical productivities, are also internal real prices of the inputs in terms of the output being maximized. They are the rates at which inputs can be exchanged for the designated output in the course of production. Similar interpretations as real prices can be given to the marginal input requirements, the rate of product transformation, and the rate of input substitution.

It is not merely linear programming that generates rates of change of the objective variable with respect to the quantities under constraint; every method of optimization subject to constraints has the same result. In the conventional theory of the firm, based on the differential calculus, the mathematical term Lagrange multiplier is used rather than dual variable, but the meaning is the same. Thus, both marginal cost and marginal revenue productivity are generated by the optimization process as Lagrange multipliers, which are also interpreted as internal prices. There is, however, a difference between the two cases in that the dual variables remain constant within a cone, permitting the ratio of quantities to vary without altering their internal prices. With smooth functions that are homogeneous of the first degree, each set of internal prices is valid only along a ray. As the input or output functions become still more general, each set of internal prices holds only for a point in input space or a point in output space.

Internal prices are a very useful device for summarizing the optimizing decisions of the firm. Input minimization generates the condition for optimality that the ratio of marginal input requirements be identical for both products. But a marginal input requirement is simply the real price of an output in terms of an input. Thus, optimality requires that both products have the same ratio of real prices in terms of the two inputs. Similarly, output maximization depends on both inputs having the same ratio of real prices in terms of the two outputs. The situation is rather like a barter economy in which there is no money to serve as a common unit of value. Real prices may be defined in terms of any commodity whose rate of exchange for each of the remaining commodities is never zero.

When market or external prices are available, showing the rate of exchange of an input or output for money, the objective of the firm can be summarized as the maximization or minimization of a money sum. If revenue is to be maximized, the various outputs contribute to that objective in proportion to their market prices. Thus, the market prices measure the relative weight or relative value to be assigned to the outputs in the attainment of the objective. Once monetary prices or relative weights are assigned to the outputs, the optimization process derives imputed or internal monetary prices for the inputs, which also represent relative weights for the inputs in the attainment of the objective. For future use, we note that the significant condition is not necessarily the availability of monetary prices but rather the assignment of relative weights in terms of a common standard.

Revenue maximization requires that fixed inputs have the same internal monetary price in all uses. If a fixed input has a different value in the production of two outputs, the input must be shifted from the less valuable to the more valuable use. The firm does this by reshuffling process levels until the input has the same value in both uses. For minimal cost each product must have the same internal monetary price in terms of each input. Otherwise the firm must redistribute the fixed output levels over the inputs. By reshuffling process levels it shifts output from the more costly to the less costly input.

When inputs as well as outputs are freely variable, the criterion for optimality in a smooth model is equality of internal and market prices for each input. Thus, the full or long-run optimum for the firm occurs only when an inflow of resources from the rest of the economy or an outflow of resources from the firm brings the internal prices of inputs into equality with the external prices. When focusing upon a single purely competitive firm, it is an acceptable first approximation to assume market prices are independent of the firm's actions. Hence, the flow of resources is determined solely by adjustment of internal prices. Attention must be given later to the determination of market prices and the process of adjustment throughout the whole economy. An alternative criterion for the long-run optimum is that the internal and external prices be equal for all products. The flow of products from the firm to the economy is expanded or contracted depending on whether long-run marginal cost falls short of or exceeds market price.

Coming chapters are casting their shadows before them. Initially we sought some method for solving the problems of how to use optimally fixed quantities of inputs or how to produce optimally fixed amounts of outputs. We then discovered that the method of optimization generated internal prices which could be used in an alternative or dual explanation of the optimal allocation of resources within a firm. In the economy as a whole, where the external relations among economic units are the focus of attention, prices or rates of exchange are the primary device for guiding the allocation of resources. A crucial question is whether the external price system achieves an allocation of resources that is, in some sense, optimal for the entire economy. This is equivalent to asking whether there is some primal optimizing process that reaches the same solution as the price mechanism. The order in which the two problems arise are reversed when we go from firm to economy. By utilizing both problems and both types of solution, the general topic of allocation of resources, which includes allocation within firms as well as allocation among firms, can be given a unified presentation.

EXERCISES

Unless otherwise specified, the exercises are based on the following numerical example:

$$v_1\begin{bmatrix}1\\2\\1\\9\end{bmatrix}+v_2\begin{bmatrix}3\\2\\12\\3\end{bmatrix}+v_3\begin{bmatrix}2\\2\\4\\8\end{bmatrix}+v_4\begin{bmatrix}7\\2\\27\\3\end{bmatrix}=\begin{bmatrix}x_1\\x_2\\z_1\\z_2\end{bmatrix}.$$

1. *Cost Minimization and Output Maximization*

(a) *Deriving an Isocost Contour*

Choose input prices of $1 each and set up the numerical example as the minimization of total cost for fixed output levels. Adjust each process to a common level of cost, such as 30 or 60, and graph an isocost contour in output space. Also graph the contour for $C = 420$. Reduce to canonical form with respect to (v_2, v_3). Write the equation for the cost function determined by those two processes and the range over which it holds.

(b) *Deriving a Product Transformation Contour*

Write the numerical example in the form shown in the text as the maximization of x_2 for constant levels of z_1, z_2, and x_1. Add slack and surplus variables as required, making sure that the signs are correct. When reduced to canonical form with respect to the first three processes, the left-hand side of the numerical example becomes

$$
\begin{array}{llll}
1v_1 & & -\tfrac{11}{7}v_4+\tfrac{3}{7}v_5+\tfrac{2}{7}v_6+2v_7 = & (z_1) \\
 & 1v_2 & +\tfrac{40}{21}v_4+\tfrac{5}{21}v_5+\tfrac{1}{21}v_6+\tfrac{2}{3}v_7 = & (z_2) \\
 & & 1v_3+\tfrac{10}{7}v_4-\tfrac{4}{7}v_5-\tfrac{3}{14}v_6-\tfrac{5}{2}v_7 = & (-x_1) \\
 & & -\tfrac{32}{21}v_4-\tfrac{4}{21}v_5-\tfrac{5}{21}v_6-\tfrac{1}{3}v_7 = & (x_2).
\end{array}
$$

Does the solution satisfy the conditions for optimality?

Complete the solution by filling in the right-hand side, using the indicated symbols for the quantities and placing each in a separate column. Identify the marginal productivities of the inputs and the rate of production transformation. Write the segment of the output function for x_2.

Set $z_1 = z_2 = 210$ and find the value of x_1 for which each process in the basis reaches zero. Verify that the range of feasibility is $(66 \leqq x_1 \leqq 75)$. Calculate the value of x_2 at each limit of the range.

Determine which process leaves and which process enters when x_1 goes below the lower limit and when it passes the upper limit. For the new solutions the columns of coefficients of the slack and surplus variables are as follows:

Below lower limit			*Above upper limit*		
$-\frac{1}{35}$	$\frac{4}{35}$	0	$-\frac{3}{11}$	$-\frac{2}{11}$	$-\frac{14}{11}$
$\frac{3}{35}$	$-\frac{1}{105}$	0	$\frac{25}{33}$	$\frac{13}{33}$	$\frac{34}{11}$
$\frac{8}{35}$	$\frac{3}{35}$	1	$-\frac{2}{11}$	$\frac{1}{22}$	$-\frac{15}{22}$
$-\frac{4}{35}$	$-\frac{22}{105}$	0	$-\frac{20}{33}$	$-\frac{17}{33}$	$-\frac{25}{11}$

In each case use the coefficients to express the processes in the basis in terms of the quantities on the right. Identify the marginal productivities and the rate of product transformation and write the segment of the output function for x_2. Verify that the respective ranges are $(0 \leqq x_1 \leqq 66)$ and $(75 \leqq x_1 \leqq 78\frac{4}{17})$. Above $x_1 = 78\frac{4}{17}$ the numerical example does not contain any further processes to bring in.

(c) *Relating the Isocost and Product Transformation Contours*

Use the segment of the cost function from (a) to determine where the three vertices of the product transformation curve, just derived in (b), lie in relation to the isocost contour for $C = 420$. Plot the product transformation curve on the isocost map including both disposal processes.

2. *Revenue Maximization and Input Minimization*

(a) *Deriving an Isorevenue Contour*

Choosing output prices of \$1 each, set up the numerical example as a revenue maximizing problem with fixed input constraints. For the cone generated by the second and third processes, derive the equation for the revenue function and the range of input ratios over which it holds. Adjust the processes to a common revenue of \$30 and plot the entire isorevenue contour in input space. Check the slope of the appropriate segment against the slope implied by the revenue function. Also draw in the contour for $R = 140$. What happens to these contours if output prices are raised to $p_1 = p_2 = 3$?

(b) *Deriving an Input Substitution Contour*

Write the numerical example in the form suggested in the text as the minimization of z_2 for constant levels of x_1, x_2, and $-z_1$. Convert the constraints to equalities identifying the added variables as slack or surplus. Reduced to canonical form with respect to the first three processes the left-hand side of the numerical example becomes

$$
\begin{array}{lllr}
1v_1 & & -\tfrac{17}{5}v_4 + \tfrac{8}{5}v_5 - \tfrac{6}{5}v_6 + \tfrac{1}{5}v_7 = & (x_1) \\
& 1v_2 & + \tfrac{8}{5}v_4 + \tfrac{3}{5}v_5 - \tfrac{1}{5}v_6 + \tfrac{1}{5}v_7 = & (x_2) \\
& & 1v_3 + \tfrac{14}{5}v_4 - \tfrac{11}{5}v_5 + \tfrac{9}{10}v_6 - \tfrac{2}{5}v_7 = & (-z_1) \\
& & \tfrac{32}{5}v_4 + \tfrac{7}{5}v_5 + \tfrac{21}{5}v_6 + \tfrac{4}{5}v_7 = & (z_2).
\end{array}
$$

Does the solution satisfy the conditions for optimality?

Complete the solution by filling in the right-hand side, using the indicated symbols for the quantities and placing each in a separate column. Identify the marginal input requirements and the rate of technical substitution. Write the segment of the input function for z_2.

Set $x_1 = 75$, $x_2 = 65$, and find the value of z_1 for which each process in the basis reaches zero. Verify that the range of feasibility is $(210 \leqq z_1 \leqq 266\tfrac{1}{4})$. Calculate the value of z_2 at each end of the range.

Determine which process leaves and which process enters when z_1 passes below the lower limit. For the new solution the coefficients of the slack and surplus variables are

$$
\begin{array}{l}
-\tfrac{8}{17}v_5 + \tfrac{6}{17}v_6 - \tfrac{1}{17}v_7 \\
\tfrac{23}{17}v_5 - \tfrac{13}{17}v_6 + \tfrac{5}{17}v_7 \\
-\tfrac{15}{17}v_5 - \tfrac{3}{34}v_6 - \tfrac{4}{17}v_7 \\
\tfrac{75}{17}v_5 + \tfrac{33}{17}v_6 + \tfrac{20}{17}v_7 .
\end{array}
$$

Use the coefficients to express the processes in the basis in terms of the quantities on the right. Identify the marginal input requirements and the rate of technical substitution. Write the segment of the input function for z_2. Verify that the range of feasibility is $(176 \leqq z_1 \leqq 210)$. Calculate z_2 at both limits.

(c) *Relating the Isorevenue and Input Substitution Contours*

Use the segment of the revenue function from (a) to determine where the three vertices just derived for the input substitution curve lie relative to the isorevenue contour for $R = 140$. Draw the segments of the input substitution curve on the isorevenue map.

3. *Combining the Solutions of Exercises* 1 *and* 2

(a) Show that Exercises 1 and 2 confirm the following results derived in the text: (1) If (q_1, q_2) lies on the product transformation curve for (b_1, b_2), then (b_1, b_2) lies on the input substitution curve for (q_1, q_2); (2) $\bar{s} = \bar{e}_{12}/\bar{e}_{22}$; (3) $\bar{e}_{22} = 1/\bar{a}_{22}$; (4) $\bar{t} = \bar{a}_{12}/\bar{a}_{22}$.

(b) If x_1 and z_1 are held constant rather than z_1 and z_2, what diagram does the output function for x_2 yield? The input function for z_2?

(c) Excluding slack and disposal processes, find $\bar{e}_{11}$ and $\bar{e}_{21}$ and write the equations for two segments of the output function for x_1. Also find $\bar{a}_{11}$ and $\bar{a}_{21}$ and write the equations for two segments of the input functions for z_1.

4. *Product Transformation Curves and an Isocost Contour*

(This exercise uses the results of Exercise 1.)

(a) In input space draw the rays corresponding to the four processes and also the cost line $C = 420 = 1z_1 + 1z_2$. Select input combinations on the segment of the cost line cut off by the second and third processes, such as (210, 210), (252, 168), and (140, 280). For each combination find the levels of the two processes and the corresponding pair of output levels. Show that these output pairs all lie on the segment of the isocost contour derived in Exercise 1a. Assuming that there are no dominated processes, state a general relationship between segments of the cost line in input space and corresponding segments of the isocost contour in output space.

(b) Choose the value of x_1 corresponding to each of the preceding input combinations and use all three quantities as constants on the right for the maximization of x_2 in Exercise 1. Calculate the levels of the three processes (v_1, v_2, v_3) and show that they are a feasible and optimal solution for the chosen values. Find the value of x_2 in each case. Show that each output pair is the vertex of a different product transformation curve and that all vertices lie on the same segment of the isocost contour.

(c) Use Exercise 1 and the preceding results to verify the following statements: (1) A basic optimal solution to the output maximization problem consists of nonnegative linear combinations of *three adjacent processes.* (2) A basic optimal solution to the cost minimization problem consists of nonnegative linear combinations of *two adjacent processes.* (3) A product transformation curve has a vertex within a segment of an isocost contour when the extra process in the output maximization problem has a level of zero. (4) A vertex of a product transformation curve coincides with a vertex of the isocost contour when the same process is the only one to appear at a positive level in both solutions.

Under what conditions do segments of both contours coincide? That is, when do combinations of three processes give the same result as combinations of two processes?

5. *Input Substitution Curves and an Isorevenue Contour*

(This exercise uses the results of Exercise 2.)

(a) In output space draw the rays corresponding to the four processes and also the revenue line $R = 420 = 3x_1+3x_2$. Select output pairs on the segment of the revenue line cut off by the second and third processes, such as (75, 65), (70, 70), (60, 80). For each output pair find the levels of the second and third processes and the corresponding input combinations required. Show that these input combinations all lie on the segment of the isorevenue contour found in Exercise 2a. Assuming that there are no dominated processes, state a general relationship between segments of the revenue line in output space and the corresponding segments of the isorevenue contour in input space.

(b) Choose the value of z_1 corresponding to each of the preceding output pairs and use all three quantities as constants on the right for the minimization of z_2 in Exercise 2. Calculate the levels of the three processes (v_1, v_2, v_3) and show that they provide a feasible and optimal solution for the chosen values of the constants. Find the value of z_2 for each set of constants. Show that each input combination is the vertex of a different input substitution curve and that all vertices lie on the same segment of the isorevenue contour.

(c) Use Exercise 2 and the preceding results to verify the following statements: (1) A basic optimal solution to the input minimization problem consists of nonnegative linear combinations of *three adjacent processes.* (2) A basic optimal solution to the revenue maximization problem consists of nonnegative linear combinations of *two adjacent processes.* (3) An input substitution curve has a vertex along a segment of an isorevenue contour when the extra process in the input minimization problem has a level of zero. (4) A vertex of an input substitution curve coincides with a vertex of an isorevenue contour when the same process is the only one to appear at a positive level in both solutions.

Under what conditions do segments of both contours coincide? That is, when do three processes at positive levels give the same result as two processes?

6. *Economic Optimization for a Smooth Model of the Firm*

For this exercise the technological conditions can be summarized in a smooth linearly homogeneous output function. Treat the numerical example as a set of four specific processes from the infinitely many processes that constitute the smooth technological conditions.

(a) Choose the combination ($z_1 = 60$, $z_2 = 120$) lying on the third ray in input space. Locate on the third ray in output space the corresponding output pair. Find the pair of output levels the first two processes produce from the same input combination. Draw a typical smooth product transformation curve through these two points. What happens to the product transformation curve as the input combination traverses its ray in input space? For a ray in output space write x_2 symbolically as a linear function of (x_1, z_1, z_2) that remains valid so long as z_1 and z_2 stay on the same ray.

(b) Draw a revenue line tangent to the product transformation curve at the point on the third ray. Show that any other output pair, such as the linear combination of the first two processes, yields less revenue from the given input combination. What happens to the optimal solution in output space when output prices remain constant and the input combination traverses its ray in input space?

Express the conditions of tangency in terms of the rate of product transformation and eliminate it from the output function. Show that the result is a linear total revenue function with the marginal revenue productivities as coefficients of the inputs. Under what conditions does the function remain valid?

Express the condition of tangency in terms of both sets of marginal input requirements. Show that tangency implies for each input identical marginal revenue productivities in the production of both inputs.

(c) For the optimal output pair draw a typical smooth input substitution contour through the original input point and also through the input combination the first two processes require to produce the optimal output pair.

Give reasons to support the following assertions. Every input combination on the substitution curve generates a product transformation curve passing through the same point on the revenue line. Only one such curve is tangent, so the others must intersect the revenue line and lie beyond it. Hence, every combination but one on the substitution curve can yield greater revenue if used differently in the production of outputs. Alternatively, proportionately smaller amounts of both inputs can be used to yield the same revenue. The isorevenue contour in input space consists of the one point from each ray whose product transformation curve is tangent to the revenue line. Alternatively, the isorevenue contour has one point in common with the family of input substitution curves generated by all points on the revenue line. It is the lower boundary or envelope. Draw a typical smooth isorevenue contour through the original input point (60, 120).

(d) Draw a cost line tangent to the isorevenue contour at the original point on the third ray. Express the condition for tangency algebraically in terms of the marginal revenue productivities. Convert to an equivalent condition involving the marginal costs of the outputs. State in economic terms the two requirements for optimality that are met by tangency of the cost line to an isorevenue contour. What else is needed? What are the long-run possibilities open to the firm under linear technological conditions?

(e) Broaden the technological conditions so that only the ratios of the marginal productivities and marginal input requirements need remain constant along rays. Explain why the preceding diagrams and conditions for optimality do not need to be modified in any essential way. State algebraically and show graphically the final requirements for a long-run optimum under nonconstant returns to scale.

7. *A Specific Function for the Smooth Version*

Exercise 4 of Chapter 9 used the specific function $x = 64z_1^{1/2}z_2^{1/2}$, and Exercise 9 of Chapter 10 employed the function $z = (x_1^2+x_2^2)^{1/2}$. With the constant omitted, the two functions can be combined as

$$(x_1^2+x_2^2)^{1/2} = z_1^{1/2}z_2^{1/2}.$$

(a) Derive an output function and an input function and check each for linear homogeneity. Choose convenient values for the variables, plot some points, and sketch in the appropriate curve in the (x_1, x_2), (z_1, z_2), (z_2, x_2), and (x_2, z_2) spaces. Identify each curve and verify that each has the required concavity or convexity.

(b) (Optional) Readers with a knowledge of differential calculus may derive the marginal productivities and marginal input requirements, introduce specific prices, and determine the optimal input and output mixes.

SUPPLEMENTARY READINGS FOR PART TWO

Readers will benefit from comparing Part Two with the treatment of the firm in any of the more widely used texts in intermediate price theory, such as the following:

Bilas, Richard A. *Microeconomic Theory: A Graphical Analysis.* New York: McGraw-Hill Book Company, 1967.

Ferguson, C. E. *Microeconomic Theory*, 2nd ed. Homewood, Ill.: Richard D. Irwin, Inc., 1969.

Leftwich, Richard H. *The Price System and Resource Allocation*, 3rd ed. New York: Holt, Rinehart and Winston, 1966.

Among the textbooks that make limited use of differential calculus, the following three are highly recommended:

Baumol, William J. *Economic Theory and Operations Analysis*, 2nd ed. Englewood Cliffs, N.J.: Prentice-Hall, Inc., 1965.

Brownlee, O. H. and Buttrick, John A. *Producer, Consumer, and Social Choice.* New York: McGraw-Hill Book Company, 1968.

Cohen, Kalman J. and Cyert, Richard M. *Theory of the Firm: Resource Allocation in a Market Economy.* Englewood Cliffs, N.J.: Prentice-Hall, Inc., 1965.

Readers with some knowledge of differential calculus will find a study of the following two books especially rewarding. Both cover the relationship of linear and nonlinear programming models of the firm to the conventional smooth version.

Naylor, Thomas H. and Vernon, John M. *Microeconomics and Decision Models of the Firm.* New York: Harcourt Brace Jovanovich, Inc., 1969.

Danoe, Sven, *Industrial Production Models.* New York: Springer-Verlag New York, Inc., 1966.

Part III

Consumer Theory

12

Preference and Utility

The classical theory of consumer's choice in economics, now about 100 years old, predicts that the consumer will choose the combination of commodities that maximizes a smooth utility function. Over the years, the concept of utility was scrutinized closely and stripped of early psychological and philosophical overtones that were found not essential to the prediction of choice. The mathematics was also refined and the theory reached essentially final form just prior to World War II in Hick's *Value and Capital* (1939) and in the work of Samuelson, later published in *Foundations of Economic Analysis* (1947).

In the classical theory of consumer's choice, utility is fundamental and preferences are derived from it. A consumer prefers one combination of commodities to another because it has a higher utility. In their now famous work, *The Theory of Games and Economic Behavior*, first published in 1944, mathematician John von Neumann and economist Oskar Morgenstern reversed the procedure and derived utility from preference. If one alternative is preferred to another, it is assigned a higher utility number. The new concept of utility was used to explain choice in situations characterized by risk and had other special features, so there has been some controversy over the wisdom of using the same name for two somewhat different concepts. The method of using preference to explain or derive utility has, however, been carried over into the theory of consumer's choice in economics and has produced greater clarity and flexibility. The new approach also required a type of mathematics different from the previously used differential calculus. Fortuitously, the mathematics of the theory of games turned out to be quite similar to that required for the theory of linear programming, a slightly later and initially independent discovery.

A third significant development dates back to Samuelson's publication in 1938 of the theory of revealed preference. The essence of the approach is to show that, conceptually, a consumer making consistent choices at various levels of prices and income reveals his preferences. In ensuing years the relationships among utility, preference, and choice have been worked out rather completely, and there is now a unified theory which can be expressed in any one of the essentially equivalent forms.

No attempt will be made to retrace the historical development of the theory. We begin with preference because it clarifies the underlying logic of consumer's choice. We then shift to the equivalent version of utility maximization for a clearer exposition of parametric variation and the resultant demand curves. The present chapter develops the logical relations between preference and utility. Chapter 13 makes the transition to demand curves and presents an appendix that briefly explains revealed preference and relates it to the other two versions of consumer's choice.

The concept of preference in economics shares certain basic logical and mathematical properties with a whole class of similar relations in many fields. In essentially the same way, all functions, including output or utility functions, possess common properties. But a function must also satisfy basic technological or economic requirements to qualify as an output or utility function. Similarly, preference in economics is a combination of generic mathematical properties and special economic requirements. The generic properties will be examined first, using an analogous but simpler example than consumer's preference.

BINARY RELATIONS AND ORDERINGS

Consider a group of men to be ranked according to height. We can measure each individual and record after his name the real number that represents his height. By so doing, we are defining a function, the height function, on a given finite set M of men. To each member m of the set M, there is associated a real number h, or in symbols: $h = f(m)$. The real numbers representing heights can be arranged in order, as has been emphasized many times in discussing the correspondence of real numbers to points on a line. Each height determines a height class to which one or more individuals belong, and these classes can be ranked unequivocally.

An alternative method of ranking the men according to height is to choose a pair of men, stand them back to back, and determine which is the taller or whether they have the same height. As usually carried out, the second method is quicker and less accurate, but this need not be so, since sophisticated equipment could be used to determine the relative heights. The basic question to be answered is this: Can we get a ranking of all men in the set simply by comparing pairs? Intuitively, we are inclined to give an affirmative answer, but the answer depends on experience and certain implicit assumptions about the nature of the comparisons. What is needed is a formal statement of the conditions that permit a ranking to be derived from pairwise comparisons. The best place to start is with the properties of real numbers that enable them to be ordered.

In ordering real numbers by size, we rely also on pairwise comparisons. The comparison of two real numbers, or of any two objects, is a special case of a binary relation. In its broadest definition, a binary relation is any statement about two objects that may or may not be true. Clearly, binary relations in general need not involve comparisons, but those in which we are interested all do. With respect to any two real numbers, a and b, either a is greater than b or it is not. The second alternative admits two possibilities: $a < b$ and $a = b$, which may be combined as $a \leqq b$. Partly by well-established convention and partly for resultant simplifications, the binary relation between real numbers is generally taken to be $\leqq$ rather than $<$ alone. We shall follow this convention after first examining each relation separately.

To find the essential properties of a relation we first attempt to apply it to any one element[1] in the set, then to any pair, and finally to any trio of elements. The results determine whether the relation does or does not possess the important attributes of *reflexivity*, *symmetry*, and *transitivity*. For any choice of real numbers a, b, c, the relations $=$ and $<$ yield the following results:

Properties of the relation $=$	*Attribute*
(1) $a = a$ *always* holds	reflexive
(2) If $a = b$, then $b = a$ *always* holds	symmetric
(3) If $a = b$ and $b = c$, then $a = c$ *always* holds	transitive
Properties of the relation $<$	
(1) $a < a$ never holds	irreflexive
(2) If $a < b$, then $b < a$ *never* holds	asymmetric
(3) If $a < b$ and $b < c$, then $a < c$ *always* holds	transitive

A relation that is reflexive, symmetric, and transitive is called an *equivalence relation*. The prototype is the relation $=$, but many other relations have the same properties. The importance of an equivalence relation is that it partitions a set into nonoverlapping classes. The familiar concept of indifference in consumer's choice also defines an equivalence relation as is shown later. The relation $<$ defines a *strong* or *strict ordering* in which there are no ties. Any other relation with the same properties also defines a strong

[1]There is an inconsistency in applying a binary relation to a single element, and some authors drop the term binary. Despite the inconsistency the use of binary relation in this context is well established, and we shall continue to use it.

ordering. It is the property of transitivity that is essential to any ordering. If it does not hold and a direct comparison shows $c<a$, no ranking is possible.

The combined relation $a \leqq b$ means either $a<b$ or $a = b$. Since both component relations are transitive, the combined relation is transitive. When a single element is chosen, $a = a$. Since one of the two component relations *always* holds, the composite relation is reflexive. Symmetry obviously does not hold when unequal elements are chosen and asymmetry does not hold for equal elements, so the composite relation is neither symmetric nor asymmetric. We can, however, extract the following information by trying to apply the composite relation both ways: If $a \leqq b$ and $b \leqq a$, then $a = b$. This property is termed *antisymmetry*. Thus, the relation $\leqq$ applied to real numbers is reflexive, transitive, and *antisymmetric*. The relation $\leqq$ determines an ordering but permits ties, so the term *weak ordering* applies.

Directly comparing men with respect to height also defines a binary relation, but between men not numbers. For "A is shorter than B," we shall modify the symbol for less than and write $\mathrm{A} \prec \mathrm{B}$. Readers may verify that the relation $\prec$ is irreflexive, asymmetric, and transitive, defining a strong ordering. For "A is as tall as B" we write $\mathrm{A} \sim \mathrm{B}$. Readers may show that the relation $\sim$ is an equivalence relation.

The combined relation "is not taller than" or $\precsim$ is obviously reflexive and transitive but neither symmetric nor asymmetric. We can, however, conclude that if A is not taller than B and B is not taller than A, then A is as tall as B. This is not antisymmetry in the strict definition given the term by mathematicians, which requires that $\mathrm{A} = \mathrm{B}$. We can only conclude that A and B are indistinguishable with respect to height, not that A and B are merely different designations for the same person. But this is as it should be. When heights are measured and the real numbers ordered, more than one individual may fall into each height class. A binary relation that is reflexive and transitive but not strictly antisymmetric is termed a *preordering* or *quasi-ordering*. It differs from an ordering in admitting ties between *distinct* members of a set.

Functions, Preorderings, and Measurement

Any real-valued function defined on a set, such as the height function defined on a set of men, implies a binary relation and a preordering on that set. If the height of A is not greater than the height of B, $h(\mathrm{A}) \leqq h(\mathrm{B})$, then A is not taller than B, $\mathrm{A} \precsim \mathrm{B}$. Conversely, does a preordering imply a function? Suppose, for example, someone measures a set of men, ranks them in order of height, and then throws away the specific measurements. How far can we get in trying to reconstruct the height function from the ranking alone?

One obstacle is that measurement of height does not require a unique real number to be assigned to each individual. Height in meters is a different real number from height in feet or in hands. But a man twice as tall as another on one scale is twice as tall on any scale. Thus, a change in units of measurement not only leaves order unchanged but also preserves the ratio of measurements.

There is a second source of uncertainty that is more pronounced in other examples. The height or altitude of an airplane can be measured from the ground below, or from sea level, or from any other point of reference. The ratio of measurements is no longer invariant, since a plane that is twice as high as another relative to the ground below will not be twice as high relative to sea level. The origin from which measurements are made may be shifted, resulting in the addition or subtraction of a constant from all previous measurements. Only in a very few cases, such as length and possibly age, is there a natural origin that is universally accepted.

Measurement requires a choice of unit and a choice of origin, both of which are arbitrary in most cases. Suppose that we are given a set of numbers and told that they are, say, the heights of mountains in a foreign country. We are not told the units of measurement nor the base from which the measurements were made. So long as the figures represent measurements, we can always convert to feet above sea level if we can find the right positive constant to multiply by and the correct positive or negative constant to add. Thus, every measurement is linearly related to every other measurement or is, specifically, a positive linear function of every other measurement. For example, if h^* represents any second measurement of the height of men, then

$$h^*(m) = th(m)+s \qquad t > 0.$$

A familiar example of the linear relation between measurements is temperature, where degrees on the Fahrenheit scale equal nine-fifths the number of degrees on the Centigrade scale plus 32. Even though we do not know the units or the origin, a given set of measurements always provides a ranking, but it is also related by a positive linear function to any other set of measurements.

The existence of different measurements is but a minor part of the problem in retrieving a function from the ranking. Actually, all traces of measurement are lost except order alone. If B is ranked higher than A in height, B $\succ$ A, all we know is that $h(\mathrm{B}) > h(\mathrm{A})$. Once numbers are assigned to represent the ranking, we can take any positive linear function of the numbers without changing the ranking they represent. But this is not all. Someone else can come along and square the numbers, take their square roots, or replace them by their logarithms. In general, the numbers can be subjected to any transformation whatsoever just so long as the larger of two numbers before the transformation corresponds to the larger of the two numbers after the transformation. Multiplication by a negative number, for example, does not satisfy the requirement.

We can express the requirement formally by means of an *increasing transformation*, which is essentially another term for an increasing function. As depicted in Figure 12–1, a function is increasing if it never becomes horizontal and never dips down. Any set of numbers h representing height may be replaced by another set of numbers h^*, so long as $h^* = F(h)$ is an increasing function. As is geometrically evident, any increasing function of h preserves the ranking or order and, hence, is called an *order-preserving* transformation. A positive linear function is an increasing function and preserves order, but it preserves measurements as well.

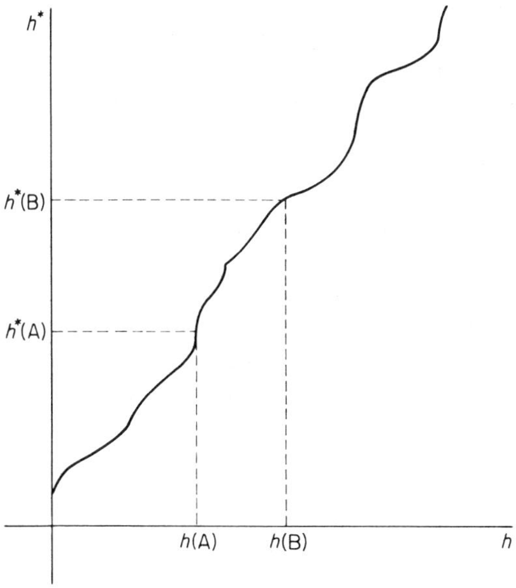

Fig. 12-1 An Increasing or Order-Preserving Function

THE PREFERENCE ORDERING OF A CONSUMER

Though logically similar, a consumer's ranking of the available alternatives is far more complex than the ranking of a set of men with respect to height. First of all, the set to be ranked is inescapably very large, and each member has many dimensions. What a consumer has to rank are combinations of commodities or commodity bundles. Each commodity bundle consists of a specified amount of every commodity available. If there are n commodities, each commodity bundle is an n-component vector,

$$\mathbf{x} = [x_1, x_2, \ldots, x_n].$$

Since each commodity has an axis along which its quantities are represented, the *commodity space* is n-dimensional, and commodity bundles are points in the nonnegative orthant of that space. It is a fact of experience that many commodities, such as tennis rackets, are sold in indivisible units and that many other commodities, such as coffee, are sold in conventional units. Relatively few commodities are like gasoline in being purchasable in almost any desired quantity. Thus, in reality, the set of all commodity bundles, called the *consumption set*, consists of unconnected points in the commodity space.

Large finite sets of isolated points are very difficult to deal with. The standard mathematical remedy is, paradoxically, to replace them with infinite sets. An example is the fitting of a straight line by least squares to a set of points or, in general, the smoothing of isolated points into a curve. The infinite set of points represented by the line or curve is much easier to work with, because it has simple general properties. This is the key to the apparent paradox. Merely enlarging sets is of no help, but enlarging sets in such a way that they acquire general properties has great power. The entire nonnegative orthant has the important property of being a convex set, whereas scattered points do not. As a reminder, a set is convex if an entire line segment lies in the set whenever the endpoints do. Thus, convexity eliminates any gaps in the set.

A standard assumption in the theory of consumer's choice is that there are no indivisible units and that every commodity is, like gasoline or electric power, available in any desired quantity. The consumption set of the consumer thus becomes the entire nonnegative orthant of commodity space. Though the main reason is mathematical, various economic justifications can be given. First of all, the aim of the theory is not to predict the precise amount of each commodity that a particular consumer will buy. Rather, the purpose is to deduce certain broad patterns of choice applicable to consumers in general. The fact that purchases can be made only in conventional units is a relatively minor qualification for most commodities, though not for durable goods, such a refrigerators, which require a somewhat different type of treatment. A second justification is that the ultimate aim of the theory is to develop market demand curves in which the demands of individuals are summed. In the aggregate, when the quantity purchased is very large relative to the size of the unit, indivisibilities are greatly reduced in importance.

The cornerstone of the theory is a binary relation known as the preference relation. With respect to two commodity bundles $\mathbf{x}^a$ and $\mathbf{x}^b$, a consumer either prefers $\mathbf{x}^a$ to $\mathbf{x}^b$ or does not. Again, the second alternative contains two possibilities: the consumer either prefers $\mathbf{x}^b$ to $\mathbf{x}^a$ or is indifferent between them. Following once again the mathematical precedent of "less than or equals," we can choose as the basic relation, "is not preferred to," and use the symbol $\precsim$. The essence of the theory is that a consumer is capable of ordering or ranking commodity bundles. Hence, the preference relation, like the height relation, must be reflexive and transitive. It seems safe to assume that a consumer is indifferent between two identical commodity bundles, so $\mathbf{x}^a \sim \mathbf{x}^a$, and the relation is reflexive. Transitivity requires that, if $\mathbf{x}^a \precsim \mathbf{x}^b$ and $\mathbf{x}^b \precsim \mathbf{x}^c$, then $\mathbf{x}^a \precsim \mathbf{x}^c$. This property is more of a problem. It need not hold if a consumer's tastes change between comparisons, or if basic tastes remain invariant but more knowledge is acquired about the commodities. Tastes and knowledge undoubtedly change as a result of experience, and present decisions are linked to prior decisions in a dynamic process. The theory of consumer's choice does not consider changes over time explicitly but examines the choices of an individual during a period of time in which knowledge and tastes are, at least temporarily, fixed. The consumer is assumed to have consistent preferences in the sense that the direct ranking of $\mathbf{x}^a$ and $\mathbf{x}^c$ is the same as the indirect ranking in which each is compared with $\mathbf{x}^b$. Transitivity is assumed to hold.

If the preference relation holds both ways—$\mathbf{x}^a \precsim \mathbf{x}^b$ and $\mathbf{x}^b \precsim \mathbf{x}^a$—we conclude that $\mathbf{x}^a \sim \mathbf{x}^b$. Strictly interpreted, $\mathbf{x}^a \sim \mathbf{x}^b$ means that the consumer is indifferent between the two commodity bundles, but usage has shortened the expression to "$\mathbf{x}^a$ is indifferent to $\mathbf{x}^b$." It is clear again that the conclusion need not hold unless changes in tastes and knowledge are excluded. Indifference is clearly not the same as equality, so the preference relation is not antisymmetric and yields only a preordering and not an ordering. However, the simpler term *preference ordering* will be used in the belief that one qualifier is sufficient warning.

Economists also use the strict preference relation and the resultant strong ordering. The decision on which ordering to use depends primarily on whether preference is being linked to utility or to choice. The conventional utility function assigns the same utility number to distinct commodity bundles, and the consumer is assumed to be indifferent between them. Linking preference to the traditional utility analysis requires a weak preference ordering. By contrast the revealed preference approach attempts to derive preference from observed choice. But choices are made in spite of indifference and not because of it. Indifference is not needed to explain choice, and choice reveals preference not indifference. In this context, then, the strong preference ordering is more appropriate. Our main concern is linking preference with utility, so we shall generally employ the weak preference ordering.

Since any two men can be compared with respect to height, we never entertained the possibility that the corresponding binary relation might not hold, one way or the other, between two members of the set. When a binary relation holds for any choice of pairs from a set, the ordering or preordering is *total* or *complete*. If there are some pairs for which the binary relation does not hold in either direction, the ordering or preordering is *partial*. There are binary relations—an example will be furnished shortly—whose very definition precludes their being applied to all members of a set. With preference there is no logical bar to its holding between any two members of the consumption set, but there are grounds for doubting the plausibility of the assumption.

Two diametrically opposed cases raise difficulties. It is doubtful that a consumer has well-defined and consistent preferences far removed from his experience and his income level. A man with only the shirt on his back may simply not know what changes he would prefer to make in a wardrobe that already contained four dozen shirts and five dozen neckties. Fortunately, for the theory, few paupers wake up as millionaires and over short periods individuals make choices in ranges with which they are familiar. For mathematical simplicity and generality, a consumer is assumed capable of ranking all possible commodity bundles even though all choices are likely to be made from a restricted subset.

The second difficulty arises from continuously divisible commodities. Taken literally, the ranking of the entire consumption set seems to imply that a consumer must be sensitive to any change in quantity, however small. Further, the sensitivity must be present even though commodities are sold only in conventional units such as pounds or quarts. Originally we recognized that most commodities are sold in indivisible or conventional units and then extended the consumption set to the entire nonnegative orthant to get a simpler mathematical model. We cannot at the same time endow the consumer with an unattainable degree of sensitivity. The consumer of reality, who buys in indivisible or conventional units and is sensitive only to discrete changes in commodities, has been replaced by a mathematical model. The issue is not whether the consumer of reality can possibly satisfy the mathematical requirements. He cannot. The issue is whether the model gives an acceptable prediction of the general characteristics of consumer's choice. Most economists believe it does. For a simple general model, then, we assume that a complete preference ordering exists on the entire nonnegative orthant of a consumer's commodity space.

THE ECONOMIC PROPERTIES OF THE PREFERENCE ORDERING

Up to this point we have merely endowed the preference relation with the generic mathematical properties common to any complete preordering. There are two basic assumptions that provide the theory of consumer's choice with nearly all of its economic content. The first describes a consumer's reaction to increases in quantities of commodities. Expressed in strong and simple form the assumption is that a consumer always prefers more to less. When there is only a single commodity, more and less simply refer to the ordering of real numbers. For commodity bundles, which are vectors, there is as yet no way of defining more and less. What is needed is an ordering of vectors.

The Partial Ordering of Vectors

The ordering of vectors rests upon pairwise comparisons of all corresponding components. So long as all comparisons go in the same direction there is no problem in ranking vectors. By the definition introduced in Chapter 6, two vectors are equal if and only if all matching components are equal. Clearly, one vector is smaller than another if all matching components are smaller. It is also reasonable to classify one vector as smaller than another if at least one matching component is smaller and none is larger. The attempt to rank vectors breaks down when one matching component is smaller and another is larger. Thus, the ordering of vectors, unlike the ordering of real numbers, is only partial.

We can define a relation $<$ for vectors as follows: If $\mathbf{x}^a$ and $\mathbf{x}^b$ are any two vectors with the same number of components, then $\mathbf{x}^a < \mathbf{x}^b$ if no matching component of $\mathbf{x}^a$ is larger and at least one is smaller. More formally, $\mathbf{x}^a < \mathbf{x}^b$ if $x_j^a \leqq x_j^b$ and $x_j^a < x_j^b$ for some j. By writing out the relationships between corresponding components, readers may easily verify that the relation $<$ for vectors is irreflexive, asymmetric, and transitive. Thus, it defines a strong, though only partial, ordering. The relation $\mathbf{x}^a \leqq \mathbf{x}^b$, permits all components to be equal and, as readers may check, satisfies the requirements for a weak ordering.

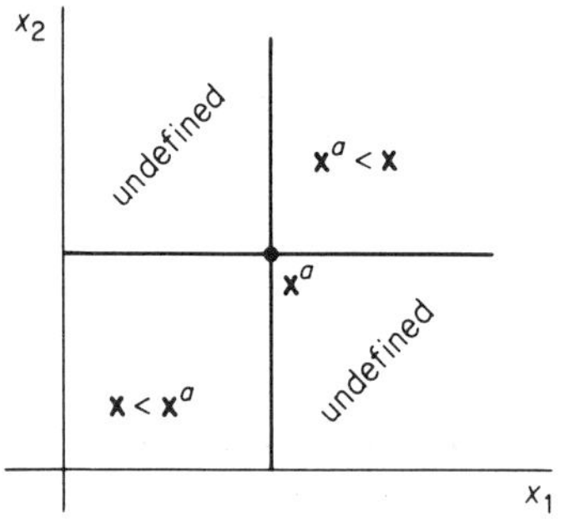

Fig. 12-2 The Partial Ordering of Commodity Bundles

The results are shown graphically in Figure 12–2. With respect to any vector $\mathbf{x}^a$, we can form four quadrants by drawing a horizontal and a vertical line through the point. In the northeast quadrant $\mathbf{x}^a < \mathbf{x}$ for every point $\mathbf{x}$ except $\mathbf{x}^a$ itself. The consumer gets more of one commodity and no less of the other. Similarly, $\mathbf{x} < \mathbf{x}^a$ in the southwest quadrant. Elsewhere the relation is not defined. The consumer gets more of one commodity and less of the other.

Nonsatiability: Preference for More over Less

Formally stated, the axiom that a consumer always prefers more to less is as follows: If $\mathbf{x}^b > \mathbf{x}^a$ then $\mathbf{x}^b \succ \mathbf{x}^a$. The expression $\mathbf{x}^b \succ \mathbf{x}^a$ means that $\mathbf{x}^b$ is preferred to $\mathbf{x}^a$, ruling out the possibility of indifference. Whenever an ordering of vectors or commodity bundles exists, the preference ordering coincides with it. A special but important case is a ray from the origin along which all commodities increase proportionately. All points can be uniquely ranked both by magnitude and by preference.

Comparisons can also be made between points on different rays. Choose a point $\mathbf{x}^a$ on a ray and draw in its four quadrants (Figure 12–3). On any second ray, $\mathbf{x}^a$ is preferred to every point on an initial closed line segment from the origin. There is also a terminal line segment every point of which is

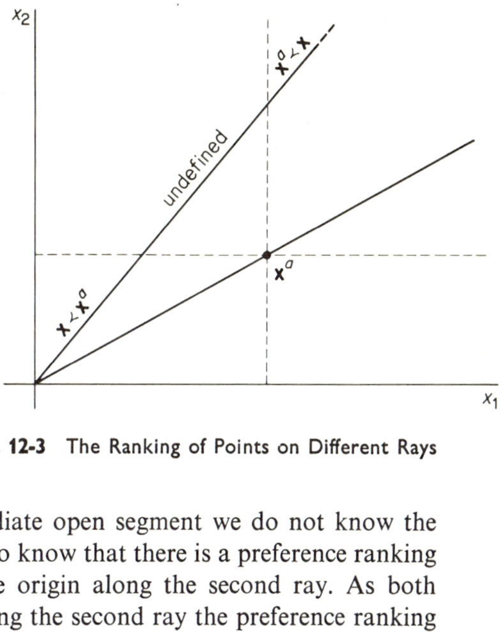

Fig. 12-3 The Ranking of Points on Different Rays

preferred to $\mathbf{x}^a$. Along the intermediate open segment we do not know the relation of any point to $\mathbf{x}^a$, but we do know that there is a preference ranking corresponding to distance from the origin along the second ray. As both quantities increase continuously along the second ray the preference ranking could jump from $\mathbf{x} \prec \mathbf{x}^a$ to $\mathbf{x} \succ \mathbf{x}^a$ without ever passing through a point of indifference. Most economic quantities cannot change continuously and, if they could, consumers would not be sensitive to infinitesimal changes. It is impossible to conduct experiments or otherwise to determine whether a jump in preference is or is not plausible. What is certain is that a discontinuity in preference, like any other discontinuity, is hard to handle mathematically. In the interest of a simpler and more tractable model, the preference relation is assumed to be continuous.

A continuous preference relation together with a preference for more over less implies a single point on each ray indifferent to $\mathbf{x}^a$. The locus of all such points is called an *indifference curve* or *indifference contour*. Readers may verify that indifference is an equivalence relation. Hence, it partitions the entire consumption set into nonoverlapping subsets, which take the form of indifference contours. Each point in the consumption set belongs to one and only one indifference contour. As a consequence of the assumption that more is preferred to less, all indifference contours must slope downward. Along any upward-sloping line both quantities are increasing, ruling out indifference. Horizontal and vertical lines also cannot form indifference contours since one quantity is increasing with the other constant. Further, the axes cannot form indifference contours. If we choose a point on the horizontal axis, all points beyond are preferred to it, and it is preferred to all points nearer the origin. Each point on the axis must lie on a distinct indifference contour, and the indifference contour must pass through its northwest quadrant. Hence, indifference curves cannot approach the axes but must intersect them.

Ruling out horizontal and vertical indifference segments and requiring that all indifference contours intersect the axes is unduly restrictive. We must, then, reexamine the axiom responsible for these results. As defined, always preferring more to less is a very strong assumption. It rules out the possibility of satiation with respect to any commodity. A consumer never has so much of a commodity that he doesn't want more. We shall weaken the assumption as follows: A consumer always prefers more of *all* commodities to less of all commodities but may be indifferent to increases in a single commodity or in a subset that contains as many as (n-1) commodities. What the theory cannot tolerate is indifference to increases in all commodities or actually preferring less to more of any commodity. In Figure 12–2, points in the interior of the northeast quadrant continue to be preferred to $\mathbf{x}^a$ but points on the axes through $\mathbf{x}^a$ need not be. The weaker form of the axiom is precisely what we need to permit horizontal and vertical indifference segments while ruling out upward-sloping segments. Also, both axes through the origin may form an indifference contour of lowest ranking, and higher ranked contours may approach but never intersect it.

Both forms of the axiom provide a unique ranking along rays where all commodities increase. Both rule out total satiation although the weaker form permits satiability with respect to some commodities. The essence of both formulations is that the consumer always prefers more to less, though the weaker axiom requires that more mean more of all. We shall generally employ the weaker form of the axiom and denote it as the preference for more over less, omitting any qualification unless specifically needed.

Convexity: Preference for Means over Extremes

Each indifference contour could consist of a single line segment. Commodity bundles on the axes, which contain only one commodity, would then be ranked equally with all intermediate combinations. Experience suggests that consumers are likely to prefer "some of each" over "all or nothing." Equally ranked intermediate combinations must then lie nearer the origin than points on the single line segment. The indifference contours bulge toward the origin and are convex. Thus, convexity of the indifference contours represents a preference for means over extremes.

An axiom that guarantees convexity is the following: A consumer who is indifferent between any two commodity bundles *always* prefers *any* weighted average of the two bundles to either alone. In symbolic form, if $\mathbf{x}^a \sim \mathbf{x}^b$, then $(1-t)\mathbf{x}^a + t\mathbf{x}^b \succ \mathbf{x}^a$ for $0 < t < 1$. When we join by a line segment two points on an indifference contour, any interior point on the line segment, or weighted average, is preferred to either endpoint. Hence, indifference contours must bend toward the origin in order to lie inside the line segment. Further, since the requirement holds everywhere, indifference contours cannot contain any line segments, however short. For isoproduct contours, we reached the same mathematical result by assuming that any weighted average of production processes was dominated by an intermediate process. Mathematically the two assumptions are equivalent, but the different forms better suit the different contexts.

A consumer with convex indifference curves prefers means to extremes, when the extremes are equally ranked. An assumption that insures concavity is as follows: If $\mathbf{x}^a \sim \mathbf{x}^b$, then $(1-t)\mathbf{x}^a + t\mathbf{x}^b \prec \mathbf{x}^a$ for $0 < t < 1$. This is the preference pattern of an extremist, one who always prefers the extremes to the mean. Consistently followed, such preferences lead to the spending of all income on one commodity. Observation of consumers reveals a general tendency toward balanced consumption and leads us to reject extremist preferences as a widely applicable pattern of consumer tastes.

To assert that a consumer always prefers the mean to either of two equally ranked extremes is a very strong statement. It is stronger than necessary to rule out extremist preferences and, in the opinion of some economists, too strong to be generally acceptable.[2] When commodity bundles are widely separated, such as points on the axes, it is plausible for consumers to prefer an intermediate combination. That they should always do so, no matter how close the commodity bundles, is harder to accept. Also, when strictly interpreted, the strong convexity axiom rules out horizontal and vertical indifference segments, including the axes. It thus negates the results we sought in weakening the nonsatiability axiom.

To exclude extremist preferences, we need only the weaker axiom: When two commodity bundles are equally ranked, a consumer *never* prefers either alone to any weighted average of the two. The weaker axiom leaves the consumer free to rank means above either extreme or to be indifferent between means and extremes. Indifference contours cannot be concave with

[2]See, for example, G. Debreu, *Theory of Value* (New York: John Wiley and Sons, Inc., 1959), p. 61.

respect to the origin but they can contain straight line segments. As yet we have not made any explicit assumption about a consumer's preference for means over extremes when the extremes are not equally ranked. As Exercise 5 shows, the assumptions already made imply that a consumer must always prefer any mean to the *lower ranked* of the two extremes.

The Indifference Map of a Consumer

The theory of consumer's choice rests upon three basic economic assumptions or axioms. The first is that a consumer is capable of ranking all commodity bundles in the consumption set. Within the theory proper, no attempt is made to account for preferences or to explain how they are formed. The starting point is a consumer who can carry out the ranking. The second assumption is a nonsatiability axiom, which states in one form or another that a consumer always prefers more to less. Finally there must be a convexity axiom, whose essential economic content is that a consumer generally, although not necessarily always, prefers a weighted average of two equally ranked commodity bundles to either alone. Also needed for a simple general model are some purely mathematical assumptions about continuity. The quantity of each commodity can be represented by real numbers and must, therefore, vary continuously. Secondly, no jump in preference can occur as the quantities are varying continuously.

To derive the implications of these axioms, we choose a ray in the consumption set and a point $\mathbf{x}^a$ on that ray. Along every ray, the preference for more over less ranks all commodity bundles in correspondence with distance from the origin. On every ray there will be points in the northeast quadrant with respect to $\mathbf{x}^a$ and points in the southwest quadrant. It follows, then, that every ray has commodity bundles preferred to $\mathbf{x}^a$ and other bundles to which $\mathbf{x}^a$ is preferred. By the two continuity assumptions, there cannot be a gap in the ranking, so each ray must have one and only one point of indifference to $\mathbf{x}^a$. There is, then, a locus of points, one to a ray, each of which is indifferent to $\mathbf{x}^a$. Further, by the transitivity of the indifference relation, any two points in the locus are indifferent to each other.

As $\mathbf{x}^a$ traverses its ray it generates a whole family of nonintersecting indifference contours. Transitivity of the indifference relation rules out intersections, since no point can be indifferent to two distinct points on another ray. Thus, the economic and mathematical axioms on consumer preference partition the consumption set into a family of indifference contours, each of which is ranked above those nearer the origin and below those farther from the origin. A smooth version of the indifference map appears in Figure 12–4.

Weaker axioms admit everything that stronger axioms allow and more besides. Conversely, if weaker axioms rule out any possibility, the stronger axioms must necessarily exclude it. The weaker forms of the nonsatiability and convexity axioms rule out upward-sloping indifference contours along which both commodities increase. They also exclude concave indifference contours or concave portions of contours which require a preference for extremes over means. Within the weaker axiom system indifference contours may have linear segments, including terminal horizontal and vertical segments, and may approach but not touch the axes. These possibilities are permitted but not required. The indifference map may consist of smooth, nowhere linear, indifference contours that either approach or intersect the axes.

Strengthening the axioms eliminates possibilities and requires results that were previously only permitted. The strong form of the nonsatiability axiom postulates that a consumer always prefers more to less, where more and less are defined by the partial ordering of vectors. It rules out terminal horizontal and vertical segments but not downward-sloping linear segments. The strong convexity axiom rules out linear segments but permits the contours to be piecewise curvilinear. The strong form of either axiom, strictly interpreted, requires intersection with the axes.

The conventional textbook version of the indifference map displays smooth, everywhere downward-sloping contours that are often drawn approaching the axes. The essential economic content is the same as the strong axioms, and the axioms need weakening only to permit an approach to the axes. However, even the strong axioms do not guarantee smoothness. As is true for isoproduct contours we must make an additional purely

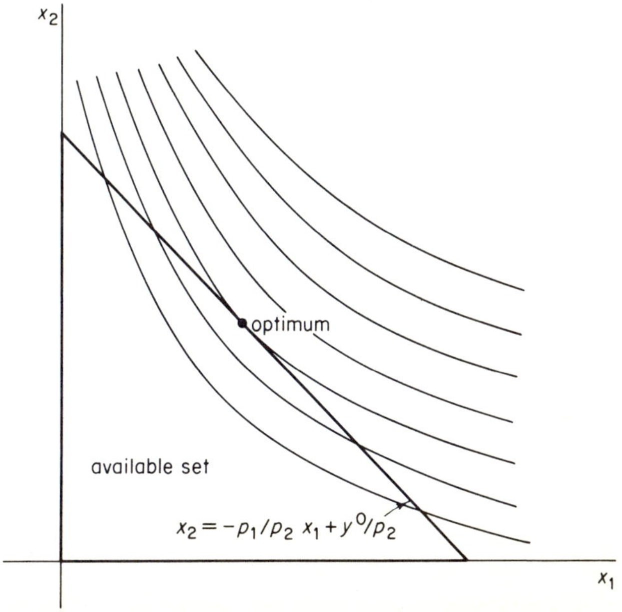

Fig. 12-4 The Choice of a Commodity Bundle

mathematical assumption. To show graphically consumer's choice with a preference relation, we select first the conventional smooth indifference map.

Preference and Optimal Choice

Once the indifference map is determined, it is easy to show graphically how a consumer decides what to buy. Each commodity has a market price, and the consumer's ability to purchase is limited by the amount of money available for spending. In the simplest first approximation, a consumer's money income is already determined and all of it is available for spending on commodities.

In deciding what to buy, an individual consumer ignores any effect that decision may have on market prices. Thus, a consumer has a fixed amount to spend at constant prices and is bound by the following constraint:

$$p_1x_1+p_2x_2 \leqq y^0,$$

where y^0 represents the fixed money income. As Figure 12–4 shows, the inequality defines a triangular region, known as the *available set*, which consists of all commodity bundles that can be bought without exceeding income. A consumer preferring more to less always chooses along the outer boundary of the available set and thus spends the entire income. When the budget line intersects a contour in two points the consumer prefers intermediate combinations. Hence, the optimal solution occurs when the budget line has only one point in common with a contour. If the contours are smooth the optimum is always a point of tangency; otherwise, it may be a vertex formed by arcs of curves.

As always, a single optimal solution is but a prelude to determining how the optimal quantities respond to variations in the parameters, which are prices and income for the consumer. The preference version of consumer's choice is ideal for revealing the logical underpinnings of the theory but is less effective in handling parametric variation. Accordingly, we shall shift over to the equivalent version, utility maximization. In earlier chapters we first set up a linear programming model for the firm and then used parametric programming to trace the effects of specified changes. A process of smoothing transformed the linear model into the conventional version of the firm, and the results of parametric programming, appropriately modified, remained applicable. We shall employ the same device for the consumer. Our aim is to show how consumer preferences are converted into consumer demand and how different patterns of preference affect demand curves. The transition from preference to demand is clearest in the linear model. We shall then smooth the indifference contours and introduce, one by one, various complexities not present in the simpler version. The previously established bridge from preference to demand permits us to show at each stage precisely how demand curves are affected.

A LINEAR VERSION OF CONSUMER'S CHOICE

A close examination and comparison of producing and consuming units reveals basic similarities that can best be brought out by employing the concept of a process. The resemblance becomes very clear once we recognize that most consuming units are families or households that possess a wide variety of fixed inputs in the form of durable consumer's goods. But even for a footloose individual satisfying his own whims, the concept of a consumption process is appropriate. A commodity is not bought to be used alone or, at the other extreme, in combination with all other commodities. A consumer generally has in mind one or more specific uses of a commodity in combination with a limited number of other commodities. Apart from the obvious case of preparing food, an evening at the theater or an afternoon at a football game requires more than one input, including, most significantly, the consumer's own time.

In Chapter 14 we shall examine more fully the meaning and implications of consumption processes, when the family is taken as the consuming unit. For the present we merely assume that there are several key ratios in which a consumer is required to use, or chooses to use, commodities. Technological requirements, similar to those for firms, may account for at least an approximation to fixed ratios. Pen and paper, desk and chair are examples. For the consumer, technology need not be the only explanation. To a perfectionist mixing cocktails the input coefficients may be more rigid than for any known technological process in home or industry.

The theory of consumer's choice has relied implicitly on the concept of a process in one special case, perfect complementarity. The consumer can use two commodities in one and only one ratio. Left and right shoes or gloves are often cited as examples, but the force of the examples is much diminished by the present practice of selling rubber gloves in packages of three, two right and one left. Along the ray determined by the fixed ratio, commodity bundles are ranked in correspondence to magnitude, or distance from the origin. The ranking can in turn be represented by assigning numbers to commodity bundles. Any assignment of higher numbers to more distant combinations is acceptable, so we can make the very special choice of numbers that are proportional to distance from the origin. The numbers assigned to represent a preference ordering are called *utility numbers.* Assigning one and only one number to each commodity bundle defines a utility function along the ray. By the very special way in which numbers are being assigned, utility increases proportionately with the size of commodity bundles along the ray.

As soon as utility is introduced, there is a temptation to equate it with consumer satisfaction. In the present context, this is incorrect. Utility is merely a convenient term for a numerical representation of a preference ranking. If a consumer prefers one commodity bundle to another, we assign it a higher number and say it has greater utility. Originally, economists took utility as primary and derived preference from it. A consumer preferred $\mathbf{x}^a$ to $\mathbf{x}^b$ *because* it had higher utility. Later in the chapter we shall discuss more fully the two approaches and show how they are related to each other. For the present, preference is always primary and utility is derived from it.

A consumer who can use commodities in only one ratio, or insists on doing so, is indifferent to any increase in one commodity alone. The indifference contours become horizontal and vertical line segments meeting on the ray. Clearly it is the weaker version of the nonsatiability axiom that is needed. The points on the horizontal and vertical segments are assigned the same utility number as the point on the ray, so the utility function is defined everywhere on the consumption set.

There is appreciably more flexibility when a consumer can use commodities in several key ratios. Each ratio determines a ray and utility numbers can be assigned to represent the ranking along each ray. There is, however, the additional requirement that points of indifference on all rays receive the same number. The utility numbers can be proportional to distance along two rays only if preferences fit a very special pattern. A consumer who is indifferent between two commodity bundles must remain indifferent when the quantities in both bundles are doubled or changed in any proportion whatsoever. More formally, if $\mathbf{x}^a \sim \mathbf{x}^b$, then $t\mathbf{x}^a \sim t\mathbf{x}^b$ for all $t > 0$. This is a simple, special pattern of consumer preference that has been analyzed in the economic literature. It is introduced to permit the use of linear programming and simplify the transition from preference to demand. The assumption will be dropped as soon as it has served its purpose.

For a specific illustration we choose six rays, including the axes, and identify on the rays the following commodity combinations with respect to which the consumer is indifferent:

$$\mathbf{a}_1 = [a_{11}, a_{21}] = [0, 10] \qquad \mathbf{a}_2 = [a_{12}, a_{22}] = [1, 6]$$

$$\mathbf{a}_3 = [a_{13}, a_{23}] = [2, 4] \qquad \mathbf{a}_4 = [a_{14}, a_{24}] = [3, 3]$$

$$\mathbf{a}_5 = [a_{15}, a_{25}] = [7, 1] \qquad \mathbf{a}_6 = [a_{16}, a_{26}] = [12, 0]$$

When the same utility number, say one, is assigned to each combination, the techniques of linear programming generate a utility function in essentially the same way as an output function. The basic difference is that technology determines the output levels, whereas the utility numbers are merely a convenient way to represent a preference ordering. Under the special assumption just made about preference, and only under that assumption, each ray represents a linear process or activity yielding utility. The first stage in deriving a utility function is the maximization of utility for given commodity levels, shown below in both symbolic and numerical form:

$$a_{11}v_1+a_{12}v_2+a_{13}v_3+a_{14}v_4+a_{15}v_5+a_{16}v_6 = q_1+0q_2$$
$$a_{21}v_1+a_{22}v_2+a_{23}v_3+a_{24}v_4+a_{25}v_5+a_{26}v_6 = 0q_1+q_2$$
$$uv_1+\ uv_2+\ uv_3+\ uv_4+\ uv_5+\ uv_6 = 0q_1+0q_2+U(\max);$$

$$0v_1+\ 1v_2+\ 2v_3+\ 3v_4+\ 7v_5+\ 12v_6 = q_1+0q_2$$
$$10v_1+\ 6v_2+\ 4v_3+\ 3v_4+\ 1v_5+\ 0v_6 = 0q_1+q_2$$
$$1v_1+\ 1v_2+\ 1v_3+\ 1v_4+\ 1v_5+\ 1v_6 = 0q_1+0q_2+U(\max).$$

The process levels, which will shortly be eliminated from the problem, represent equiproportional changes in both commodities. If v_3 and v_4 turn out to be the optimal solution, as they do with $q_1 = 5$ and $q_2 = 7$, reduction to canonical form converts the objective function to the following linear function of the commodity levels:

$$U = \bar{u}_1 q_1 + \bar{u}_2 q_2 = \tfrac{1}{6}q_1 + \tfrac{1}{6}q_2.$$

The coefficients of q_1 and q_2 are the rates of change of utility with respect to each of the commodities, or their respective marginal utilities. The marginal utilities are the dual variables of the problem and, like all dual variables, can be interpreted as prices. They represent internal prices or valuations placed upon the commodities by the consumer's preferences.

The equation shown above holds for all values of x_1 and x_2 within the cone of the third and fourth rays. It forms one segment of a piecewise-linear utility function, and every other pair of adjacent rays determines another segment. By using parametric programming readers may verify that the numerical example yields the utility function presented in Table 12–1 and graphed in Figure 12–5.

For each value of U the equations trace out a piecewise-linear iso-utility contour. Along each segment the slope is the negative ratio of the marginal

TABLE 12–1

A Piecewise-Linear Utility Function

Processes	*Range of* x_2/x_1	*Linear equation*	*Slope*
		$U = \bar{u}_1 x_1 + \bar{u}_2 x_2$	$-\bar{u}_1/\bar{u}_2$
(v_1, v_2)	6 and over	$U = \frac{4}{10}x_1 + \frac{1}{10}x_2$	-4
(v_2, v_3)	6 to 2	$U = \frac{1}{4}x_1 + \frac{1}{8}x_2$	-2
(v_3, v_4)	2 to 1	$U = \frac{1}{6}x_1 + \frac{1}{6}x_2$	-1
(v_4, v_5)	1 to $\frac{1}{7}$	$U = \frac{1}{9}x_1 + \frac{2}{9}x_2$	$-\frac{1}{2}$
(v_5, v_6)	$\frac{1}{7}$ to 0	$U = \frac{1}{12}x_1 + \frac{5}{12}x_2$	$-\frac{1}{5}$

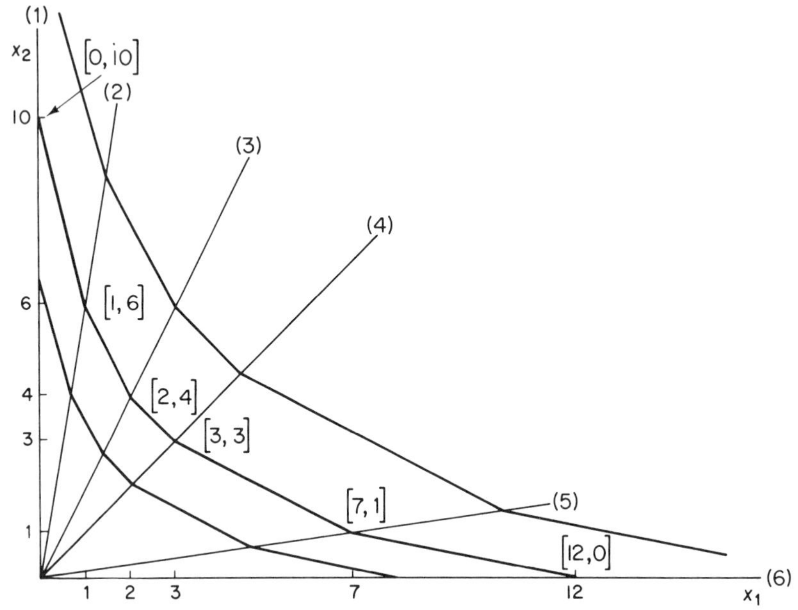

Fig. 12-5 Indifference Curves that are Piecewise-Linear and Parallel Along Rays

utilities $-\bar{u}_1/\bar{u}_2$ and the intercept is $U/\bar{u}_2$. The assignment of utility coefficients to the processes is arbitrary, and we can multiply them by any positive number, say t. Both the utility index and the marginal utilities are also multiplied by t, leaving the slope and intercept of each segment unchanged. The contours are renumbered but are otherwise unaffected.

The marginal utilities, being dual variables, represent internal prices or valuations in terms of utility. Since the level of utility is arbitrary, only the ratios or relative valuations matter. As x_1 increases relative to x_2 along a contour, the relative valuation of x_1 declines from segment to segment. The decline merely expresses quantitatively the consumer's preference for the mean over widely separated but equally ranked extremes. The indifference contours intersect the axes, contrary to the figures drawn in any textbooks. The reason is that either commodity can be used alone, as the first and sixth processes attest. Since the consumer would never choose a slack process, we have excluded them from the problem. If a consumer cannot use either commodity alone, as in the case of perfect complementarity, the contours must have terminal horizontal and vertical segments representing slack processes and will not intersect the axes. The axes themselves then form an indifference contour with zero utility. The conclusions carry over to smooth indifference contours; drawing such contours with no points on the axes implies that either commodity alone has no utility.

The preceding example does not reveal the full importance of consumption processes. In the case of the firm, maximizing output for given inputs is a device for eliminating inferior or dominated technological processes. The theory of the firm, as customarily presented in economics, assumes that the elimination of inferior methods has already been carried out and that the entrepreneur has an output function showing the maximum attainable output for each combination of inputs. Though it has not been generally recognized, the established theory of consumer's choice rests upon an analogous simplification.

There are, of course, many inferior consumption processes that are ruled out in one way or another. Books could be used for a fire in the fireplace and, in extreme cases, might be so used. Generally, though, enjoying a fire is but one of many consumption processes and the available inputs must be allocated over all processes in an optimal way. With cordwood available no literate consumer is likely to burn books. For each combination of commodities a consumer determines the optimal way of allocating them over the various consumption processes. In the traditional theory, a consumer going forth to market has already made all optimizing decisions that do not require the information provided by market prices. The results of these decisions are embodied in a consistent preference ranking or, alternatively, in a utility function. The final step is to make an optimal choice within the budget constraint.

Economic theory has been market oriented. It has focused upon the interaction of buyers and sellers in markets and upon the consequent allocation of resources. Consumers and firms are assumed to be equipped with just the information needed for making optimizing decisions as buyers or sellers. As we have seen, a firm, particularly one with many plants and many products, has formidable problems of internal allocation to solve. The solution of these internal problems provides the technological information summarized in an output function. The consuming unit faces similar internal problems, particularly when it is a family or household consisting of several persons. Interpreted more broadly, economics includes not merely market behavior but the internal allocative decisions within producing and consuming units.

It has been only fairly recently that economists have begun to look into the allocative decisions of consuming units, and the implications are not as yet clear. In Chapter 14 we shall take up the family and the problems it poses for the theory of consumer's choice.

SUMMARY AND HISTORICAL NOTE ON PREFERENCE AND UTILITY

Just as we did for the firm, we can, conceptually, insert between any two consumption processes a process that dominates their linear combination.

This is one specific way of establishing that a consumer always prefers the mean to either of two equally ranked extremes. The conventional theory of consumer's choice does not try to account for preferences but simply posits that the preferences satisfy a set of axioms. It leaves open an explanation in terms of consumption processes, where such an explanation is appropriate, but does not require any such explanation. We have taken advantage of the opening to use the consumption process as a simple device for showing the relation between preference and utility and, later, between preference and choice. There are other reasons as well, as just explained. Once we go below the surface of preference, consumption processes, though not necessarily linear processes, have a definite place in consumption theory. The recent introduction of consumption processes may in time lead to significant revisions of the theory.

One result of using linear processes is very special and must be dropped; another carries over and holds generally. Linear processes, no matter how large the number, generate indifference contours that are parallel along rays, a restriction that is abandoned in the following chapter. Secondly, the line segments in the piecewise-linear contours have slopes that equal the negative ratio of the marginal utilities. The result remains valid when cones shrink to rays and the line segments to points. If the contours are smooth, the tangent line at every point has its slope equal to the negative ratio of marginal utilities. At vertices, if they exist, the ratio of marginal utilities lies within a range and does not have a unique value.

For a very special case, we have shown that utility numbers can be assigned and a utility function derived to represent preferences. Indifferent combinations receive the same number and preferred combinations higher numbers. This important result also holds generally. The axioms set forth earlier in the chapter, including the continuity of the preference relation, are sufficient to prove the existence of a continuous utility function that represents preferences. Thus, any pattern of preferences that satisfies the axioms, in either the weak or the strong form, can be represented by a continuous utility function.

We must ask next whether there is only one such function, and the answer should be clear by now. In the case of height we saw that we could not retrieve a unique height function from a ranking alone. If two numbers are chosen to represent height classes, any other numbers with the same order will do as well. The conclusion holds for a utility index derived from a preference ranking. If one index represents the ranking so does any increasing function of that index. An increasing function, illustrated in Figure 12–1, is a function that constantly rises, never becoming horizontal and never dropping down. Specifically, once a utility index or utility function is chosen, someone can come along and multiply all numbers by a positive constant, square them, take their logarithms, or make any other transformation, so long as the larger of two numbers before the change becomes the larger afterward.

In technical mathematical language, utility is unique up to a continuous, increasing transformation.

In our discussion preference is basic and utility follows from it. Historically, utility preceded preference, and the indifference map was first derived from a utility function rather than being built up from a preference relation. Utility was expressed as a function of the commodities consumed,

$$U = f(x_1, x_2, x_3, \ldots, x_n).$$

The function was endowed with the necessary properties to ensure that utility increased along rays and that the iso-utility contours were downward sloping, convex, and continuous. The main reason for introducing the utility function was to predict consumer's choice by using the maximizing techniques of the differential calculus. Since the calculus abhors corners, the function and the contours had to be smooth, as the term was explained in Chapter 9. There is no economic reason why indifference contours should be smooth, so the assumption has to be justified as a sufficiently close approximation that permits an easier derivation of valid general results.

The use of the differential calculus in the traditional theory of consumer's choice has been retained and, indeed, refined, but other aspects of the original formulation have been modified drastically. Before the concept of utility appeared in economics around 1870, demand was explained in terms of basic needs and wants and the ability of each commodity to satisfy specific needs. It was a considerable feat of unification and generalization to introduce utility as a general measure of the want-satisfying capability of diverse combinations of commodities. The term itself and some of its meaning were taken over from the social philosophy of Utilitarianism that flourished in the first half of the nineteenth century. Early utility theorists in economics believed that utility, though a subjective or introspective quantity, was clearly felt or recognized by an individual and served as a guide to choice. Samuelson has epitomized the state of mind by remarking that to Edgeworth, a famous nineteenth century economist, utility was "as real as his morning jam."

By the end of the nineteenth century, some economists, notably Pareto, had come to recognize that the assumption of a unique utility function for an individual was unnecessary and, probably, unwarranted. As they saw it, the essential information was embodied in the indifference contours, and the utility numbers assigned to the contours were of no significance. Hence, if one utility function or index has the desired properties, an increasing function of that index will do as well. Partly out of tradition but mainly for mathematical convenience, the modern theory of consumer's choice, as customarily presented, begins with the assumption of a utility function, but the theory accepts as valid only those economic results that follow from a preference ordering.

A utility index that is not unique but subject to an increasing transformation is called *ordinal*, since such an index imparts only an ordering to the commodity bundles. By contrast, the term *cardinal* is applied to the earlier concept of utility as a unique function. In this context, cardinal means that the real numbers representing utility retain all of their arithmetic properties as well as order. It is doubtful that the early theorists regarded utility as measurable in the sense of being subject only to increasing linear transformations that change units and shift the origin. In any event, the issue was not explicitly raised until much later, in the early 1940's, when a different concept of utility was developed for the theory of games. There are some economists who still believe in the existence of an introspective cardinal, or at least measurable, utility. The majority of economists either doubt the existence of subjective utility or question the need for it. The modern theory of ordinal utility represents a consensus; it preserves the portion of the original theory on which nearly all can agree, its correspondence with a preference ordering.

To most economists the main justification for employing a utility function is that the differential calculus, like linear programming, contains a highly useful technique for varying parameters and calculating the response of the optimal quantities to the changes. The price that has to be paid is an additional assumption, beyond those required for preference, that the utility function has smooth iso-utility or indifference contours. Since the purpose is to derive general properties of demand, the price is certainly not too high. In Chapter 13 we shall, as an alternative method, use parametric programming followed by a process of smoothing to derive the same general results.

EXERCISES

1. *Relations and Their Properties*

For the following relations choose some appropriate large set, such as the population of the United States, on which each is defined, that is, on which it has meaning. By trying to apply each relation to one, to two, and then to three typical members, determine whether each relation is reflexive, irreflexive, or neither; symmetric, asymmetric, or neither; transitive, intransitive, or neither.

(a) "is a first cousin of"
(b) "is a son of"
(c) "is a relative of"
(d) "is a friend of"
(e) "is richer than"
(f) "is not older than"
(g) "is as old as"

Identify any equivalence relations and any relations that determine strong or weak orderings or preorderings. State whether each ordering or preordering is complete or partial on the set you have chosen for it.

2. *The Partial Ordering of Vectors*

(a) Define the relation $<$ for vectors and the relation $\leqq$. Explain why each is necessarily partial rather than complete. By comparing components show that the relation $<$ for vectors determines a strong partial ordering and that the relation $\leqq$ for vectors determines a weak partial ordering.

(b) Rank each of the following vectors with respect to as many other vectors as possible: [2, 2], [3, 0], [$\frac{3}{2}$, $\frac{1}{2}$], [1, 6], [2, 3], and [4, 3]. Use the property of transitivity to find the largest subset that can be unequivocally ranked. Check by graphing.

(c) The relation $<$ for vectors, unlike that for real numbers, permits differences of degree. We can give separate recognition to the case where *all* matching components are smaller and use the stronger symbolic notation, $x^a \ll x^b$. Nonsatiability may be expressed by the following two conditions:

$$x^a \prec x^b \quad \text{whenever} \quad x^a \ll x^b$$

$$x^a \precsim x^b \quad \text{whenever} \quad x^a < x^b.$$

Show that these two conditions express the *weaker* form of the nonsatiability axiom presented in the text. Illustrate graphically the difference between the strong and the weaker forms of the axiom.

3. *Satiation and the Preference for More over Less*

In this exercise "more" and "less" are defined by the partial ordering of vectors as presented in the text. The following three axioms describe possible patterns of consumer reaction to increases in commodities:

(A) (Strong): A consumer always prefers more to less.

(B) (Weakest): A consumer never prefers less to more.

(C) (Intermediate or weaker): A consumer never prefers less to more and always prefers more to less with respect to at least one commodity.

Show that the intermediate axiom (C) is almost, but not quite, equivalent to the weaker form of the axiom, as stated on page 294. Consider perfect complements. Which statement of the axiom permits and which does not? Are they otherwise equivalent?

(a) Along a ray in commodity space, do all three axioms require that more distant points have higher ranking? Do any permit an equal ranking? A lower ranking? Specifically, what does each axiom permit and require in the assignment of utility numbers along rays?

(b) The possibility of satiation exists if there is at least one commodity bundle with no other bundle preferred to it; that is, if there is an $\mathbf{x}^s$ such that $\mathbf{x} \precsim \mathbf{x}^s$ for all commodity bundles x in the consumption set. Which of the preceding axioms rule out satiation and which do not?

(c) Show with the aid of a graph that the strong axiom requires the indifference curve through any point to be downward sloping. Show further that all indifference curves must intersect the axes.

Does the weakest axiom permit indifference curves to slope upward? Demonstrate that the weakest axiom permits bands of indifference and does not require one point of indifference on every ray.

Does the intermediate or weaker axiom permit bands of indifference? Demonstrate that the weaker or intermediate axiom allows indifference contours to have vertical or horizontal segments. Show why it also permits indifference curves to approach the axes without touching them. Do the results hold for the axiom of page 294?

4. *Consumer's Choice under Different Convexity Axioms*

(a) Define the available set and write as the intersection of closed half-spaces in two dimensions. How does the available set change when one commodity price is zero? Is there any difference between the available set and the constraint set or feasible set?

(b) Show that under both the strong and the *weaker* or *intermediate* nonsatiability axiom a consumer always makes a choice on the outer boundary of the available set. When one price is zero, do the two versions lead to different results? Check your answer by graphing. In the remaining parts of the question rule out zero prices.

(c) Suppose that a consumer *always* prefers either of two equally ranked extremes to any weighted average of the two. Use the axiom to predict the consumer's choice. Show graphically.

(d) A consumer *never* prefers either of two equally ranked extremes to their mean. Can you predict choice from the preference ordering? Illustrate by a graph.

(e) A consumer *always* prefers the mean to either of two equally ranked extremes. Use the axiom to show that there must be a unique highest ranked bundle in the available set whenever prices and income are positive. Can choice be predicted?

(f) Suppose that the indifference contours are smoothed. Part (e) established that every set of positive prices and income determines a unique highest ranked bundle. Show that smoothing implies the following: For every commodity bundle there is one and only one ratio of positive prices at which it can have highest ranking.

5. *Unequally Ranked Extremes*

The weaker version of the convexity axiom merely states that a consumer never prefers either of two equally ranked extremes to any weighted average. It is silent about the preference for means when the extremes are not equally ranked. This exercise examines the various possibilities. Let $\mathbf{x}^m = (1-t)\mathbf{x}^b + t\mathbf{x}^a$, $0 < t < 1$.

Two of the possibilities are as follows:

(a) If $\mathbf{x}^b \succ \mathbf{x}^a$, then $\mathbf{x}^m \succsim \mathbf{x}^a$. This condition may be paraphrased as follows: "If one loaf is better than no loaves, then half a loaf is not worse than none at all."

(b) If $\mathbf{x}^b \succ \mathbf{x}^a$, then $\mathbf{x}^m \succ \mathbf{x}^a$. The paraphrase is as follows: "If one loaf is better than no loaves, then half a loaf is better than none."

By selecting points on a ray, show that (a) permits bands of indifference but (b) does not. Show that the weaker or intermediate version of the nonsatiability axiom makes (b) the only effective possibility.

The convexity axiom is often stated in the form of (b), without reference to equally ranked extremes. Show that (b) rules out concavity and hence implies the weaker convexity axiom as stated in the text.

There is a third possibility: (c) If $\mathbf{x}^b \succ \mathbf{x}^a$, then $\mathbf{x}^m \succ \mathbf{x}^b$. Readers who are curious may show, by choosing points on a ray, that (c) violates transitivity as well as nonsatiability.

6. *A Linear Model of Utility Maximization*

The following numerical example represents the maximization of utility for given commodity levels:

$$\begin{aligned}
0v_1 + 3v_2 + 4v_3 + 6v_4 + 12v_5 + 20v_6 &= q_1 + 0q_2 \\
36v_1 + 12v_2 + 6v_3 + 4v_4 + 2v_5 + 0v_6 &= 0q_1 + q_2 \\
10v_1 + 10v_2 + 10v_3 + 10v_4 + 10v_5 + 10v_6 &= 0q_1 + 0q_2 + U(\max).
\end{aligned}$$

(a) What general assumptions and what special assumption about consumer preference are required to justify the model?

(b) Graph an iso-utility contour or indifference curve. What assumptions about preference rule out the possibility of a dominated process such as [10, 10, 10]? What assumptions about preference assure that linear combinations of adjacent processes will always form the line segments of a contour?

(c) Write utility in symbolic form as a linear function of the commodities. What is the meaning of the dual variables? Find the piecewise-linear utility function and present in the form of Table 12–1. How do proportional changes in all utility coefficients affect the utility function and the iso-utility map?

7. *An Alternative Linear Minimization Problem*

Exercise 6 develops what may be called the technological maximization problem for a consumer. By analogy with the firm set up the technological minimizing problem for a consumer. To what extent do the results of the two problems coincide? Express the objective function symbolically after reduction to canonical form using the same coefficients as for the firm. What is the economic meaning of the coefficients in this context?

8. *The Preference Relation Determined by a Utility Function*

A utility function is defined on the consumption set if it assigns to every commodity bundle one and only one real number, called its utility number. Define the relations: $x^a \prec \mathbf{x}^b$ if $U(\mathbf{x}^a) < U(\mathbf{x}^b)$; $\mathbf{x}^a \sim \mathbf{x}^b$ if $U(\mathbf{x}^a) = U(\mathbf{x}^b)$. What properties does each relation possess? What properties does the combined relation $\precsim$ possess?

Suppose that we choose a new utility index U^* that is a function of the original index U. The new index also assigns one and only one utility number to each combination, the number determined by the function $U^* = F(U)$. For each of the following specific functions or transformations of U, determine whether the new index U^* gives the same ranking: $U^* =$ (a) U^2; (b) $U^2 - U + 3$; (c) $1/U$; (d) $3 + 2U$; (e) $-6 + 5U$; (f) $6 - 5U$. Explain what is meant by a function that preserves measurements. Which of the preceding qualify?

9. *Utility Functions and the Preference Axioms*

Each of the following candidates for a utility function assigns one and only one utility number to each commodity bundle in the consumption set: $U =$ (a) $x_1^2 + x_2^2$; (b) $x_1 x_2$; (c) $x_1 + x_2$; (d) $1/x_1 x_2$; (e) $(x_1 - 1)^2 + (x_2 - 1)^2$; (f) $-1/x_1 x_2$.

For each function describe the behavior of utility along rays and state what it implies about preferences for more and less. Describe in general terms the iso-utility contours for each function and state what the shape of these contours implies about preferences for means and extremes. Which are acceptable utility functions in the sense of satisfying the preference axioms in either strong or weak form?

13

Choice and Demand

The reason for introducing either preference or utility is to explain or predict consumer's choice. The presence of a budget constraint limits choice to members of the available set. The basic assumption about consumer motivation, which forms the link between preference and choice, is that a consumer never chooses one member of the available set while preferring another. If a commodity bundle is chosen, no other bundle in the available set is preferred to it. So long as more is preferred to less, choice must be made from commodity bundles on the budget line or outer boundary of the available set.

Uncertainty arises when the indifference contours contain line segments and a line segment coincides with the budget line. Preference narrows the range of choice but does not shrink it to a single commodity bundle. Unless some additional criterion is introduced, choice cannot be predicted. We cannot rule out the possibility that a consumer may be truly indifferent between distinct commodity bundles, but we can minimize its significance. Since any choice is better than none at all, the consumer is not likely to agonize indefinitely over which to choose. Further, the probability that a line segment will coincide with the budget line is vanishingly small. It can occur for only a few specific price ratios out of an infinity of such ratios. Since ties are a rare phenomenon, we shall not attempt to explain how they are broken. At worst, the existence of ties is a minor qualification to general conclusions about consumer's choice. Once the transition is made to smooth contours, choice is unique, and the minor qualification disappears.

When preferences are translated into a utility function, choice can be predicted by the maximization of utility. A consumer will not choose one bundle when another is available that yields greater utility. The advantage of the alternative utility maximization model is that it provides techniques for predicting how the optimal quantities change in response to variations in income and prices. Thus, patterns of preference can be converted into properties of the demand functions. As usual, we shall employ a linear model first and then smooth the results.

PARAMETRIC VARIATION: ENGEL CURVES AND DEMAND CURVES

To derive a utility function, as in Chapter 12, utility is maximized for constant amounts of the commodities. In predicting choice, utility is maximized subject to a budget constraint. Both commodities become variables but their amounts are limited by prices and the available money income, as in the following reformulation:

$$\begin{aligned}
a_{11}v_1+a_{12}v_2+a_{13}v_3+a_{14}v_4+a_{15}v_5+a_{16}v_6-x_1 \quad &= 0\\
a_{21}v_1+a_{22}v_2+a_{23}v_3+a_{24}v_4+a_{25}v_5+a_{26}v_6 \quad -x_2 &= 0\\
p_1x_1+p_2x_2 &= y^0\\
1v_1+\ 1v_2+\ 1v_3+\ 1v_4+\ 1v_5+\ 1v_6 \quad &= U(\max).
\end{aligned}$$

The first two equations can be used to replace x_1 and x_2 in the third equation with the resultant simplification:

$$\begin{aligned}
(p_1a_{11}+p_2a_{21})v_1+(p_1a_{12}+p_2a_{22})v_2+(p_1a_{13}+p_2a_{23})v_3+\cdots &= y^0\\
1v_1+ \qquad\qquad 1v_2+ \qquad\qquad 1v_3 \qquad\qquad &\\
+\cdots &= 0y^0+U(\max).
\end{aligned}$$

Since each process is scaled to yield one unit of utility, the optimal solution is the process with lowest cost at the current levels of prices. Ties are possible but highly improbable, since they occur only for several specific price ratios out of the infinity of possible ratios. Thus, the optimum is almost certain to lie at a vertex rather than along an entire line segment.

Reduction to canonical form converts utility to a function of income or expenditure, $U = \bar{u}y^0$, the coefficient being the marginal utility of income or expenditure. It is the dual variable of the maximization problem and gives the rate of change or of exchange between utility and money for one consumer.[1] If, say, the third process is the least costly, reduction to canonical form shows that

$$U = \frac{1}{p_1 a_{13} + p_2 a_{23}} y^0 = \bar{u} y^0.$$

As expected, the marginal utility of expenditure is the reciprocal of the marginal cost of utility. When market prices increase with income constant, the marginal cost of utility becomes greater and the marginal utility of money becomes proportionately smaller.

There are two sets of prices, the internal prices determined by the assignment of utility numbers to represent preference and the market prices. The situation is not unlike trade between two countries, where a foreign exchange rate develops between the two currencies or standards of value. The marginal utility of income or money represents the rate of conversion between the internal and external standards of value. The flaw in the analogy is that the internal standard of value is completely arbitrary. We can multiply utility and, hence, the marginal utility of money by any positive number whatsoever. The only conclusion that remains valid is that the marginal utility of income is some positive number.

Engel Curves

With both prices constant, the parametric variation of income, which represents a parallel shift of the budget line, does not affect the optimal solution. As readers may verify geometrically, the optimal solution continues to be found at a vertex on the same ray or along parallel line segments. When income varies with prices constant, the locus of all optimal solutions is a ray in commodity space.[2] Such a locus is called an *Engel curve or income-consumption curve*. When plotted separately against income, each commodity also lies on a straight line through the origin. The income-consumption curves take the simple form of rays only when the indifference contours are parallel along rays, a limitation that is soon to be dropped.

A proportional change in both prices causes the same proportional change in all cost coefficients and does not affect the choice of process. If both prices are cut in half, the effect is the same as a doubling of money income with prices constant. When prices and income increase or decrease together in the same proportion, the effects cancel each other and the con-

[1]Readers familiar with constrained optimization by the differential calculus will note the resemblance of $\bar{u}$ to the Lagrange multiplier. There is a very close connection, almost an identity, between dual variables and Lagrange multipliers. Both measure the rate of change of the objective variable with respect to a quantity in constraint.

[2]In the improbable case where a line segment coincides with the budget line, the locus is the entire cone formed by two distinct rays. We shall ignore this unlikely possibility since it disappears when contours are smoothed.

sumer continues to buy the same quantities. Geometrically, such changes are not even discernible, since the budget line,

$$x_2 = -\frac{p_1}{p_2}x_1 + \frac{y^0}{p_2},$$

retains the same slope and the same intercept. The conclusion does not depend on any special pattern of consumer preference but is traceable to the budget constraint. So long as expenditure always equals income or, more generally, always bears the same ratio to income, equiproportional changes do not affect the amounts a consumer buys. A consumer who seeks to maximize utility, and has succeeded in doing so before the change, must remain unaffected by the change.

The phrase "absence of money illusion" is generally used to characterize the lack of response to proportional changes in prices and money income; the consumer sees through the monetary changes to the underlying real or nonmonetary situation. In the present case, a consumer who is not fooled by price changes does not alter his purchases, but such a response need not be correct in all cases. As we shall see later, when expenditure is not always equal or proportional to money income, price changes do make a difference even when income varies in the same ratio as prices. A consumer *is* fooled by price changes unless he does alter the quantities bought.

Price-Consumption Curves

When one price alone varies, the cost coefficients do not change proportionately, and one solution cannot remain optimal indefinitely. So long as the current solution does remain optimal, the consumer continues to buy both commodities in the same ratio, but the lower price of one permits him to buy more of both. The effect on each commodity is the same as that of a change in income and is called the *income effect of a price change.* As one price changes continuously, a tie between processes emerges, followed by an abrupt shift to a new process. The numerical example of Chapter 12, with p_2 set at 5 and y^0 at 50, provides the following specific problem:

$$50v_1 + (p_1+30)v_2 + (2p_1+20)v_3 + (3p_1+15)v_4 + (7p_1+5)v_5 + (12p_1)v_6 = 50$$

$$1v_1 + 1v_2 + 1v_3 + 1v_4 + 1v_5 + 1v_6 = U(\max).$$

So long as p_1 remains above 20, the first process is the least costly, and the consumer spends the entire income on x_2. At any price below 20, x_1 is also bought. By equating the coefficients of adjacent processes, readers may determine the critical values of p_1 at which ties occur and shifts are about to take place.

The results of a continuous decline in p_1 are graphed in Figure 13–1. When the first price alone varies, the slope of the budget line changes but the vertical intercept does not since it represents the maximum amount of x_2 the fixed money income will buy at the constant price. As p_1 decreases, the budget line remains anchored on the vertical axis and swings upward, approaching the horizontal as p_1 approaches zero. When p_1 is above 20, the budget line is steeper than any segment of the indifference contours, and the solution occurs on the vertical axis, which represents the first process. As soon as p_1 drops below 20, the optimal solution shifts to the second ray or process, continuing along it until p_1 reaches the next critical value and the budget line coincides with a line segment of a contour. With a further reduction in p_1, the optimal solution shifts to the next lower ray.

In the linear model, a decline in price produces an alternation of outward movements along rays and downward movements along contours. The outward movement along rays, during which a single solution remains optimal, is the income effect of a price change. When contours are parallel along rays, both commodities increase proportionately. During the downward movement along contours, one commodity increases at the expense of the other or is substituted for it. Since it is unalloyed with any income effect, the response of quantities along the same contour is called the *pure substitution effect of a price change.*

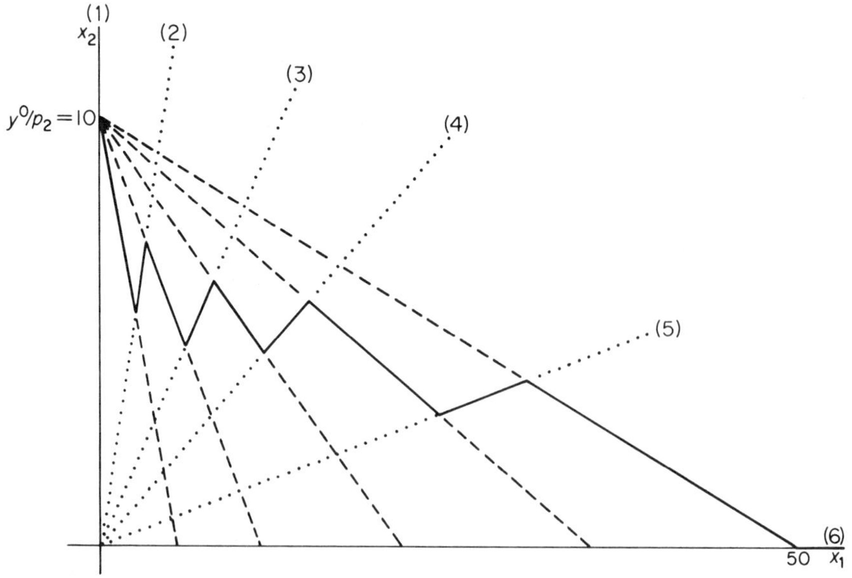

Fig. 13-1 A Price-Consumption Curve for the Linear Model

When one price changes, the locus of all optimal combinations in commodity space is called a *price-consumption curve.* It is an intermediate step in the derivation of demand curves. At each value of p_1 we can find the optimal solution, select the value of x_1 in that solution, and plot the pair of values as a point in price-quantity space. Such a procedure is obviously tedious, so we should like to have some general way of transferring or mapping the results from commodity space into price-quantity space. So long as the optimal solution lies on, say, the third ray, it is the point of intersection of the budget line and the ray or the solution of the following equations:[3]

$$p_1x_1+p_2x_2 = y^0$$

$$a_{23}x_1-a_{13}x_2 = 0.$$

The solution is

$$x_1 = \frac{a_{13}y^0}{p_1a_{13}+p_2a_{23}} \qquad x_2 = \frac{a_{23}y^0}{p_1a_{13}+p_2a_{23}}.$$

If we set $y^0 = 50$, $p_2 = 5$, and choose $\mathbf{a}_3 = [a_{13}, a_{23}] = [2, 4]$ from the numerical example, the solution becomes

$$x_1 = \frac{50}{p_1+10} \qquad x_2 = \frac{100}{p_1+10}.$$

As p_1 varies, x_1 traces out the curve in price-quantity space shown in Figure 13–2b. When $p_1 = 0$ the curve intersects the horizontal axis and x_1 has its greatest value, 5. In commodity space, the budget line is horizontal. As p_1 increases and the budget line rotates downward, x_1 decreases along the curve, approaching zero as p_1 increases without limit and the budget line approaches a vertical position. If we reverse directions, any outward movement along the specified ray in commodity space generates a downward movement along the corresponding curve in the price-quantity space for x_1.

Demand Schedules and Demand Curves

If the two commodities are perfect complements, all optimal solutions do lie on the same ray, and Figure 13–2b represents the demand curve for x_1. In general, the optimal solution shifts from ray to ray as p_1 declines. Each ray generates a distinct curve in price-quantity space, which we shall call its image curve. The smaller the slope of a ray, the farther to the right its image curve must lie. The reason is that a given budget line always intersects a lower ray at a larger value of x_1. The lowest ray of all is the horizontal axis, when all income is spent on x_1 alone. The corresponding image curve is the

[3]Along the third ray, the ray generated by $\mathbf{a}_3 = [a_{13}, a_{23}]$, the variables are in the ratio $x_2/x_1 = a_{23}/a_{13}$. Crossmultiplication gives the equation in the text.

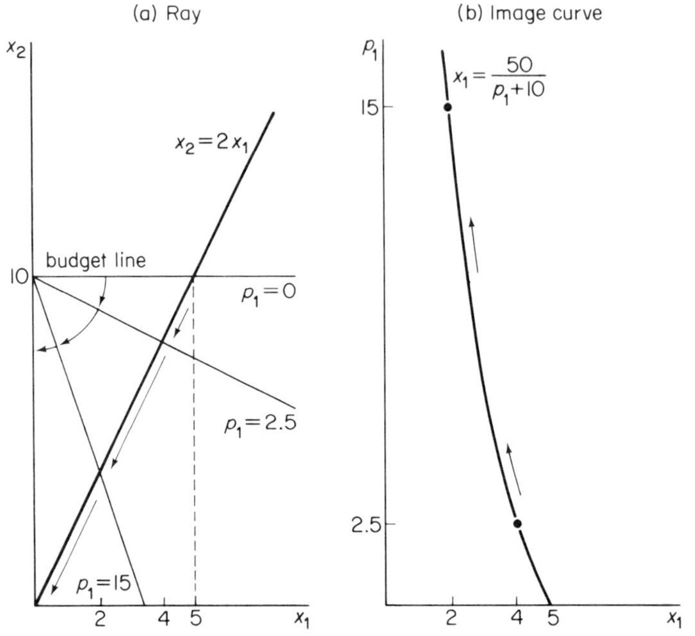

Fig. 13-2 The Image Curve of a Ray

rectangular hyperbola $p_1x_1 = y^0$ which lies farthest to the right. The steepest ray is the vertical axis, where $x_1 = 0$. The image curve is the vertical axis in price-quantity space. Downward shifts to a lower ray become horizontal rightward shifts to the corresponding image curve.

Table 13–1 displays the demand schedule for x_1. To construct it we need to know the image curve for each of the six rays in the numerical example and the range of p_1 over which it remains effective. To get the equation of each image curve we can solve the appropriate pair of linear equations or simply replace a_{13} and a_{23} by the corresponding numbers for each ray. An image curve holds over a range of p_1 for which the corresponding ray or process remains optimal. Alternatively, the range is determined by the values of p_1 at which the budget line has the same slope as each of two successive line segments in the contours. Column (3) shows the income effect of the price change, the extent of the change in x_1 along each of the image curves. Column (4) records the size of the shift from one curve to the next, which is the pure substitution effect. Figure 13–3 graphs the results as the demand curve for x_1.

We can now see how the shape of the indifference contours affects the demand curve for a commodity. With perfect complementarity and right-angled contours, the demand curve coincides with a single image curve, and the quantity demanded shows relatively little response to price changes. The

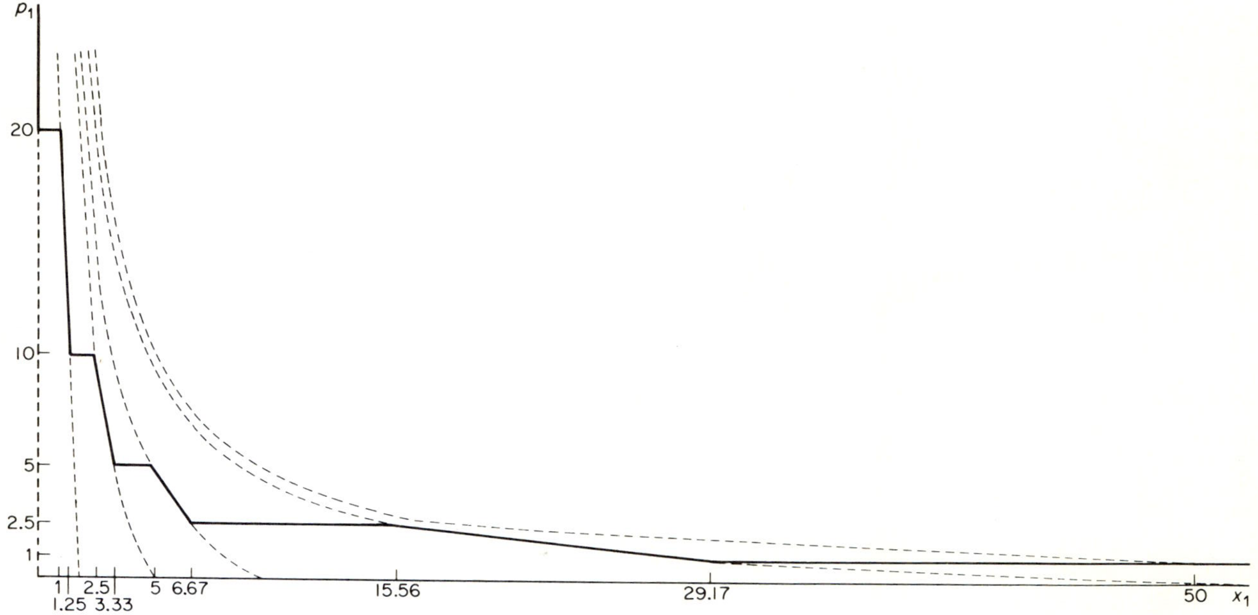

Fig. 13-3 The Demand Curve for a Commodity

TABLE 13–1

Demand Schedule for Commodity 1 ($p_2 = 5$; $y^0 = 5.0$)

Image curve for x_1 (1)	Range of p_1 (2)	Range of x_1: Income effect (3)	Range of x_1: Pure substitution effect (4)
$x_1 = 0$	$p_1 \geqq 20$	none	
			0 to 1
$\frac{50}{p_1+30}$	20 to 10	1 to 1·25	
			1·25 to 2·5
$\frac{50}{p_1+10}$	10 to 5	2·5 to 3·33	
			3·33 to 5
$\frac{50}{p_1+5}$	5 to 2·5	5 to 6·67	
			6·67 to 15·56
$\frac{50}{p_1+\frac{5}{7}}$	2·5 to 1	15·56 to 29·17	
			29·17 to 50
$\frac{50}{p_1+0}$	1 to 0	50 to no upper limit	

response to a given price change is greater when the downward movement along any one image curve is relatively short. If the line segments meeting in a vertex have nearly equal slopes, the outward expansion along that ray will not last very long. In the limiting case where all segments have the same slope, there is no income effect along any ray but the horizontal axis. At the

TABLE 13–2

The Cross-Demand Schedule for Commodity 2 ($p_2 = 5$; $y^0 = 50$)

Image curve for x_2 (1)	Range of p_1 (2)	Range of x_2: Income effect (3)	Range of x_2: Pure substitution effect (4)
$\frac{500}{0+50}$	$p_1 \geqq 20$	none	
			10 to 6
$\frac{300}{p_1+30}$	20 to 10	6 to 7·5	
			7·5 to 5
$\frac{100}{p_1+10}$	10 to 5	5 to 6·67	
			6·67 to 5
$\frac{50}{p_1+5}$	5 to 2·5	5 to 6·67	
			6·67 to 2·45
$\frac{50}{7p_1+5}$	2·5 to 1	2·45 to 4·17	
			4·17 to 0
0	1 to 0	none	

critical price ratio, the consumer jumps from spending all income on x_2 to spending all income on x_1. The demand curve consists of the vertical axis above the critical price and a rectangular hyperbola below. The two commodities are termed *perfect substitutes*, since the consumer is indifferent between either commodity alone or any weighted averages of the two. Depending on which extreme the contours resemble most closely, the demand curve will be relatively steep or relatively flat between the axis and the hyperbola.

Cross-Demand Curves

From the price-consumption curve in commodity space we can also derive pairs of values for x_2 and p_1 by first finding the equation for x_2 in terms of p_1 along each ray. The results are summarized in Table 13–2 as the cross-demand schedule for x_2. Along a contour, a decline in p_1 always causes a decline in x_2. The income effect of the price change goes in the opposite direction, since a decline in p_1 permits the consumer to buy more of both commodities. So long as the indifference contours are parallel along rays, changes in the other commodity's price have offsetting income and pure substitution effects. By contrast, changes in a commodity's own price have reinforcing income and pure substitution effects. Such relationships are normal but by no means universal once we drop the simplification of parallel indifference contours. Figure 13–4 graphs the cross-demand curve for x_2.

PARAMETRIC VARIATION WITH SMOOTH INDIFFERENCE CONTOURS

With smooth indifference contours, the optimal solution, except when it lies on an axis, always occurs at a point of tangency between the budget line and a contour.[4] So long as the contours, after smoothing, remain parallel along rays, a change in income with prices constant continues to generate Engel curves that are rays. With income constant, any change in p_1, however small, causes the point of tangency to shift to a different ray as well as a different contour. The income effect along a ray and the pure substitution effect along a contour take place simultaneously not consecutively. The relative strengths of the income and pure substitution effects are no longer shown by the durations of the outward movement along rays and the downward movement along contours. The two effects combine to determine at each point the direction the price-consumption curve takes in Figure 13–5a.

As demonstrated for the linear model, every ray on the indifference map

[4]As explained earlier, the axioms on preference, even in the strongest version, do not imply smooth indifference contours, but leave open the possibility of vertices formed by arcs of curves. The presence of such vertices has a negligble effect on the economic content of the theory and affects mainly the mathematical formulation. The main effect is to produce corresponding vertices or kinks in the demand curve.

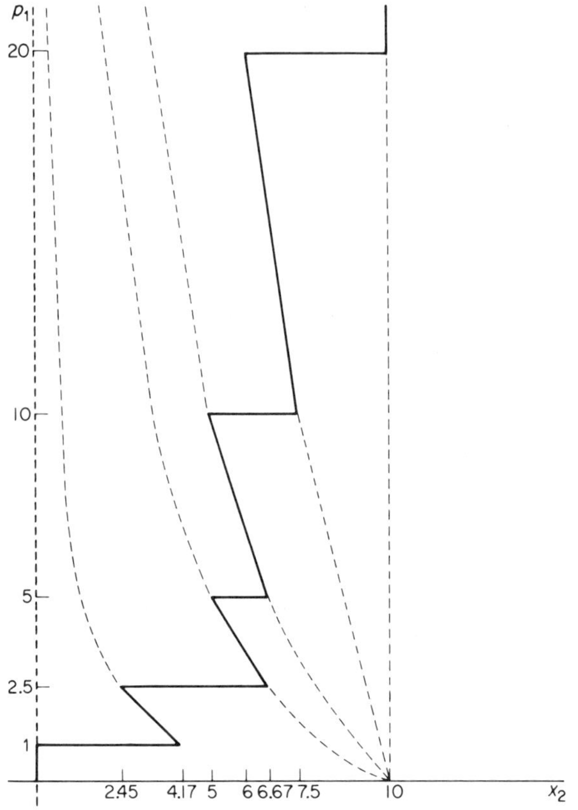

Fig. 13-4 The Cross-Demand Curve for a Commodity

determines one member of an infinite family of image curves in the price-quantity space. With parallel contours, there is one and only one optimal solution on each ray, except for the axes, and only one point on the corresponding image curve. The demand curve (Figure 13–5b) cuts across the whole infinite family of image curves, having only one point in common with each member except the first and last. At high prices, x_1 is not bought and the vertical axis represents the demand curve. At sufficiently low prices, x_1 is bought exclusively and the demand curve coincides with the rectangular hyperbola, $x_1 = y^0/p_1$. With smooth contours, the demand curve is also smooth, except for the corners at the initial and terminal portions. The direction or slope of the demand curve depends on the relative strengths of the income and pure substitution effects. The income effect is a movement down a single image curve and contributes to steepness of slope. The pure substitution effect is a right-ward shift and contributes solely to flatness.

The indifference contours of Figure 13–5a intersect both axes, implying that either commodity alone has some utility to the consumer. The consumer does not buy x_1 when its price is too high and buys it exclusively when the price drops sufficiently. To refrain from buying at very high prices is plausible but to buy one commodity exclusively is not. Yet, with only two commodities, one requires the other. The source of the difficulty is restricting the number of commodities for a convenient geometric representation. The restriction is removed later. If indifference curves merely approach but do

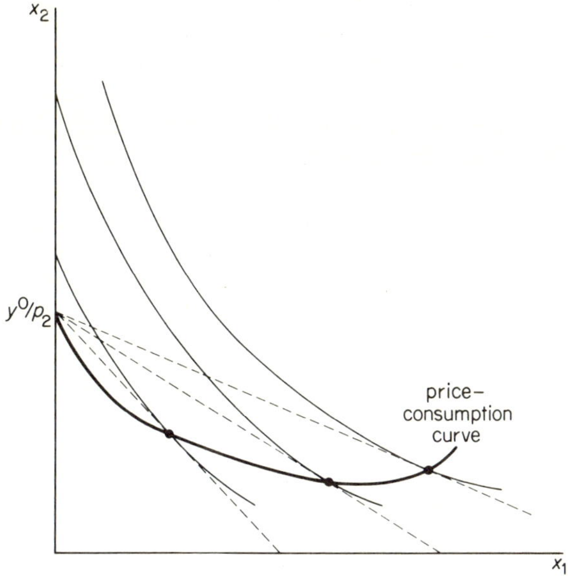

Fig. 13-5a The Price-Consumption Curve

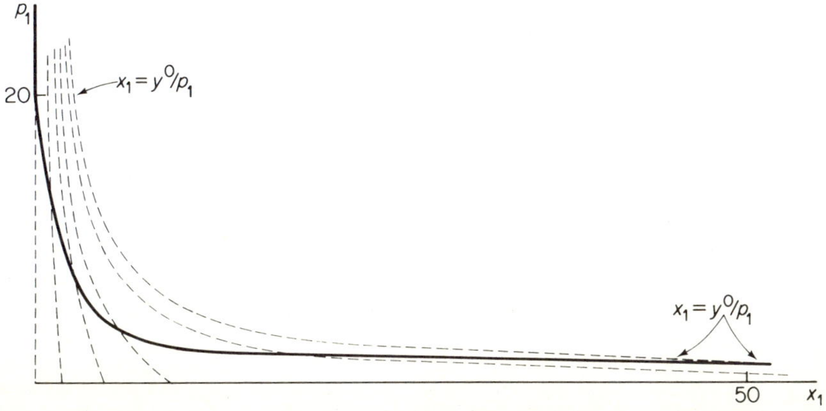

Fig. 13-5b A Smooth Demand Curve

not intersect the axes, the demand curve approaches but does not touch either the vertical axis or the rectangular hyperbola that represents exclusive purchase of x_1.

INDIFFERENCE CONTOURS THAT ARE NOT PARALLEL

Since it has served its purpose, we now drop the simplification that indifference contours are parallel along rays. We do, however, wish to retain one important result from the linear version. The maximization of utility for constant amounts of the commodities generates dual variables or internal valuations of the commodities in the form of marginal utilities. Along each line segment in a contour, the marginal utilities remain constant. As shown for the firm, the results obtained from the linear formulation carry over when the contours are smoothed and the line segments shrink to points. At every point, then, a smooth utility function determines internal valuations or marginal utilities for each commodity. Since the utility index is not unique, only the relative valuations or ratios of marginal utilities are significant.

There is another way of measuring the relative value of the commodities. What is the maximum amount of the second commodity a consumer will give up for an additional unit of the first commodity? A consumer will not part with so much of x_2 as to drop to a lower indifference contour, so the changes must take place along one contour. In the linear version, when a consumer stays on the same line segment, the amount of x_2 that will be given up for an additional unit of x_1 is measured by the slope of that segment. The slope of the segment is negative, but the positive form of the relationship gives a better expression of the economic meaning.[5] Hence, we define *the rate of commodity substitution* of x_2 for x_1 as the negative of the slope along an indifference contour. As derived on page 301, the negative of the slope along a line segment equals the ratio of the marginal utilities. The two methods of valuation yield the same result:

$$-\frac{\Delta x_2}{\Delta x_1} = \text{rate of commodity substitution} = \frac{\bar{u}_1}{\bar{u}_2}.$$

If x_1 is the more valuable commodity ($\bar{u}_1 > \bar{u}_2$), then more than one unit of x_2 must be given up for each unit of x_1 ($-\Delta x_2 > \Delta x_1$). Even though utility is not used to represent preference, a preference ordering implicitly determines how valuable one commodity is relative to the other.

[5]In mathematics, when two quantities change in opposite directions, the changes are given different signs. By their very definition certain economic concepts, such as exchange and substitution, imply changes in the opposite direction. The negative sign is not needed so rates of exchange or substitution can be expressed in the more convenient positive form.

When contours are smoothed, the slope of the line segment is replaced by the slope of the tangent to the contour. Hence, the rate of commodity substitution becomes the negative of the slope of the tangent line at each point. With no vertices there is only one relative valuation or rate of commodity substitution at each point, and the rate of commodity substitution changes from point to point. We cannot accurately express the rate of commodity substitution at a point as the amount of x_2 that will be given up for one additional unit of x_1. Such discrete changes take the consumer along the tangent line to points below the indifference curve. The rate of commodity substitution represents merely a tendency or inclination to interchange the commodities in the specified ratio. The concrete form of the concept is, however, too convenient to drop entirely. We shall use it on occasion, trusting readers to make the correct interpretation.

If each indifference contour consists of a single line segment, the relative amounts or ratios of the commodities have no effect on their relative valuations or rate of commodity substitution. Similarly, if the contours have the same slope along rays, the absolute amounts of the two commodities do not affect their relative valuations. Contours that are convex to the origin imply that the relative value of a commodity goes down as the relative quantity goes up; the greater the amount of x_1 already possessed, the smaller the quantity of x_2 the consumer is willing to sacrifice for an additional unit of x_1. This conclusion follows directly from the axiom that a consumer always prefers means over equally ranked extremes.

The axioms on preference do not yield any specific inferences about the effect of proportional increases in both commodities on their relative valuations. Any pattern is acceptable so long as it does not contradict the axioms. There is, however, plenty of empirical evidence to show that the contours need not be parallel along rays. For obvious reasons, a consumer with rising income does not increase the amount of food consumed proportionately with other items in the budget. Once the simplification of parallel contours is dropped, there are many possible patterns of consumer preference. As increasing income permits higher purchases, a consumer could vacillate, at one stage shifting toward one commodity and then switching back to the other. The example of food illustrates a more plausible general pattern, which has received much attention in economics, a persistent decline in the relative valuation of one commodity as both increase. If indifference curves flatten out as both quantities increase along rays, the rate of commodity substitution of x_2 for x_1 is declining. The consumer gives up progressively smaller amounts of x_2 to acquire a unit of x_1. A unit of x_1 is becoming relatively less valuable.

With the rate of commodity substitution declining along rays, the income-consumption curve no longer coincides with a ray. When income increases at constant prices, a consumer can buy proportionately more of both commodities but chooses, instead, to shift purchases toward the relatively more valuable second commodity (Figure 13–6a). The income effect can be broken down into an outward expansion along a ray and a movement along the budget line to adjust expenditure to the change in relative preference. When income changes continuously, the two movements occur simultaneously and combine to determine the direction in which the income-consumption curve is moving. As indifference curves flatten out along rays the income-consumption curve cuts upward across the rays (Figure 13–6b).

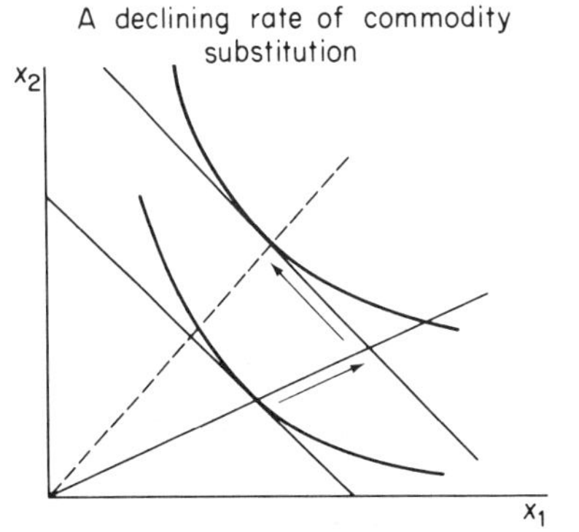

Fig. 13-6a

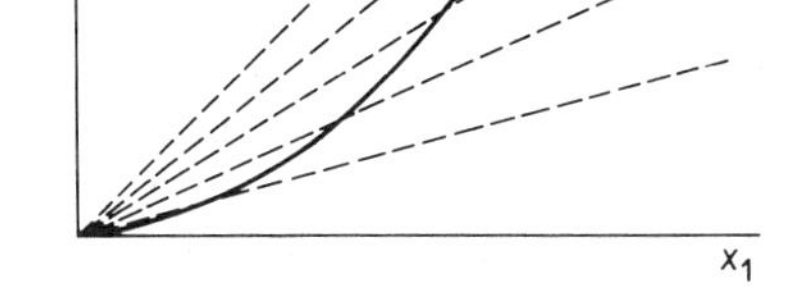

Fig. 13-6b

If the change in the slope of the contours is gradual, the outward movement along rays predominates and the slope of the income-consumption curve is but little greater than that of the ray it is crossing. Conversely, contours could conceivably flatten so rapidly that the outward movement was relatively insignificant and the net effect of a higher income on x_1 was zero or negative. Such a rapid change might, however, be inconsistent with the basic requirements that the indifference contours be nonintersecting, downward sloping, and convex. What we must now determine is just how rapidly the contours can flatten out without violating any of the basic assumptions about consumer's preference.

NORMAL AND INFERIOR COMMODITIES

The intermediate case that separates normal from inferior commodities is a commodity that does not respond at all to increases in income. The income-consumption curve is a vertical line, and the contours must be parallel along vertical lines. A zero income effect is obviously consistent with the axioms on preference, since we need only draw one smooth, convex indifference curve and then shift it vertically upward to obtain higher indifference contours (Figure 13–7a). As the budget line also shifts upward in parallel fashion, the same amount of x_1 is chosen.

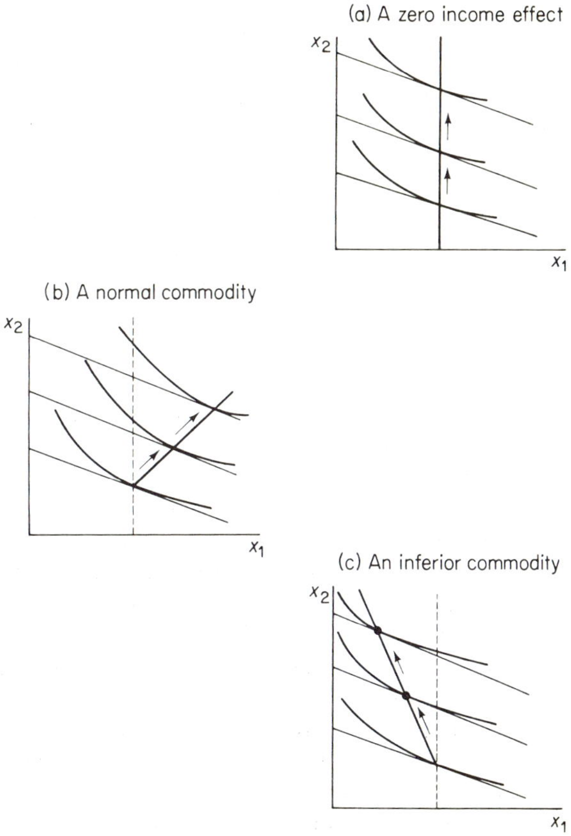

Fig. 13-7 Normal and Inferior Commodities

When indifference curves are parallel along vertical lines, the rate of commodity substitution or relative valuation of the commodities depends on x_1 alone and is independent of x_2. Thus, an increase in x_1 along a ray, with x_2 increasing, has the same effect on the rate of commodity substitution as an equal increase in x_1 along a contour, with x_2 decreasing. For a zero income effect, the rate of commodity substitution must decline along rays exactly as fast as it declines along contours.

One normally expects that increases in x_2 with x_1 constant will decrease the relative value of x_2 or, what amounts to the same thing, increase the rate of substitution of x_2 for x_1. If so, the contours become steeper along vertical lines as x_2 increases. As income increases with prices constant, the point of tangency shifts to the right along the budget line, implying an increase in x_1. (Figure 13–7b). A commodity is classified as *normal* if the quantity purchased increases with income. There may be wide differences among normal commodities in the degree of response to income but all share the common property of having positive income effects.

For income to have a negative effect on x_1, the indifference contours must flatten out along vertical lines, causing the point of tangency to shift to the left along the budget line. As x_2 increases with x_1 constant, the rate of substitution of x_2 for x_1 declines. The second commodity rises in relative value even as its quantity increases. Such a pattern is consistent with the axioms, since we need only draw one contour and shift it parallel to itself along a line or curve sloping back toward the vertical axis (Figure 13–7c). A commodity whose quantity declines as income rises is classified as *inferior*. For a commodity to be inferior, the contours must flatten out at a rapid rate along rays.

In explaining zero and negative income effects, we purposely considered only parallel *upward* shifts of a contour. If all indifference curves are parallel along a vertical or a backward-sloping line, the income-consumption curve for a decline in income must coincide with that line until it reaches the horizontal axis. At still lower levels of income, the optimal choice consists of corner solutions along the horizontal axis, as readers may verify by completing the pattern of parallel indifference curves in Figures 13–7a and 13–7c. Along the horizontal axis the income effect on x_1 is positive. The income effect cannot be zero or negative everywhere or the commodity would never be consumed at all. A commodity can become inferior only after it is purchased in some positive amount. Further, the transition from a normal to an inferior commodity is likely to be gradual rather than abrupt. Under the assumptions of Figure 13–7, a consumer first spends every additional dollar on x_1 and then buys no more of it or reduces purchases while income continues to rise.

For a gradual transition to inferiority, the indifference contours must flatten out along rays slowly at first but then at a steadily increasing rate. The income-consumption curve bends gradually upward until it becomes vertical and then bends backward toward the vertical axis. Though it need not do so, the income-consumption curve may continue on to an intersection with the vertical axis. There is no reason why a consumer must continue to buy at high levels of income a commodity that was attractive at low levels. However, the income-consumption curve cannot intersect the vertical axis unless the indifference contours do.

DEMAND CURVES FOR INFERIOR COMMODITIES

The flattening of contours along rays affects both the price-consumption curve and the demand curve. A decline in p_1 causes the budget line to rotate upward and become flatter. In the linear version, the optimal solution remains on a ray until the budget line coincides with the lower and flatter line segment through a vertex. If the line segments are themselves flattening out, the solution remains on the ray for a longer interval, and the demand curve coincides with that particular image curve for a greater price range. The general effect is a steeper demand curve. In the smooth version, the income and pure substitution effects of a price change occur simultaneously, but flattening contours partially offset the pure substitution effect and produce steeper demand curves.

So long as a commodity remains normal, both the pure substitution and the income effects of a price change must go in the same direction. A reduction in p_1, like an increase in income, permits a consumer to buy more of both commodities. If an increase in income induces a larger purchase of x_1, so will a decline in price. When a commodity becomes inferior, the pure substitution and income effects of a price change go in opposite directions, and demand curves are necessarily steeper. A possibility that has long intrigued economists is that the negative income effect could offset or outweigh the pure substitution effect, causing demand curves to become vertical or even slope upward. For a vertical demand curve the price-consumption curve must also be vertical. This in turn implies that the indifference curves must have the same slope as the rotating budget locus along a vertical line. The tangent lines to the indifference curves as they intersect the same vertical line must all be drawn from the same point, and that point must be the vertical intercept of the budget line. Obviously we can draw a set of curves with the desired property along at least one vertical line but the key issue is whether the resultant indifference map satisfies the axioms on preference.

Clearly, we must permit satiation with respect to one of the commodities. If the indifference curves intersecting a vertical line have tangents drawn from the same vertical intercept, one such indifference curve must have a horizontal tangent line. The marginal utility or personal valuation of the first commodity falls to zero, denoting satiation. But satiation with one commodity does not violate the axioms. We must, however, continue the indifference curve as a horizontal line segment beyond the point of satiation. We can provide an explicit justification for the horizontal extension by positing that excess amounts of x_1 go costlessly to waste and introducing a costless slack process.

The convexity axiom requires that smooth indifference curves become steeper as x_1 decreases. Hence, as an indifference curve crosses vertical lines nearer the vertical axis it must have tangent lines with higher intercepts. This suggests a method for constructing an indifference map satisfying the convexity axiom: For every vertical line in the consumption set choose a single point on the vertical axis, but for vertical lines drawn to smaller values of x_1 choose higher points. Each indifference curve has the same slope at every point as the line drawn to the corresponding vertical intercept, and the numerical value of the slope declines as x_1 increases, up to the point of satiation. Satiation with x_1 occurs along each vertical line at the height of the vertical intercept but we can make satiation a remote possibility, if we wish, by choosing large values for all vertical intercepts. Exercise 6 illustrates the method of construction for the piecewise-linear case.

The geometric device for deriving contours, just described, will generate an entire indifference map satisfying the axioms on preference. As proof we present the following smooth utility function which has been obtained by an application of the method:

$$U = \frac{x_2}{x_1} - 200x_1^{-2}.$$

It is a specific member of a general class of utility functions that generate vertical price-consumption curves and demand curves.[6] Figure 13–8 graphs the iso-utility contours. Each contour becomes horizontal at a point on the rectangular hyperbola $x_1 x_2 = 400$. If the constant in the utility function has higher values than 200, satiation will not occur until correspondingly higher levels of x_1. The contours are obviously nonintersecting, downward sloping to the point of satiation, continuous, and convex, thus satisfying the axioms on preference. Exercise 7 verifies that both the price-consumption and demand curves are vertical. For example, with $y = 40$ and $p_2 = 1$, the consumer continues to buy 10 units of x_1 as p_1 declines toward zero.

There are also lower indifference contours, not shown in the figure, that

[6]The function,

$$U = \frac{1}{1+n}\frac{x_2^{1+n}}{x_1} - \frac{k}{1-m}x_1^{m-1},$$

with $k>0$, $m<0$, generates demand curves whose slope depends on the sign of n. The demand curves slope downward when n is negative, upward when n is positive, and are vertical when $n = 0$, as in the text. When $n = 0$, satiation occurs along the rectangular hyperbola $x_1 x_2 = k$. If k is very large, satiation occurs only at high levels of x_1.

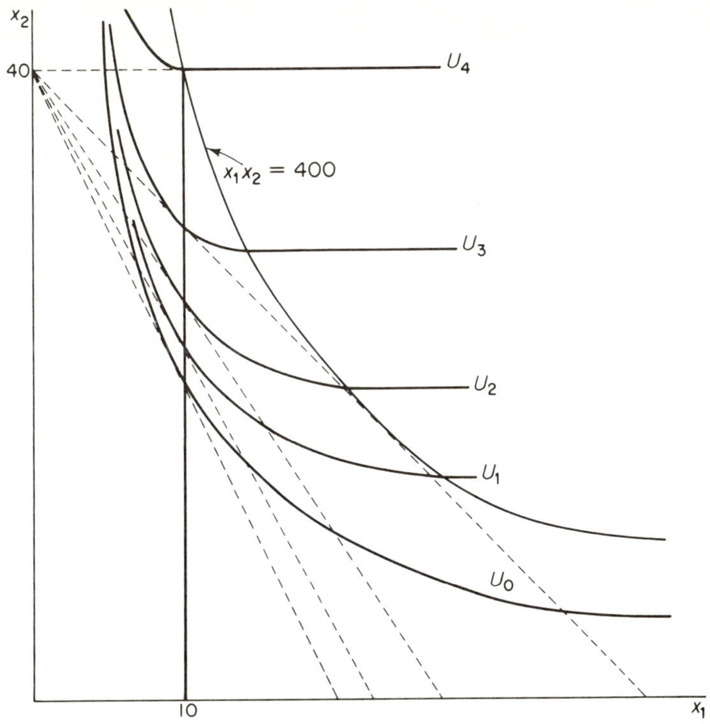

Fig. 13-8 A Vertical Price-Consumption Curve

intersect the horizontal axis. As p_1 continues to increase, the vertical price-consumption curve reaches the horizontal axis, makes a right-angled turn, and thereafter coincides with the axis to the origin. Obviously, the effect of price on consumption, like the effect of income, cannot be everywhere zero, or the commodity will not be consumed at all. The very special conditions that yield vertical demand curves are appropriate only for a portion of the indifference map. We shall show shortly how they fit into a broader pattern of consumer preference.

Backward-Sloping Price-Consumption Curves

When the contours flatten out as rapidly as the budget line along vertical lines, the rate of substitution of x_2 for x_1 or the relative valuation of x_1 must be declining very fast along rays. In fact the decline must be fast enough to offset both the income effect and the pure substitution effect of the fall in p_1. A lower price permits the consumer to have more of both commodities. But having more of both commodities so lowers the relative value of x_1 that the consumer is willing to trade the entire increase in x_1 for an even larger quantity of x_2.

The decline in the relative value can be even greater and cause the consumer to buy less of x_1 when its price falls. Instead of vertical lines we choose a family of parallel lines sloping backward toward the vertical axis. As indifference contours intersect one of these backward-sloping lines, they must all have tangent lines with the same vertical intercept. Also, the nearer a line is to the origin, the higher its intercept must be, insuring convexity of the contours. The geometric method generates an acceptable indifference map but only away from the origin. The contours are essentially the same as those in Figure 13-8 except that they must have somewhat more curvature and reach the point of satiation sooner. Footnote 6 explains how to modify the smooth utility function for the desired contours. Price-consumption curves that slope toward the vertical axis imply demand curves that tail off toward the vertical axis as the price falls.

SUMMARY AND SYNTHESIS

For expository purposes a consumer's response to a decline in price can be separated into three distinct movements on the indifference map (Figure 13–9). The first movement from a to b along the original contour is the pure substitution effect. It shows the consumer's reaction to a change in the commodity mix when that change leaves the consumer neither better nor worse off. The contour has the same slope as the new price ratio, and point

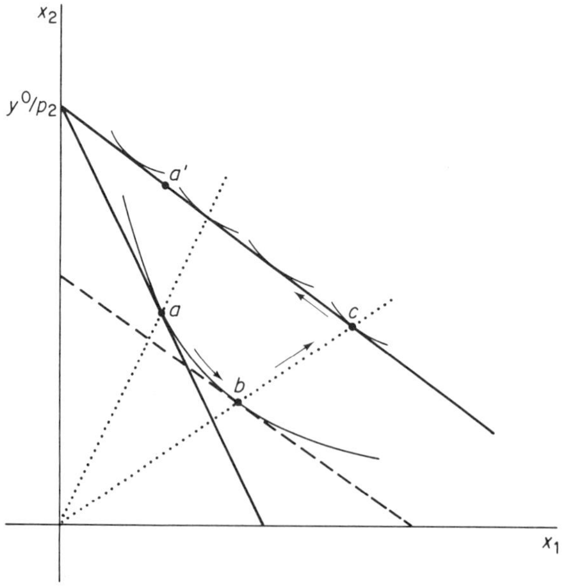

Fig. 13-9 The Effect of a Decline in the Price of a Commodity

b would be the new optimal solution if income were reduced by just enough to offset the decline in p_1. If the slope changes gradually along a contour, the pure substitution effect is large.

The lower price for one commodity permits a consumer to buy more of both, but proportional expansion along the ray from b to c takes place only if the absolute amounts of the commodities do not affect their relative valuations and the contours are parallel along rays. If the relative valuation of x_1 decreases, the consumer moves backward along the budget line to the highest indifference contour. Customarily, the two separate movements along the ray and along the new budget line are combined into a single net effect and called the income effect of a price change. The extent of the backward movement along the new budget line depends on the rate at which the indifference contours flatten out along rays. Tangency to the left of a' means a positive-sloping demand curve. Conversely, if the relative valuation of x_1 increases along rays, the income effect reinforces the pure substitution effect and the optimum occurs at points below c on the budget line.

When p_1 changes continuously, all three movements occur simultaneously and combine to determine the direction which the price-consumption curve takes as it passes through the point a. The axioms on preference leave open a wide range of possibilities. The price-consumption curve must cut across the indifference contour at a, but it may slope downward, upward, or backward toward the vertical axis. A decline in p_1 may induce a consumer to increase x_1 at the expense of x_2, to buy more of both, or to decrease purchases of x_1.

A Pattern of Increasing Inferiority

Consumers chosen at random may react in any of the alternative ways, but a single consumer observed in many different price-income situations is likely to reveal a pattern of reaction. A commodity cannot be inferior at all levels of income. Inferiority, when it occurs, is likely to be the result of a gradual but increasingly rapid decline in the rate of commodity substitution along rays. Figure 13–10 shows such a pattern in both price-consumption and demand curves. Though the contours are not drawn, they are assumed to be parallel along rays or flattening slightly at low levels of utility. With contours parallel along rays a rotating budget line with declining slope must find its point of tangency on successively lower rays. So long as the contours do not flatten out rapidly enough for all optimal solutions to lie on a single ray, the price consumption curve continues to cross successively lower rays. As soon as the rate of commodity substitution declines more rapidly than the price ratio along a ray, the price consumption curve cuts upward across the rays. The point of tangency with one ray marks the change from the first pattern to the second. The price-consumption curve bends backward and, when p_1 reaches zero, terminates in a point of satiation at the same height as the vertical intercept of the budget line.

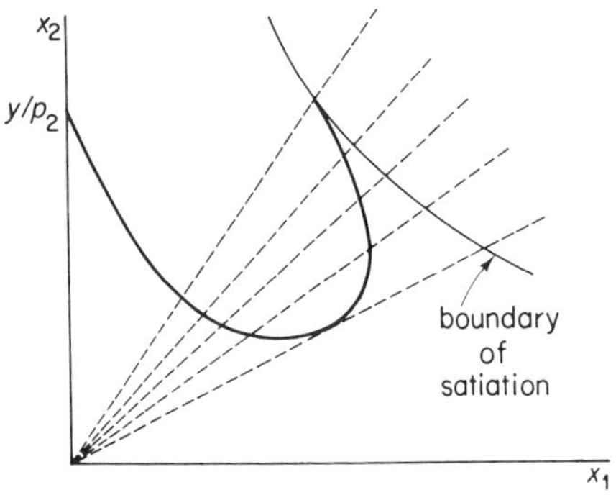

Fig. 13-10a A Backward-Rising Price-Consumption Curve

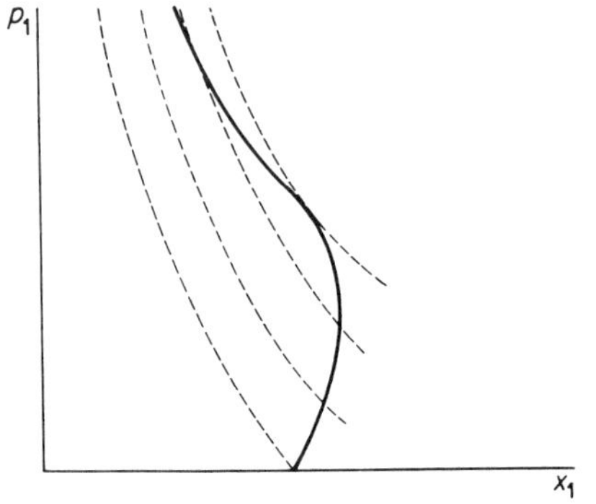

Fig. 13-10b A Backward Sloping Demand Curve

When the price-consumption curve is tangent to a ray, the demand curve is tangent to the image curve of that ray. The demand curve then curve curls backward and attains a positive slope before reaching the point of satiation on the horizontal axis. When incorporated into the general pattern of a progressively more rapid decline in the rate of commodity substitution, a positive-sloping demand curve becomes the next-to-last stage before satiation.

The possibility of satiation, by itself, is neither sufficient nor necessary for an upward-sloping demand curve. When indifference curves flatten out gradually along rays the price-consumption curve reaches the boundary of satiation without curling backward. The essential ingredient for an upward-sloping demand curve is the rapid decline in the rate of commodity substitution. After a phase of rapid decline the consumer's attitude toward the commodity could change, and the indifference curves could gradually become parallel along rays. After curling backward toward the vertical axis, the demand curve would reverse its slope and approach the horizontal axis without touching it.

The theoretical possibility of upward-sloping demand curves has been proved mathematically, but their actual occurrence remains an open question. For a plausible empirical example, economists often cite the Giffen paradox, for which the essential condition is extreme poverty such as prevailed in nineteenth century Ireland and forced the peasants to satisfy their minimal caloric needs by consuming potatoes almost exclusively. A diet of potatoes may well have been the least costly way of obtaining calories but it certainly did not satisfy other nutritional needs or provide the gourmet pleasures of dining. A fall in the price of potatoes enabled the peasants to fulfill their basic caloric needs with some income left over for the purchase of other foods. But all foods provide calories, and variety is desirable in any diet, so a lower price for potatoes could well have reduced the quantity purchased. What Giffen's paradox does is to posit a set of extreme conditions under which indifference curves may flatten out very rapidly even at low levels of income.[7] A consumer who has been living on potatoes is certainly likely to have a precipitously declining rate of substitution when offered more potatoes, although it is not clear whether this represents a transient or permanent state of preference. The Giffen conditions also explain how the aggregate demand curve could slope upward, since most consumers are simultaneously in the same situation.

The Law of Consumer Demand

The very general axioms on consumer preference are almost, but not quite, strong enough to establish, as a law of consumer demand, that all individual demand curves must slope downward. The axioms do not rule out the increasingly rapid decline in the rate of commodity substitution that ultimately causes a demand curve to bend backward toward the vertical axis. As yet, there is no firm empirical evidence for positive-sloping individual demand curves, so we do not know whether the phenomenon has actually occurred. However, when individual demand curves are aggregated to form market demand curves, there is little likelihood of a positive slope. Tastes and income differ, and extreme inferiority is a localized condition on any one indifference map. Even though some individual demand curves slope upward, they are unlikely to predominate in the aggregate.

[7]An upward-sloping demand curve requires that the income effect of a price change be positive and outweigh the always negative pure substitution effect. Since it is a decline in price that frees money for increased expenditure, the *income effect of a price change* is opposite in sign to the *income effect*. For the income effect to have a large negative value the rate of commodity substitution must be declining rapidly along rays. Many economics texts attribute the Giffen paradox directly to the large fraction of income being spent on one commodity. It is true that the income effect of a price change is greater when the consumer is buying many units of a commodity; a given price change frees more dollars. But a large value for x_1 also means that the consumer is on a flatter portion of an indifference curve and that the pure substitution effect is also larger. It is the general pattern of consumer preference that is essential, not the fraction of income spent on a commodity, which may have offsetting effects.

The sign and size of the income effect influence the slope of demand curves but are also important in another way. A change in income with p_2 constant shifts the intercept of the budget line and generates both a new price-consumption curve and a new demand curve for x_1. If the income effect is negative, less is bought at each price, and the demand curve shifts to the left. In the normal case of a positive income effect, the demand curve shifts to the right as income rises.

The Extension to Many Commodities: Composite Commodities

To be significant, results derived from the two-commodity simplification must also hold when there are many commodities. The extension of the results can be achieved by formal mathematical methods, but there is also a device that accomplishes part of the generalization while retaining two-dimensional diagrams. Any subset of commodities whose prices are constant or change proportionately can be treated as a composite commodity. Thus, x_2 in the previous diagrams may be regarded as a composite of $(n-1)$ commodities, with the price of any one commodity serving as the price of the composite commodity.

When the remaining $n-1$ prices do not change proportionately, each commodity must be treated separately in a more general model. If, say, a third commodity is present, the amount of that commodity is likely to affect the preference for x_1 and x_2. A consumer who acquires a record player is not likely to retain the same preference for records and books. The existence of complements and substitutes is familiar and important, but there are problems in defining each satisfactorily.

Substitutes and Complements

To see the issues clearly, assume that the consumer receives the third commodity without having to buy it, say as a gift. After the consumer has allocated his income optimally between the first two commodities, he receives more of the third. The increased amount of the third commodity can affect his purchases only by changing the slopes of the contours relative to the fixed budget line. If the contours become flatter, the consumer moves backward along the budget line, buying less of x_1 and more of x_2. Since an increase in x_3 induces the consumer to buy more of x_2, we call x_2 a complement of x_3, and x_1 a substitute. Formally, then, x_2 is classified as a complement of x_3, and x_1 as a substitute if an increase in x_3 lowers the rate of substitution of x_2 for x_1.

When x_3 is also included in the budget, complications arise. A fall in p_3, which nearly always causes an increase in x_3, also has an income effect. Less of x_1 may be bought because it is an inferior good and not just because it is a substitute for x_3. To get a pure measure of substitution and complementarity, unalloyed with an income effect, the consumer must remain on the same three-dimensional indifference contour. Since the consumer has no incentive to remain on the same contour, he must be induced to do so by taking away just enough income to nullify the income effect of the price change. Conceptually this is possible, but there is no feasible way of carrying it out, even for experimental purposes, and there is no way of removing the income effect from statistical data. When the consumer is buying many commodities and the fraction of income spent on each is relatively small, the income effect of a price change is not likely to be significant. In general, little error is introduced by classifying x_1 as a substitute of x_3 if its demand curve shifts to the left when p_3 falls, and x_2 as a complement of x_3 if its demand curve shifts to the right. As a warning that income effects have not been removed, the terms *gross substitute* and *gross complement* are used.

The demand for any one commodity is influenced not only by its own direct substitutes and complements, but also indirectly by the substitution and complementarity that prevails among other commodities. Both the position and the shape of the demand curve are affected, but it still remains true that only a strongly negative income effect provides an exception to the generalization that quantity demanded varies inversely with price.

APPENDIX: REVEALED PREFERENCE

Neither utility nor preference are observable directly. Preferences could be determined by interviewing, but answers to hypothetical questions are notoriously unreliable, and there is a general belief that "actions speak louder than words." What is observable is the choice that a consumer makes under a given set of prices and income. A sequence of choices under different conditions gives considerable evidence about a consumer's preferences. An intriguing question is whether a sufficiently prolonged sequence of choices could, at least conceptually, reveal the entire indifference map. The primary concern of economists to date has not been the empirical determination of individual indifference maps but rather the logical relationship between choice and preference.

The relationship between choice and preference has counterparts in two previously discussed cases. In an example early in the chapter, a set of men was measured and ranked according to height. The measurements were then assumed to have been destroyed, and the problem was to retrieve as much of the measurement as possible from the ranking alone. The second case is the relationship between utility and preference. A utility function that increases along rays and has strictly convex iso-utility contours implies a complete preference ordering in which more is always preferred to less and the mean is always preferred to either of two equally ranked extremes. We then turn the problem around and ask: Given a preference ordering with the stipulated properties, how far can we go in retrieving the utility function from which it was derived? If the preference relation is continuous, as assumed earlier, a continuous utility function can be constructed to represent preferences by assigning the same number to indifferent combinations

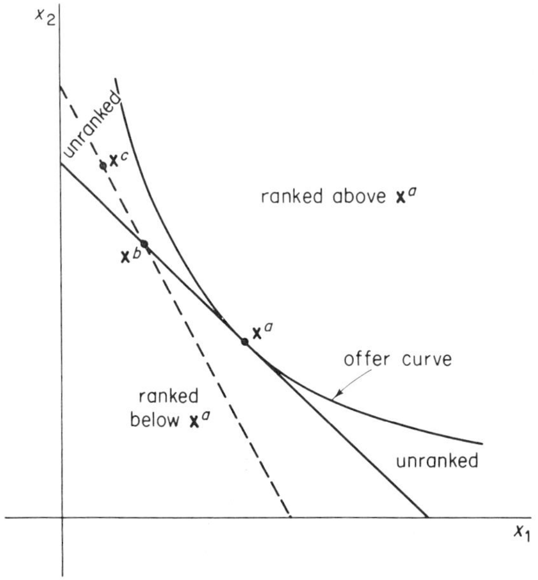

Fig. 13-11 Ranking of Commodity Bundles by Choice

and higher numbers to preferred combinations. The function is also increasing along rays and has convex contours. What cannot be retrieved is any specific assignment of utility numbers; if one function represents preferences, any increasing transformation of that function will do as well. Thus, cardinal utility is superfluous, and the term ordinal is used to denote those properties of utility that are just sufficient to determine the desired preference relation.

Preference itself is introduced as a means of explaining or predicting choice. The assumptions made about preference are sufficient to predict a unique choice in every price-income situation. But are they all strictly necessary, or can we drop or weaken an assumption and still be able to predict a unique choice in every price-income situation? To answer this question we must see if we can retrieve the preference ordering from the choices made.

When a consumer chooses $\mathbf{x}^a$ at a particular set of prices and income, he could have chosen any other commodity bundle that does not cost more than $\mathbf{x}^a$. The choice of $\mathbf{x}^a$ when $\mathbf{x}^b$ is available will be taken as a ranking of $\mathbf{x}^a$ above $\mathbf{x}^b$. The binary relation is usually defined as "$\mathbf{x}^a$ is revealed preferred to $\mathbf{x}^b$," but to keep preference and choice distinct from each other it is better to express the relation as, "$\mathbf{x}^a$ is chosen over $\mathbf{x}^b$," or, "$\mathbf{x}^a$ is ranked (by choice) above $\mathbf{x}^b$." As shown in Figure 13–11, the choice of $\mathbf{x}^a$ ranks it above every other member of the available set.

If there are commodity bundles that will not be chosen at any set of prices and income, it is impossible to derive a complete ranking. There must be at least one set of prices and income at which each bundle will be chosen. The set of prices and income at which a bundle is chosen can never be unique, since proportional changes leave the budget line unchanged. More important, there need not even be a unique budget line at which a commodity bundle is chosen. However, when this is the case, the exposition is greatly simplified without materially affecting the conclusions.[8]

[8]To satisfy this condition, the indifference contours must have a tangent at every point and must not intersect the axes.

We now have the first important assumption about consumer's choice. Except for proportional changes, there is one and only one set of prices and income at which each commodity bundle is chosen.

If $\mathbf{x}^a$ is chosen over $\mathbf{x}^b$, then, for a ranking to exist, $\mathbf{x}^b$ must never be chosen over $\mathbf{x}^a$. But, by the first assumption, there is some set of prices and income at which $\mathbf{x}^b$ will be chosen. Hence, when $\mathbf{x}^b$ is chosen, $\mathbf{x}^a$ must not be available; its cost must exceed income. We now have the second assumption about consumer's choice: if $\mathbf{x}^b$ can be purchased when $\mathbf{x}^a$ is chosen, then $\mathbf{x}^a$ must not be purchasable when $\mathbf{x}^b$ is chosen. If we let $[p_1^a, p_2^a]$ and $[p_1^b, p_2^b]$ be the sets of prices at which $\mathbf{x}^a$ and $\mathbf{x}^b$ are chosen, the assumption becomes

$$\text{If} \qquad p_1^a x_1^b + p_2^a x_2^b \leqq p_1^a x_1^a + p_2^a x_2^a,$$

$$\text{then} \qquad p_1^b x_1^b + p_2^b x_2^b < p_1^b x_1^a + p_2^b x_2^a.$$

The foregoing assumption is known as the *weak axiom of revealed preference.*

The two properties or assumptions about choice provide a ranking for much of the consumption set. All members of the available set are placed below $\mathbf{x}^a$. All combinations in the northeast quadrant cost more than $\mathbf{x}^a$ at any set of positive prices. But each commodity bundle must be bought at some set of positive prices. Hence, $\mathbf{x}^a$ is available when each of these commodity bundles is chosen and ranks below all of them. The same conclusion holds for any other commodity bundle and provides a ranking of commodity bundles along every ray from the origin. As in the case of preference, more is always ranked above less.

By selecting all possible sets of positive prices, the budget line can be rotated about the point $\mathbf{x}^a$. At every price ratio but one, the consumer chooses some other commodity bundle that costs as much as $\mathbf{x}^a$, and thereby ranks it above $\mathbf{x}^a$. The locus of all such points is known in other contexts as the *offer curve*, since the difference in quantities between $\mathbf{x}^a$ and a point on the curve shows how much of one commodity the individual is willing to offer in exchange for the other commodity. By drawing rays through each point on the offer curve, we can establish that every commodity bundle beyond the offer curve is also ranked above $\mathbf{x}^a$.

The consumption set in Figure 13–11 is partitioned into three regions: the available set in which points are ranked below $\mathbf{x}^a$, the region bounded by the offer curve where points rank above $\mathbf{x}^a$, and an intermediate region in which points are not ranked relative to $\mathbf{x}^a$. Further, these intermediate points can never be ranked by direct choice; any such point $\mathbf{x}^c$ is not available when $\mathbf{x}^a$ is chosen and $\mathbf{x}^a$ is not available when $\mathbf{x}^c$ is chosen. For at least some unranked points, indirect comparisons are possible. Point $\mathbf{x}^b$ on the budget line ranks below $\mathbf{x}^a$ and must be chosen, as shown, at a set of prices such that $\mathbf{x}^a$ is not purchasable. Any such budget line cuts into the intermediate region. All points on the line and all points on rays nearer the origin are ranked below $\mathbf{x}^b$. The ranking can be extended into the intermediate zone by accepting the evidence of indirect comparisons. We can say that $\mathbf{x}^a$ is indirectly ranked above $\mathbf{x}^c$ if there is a commodity bundle $\mathbf{x}^b$ such that $\mathbf{x}^a$ is chosen over $\mathbf{x}^b$ and $\mathbf{x}^b$ is chosen over $\mathbf{x}^c$.

Points can be indirectly related to each other not just by a third point but by a whole sequence of points, each of which is chosen over its immediate successor. If $\mathbf{x}^a$ occurs at the beginning of any such finite sequence of points and $\mathbf{x}^c$ appears at the end, then $\mathbf{x}^a$ is indirectly chosen or indirectly ranked over $\mathbf{x}^c$. Between any two points, many indirect comparisons exist, but if there is to be a ranking, all must go in the same direction. Hence, we need the assumption: If $\mathbf{x}^a$ is indirectly chosen over $\mathbf{x}^c$, then $\mathbf{x}^c$ must *never* be indirectly chosen over $\mathbf{x}^a$. This is the *strong* axiom of revealed preference, which supersedes the weak axiom since it implies everything the weak axiom does and more besides. A consumer with a preference ordering would make choices that satisfied the strong axiom, but it is now being put forth as an independent assumption about choice regardless of how choice is explained.

How far do indirect comparisons go in eliminating the zone of points that are unranked relative to $\mathbf{x}^a$? Although it has taken many years and much intellectual effort to devise a satisfactory proof, particularly for the n-commodity case, the answer is simple and not unexpected: On each ray every point but one can be ranked relative to $\mathbf{x}^a$. Further, these points must lie on a curve that is convex to the origin. Readers may use the weak axiom to show that, if $\mathbf{x}^b$ and $\mathbf{x}^c$ are unranked relative to $\mathbf{x}^a$, any point on the line segment joining them must be ranked above $\mathbf{x}^a$. The temptation to identify these unranked points as an indifference contour is compelling but must be resisted. All we know and all we can ever know from choice alone is that the consumer's decisions will never provide evidence for ranking relative to $\mathbf{x}^a$ one point on each ray. After a moment's reflection, the result is not surprising; choices are made in spite of indifference and not because of it.

Just as cardinal utility was a casualty in the transition from utility to preference, so is indifference a casualty in the transition from preference to choice. So long as an individual can express a preference, in either direction, between any point $\mathbf{x}^a$ and all points but one on each ray, he is equipped to make all choices he will ever be called upon to make as a consumer. The choice will be the same regardless of whether the consumer is indifferent between $\mathbf{x}^a$ and the remaining point, has a preference, or simply has not made up his mind. For consistency with choice, indifference can be dropped, and a partial ordering constructed in terms of strict preference alone. One difficulty with this solution is that, when indifference is dropped, ordinal utility in its conventional formulation also becomes a casualty. Iso-utility contours, if they are to have any meaning, must imply indifference between points on the same contour.

Although indifference contours are not strictly necessary to explain choice, there are advantages in retaining the concept. They permit the preservation of the traditional theory of ordinal utility and make possible a unified presentation of the various formulations of consumer's choice. The consumer of economic theory can then be defined in three essentially equivalent ways: as an individual who possesses the previously described type of utility function and makes choices by maximizing utility, as an individual with a complete preference ordering who always chooses the highest commodity bundle on his preference scale, and as an individual whose choices always satisfy the strong axiom of revealed preference. Because of their unifying power, it is convenient to assume indifference contours, as was done earlier in the chapter, but we must be careful not to accept any results that do not follow from the evidence of choice alone. All earlier conclusions about demand do follow from the two assumptions about choice. Thus, there are three essentially equivalent versions of consumer's choice, each of which is almost but not quite sufficient to prove that all individual demand curves must be downward sloping.

EXERCISES

1. *A Numerical Example of the Linear Model*

Set up the numerical example of Exercise 6 in Chapter 12 as the maximization of utility for a given budget constraint. Choose $p_2 = 4$ and $y^0 = 24$.

(a) Let p_1 vary through the positive range and find the critical levels of p_1. Determine the solution that is optimal at each value of p_1 and graph the price-consumption curve as in Figure 13–1.

(b) Find the image curve of the third ray, plot a few points and sketch. Under what conditions would the image curve become the demand curve for x_1?

(c) Derive the demand schedule for x_1 and present in the form of Table 13–1. Plot the critical values of (x_1, p_1) and draw in the demand curve. You need not try to draw exact image curves. Explain in economic terms why the income effect of a given price change increases as the price falls.

2. *The Cross-Demand Curve*

For the numerical example of Exercise 1 find the effect on x_2 of changes in p_1 and present a cross-demand schedule in the form of Table 13–2. Plot the critical values of (x_2, p_1) and sketch in the cross-demand curve. What special feature of the linear model guarantees that the income and pure substitution effects must be offsetting in the cross-demand curve and reinforcing in the demand curve?

3. *The Expenditure Minimizing Model*

Chapters 8 and 9 showed that the theory of a single-product firm could be developed in two different ways: by maximizing output or revenue for a given level of cost and by minimizing cost for a given level of output. For the consumer, utility corresponds to output or revenue and commodities correspond to inputs. We can, then, develop an alternative model of the consumer by minimizing cost, or expenditure on commodities, subject to a given level of utility. Each linear segment of the utility function determines a constraint of the form $\bar{u}_1x_1+\bar{u}_2x_2 \geqq U^0$. The objective is to minimize $E = p_1x_1+p_2x_2$. Income y is no longer appropriate.

(a) Use the piecewise-linear utility function of Table 12–1 to set up a numerical example of the expenditure or cost minimizing version of consumer's choice. What is the economic meaning of the dual variable or the coefficient of U in the objective function after reduction to canonical form?

(b) Graph the expenditure minimizing problem, identifying the feasible set. Demonstrate that, when prices are the same and both U^0 and y^0 are appropriately chosen, both the maximizing and minimizing versions have the same optimal solutions.

(c) Assume that both problems have the same solutions when $p_1 = 5$, $p_2 = 5$, and $y^0 = 50$. Let p_1 vary parametrically in the expenditure minimization problem. What is the locus of all possible optimal solutions as p_1 varies through the entire nonnegative range? Compare with the price-consumption curve. Are the values of x_1 larger or smaller for the same levels of p_1?

(d) Find the critical values of (x_1, p_1) and plot. Draw the demand curve for x_1 when p_1 varies with the utility constant. How does it compare with the demand curve when income is constant? What feature of the demand curve shows the absence of an income effect?

(e) When a price changes with income constant, utility must vary. When a price changes with utility constant, income must vary. Find the precise amount by which income must change to offset the income effect along each ray and keep the consumer on the same iso-utility contour.

4. *A Zero Income Effect: Piecewise-Linear Version*

For the required piecewise-linear indifference map all contours must have the same slope between vertical lines drawn at specific values of x_1. Choose the integral values $x_1 = 0, 1, 2, 3, 4, \ldots$. Let the slope of the indifference curves over each interval be $m = -k/d = -4/d$, where d is the largest value of x_1 in the interval. Thus, in the interval $0 \leqq x_1 \leqq 1$, the slope is constant and determined by $d = 1$. A similar relation holds for all subsequent intervals.

(a) Present a graph showing several indifference contours over the first four intervals. What happens to the slope of the contours on subsequent intervals as x_1 continues to increase? Does satiation occur? How does the rate of commodity substitution change along rays?

Is the indifference map consistent with the axioms on preference? For each axiom state the strongest version that applies.

(b) Let $p_1 = 5$ and $p_2 = 3$. Find and indicate on the graph the entire income-consumption locus as income varies from zero upward. What is special and extreme about the pattern? Explain how to modify consumer preferences to yield a more plausible result.

(c) Take $p_2 = 3$ and $y^0 = 36$. To what level must p_1 fall before the consumer is on the verge of buying it? Show on the graph the price-consumption locus as p_1 continues to decline.

Calculate the critical values of (x_1, p_1) and plot as points in price-quantity space. Distinguish between income and pure substitution effects. Draw in the demand curve for intervening prices.

(d) When indifference curves are parallel along rays, the income effect takes place along the image curves of the rays. Does a similar conclusion hold in the present example? What is the image in price-quantity space of a vertical line in commodity space? Explain how the income and pure substitution effects show up in the demand curve when the indifference curves are smoothed but remain parallel.

5. *The Indifference Map for an Inferior Commodity*

(a) Draw a set of parallel straight lines in commodity space sloping backward toward the vertical axis. Between each pair of lines the segments of all indifference contours have the same slope. As x_1 increases through the successive intervals each segment has a slope less than that of the preceding segment, say one-half of it. Sketch in several indifference contours. Need satiation ever occur? Verify that the resultant indifference map satisfies the axioms on preference. For each axiom state the precise version required.

(b) For a simple numerical illustration, choose parallel lines with a slope of -4 intersecting the horizontal axis in integral values of x_1. The equation of the lines is $x_1 = -\frac{1}{4}x_2 + d$, where the horizontal intercept d is assigned the values of the successive integers. Consider only $d = 3$, 4, 5, 6. Assign to the successive indifference segments slopes of -3, -2, and -1. Select for graphing the contour with vertical intercept (0, 14). By solving the appropriate linear equations find the critical values of (x_1, x_2) and graph the first three segments of the contour. Draw in some higher and lower contours.

(c) Let $p_1 = 3$, $p_2 = 2$, and identify on the graph the income-consumption curve as income increases from $y = 9$. Omit the curve in the vicinity of the origin. Express in economic terms how the consumer reacts to increases in x_2 with x_1 constant. Plot x_1 against y.

(d) With $y^0 = 28$ and $p_2 = 2$, let the price of x_1 decline from levels above $p_1 = 6$. Find the critical values of (x_1, p_1) and show the price-consumption curve on the graph. Also graph the critical points in price-quantity space. Identify the income and pure substitution effects of a price change.

(e) Drawing the precise demand curve requires the image curves of the backward-sloping lines. Solve simultaneously the budget equation and the equation for the lines, getting x_1 as a function of p_1. Choose a value for d and select prices in the appropriate range. Show that x_1 and p_1 both decrease along the segment of the image curve. Sketch the demand curve. Explain how the income and pure substitution effects combine to form the demand curve when the indifference curves are smoothed.

(f) What happens to the demand curve if income increases, say to $y^0 = 32$?

6. *Vertical and Backward-Sloping Price-Consumption Curves*

Choose equally spaced values on the horizontal axis, $d = 0, 5, 10, 15, 20, \ldots$. Over each interval the segments of the indifference contours have the same vertical intercept. Select the vertical intercepts by the formula $b = 300/d$. On each horizontal interval the larger value of d determines the vertical intercept. Hence, on the interval $0 \leqq x_1 \leqq 5$, the vertical intercept is $300/5 = 60$.

(a) For the contour that passes through the point (5, 20) find the slope of each segment and graph. Also graph the contours that pass through the points (5, 25) and (5, 15). On the assumption that a contour continues as a horizontal line once a horizontal segment appears, show that the indifference map satisfies the axioms of consumer preference. State the strongest permissible version of each axiom.

(b) Set $p_2 = 4$ and $y^0 = 100$. Find the price-consumption locus as p_1 declines steadily from a high level to zero. Graph the demand curve for x_1.

What happens to the price-consumption locus and the demand curve for x_1 if income is higher ($y^0 = 160$) or lower ($y^0 = 72$)? State the geometric condition that determines what the locus will be.

(c) Set $p_1 = 2$, $p_2 = 4$, and let y vary from zero upward. Present a graph of the income-consumption locus. What are the critical values of y at which a shift is about to occur?

(d) Replace the vertical lines with the family of parallel lines, $x_1 = -\frac{1}{20}x_2 + d$, that slope backward from the same points on the horizontal axis. Retain the same vertical intercepts to determine the line segments in each interval formed by successive parallel lines. Draw the three contours that pass through the points (4, 20), (0, 10), and (9, 20). You need not calculate the values of (x_1, x_2) on each line. On the assumption that a contour continues as a horizontal line once a horizontal segment appears, show that the indifference map satisfies the axioms on preference.

(e) Set $p_2 = 4$ and $y^0 = 100$. Determine graphically the price-consumption locus as p_1 declines steadily from a high level to zero.

Write the equation for each segment of the price-consumption locus. Find x_1 as a function of p_1 by substituting for x_2 in the budget equation. Graph the demand curve for x_1.

What happens to the price-consumption locus and the demand curve for x_1 if income is higher ($y^0 = 160$) or lower ($y^0 = 72$)?

7. *Smooth Utility Functions and Vertical Demand Curves*

The smooth utility function presented in the text is a member of the class of functions

$$U = \frac{1}{1+n}\,\frac{x_2^{1+n}}{x_1} - \frac{k}{1-m}x_1^{m-1}.$$

With $k > 0$ and $m < 0$, the functions generate demand curves that are vertical when $n = 0$ and slope upward when $n > 0$. To confirm the first part of the statement choose $n = 0$, $m = -1$, $k = 400$ as in the text.

(a) Choose convenient values for U such as $0, \frac{1}{4}, \frac{1}{2}, 1, 2$ and also set $y = 40$, $p_2 = 1$. For a specific value of p_1 the budget line does not intersect a given iso-utility contour, intersects in two points, or is tangent. To find the values of p_1 and x_1 at which tangency occurs, use the budget equation to eliminate x_2 from the equation for the contour. Tangency occurs when the resultant quadratic equation has real and equal roots. (See the Workbook for further details.) Verify that tangency of the budget line with the contours occurs at $x_1 = 10$.

(b) For the values of U chosen in (a), find the values of x_2 and x_1 at which each contour is tangent to a horizontal line. That is, choose x_2 in such a way that the quadratic equation in x_1 representing the contour has equal roots. Verify that the points lie on the rectangular hyperbola $x_1x_2 = 2k = 400$. What happens if larger values are chosen for k?

(c) Set $p_1 = p_2 = 1$ and let y vary. For each of the previously chosen contours find the values of y and x_1 at which tangency occurs. Describe the salient features of the income-consumption locus.

(d) (Optional) Readers familiar with analytic geometry may show that each contour is a hyperbola that approaches as asymptotes the vertical axis and a ray through the origin that depends on the value of U. For a given value of U, how do changes in k affect the contours?

14

The Theory Extended: Inputs Supplied and the Family as Consuming Unit

The consuming sector does not consist solely or even predominantly of individuals who are free to satisfy their own tastes and preferences independently of other persons. Most individuals are members of families, and their consumption decisions are influenced in varying degrees by membership in a family. When closely scrutinized, the family or household turns out to be a highly complex economic unit that mirrors in microcosm most of the economic problems of society as a whole. There are joint consumption and joint production processes, variable and fixed inputs, private and public goods, and the knotty problems of reconciling short-run with long-run goals as well as the interests of individuals with the group or public interest. Limitations of space do not permit detailed consideration of family decision making. Besides, the formal investigation of the family as a consuming unit is of relatively recent origin, and the results are as yet incomplete and tentative. We shall examine only those decisions that most closely parallel the process of short-run allocation in the economy as a whole. Since the family does mirror society as a whole, it provides a convenient setting for investigation in a somewhat simpler form certain problems and solutions that constitute part of the allocative model for the economy.

For the family and for the individual, the most important decisions are those that determine the level of income itself. So far, we have simply taken income as given and examined only the allocation of a fixed money income over the available commodities. Before taking up allocation within the family, we shall drop the restriction of a fixed income and extend the previously developed theory to cover the supply of inputs by an individual.

THE SUPPLY OF PRIMARY INPUTS

The predominant source of income for most persons is the supply of labor hours. Initially, we shall take it to be the sole source. The amount that an individual can earn in the present depends heavily on past decisions, particularly on his previously acquired education, training, and skill. Further, the amount of time that an individual is allowed to work is generally limited by law, by union contract, or by various other restrictions. There remains, however, some scope for individual choice even in the short run. Further, the economic significance of restrictions on hours of work can be evaluated only by contrast with what workers would have chosen in the absence of the constraints. In the initial presentation, then, each individual can choose freely the number of hours to work.

An Indifference Map for Time and Commodities

As noted earlier, a consumer's time is an important ingredient in all consumption processes and should be regarded as one of the inputs along with commodities. Even if all of a consumer's time is available for consumption, it is limited in total amount and must enter as a constraint in the choice of consumption processes. For most persons, there is the further limitation of having to exchange a portion of the available time for money income in order to acquire commodities. To achieve an optimal consumption pattern, an individual must make the correct division between the personal use of time and work or, what amounts to the same thing, must choose the highest ranked combination of consumption time and commodities. It is not intrinsically more difficult for a consumer to rank combinations consisting of time and commodities than it is to rank commodity bundles alone. With time included, consumers are, if anything, more likely to prefer more to less and generally to prefer intermediate combinations over much time and few commodities or over large amounts of commodities with little time to enjoy them. We shall assume, then, that a preference ranking exists for combinations of consumption time and commodities, and that the ranking satisfies the basic axioms of consumer preference.

For a graphical presentation we limit the number of commodities to one, which can be regarded as a composite commodity when all prices change proportionately. With consumption time on one axis and the composite commodity on the other, there is a set of convex, nonintersecting indifference contours similar, except in one respect, to the indifference map for two commodities. If prices fall low enough all commodity combinations are attainable and must, for generality, be included in the indifference map. By contrast, consumption times in excess of 168 hours a week are unattainable and can be excluded. With time on the vertical axis all indifference contours terminate on the horizontal line representing the total available time for the period chosen. The contours must be downward sloping at the upper terminus, but otherwise there is wide scope for differences among individuals. Consumption times in the vicinity of zero are also unattainable though for a different reason; human technological or physiological conditions do not permit incessant work. In this respect, consumption time is no different from food. As the remaining consumption time dwindles, its value rises rapidly; the consumer is ultimately unwilling to give up more time for any increase in the composite commodity, however large. Hence, all indifference contours approach the horizontal at some positive, but not necessarily identical, level of consumption time.

Economists generally employ the terms work and leisure to designate the two uses of time. Leisure must not, however, be interpreted solely as idleness or even as time spent in amusement or recreation. The basic distinction is between the portion of time exchanged in the labor market for wages and the portion that the individual retains for personal use, be it sleep, recreation, study, or do-it-yourself projects. When convenient we shall use the term leisure to denote the personal use of time.

The constraint that the consumer faces is no longer a fixed amount of money income but the upper limit of the available time. With x_2 the amount of time reserved for personal use and z_2 the amount supplied as labor hours at the wage rate c_2, the conditions under which the consumer must operate are

$$x_2+z_2 = T \text{ (total time)} \qquad y = c_2 z_2 = p_1 x_1.$$

After multiplication by c_2, the first equation can be combined with the second to give

$$c_2 x_2 + p_1 x_1 = c_2 T \qquad \text{or} \qquad x_2 = -\frac{p_1}{c_2} x_1 + T.$$

For each hour of time devoted to personal use, the consumer must pay—that is, give up—the amount of money at which an hour of time can be sold in the labor market. Thus, c_2 represents the price or value to the consumer of consumption time.[1] The optimal solution in the smooth case is again the sole point of tangency between the constraint and a contour (Figure 14–1a). Figure 14–1b is simply Figure 14–1a looked at from the side, with working time increasing to the right from zero instead of downward from T. For later purposes, it is sometimes the more useful diagram.

As p_1 declines, the constraint swings upward and the locus of points of tangency traces out the price-consumption curve for x_1, in essentially the

[1]The statement is correct only for an individual who decides to work a positive amount of time. If a consumer has an alternative source of income and decides not to work, an hour of consumption time has a greater value or price than an hour of working time.

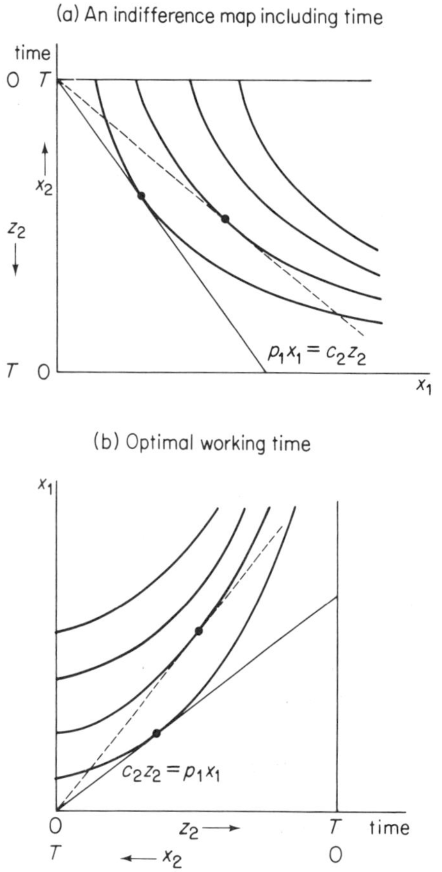

Fig. 14-1

same way as shown previously. However, when it is c_2 that changes, differences appear. A change in any price has an income effect, but the effects go in the opposite direction when the commodity is sold rather than bought. It is a rise in c_2 that increases income, not a fall. When x_2 is a purchased commodity, the budget constraint is

$$x_2 = -\frac{p_1}{p_2}x_1 + \frac{y^0}{p_2}.$$

A rise in p_2 both flattens the budget line and causes it to shift downward. When x_2 is consumption time, a rise in c_2 flattens the constraint line but has no effect on the vertical intercept T, as shown in the earlier constraint equation for time. An increase in c_2 with p_1 constant affects the consumer in precisely the same way as a decline in p_1 with c_2 constant; both alter identically the rate of exchange between time and the composite commodity.

The Demand for Consumption Time and the Supply of Labor

The demand curve for consumption time differs from the demand curve for a commodity in that the pure substitution and income effects of a price change *normally* go in opposite directions. Along a given contour, a rise in c_2 causes a consumer to conserve on time and choose combinations that require less time and more of the composite commodity. But a rise in c_2 also permits a consumer to enjoy more of both. If a consumer regards time for personal use as an inferior good, the high income induces a further reduction in consumption time. Conversely, if a consumer wishes to enjoy a high income partly in the form of more leisure, the two effects tend to cancel each other. Since a decline in p_1 has the same effect on x_2 as a rise in c_2, the cross-demand curve for x_2 with p_1 falling is identical with the demand curve for x_2 with c_2 rising. The relationship is shown in Figure 14–2, which also displays the supply curve for labor hours, $z_2 = T - x_2$. The amount of work a consumer chooses to supply at each wage rate is simply the horizontal difference between total available time and the amount optimally reserved for personal use.

We have purposely not drawn a supply curve of labor at low levels of the wage rate. When the wage rate is at or near the subsistence level, and there is no other source of income, it makes little sense to explain the willingness to work in terms of preferences for leisure time. Only at higher levels of the wage rate can a consumer be expected to balance off the relative contributions of time and commodities to a consumption pattern. For a commodity the axioms of consumer preference are almost, but not quite, sufficient

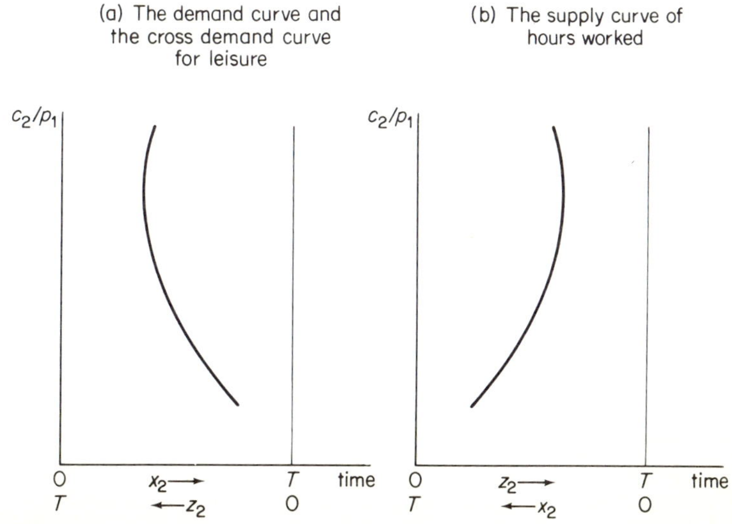

Fig. 14-2

to prove the negative slope of a demand curve. With respect to the supply curve of labor hours the axioms do not permit any conclusion about the probable sign of the slope. Individuals may differ widely in their attitudes toward the personal use of time. Some may respond avidly to the opportunity for higher income, whereas others may prefer to work the minimum number of hours necessary to finance study, cultural pursuits, or recreation. The first group will have upward-sloping supply curves, the second backward-bending supply curves. The normal opposition of income and pure substitution effects does, however, establish a presumption that, at least in intermediate ranges, the typical supply curve will not show very much sensitivity to changes in the wage rate.

Optimal Choice with More than One Input

While most persons have only a single input, labor services, to offer, there are some individuals who are in a position to supply a second input, such as the services of land. Like time, land can also be devoted to a consumer's personal use in various ways, such as hunting, gardening, or the enjoyment of ample space. Land can also be leased or rented to provide income. The sale of land is a transfer of assets from one form to another and does not enter directly into the determination of current income. Land differs from time in that the total amount can be offered in the market at the current rental prices. As is shown later, this special result fits readily into the general analysis.

To make the model more complete, we shall also include two commodities and develop the conditions for optimality when there is choice both in the supply of inputs and in the purchase of commodities. A consumer must now make three decisions. The first has already been explained in preceding chapters and is illustrated in Figure 14–3a. Whatever its level, money income must be optimally distributed over the available commodities, as shown by tangency of the budget line to an indifference contour.

Second, each level of income must be optimally earned by supplying each input in the correct amount. Figure 14–3b shows the total amounts of the two inputs as horizontal and vertical lines meeting in the point $0'$. The amounts retained by the consumer for personal use are measured rightward and upward from the conventional origin 0 and are designated by x_1 and x_2. The amounts sold, z_1 and z_2, are measured leftward and downward from the origin $0'$. With fixed prices c_1 and c_2, the income from the sales of inputs, $y = c_1z_1 + c_2z_2$, is represented by parallel straight lines. Greater distances from $0'$ show higher levels of income but smaller amounts of the inputs retained for personal use. Any prescribed level of income y^0 can be obtained by selling any combination of inputs on the corresponding straight line. The optimizing consumer chooses to supply inputs in such a way that the amounts remaining form the highest ranked combination. The highest ranked combination lies on the farthest attainable indifference contour from the conventional origin 0, and is identified by the point of tangency. Alternatively, we may flip the diagram over, as also shown in Figure 14–3b, and display the indifference contours relative to the origin 0′. The nearest attainable concave contour represents the optimum.

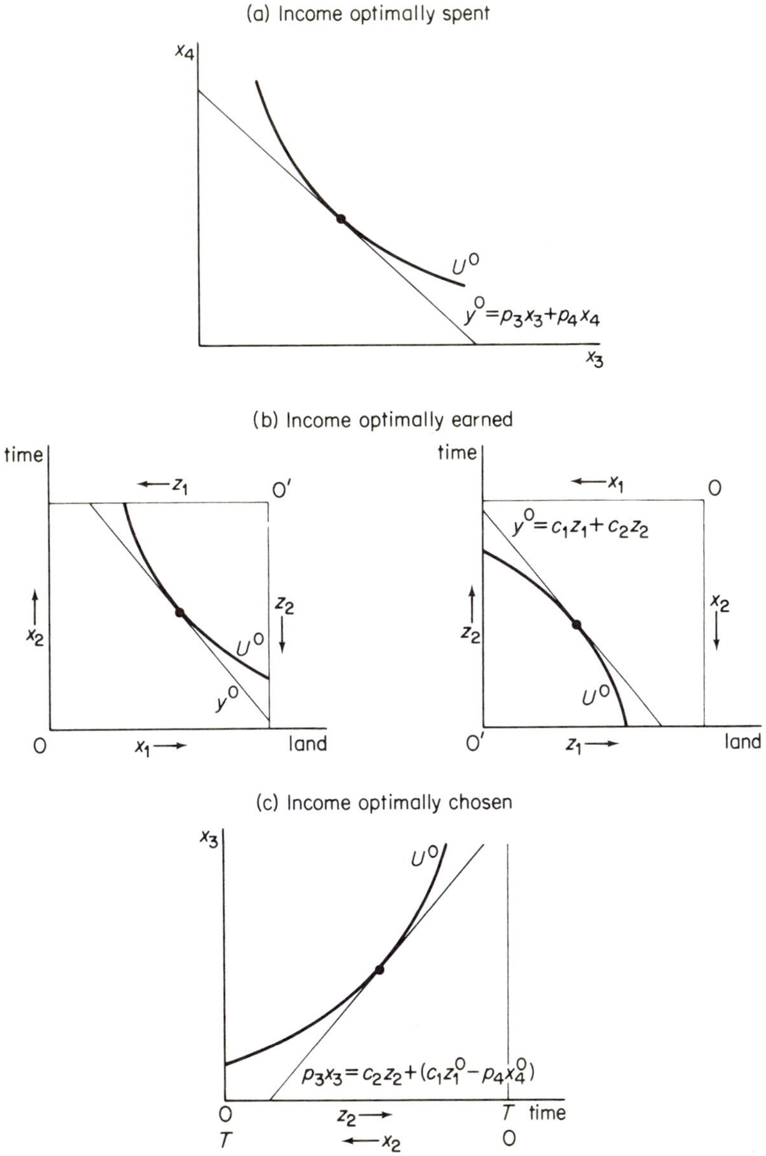

Fig. 14-3

It is not quite enough that any given level of income be optimally earned and optimally spent; the level itself must also be optimal. As shown earlier in the chapter, a consumer must find the best attainable combination of commodities purchased and inputs retained for personal use. So long as a correct balance is maintained at each level of income between the inputs supplied and between the commodities purchased, it is only necessary to show that one input and one commodity are optimally related to each other. If z_2 designates labor, then Figure 14–3c is essentially the same as Figure 14–1b, derived earlier in the chapter, with one minor exception. When x_4 and z_1 are constant at x_4^0 and z_1^0, the equality of income and expenditure is:

$$p_4 x_4^0 + p_3 x_3 = c_2 z_2 + c_1 z_1^0$$

or

$$p_3 x_3 = c_2 z_2 + (c_1 z_1^0 - p_4 x_4^0).$$

The expenditure on x_3 can differ by a constant amount, positive or negative, from the wage income. The income constraint need not go through the origin $0'$ but may have an intercept either above or to the right of it. However, tangency of the income line to an indifference curve remains the condition for optimality. When there are two inputs and two commodities, a total of four variables, three diagrams in two-dimensional space are needed for the full optimal solution.[2]

If land devoted to personal use has no value to a consumer, the entire amount will be offered for lease at any positive price. So long as a consumer is not satiated with respect to all commodities, more income is better than less, so there is a gain but no offsetting loss in leasing out all available land. Since $\bar{u}_1 = 0$, the indifference curves in Figure 14–3b are horizontal, and there is always a corner solution where $x_1 = 0$ or z_1 equals the total amount available. There is no longer any problem of balancing the supply of inputs, so Figure 14–3b can be dropped. The decision to supply or retain time remains and is affected by the availability of income from the rental of land. The consumer can have both more leisure and more commodities, but there is

[2]For any pair of the four variables, be they inputs retained, x_1 and x_2, or commodities purchased, x_3 and x_4, the ratio of internal prices must equal the ratio of the market prices. Four variables can be combined into six distinctive pairs. Let the internal and external price ratios be equal for any three pairs, such as:

$$\frac{\bar{u}_1}{\bar{u}_2} = \frac{c_1}{c_2} \qquad \frac{\bar{u}_3}{\bar{u}_4} = \frac{p_3}{p_4} \qquad \frac{\bar{u}_2}{\bar{u}_3} = \frac{c_2}{p_3}.$$

It is easy to show that equality of ratios holds for any other pair, specifically:

$$\frac{\bar{u}_3}{\bar{u}_4} \times \frac{\bar{u}_2}{\bar{u}_3} = \frac{p_3}{p_4} \times \frac{c_2}{p_3} \qquad \text{or} \qquad \frac{\bar{u}_2}{\bar{u}_4} = \frac{c_2}{p_4}.$$

In general, when the consumer has n quantities to determine optimally, $(n-1)$ diagrams or $(n-1)$ equalities between ratios of internal and external prices are sufficient.

great latitude depending on preferences. Figure 14–3c remains essentially unchanged.

Consumers may also receive nonlabor income from the ownership of financial assets such as stocks, bonds, or deposits in various savings institutions. Such income affects the result in a similar way to income from the ownership of land. More significant than the present ownership of such assets is their acquisition through current saving, a topic to be included in the following section.

CONSUMER DECISION MAKING: A BROADER PERSPECTIVE

As a little experience soon shows, it is simply not effective to try to solve all problems at once or to seek initially the most general solution. "I'll cross that bridge when I come to it" is a bit of folk wisdom that has relevance to problem solving. It pays to break complex problems down into simpler subproblems to be solved separately. For a complete solution the separate decisions must fit into a consistent overall pattern. As later chapters bring out, a purely competitive economic system is a form of decentralized decision making that achieves an optimum through separate optimizing decisions by individual economic units. The theory of consumer's choice, broadly viewed, is an example of suboptimization.

In the preceding section, we broke the consumer's problem down into two simpler subproblems: how to allocate a predetermined level of income optimally over the available commodities and how to obtain optimally any prescribed level of income. The two separate decisions were then linked into an overall optimal solution by determining the level of income. For a more complete model of consumer's choice an additional basic decision must be included: How much of any given income is to be devoted to consumption and how much to saving? Once the division has been made, an individual faces a suboptimization problem similar to buying commodities. There is a wide variety of financial assets such as stocks, bonds, deposits in various savings institutions, and cash itself. The individual, qua investor, must allocate the given sum optimally over the available financial assets. Since most persons already hold some financial assets, the problem is actually to allocate optimally the total value of financial assets and not just the current increment represented by saving.

The portfolio problem, or investor's choice, has great fascination as well as economic importance. It bears a generic resemblance to the choice of commodities since it is a constrained optimizing problem in which the investor seeks the combination of financial assets with the best mixture of liquidity, safety, and earnings. The problem is, however, inescapably dynamic or speculative; decisions cannot be based solely on present prices but must involve anticipations of future prices. Also required are preferences with respect to the pattern of income or consumption over time.

There are, then, three subproblems to be solved: consumer's choice, investor's choice, and the choice of the input combination to be supplied. Additionally, an individual must determine the optimal amounts to be taken as given for each suboptimization. In its full generality, the problem is probably too complex for an individual to solve in any precise way, and it is too complex to incorporate into models of the whole economic system. It is both realistic and necessary to introduce such simplifications as individuals are themselves likely to make.

A simplification frequently used is that the prices of inputs have little or no effect on the amounts supplied in the short run. There is no choice in the supply of inputs, so one of the subproblems disappears. Further, since market prices determine what income will be, an individual no longer has to decide what is the optimal level. As shown earlier, the normal opposition of the pure substitution and income effects support the conclusion that hours worked are not likely to be highly responsive to the wage rate. Legal, conventional, and institutional restrictions on hours of work reinforce the conclusion. For inputs other than time, the short-run supply is also likely to be highly inelastic. For example, changes in the rental price of land are not likely to have immediate effects on the division between personal use and rental to the producing sector.

The problem of dividing income between consumption and saving is often solved by omitting it; all income is assumed to be spent on commodities. The reason for the simplification is that it permits economists to analyze and to explain the allocative function of the economy in the simplest possible setting, where allocation of given resources is essentially the only function the economy has to perform. A more realistic simplification is the consumption function of national income analysis. In dividing money income between consumption and saving, an individual relies solely on the level of income itself and on the level of commodity prices, or succinctly, on the level of real income. More advanced versions of the consumption function allow financial assets to affect the division of income either through asset prices, usually expressed by yields or interest rates, or through the total value held. Once the division between saving and consumption is made, commodities and financial assets are chosen independently.

In national income analysis, which emphasizes the saving-investment process and its effects on aggregate income and output, consumer's choice receives little attention. Choice is restricted to a single composite commodity by neglecting relative price changes, or even eliminated entirely by positing only one commodity. By contrast, price and allocation theory focuses upon commodity and input markets and often simplifies to the point of elimination of the saving-investment process. Individuals must simplify their problems in order to solve them, and models of economic decision making for both firm and consumer incorporate such simplifications. But economists also have to simplify their problems in order to solve them and have developed various special models of the economic system, each emphasizing only certain functions of the economy and neglecting the rest. Important examples are the short-run allocative, the national income or macroeconomic, and the long-run growth models. Ideally there should be only one model which simulates all relevant aspects of the economy, but the economic system is so complex that the ideal has not yet been attained and may never be. Economists generally believe that a set of partial models, each emphasizing special functions, yields more insight than a detailed description of the economic system without a formal model.

In the chapters that follow we shall be developing the short-run allocative model of the economy and shall use the simplification that saving and investment are zero. National income analysis shows how the decisions to save and the decisions by business to increase capacity interact to determine the level of employment for existing resources, particularly labor. Whatever the levels of investment and employment of resources, the short-run allocative mechanism is at work guiding resources into the various industries and determining the output of commodities. Investment, of course, adds to productive capacity, but short-run national income models consider only the effects of constructing capacity and not its subsequent use. To allow for the effects of present investment upon future output, we must employ a long-run growth model, in which the population is also free to vary. In concentrating on growth, many long-run growth models eliminate short-run problems by assuming all resources both fully employed and optimally allocated at every point of time. The focus becomes rates of growth of the productive resources, how they vary relative to each other, and what the consequences are. Allocation, level of employment, and growth of productive resources are all vitally important aspects of economic activity. Each receives detailed analysis in special, simplified versions of the economic system.

THE FAMILY AS CONSUMING UNIT

An individual consumer has only a single preference ranking or utility function to guide the purchase of commodities. When two or more individuals share the same income, there is more than one preference ranking for the available commodity bundles. Sharing a common income is the minimal economic requirement for a family to be the consuming unit. Since income is derived primarily from the sale of inputs, the more fundamental economic characteristic of the family is the sharing of productive resources that may either be used internally in consumption processes or exchanged in the market for commodities. Family members also share consumption processes either directly through cooperation or indirectly, as when one member's purchase of, say, bongo drums affects the rest of the family. Finally, the family generally has joint goals or objectives in addition to the personal objectives that individual members have. We shall explore mainly the consequences of sharing income under the simplifying assumption that both the consumption processes and the objectives of the family members are independent.

The Utility Transformation Contour

A family is not likely to use its income unrestrictedly to maximize the utility of one member but it certainly can use its income to maximize the utility of one member subject to constant levels for the other members. In fact, as we shall see, any solution that does not satisfy this minimal requirement is wasteful and inefficient. With two members in the family and two commodities available, the problem can be expressed in the following linear programming form:

$$\begin{aligned}
a_{11}v_1+a_{12}v_2+a_{13}v_3+a_{14}v_4+a_{15}v_5+a_{16}v_6 &\leqq q_1\\
a_{21}v_1+a_{22}v_2+a_{23}v_3+a_{24}v_4+a_{25}v_5+a_{26}v_6 &\leqq q_2\\
v_1+\quad v_2+\quad v_3 \qquad\qquad\qquad\qquad\qquad &\geqq U_1^0\\
v_4+\quad v_5+\quad v_6 &= U_2(\max).
\end{aligned}$$

The quantities on the right represent total family purchases of the two commodities. The first three columns contain consumption processes for the first family member, and the next three columns consumption processes for the second member. Neither individual is affected by the consumption processes of the other; U_1 depends solely on the first three processes and U_2 on the next three.

As in all previous problems, the optimal solution in canonical form displays the objective variable as a linear function of the quantities in the constraints, which may be written as follows:

$$U_2 = -\bar{t}U_1+\bar{u}_{21}q_1+\bar{u}_{22}q_2.$$

The coefficients $\bar{u}_{21}$ and $\bar{u}_{22}$ are the rates of change of U_2 with respect to each commodity, or the marginal utilities of the respective commodities to the second consumer. Being dual variables, they can also be interpreted as the valuations that the second member places on a unit of these commodities.

Before interpreting $\bar{t}$, we note that the problem is similar in structure to the model of a two-input, two-output firm presented in Chapter 11. The commodities serve as inputs to the consumption processes, whose outputs are not physical quantities but levels of utility for the two family members. The internal or technological optimizing problem for the firm is to use any given combination of inputs in such a way as to maximize one output for any specified level of the other. Parametric variation of the second output with both inputs fixed traces out the product transformation contour of Figure 11–1a. For the firm the coefficient $\bar{t}$ is the rate of change of one product with respect to the other, which is the rate of product transformation or the negative of the slope along the transformation contour.

Parametric variation of U_1 with both commodities constant traces out a utility transformation contour whose slope is $-\bar{t}$.[3] There is an important difference between the two cases in that output levels are observable and measurable objectively, whereas utility levels are not, a problem to be taken up shortly. We wish first to exploit the similarities between firm and family. With utility levels on the axes, Figure 14–4 displays a piecewise-linear utility transformation contour, whose slope is the negative of the rate of utility transformation. Each point on the contour represents a different distribution of the available commodities between the two family members. A utility transformation contour, like its analogue for the firm, must be concave to the origin rather than convex. Otherwise intermediate combinations would represent higher utility levels for both members and the requirements for a maximum would not be met.

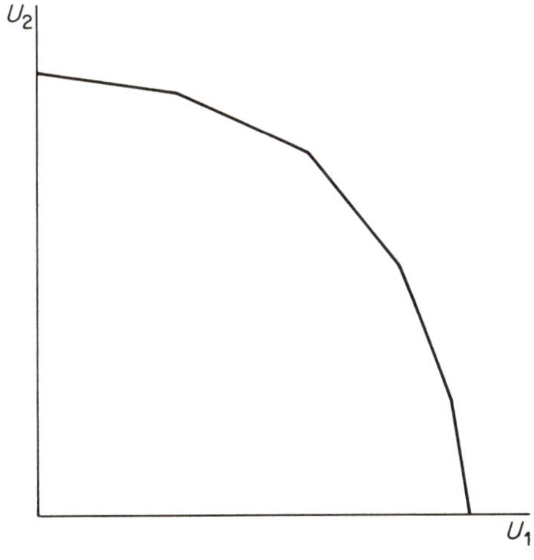

Fig. 14-4 A Piecewise-Linear Utility Transformation Contour

The Edgeworth Box Diagram and Contract Locus

The utility transformation contour can be smoothed by the familiar conceptual device of letting the number of consumption processes increase without limit. There is also a very instructive diagrammatic method for

[3]The negative sign before $\bar{t}$ arises when we change signs and reverse the inequality to make the third constraint conform to the first two.

deriving a smooth transformation contour directly from smooth indifference curves. The total amounts of both commodities are shown in Figure 14–5a by the vertical and horizontal lines intersecting in 0′. The amounts going to the first family member, x_{12} and x_{11}, are measured upward and rightward from 0. The curve U_1^0 contains all available combinations that yield the prescribed utility level for the first consumer. The portion of the rectangle beyond U_1^0 is the available set for the second member, as shown explicitly in Figure 14–5b. Curve U_2 is maximized when the second member receives the commodity bundle at the point of tangency. The maximum U_2 and the preassigned U_1^0 plot as one point on the utility transformation contour.

To generate the entire transformation contour we must repeat the procedure for every level of U_1 that is attainable within the rectangle. Every indifference curve for the first member, drawn relative to the origin 0, must be tangent to an indifference curve for the second member, drawn relative to 0′. Figure 14–5c, which shows the configuration, is called an *Edgeworth box diagram.* The locus of all points of tangency between the two sets of

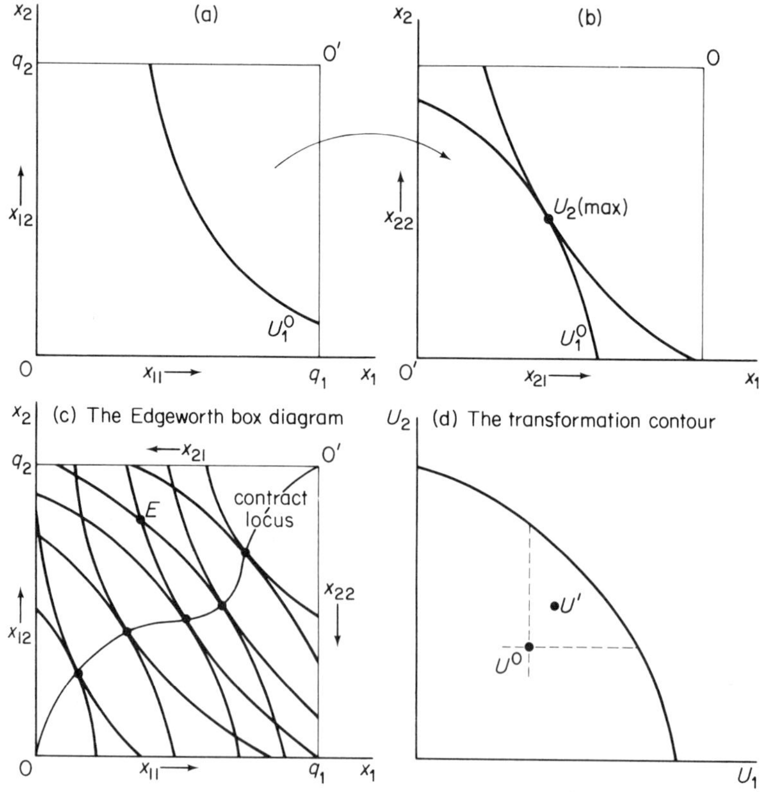

Fig. 14-5 Derivation of a Utility Transformation Contour

indifference curves identifies all pairs of utility levels lying on the utility transformation curve of Figure 14–5d.

Besides generating a utility transformation curve, the locus of points of tangency has an important role in explaining trade or bargaining between two individuals. For this reason it is called an *Edgeworth contract locus.* Every point in the Edgeworth box represents some specific division of the available commodities between the individuals. At any point off the contract locus, such as E, there is always a redistribution of the commodity holdings that makes at least one individual better off and neither worse off. By following each indifference curve from the intersection at E to the contract locus, we see that both individuals could be as well off as at E with commodities left over. Any assignment of the excess commodities to the two individuals makes at least one better off. A downward-sloping line in the box diagram represents a constant rate of change or of exchange between the two commodities, or a fixed trading ratio. Any straight line from E that passes through the gap on the contract locus determines a ratio at which both can trade and both be better off. How the gain from trade is split depends on the specific trading ratio.

Points off the contract locus correspond to utility pairs inside the transformation contour. One individual can become better off without making the other worse off. Once the contract locus or contour is reached, one person can gain only at the expense of the other. A situation in which no one can gain unless someone else loses is said to be *Pareto optimal* or to satisfy the criterion of *Pareto optimality.* Pareto optimality is a relatively weak criterion that permits us to rank a given situation or combination relative to some other situations but not all. When closely examined, it turns out to be a special application of the partial ordering of vectors. Points in utility space are vectors of the form $\mathbf{u} = [U_1, U_2]$. If one vector is larger than another, $\mathbf{u}^1 > \mathbf{u}^0$, no matching component can be smaller and at least one must be larger. But this is the same as saying that no individual can be worse off (have lower utility) and at least one must be better off. Geometrically, $\mathbf{u}^1$ must be in the northeast quadrant relative to $\mathbf{u}^0$. If $\mathbf{u}^0$ lies inside the contour, all attainable utility pairs in its northeast quadrant represent an improvement. When $\mathbf{u}^0$ lies on the contour there is no attainable vector in the northeast quadrant, so $\mathbf{u}^0$ is Pareto optimal.

COMMODITY SUBSTITUTION OR SCITOVSKY CONTOURS

Utility transformation contours give valuable insight into the problem of optimization for the family, but they suffer from the defect of not being expressed directly in terms of commodities. What we should like to have are contours in commodity space, which is analogous to input space for the firm.

We were able to derive input substitution contours by first minimizing one input subject to constant levels for the other input and both outputs. The analogous problem for the family, shown below, is to hold utility levels and one commodity constant and to minimize the amount of the other commodity.

$$\begin{aligned} v_1 + v_2 + v_3 \qquad\qquad\qquad &\geqq U_1^0 \\ v_4 + v_5 + v_6 &\geqq U_2^0 \\ a_{11}v_1 + a_{12}v_1 + a_{13}v_3 + a_{14}v_4 + a_{15}v_5 + a_{16}v_6 &\leqq q_1 \\ a_{21}v_1 + a_{22}v_2 + a_{23}v_3 + a_{24}v_4 + a_{25}v_5 + a_{26}v_6 &= x_2(\text{min}). \end{aligned}$$

After changing signs in the third constraint, reduction to canonical form for the optimal solution yields the commodity minimized as the following linear function of the quantities under constraint:

$$x_2 = -\bar{s}x_1 + \frac{1}{\bar{u}_{12}}U_1^0 + \frac{1}{\bar{u}_{22}}U_2^0.$$

The coefficients of U_1^0 and U_2^0 are the reciprocals of the marginal utilities of x_2 to the respective family members. For the firm the corresponding coefficients were shown to be the reciprocals of the marginal physical productivities in the two products. As x_1 varies it traces out a piecewise-linear contour in commodity space, which is shown in Figure 14–6 and then transformed into a smooth curve. The contour must be convex to the origin like an indifference curve; otherwise intermediate combinations of commodities would be nearer the origin, indicating that the same utility levels could be attained with smaller amounts of the commodities. Commodity substitution contours are generally called *Scitovsky contours* in honor of the economist who introduced them.

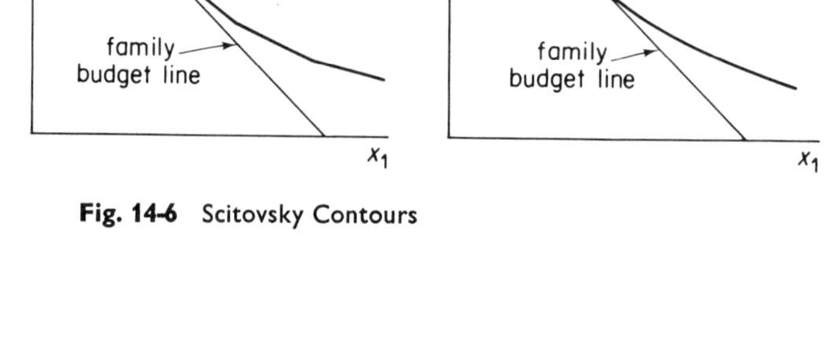

Fig. 14-6 Scitovsky Contours

As shown earlier for the firm, maximizing an output and minimizing an input yield the same information so long as the marginal physical productivities are neither zero nor infinite. By ruling out similar extreme values for the marginal utilities we can conclude that the utility maximizing and commodity minimizing versions for the family give consistent results. If a commodity bundle is yielding maximum utility levels, it will not be possible to reduce one commodity and keep both levels constant. Since $\bar{u}_{22}$ cannot become zero, we can divide by it and rewrite the utility transformation equation in the following form:

$$x_2 = -\frac{\bar{u}_{21}}{\bar{u}_{22}}x_1 + \frac{\bar{t}}{\bar{u}_{22}}U_1^0 + \frac{1}{\bar{u}_{22}}U_2^0.$$

The coefficient of x_1 is the ratio of marginal utilities of x_1 and x_2 to the second family member, or the rate of commodity substitution. A similar equation holds for the other member when U_1 is maximized for a constant U_2. Comparing coefficients of x_1 in the commodity substitution equation and in the revised transformation equations shows that

$$\bar{s} = \frac{\bar{u}_{21}}{\bar{u}_{22}} = \frac{\bar{u}_{11}}{\bar{u}_{12}}.$$

Along a Scitovsky contour, $\bar{s}$ is the rate at which the family can substitute x_2 for x_1 and maintain constant utility levels for both members. To satisfy Pareto optimality, the family's rate of commodity substitution must equal the rate for each of its members. The Edgeworth box diagram confirms the result by showing that tangency of the indifference curves, or equal rates of commodity substitution, is the requirement for Pareto optimality.

The Efficient Spending of Family Income

An important conclusion follows from the preceding equality. Suppose that the family simply divides its income between the two members and lets each make an independent optimizing decision. So long as both members base their decisions on the same set of market prices, the individual rates of commodity substitution will be equal to the same price ratio and, hence, equal to each other. The purchases of the two members add up to a point on the family income line whose slope is the negative ratio of the market prices. Further, the price ratio, being equal to both individual rates of commodity substitution, must also be equal to the family's rate of commodity substitution. Hence, the family income line must be tangent to a Scitovsky contour that passes through the point of total family purchases.

Here the similarity to individual indifference curves ends. There are infinitely many ways of allocating family income between the members. Different distributions result in different total purchases, except in the extreme case where both consumers have identical indifference maps that are also parallel along rays through the origin. Each distribution produces a Pareto optimal solution but at a different point on the family income line. Thus, at virtually every point along the family income line there can be tangency to some Scitovsky contour. Unlike individual indifference curves, Scitovsky contours do not determine a unique optimal commodity bundle for the family to purchase.

Instead of apportioning income, the family may employ some collective decision process to purchase a particular commodity bundle and then distribute it among the members. If the distribution does not satisfy Pareto optimality and the individual rates of commodity substitution are not equal, the family members can improve the distribution by trading with each other, as the children in the family often do at Christmastime. Internal trading will equate the individual rates of commodity substitution to each other, but will not in general equate them to the market price ratio. Hence, the Scitovsky contour for the levels of utility attained by internal trade intersects the family income line. The family can spend less money and still attain the same levels of utility for its members. Even though the distribution of commodities satisfies Pareto optimality, the family is not spending its income efficiently.

If family members are free to trade with outsiders at the going prices, they will do so until each individual rate of commodity substitution equals the market price ratio. By trading with outsiders and altering the quantity of each commodity, the members move the family to a different point on the income line, where it is tangent to a Scitovsky contour. A given commodity bundle can be distributed among the family members in infinitely many Pareto optimal ways, each corresponding to a point on the contract locus. But the family can spend its income efficiently only if it chooses the point on the locus at which both individual rates of commodity substitution equal the market price ratio. The decision to buy a commodity bundle also determines how it is to be distributed. Conversely, if the family decides in advance on a formula for distribution, it is also deciding what commodity bundle to purchase out of a given income. To spend income efficiently the family must coordinate the purchase of commodities with their subsequent distribution.

Members of the consuming sector are like members of the family in that they share a common aggregate income. In Chapter 19 we shall show that the market mechanism so links together all members of the consuming sector that the conclusions just reached for the family carry over to an entire sector of independent consuming units. A given total quantity of goods can be distributed among all consumers in infinitely many Pareto optimal ways. But aggregate income is being efficiently spent only when all individual rates of commodity substitution equal the price ratio.

A FAMILY WELFARE FUNCTION

Virtually every point on the family income line is tangent to some Scitovsky contour, so it is obvious that such contours must intersect. Furthermore, there is a general pattern to their intersection. A commodity bundle, which is a point in commodity space, can be apportioned between the family members in infinitely many ways, each corresponding to a point on the contract locus and to a point on the utility transformation curve. A pair of utility levels, which is a point in utility space, can be efficiently attained by any one of the infinitely many bundles on a commodity substitution contour. Since each point on the transformation curve generates a distinct Scitovsky contour, the entire transformation curve generates an infinite family of Scitovsky contours. The common characteristic that determines membership in the family is that each contour passes through the original point in commodity space that generates the utility transformation curve.

The conclusion is confirmed by the Edgeworth box diagram which is drawn for fixed quantities of the commodities and, hence, for a single point in commodity space. Each point on the contract locus corresponds to a point on the utility transformation contour. Further, at each point on the contract locus, the individual rates of commodity substitution are equal to each other and, hence, equal to the rate of substitution along some Scitovsky contour. Thus, each point on the contract locus identifies both a point in utility space and the slope of the corresponding Scitovsky contour passing through the given point in commodity space. Since infinitely many Scitovsky contours pass through each point, there is a range of price ratios for which the income line can be tangent to a contour. With market prices given, the income line will be tangent to one contour, which in turn corresponds to one pair of utility levels. When the family buys the particular commodity bundle, it is spending income efficiently only if the distribution of the commodities permits each member to attain the corresponding utility level.

Intersecting contours are not something peculiar to the family but are inherent in the type of problem; the input substitution contours of the multiproduct firm intersect in a precisely similar way. Despite the indeterminacy the firm is able to make a unique optimizing decision. Any given input combination can produce any output pair on an entire product transformation contour. As soon as output prices or revenue coefficients are introduced, all output combinations can be ranked with respect to the revenue they yield. Along each contour the firm chooses an output pair that yields maximum revenue. With revenue coefficients constant, all input combinations can be ranked with respect to the maximum revenue each produces. As shown in Chapter 11, the result is a partitioning of input space into a set of isorevenue contours that do not intersect and are convex to the origin.

Without a revenue function a firm cannot compare outputs and decide whether a unit of one output or a unit of the other should be produced. It has two objectives, maximizing the level of x_1 and maximizing the level of x_2. The goals are partially in conflict with each other, since more of one output generally means less of the other. If the firm cannot assign relative values to the two outputs, the only clearly justified policy is to maximize one output for some constant level of the other. An explicit revenue function provides a single consistent objective in place of the previous partially conflicting objectives. The relative importance of each output with respect to the new objective is the rate at which each contributes to total revenue. A special simple case of a revenue function, appropriate for pure competition, is a linear function with fixed weights in the form of price or revenue coefficients. When the revenue function is not linear, as it would not be under monopolistic conditions, the weights vary with the amounts sold.

Whenever conflicting goals exist, the formally correct and logically rigorous solution is to assign weights to the conflicting goals and combine them into a single objective. The utility function for a single consumer, introduced over 100 years ago, represents precisely this type of solution. Previously, consumer's choice had been analyzed in terms of a limited number of basic needs and wants, toward whose satisfaction commodities contributed. As a generalized measure of want satisfying capacity, utility provided a single objective in place of the separate objectives of satisfying specific needs and wants. Hence, when we posit a utility function or complete preference ranking, we assume implicitly that the consumer has successfully reconciled diverse goals. Even though each family member has a single goal, the maximization of individual utility, the family has a multiplicity of partially conflicting goals, since it seeks to maximize the personal utility of all members.

Isowelfare or Bergson Contours

What is required for a formal solution is that weights somehow be assigned to the utility levels of the family members. The simplest solution, analogous to that for a purely competitive firm, is to assign fixed weights and define the following family welfare function:

$$W = r_1 U_1 + r_2 U_2.$$

A given commodity combination generates an entire concave utility transformation contour, but only one point on the contour is tangent to a family welfare line and represents maximum family welfare. We can then label the original point in commodity space with the unique maximum family welfare it can produce. The procedure is repeated conceptually for all points in commodity space. As is true in input space for the firm, the result is a partitioning of commodity space into a set of convex, nonintersecting contours. These isowelfare contours in commodity space are generally called *Bergson contours*, once again in honor of the economist who introduced them.

The relationship between Bergson contours and Scitovsky contours is formally similar to the previously explained relationship between isorevenue contours and input substitution contours. Each point on a welfare line in utility space generates a Scitovsky contour in commodity space. Taken together all such contours form a region in commodity space, every point of which represents the same family welfare. But some points lie nearer the origin than others and represent more efficient ways of attaining a given state of well being for the family. To find the lower boundary, we minimize x_1 subject to a constant amount of x_2 and a constant level of welfare. The resultant leftmost point lies on the lower boundary or Bergson contour. Letting x_2 vary parametrically traces out the entire lower boundary. A Bergson contour, like an isorevenue contour, is an envelope curve tangent at every point to a different Scitovsky contour.

Tangency of the income line to a Bergson contour determines both the family's choice of a commodity bundle and its distribution among the members. Every point on the family income line is tangent to a Scitovsky contour, but each contour is generated by a different pair of utility levels. Without an explicit welfare function there is no way of choosing one particular utility pair over another. The welfare function ranks the utility pairs attainable along the family budget line and identifies the highest ranking pair. The commodities are so apportioned among members as to attain the desired utility levels.

Properties of a Welfare Function

A welfare function resembles a revenue function in being the formally correct method of reconciling conflicting multiple objectives. But there is an important difference in that welfare and utility are not observable or measurable. What a welfare function does is to provide a ranking of vectors or ordered pairs of utility levels. As is true for any ranking there is nothing immutable about the numbers that represent it. Once a particular welfare function has been chosen, any increasing transformation of that index will do as well.

In other respects also the ranking of utility levels resembles the ranking of commodity bundles. We should expect the welfare ranking to satisfy the condition that more is preferred to less; the family is better off when at least one member is better off and none is worse off. But this simply means that the welfare ranking coincides with the partial ordering of utility vectors. As shown earlier, it is equivalent to the criterion of Pareto optimality. Family welfare must be an increasing function of the utility levels, but the form the function may take is not otherwise restricted. A linear welfare function implies that the family ranks equally intermediate combinations and extreme vectors in which one member receives no commodities and has zero utility. Much more plausible are convex welfare contours that express in some degree a preference for narrow over wide differences in utility.

The utility levels of the members merely represent rankings and are themselves subject to increasing transformations, which cause both the utility transformation curves and the isowelfare contours to shift about in utility space. But curves and contours that are tangent before the shift remain tangent after. In commodity space, the Bergson contours remain fixed and are merely relabeled with different welfare numbers, so decisions are unaffected.

We have introduced the family welfare function not as a practical method but as the formally rigorous method of resolving indeterminacy in family choice. As such, it clarifies the problem and provides an evaluation of other solutions. Suppose that the family meets each price-income situation as it arises and makes ad hoc decisions. Efficient expenditure of income requires that the commodity bundle purchased be distributed in only one way, thus determining utility levels. By its action the family is implicitly ranking that particular utility vector over all other pairs that could be attained at the given level of income and prices. Repeated ad hoc decisions are not likely to provide a consistent welfare ranking. Nor do consistent results follow from dividing money income in a fixed ratio between the members and letting each make individual optimizing decisions. Suppose that at the going prices the division of income results in equal utility levels, based on a specific utility index for each member. The first member buys large amounts of one commodity and the second member buys large amounts of the other. A change in relative prices will have different effects on the two utility levels, which could be offset by a change in the distribution of income. Thus, by adhering to a fixed distribution of income the family implicitly chooses equal utility levels when it could have unequal levels, and chooses unequal levels when it could have equal levels. When family members have different tastes, changes in relative prices have diverse effects on their utility levels. No single distribution of income can achieve maximum family welfare when prices are changing.

INTERDEPENDENCE OF CONSUMPTION PROCESSES

Not only within the family but also in the consuming sector as a whole, the consumption processes of one individual affect the well being of other persons. The terms *external effect*, *externality*, and *spillover effect* are applied when the decisions of one economic unit have repercussions upon other distinct economic units. Population growth and technological and cultural changes have forced us all to live in closer quarters than before, and externalities are acquiring ever greater significance. The unfavorable effects, such as air and noise pollution, have received most attention, but there are also benefits, which partly explain migration to cities. Later chapters will take up externalities in the economy, but the family reveals in particularly clear and simple form some of the implications.

To see the problem in explicit form, we modify the linear model of the family on page 354. The consumption processes of one individual no longer have zero effect on the well being of the other, so we must introduce coefficients, which may be positive or negative, to show the interdependence. The revised linear utility functions are

$$u_{11}v_1+u_{12}v_2+u_{13}v_3+u_{14}v_4+u_{15}v_5+u_{16}v_6 = U_1$$

$$u_{21}v_1+u_{22}v_2+u_{23}v_3+u_{24}v_4+u_{25}v_5+u_{26}v_6 = U_2.$$

Since the first three processes are those of the first consumer, readers can readily identify the coefficients that show cross-effects. By setting up as a utility maximizing problem or as a commodity minimizing problem, we can derive utility transformation contours and commodity substitution contours in essentially the same way as before.

The family's rate of commodity substitution will again be equal to the ratio of marginal utilities for each member, but only when each marginal utility includes the gain or loss that results from the other member's purchase of the commodity. Utility levels in consumption processes are formally similar to output levels in production processes, and interdependence of utility levels is analogous to joint products. There is one notable difference. A negative coefficient in a production process implies that the product is being used as an input. A negative coefficient in a consumption process implies an actual reduction in the other member's level of utility. A firm could ignore joint products by treating each process as if it turned out only the principal product. All other outputs arbitrarily receive coefficients of zero. With part of their output ignored, the inputs cannot have the same marginal productivities. Except in the very unusual case where the ratio of the marginal productivities happens to remain the same, the firm cannot make the correct decision about use of inputs. Similarly, when cross effects are present but ignored within the family, commodities are not likely to have the same ratio of marginal utilities to either family member as when cross-effects are taken into account.

The family can no longer spend its income efficiently by apportioning income among the members and letting each make an independent optimizing decision. If each member buys books without realizing that the rest of the family can also read them, there will be duplicates and a general lack of balance. Efficient spending requires the market price ratio to equal the family rate of commodity substitution, which in turn equals the ratio of each individual's marginal utilities with cross effects included. Family purchases must be distributed among members, and the distribution represents one point on each member's private indifference map. There is a set of prices and income at which each member would independently choose the commodity bundle that is optimal for the family. Unfortunately, these prices cannot be the same as the market prices and must in general be chosen separately for each family member.

These conclusions acquire broader significance when applied later to an entire sector of independent consuming units. When externalities are present, the sector's aggregate income will not be spent efficiently if all units make independent optimizing decisions based on the same market prices. But it is extremely difficult to establish a system of different price ratios for each unit.

SUMMARY

We have completed our analysis of consumer's choice and shall move on to constructing a model for the economy as a whole. For individual consumers, demand curves for commodities were first derived, and the method was then extended to the supply of primary inputs. In the following chapter individual demand curves are combined to form the aggregate or market demand curves of all consumers for a single commodity. For later use we shall consider briefly at this stage the aggregate supply of primary inputs. As shown earlier, the normal opposition of pure substitution and income effects implies that individual supply curves for labor may slope upward or bend backward and are likely in either case to be relatively steep. Since attitudes toward work and leisure differ considerably, we should expect the upward-sloping supply curves of some individuals to be offset in the aggregate by the backward-bending curves of other individuals. Hence, even if hours of work were not regulated, we should not expect the aggregate supply of labor to show much response to short-run changes in wage rates. For other primary inputs, such as land, short-run changes in rental prices are not likely to affect appreciably the division between personal use and renting to the producing sector. We shall feel free, then, to employ, when convenient, the simplification that the total supply of primary inputs is constant. In other contexts, allowance will be made for some response of supply to price.

The present chapter took a brief look at decision making by the family. The basic problem is that any commodity bundle may be distributed among the members in infinitely many ways, each corresponding to a Scitovsky contour through the point in commodity space. Only when utility levels are prescribed for all members is there a single contour through the point. The same indeterminacy also extends to the supply of inputs. If the time of the family members is the only primary input, the problem is the same as for a single consumer, dividing time optimally between personal use and sale as labor services. But there is an additional complication: Who does the work and who enjoys the leisure? The same level of income can be attained by infinitely many combinations of work and leisure for the two members, each determining a different pair of utility levels. Only by holding the levels constant can we set up a minimizing problem and derive a Scitovsky contour between leisure and the composite commodity. Tangency between the desired income line and a Scitovsky contour is the condition for efficient earning of income, but unfortunately it can occur almost anywhere along the income line.

The purpose of constructing a model for the economy is to show how economic units interact with each other and determine the pattern of economic activity. But it is futile to try to analyze how economic units interact unless we can first state with reasonable accuracy how each economic unit is likely to act. The family presents something of a problem, but what is usually done, implicitly or explicitly, is to accept the model for an individual consumer as a sufficiently accurate first approximation. Under some family decision processes, the assumption is strictly correct. If income is simply distributed among members in fixed ratio, the solution may not be optimal for the family but it does result in individual decision making. With an explicit family welfare function the Bergson contours are similar to individual indifference curves and result in similar demand and supply curves. Finally, one member may make the decisions for the family in a dictatorial but consistent way. We shall, then, go along with the customary assumption that no appreciable error results from treating the consuming sector as if it were composed solely of individual consumers.

EXERCISES

1. *A Linear Model for Leisure and Hours Worked*

With x_2 representing consumption time, a linear model for the consumer takes the following form:

$$\begin{aligned} a_{11}v_1+a_{12}v_2+a_{13}v_3+a_{14}v_4-x_1 \qquad &= 0\\ a_{21}v_1+a_{22}v_2+a_{23}v_3+a_{24}v_4 \qquad -x_2 &= 0\\ x_2 &\leqq T\\ u_1v_1+u_2v_2+u_3v_3+u_4v_4 \qquad &= U(\max). \end{aligned}$$

As the problem is formulated working time z_2 is a slack variable, and the third constraint is $x_2+z_2 = T$. After using the third constraint to eliminate x_2 we can drop it. Assigning fixed values to x_1 and z_2, and inferentially to x_2, sets up the problem for solution.

(a) For a numerical example use Exercise 6 of Chapter 12. The sixth process in that example uses only x_1. What type of solution does this permit? Explain why it is not acceptable in the present application. Replace the sixth process by a slack process with a zero objective coefficient. State precisely what such a process implies about the consumer's reaction to x_1. What is the effect on the indifference map?

The first process uses x_2 alone. Can this process be interpreted as the enjoyment of pure leisure? Need it be dropped?

(b) Set $T = 24$ and find the piecewise-linear utility function. You may use previously obtained results. What is the economic meaning of the dual variables or coefficients of x_1 and $x_2 = (T - z_2)$ in the objective form? Graph a contour for some convenient level of U.

(c) Introduce prices p_1 and c_2 for the first commodity and for hours worked. Set the problem up in symbolic form as the maximization of utility subject to a single constraint. Verify that the constraint may be either total time or the monetary value of total time without affecting the optimal solution or the value of U. Show that the following relation must hold: $U = \bar{u}_T(T) = \bar{u}_y(c_2 T)$. Interpret the two coefficients as internal prices. Equate the internal and external rates of exchange between time and money.

(d) Choose a convenient value for c_2 and let p_1 decline from relatively high levels. Use the previously constructed graph to show the price-consumption locus, identifying the income and pure substitution effects. Hold p_1 constant and let c_2 increase from relatively low levels. How does the price-consumption locus compare with that generated by changes in p_1? Calculate the critical values of c_2 and x_2. Plot in price-quantity space and sketch in the demand curve for x_2. Convert to a supply curve for z_2.

(e) What does the model predict at low levels of c_2? Explain why this prediction is not acceptable. What does the model predict the consumer will ultimately do as c_2 continues to increase? Does this pattern seem plausible?

(f) From the method of constructing the demand curve for x_2 and the supply curve for z_2, describe the likely consequences if x_1 is an inferior good or if x_2 is an inferior good.

2. *A Linear Model for Two Inputs and Two Commodities*

Let x_1 be the services of land devoted to personal use and x_2 be consumption time. There are also two commodities x_3 and x_4 purchasable in the market. Set up in symbolic form a linear utility maximization model. You need show only two processes and dot in the rest. Introduce slack processes for the commodities. For the inputs write the additional constraints $x_1 + z_1 = L$, $x_2 + z_2 = T$. Drop the constraints after using them to eliminate x_1 and x_2.

(a) Set z_1, z_2, x_3, and x_4 constant. Assuming that the problem has been reduced to canonical form with respect to an optimal solution, express utility symbolically in terms of the quantities under constraint. Explain the meaning of each coefficient or dual variable.

(b) For a given level of utility hold the quantities constant in pairs and let the other pair vary parametrically. Draw the piecewise-linear equivalents of the diagrams in Figure 14–3.

(c) For each diagram write the slope of the contours along segments in terms of the coefficients in the objective form. Introduce market prices and show graphically an optimal solution in each diagram. When the optimum lies at a vertex, express the conditions for optimality in each diagram as a relation between internal valuations or prices and external or market prices. What are the corresponding conditions when an optimum lies along a segment or the contours are smooth?

(d) Let z_1, z_2, x_3, and x_4 be variable. Use their market prices to combine the four constraints into a single constraint with the right-hand side equal to c_1L+c_2T. What condition determines the optimal solution or an optimal solution? Explain how an optimal solution so obtained is related to the optimum shown by the three diagrams.

3. *A Two-Plant Firm and a Two-Member Family*

(Readers will find a review of Chapter 11 very helpful for this exercise.)

A firm has two plants, each of which has independent production processes and turns out a single product different from that of the other plant. Both plants use the same two inputs, which are supplied by the firm. There are no inputs fixed within plants.

(a) *The Maximization of One Plant's Output or One Member's Utility*

Set up in symbolic form the problem of maximizing one plant's output for a constant level of the other plant's output and constant amounts of both inputs. Assign three processes to each plant. If you wish to have a numerical example as a guide, combine the numerical examples in the text and Exercise 1 of Chapter 8, dropping a process from each plant.

Express in symbolic form an output function for the firm in terms of the remaining output and both inputs. Hold both inputs constant and sketch a product transformation curve for the firm.

Write down in symbolic form the problem of maximizing one family member's utility for a constant level of the other member's utility and constant total amounts of both commodities. Show that the optimizing problems of the family and the firm are formally similar and that one can be derived from the other by substituting utility levels for output levels and commodities for inputs. Reinterpret the output function and the transformation curve so as to be appropriate for the family.

(b) *The Minimization of One Input or One Commodity*

Set up in symbolic form a corresponding input minimization problem for the firm and write an input function. Hold both outputs constant and sketch an input substitution contour for the firm.

Treat the preceding problem as a commodity minimization problem for the family and give appropriate reinterpretations of the input function and input substitution contour. What special term is given to this contour?

(c) *Marginal Productivities and Marginal Utilities*

As was done in Chapter 11, use both input and output functions to express the rate of product transformation and rate of input substitution in terms of marginal input requirements and marginal productivities. Confine the results to segments that are neither horizontal nor vertical. Make the appropriate reinterpretations for the family.

(d) *A Budget Constraint for the Firm and the Family*

The firm has a budget constraint and cannot spend more than some maximum amount on inputs. The firm spends the maximum amount on some particular combination of inputs and then seeks to allocate them optimally between the plants. What criterion for optimality can the firm use in the absence of output prices? State and illustrate graphically the specific requirement for optimality in the *smooth* version of the firm.

Instead of allocating inputs the firm assigns each plant a share of the sum available for purchase of inputs. Each plant buys its own inputs in the market. Draw separate *smooth* diagrams for each plant illustrating the optimal solution. Explain why the two alternative plans must lead to the same result. Reinterpret for the family.

(e) *Isocost Contours*

Following the method outlined in Chapter 11 explain how to derive an isocost contour for the firm. How are product transformation curves and isocost contours related for a smooth version of the firm? Illustrate graphically. Reinterpret the results for two members of a consuming unit. What information does the isocost contour give for the consuming unit?

4. *Superimposing Isoproduct Maps*

(a) Figure 14–5 illustrated the derivation of a utility transformation contour by use of the Edgeworth box diagram, which superimposes the indifference map of one consumer upon that of the other. By using essentially the same reasoning and by drawing analogous diagrams demonstrate that the same method yields a product transformation contour for a firm each of whose two plants use the same inputs but turn out a different product.

Chapter 8 analyzed the allocation of a single input between two plants producing the same output. Figure 8–7 displayed the results graphically. Show that the technique of the Edgeworth box diagram is simply the extension to the two-input, two-output case of the method used in constructing Figure 8–7.

(b) Under what analogous conditions could we superimpose iso-input maps in output space and derive an input substitution contour?

(c) Explain why the Edgeworth box diagram cannot be employed when there are joint products or joint consumption processes.

(d) Construct an Edgeworth box diagram for piecewise-linear input substitution contours.

5. *Revenue Functions and Welfare Functions*

(A continuation of Exercise 3.)

(a) Demonstrate that a linear total revenue function with both prices constant determines a complete quasiordering of the output pairs produced by two separate plants owned by a firm. By comparison with the preference ordering, what are the economic properties of the revenue ordering? What is the effect on the ordering of a proportionate change in both prices, a disproportionate change?

(b) Set up the model of the two-plant firm specified in Exercise 3 as the maximization of revenue subject to two input constraints. Write the objective function in symbolic form and identify the coefficients of the inputs. What contour results from holding revenue constant and letting both inputs vary? Write the algebraic expression for the slope of the contour along line segments. For the smooth version of the firm draw a typical contour and illustrate the relationship to input substitution curves.

(c) Choose a linear welfare function for a two-member family and make the appropriate reinterpretation of all preceding results. Identify Bergson and Scitovsky contours and explain how they are related graphically to each other.

(d) Introduce input prices and a budget constraint for the firm. Show graphically the optimal solution for the firm and write the algebraic conditions for optimality. Reinterpret the diagram and the algebraic conditions for a two-member family. Explain precisely what the optimal solution means or implies for the family and each of its members.

6. *Technical Efficiency, Pareto Optimality, and Welfare*

(a) Define the criterion of technical or technological efficiency for a two-product firm. Define the criterion of Pareto optimality for a two-member family. Show that both criteria are alike in being special cases of the partial ordering of vectors. Illustrate graphically.

(b) Develop a welfare ordering for a two-member family by analogy with a preference ordering. First, what is the set to be ordered? Is it the set of family members or the set of utility levels of family members? Decide on some appropriate verbal designation for the family welfare relation. Make the same continuity assumptions as for the preference relation and explain what they mean in this application. Consider various axioms similar to those for preference and decide upon a reasonable set. Do the axioms you have chosen imply Pareto optimality? Draw a typical isowelfare contour and describe the properties of the isowelfare map.

(c) By analogy with preference show that a welfare ordering implies a welfare function. Use a piecewise-linear example.

Write the equation for the slope of a utility transformation contour in terms of the marginal utilities of both consumers for both commodities. Find the slope of a linear welfare function. Show what happens to each slope when the second consumer's utility is multiplied by some positive constant k Graph. Show also that the welfare function may be multiplied by any positive number whatsoever without affecting the optimum.

The preceding results constitute a demonstration, although not a proof, that results are unchanged when utility levels and welfare are all subjected to increasing transformations.

7. *Joint Consumption Processes*

The following numerical example contains three joint consumption processes for each of two family members:

$$\begin{aligned}
3v_1+4v_2+8v_3+4v_4+6v_5+12v_6 &= x_1\\
12v_1+6v_2+4v_3+8v_4+4v_5+3v_6 &= x_2\\
8v_1+8v_2+8v_3-2v_4-2v_5+4v_6 &= U_1\\
4v_1-1v_2-2v_3+8v_4+8v_5+8v_6 &= U_2.
\end{aligned}$$

(a) Choose $U_1 = 64$, $U_2 = 56$, $p_1 = p_2 = 1$. Set up as the minimization of expenditure, $p_1x_1+p_2x_2$, for constant levels of utility. Find the optimal solution and the combination of commodities allocated to each consumer. Calculate at current market prices the value of commodities each member receives.

(b) The family assigns to each member a money sum equal to the value of commodities received in (a). Each member maximizes utility independently of the other, ignoring cross-effects. Find the two independent optimal solutions. Compared with (a), what is the *net* effect on the utility level of each member?

Find the amounts of the commodities each member chooses to purchase. Compare the amounts each member obtains and the total family purchases with the results of (a). Use the specific values of the original utility coefficients to explain the difference. Find a separate set of prices for each family member at which individual optimizing decisions by each member add up to the optimum for the family.

SUPPLEMENTARY READINGS FOR PART THREE

Readers will find it instructive to compare Part Three with the treatment of consumer demand in any of the first five textbooks listed in the Supplementary Readings for Part Two. Also recommended:

Kuenne, Robert E., *Microeconomic Theory of the Market Mechanism*, New York: The Macmillan Company, 1968.

Each of the following books contains an excellent alternative or more advanced presentation of the axiomatic approach to consumer theory through a preference relation:

Lloyd, Cliff, *Microeconomic Analysis*, Homewood, Ill.: Richard D. Irwin, Inc., 1967.

Newman, Peter, *The Theory of Exchange*, Englewood Cliffs, N.J.: Prentice-Hall, Inc., 1965.

Debreu, Gerard, *Theory of Value*, New York: John Wiley and Sons, Inc., 1959.

The third of the books, which contains a most rigorous and definitive presentation, assumes a substantial background in mathematics.

A book that effectively presents and compares all these approaches to consumer theory is

Wu, Sheh-Yen and Pontney, Jack A., *An Introduction to Modern Demand Theory*, New York: Random House, 1967.

The authors assume some knowledge of matrix algebra and differential calculus.

To date, discussion of consumption processes and analysis of the family as a consuming unit have appeared almost exclusively in journal articles. Some of the more significant articles are:

Samuelson, Paul A. "Social Indifference Curves," *Quarterly Journal of Economics* (February 1956).

Becker, Gary S. "A Theory of the Allocation of Time," *Economic Journal* (September 1965).

Lancaster, Kelvin. "Change and Innovation in the Theory of Consumption," *American Economic Review* (Papers and Proceedings) (May 1966).

Muth, Richard F. "Household Production and Consumer Demand Functions," *Econometrica* (July 1966).

Part IV

Markets, Industries, and the Economy

15

Purely Competitive Markets

The private economy consists of a myriad of economic units, each of which makes independent decisions regarding its own economic welfare. To maximize net revenue, firms must determine simultaneously what outputs to produce and in what quantities, what inputs to employ and in what amounts. Consumers are striving to allocate income optimally over the available commodities and are also making basic decisions on the supply of inputs and the desired level of income. If chaos is to be forestalled, there must be a mechanism, and a reasonably effective one, that reconciles the complex of individual decisions and shapes them into a mutually consistent pattern. As the first stage in explaining the process of mutual reconciliation, the present chapter focuses upon the interaction of buyers and sellers in the market for a single commodity.

AGGREGATE OR MARKET DEMAND FUNCTIONS

Any general model of the economic system must ultimately explain how the incomes of consumers are determined and must, therefore, include decisions by individuals or families as to the amounts of the primary inputs they wish to supply. In the present section we shall temporarily revert to the simpler analysis of consumer's choice as the allocation of fixed money income or fixed total expenditure over the set of available commodities. For each level of money income and each set of commodity prices, a consuming unit is able to decide what amount of each commodity it wishes to buy. Thus, to each set of prices and money income there is associated one and only one quantity of any specified commodity, say the first. In mathematical language, a function is defined as the choice or demand function of the particular consumer for the first commodity. Symbolically, for the case of only two commodities,

$$x_{1j} = d_{1j}(p_1, p_2, y_j).$$

The mnemonic symbol d is used for demand functions. The first subscript on the quantity and subscripts on the prices denote commodities. The second subscript on the quantity and the subscript on income specify the consumer. The symbol j indicates simply that the demand function belongs to one of the consuming units but does not identify it. The demand function of the jth consumer for the second commodity is

$$x_{2j} = d_{2j}(p_1, p_2, y_j).$$

Each consuming unit has a set of demand functions, one for each commodity. In general, when the number of commodities is the indefinitely large n rather than the specific 2, there are n distinct demand functions, and each must include the prices of all n commodities. Further, every consuming unit has its own set of n distinct demand functions. This is the inevitable consequence of permitting individuals to make their own choices. Even if one rejects the specific optimizing model of consumer's choice developed in economics, it still remains true, so long as there is freedom of choice, that the economic system must adjust to the complex of decisions by individual consumers.

One simplification that may be made is to add up the demands of the individual consumers commodity by commodity. To give the process a precise but fictitious embodiment, imagine that there is a central data processing agency in telephonic contact with every consuming and producing unit. The central agency chooses a set of prices for all commodities and transmits them to each consuming unit along with a figure representing its money income. To each consumer the question is put: At the given set of prices and money income, what quantity do you wish to purchase of each commodity? The existence of the demand functions guarantees that each consumer will always be able to supply the answer. By summing the amounts reported for each commodity, the central agency gets the aggregate amount demanded at a given level of prices and for a specified amount of income received by each consuming unit. Conceptually, the process of interrogation can be repeated for all sets of nonnegative prices and for all possible levels and distributions of income among consumers. The result is a set of aggregate or market demand functions that show for each commodity the aggregate amount demanded at all sets of prices and all possible levels and distributions of money income. If the total number of consuming units is denoted by M, the aggregate demand for the first commodity is

$$\begin{aligned}
x_1 &= \quad x_{11} \quad + \quad x_{12} \quad + \cdots + \quad x_{1M} \\
&= d_{11}(p_1, p_2, y_1) + d_{12}(p_1, p_2, y_2) + \cdots + d_{1M}(p_1, p_2, y_M) \\
&= \sum_{j=1}^{M} d_{1j}(p_1, p_2, y_j) \\
&= D_1(p_1, p_2, y_1, y_2, \ldots, y_M).
\end{aligned}$$

Strictly interpreted, the aggregate demand function, for which the symbol D is used, must depend on the specific money income of each consumer. Even though the total money income remains the same, aggregate demand will change when the total is redistributed among consumers. If, however, the distribution of income among consumers remains constant, a simplification can be made. It is only necessary to specify aggregate income and the income of each consumer will be determined as a constant relative share. The central agency must still supply each consumer with a figure representing income but, so long as aggregate income is constant, each consumer receives the same income and buys the same amounts. Market demand can be rewritten, as follows, as functions of Y, the aggregate disposable income:[1]

$$\begin{aligned}
x_1 &= D_1(p_1, p_2, Y) \\
x_2 &= D_2(p_1, p_2, Y).
\end{aligned}$$

In reality, the distribution of income does not change appreciably, particularly over short periods, so the simplification is not likely to be a significant source of error.

There will in general be n market demand functions, each dependent on all n prices as well as on aggregate disposable income. Whenever possible, we shall for a simpler exposition consider only two commodities. As explained in Chapter 13 any subset of commodities whose prices do not change or change only proportionately can be regarded as a composite commodity. In much of the present chapter, the requirement is satisfied, so the second commodity may be taken as a composite of the remaining $(n-1)$ commodities.

The aggregate demand functions inherit their economic and mathematical properties from the individual demand functions. Since consumers have been assumed to be free of money illusion and to be able to see through proportional changes in prices and money income, market demand is also unaffected by equiproportional changes in all variables. When aggregate income and the prices of all but one commodity are held constant, the

[1]In a simplified model of the private economy, in which taxes, transfer payments, and retained earnings by business are left out, disposable income = personal income = national income.

demand function becomes a demand curve with a graph in two dimensions. In mathematical terminology, the demand curve is a *restriction* of the demand function and is shown symbolically by

$$x_1 = D_1(p_1|p_2,\ Y = \text{constant}).$$

The variables held constant are placed behind a bar, or sometimes a colon, and their constancy is sometimes stated explicitly, sometimes understood.

The individual demand curves may be the discontinuous, piecewise-curvilinear type derived from a linear model in Chapter 13. Since tastes differ, the jumps in quantity demanded are unlikely to occur at the same critical prices for all or even very many consumers. Adding the curves reduces the significance of the discontinuities, so smooth curves may be satisfactory first approximations to market demand curves even when not to individual demand curves. Chapters 15–17 employ smooth curves.

From preceding chapters, an individual demand curve that slopes backward toward the vertical axis as price falls is a possibility but requires a rather special indifference map. It is highly unlikely that a large number of consumers will have upward-sloping demand curves in the same price range. Thus, a rare phenomenon becomes even rarer in the aggregate and will not be mentioned again. All market demand curves are, then, downward sloping, but different commodities display widely diverse responses to changes in price. It is important to have some measure that summarizes the characteristic response of a commodity to variations in its own price. Such a measure will now be developed.

ELASTICITY OF DEMAND

If all demand curves were linear, the slope would do very well as a measure of the response to changes in price, but the implication of a constant slope is that a given cut in price has the same effect whether the initial level is \$1 or \$100. Personal experience, the theory of consumer's choice, and statistical evidence all tend to refute this implication except as an approximation over fairly narrow ranges. A measure that takes into account the initial level from which changes are made is the *price elasticity of demand*, defined as the ratio of the relative change in quantity to the relative change in price. In symbols the elasticity of the first commodity with respect to its own price is

$$s_{11} = \frac{\Delta x_1/x_1}{\Delta p_1/p_1} = \frac{p_1/x_1}{\Delta p_1/\Delta x_1} = \frac{\text{slope of ray}}{\text{slope of tangent}}.$$

Elasticity can be illustrated graphically in a very simple way (Figure 15–1). The slope of the ray to any point on the demand curve is p_1/x_1, and the slope of the tangent at that point is $\Delta p_1/\Delta x_1$. Elasticity is thus the ratio between the slope of the ray and the slope of the tangent to a point on the demand curve. If the two slopes are equal in magnitude, the elasticity is -1, since the slope of the tangent is negative. The ray and the tangent line, having equal slopes, form with the horizontal (or the vertical) axis an isosceles triangle. The horizontal distance from the vertical axis to the chosen point on the demand curve is equal to the horizontal distance from the point to the intersection of the tangent line with the horizontal axis. With an elasticity of -2, the horizontal distance beyond the point on the curve is twice the distance from the origin to the point. We can depict any other degree of elasticity in the same way.

When a demand curve is linear, the slope of the tangent is the same at all points, but the slope of the ray varies from point to point. Near the vertical axis, the slope of the ray and the numerical value of elasticity become very large; at points near the horizontal axis, the slope of the ray and the elasticity approach zero. At the midpoint on the demand curve, the ray and the tangent line, which is the demand curve itself, form an isosceles triangle, and the elasticity is -1.

Two conclusions can be drawn. The first is that elasticity is not an

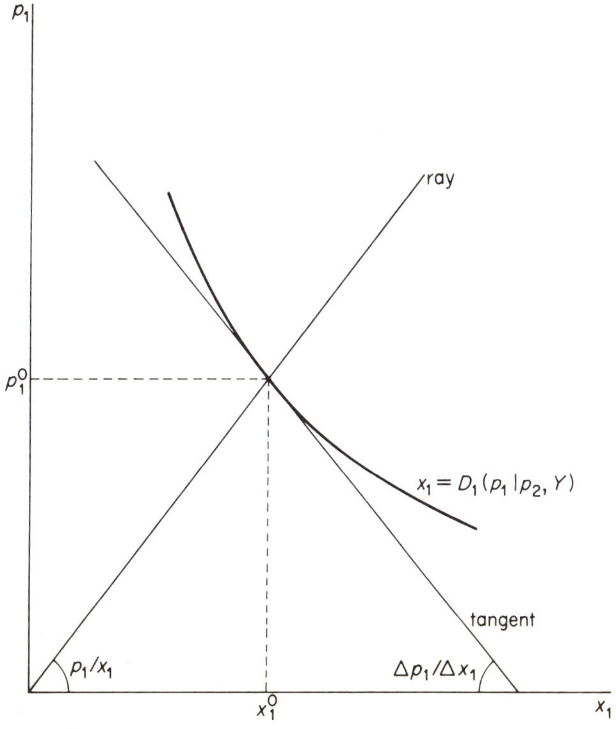

Fig. 15-1 Geometric Illustration of Price Elasticity

appropriate measure for the characteristics of a linear demand curve. Since elasticity varies from minus infinity to zero along every linear demand curve, it is not a satisfactory way of distinguishing between two such curves. Straight lines are best distinguished by slope and intercept, which are invariant for each line. A second inference is that any demand curve with constant elasticity at every point cannot contain any straight line segments. The slope of the ray varies along line segments but the slope of the tangent line does not.[2] For a demand curve of constant elasticity, the slope of the tangent must vary from point to point in such a way as to match the changing slope of the ray. Demand curves with constant elasticity have the general form

$$x_1 = k_1 p_1^{s_{11}} \qquad k_1 > 0.$$

The exponent of p_1 is the constant price elasticity of demand, and k_1 is some positive constant that measures the strength of the demand at any price. In a market demand curve, the constant k_1 is influenced by the number of consuming units, their preference patterns, and their incomes, as well as by various other factors. From the definition of elasticity, all demand curves with the same elasticity must be parallel along rays, so k_1 measures the distance from the origin along any chosen ray.

Price Elasticity and Total Revenue

The most important property of price elasticity is that it predicts accurately how total revenue responds to changes in price or in quantity sold. Total revenue or total value of sales is

$$R = p_1 x_1 = p_1(k_1 p_1^{s_{11}}) = k_1 p_1^{1+s_{11}}.$$

If we choose as illustrative values of the price elasticity $s_{11} = -\frac{1}{2}, -1, -2$, revenue is, respectively,

$$R = k_1 p_1^{1/2} \qquad R = k_1 p_1^0 = k_1 \qquad R = k_1 p_1^{-1} = \frac{k_1}{p_1}.$$

The three revenue functions and the three demand curves from which they are derived are graphed in Figure 15–2. A demand curve whose elasticity has a numerical value of 1 (i.e., $-s_{11} = 1$) is called a *demand curve of unit elasticity* and shows no change in revenue as the price varies. When the

[2]There is also the occasionally used concept of *arc elasticity*, based upon the finite changes in price and quantity between two distinct points on a demand curve. The effect is to replace the arc of the curve between the two points by a line segment. The slope of the line segment is determinate, but we can choose the ray through either point or any ray in between. In general, there is no unique value for arc elasticity. For smooth curves the concept of *point elasticity*, as defined in the text, is more appropriate.

numerical value of the elasticity is $\frac{1}{2}$ or, more generally, any number less than 1 (i.e. $0 \leqq -s_{11} < 1$), the demand curve is classified as *inelastic.* Along inelastic demand curves, higher prices draw in higher revenue. A demand curve whose elasticity exceeds 1 in numerical value ($1 < -s_{11}$) is termed *elastic.* Revenue declines as price increases along elastic demand curves.

Demand curves of constant elasticity can be rewritten, as follows, with price as a function of quantity:

$$x_1 = k_1 p_1^{s_{11}}$$

$$x_1^{1/s_{11}} = (k_1 p_1^{s_{11}})^{1/s_{11}}$$

$$x_1^{1/s_{11}} = k_1^{1/s_{11}} p_1$$

$$p_1 = \left(\frac{1}{k_1}\right)^{1/s_{11}} x_1^{1/s_{11}} = k_1^{-1/s_{11}} x_1^{1/s_{11}}.$$

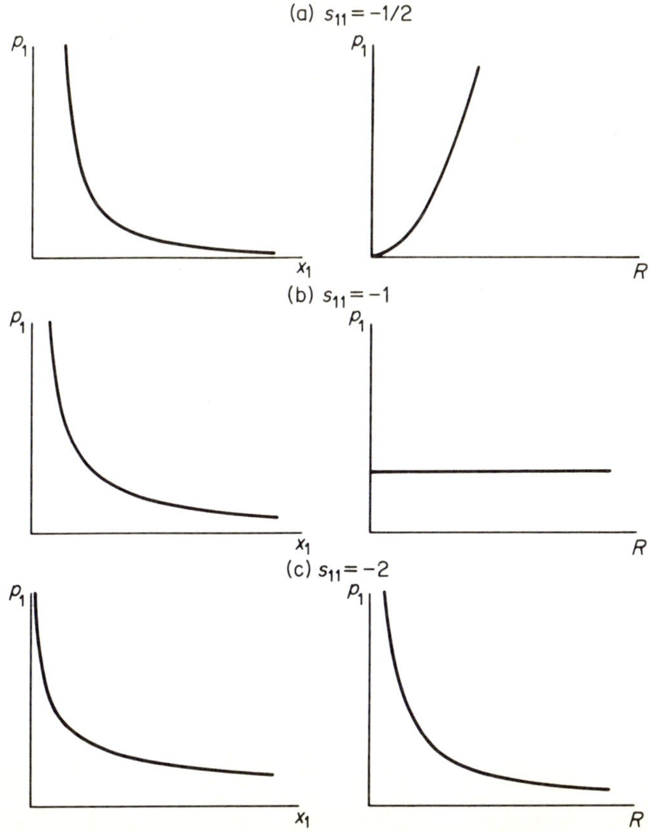

Fig. 15-2 Demand and Total Revenue Curves for Different Elasticities

Total revenue as a function of quantity is

$$R = p_1 x_1 = (k_1^{-1/s_{11}} x_1^{1/s_{11}}) x_1 = k_1^{-1/s_{11}} x_1^{1+1/s_{11}}$$

For the three previously used values of elasticity, total revenue is, respectively,

$$R = k_1^2 x_1^{-1} \qquad R = k_1 \qquad R = k_1^{1/2} x_1^{1/2}.$$

Since price and quantity are inversely related, an increase in quantity causes revenue to decrease along inelastic curves and to increase along elastic demand curves.

Elasticity cannot be expected to remain constant everywhere along an actual demand curve,[3] but it is still a useful property, provided that its value remains within a range. As just demonstrated, a numerical value of 1 divides elasticity into two broad ranges characterized by diametrically opposed responses of total revenue. Within these broad ranges, one curve may be described as more elastic or more inelastic than another curve if its elasticity is everywhere greater numerically or everywhere less than that of the other curve.

Cross Elasticity of Demand

The effect on x_1 of a change in p_2 is summarized by the cross elasticity of demand, which is expressed symbolically by

$$s_{12} = \frac{\Delta x_1/x_1}{\Delta p_2/p_2} = \frac{p_2/x_1}{\Delta p_2/\Delta x_1} = \frac{\text{slope of ray}}{\text{slope of tangent}}.$$

Income, p_1 and the prices of any other commodities are assumed to be constant. Since p_1 remains constant, the demand curve for x_1 must shift, and cross elasticity compares the relative size of the shift with the relative change in price that causes it. Again, the rationale underlying the concept is that there is likely to be a more stable relationship between relative changes, where the initial levels are considered, than between absolute changes. If the cross elasticity is positive, a rise in p_2 causes an increase in demand for x_1, so the two commodities are classified as substitutes. Similarly, a negative value implies a leftward shift and complementarity. As explained in Chapter 13, these effects are not pure but include the income effect of the price change. Hence, commodities with positive cross elasticities are called *gross substitutes*, and commodities with negative cross elasticities are called *gross complements*.

[3]Demand curves of constant elasticity do not intersect either axis and become improbable at very high or very low prices. With income constant, there is a price above which all consumers will cease to buy any commodity, and a zero price need not induce unlimited acquisition. But extreme prices are themselves improbable, so the failure to intersect the axes is not a sufficient reason for rejecting iso-elastic demand curves in statistical investigations.

Income Elasticity of Demand

The effect of a change in income can also be summarized by the following measure of income elasticity:

$$s_{1y} = \frac{\Delta x_1/x_1}{\Delta Y/Y} = \frac{Y/x_1}{\Delta Y/\Delta x_1} = \frac{\text{slope of ray}}{\text{slope of tangent}}.$$

Inferior commodities have negative income elasticities; normal commodities have positive income elasticities. Since p_1 and all other prices are constant, the effect of an increase in income is a rightward shift of the demand curve for a normal commodity and a leftward shift for an inferior commodity.

The three measures of elasticity, if constant, can be incorporated into a demand function of the following type:

$$x_1 = h_1 p_1^{s_{11}} p_2^{s_{12}} Y^{s_{1y}}.$$

When p_2 and Y are held constant to obtain the demand curve, they simply combine with the constant h_1. If, say, $s_{1y} = -\frac{1}{2}$, $s_{12} = \frac{2}{3}$, the demand curve for x_1 is

$$x_1 = \left(\frac{h_1 p_2^{2/3}}{Y^{1/2}}\right) p_1^{s_{11}} = k_1 p_1^{s_{11}}.$$

Because x_1 is an inferior good ($s_{1y} = -\frac{1}{2}$), the larger the value at which Y is held constant, the smaller the constant term in the demand curve. As is now clear, the constant k_1 in the demand curve is a composite expression that includes all variables being held constant.

Chapter 13 demonstrated that a negative income effect, which represents a shift in relative preference away from a commodity, partially offsets the pure substitution effect and causes a smaller response of quantity to a change in price. Consequently, we have reason to expect that a negative income effect will also impart a lower value to the price elasticity. The precise relationship among elasticities is as follows:

$$s_{11} = -(s_{12}+s_{1y}).$$

When the income elasticity has a large positive value, s_{11} tends to have a large negative value, and the demand curve is highly elastic. Similarly, when income elasticity is negative, s_{11} becomes a smaller negative number and can even turn out to be positive.[4]

[4]The formula does show the precise relationship among the various elasticities but it does not isolate the income and pure substitution effects of a price change. The cross elasticity is not a pure measure of substitution or complementarity but contains as well the income effect of a price change. If the income effect on x_1 is positive, a decline in p_2 will stimulate purchases of x_1 by way of the income effect, partially offsetting the pure substitution effect and causing s_{12} to be smaller or even negative. Hence, the elasticities do not measure exactly the pure substitution and income effects.

To summarize, the optimizing decisions of all consumers determine a set of aggregate or market demand functions, one for each commodity. If income and all prices but one are constant, the demand function for one commodity can be portrayed in two dimensions as a demand curve. As the price varies and the quantity demanded moves along this curve, the demand curves for all other commodities must in general be shifting. The direction and extent of each shift is determined by the appropriate coefficient of cross elasticity. The set of demand functions represents only one side of the market for commodities. A corresponding set of supply functions must also be derived to complete the general model of the economic system.

GENERAL AND PARTIAL EQUILIBRIUM ANALYSIS

The optimizing decisions of a single firm have already been analyzed in great detail. Given the input and output prices, each firm is capable of deciding what commodities to produce and in what amounts. We can again imagine that our hypothetical central data processing agency supplies a set of input and output prices and interrogates every firm as to the quantity of each commodity it wishes to produce. Most firms are highly specialized, so the replies will contain a great many zeros. The reported quantities can then be aggregated for each commodity, and the interrogation repeated for all possible combinations of output and input prices. Since each combination of prices brings forth a unique amount for each commodity, the result of the interrogation is a set of supply functions, one for each commodity, showing the dependence of the quantity supplied on all output and all input prices.

We established earlier that the central agency, by choosing a set of prices for all commodities and a set of money incomes for all consumers, can determine the aggregate amount demanded for each commodity. By adding a set of input prices and interrogating producers, the agency also obtains the aggregate quantities producers wish to supply of each commodity. Readers may have spotted an inconsistency in the model. The central agency submits input prices to firms and receives information on output levels. But the quantities produced determine the amounts of the inputs used, and the amounts of the inputs employed together with their prices determine the incomes of consumers. As an initial simplification in deriving aggregate demand functions, each consuming unit was assumed to have a fixed level of money income. In the broader model of the economic system, consumers must know the prevailing input prices and make their own decisions as to the amounts of the inputs, primarily labor services, they wish to supply. At a given set of prices for both commodities and inputs, each consuming unit decides how much of each input it wishes to supply. The central agency may sum these quantities input by input. Similarly, the optimizing decisions by firms determine the amounts they wish to buy, which can also be aggregated input by input. By repeating the conceptual experiment for all sets of nonnegative input and output prices, the agency may derive for each input aggregate supply and aggregate demand as functions of all prices.

In the broader model, income disappears from both the individual and the aggregate demand functions for commodities, being replaced by the set of input prices. The income of a consuming unit depends on the quantities of the various inputs it supplies at the prevailing prices. The amount supplied depends upon the total amount available and upon the optimizing decision as to how much to use within the unit and how much to sell. At each full set of prices every consuming unit is assumed capable of making the requisite decision and is, therefore, able to supply the central agency with the data it needs.

The preceding discussion has focused upon the supply of inputs by consumers, but every firm also obtains inputs from other firms. The economic system does not consist solely of markets in which producers confront consumers but contains many markets, actually many more markets, in which producers confront producers. The goods and services that producers exchange with each other are both inputs and outputs. From one point of view, they are *intermediate* outputs or *intermediate* goods and services as distinguished from the *final* goods and services sold to consumers. From the other point of view they are *intermediate* inputs or produced means of production as distinguished from the *primary* inputs supplied by consumers. In either case the distinction is functional and not absolute; the same good or service, such as stationery or electric power, may be either final or intermediate depending on whether it is sold to consumers or to other firms. The presence of intermediate goods and services does not alter appreciably the basic model of the economic system, although it does expand greatly the amount of detail. Each firm can make an optimizing decision if it knows the prices of the outputs it can sell, whether final or intermediate, and if it knows the prices of the inputs it buys, intermediate or primary. By providing firms with a set of prices for all outputs and inputs, the central agency can conceptually obtain the aggregate amount firms wish to buy and wish to sell for every good, service, or input.

The central agency may choose a set of prices, obtain from each economic unit the amounts it wishes to buy or sell, and then sum the amounts to get the aggregate demand and the aggregate supply. The next step is to match up the quantities buyers wish to buy and sellers wish to sell for each input and output. It would, indeed, be miraculous if the prices the agency happened to choose equated supply and demand for all outputs and inputs. In fact, it is exceedingly difficult to prove that there is any set of nonnegative prices capable of bringing demand and supply everywhere into equality. A state in which the quantity demanded equals the quantity supplied for all inputs and all outputs is termed the *general equilibrium* of the economic system.

The question at issue, then, is the very existence of general equilibrium; whether there is even one set of prices that will reconcile demand and supply for every output and input. Economists have long believed in the existence of general equilibrium and have made repeated attempts to prove its existence, but it took nearly 80 years, from the mid 1870's to the early 1950's, to come up with a satisfactory general proof. The issue is now settled for a purely competitive economic system—that is, for an economic system in which every consuming and producing unit takes prices as given and chooses to neglect any effect its decisions may have on prices. For such an economy there exists at least one set of prices at which all economic units will make mutually consistent decisions.

The existence of general equilibrium does not depend on the actions that buyers and sellers take in markets nor even upon the existence of markets. The device of the central data processing agency serves to emphasize this point. It is only necessary that independent decisions by producers and consumers add up to the same total amounts. But if general equilibrium is to have any significance and if the economic system is to be regarded as an efficient mechanism, prices must move toward their equilibrium levels. To explain changes in prices requires not merely the existence of markets but also some additional hypotheses as to how buyers and sellers react when demand does not equal supply at existing prices. An economic system is said to be *globally stable* whenever prices approach their equilibrium values from any initially prevailing levels. We shall investigate the conditions for stability of the economic system, beginning with the stability of a single market in the present chapter.

Having sketched out the broad outline of the next several chapters, we must now get down to details. Each consuming and producing unit has hitherto been assumed to take prices as given and to act as if its decisions had no effect on prices. Yet, collectively, their decisions must determine prices. The first stage, then, in proceeding from individual producers and consumers to a model of the whole economy is to show how the price is determined in the market for a single product. While studying the determination of price for a single commodity, we shall initially insulate that market from changes in other markets. All other commodity prices and all input prices are assumed not to change, and individual incomes remain fixed. Hence, the aggregate demand and supply curves for the commodity under study do not shift.

When a price changes in one market, it causes the demand curves and supply curves for other products to shift. If these markets had been previously in equilibrium, they will no longer be. The ensuing process of adjustment has repercussions on the original market. When the feedback is ignored and one market is studied as if isolated, the term *partial equilibrium analysis* applies. Repeated applications of partial equilibrium analysis to each market in turn will never give a satisfactory model of the whole economy; the economic system cannot be put together piece by piece like a jigsaw puzzle. The interactions between markets must be taken into account in general equilibrium analysis. On the other hand, it is virtually impossible to learn how markets operate if all repercussions through all markets must be considered simultaneously. The economist needs a counterpart to the experimental techniques of physical science in which external conditions can be held rigidly constant. Developing a satisfactory model of the economic system requires both general and partial equilibrium analysis.

THE SINGLE-PRODUCT, PURELY COMPETITIVE INDUSTRY

In general, the aggregate supply function for a commodity depends on all input and output prices. But most firms are highly specialized, being technologically capable of producing only a relatively few commodities and of utilizing but a small fraction of the available inputs. Firms simply ignore the prices of most outputs and inputs, particularly in the short run. The extreme case of specialization is the single-product firm, whose supply function depends on only one output price. It is analyzed first. Also, we shall, through Chapter 17, portray equilibrium by the intersection of smooth curves rather than by a line segment passing through a gap.

The precise definition of an industry is hard to pin down, particularly when multiproduct firms turn out a wide variety of products. There is, however, no difficulty in designating as an industry a subset of firms producing identical outputs. The adjective "identical" is stronger than required and can be weakened. It is not necessary that the outputs of the different firms be indistinguishable from each other when subjected to a battery of scientific tests. It is not even necessary that the outputs be indistinguishable to consumers, although this helps. What is required is that, between any two outputs, every consumer always stands ready to buy the one selling at the lower price, no matter how small the difference in price. Thus, between the outputs of any two firms, every consumer has indifference contours with a slope of -1, implying that the two outputs are perfect substitutes for each other. The firms are then producing what is called a *homogeneous* or *undifferentiated* product, even though the outputs are not necessarily identical or indistinguishable.[5]

A homogeneous product has an aggregate demand curve showing the total amount all producers together can sell at each level of price. Although the demand curve exists, it is unknown to the firms in the industry except to the extent that past experience may have provided some rather vague

[5]Logically, outputs may have distinguishing characteristics without affecting the definition. In reality, at least a few consumers are likely to develop preferences whenever any differences, however inessential, exist. The industry then slips over into the classification of monopolistic competition, to be considered later.

impressions of the curve's general properties. Further, even exact knowledge of the market demand curve would not be of much use to a single firm, since its decisions are so greatly influenced by the actions of its competitors. Decisions can be based directly on the market demand curve only if firms do not act independently but enter into some collusive agreement, such as a cartel.

If a firm is to decide independently on the price to charge, it needs to know the amounts of its own output that can be sold at different prices. But the required demand curve for a single firm's output simply does not exist when the product is homogeneous. If a single firm quotes a price higher than any of its rivals, it cannot expect to sell anything. If the firm undercuts, the rivals cannot expect to sell anything. When all firms charge the same price, consumers are indifferent with respect to the amount purchased from any one firm. Thus, as shown in Figure 15–3, the demand curve for one firm's output consists of the vertical axis above the common price and the aggregate demand curve below it. At the common price no quantity can be specified. The horizontal gap at the common price has sometimes been misinterpreted as a horizontal demand curve and then further misinterpreted to imply that a producer can sell "as much as he pleases at the going price." As emphasized in earlier chapters, a demand curve gives quantity as a function of price. With price on the vertical axis, any horizontal line simply means that a unique quantity cannot be associated with price and, hence, that a demand curve does not exist.

Once again, the basic difficulty is that optimization does not predict choice when there are ties. Some additional criterion needs to be introduced. When truly indifferent between the output of one firm and the output of

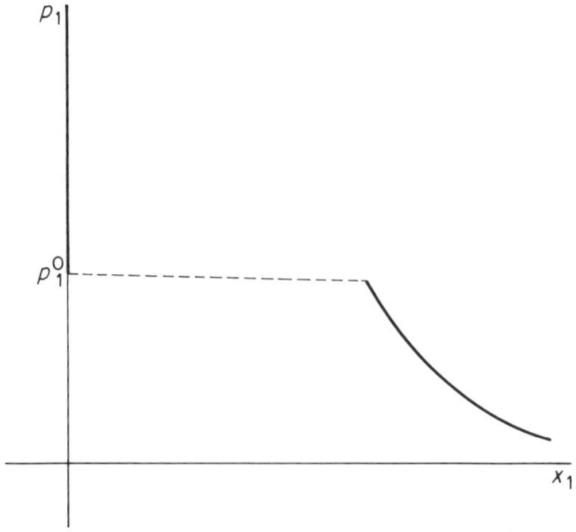

Fig. 15-3 The Demand Curve for a Purely Competitive Firm

another firm, a consumer would presumably seek to minimize the cost, psychic or other, of making a choice, possibly by choosing at random. An even better solution is not to be offered the choice at all, which occurs when a homogeneous product is sold without identification of producers. Anonymity of producer is, however, optimal only if quality is truly invariant or is independently certified. Otherwise identification of producer may be required as insurance against deterioration of quality.

If buyers are fully informed about price quotations, then at any given time and place there is only one price at which a homogeneous product can be sold. When there are many producers, as is true of agricultural products, some organized marketing institution is likely to develop for the purpose of determining the price at which the product is sold. With relatively few sellers of a homogeneous product, formal markets, such as the wheat and cotton exchanges, are not likely to emerge. In such industries, which are classified as *pure oligopolies*, a frequent solution has been price leadership, where one firm customarily takes the lead in announcing a new price, and other firms follow by quoting the same price. Price leadership has existed in such industries as steel, newsprint paper, and cigarettes, even though the product is not quite homogeneous in the strict sense of the term.

Neither of the two preceding cases accurately portrays the conditions under which most sales are made, particularly sales to ultimate consumers. Most firms turn out products that are to some degree differentiated from those of their competitors, at least in the image that advertising has created in the minds of buyers. Such firms typically set prices for their products and have some limited power to vary prices without pricing either themselves or their competitors out of the market. A model of an industry or a model of the economy is more difficult to construct and to understand when each firm is capable of setting prices. To give the simplest and clearest explanation of general equilibrium for the whole economy, economists have chosen, as a first approximation, a model in which consumers and producers deal directly with each other in organized markets similar to the commodity and stock exchanges. An industry is termed purely competitive when many firms produce a homogeneous product, and no one firm turns out an appreciable share of the total. A market is purely competitive when there are many buyers and many sellers of a homogeneous product, and no one participant can appreciably affect the price. The purely competitive model for the industry and for the economy will be developed first.

PRICE DETERMINATION IN A COMPETITIVE MARKET

In the preceding section we showed that a firm selling a homogeneous product does not have a usable demand curve for its own output. Yet the optimum of a purely competitive firm is shown conventionally by the intersection of the marginal cost curve with a horizontal line that is called the demand curve of the firm. The horizontal line is not a demand curve but a special case of a *market reaction curve*, which gives market price as a function of the firm's output. A horizontal market reaction curve indicates that a single firm can vary its output without having any effect on the market price. Taken literally, as it must be in any theoretical model, the assumption that one firm has a zero effect on the market price leads to logical difficulties. If any one firm has a zero effect on market price, so does any finite number of firms, however large, since the sum of any finite number of zeros is still zero. We are left with the untenable implication that all firms in the industry cannot affect the price. The correct statement is that each firm has some effect on the market price but the effect is so small the firm chooses to ignore it. This approach also gives rise to a problem: How can the industry ever come into equilibrium when each firm is acting upon an objectively false assumption? Fortunately, the question can be answered and will be answered at the beginning of Chapter 16. Until then, we shall continue to portray the optimum output of the firm as the intersection of the marginal cost curve with a market reaction curve that the firm takes to be horizontal.

With all other prices constant there is, then, for a specific commodity an aggregate supply curve and an aggregate demand curve that intersect in a market clearing price. The intersection of the two curves merely shows that an equilibrium price exists but does not explain how the price is established. Specifically, if a number of sellers should drop out of the market there would be a new market clearing price whose level was unknown to the remaining participants. Who does what to cause the market price to attain the new equilibrium level?

The previously developed models of the consumer and of the purely competitive firm are not sufficient by themselves to explain the determination of market prices. The theory of consumer's choice portrays the consumer as a passive optimizer who can decide how much to buy out of a given income once the prices are known. The theory does not predict how a consumer will react when unable to buy at a given price the quantity determined to be optimal. Similarly, the purely competitive firm emerges as a passive optimizer capable of determining output levels when both input and output prices are given. There is nothing in the theory that directly predicts what the firm will do if the output cannot be sold at the expected price. If the typical consumer enters the market with a conventional demand curve and the typical producer with a conventional supply curve, each is in effect waiting for the other to quote a price to which he can react.

Passive maximizers do not take on the role of active traders easily. Hence, it is not surprising that, when actual conditions approximate the purely competitive, an elaborate marketing institution develops, in which brokers and other specialists furnish much assistance to buyers and sellers. Also, a class of professional traders appears, who seek to make a profit by buying or selling whenever they believe the current price to be too low or too high. The idealized competitive market of economic theory carries these activities a bit further and assigns to an outside agency an active role in the determination of market prices. An auctioneer—or it could be our central data processing agency—assumes the role of quoting a price and determining the total amount buyers wish to buy and sellers wish to sell at that price. If the amount demanded exceeds the amount sellers wish to supply, no transactions take place but a new higher price is quoted. The process is continued until the market clearing price is reached. Should supply exceed demand at a given price, a lower price would be tried.

The foregoing explanation of how the market clearing price is attained is known as a *tâtonnement process* and was introduced in 1874 by Léon Walras, the first economist to develop a full model of general equilibrium. The essence of the process is that the existence of excess demand tends to raise prices and the existence of excess supply tends to depress prices. In actual markets excess demand and supply operate through the decisions and actions of individual traders, and the external agent or auctioneer is simply a device for expressing these market forces in precise and idealized form. Before going on we shall consider briefly how excess demand and supply operate through individual traders to affect the level of the market price.

In an actual market, the prices quoted by the sellers may vary considerably, but each buyer may know only the quotations of a few sellers and be ignorant of the remainder. Also, all transactions need not be concluded at the same time but may be strung out over time. Buyers must decide whether to buy here and now or to hold off in the hopes of concluding a better bargain later. A buyer is likely to snap up an offer if he believes that few sellers will make an equally low offer. He will also act fast if he believes other buyers will accept the offer quickly and deprive him of a second chance. Sellers will also be making analogous decisions about the best price to quote. In this indirect way an assessment of the relative strength of demand and supply exerts its influence over the price. If they were not sure of the relative strengths to begin with, informed and experienced traders would be able to get a reading of the market from a relatively few initial transactions. As experimental simulations of markets have confirmed, there is a tendency for the price to gravitate toward the market clearing level, although the result is neither swift nor certain. Within general equilibrium models what is actually only a strong tendency is assumed to be realized fully and quickly.

With a downward-sloping demand curve and an upward-sloping supply curve, a price that rises in response to excess demand is moving toward its equilibrium level. Also, if we regard excess demand as a force operating on the price, the force diminishes as the price rises toward the market clearing level. An explicit dynamic model can be constructed in which the rate of change of price over time is a function of the excess demand, say, proportional to it. When supply exceeds demand, both excess demand and the rate of change of price over time are negative.

If price responds continuously to excess demand, the dynamic market process is stable, and the price inches toward the equilibrium level without ever exceeding it. The reason is that the continuously rising price continuously reduces excess demand and relieves the pressure for further price rises. The rate of increase in price over time continues to decline and approaches zero as the excess demand dwindles. When the price is initially too high the same process operates downward.

A continuous response of price to excess demand can only be an approximation of actual processes. Some lag in response, however short, is likely to occur. With lags present, the degree of responsiveness of price to excess demand affects the stability of the dynamic market process. If sellers respond with wild enthusiasm to a slight amount of excess demand, they may raise the price in the next trading period farther above the market clearing level than it is currently below. An excess of pessimism then carries the price below its original level. The result is possible but unlikely. People who live beneath towering, snow-covered mountains learn not to fire cannon. Similarly, we can expect that relatively flat demand and supply curves will in time teach traders to respond moderately when excess demand appears. So long as the response of price to excess demand is appropriate for the underlying supply and demand conditions, the dynamic market price will be stable and the price will approach its equilibrium level. As Exercise 6 shows, the convergence to equilibrium may be oscillatory, the price being alternately above and below the equilibrium by successively smaller amounts.

With a continuous or a moderate response of price to excess demand, the equilibrium price is stable under a tâtonnement process if the demand curve slopes downward and the supply curve slopes upward. Readers may verify geometrically that there is also a stable equilibrium price when the supply curve is downward sloping but steeper than the demand curve. There is excess demand below the intersection and excess supply above. Conversely, a steeper demand curve causes the price to diverge from the intersection, but neither of these cases has much significance since it is difficult to give a plausible economic rationale for a downward-sloping supply curve under purely competitive conditions.

COBWEB CYCLES

The short-run supply curve of a purely competitive firm represents amounts that the firm is willing to produce and supply out of existing capacity. But production takes time, so the indicated quantities cannot be supplied instantaneously or on the spot. Thus, the market is essentially a market for future delivery, or futures market, rather than a spot market. What it determines is a rate of production by the industry that can be maintained indefinitely under unchanging conditions. The amount that can be supplied on the spot depends on past production, which is a fixed quantity. With no possibility of storage and no cost of selling, the supply curve of each firm and of the industry becomes vertical. The past decision to produce cannot be reversed; all a firm can do is try to get the best price for the quantity on hand. The market clearing price lies at the intersection of the demand curve and the vertical supply curve. Since excess demand is positive below the intersection and negative above, the equilibrium spot price is stable under a tâtonnement process in the spot market.

For many commodities there do exist markets in which future output levels are adjusted to future orders. The market price as determined by past production becomes the guide to future production, which in turn determines the next period's spot price. If the spot price happens to equal the short-run equilibrium price, and conditions do not change, firms will continue to produce the same amount period after period. The vertical market supply curve and the short-run or future supply curve both intersect the demand curve in the same point. But if, say, the demand curve shifts between one period and the next, the spot price will no longer be equal to the short-run equilibrium price. We must investigate whether there is a dynamic process through which the spot price converges to the new short-run equilibrium price.

Figure 15–4a shows the divergence between the spot price and the short-run equilibrium price after an increase in demand. Each firm accepts the spot price as the guide to future production and chooses the appropriate output along its short-run supply curve. As graphed in Figure 15–4a, the aggregate output of all firms determines a new spot price at the point of intersection with the market demand curve. Since the spot price is initially above the short-run equilibrium price, firms overproduce, cause the price to fall

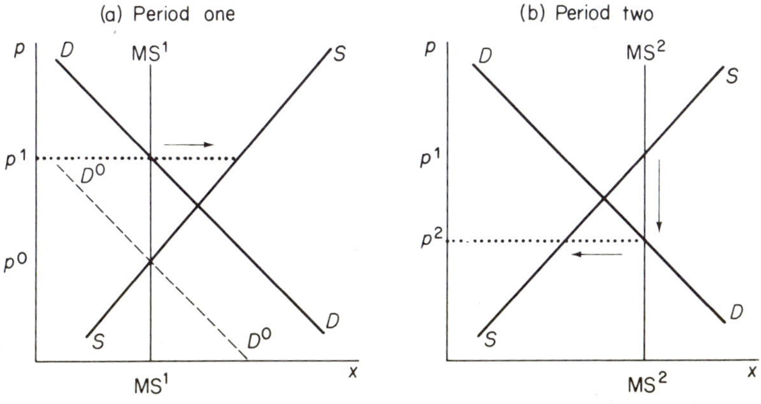

Fig. 15-4 A Lagged Response of Supply to the Spot Price

below the equilibrium level, and then contract output. Naturally, the price then rises above the equilibrium level again, and the process continues. The crucial question is whether the rise in price does or does not carry it above the initial level. If it does, the next rise will go still higher, and the price is diverging from the equilibrium level.

What causes instability is an overresponse of the quantity supplied to a change in price. Specifically, if both the demand and supply curves are linear and the rate of change of quantity with respect to price is numerically greater along the supply curve than along the demand curve, the price diverges from the equilibrium level. Algebraically the condition for divergence is

$$\left(\frac{\Delta x_1}{\Delta p_1}\right)_{\text{supply}} > -\left(\frac{\Delta x_1}{\Delta p_1}\right)_{\text{demand}},$$

which implies that

$$\left(\frac{\Delta p_1}{\Delta x_1}\right)_{\text{supply}} < -\left(\frac{\Delta p_1}{\Delta x_1}\right)_{\text{demand}},$$

or that the demand curve is relatively steeper than the supply curve. If the inequality is reversed, supply is less responsive to a change in price, and the price converges. In the improbable case of numerically equal slopes, the same pattern is repeated indefinitely, and the price neither converges nor diverges. The three patterns are shown in Figure 15–5. For obvious reasons, the pattern of reaction is known as a *cobweb cycle.*

When the cobweb cycle is convergent, the price approaches the short-run equilibrium level, as it does under a tâtonnement process in the futures market. However, a continuous or moderate tâtonnement process is convergent whenever the supply curve slopes upward but the cobweb cycle is not. The result emphasizes a significant, general conclusion about the stability of equilibria. We can classify an equilibrium as stable or unstable only if we specify the dynamic process by which the variables change over time when not in equilibrium.

The tâtonnement process is stable under more general conditions because it permits mutual adjustment by both buyers and sellers. The cobweb cycle consists of action by sellers followed by reaction from buyers. Such processes are basically less stable, but the simple geometric version just presented exaggerates the instability. Sellers are assumed to react in unison but differences in speeds of reaction are much more probable. The increased supply will come on the market gradually permitting a reaction that is closer to that of the tâtonnement process. Correct anticipations may also mitigate the swings of the market. Finally, limitations of capacity will cause the short-

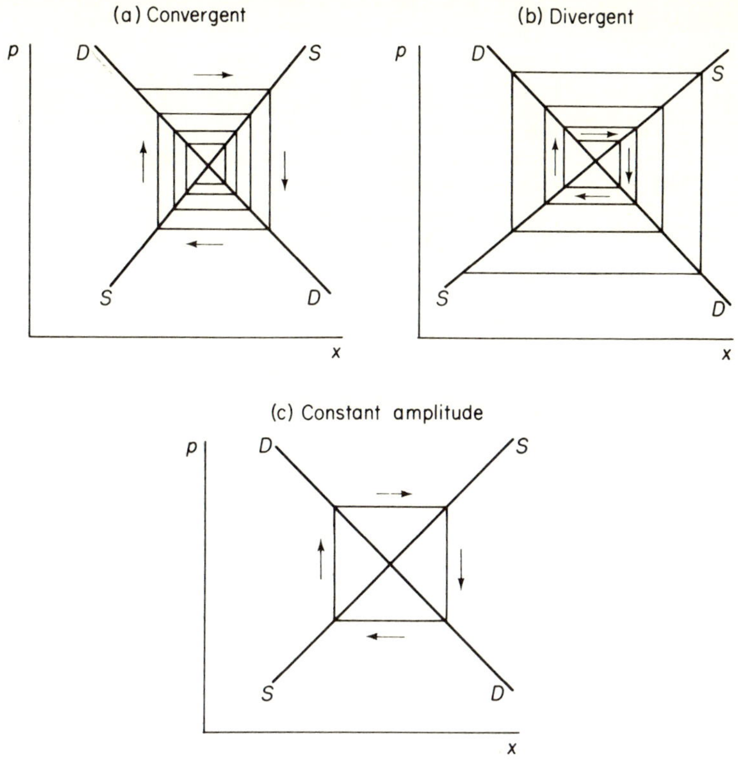

Fig. 15-5 Three Types of Cobweb Cycles

run supply curve ultimately to become very steep, reducing the response of supply. Except in a few cases, where the adjustment of supply takes a long time, it is not generally believed that cobweb cycles of any appreciable amplitude are present in the economy.

In constructing a model of general equilibrium for the whole economy, economists usually assume that the market for each commodity is stable when all other prices and income are constant. The dynamic process most often specified is a tâtonnement process in the futures market. If a market is stable under a cobweb process, it is also stable under a tâtonnement process. As we observed earlier, it is not possible to show the existence of general equilibrium in piecemeal fashion by finding the equilibrium in each market with all other prices constant. Similarly, the stability of the whole economic system cannot be demonstrated by showing that each individual market is stable when all other prices are constant. The chain reaction or feedback through other markets may cause instability. Attention will be given in Chapter 17 to the conditions under which the whole system of markets is stable.

EXERCISES

1. *Constructing Market Demand Curves*

(a) The consuming sector consists of four independent consuming units. There are three commodities. How many distinct individual demand functions are there? With rows denoting commodities and columns denoting consumers, draw up a table showing the set of all individual demand functions in symbolic form. Make the simplifying assumption that each consumer has given money income and spends all of it.

(b) For one of the commodities illustrate the procedure for obtaining the aggregate demand function. Write the aggregate demand functions in symbolic form as column 5 of the table.

Multiply each row or quantity demanded by its market price. Identify total expenditure, which equals income, for each consuming unit. Explain why aggregate expenditure must equal aggregate income at any set of positive commodity prices.

(c) Assume that all prices but one are constant. Draw typical individual demand curves for the commodity whose price is variable, and illustrate geometrically the procedure for getting the market demand curve.

(d) The individual consumer incomes are, say, $y_1 = 40$, $y_2 = 30$, $y_3 = 20$, $y_4 = 10$. We wish to substitute aggregate income for the individual incomes in the market demand functions. What condition provides a rigorous justification for such a substitution? Explain why.

(e) There are two primary inputs. Each consumer supplies fixed amounts of each regardless of prices. How is each consumer's income determined? Do these conditions permit the substitution of aggregate income for individual incomes in the market demand functions? Suppose there is only one primary input supplied in fixed amount by each unit. Can the substitution be made?

2. *Iso-elastic Demand Curves*

(In this exercise all demand curves are assumed to be iso-elastic, i.e., to have the same elasticity at every point.)

(a) A demand curve shifts but remains parallel to its original position along rays. Prove that the elasticity remains the same. Does the numerical value of the elasticity increase or decrease if the curves, in shifting, becomes flatter along rays, steeper along rays?

(b) Choose some constant level of price. Two distinct demand curves with the same elasticity intersect the horizontal line. Demonstrate that the tangent lines to both points of intersection must be drawn from the same vertical intercept. Show, conversely, that the elasticities cannot be the same if the vertical intercepts are different points.

(c) Set $k_1 = 1$ in the equation on page 380 and write the equations for demand curves with elasticities $-\frac{1}{2}$, -1, -2. Find the point of intersection of the curves and identify the ray.

Compute the quantity demanded along each curve when $p_1 = 4$. Identify the ray that each curve is intersecting and calculate the slope each demand curve must have. Repeat for $p_1 = \frac{1}{4}$. Use the results to sketch on separate diagrams the three demand curves.

When demand curves of constant but different elasticities intersect, explain in general how quantities must be related to elasticities at prices above the intersection and at prices below.

(d) For each specific demand curve of (c), write total revenue as a function of price. Find the total revenue associated with each curve at each of the specific prices. Plot the points on a single diagram and sketch the total revenue curves. Use the results of (c) to explain the relationships of the revenue curves to each other.

(e) Follow the instructions of (d) for total revenue as a function of quantity.

3. *Cross Elasticity of Demand*

(a) Relate negative, zero, and positive cross elasticities of demand to substitution and complementarity of commodities. Draw demand curves for x_1 and x_2. For each type of cross elasticity show how the demand curve for x_1 shifts as p_2 moves along the demand curve for x_2.

(b) A cross-demand curve has constant negative cross elasticity. Show that, except for a relabeling of the vertical axis, the cross-demand curve is indistinguishable from a demand curve with the same elasticity.

When the cross elasticity is zero, what is the value of $\Delta x_1/\Delta p_2$? Draw the curve. Rewrite the formula for cross elasticity in terms of $\Delta x_1/\Delta p_2$ and show that the formula is consistent with the curve.

(c) When $s_{12} = 1$, how must the slope of the tangent line at each point be related to the slope of the ray? Draw a typical curve.

If $s_{12} > 1$, say $s_{12} = 2$, describe the relationship of the cross-demand curve to each successive ray it crosses. What is the relationship when s_{12} is positive but less than 1, say $s_{12} = \frac{1}{2}$?

(d) Take the cross-demand curve in the simple form, $x_1 = p_2^{s_{12}}$. Let $s_{12} = \frac{1}{2}$, 1, 2. Find the point of intersection of the three curves. Choose $p_2 = 4, \frac{1}{4}$. Find the values of x_1. From the slope of the rays find the slopes of the tangent lines. Use the information to sketch the curves on a single diagram with p_2 on the vertical axis.

4. *Income Elasticity of Demand*

(a) From the analysis in Chapter 13, describe the general patterns o. indifference maps that give rise to positive, zero, and negative income elasticities. Relate the sign of the cross elasticities to the classification of commodities in Chapter 13. Can a commodity have a negative or zero income elasticity at all levels of income?

(b) When $s_{1y} = 1$, how must the slope of the tangent line at each point be related to the slope of the ray? Draw a typical income demand curve for this case with Y on the vertical axis.

If $s_{1y} > 1$, say $s_{1y} = 2$, describe the relationship of the income-demand curve to each successive ray it crosses. Do the same for $0 < s_{12} < 1$.

(c) Assume income to be measured in sufficiently small units and take the income-demand curve in the simple form: $x_1 = Y^{s_{1y}}$. Let $s_{1y} = \frac{1}{2}$, 1, 2. Find the point of intersection of the three curves. Choose $Y = 4$, $\frac{1}{4}$. Find the values for x_1 on the three curves. From the slopes of the rays find the slopes of the tangent lines and use the information to sketch the three curves on a single diagram.

With only two commodities, what are the implications of an income elasticity that everywhere exceeds 1? Are the implications acceptable on economic grounds?

5. *Demand Functions and Demand Curves*

(a) Write in symbolic form the demand *function* for x_1 when only one other commodity is available and the distribution of income is constant.

Write, also in symbolic form, the restrictions of the demand function that define the three different demand *curves* for x_1.

(b) Take the demand function in the specific form: $x_1 = p_1^{s_{11}} p_2^{s_{12}} Y^{s_{1y}}$. Write the general relationship to which the elasticities must conform. Choose simple numerical values for the elasticities that satisfy the general relationship and are economically plausible. Also assign specific numerical values to the independent variables in pairs. Write the equations for the resultant demand curves.

(c) Over some intermediate range of income, let s_{1y} have the three separate values $-\frac{1}{2}$, 0, $\frac{1}{2}$. Set $s_{12} = \frac{3}{4}$. Find the corresponding value for s_{11} and state the effect of income elasticity on price elasticity. Choose convenient numerical values for p_2 and Y. Write the equations for the three separate price-demand curves. What happens to each of these demand curves as Y increases or decreases?

(d) Set $s_{1y} = \frac{1}{2}$ and $s_{12} = -\frac{1}{2}, 0, \frac{1}{2}$. Find the corresponding values for s_{11}. Summarize the relation of cross elasticity to price elasticity. Choose convenient values for Y and p_2 and write the equations for the three price-demand curves. What happens to each of the curves as p_2 rises or falls?

6. *The Walrasian Tâtonnement Process*

For a simple illustration choose the linear market supply and demand curves: $p^s = a+(1/h)x^s$; $p^d = b+(1/k)x^d$; $h > 0$, $k < 0$, $b > 0$, $b > a$.

(a) Explain the meaning of and the necessity for the restrictive inequalities. Do the restrictive inequalities guarantee an intersection at a positive quantity, at a positive price? To answer, solve for x and p. Write down any further restrictions that may be needed and assume they are always satisfied.

Draw a typical pair of curves. How do quantity demanded and quantity supplied compare at prices above equilibrium and at prices below equilibrium?

(b) Write an alternative set of restrictive inequalities that will insure both equilibrium in the positive ranges and the same pattern of excess demand above and below the equilibrium price. Draw a typical pair of such linear demand and supply curves.

(c) Express the demand and supply curves of (a) in inverse form with x^d and x^s as explicit functions of p^d and p^s. Define excess demand as $E = E(p) = x^d - x^s$, when $p^d = p^s = p$. Write the excess demand function for (a).

Find the expression for the rate of change of excess demand with respect to the market price, $\Delta E(p)/\Delta p$. What is its sign? How is its magnitude related to the steepness or flatness of the demand and supply curves?

(d) For a simple example set $a = 0$, $b = 64$, $h = 1$, $k = -1$. Find the equilibrium price and quantity. Write the excess demand function. What is the amount of the excess demand when $p = 16$?

(e) To provide a numerical illustration of a tâtonnement process we must specify precisely the response of price to excess demand. The price could respond continuously to excess demand or only after a lag. We choose the latter and state that the price in the next trading period depends upon both the price and the excess demand in the present period. Further, we require that the change in price have the same sign as the excess demand and be proportional to it. With subscripts denoting successive trading periods, the pattern of response is $p_{t+1} - p_t = rE_t$, $r > 0$.

To denote different degrees of response choose $r = \frac{1}{4}, \frac{1}{2}, \frac{3}{4}, 1, \frac{5}{4}$. Set $p_0 = 16$ and for each value of r calculate successively E_0, p_1 and E_1. Continue the calculations until you have p_4 and E_4. Summarize the results in a table showing for each value of r the successive values of p_t and E_t. In each case determine whether convergence to equilibrium is occurring and by what pattern.

In general, how must the degree of response be related to the slope of the excess demand function to insure convergence?

7. *A Cobweb Process*

In the present model the quantity supplied in the next period depends on the price in the present period, and the price in each period is at the market clearing level for the specific quantity supplied. The linear supply and demand curves, explained more fully in Exercise 6, are $p^s = a + (1/h)x^s$; $p^d = b + (1/k)x^d$; $h > 0$, $k < 0, b > 0, b > a$.

(a) Verify the following results. In each period the price is determined by $p_{t+1} = b + (1/k)x^s_{t+1}$. The quantity supplied depends upon $x^s_{t+1} = -ah + hp_t$. The two equations combine to form the following equation for the variation of market price over time:

$$p_{t+1} = \frac{bk - ah}{k} + \frac{h}{k} p_t.$$

(b) Carry out the following instructions for each of the sets of specific values shown below. Write the specific equation for p_{t+1}. Find the successive market prices up to p_4. At each level of price determine the quantity sellers have supplied and the quantity they wish to supply. Investigate whether the market is converging toward equilibrium. Draw the cobweb diagram in each case.

(1) $a = 0, b = 64, h = 1, k = -1, p_0 = 16.$

(2) $a = -32, b = 64, h = \frac{1}{2}, k = -1, p_0 = 16.$

(3) $a = 16, b = 64, h = 2, k = -1, p_0 = 30.$

16

Equilibrium and Optimality for Purely Competitive Industries

Earlier chapters developed in detail the process of allocation within the purely competitive firm, culminating in the generalization of Chapter 11, which should be reviewed before going on. The present chapter resumes the treatment of allocation of inputs and extends it to purely competitive industries. We take up first industries composed of single-product firms and then extend the analysis to industries where all firms are technologically capable of producing the same set of two or more products. Each product is sold and each variable input is purchased in a purely competitive market, which is assumed to be stable under a tâtonnement process. The prices of all commodities not produced by the industry and the prices of all inputs not used by the industry are held constant. Since the equilibrating mechanism is temporarily suspended, these markets are in disequilibrium. The process of adjustment and the repercussions it generates appear in Chapter 17 in the model of the economy as a whole. Before taking up the allocation of resources, we shall first clear up the minor difficulty of reconciling each firm's neglect of influence with equilibrium for the industry.

MARKET REACTION CURVES AND THE ADJUSTMENT PROCESS

With m firms selling a homogeneous product, the exact effect of any one firm on the market price can be determined conceptually by first finding at each price the horizontal difference between the market demand and the amount the remaining $m-1$ firms wish to supply. Figure 16–1 shows on one graph the market demand curve and the supply curve of $(m-1)$ firms, and on

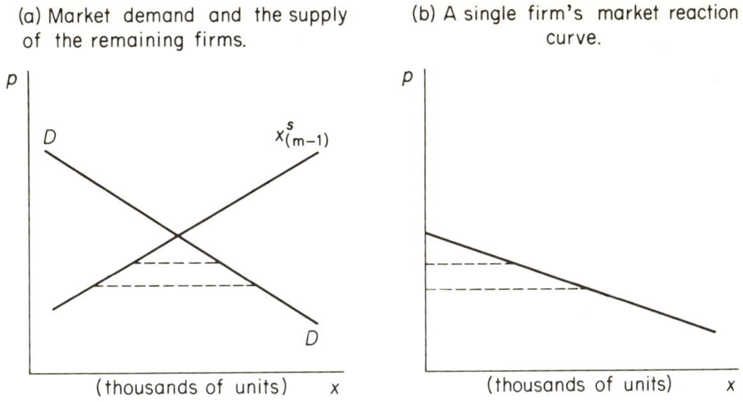

Fig. 16-1 Derivation of a Firm's Market Reaction Curve

a second graph the horizontal difference between them. We are, in effect, assuming that each one of the $(m-1)$ firms can be interrogated with respect to the amount it wishes to supply and that the replies trace out an upward-sloping supply curve.[1]

If the mth firm supplies no output, the market price lies at the intersection of the demand curve and the supply curve of the remaining firms. As the mth firm increases its output above zero the market price must fall to the level at which the output of the mth firm equals the horizontal gap between the industry demand and the supply of the remaining firms. Thus, Figure 16–1b shows how the market price responds to the output of the mth firm, and is called the *market reaction curve* of the firm. Despite superficial resemblances, a market reaction is not a demand curve, since it shows price as a function of quantity supplied rather than quantity demanded as a function of price.

In order to confine market demand and supply curves to a single page, we must measure the quantity on the horizontal axis in something like thousands or millions of units. Thus, these curves show how quantity in thousands or millions of units responds to a change in the price of a single unit. The slopes become much steeper than they are in terms of single units. A line with a slope of 1 in thousands of units is a line with a slope of 1/1000 in single units, which differs little from a horizontal line. As drawn in Figure 16–1b, the market reaction curve for the mth firm is also measured in terms of thousands of units and appears much steeper than it actually is to a firm that varies its output by single units.

[1]The supply curve will be upward sloping if it coincides with the marginal cost curve, but the reasoning of the present section becomes circular if the assumption is made. What we are trying to do is develop the rationale for a firm's neglecting its influence on market price and, hence, adopting the marginal cost curve as its supply curve. To avoid circularity, we simply assume initially that the supply curve of a firm, however derived, is upward sloping.

A Decision Model for a Purely Competitive Firm

If a slight reduction in market price causes a large increase in quantity demanded and a large decrease in quantity supplied by the remaining firms, the market reaction curve is very flat, and the output of the mth firm has little effect on the market price. With many firms in an industry, the response of supply to a given price change is likely to be large. If a \$1 increase in price causes one firm to expand output by g units, it will induce $(m-1)$ identical firms to expand by $(m-1)\ g$ units. Expressed more precisely, the relationship is

$$\Delta x^S_{(m-1)} = (m-1)g\ \Delta p.$$

For simplicity of exposition, but without affecting the conclusions, the market demand curve may also be represented by a straight line, and the response of quantity to a change in price written as

$$\Delta x^D = d\ \Delta p.$$

When the mth firm varies its output, the market price must change by just the right amount to create the appropriate gap between the quantity demanded by consumers and the quantity supplied by the remaining firms. In symbols,

$$\Delta x_m = \Delta x^D - \Delta x^S_{(m-1)} = d\ \Delta p - (m-1)g\ \Delta p = [d-(m-1)g]\ \Delta p,$$

or

$$\frac{\Delta p}{\Delta x_m} = \frac{1}{d-(m-1)g}.$$

The final expression is the slope of the mth firm's market reaction curve, which will clearly be negative whenever the market demand curve slopes downward ($d < 0$) and the supply curve of each firm slopes upward ($g > 0$). Also, since m appears in the denominator, the slope will be numerically smaller and the market reaction curve flatter, the larger the number of firms in the industry.

If a purely competitive firm knew with certainty its exact market reaction curve, the firm would use it to determine the optimal output. The gain may be small but, if the gain is there for the taking, the firm has not achieved an optimum unless it takes the gain.[2] Of course, a purely competitive firm does

[2]The optimal output occurs at the intersection of marginal cost with a marginal revenue curve derived from the market reaction curve and lying below it. The result is similar to monopoly or monopolistic competition, except that the firm has no power to set a price independently and can only affect the common market price by varying output.

not know its exact market reaction curve, but any entrepreneur with many rivals would soon learn, if he did not know to begin with, that his decisions have an almost imperceptible effect on the market price. The entrepreneur is almost certain to decide that he will be better off ignoring the effect than spending any time or money trying to estimate it, particularly when any estimate will be subject to a large standard error. By ignoring the effect, he approximates the true market reaction curve by a horizontal line at the going price and produces at the point where the marginal cost curve intersects the horizontal approximation.

One of the requirements for pure competition is a large number of firms, but the size of the number is never specified, and it is now clear why no specific number can ever be given. What pure competition really represents is a hypothesis about economic behavior or decision making under specified conditions. It is not possible to establish this hypothesis deductively by proving that it must hold whenever the number of firms equals or exceeds a specific figure. What we can show deductively is that, other conditions being the same, the influence of one firm on the market price declines as the number increases. By contrast, the difficulty or cost of estimating the influence certainly does not decline with an increase in the number of firms. The hypothesis is that, other conditions being the same, a firm is more likely to ignore its effect on market price, the larger the number of rivals. We cannot prove that a firm must neglect its influence no matter how many rivals it has. All we can do is show that neglect of influence becomes an objectively more attractive choice when the number of firms is large, and then predict that firms will choose it.

A firm with only a few rivals selling a homogeneous product cannot afford to neglect its influence on the other firms, but this does not mean that the firm adjusts output along a market reaction curve. For a market reaction curve to exist, there must be a formal market in which the price is established, and rivals must react only to the changes in the market price. Neither of these conditions is likely to be fulfilled when there are few firms. In particular, a firm is likely to keep a close watch on each rival and respond directly to the rival's decisions rather than indirectly by way of the effect on the market price. Either acute rivalry or some form of cooperation is likely to emerge, or one followed by the other.

The Internal Adjustment Process of the Industry

For a single, purely competitive firm we can construct a plausible decision model in which the firm simplifies its optimizing problem by treating market price as a parameter and neglecting any effect its output may have. But so long as there is any effect, however slight, we cannot ignore it when we construct a model for the industry. In Figure 16–2, the solid horizontal line is drawn at the market price before the *m*th firm enters the market. The firm

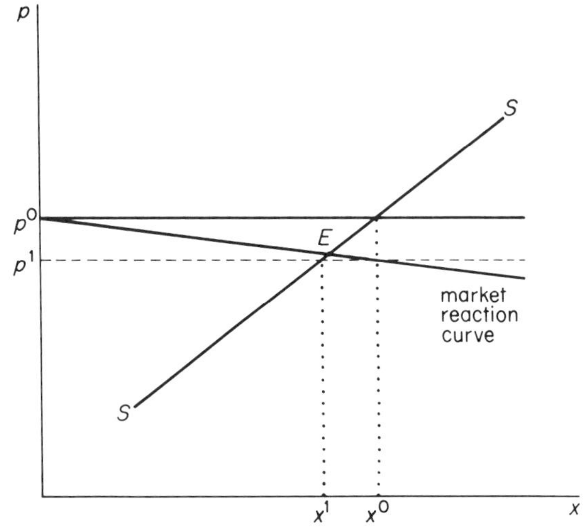

Fig. 16-2 The Adjustment Process When One Firm Varies Output

chooses its optimal output at the intersection of the marginal cost curve with the horizontal approximation to the market reaction curve. But when that quantity is supplied the market price drops to the level shown by the true market reaction curve directly below. The dashed line is the horizontal approximation at the new market price. Output is cut back to the intersection with the marginal cost curve, and the price rises, but not to the pre-entry level. There is, then, a small cobweb process that converges to the intersection of the marginal cost curve with the market reaction curve. Not only is the process virtually certain to converge but the price is also likely to approach the equilibrium level very rapidly since the market reaction curve is almost certain to be much flatter than the marginal cost curve. The adjustment is even smaller when the firm varies its output from some previously attained positive level.

Equilibrium for both firm and industry occurs at the point E when the horizontal approximation at the current price passes through the intersection of the marginal cost curve with the true market reaction curve. A firm that does not correctly assess its own effect on the market price encounters some small feedback from changes in its output level. Thus, if the firm does not make the correct decision initially, it must make a sequence of minor corrections leading to the same result. The firm does not identify this feedback as a consequence of its own action but simply reacts in the same way as it does to a change in market price caused by the actions of other firms or by forces external to the industry. An industry that is stable under external changes will be stable when a single firm varies its output. Hence, a stable equilibrium exists even though every firm acts on objectively false information.

SHORT-RUN DEMAND AND SUPPLY CURVES

The standard textbook version of a single-product industry uses only two inputs, one variable and one fixed in the short run. With the output price given, the optimizing decision of each firm determines marginal revenue productivities or internal prices for each combination of inputs. When an input can be purchased, a firm will continue to purchase and use the input up to the point at which the marginal revenue productivity, or variable internal price, comes into equality with the given external price. Alternatively, the given price for the variable input determines the marginal cost or internal price at each level of output. To maximize net revenue the firm increases production up to the point at which the variable internal price for the output equals the external or market price. The conditions are not independent but equivalent; either implies the other.

If the market price for the input remains constant but the market price of the product varies, every firm optimizes by choosing at each output price the appropriate quantity on the upward-sloping portion of the marginal cost curve beyond minimal average variable cost, which thus represents the supply curve of the firm. The supply curve of the industry is the horizontal summation at each price of the quantities on the supply curves of the individual firms. Hence, at every point on the aggregate supply curve all firms have identical marginal costs or internal prices for the product. Alternatively, when the market price of the product is constant but the price of the input varies, each firm optimizes by choosing the appropriate quantity on the downward-sloping portion of the marginal revenue productivity curve below maximum average revenue product, which becomes the demand curve of the firm for the variable input. The demand curve of the industry for the input is the horizontal summation at each input price of the quantities the individual firms wish to purchase. At every point on the aggregate demand curve all firms have identical marginal revenue productivities or internal prices for the variable input.

A short-run aggregate supply curve for the product can be derived when the price of the variable input is constant, and a short-run aggregate demand curve for the variable input exists when the output price is constant. In general neither of these restrictions is valid. When all firms in the industry expand or contract the output produced and the input utilized, both output and input prices vary. The output price varies along the demand curve for the product, and the input price varies along the supply curve of the input to the industry, a concept which must now be examined.

The Supply Curve of an Input to an Industry

We need to distinguish between inputs used exclusively or almost exclusively by the industry under study and inputs in demand by other industries as well. A second distinction, which will be examined more fully in Chapter 18, is between primary inputs supplied by consumers and produced inputs supplied by other industries. The supply curve of an input to an industry is not a clearly defined concept when the input is purchased by more than one industry. Consequently, the first case to be taken up is an input that is specific to the industry under study.

For a produced input, the supply curve to the industry using the input is simply the aggregate supply curve of the industry producing it. For a primary input used exclusively by one industry, the supply curve shows the amounts consumers are willing to supply at each price. This information is potentially retrievable by submitting to consumers sets of prices in which only the input price varies and then interrogating them as to the amounts they wish to supply. The supply curve is taken to be upward sloping, although the opposite possibility cannot be ruled out completely. When the choice open to consumers is simply work or leisure, the supply curve for labor services may bend backward toward the vertical axis as the wage rate rises. Consumers may choose more leisure over more income once the rising wage rate has lifted income to a satisfactory level. When there are alternative occupations, as is assumed here, a rising wage rate in one occupation is likely to attract workers from other occupations, imparting an upward slope. When the input is produced by another purely competitive industry, the supply curve is always upward sloping in the short run.

Reaction Curves in the Input Markets

The supply curve of an input to a purely competitive industry, like the demand curve for the product, is unknown to the firms and does not enter directly into their decision making. So long as suppliers of the input have no preferences among firms and are always ready to sell to the highest bidder, there is no meaningful supply curve of the input to an individual firm. If one firm offers a higher price than its rivals do, it can corral the entire supply; a firm quoting a lower price gets nothing. When all firms quote the same price, the allocation of the supply among firms becomes indeterminate. So long as the market for the input is purely competitive, the decision of each firm must be based on a market reaction curve.

The true market reaction curve for the mth firm is the horizontal difference at each price between the supply curve to the industry and the demand curve of the remaining $m-1$ firms. The demand curve of the remaining $m-1$ firms, being the summation of downward-sloping curves for all firms, must slope downward. Since the supply curve to the industry almost certainly slopes upward, so does the market reaction curve. Suppose that $m-1$ firms are buying the entire supply at the going price. When the mth firm enters and tries to buy some of the input, there is excess demand and the price must rise. The price must continue to rise until the quantity the mth firm wishes to buy equals the horizontal gap between the supply curve to the industry and the demand curve of the $m-1$ firms. By plotting the horizontal gaps against the price that causes them we get the upward-sloping market reaction curve for the mth firm, which shows the effect on the market price of each quantity demanded by the mth firm. Since the precise slope is difficult to determine but probably differs little from zero, the firm chooses a horizontal approximation at the going price. The assumption is not quite correct, so there must be a minor, but almost certainly stable, adjustment process in the input market. Equilibrium for both firm and industry prevails when each firm's input demand curve intersects its true market reaction curve at the prevailing price. When changes occur that affect all firms simultaneously, it is not necessary to consider the minor process by which markets adjust to changes initiated by one firm. The analogy to the market reaction curve in the output market should be clear.

Short-Run Equilibrium for Both Input and Output

To provide a simple introductory case, we shall choose an input that is not only specific to the industry under study but also fixed in total amount in the short run. An agricultural commodity that is not storable provides a reasonably apt example. So also does some special type of labor skill, such as glass blowing, for which training may be required to increase the supply. Initially, then, the supply curve of the input to the industry is simply a vertical line, but this is a prelude to a more general treatment of the problem.

Full equilibrium for the industry exists only when the market clearing price prevails in both the input and the output markets. Prices are assumed to be established by separate tâtonnement processes in each market. The added complication is that a price change in one market causes a curve to shift in the other. As displayed in Figure 16–3, each price for the product determines a different derived demand curve DD for the variable input, high prices causing a shift upward and to the right. Similarly, each input price in Figure 16–3b generates a new derived supply curve DS for the product, higher prices causing a shift upward and to the left. Any initially prevailing output price determines successively a derived demand curve for the input, an equilibrium price in the input market, and a derived supply curve for the output. For equilibrium to prevail simultaneously in both markets, the derived supply curve must intersect the demand curve at the initially prevailing price. Readers may verify that only p_1^1 satisfies the requirement in Figure 16–3.

Suppose that the price happened to jump to the level of p_1^2. Would the market forces bring it back to the equilibrium level? The derived demand curve for the input shifts to the right, creating excess demand at the previously prevailing price, c_1^1. The input price rises to c_1^2 and the derived supply curve becomes DS^2. The crucial question is whether the derived supply curve can

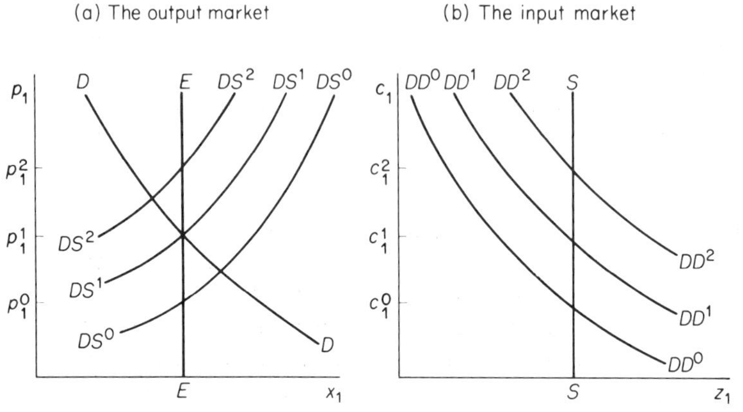

Fig. 16-3 Simultaneous Equilibrium in Both Output and Input Markets

shift so far to the left as to create excess demand at the price p_2^2. If so, the output price would move farther away from its equilibrium level. This cannot occur. Equilibrium in the input market implies that the marginal revenue productivity of the input to every firm is equal to the market price.

$$p_1\bar{e}_1 = c_1.$$

But the height of the derived supply curve, which equals marginal cost, is $c_1/\bar{e}_1$. With the amount of the input fixed, $\bar{e}_1$ is constant, so the marginal cost curve shifts in proportion to the change in c_1, which is in turn proportional to the change in p_1. Hence, a rise in output price above its equilibrium level induces, by way of the input market, a proportional upward shift of the derived supply curve. The rise in output price, since it causes a proportional rise in the input price, does not affect the quantity firms wish to supply. Since the quantity demanded falls off, there is excess supply at p_1^2, and the output price falls. The fall in price sets into motion a succession of downward shifts in the derived supply curve converging to the equilibrium position.

It is sometimes convenient to summarize the adjustment process in one diagram. For each input price there is an entire curve showing the amounts of the output that firms wish to supply at various levels of the output price. But there is only one amount that can be produced and supplied if demand is to equal supply in the input market. When the amount of the input is fixed, there is only one level of production that utilizes the full amount of the input. Hence, we may draw through the family of derived supply curves a vertical line showing the maximum output. The vertical line EE shows for each derived supply curve the only amount that can be supplied when the input market is in equilibrium. The vertical line intersects the demand curve at p_1^1. The equilibrium is stable since there is excess supply above p_1^1 and excess demand below.

An Upward-Sloping Input Supply Curve

Figure 16–4 shows the adjustment of both markets when the supply curve of the input is upward sloping but not vertical. As before, each level of the output price generates a different derived demand curve for the input, and each level of the input price determines a distinct derived supply curve for the output. As the dashed line shows, when the output price is high, equilibrium is possible in the input market only if a large amount of the input is used. But the use of a large amount of the input means a high level of production and an excess of supply. Output price falls to the intersection of the demand curve with the derived supply curve DS^2 and causes successively a leftward shift of the derived demand curve, a decline in the input price, and a downward shift of the derived supply curve. The process continues with the derived supply curve converging toward DS^1, when equilibrium prevails in both markets.

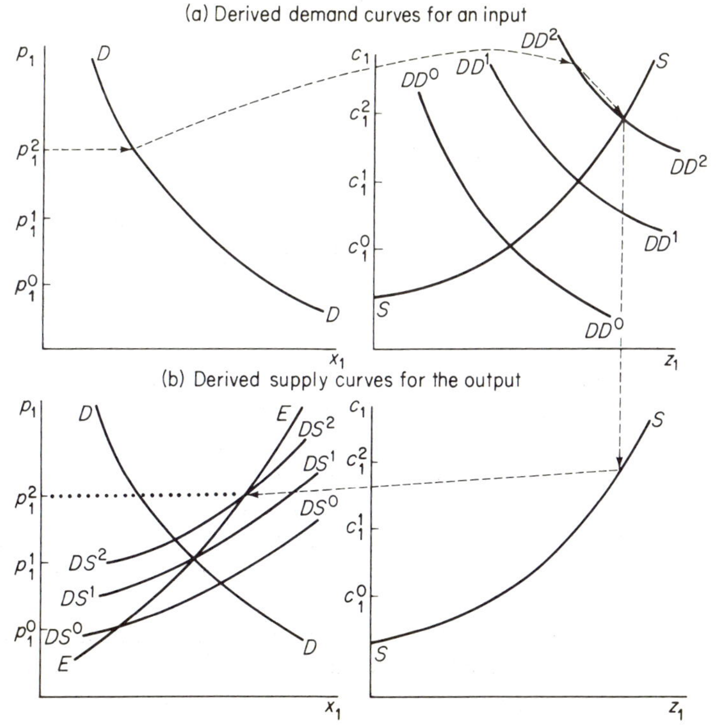

Fig. 16-4 Simultaneous Equilibrium with a Rising Input Supply Curve

The adjustment process can be summarized in the output market alone by using the curve *EE*. Each input price determines both a derived supply curve for the output and the amount of the input that will be supplied. Equilibrium prevails in the input market only if the amount supplied is actually used. Hence, for each input price there is only one level of output and only one point on the corresponding derived supply curve at which the input market is in equilibrium. The curve *EE* is drawn through these points and thus transfers to the output diagram the condition of equilibrium in the input market. Both markets are in adjustment where the *EE* curve intersects the demand curve for the product. An alternative possibility is to portray the adjustment solely in the input market by choosing on each derived demand curve the amount of the input firms must utilize to ensure that supply equals demand in the product market.

The *EE* curve is sometimes called a supply curve, but this designation is hard to justify. As generally used in economics, supply and demand curves are based on the decisions of economic units as to the amounts they wish to sell or buy as one price changes with all others constant. The *EE* curve shows not just the amounts firms wish to supply but the amounts they have to supply to keep the input market in equilibrium. Equilibrium in the input market results from the action of all firms; a single firm cannot determine how much to supply in order to bring the market into equilibrium.

OPTIMALITY FOR THE SINGLE-PRODUCT INDUSTRY

The firm in economics is a decision-making unit seeking solutions that are optimal in terms of some generally acceptable goal or objective. Depending on the situation, maximizing net revenue or the level of an output, minimizing cost or the use of an input are taken to be the objectives of the firm. Although many individuals and many different plants or divisions may be involved, the decisions made and the policies followed are assumed to be governed by and directed toward achievement of the broad objectives of the firm. The purely competitive industry is, by contrast, a collection of independent firms, each pursuing goals that are in conflict with those of the other firms. When we raise the question of optimality for a purely competitive industry, we are asking whether the independent and antithetical decisions of the individual firms unintentionally produce results that are in some sense optimal.

The key to the answer is to be found in the relationship between the primal and dual optimizing problems for an individual firm. Every primal optimizing problem for the firm generates dual variables that are measured in the same units as prices and can be given a significant economic interpretation as prices. As has been shown repeatedly, the necessary and sufficient conditions for an optimal solution to the primal can always be formulated in terms of dual variables or internal prices. Further, the use of a system of internal prices has often been proposed, and sometimes adopted, as a decentralized method for achieving the optimal solution for a firm.

For the industry and for the economy as a whole, it is the pricing mechanism that guides the allocation of resources. Buyers and sellers competing among themselves and trading with each other within the market system establish equilibrium levels of prices. These prices determine mutually consistent decisions as to the amounts of the inputs supplied to each firm and the quantities of the outputs produced. As is true for internal prices within the firm, the market prices by themselves cannot be judged optimal or nonoptimal. They acquire significance in this respect only if they indicate that the relevant quantities are at optimal levels. What we need to find, then, is the corresponding primal optimizing process. The pricing mechanism of purely competitive markets is a dual in search of a primal.

When we first encountered the dual problem within the firm, we likened it to the pricing mechanism within the economy at large. To find the primal problem for the industry, we shall reverse the procedure, liken the industry to a giant firm, and analyze its problems of allocation. The single-product, purely competitive industry consists of a large number of firms, each possessing a set of production processes or an equivalent output function. In the short run, each firm has trapped within it one or more fixed inputs whose quantities cannot be altered either by new production or by trade with other firms. There may be, and we shall assume that there is, at least one input specific to the industry. For the present, we return temporarily to the earlier assumption that any input specific to the industry is also fixed in total supply. Rising supply curves for specific inputs as well as the purchase of inputs in competition with other industries will be brought in later. Thus, each firm possesses fixed, nontransferable inputs and also shares with other firms inputs that are in constant supply for the industry as a whole. The problem of allocation is essentially that of a multiplant firm, in which each plant has fixed inputs of its own and shares fixed inputs with the remaining plants.

Chapter 8 established the conditions for optimality in a firm of the type just described. Solving the technological maximum problem, or maximizing output for given levels of the inputs, generates marginal productivities or internal real prices for the inputs. The allocation of a shared input to plants is unique and optimal when the firm-wide internal price passes through vertical gaps in the marginal productivity curves of all plants except one. Under smooth technological conditions vertical gaps disappear and the marginal productivity of a shared input within each plant must equal the common value in the firm as a whole. Hence, the marginal productivity must be equal in all plants. The firm has then attained the maximum output from given inputs, since transferring the shared input from one plant to another causes offsetting gains and losses. The maximization of revenue from given inputs requires the marginal revenue productivity of a shared input to be equal in all plants. With only a single product, output is maximized whenever revenue is, and the equality of marginal revenue productivities implies the equality of marginal physical productivities.

For the single-product, purely competitive industry, competition of buyers and sellers establishes uniform market prices for the output and the shared inputs. So long as all firms accept the market prices and produce at the point where the marginal revenue productivity equals the input price, a shared input is distributed among firms in such a way as to equalize its marginal physical productivity and, hence, to maximize output. For the industry as a whole, the maximization of output does not necessarily imply the maximization of total revenue. If the demand curve for the product is inelastic in the neighborhood of the equilibrium price, total revenue can always be increased by restricting total output and causing the price to rise. It is only at a constant price that output and revenue can be interchanged in the maximization process. Thus, the appropriate primal optimizing process for the industry is the maximization of output. The equality of marginal revenue productivities from firm to firm is significant mainly because it implies equality of marginal physical productivities.[3] Even though no one consciously strives to attain the goal, the competition of firms within the market system so allocates inputs as to yield the greatest possible output. This is an example of the "invisible hand," a graphic phrase that Adam Smith used to describe the working of competition.

The attainment of equilibrium also determines marginal revenue productivities or internal prices for the inputs trapped within each firm. If these inputs are heterogeneous, varying in quality from firm to firm, nothing further can be said about their allocation. Suppose, instead, that the inputs are of uniform quality. If the internal prices happen to be equal from firm to firm, the distribution of the fixed inputs is also optimal in the sense of yielding the greatest possible output from the given total amounts of the inputs. Whenever all firms have an identical set of linear processes or identical linear and homogeneous output functions, identical internal prices will be established whenever the fixed inputs are present *in the same ratio* in every firm. Thus, the optimal distribution is independent of the size of the firms. If the output function shows diminishing returns to scale, the absolute amounts of the inputs as well as the relative amounts influence the marginal productivities. With identical functions, all firms must have the *same amounts* of the fixed inputs for output to be maximized. When firms have different technologies, there is no simple pattern for optimal distribution of the fixed inputs, except that more efficient firms must get a larger share.

[3]If, by reason of ignorance, time lags, or other market imperfections, all firms do not base their decisions on the same output price, then equality of marginal revenue productivity to a common input price does not imply equality of the marginal physical productivities.

The foregoing result emphasizes the importance of marketing arrangements for the sale or lease of such inputs as can be shifted from firm to firm in the short run. When inputs are trapped within firms, the marginal revenue productivity may differ widely from firm to firm, and the criterion of maximum output will not be satisfied. Fortunately, both the entrepreneurs themselves and enterprising outsiders have an interest in developing to the utmost methods for shifting inputs among firms. It is interesting to note, also, that decentralized decision making by fully informed entrepreneurs combined with perfectly functioning markets achieves the same allocation of the shared input as a fully informed central planning agency combined with a perfectly operating administrative organization to carry out its decisions. Hence, the superiority of one method over the other in a given situation depends on the degree of effectiveness with which the different types of organization operate.

When an input specific to an industry has an upward-sloping but not vertical supply curve, the market mechanism determines both the allocation among firms and the total amount the industry receives. So long as every firm bases its optimizing decisions on the same set of prices, the marginal physical productivity of the specific input will be the same in all firms. Hence, whatever amount the industry obtains will be so distributed among firms as to yield the greatest possible output. Whether the amount the industry receives is also optimal cannot be determined at this stage. So long as any input, specific or not, is limited in total supply, the more one industry receives the less there is for other industries or for the use of consumers. The correct amount for any one industry can only be found within a pattern of optimal allocation in the economy as a whole, a topic for subsequent chapters.

INPUTS PURCHASED IN COMPETITION WITH OTHER INDUSTRIES

To round out the short-run equilibrium of a single-product, purely competitive industry we must take up inputs purchased in competition with other industries. So long as both buyers and sellers have no preferences as to whom they deal with and are motivated solely to conclude the best bargain, there is the same indeterminacy in defining a supply curve to an industry as was encountered previously in defining a supply curve or a demand curve for a purely competitive firm. At a higher price one industry corrals the whole market, and at a lower price the industry gets nothing. If all industries offer the same price, the allocation among them is indeterminate. It is not correct to interpret this indeterminacy as a horizontal supply curve to each industry; the analysis must be based on market reaction curves.

When many industries use an input, the demand curve is the sum of the amounts demanded by every firm in all industries. For any one industry, the true market reaction curve is the horizontal difference at each price between the total supply and the total amount demanded by the remaining industries. Thus, the equilibrium for one industry can be portrayed as the intersection of its demand and market reaction curves. The objection to this procedure is that it is a tail-wagging-the-dog solution. To show the equilibrium of one industry we must assume that all other industries using the input are in adjustment at each level of the input price. Only in this way are their demands for the input determined. Since the purpose of analyzing one industry at a time is to pave the way for general equilibrium analysis, this procedure comes uncomfortably close to assuming what is to be proved.

What is often done is to approximate the market reaction curve for an industry by a horizontal line at the going price. The approximation is the more accurate the larger the number of industries using the input and the smaller the relative size of the industry under study. Nonetheless, the simplification is objectively incorrect, since the market for an input cannot remain in equilibrium while one industry varies its production levels. The disequilibrium and the feedback it causes are, however, temporarily ignored. An equivalent but artificial assumption is that some outside agency supplies at the going price any increased demand by the industry under study and buys up any amounts that would otherwise be unused. The use of a horizontal market reaction curve is a valid simplification so long as the temporarily neglected feedback is later shown not to cause instability.

The preceding simplification for the industry bears a resemblance to the earlier treatment of the purely competitive firm, but there is one important difference. In developing the model of the purely competitive firm economists are advancing a hypothesis about economic behavior under the specified conditions. The hypothesis is that an entrepreneur in the purely competitive situation will simplify his decision making by choosing to neglect any effect his decisions may have in the markets where he buys and sells. When economists assume that the market reaction curve of an industry is horizontal, they are simplifying their own problems, not setting up hypotheses about economic behavior. The market reaction curve for an industry does not enter into the decision making of individual firms. Although the final results differ, firms make their decisions in the same way regardless of the slope of the industry's market reaction curve. The assumption of a horizontal market reaction curve permits the economist to ignore temporarily any repercussions on other industries that originate in the input market. It also simplifies the process of adjustment within the industry under study. If the prices of all variable inputs remain constant, there is only one derived supply curve for the product. During the process of adjustment only the derived demand curves for the inputs shift.

A horizontal market reaction curve for an industry implies that each firm can buy at the given price whatever amount of the input it needs. Since there is no limitation of supply, there is no true problem of allocation within the industry. However, from the equality of each firm's marginal revenue productivity to the given price, it follows that any amount obtained by the industry will in fact be optimally distributed. The significant question, to be examined later, is whether the inputs could be used more productively in other industries.

SHORT-RUN EQUILIBRIUM FOR A MULTIPRODUCT INDUSTRY

Most firms are technologically capable of producing more than one output and utilize a variety of inputs. For the simplest version of a multiproduct, purely competitive industry we shall assume the existence of many firms, each capable of turning out the same two products and each utilizing the same two inputs, which are variable to the firms but specific to the industry. Each firm has in addition its own productive capacity in the form of inputs that are fixed in amount and nontransferable in the short run. Equilibrium for the industry requires a set of output and input prices that simultaneously equate quantity demanded and quantity supplied in all four markets. The added complication is that a change in price in one market induces a shift in all pairs of supply and demand curves in the remaining markets.

As an illustration, take the industry initially in equilibrium and allow the price of the first product to rise. A multiproduct firm can and will divert the services of the fixed inputs into the production of a commodity that has risen in price. As shown in Chapter 5 for the linear model, a rise in price of one product brings into the basis processes that are complementary with it. The resources that are most needed for the more valuable product are thus freed to expand its production. The same general tendency remains when the model is smoothed.

We can also explain the shift of resources by the variation in the imputed prices. The height of a firm's supply curve for any product depends in part on the imputed unit cost. A rise in price of one product changes the internal prices of the fixed inputs and has the general effect of raising the supply curves for the remaining products, reducing the amounts supplied at given prices.[4] Thus, the supply curve of each output in a multiproduct firm depends on the prices of the other products.

If the goal is the construction of simple models for industries and the economy, multiproduct firms represent an unwanted complication. But, as usual, there is another side. So long as firms specialize on a single product,

[4]With only two products, a rise in one price invariably causes the supply curve for the other product to shift upward. When there are more than two products, every supply curve need not shift upward; there may be complementarity on the supply side. The possibility will not be considered further.

fixed inputs are not shiftable from product to product in the short run and part of the allocative mechanism is lost. The inputs trapped within multi-product firms can be partially reallocated in response to price changes. The mechanism that accomplishes it is the dependence of one product's supply curve on the price of the other product.

As is true for a single-product firm, a rise in the price of a product affects the marginal revenue productivities of the inputs and causes their demand curves to shift. Because of substitutability or possibly complementarity, a change in the price of one input affects the demand for the others. At the same time, a change in an input price shifts the supply curves of the products. The interdependence of the various curves can be shown formally by writing the following supply and demand functions for a two-output, two-input industry:

$$x_1^S = S_1(p_1, p_2, c_1, c_2) \qquad z_1^D = D_1(c_1, c_2, p_1, p_2)$$
$$x_2^S = S_2(p_1, p_2, c_1, c_2) \qquad z_2^D = D_2(c_1, c_2, p_1, p_2).$$

Given all four prices the firms in the industry can make optimizing decisions and thus determine the aggregate amount supplied of each product and aggregate amount demanded of each input. Fixing three prices determines a demand or supply curve for the remaining quantity, but a change in any one of the three prices causes the curve to shift.

There are also demand functions for the two products and supply functions of the two inputs. These, however, depend largely on variables external to the industry, and we have some discretion as to how much of the rest of the economy we bring into a simple model for the industry. Minimally, the demand for each product must depend on the prices of both products and the supply of each input on the prices of both inputs. We can, however, eliminate interdependence of inputs by taking both supply curves vertical. The effects of commodity prices on inputs supplied or of input prices on commodities demanded occur by way of optimizing readjustments by consumers and can be ignored in the partial analysis of a single industry.

The adjustment process for a multiproduct, multi-input industry resembles that of the economy as a whole. It will be merged with the general discussion of that topic in Chapter 17. For the present we merely take for granted that a stable equilibrium exists and proceed to examine its optimality.

OPTIMALITY OF EQUILIBRIUM FOR A MULTIPRODUCT INDUSTRY

A multiproduct industry has essentially the same short-run problem of allocation as does a firm that produces a variety of products in each of its plants. Chapter 11 analyzed a firm that produces the same two products in both plants and has two inputs fixed in amount to the firm but shared by the plants. With smooth technology, the optimal allocation requires that each shared input have the same marginal productivities in every plant. Otherwise, the firm could shift an input between plants and get more of one product without giving up any units of the other product. Each plant must use whatever amounts of the shared inputs it receives in such a way as to maximize one output for a constant level of the other. The required conditions are

$$\frac{\bar{a}_{21}}{\bar{a}_{22}} = \frac{\bar{a}_{11}}{\bar{a}_{12}} \quad \text{or} \quad \frac{\bar{e}_{22}}{\bar{e}_{12}} = \frac{\bar{e}_{21}}{\bar{e}_{11}}.$$

Since the marginal productivities are the same in all plants, the conditions for optimality hold throughout the firm, and the multiplant firm has solved its technological maximizing problem. Each product is maximized for any assigned level of the other, generating a product transformation curve for the firm. Market prices for the outputs determine the revenue maximizing output pair and also establish internal monetary prices for all inputs. The solution is optimal only when the shared inputs have the same internal price or marginal revenue productivity in all plants and in all products within plants.

The results carry over directly to a multiproduct industry composed of single-plant firms. For any input specific to the industry, the market establishes a uniform price that takes the place of the common internal price. So long as all firms base their optimizing decisions on the same set of input and output prices, the marginal revenue productivity of each shared input will be equal from firm to firm. At the given level of prices, but only at that level, net revenue is being maximized for the industry. Firms in an industry can act collectively and determine the selling prices by jointly controlling total output. So long as this option is open, it is not appropriate to say that the industry has solved the net revenue maximizing problem. When the marginal revenue productivity of an input within each firm is equated to a common market price, the marginal physical productivities of that input must be the same from firm to firm. Also, as shown below, the equality of the marginal revenue productivities in different products within firms implies equal ratios of the marginal physical productivities:

$$\frac{p_2\bar{e}_{22}}{p_2\bar{e}_{21}} = \frac{p_1\bar{e}_{12}}{p_1\bar{e}_{11}} \quad \text{implies} \quad \frac{\bar{e}_{22}}{\bar{e}_{12}} = \frac{\bar{e}_{21}}{\bar{e}_{11}}.$$

Hence, all requirements for a technological optimum are met. When independent firms base their optimizing decisions on the same set of market prices, they succeed in solving the technological maximum problem for the industry as a whole. Once the industry has reached equilibrium it can increase one product only by reducing the other.

When an industry consists of multiplant firms, the allocative process operates at three levels rather than two. Within each plant, the fixed, non-transferable resources must be correctly allocated among products. Secondly, the inputs that are fixed to the firm but shared by plants must be optimally distributed among plants and correctly allocated within plants to products. Finally, the inputs shared by firms must be correctly assigned to firms, to plants owned by firms, and then to products within plants. If firms make no errors in attempting to maximize net revenue and if markets function properly, the industry achieves the optimal allocation at all three levels. The process of allocation for the industry operates in essentially the same way with single-plant as with multiplant firms. In the interest of a simpler exposition, the subsequent analysis deals only with single-plant firms and drops the lowest level of allocation within separate plants.

The inputs that are fixed in amount within firms in the short run will be optimally allocated only if the internal prices happen to be equal from firm to firm. If the technology consists of linear processes or of a linear and homogeneous output function, proportionate changes in inputs within a firm leave their marginal revenue productivities unchanged. Hence, with identical linear processes or identical linear and homogeneous output functions for all firms, the fixed inputs are optimally distributed whenever they are present *in the same ratio* in every firm. The optimal distribution of fixed inputs in the short run should not be confused with long-run optimality. An optimal distribution of fixed inputs is necessary for optimality of the industry in the long run, but it is not sufficient. We must also show that the industry has optimal total quantities of those inputs that are fixed in the short run.

An Output Function for the Industry

Under constant returns to scale and an optimal distribution of the fixed inputs, the industry has the same productive capacity as if all inputs were concentrated in a single firm. In Chapter 11 we derived an output function for the firm by maximizing one output subject to constant levels for the inputs and the other output. Parametric variation of the remaining output traced out a product transformation curve or efficiency frontier beyond which production could not occur. Since the equilibrating mechanism for an industry also maximizes one product for each level of the other, it defines an output function for the industry and traces out a product transformation curve. With two fixed inputs, b_3 and b_4, and two variable inputs specific to the industry but in constant supply, b_1 and b_2, the output function becomes

$$x_2 = -\bar{t}x_1 + \bar{e}_{21}b_1 + \bar{e}_{22}b_2 + \bar{e}_{23}b_3 + \bar{e}_{24}b_4.$$

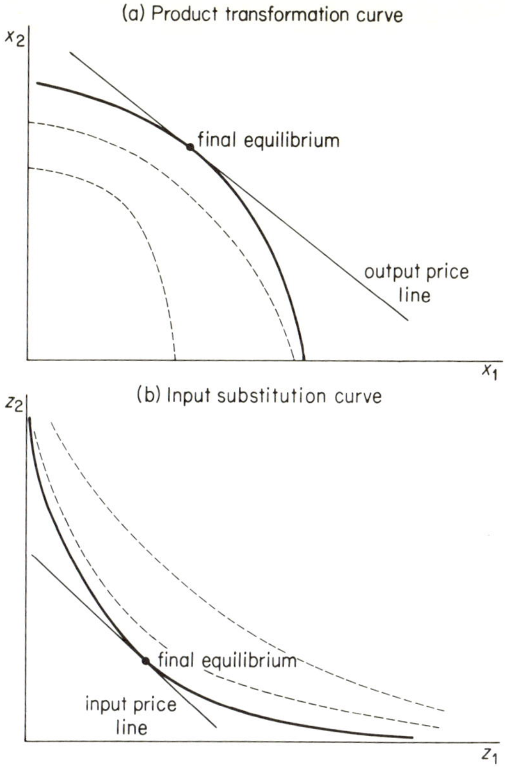

Fig. 16-5 Optimality of Equilibrium for a Multiproduct Industry

As x_1 varies, it traces out the efficiency frontier shown in Figure 16–5a. For nonoptimal distributions of the fixed inputs among firms, there are also efficiency frontiers, but, as the dotted curves in Figure 16–5a show, they always lie inside the optimal curve. The greater the disparity of the internal prices for the fixed inputs, the nearer the origin the nonoptimal curves must lie.

The final equilibrium for the industry lies on the product transformation curve at a point where the rate of product transformation, the negative of the slope, equals the ratio of output prices.[5] Algebraically, the condition for tangency is $\bar{t} = p_1/p_2$. If output prices, or even their ratio, were constant the equilibrium of the industry could be portrayed as the maximization of revenue. But, of course, prices do change during the process of adjustment before settling down to their final equilibrium levels. All we can say, then, is that the product transformation curve is the locus of all possible equilibria

[5]Equilibrium will always occur on the product transformation curve and not inside it, provided that the demand for each product is sufficiently large at a zero price.

for the industry and that the demand for the two products must determine where the equilibrium is to be.

Input Functions and Substitution Contours

For a single firm we can also derive input functions by minimizing the quantity of one input subject to constant levels for the outputs and the remaining inputs. Parametric variation of a second input then traces out an input substitution contour below which no combination of inputs is capable of yielding the specified output levels. A similar curve exists for the industry. Each input has equal marginal revenue productivities everywhere in the industry, so equations like the following hold for any pair of inputs:

$$p_1\bar{e}_{11} = p_2\bar{e}_{21}$$
$$p_1\bar{e}_{12} = p_2\bar{e}_{22}.$$

Division of the first equation by the second gives the condition for input minimization presented on page 258. We can carry out the division provided that prices and marginal productivities are not zero. Figure 16–5b shows substitution curves for the two variable inputs *specific* to the industry. Along the curve nearest the origin the inputs *fixed within firms* have equal internal prices and are optimally distributed. The dotted contours show that a non-optimal distribution of fixed inputs requires greater amounts of the variable, specific inputs to achieve the same output levels. We can convert the previously derived output function for the industry into an input function, provided that neither specific input is in excess supply and neither output exceeds demand at a zero price. The same function also yields a total product contour and an input requirement contour when x_1 is held constant and one of the inputs specific to the industry varies. Thus, the equilibrating mechanism for the industry generates essentially the same set of functions and the same set of diagrams as the technological optimizing decisions generate for the multi-product firm of Chapter 11.

Output maximization implies input minimization, and conversely. If a combination of inputs and a pair of output levels satisfy the conditions for output maximization, they must also fulfill the conditions for input minimization. Both sets of conditions depend upon each input having the same marginal revenue productivity in every use. Either set can be derived from the other simply by a rearrangement of terms. A single combination of inputs yields every pair of output levels on a product transformation curve. But each point or pair of output levels can be optimally produced by every input combination on an entire input substitution curve. There is, then, an entire family of input substitution curves, one for every point on the product transformation curve. But the original input combination that generated the transformation curve must lie on every one of the input substitution contours, since it can produce optimally every pair of output levels. Each member of the family of input substitution curves passes through the original input point and, under smooth technological conditions, has a different slope from every other member. A similar relationship holds in the opposite direction. A pair of output levels generates an entire input substitution contour. Each point on the contour in turn determines a product transformation curve that passes through the original output point with a unique slope.

The product transformation contours and the input substitution curves depend upon technological conditions, upon the total amounts of the variable inputs, and upon both the total quantities of the fixed inputs and their distribution among firms. In the short run, only the variable inputs may change, but these inputs may also be fixed in total supply to the industry, although not to individual firms. The industry operates in an economic environment consisting of the demand conditions for outputs and the supply conditions for inputs. As a first approximation, partial equilibrium analysis assumes that the adjustment of the industry has no effects on the economic environment in which it operates. Optimization by individual firms within the market mechanism brings the industry into adjustment with its external economic environment. Product transformation and input substitution contours are ideal for showing the final equilibrium for the industry and for appraising its optimality. They are less effective in analyzing the dynamic process by which the equilibrium is attained. The stability of the dynamic process and of the resultant equilibrium depends on the reaction of market prices to excess demand and can be analyzed best by the use of the supply and demand curves. Accordingly, in Chapter 17 we shall shift back to supply and demand functions to derive the conditions for stability of equilibrium.

LONG-RUN EQUILIBRIUM

For firms and industries the long run is defined not as some fixed period of chronological time but rather in an operational sense as a period of time sufficiently long so that no inputs remain fixed to the firm. In general, also, inputs that are specific to the industry but fixed over short periods become variable. But for some inputs the quantity available to the industry may remain constant even in the long run, when there is a basic limitation of supply. In the long run, then, each firm may alter at will the amount of any input. This does not mean simply sale or lease of equipment between firms; such a reshuffling of productive capacity is included in the short run. The result is achieved through the replacement of existing facilities by new productive capacity better suited to prevailing conditions. To explain most clearly and simply the underlying process of attaining long-run equilibrium, we shall confine the analysis to single-product firms.

An alternative designation of the long run is the planning period, in which each firm is assumed free to design new plant capacity. We shall again utilize the device of a central data processing agency that submits sets of prices to firms and interrogates them as to the amount of the product they plan to produce and the amount of each input they plan to utilize. By combining technological information with the economic data supplied by the agency each firm can find its optimal solution. Note that the solution involves choosing the optimal size of firm as well as the optimal rate of production within the firm. If the agency varies the output price only, the long run marginal cost curve is the locus of optimal solutions for each firm. As pointed out on pages 217–18, we cannot predict that a firm will have long-run decisions solely on present conditions and that it will build a plant for the optimal level of output under current prices. To complete the model for the industry we shall, for the present, go along with the frequently used assumption that the supply curve of each firm coincides with the long-run marginal cost curve beyond minimal average cost. If the output function shows constant returns to scale, the long-run marginal cost and average cost curves are coincident horizontal lines. One size of firm is as efficient as any other, so entrepreneurs cannot decide on the basis of price and cost data alone how far to expand. Constant returns to scale over an indefinitely wide range of output are highly improbable and can be justified only as a convenient first approximation in economic model building. What is more likely is that diminishing returns ultimately set in. For the number of firms to remain large and the industry to be purely competitive, minimal average cost for the firm must occur at a level of output that is small relative to the total quantity demanded at a price equal to minimal average cost.

There is a temptation to follow the precedent of adding the supply curves of the firms horizontally and calling the result the long-run supply curve for the industry. Such a procedure implies that the number of firms in the industry must remain fixed. In the long run or planning period there is no justification for limiting the roster of firms to those already in the industry. Unless there are sufficiently high barriers to entry and to exit, firms may move into or out of the industry. The difficult problem is to identify potential entrants and to determine the amounts of the given product they will choose to produce after entry. One possibility is to interrogate all firms as to the amounts they wish to produce of every product at given sets of prices. Even this solution is not entirely satisfactory since it limits potential entrants to the existing population of businesses. New firms may spring up to take advantage of the opportunities for profit. However, when analyzing one industry, the existing population of firms does provide a sufficiently large supply of potential entrants, so we shall not consider the formation of new firms.

What attracts firms into an industry is the prospect of profits. This tendency is sometimes formalized by introducing the concept of the normal rate of profit, the minimal level below which firms would not choose to enter. Entry is then explained by the difference between the prospective rate of profit and the normal rate. Unless the normal rate is defined and measured independently, the reasoning is clearly circular. One way of fixing the normal rate is to equate it to the rate that can be earned in other industries. Generally, the rate of profit will vary from industry to industry and firm to firm, so some form of averaging has to be used. To keep the model simple and to focus attention on the essentials of entry, we shall make the simplifying assumption of a uniform rate of profit prevailing elsewhere in the economy. In reality, industries may differ significantly in degree of risk or other factors, and the industry under study may attract entrants only if the prospective rate of profit is considerably above the rate prevailing elsewhere. To show in precise form what is only a general tendency, we shall take the difference between prospective profits in the industry under study and the rate earned in other industries to be the sole motive for the migration of firms.

In interrogating firms already in the industry and potential entrants, the central agency includes the normal rate of profit in the economic data. Each entrepreneur, knowing the rate of profit he can expect elsewhere, can decide whether he wishes to enter or remain in the industry under study. In the process of deciding, each entrepreneur must determine the most profitable size of firm and most profitable rate of output within that firm. To generate the long-run supply curve for the industry, the price of the product is varied systematically with input prices and the normal rate of profit held constant. The long-run supply curve shows the aggregate amounts that all present firms and all potential entrants wish to supply from optimally designed productive facilities.

If all firms, actual or potential, have the same technological conditions, difficulties arise. Depending on the output price, the rate of profit for all firms in the industry under study exceeds, equals, or falls short of the normal rate. When the normal rate of profit is treated as an opportunity cost and included in total cost, as it properly should be, the equivalent relationships are that the market price exceeds, equals, or falls short of minimal average cost. The three possibilities are that all firms wish to enter, all are indifferent about entering, or none wishes to enter. As in the case of constant returns to scale, there is no meaningful long-run supply curve, only the indeterminacy of a horizontal line at a price equal to minimal average cost. Here, however, the horizontal line portrays variations in the number of equally efficient firms.

The process of entry can be very unstable if firms react quickly. Fortunately, the seriousness and short-run irreversibility of the decision slows down the reaction of firms. Also, it is clear that the tâtonnement process, which portrays short-run market behavior, is not appropriate for long-run variation in the size and number of firms, since excess supply is virtually unlimited above the equilibrium price. Instead of making the price dependent on the difference between quantity demanded and quantity supplied, we must make the entry of new firms depend on the difference between the selling price and minimal average cost. The larger the difference, the greater will be the excess of prospective over normal profits, and the higher the incentive to enter. If potential entrants respond moderately to high prospective profits, the excess of price over minimal average cost will decline gradually instead of being reversed by a sudden influx of firms. The decline in price reduces the incentive to enter and the rate of entry, so the industry may ease toward the long-run equilibrium in which price equals minimal average cost for every firm. The results for both firm and industry are graphed in Figure 16–6. The equilibrium could also be attained, as in a stable cobweb process, by a moderate overshoot of the equilibrium point followed by the exit of firms. Observation of our economic system shows that this does occur, but the subsequent liquidation or shift of capacity makes the attainment of equilibrium more difficult.

The long-run equilibrium of the industry shows all firms of optimal size having been designed to produce at the minimum point of the average cost curve. The process of entry does not explain how this result is achieved. Consider the case of an early entrant who decides to come in when the output price is still high. Under prevailing conditions, the most profitable scale of firm occurs beyond minimal average cost, where long-run marginal cost

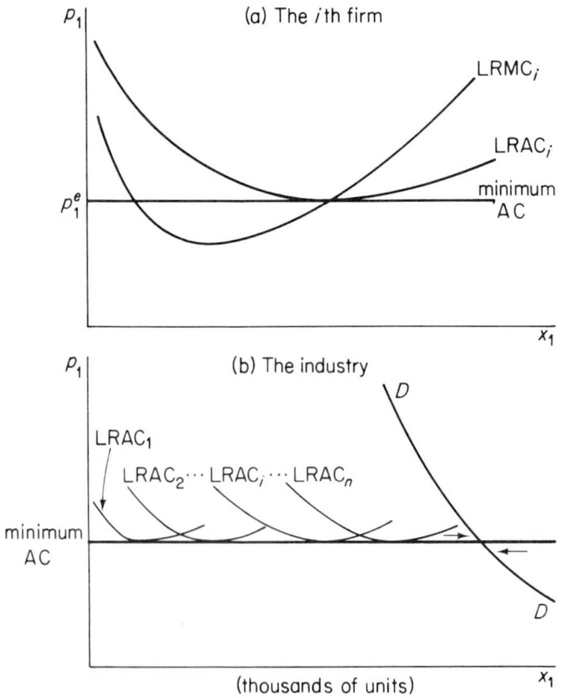

Fig. 16-6 Long-Run Adjustment of Number of Firms to Difference Between Minimum Average Cost and Price

equals the high price. If early entrants choose the currently most profitable scale of firm, they will be overly large and inefficient. Equilibrium can only come when this capacity is scrapped and replaced. Firms entering an industry or building new capacity cannot base decisions on current prices alone but must try to assess the conditions they are likely to face over the life of the venture. So long as they are aware that other firms can also enter, they will not expect present prices to persist. One effective way of hedging against future declines in price is to choose initially the optimal or most efficient scale. In so doing, an entrepreneur foregoes short-run profits but avoids any unnecessary losses and minimizes such losses as may be unavoidable. Under such conservative decision making, which is plausible in the highly risky situation of entering a new industry or building new capacity, the long-run equilibrium can be attained without waiting for the scrapping or withdrawal of productive capacity, provided that input prices do not change during the process of entry. Supply, however, does not coincide with marginal cost.

The foregoing long-run model for a purely competitive industry rests on the simplifying assumption that all inputs have horizontal market reaction curves. The treatment of profits and entry also implies a horizontal market reaction curve for entrepreneurship or the number of firms. Expansion or contraction of the industry under study is regarded as having no effect on the profit earned in other industries. For all inputs, including entrepreneurship, the uniform internal prices within the industry are equated to the given external prices. The amount of any input going to one firm does not affect the amounts available to other firms, so there is no problem of allocating scarce inputs within the industry. Whether the amounts of the inputs garnered by the industry are in any sense optimal can be determined only by examining the overall pattern of allocation in the economy as a whole. To do this we must drop the assumption of constant external prices and allow all markets to adjust in a model of general equilibrium.

The significance of long-run equilibrium for a purely competitive industry needs careful examination. What has been shown is that the economic model of the industry does possess a long-run equilibrium under the highly simplified conditions of constant prices for all inputs and an invariant demand curve for the product. If the model did not possess an equilibrium under such conditions, its validity would be questionable. Hence, the demonstration that an equilibrium exists provides some very minimal assurance of the correctness of the model.

Although the equilibrium exists, the possibility of its attainment is negligible. Even under the highly simplified conditions, it may be necessary for long-lived capacity to depreciate, be scrapped, and be replaced. With varying prices for the inputs, the problem becomes greater. At any stage in the expansion of the industry, the price for any specific input with rising supply curve will be less than the final equilibrium price. Firms entering during early stages will have no way of knowing what will prove ultimately to be the optimal size. They will be induced by the low input price to build what will prove to be uneconomically large facilities. The difficulty is compounded by changes elsewhere in the economy, which may be the result of the industry's own expansion. The attainment of equilibrium would be plausible only if past decisions could be wiped out more quickly than by waiting for plants to be scrapped.

What has been shown, then, is that, with constant external prices, an invariant demand curve, and unchanging technology, there exists a long-run equilibrium for a purely competitive industry. With no barriers to entry, the search for profits impels firms toward it. Obviously, the equilibrium is unlikely to be attained since conditions will not remain unchanged for a long enough time. The industry is at best taking aim on a moving target. What is most likely is that growth factors will be present—rising population and income and improving technology. The equilibrium output then shows a rising trend over time. The long-run equilibrating tendency acquires new significance. An industry that adjusts toward its long-run equilibrium under stationary conditions is more likely to move toward rather than away from the long-run equilibrium growth path.

EXERCISES

1. *The Market Reaction Curve for an Output*

(a) All m firms in a purely competitive industry have identical output supply curves of the form $x_j^S = gp = 1p$, where x_j^S denotes the amount supplied by a typical firm. Write the supply curve of $m-1$ firms and the rate of change of quantity supplied with respect to price.

(b) The total number of firms is $m = 100$. The market demand curve is $x^D = 1000-1p$. Find the equilibrium price and quantity when only $m-1$ firms supply output. Derive the equation for the market reaction curve of the mth firm. Show graphically the derivation of the market reaction curve. Write in both symbolic and numerical form the rate of change of market price with respect to the mth firm's output.

(c) If the mth firm takes the market price as given and enters the market, how much will it supply? To what level will the market price fall? Find the equilibrium price when all m firms produce and calculate the amount of the adjustment that must occur to reach equilibrium.

(d) Find the slope of the mth firm's market reaction curve under the following sets of conditions: $m = 200$, $x^D = 2000-p$; $m = 1000$, $x^D = 10000-p$.

(e) To show the influence of demand elasticity on the market reaction curve first go back to (b) and calculate the elasticity of demand at the equilibrium price and quantity supplied by $m-1$ firms. What must the slope of the market demand curve be for an elasticity of -1? What is the effect on the slope of the market reaction curve for the mth firm?

(f) Summarize the hypothesis about the decision making of the purely competitive firm and relate it to the relevant conditions, including the slope of the typical firm's supply curve.

2. *The Market Reaction Curve for an Input*

(a) All m firms in a purely competitive industry have identical demand curves for an input of the form $z_j^D = a - hc = 10 - 1c$, where j denotes a typical firm and c is the input price. Write the demand curve for $m-1$ firms and the rate of change of quantity demanded with respect to price.

(b) The number of firms is $m = 101$. The input is specific to the industry and the supply curve is $z^s = sc = 100c$. Find the equilibrium price and quantity when only $m-1$ firms demand the input. Derive the equation for the market reaction curve for the mth (101st) firm. Show graphically the derivation of the market reaction curve for an input. Write in both symbolic and numerical form the rate of change of the market price with respect to the quantity demanded by the mth firm.

(c) Explain how changes in the number of firms, changes in the slope of the supply curve, and changes in the slope of the demand curve for the typical firm affect the market reaction curve for the mth firm.

(d) Assume that the input is shared by many industries and that the demand curves of part (a) applies to industries rather than firms. Explain how to derive a market reaction curve for an industry. What are the implications of replacing an industry's market reaction curve by a horizontal approximation at the going price? In what significant ways does a market reaction curve for an industry differ from that of a firm within an industry?

3. *Equilibrium and Optimality with a Constant Input Price*

A single-product, purely competitive industry uses one variable input z_1, which is available at a constant price. That is, we assume, as a first approximation, that the industry has a horizontal market reaction curve.

(a) Let $\bar{a}_1$ be the typical firm's marginal requirement for the first input and $\bar{e}_1$ be the marginal productivity. How are the two related? If c_1 is the input price and p is the output price write the expressions for marginal cost w and marginal revenue productivity y_1. Express the optimality condition for the firm in two equivalent ways.

(b) For all firms the marginal requirement for the input is the same linear function of output: $\bar{a}_1 = kx$. Write the equation for the marginal cost curve of one firm. Explain precisely how to convert the marginal cost curve into a supply curve, expressing quantity supplied as an explicit function of price.

Write the equation for the supply curve of the industry. Show graphically for a few firms the procedure for deriving the industry supply curve. Explain why all firms must have the same marginal cost at all points on the industry supply curve.

(c) If all firms in the industry were plants owned by a single firm, what could you infer from equal marginal cost about the allocation of output quotas among plants? About the total amount of the variable input employed by the firm? Suppose that the firm kept total output constant but varied the assignment of output quotas to plants. What would happen to the use of the variable input by the firm?

Transferring the results to the industry, what optimizing problem for the industry does the attainment of equilibrium solve? Assume that the demand curve for the product shifts over the entire permissible range and that the industry attains equilibrium at every position of the demand curve. What function for the industry as a whole does the locus of all equilibria implicitly generate?

(d) All firms in the industry are taxed at the same rate of t dollars per unit supplied. Show that the optimum for a typical firm can be expressed either by adding the tax to marginal cost or subtracting it from the market price. What happens to the aggregate output? Does the allocation of the new total output among firms become nonoptimal?

The firms are taxed at different rates but in such a way as to cause the same change in the aggregate output. What can you infer about the allocation of output among firms and the use of the variable input by the industry?

4. *Equilibrium and Optimality with a Specific Input*

A single-product, purely competitive industry uses one variable input z_1 that is specific and in vertical supply.

(a) Let $\bar{a}_1$ be the typical firm's marginal input requirement and e_1 be the marginal productivity. How are the two related? If c_1 is the input price and p is the output price, write the expression for marginal cost w and the marginal revenue productivity y_1. Express the optimality conditions for the firm in two equivalent ways.

(b) For all firms the marginal productivity of the variable input is the same linear function of the amount used: $\bar{e}_1 = b - dz_1$. Write the equation for the marginal revenue productivity curve. Explain precisely how to convert the marginal revenue productivity curve into a demand curve, expressing quantity demanded as a function of the input price.

Write the equation for the input demand curve of the industry. Show graphically for a few firms the procedure for deriving the industry demand curve. Explain why the marginal revenue productivity must be equal in all firms at every point on the demand curve.

(c) If all firms in the industry were plants owned by a single firm, what could you infer from the equality of the marginal revenue productivity about the allocation of the input among plants? About the total output produced by the firm? Suppose that the firm chose a different allocation among plants of the same total supply of the input. What would happen to the output produced?

Transferring the results to the industry, what optimizing problem for the industry is solved when equilibrium is attained in the input market? Assume that the quantity of the specific input varies over the entire usable range and that the industry reaches equilibrium at each quantity. What function for the industry as a whole does the locus of all possible equilibria implicitly generate?

(d) All firms in the industry pay a tax of t dollars for every unit of the input used. Show that the optimality condition for a single firm can be expressed either by subtracting the tax from the marginal revenue productivity or adding it to the market price. What is the effect on the equilibrium of the industry and the optimality of the allocation of the input?

The firms are taxed for their use of the input but at different rates. What can you infer about the allocation of the input among firms and the aggregate output?

5. *The Adjustment Process for an Industry*

A single-product, purely competitive industry uses one fixed and one variable input. It is initially in equilibrium when the demand for the product increases. Describe the process of adjustment under each of the following supply conditions for the variable input:

(a) The market reaction curve for the industry is assumed to be horizontal.
(b) The input is specific to the industry and in vertical supply.
(c) The input is specific and has a rising but not vertical supply curve.

6. *Optimality of Equilibrium for a Multiproduct Industry*

(a) A single-plant firm jointly requires two inputs and jointly produces two outputs. With both inputs fixed, what condition has to be satisfied for a solution to the technological optimizing problem? What function does the set of all solutions generate and what is its graph? Write in full the expression for the slope of the contour.

Extend the results to a firm that produces jointly the same two outputs in each plant, and utilizes two inputs fixed in amount to the firm. What function for the firm as a whole does the set of all optimal solutions generate? What is the effect on the function of nontransferable inputs fixed within plants?

Show how the equilibrating mechanism for the industry extends to an industry of single-plant firms the results obtained previously for a multiplant firm.

(b) Hold both outputs constant and write the results of the technological optimizing problem for a single-plant firm. Explain how the results can be extended successively to a multiplant firm and a multifirm industry.

(c) Follow the general instructions of (a) and (b), holding one input and one output constant.

17

General Equilibrium for the Economy: Existence and Stability

In the partial equilibrium analysis of a single industry, we hold constant the prices of all products not sold by the industry and the prices of all inputs either not used by the industry under study or shared by it with other industries. Even if the markets for the remaining products and for the inputs are in equilibrium initially, they will not remain in that state. In partial equilibrium analysis the adjustment processes in these markets are suspended temporarily while the market or markets under study come into equilibrium. But this equilibrium cannot persist when adjustment does take place in the remaining markets, since the demand and supply curves shift. One market can be truly and permanently in equilibrium only if all are. Thus, we are inevitably led to ask whether all markets can be in equilibrium. Does there exist any set of prices at which supply simultaneously equals demand in every market? This is the problem of *existence of equilibrium.* Related to it is the question of *stability of equilibrium.* If prices are not at equilibrium levels, will they change in such a way as to converge toward those levels?

In the present chapter we continue to use a simplified version of the economy in which all firms buy only primary inputs from consumers and sell their outputs only to consumers. Chapter 18 analyzes the Leontief input-output system, which focuses primarily upon the sale of intermediate commodities, or produced inputs, from one firm to another. The two chapters fit together into an expanded and more realistic model of the economy. But it will also be shown that, in equilibrium, the intermediate transactions cancel out and leave only the transactions between producers and consumers. Thus, the results of the present chapter remain valid when the economy is expanded to include sales between firms.

THE INTERRELATION OF ALL MARKETS

In studying the allocation of inputs among industries, we shall take advantage of certain simplifications in the model for each industry. Diversity of technological conditions and diversity in the ratio of fixed inputs from firm to firm affect the actual *pattern of allocation*, but these diversities do not alter the *process of allocation*. To focus attention on the process, we make the simplifying assumptions that each industry has a single constant-returns-to-scale output function and that the inputs fixed within firms are distributed among them in the same ratio. By the operation of the market mechanism, all inputs variable to the firms but specific to the industry are then allocated among firms in an identical ratio and in amounts proportional to the size of the firms. The criterion of maximum efficiency is satisfied for both types of inputs. There is no possible redistribution of these inputs that will increase output in a single-product industry or increase one output, except at the expense of the others, in a multiproduct industry.

There remain the primary inputs shared by most or all industries. The prices of these primary inputs are the major determinant of the level and distribution of income. In the partial analysis of a single industry we could allow the effects of price changes to seep into the rest of the economy and disappear. But changes in the prices of primary inputs have a feedback too significant to be ignored. We must deal instead with an interrelated system of markets in which any change in one market is also recorded in other markets. Every economic unit sells in some markets and buys in others. Any increase in receipts as seller returns to the system as increased purchases. The fact that every buyer is a seller ties the system of markets together into a consistent general pattern. Economic units carry out their roles as buyers and sellers regardless of whether the entire economic system is or is not in equilibrium. The general pattern of interdependency of markets is inherent in the basic nature of the economic system and does not depend on its ability to attain simultaneous equilibrium in all markets.

For a simple illustration of the general relationship among markets we take a model with two final outputs and two primary inputs. A purely competitive industry composed of single-product firms turns out each product separately but uses both primary inputs jointly. There are four interdependent markets in which buyers and sellers confront each other. In general, the quantity demanded and the quantity supplied of each input and output depends on all prices in the system. The demand and supply curves for any one commodity require fixed levels for all remaining prices. Specifically, once prices are determined for both outputs and for the second input, the demand and supply curves for the remaining first input fall into place. As the price of the first input varies, all other prices remaining constant, consumers make successive optimizing decisions to determine the amounts they wish to supply at each price. Similarly, the demand curve is the aggregate of the quantities deemed optimal by each firm.

The demand and supply curves for the two inputs, shown in linear form in Figure 17–1, constitute an interrelated system. A change in one price shifts both curves for the other input. If, in turn, input or factor prices are given, each firm can make optimizing decisions on the amount to produce at each level of the output price. Since each firm chooses the output level at which marginal cost equals price, the marginal cost curve becomes its supply curve. The supply curve for the industry is the horizontal summation of the marginal cost curves, so all firms have the same marginal cost at every point on the supply curve for a product. In the special case of single-product firms, the prices of other products do not affect their decisions in the short run. Consequently, the output supply curves do not shift with changes in output prices. The demand curve for a product does, of course, depend on prices of other products as well as input prices. Figure 17–1 also displays pairs of supply and demand curves for the products.

A change in any one price shifts curves in all other markets and generates a chain reaction of further shifts. For the present, though, we are not interested in the shifts of the curves but rather in the positions they must assume relative to each other at any set of prices, however chosen. Any choice of prices for three commodities, or in general for $n-1$ commodities,

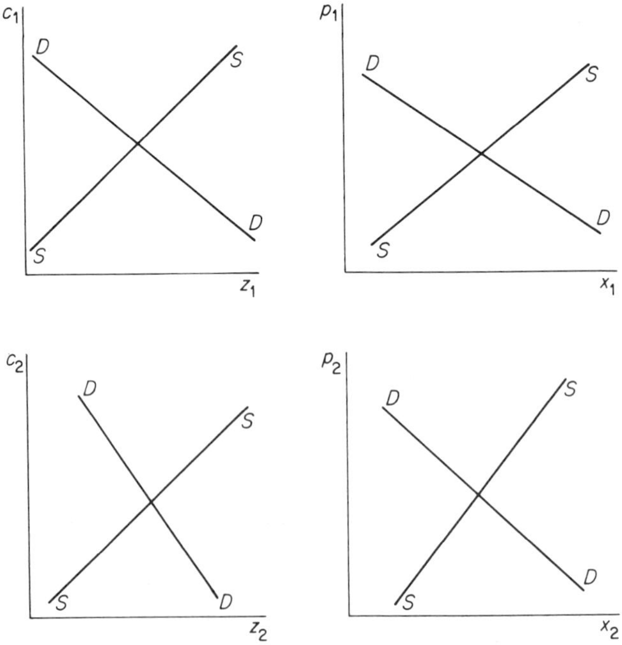

Fig. 17-1 Interrelated Supply and Demand Curves

fixes the positions of the demand and supply curves for the remaining commodity. The choice of its price determines the amount of excess demand or excess supply in its market. If our hypothetical central agency passes along a set of prices to firms and consumers, their independent optimizing decisions collectively determine a pattern of excess demand and supply in all markets. Regardless of the prices chosen, the pattern of excess demand must conform to the same general rule or law.

Walras' Law: An Accounting Identity

At any set of input and output prices, each firm decides how much to produce and what quantities of the variable inputs to employ. Under present assumptions, firms do not retain any part of the receipts but pay everything out to those who provide the inputs. Market prices determine the amounts going to variable inputs, and the remainder is paid to owners of the fixed inputs. The optimizing decision that each firm makes at a particular set of prices can be summarized in a simple account. The right-hand side shows receipts from the output it wishes to supply and the left-hand side lists the payments to the inputs the firm plans to hire. Since there are no transactions between firms, the accounts of all firms can be simply added or combined to give the following account for the producing sector as a whole.

Producing Sector

Expenditures or payments	*Receipts*
$c_1 z_1^d$	$p_1 x_1^s$
$c_2 z_2^d$	$p_2 x_2^s$
Total: $c_1 z_1^d + c_2 z_2^d$	Total: $p_1 x_1^s + p_2 x_2^s$

The account can obviously accommodate any number of outputs and any number of inputs. Since the number does not affect the nature of the results, the account omits the inputs specific to industries or fixed within firms. The decisions of each consumer at given prices also fit into a simple account. With no transactions between consumers, the individual accounts combine into the following account for the consuming sector.

Consuming Sector

Expenditures	*Receipts (income)*
$p_1 x_1^d$	$c_1 z_1^s$
$p_2 x_2^d$	$c_2 z_2$
Total: $p_1 x_1^d + p_2 x_2^d$	Total: $c_1 z_1^s + c_2 z_2^s$

The two accounts yield the following equalities of total receipts and expenditures for each sector:

$$p_1 x_1^d + p_2 x_2^d = c_1 z_1^s + c_2 z_2^s$$
$$p_1 x_1^s + p_2 x_2^s = c_1 z_1^d + c_2 z_2^d$$

Subtracting the second equality from the first gives

$$p_1(x_1^d - x_1^s) + p_2(x_2^d - x_2^s) = c_1(z_1^s - z_1^d) + c_2(z_2^s - z_2^d)$$

or

$$p_1(x_1^d - x_1^s) + p_2(x_2^d - x_2^s) + c_1(z_1^d - z_1^s) + c_2(z_2^d - z_2^s) = 0.$$

The value of the aggregate excess demand in all markets must be zero. The general relationship is known as *Walras' law*. From the method of derivation, Walras' law is clearly an accounting identity, valid for all sets of prices.

At any set of prices the demand and supply curves must shift into positions that satisfy Walras' law. If businessmen are planning to spend less on inputs than consumers expect to receive, then business must also be planning to supply a smaller total value of products than consumers are expecting to buy. For both consumers and firms, supplying less in one set of markets means demanding less in the other set, so the aggregate value of excess demand in all markets must equal the aggregate value of excess supply.

Various special results follow from the general relationship. If the aggregate value of excess demand is zero in $n-2$ markets, it must be zero also in the two remaining markets. Thus, any excess supply in one market must be matched by an equal value of excess demand in the other. If the condition of zero excess demand is extended to $n-1$ markets, the only possibility is zero excess demand in the remaining market. A very special case is equilibrium or zero excess demand in each of the first $n-1$ markets. The remaining market must also be in equilibrium. This does not imply that demand must equal supply in the nth market regardless of price. As shown previously, the demand and supply curves for any one commodity require the fixity of all other prices. The excess demand for each of the first $n-1$ commodities depends on the prices of all remaining commodities, specifically the nth. The nth price has already been specified and does not need to be determined. What Walras' law tells us is that we don't have to look at the demand and supply curves for the nth commodity to find the excess demand at the specified price. We already know that it is zero.

Zero Homogeneity and the Indeterminacy of the Price Level

There is indeterminancy in the level of prices, but it is not a consequence of Walras' law. An equiproportional change in all prices leaves the quantities demanded and supplied unchanged. To see why quantities demanded and supplied do not respond to equiproportional changes in all prices, we must go back to the optimizing decisions by consumers and firms. For consumers the budget constraint is

$$y = p_1x_1+p_2x_2 \qquad \text{or} \qquad x_2 = -\frac{p_1}{p_2}x_1+\frac{y}{p_2}.$$

Inputs are not shown explicitly, but a change in y represents an equiproportional change in input prices. If all prices change proportionately, neither the slope, $-p_1/p_2$, nor the intercept, y/p_2, is affected, and the budget line does not move. The consumer optimizes subject to the same constraint, so what was optimal before the price change remains optimal after. For firms the optimizing conditions take the form $p_1\bar{e}_{11} = c_1$, equality of marginal revenue productivity and market price for each variable input in every use. When input and output prices change proportionately, firms have no incentive to vary the amount of any input or any output.

In terminology borrowed from mathematics, the demand and supply functions are *homogeneous of degree zero* in all prices. As explained in Chapter 9, an output function is homogeneous of the first degree when proportional changes in all independent variables, which are the inputs, result in the same proportional change in the dependent variable, the output. A demand or a supply function shows either the quantity demanded or quantity supplied as dependent on all prices. Each demand or supply function is homogeneous of the zeroth degree since equiproportional changes in all independent variables, the prices, have zero effect on the dependent variable, the quantity demanded or supplied.[1]

The zero homogeneity of the demand and supply functions has several important consequences. If one set of prices reduces excess demand to zero in all markets, any positive multiple of those prices has the same effect. More generally, equiproportional changes in any set of prices leaves the *amount* of the excess demand unchanged in every market and causes the *value* of excess demand to vary in the same ratio as prices. Finally, equiproportional changes in $n-1$ prices must cause both the demand curve and the supply curve for the nth commodity to shift upward or downward by an amount proportional to the change in prices. Otherwise, the subsequent proportional change in the nth price would not leave unchanged the quantity demanded and the quantity supplied.

We do not yet know whether an equilibrium set of prices exists but we do know something about such a set, if one happens to exist. Any set of n prices that reduces excess demand to zero in $n-1$ markets must also eliminate

[1]In general, a homogeneous function satisfies the condition $f(tx_1, tx_2, \ldots, tx_n) = t^kf(x_1, x_2, \ldots, x_n)$. The degree of homogeneity is shown by k. When $k = 0$, $t^k = 1$, and proportional changes in all independent variables have no effect.

excess demand in the remaining market. An equilibrium set of prices has to satisfy only $n-1$ independent conditions. Second, there cannot be a unique set of equilibrium prices, since any positive multiple of those prices also clears all markets. Though usually presented together, Walras' law and the zero homogeneity property are traceable to quite distinct features of the economic system. Walras' law is a direct consequence of the interrelated character of the market system. It holds regardless of the way in which economic units make their decisions. By contrast, zero homogeneity depends on special features of the decision models for economic units. As we shall show in a later section, Walras' law may hold even though zero homogeneity is not present.

THE EXISTENCE OF GENERAL EQUILIBRIUM

The existence of equilibrium, as distinguished from its stability, does not require prices to respond in any specific way to market conditions. In essence, it does not even require the existence of markets. We can illustrate by the device of a central data processing agency that submits sets of prices to consumers and firms, receives data on quantities demanded and supplied, and tabulates the results. Equilibrium exists if it is somehow possible for the agency to hit upon a set of prices that elicits equal totals for the quantity demanded and the quantity supplied of every commodity. The existence of equilibrium means that at least one set of market clearing prices is there for the choosing. Of course, if one set of prices satisfies the requirements, so will any positive multiple of that set. In this sense, the equilibrium set of prices cannot be unique. But it may also be true that more than one set of *relative prices* clears all markets.

The basic problem in proving the existence of general equilibrium is the interrelatedness of the system. The demand and the supply curves for one commodity stay put only if all remaining $n-1$ prices remain constant. There is no possibility of obtaining the equilibrium set of prices by finding the market clearing price for each market in succession. As remarked earlier, the economic system does not resemble a jigsaw puzzle that is built up from pieces of fixed size and shape. As soon as we select the second piece, the first piece assumes a new size and shape.

A Linear Model of the Economy

For a set of two inputs and two outputs, equilibrium in the four markets can be illustrated by drawing geometrically simple and convenient curves, as in Figure 17–1. But the economic system contains many more than four commodities, and drawing geometrically convenient curves is a long way from providing a proof. The earliest attempts at proving the existence of equilibrium amounted to little more than showing that the equations and unknowns were equal in number. Such a method does have some validity for linear equations, so we shall initially take the demand and supply functions to be linear. The following equations are linear demand and supply functions for the first commodity:

$$x_1^d = d_{11}p_1 + d_{12}p_2 + d_{13}p_3 + d_{14}p_4$$

$$x_1^s = s_{11}p_1 + s_{12}p_2 + s_{13}p_3 + s_{14}p_4.$$

For a uniform terminology we are classifying both inputs and outputs as commodities and using the symbols x for quantity and p for price in all cases. The primary inputs become the first and second commodities, the final outputs the third and fourth. With all prices but the first constant, the equations become linear demand and supply curves for x_1, like those in Figure 17–1. The coefficients of the other prices, such as d_{12} and s_{13}, show how much the respective curves shift when those prices vary.

The condition for equilibrium is

$$x_1^d = x_1^s \qquad \text{or} \qquad x_1^d - x_1^s = 0.$$

Subtraction of supply from demand gives the excess demand function, whose coefficients are of the form $(d_{11} - s_{11})$. For the sake of a simpler and more familiar notation, we make the substitution $(d_{11} - s_{11}) = a_{11}$ for all coefficients. The excess demand functions for all commodities form the following set of equations:

$$a_{11}p_1 + a_{12}p_2 + a_{13}p_3 + a_{14}p_4 = 0$$

$$a_{21}p_1 + a_{22}p_2 + a_{23}p_3 + a_{24}p_4 = 0$$

$$a_{31}p_1 + a_{32}p_2 + a_{33}p_3 + a_{34}p_4 = 0$$

$$a_{41}p_1 + a_{42}p_2 + a_{43}p_3 + a_{44}p_4 = 0.$$

The economy is in equilibrium if a set of prices can be found that equates supply and demand or, equivalently, makes excess demand zero in all markets.

The excess demand functions are a system of four homogeneous linear equations in four unknowns. A special feature of homogeneous linear equations is that they always have a *trivial solution* in which all variables are zero. What we seek is a *nontrivial* solution. The linear excess demand equations satisfy the zero homogeneity condition. If one set of prices is a solution, so is any multiple t of those prices, since t factors out in each equation. The most that we can do is to solve for three prices in terms of the remaining price. When one variable, say the fourth price, is transferred to the right-hand side, the left-hand side consists of four equations in three unknowns. As demonstrated in Chapter 2, such a system has a solution only if the excess equation is redundant. Walras' law comes to the rescue and assures us that the fourth equation is indeed redundant. Any set of prices that eliminates excess demand in the first $n-1$ markets also equates excess demand to zero in the nth market and satisfies the nth equation. With the fourth equation dropped, the system becomes

$$\begin{aligned} a_{11}p_1+a_{12}p_2+a_{13}p_3 &= -a_{14}p_4 \\ a_{21}p_1+a_{22}p_2+a_{23}p_3 &= -a_{24}p_4 \\ a_{31}p_1+a_{32}p_2+a_{33}p_3 &= -a_{34}p_4. \end{aligned}$$

Unless the coefficients in one equation happen to be a linear combination of the coefficients in the other equations, the system can be reduced to diagonal form and solved. For the coefficients to be linear combinations of each other there must be an improbable degree of uniformity in the responses of all consumers and all firms. This we rule out, so the equality of equations and unknowns guarantees a unique solution. The existence of a unique solution depends only upon the coefficients on the left and not at all upon the constants on the right. Hence, p_4 may be assigned any value whatsoever, and the first three variables have unique values.

Nonnegative Prices and Quantities

One glaring difficulty remains. While two straight lines, if they are not parallel, must always intersect, they can intersect anywhere in two-dimensional space. The existence of solutions for any system of linear equations does not guarantee that all solution values will be nonnegative. Further, even if all prices are positive, they may equate demand and supply at a negative quantity. The nonnegativity of prices can be guaranteed, as in linear programming, by using inequalities, that is, by merely requiring that quantity demanded be less than or equal to the quantity supplied. When the strict inequality holds, the commodity becomes a free good with a zero price. This is as it should be. Which commodities, if any, are to be free goods can be specified only after equilibrium is attained. We can also borrow from linear programming a solution to the problem of negative output levels; commodities that require subsidies are not produced. Hence, a commodity is dropped if its supply curve or supply price lies above its demand curve or demand price at all positive levels of output.

For a meaningful economic equilibrium, we must replace the excess demand equations by inequalities and seek a feasible solution to the system. The problem resembles Phase I of the simplex method, which determines whether there is any set of nonnegative variables satisfying the constraints. (See the last part of Chapter 3.) Feasible solutions may exist even though the variables and the constraints are not equal in number, so the equality of variables and constraints no longer provides even a prima facie condition for the existence of economic equilibrium. We cannot actually apply Phase I of the simplex method to find a solution since the values of the coefficients are unknown and the number of commodities in an actual economic system still exceeds the capacity of computers. Further, any such solution would only show that an equilibrium exists for a particular set of coefficients. What is required is a proof that a feasible solution exists for any economically admissible values the coefficients may take. We also must recognize that linear demand and supply functions are a drastic and probably unwarranted simplification. Even if firms and consumers fit the linear programming model, supply and demand curves are not linear. The existence of equilibrium must be proved under more general assumptions that include linear models as a special case.

General Conditions for the Existence of Equilibrium

As soon as linearity is abandoned, the difficulties become much greater. While two nonparallel straight lines must always intersect once, two circles may meet once, twice, or not at all. Even with the simplest of nonlinear functions, the equality of equations and unknowns does not guarantee any solution, even a negative one. The exact mathematical form of the demand and supply functions is not known. All that is known about them is what can be inferred from the optimizing decisions of firms and consumers. What must be done is to prove the existence of equilibrium with essentially no more information than is provided by the assumption that firms and consumers are able to reach optimal solutions. The proof itself involves considerable mathematical complexity and subtlety and cannot be reproduced here. We can, however, outline briefly a set of conditions under which a purely competitive equilibrium can be proved to exist no matter how large the number of consumers, firms, outputs, and inputs.

All consumers must fit the broad pattern developed earlier, generally preferring more to less and preferring the mean to equally ranked extremes. It is not necessary that a consumer always prefer more to less with respect to every commodity but only that a consumer prefer more to less with respect to at least one commodity. There is, then, no commodity bundle that is preferred to all others and no satiation for the consumer. The indifference contours must be convex to the origin but can contain vertices and straight line segments. The penalty for allowing vertices and straight line segments is likely to be lack of uniqueness in the equilibrium prices or quantities. The amount of each commodity can vary continuously, being measured in real numbers, and the consumption set of each individual is closed, convex, and lower bounded. Either a preference relation or a utility function can represent the tastes of each consumer, but whichever one is used must satisfy the requirement of continuity. There are also certain not very stringent conditions imposed on the supply of inputs. No individual has an unlimited amount of any input, and no individual has zero income either because he has no inputs to supply or because those he can supply have zero value. Each consumer must of course choose optimally within the constraints imposed by the initial holdings of primary inputs and the prices established for these inputs.

On the production side, the most significant limitation is that there be no increasing returns to scale. If there are increasing returns to scale up to a point, equilibrium can exist provided that all firms operate beyond this point. The isoproduct contours must be convex to the origin but they can be piecewise linear, with the likely consequence of lack of uniqueness in the equilibrium prices or quantities. The quantities of both outputs and inputs must be continuous variables, and the output or input functions also must be continuous. There are also the easily satisfied conditions that production processes cannot be reversed, converting outputs into inputs, and that there can be no output without the use of inputs. The producing sector as a whole must satisfy the rather special requirement that net output may be zero for all products; all output may be used up as intermediate inputs within the sector. The reason for the requirement is to fill out a set, not to provide a likely outcome. Firms are assumed always to seek maximum net revenue and to pay to owners of inputs the entire revenue received.

Under the foregoing conditions, there must exist at least one set of non-negative prices that clears all markets. Since zero homogeneity is present, it is always possible to multiply any equilibrium set of prices by a positive constant and obtain another such set. Only relative prices are established. In addition there may be many distinct sets of relative prices that clear all markets.[2]

THE STABILITY OF GENERAL EQUILIBRIUM

Proving the stability of general equilibrium requires all assumptions needed to establish its existence. To these we must add the further condition that excess demand tends to raise the price in each market, excess supply to lower it. Any set of prices establishes a pattern of excess demand in all markets. The next set must have higher prices where there is excess demand, lower prices where there is excess supply, and unchanged prices where excess demand is zero. Except for the necessary addition of a market process, economists would like to be able to prove the stability of equilibrium with

[2]As noted earlier, it took about 80 years for a satisfactory proof to be constructed for the existence of competitive equilibrium. Although earlier efforts came close, the first generally satisfactory proof was that of Kenneth Arrow and Gerard Debreu in 1954. The conditions given in the text, although paraphrased in nonmathematical language, are essentially their conditions as simplified in later publications, particularly Gerard Debreu, *Theory of Value* (New York: John Wiley and Sons, Inc., 1959).

no stronger assumptions than are required to establish its existence. The aim has not been achieved and is not likely to be; some additional restriction, not deducible from the decision models of economic units, has to be placed on the relationships among commodities.

What economists have been able to do is to establish that a purely competitive economic system is necessarily stable if one very specific requirement is met. Between any two commodities the cross elasticity must be positive, and they must, therefore, be gross substitutes. There is one general pattern of reaction in all markets: a rise in any one price, with all other prices constant, increases the demand for every other commodity. A further consequence is that all demand curves must slope downward. All commodities will be gross substitutes if, for every consumer, the pure substitution effect dominates the income effect whenever they have opposite signs. But the condition can hold in the aggregate without holding for every consumer.

When a second commodity is being supplied rather than demanded, the effect of a price change goes in the opposite direction. For example, if commodities consumed and leisure are gross substitutes, a rise in price of a commodity increases the demand for leisure and reduces the number of hours worked at a given wage rate. Thus, the supply curve for labor shifts leftward. Rightward shifts of demand curves and leftward shifts of supply curves have the same effect; both increase excess demand or, what amounts to the same thing, reduce excess supply. In general, then, whenever two commodities are gross substitutes, a rise in one price raises the excess demand for the other commodity.

Proofs of stability are very lengthy and make use of rather advanced mathematics. In lieu of a proof we shall discuss in a general way the sources of instability and show why gross substitutability is an effective way of removing them. Historically, proofs of stability grew out of attempts to answer a related but simpler question: Can repercussions through the remaining markets destabilize an otherwise stable market?

The Feedback through Other Markets: Hicksian Stability

The starting point is a system of n markets originally in equilibrium. The price in one market, say the first, rises above the equilibrium level. Alternatively, the price could remain the same but either demand or supply conditions change in such a way as to leave the price above its new equilibrium level. The rise in the first price creates excess supply or negative excess demand in its own market. At the same time, the rise in the first price creates excess demand for the remaining $n-1$ commodities, each of which is a gross substitute. The effect may occur through a reduction in supply. When leisure and a commodity are gross substitutes, a rise in the commodity price increases the demand for leisure and reduces the supply of labor hours. By Walras' law any set of prices creates a pattern of excess demand whose total value is zero. The total value of excess demand for the remaining $n-1$ commodities equals the total value of excess supply for the first commodity. Further, every one of the $n-1$ commodities has a value of excess demand less than the total amount and, therefore, limited in size.

Suppose, instead, that there are some gross complements among the $n-1$ commodities. All cannot be, or the value of excess demand would not sum to zero. The total value of excess demand is still limited, but there is no longer the same limit on the individual components. A large negative excess demand for one commodity balances a large positive excess demand for another. The magnitude of the disequilibrium in any one market may be much larger.

Under universal gross substitutability the rise in the first price creates excess demand in all other markets. When any one of these markets adjusts under its own tâtonnement process, the price rises. The rise in price of each of the $n-1$ commodities increases the excess demand for each of the others, since they too are gross substitutes. In analyzing the reaction we may first allow one of the remaining markets to adjust, then two, then three, and finally all $n-1$. Although the specific results differ with the number of markets, the general effect is always a rise in prices.

At each stage of the adjustment of the remaining markets we can check the effect on the first market. Rises in any combination of the $n-1$ prices increase excess demand for the first commodity and reduce the excess supply. The crucial question is whether these induced price rises can turn the excess supply in the first market into excess demand and cause its price to diverge from its equilibrium level. From the zero homogeneity property we know that, say, a 10% rise in all $n-1$ prices will cause the demand and supply curves for the first commodity to shift upward by 10%. If, then, the first price had originally risen by 10%, the excess supply would be reduced to zero. The crucial question thus becomes: Can a 10% rise in the first price induce all remaining prices to rise, on balance, by more than 10%? Under universal gross substitutability, it cannot.

With some gross complementarity present, some of the $n-1$ prices may rise and others may fall. The magnitude of the changes may also be greater. Further, both the prices that rise and the prices that fall may increase the excess demand for the first commodity. This will occur if the commodities with rising prices are gross substitutes for the first commodity and the commodities with falling prices are gross complements. Thus, the repercussions on the first market may be much greater with gross complementarity present and can in fact be large enough to destabilize it.

In his pioneering treatment of multimarket stability in *Value and Capital* (1939), Hicks used the foregoing analysis as a basis for a definition of *perfect stability*. Specifically, an equilibrium is perfectly stable if a rise in one price creates excess supply for the commodity, and the excess supply persists as each of the remaining markets comes successively into equilibrium.

For a fall in one price there must be persistent excess demand. The term *imperfect stability* was applied if the adjustment of some of the remaining markets converted the excess supply to excess demand but the final adjustment of all remaining $n-1$ markets restored the excess supply. Perfect stability has turned out to be the more useful concept and has been the subject of much of the subsequent analysis.

Hicksian perfect stability gives theoretical validity to the method of partial equilibrium analysis. The reaction of a single industry or a single market to changes can be studied without attempting to trace the repercussions through other markets. When the feedback does impinge on the industry, it does not prevent the industry from attaining an equilibrium and, besides, the response of the industry to the feedback is no different from its response to any other change. We can go further and make predictions about the consequences of a change. A decrease in demand for a product or a cost reducing technological change both have the effect of creating excess supply at the price prevailing previously. By the method of partial equilibrium analysis we predict that the price will fall. Given perfect stability, the prediction of a fall in price holds up no matter how many other markets respond to the change.

Global Stability of the Economy

Despite its usefulness, Hicksian perfect stability is oriented toward a single market and toward changes that arise in a single market. A more general concept is global stability of the entire system of markets. Global stability means that, if all markets are thrown into disequilibrium simultaneously by any initial choice of prices, all markets together approach their equilibrium levels. So long as gross substitutability is everywhere present, there is no problem; the economic system is necessarily both perfectly stable in the Hicksian sense and globally stable.

Universal gross substitutability and balanced budgets, or some equivalent requirement, are very important conditions for stability in the economic system, and the reason is easy to grasp intuitively. Balanced budgets hold down the transmission of changes through the economic system. If a substantial number of economic units stepped up expenditures by more than the increase in receipts, the effects of a disturbance in one market could snowball as they passed through the economic system. It is well known that in national income models marginal propensities to consume greater than one have a destabilizing effect. Universal gross substitutability has the useful property of diffusing effects rather than concentrating them. A rise in price of a primary input that increases income also induces consumers to spread the higher income over all commodities. Additionally, by reducing the amount supplied of other inputs it holds the net increase in income to less than the amount provided by the initial price rise. Since any increase in income is allocated over all commodities, it is impossible for the increase in expenditure on any one commodity to exceed the rise in income. There is no possibility of greatly reinforced effects impinging on a single market in a way similar to the resonance effect that may occur when soldiers march in uniform cadence over a bridge and set it into violent vibration.

The preceding statements about the importance of gross substitutability and balanced budgets must not be misinterpreted. We are not implying that the economic system will be unstable under a tâtonnement process if one consumer spends a little more than his income or if gross complementarity is present somewhere in the system. Examples have, however, been constructed in which gross complementarity does destabilize the model, and the potential destabilizing effects of unbalanced budgets are clear from national income analysis. The system may be unstable, but does not have to be unstable, when gross complementarity or unbalanced budgets are present. As yet no way has been found to specify precisely the permissible amount of gross complementarity or budgetary freedom. What can be rigorously proved is that balanced budgets and universal gross substitutability do insure global stability under a tâtonnement process in every market.

When the equilibrium is not unique, the definition of stability has to be broadened. The system is globally stable if it approaches any one of its equilibrium levels from any initial set of prices. Lack of uniqueness due to zero homogeneity is easy to handle, since we may choose any one price and thus fix the level of all. More than one set of relative prices could raise complications but, under universal gross substitutability, the difficulties do not arise. When all commodities are gross substitutes there is only one set of relative prices that will clear all markets.

The existence of a unique, stable set of market clearing prices means that the dual pricing process always converges to a solution. Once again, the next step is to uncover the implied primal optimizing process or processes for both the consuming and producing sectors. The first stage is to extend the results obtained previously for a single industry to an entire producing sector composed of many industries. The Leontief input-output system is essentially a short-run linear model of the producing sector and permits a simple and specific determination of basic relationships, which we can then extend to more general models. Because the Leontief model is important by itself and because it is the most convenient introduction to a more general formulation, we shall explore the input-output system in Chapter 18.

THE PRICE LEVEL AND THE SUPPLY OF MONEY

In developing decision models for firms and consumers we first assume prices are constant and then let them vary to determine demand and supply functions. When concentrating on an industry, we take all other prices as constant. At each stage in building a model of the economy there is some prevailing level of prices to which the economic units can adjust. Once the pinnacle of general equilibrium is reached, all prices become variable; the problem of the absolute price level suddenly looms, and the carefully constructed model of the economy provides no solution. So long as all prices change proportionately, the absolute level of prices has no effect at all on the decisions of firms and consumers. Faced with this difficulty, nineteenth century economists sought a solution from outside the formal general equilibrium model, essentially by tacking on an additional equation to determine the absolute level of prices. Such a solution runs grave risks of inconsistency with the carefully elaborated general equilibrium model, and the economic literature contains a lengthy controversy on this topic. We shall not attempt to recapitulate the controversy but shall merely try to summarize the principal results that have emerged from it.

One solution to the indeterminacy of absolute prices can be quickly disposed of. In the linear model of the second section of the chapter, fixing one price determines all. Any one of the n commodities may be selected, and its price can be pegged at any positive level. The simplest procedure is to set the price equal to one and thus add the simplest of all possible equations, $p_j = 1$, to the system. The same method also works when the equations are not linear. The price of any one of the commodities can be fixed, but the commodity that happens to be chosen is called the *numéraire*. For every other commodity the price per unit becomes the number of units of the numéraire for which it can be exchanged. The use of a numéraire should be recognized for what it is, a simple device by which economists arbitrarily eliminate the indeterminacy of absolute prices from models of the economic system. Most especially, the commodity chosen as the numéraire should not be confused with money in the usual sense of circulating medium, means of payment, and store of value.

A second method, often used, is to add an equation relating the price level to the supply of money. The equation undoubtedly identifies an important determinant of the price level, but merely adding another equation is not the basically correct method of solution. What must be done is to reformulate the decision models of consumers and firms in such a way that the level of prices enters into their decisions either directly or indirectly. The general equilibrium model determines relative prices because changes in relative prices do influence the decisions of economic units. So long as the level of prices has no effect on the decisions of the individual units that make up the economic system, their decisions cannot determine the level. If a given change does not affect the objective function and does not affect the constraints, it leaves the optimal solution unchanged. The remedy, then, is to modify objective functions or constraints or both in such a way that changes in the absolute level of prices influence the optimizing decisions.

The absolute level of prices enters the utility function by way of real balances, which are the cash holdings of a consumer divided by some price index or, possibly, by the total value of expenditures. There are many reasons why an individual benefits from holding cash balances. Basically, an individual with no credit and no cash has to sell something before he can buy. He is not free to buy when he needs to or wishes to and is restricted from choosing the optimal temporal pattern of expenditures. Any binding constraint represents a cost and any easing of that constraint has a positive value. A typical consumer is likely to accept some slight reduction in total consumption in order to have greater freedom in buying.

The amount of cash a consumer requires depends on the prices of the things he buys. This is the justification for including real balances in the utility function. A fall in prices increases the size of the real balances, so a consumer can attain the same level of utility with part of the cash balances left over. The cash can be spent like income to attain a higher level of utility. Part may in fact go into slightly higher real balances in the new optimal solution. Proportional changes in all prices no longer leave consumers unaffected. If all prices rise with cash balances constant, a typical consumer spends less than income in order to build up cash balances. Conversely, a fall in the price level stimulates dissaving.

Expanding the utility function to include real balances and other financial assets[3] would take us far afield from our main purpose of developing the allocative model of the economy. We shall assume instead that the consumer recognizes the utility of cash balances but determines the amount to hold by a simple rule of thumb rather than by a formal optimizing decision. The simple rule is to maintain cash balances at some fraction of money income. The result is essentially the same as including real balances in the utility function and positing elasticities of 1 and -1 with respect to income and the price index. When cash balances are a constant fraction of income, the absolute level of prices affects the budget constraint, as will be shown shortly. To prepare the way for the treatment of cash balances and their relation to the price level, we wish first to introduce a system of monetary transfers among consumers and analyze the effects.

Monetary Transfer Payments and the Price Level

Whenever all individual budgets are balanced, both the accounting identity known as Walras' law and the zero homogeneity of the excess demand functions with respect to prices must hold. Under a system of fixed monetary transfer payments, Walras' law continues to hold but zero homogeneity does not. A system of fixed monetary transfer payments means that each consumer either receives in each period a fixed monetary supplement from other

[3]The topic is explored thoroughly in Don Patinkin, *Money, Interest, and Prices*, 2nd ed. (New York: Harper and Row, 1965).

consumers or pays a fixed amount to other consumers. The budget constraint for a typical consumer now becomes

$$y+t = p_1x_1+p_2x_2 \qquad \text{or} \qquad x_2 = -\frac{p_1}{p_2}x_1+\left(\frac{y}{p_2}+\frac{t}{p_2}\right).$$

Since the vertical intercept is $(y/p_2)+(t/p_2)$, proportional changes in prices do have an effect. If a consumer *receives* a payment, t is positive. A rise in prices reduces t/p_2 and lowers the vertical intercept. If t is negative, a rise in price reduces the amount subtracted from y/p_2 and raises the intercept. The budget constraint shifts and, as displayed in Figure 17–2, the amounts bought are not the same as before. So long as a consumer pays or receives fixed monetary amounts, the absolute level of prices does matter. A system of governmentally imposed tax and transfer payments furnishes an example, as does the well-known case of debtors and creditors, the monetary transfers being the interest payments. To be realistic, however, the latter example must also be expanded to include the repayment of debt, increases in indebtedness, and the effect of prices on the real value of financial assets and liabilities.

We now make use of the simple accounts introduced earlier in the chapter. Each consumer receiving a transfer payment enters it along with receipts of income on the right-hand side of the account. Each consumer

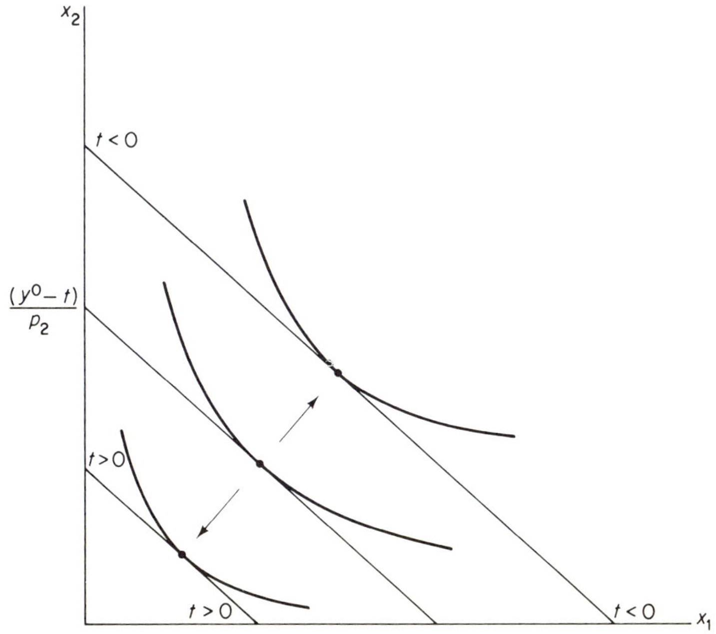

Fig. 17-2 Transfer Payments and the Budget Line

making a payment enters it on the left under expenditures or payments. When the individual accounts are summed into an account for the consuming sector, the total amount of transfers received on the right equals the total amount of transfers paid on the left. The two totals cancel, leaving total receipts of income equal to total expenditures on goods and services. Walras' law, which is derived from the equality of receipts and expenditures for the sector, continues to hold. But the market demand functions are no longer homogeneous of the zeroth degree. Zero homogeneity must be present in each individual demand function in order to be present in their sum.

A system of monetary transfer payments changes the distribution of income within the consuming sector. A different distribution of income also results from any change in the holdings of primary inputs. The earlier section on the existence of general equilibrium established the following conclusion: for any distribution of primary inputs that does not deprive any individual of income, there exists at least one equilibrium set of relative prices for the economy. But the set will in general differ with the distribution of income. Hence, for any set of monetary transfer payments that does not deprive any individual of his entire income, an equilibrium set of relative prices exists. But if all prices are doubled consumers no longer continue to buy the same amounts as before. Some buy less and others more of each commodity. There is no reason to expect that the changes will offset each other exactly, leaving excess demand unchanged in all markets. With fixed monetary transfer payments present, the absolute level of prices affects the constraints and, by affecting the constraints, changes the optimal solution. To each set of transfer payments there corresponds at least one set of equilibrium prices, but the set may not be unique. We shall, however, assume uniqueness since it simplifies the subsequent discussion without affecting its general validity.

Cash Balances and the Price Level

We shall now show that the introduction of cash balances has consequences similar to those of monetary transfer payments. An individual who makes a transfer payment must spend less than income, or save. So does an individual whose cash balances are below the desired level. Conversely, individuals who receive transfer payments or individuals who have excess cash balances spend more than income, or dissave. With cash balances introduced the budget constraint for a typical consumer becomes

$$p_1x_1+p_2x_2+(m^d-m^s) = y = c_1z_1+c_2z_2.$$

The expression (m^d-m^s) is the difference between the desired and actual levels of cash balances or the difference between the demand and the supply of cash balances for the individual consumer.

If the typical consumer always desires cash balances to be a constant fraction of income, say $m^d = dy$, the budget constraint becomes

$$p_1x_1+p_2x_2 = (1-d)y+m^s \qquad \text{or} \qquad x_2 = -\frac{p_1}{p_2}x_1+\frac{(1-d)y+m^s}{p_2}.$$

The final term is the intercept of the budget line. Equiproportional changes in all prices, or equivalently, in commodity prices and income, change the intercept and shift the budget constraint. The consumer's optimal solution does not remain the same, so the individual demand functions are not homogeneous of zero degree in all prices. The consumer continues to demand the same amounts of commodities only when each change in the price level is accompanied by a simultaneous proportional change in cash holdings (m^s).

We must next investigate what has happened to Walras' law. For this purpose simple accounts are again helpful. As before, each individual account shows on the right-hand side the receipts from sale of primary inputs, or money income. The left-hand side now contains, in addition to expenditures on goods and services, the current saving or dissaving of the individual consumer. With only one financial asset available, the current saving or dissaving of a consumer equals the difference, positive or negative, between the desired cash holdings and the actual amount. The individual accounts can be summed into the following account for the consuming sector.

Consuming Sector

Expenditures and saving	*Receipts (income)*
$p_1x_1^d$	$c_1z_1^s$
$p_2x_2^d$	$c_2z_2^s$
$M_c^d-M_c^s$	
Total: $p_1x_1^d+p_2x_2^d+M_c^d-M_c^s$	Total: $c_1z_1^s+c_2z_2^s$

The subscript c on the supply and demand for money denotes the consuming sector. The aggregate demand for cash by the sector, M_c^d, is the sum of the individual demands, and M_c^s represents the total amount of money held by all consumers. Firms may also find their actual cash balances larger or smaller than desired. For each firm the difference between desired and actual balances appears on the left-hand side along with payments for primary inputs. When the individual accounts are combined into an account for the producing sector, the aggregate difference between desired and actual cash holdings, $M_b^d-M_b^s$, appears on the left with the total payments for primary inputs. Readers may draw up the account. The equality of totals for each sector becomes

$$p_1x_1^d+p_2x_2^d+M_c^d-M_c^s = c_1z_1^s+c_2z_2^s$$
$$p_1x_1^s+p_2x_2^s = c_1z_1^d+c_2z_2^d+M_b^d-M_b^d.$$

By subtracting the second line from the first and rearranging terms, we get

$$p_1(x_1^d - x_1^s) + p_2(x_2^d - x_2^s) + c_1(z_1^d - z_1^s) + c_2(z_2^d - z_2^s) + M^d - M^s = 0.$$

The accounting identity known as Walras' law continues to hold but only when the aggregate demand and supply of money are included. It is no longer necessary for the aggregate value of excess demand to be zero in the commodity markets alone.

Since the demand for cash depends on income and through income on prices, the individual demand functions are no longer homogeneous of the zeroth degree in all prices. An equiproportional change in all prices causes an individual to save or dissave. The amount budgeted for expenditures changes, and the budget constraint shifts into a different position on the indifference map. If each change in a consumer's demand for money is matched somehow by a change in his own personal supply, expenditures always equal income and zero homogeneity is restored to the individual demand and supply functions. The restoration of zero homogeneity to the market demand and supply functions requires that every change in the demand for money by an economic unit be balanced by a change in that unit's own supply. Balancing changes in total demand and total supply are necessary but not sufficient. What equality between the total demand and total supply of money implies is that the aggregate value of excess demand is zero in all commodity markets.

General Equilibrium and the Excess Demand for Money

General equilibrium requires that excess demand be zero in all input and output markets. Hence, a necessary condition for general equilibrium is that the aggregate demand for money equal the aggregate supply. But this equality can come about in two ways. Every economic unit may have exactly the amount of cash it desires. Being zero everywhere, the excess demand for money is necessarily zero in the aggregate. Alternatively, the excess demand for cash by some economic units may balance exactly the excess supply of other units. Aggregate demand may equal aggregate supply even though no single economic unit is satisfied with its cash balances.

Although general equilibrium can exist under both types of zero excess demand for money, there are basic differences. Assume that the central agency not only submits a set of prices to each economic unit but also provides each unit with a figure representing its cash balances. When the agency finds a set of prices that clears all markets, that set of prices also determines the demand of each unit for cash balances. By selecting a total supply of money equal to the total demand and by supplying each economic unit with an amount equal to its own demand, the agency guarantees general equilibrium for the economy. Hence, general equilibrium exists in the sense that there is a set of prices, a total supply of money, and a distribution of that supply such that all economic units can make mutually consistent decisions. If the total supply of money is not at the correct level, equilibrium can be brought about by a proportional change in all prices, which does not affect the excess demand for commodities but causes the demand for money by each unit to change in the same proportion. Similarly, once an equilibrium level of prices has been found, a proportional rise in those prices will increase every unit's demand for cash. With the supply of money and its distribution unchanged, each unit tries to save and reduces expenditures, creating excess supply in every market. Thus, the level of prices is tied to the total supply of money.

The link just developed between the level of prices and the supply of money rests on a very special assumption. The supply of money must be distributed among economic units in the same pattern as the demand for money; the ratio of desired to actual cash balances must be the same everywhere. Only then can a proportional change in prices eliminate every unit's excess demand for cash balances. Suppose that the central agency has found a set of prices and a distribution of cash holdings that clears all markets and eliminates the excess demand for cash everywhere. It then changes the distribution of the cash balances. At the previously prevailing set of prices, some units now have insufficient cash and reduce expenditure on goods and services; others have excess cash and increase expenditures. There is no reason to expect that these changes will offset each other exactly, leaving excess demand zero in all commodity markets. If equilibrium is to exist, the agency must choose a new set of prices that is not a positive multiple of the old set. Any new set of prices cannot eliminate the excess demand for money everywhere. The most it can do is to bring the aggregate demand into equality with the aggregate supply.

Does such an equilibrium set of prices exist? To show that it does we rely on the previously discussed system of monetary transfer payments. Saving by an economic unit has the same effect on that unit as making a transfer payment, and dissaving is equivalent to receiving such a payment. An equilibrium set of prices exists for every system of transfer payments that does not deprive any individual of all income. For the same pattern of saving or dissaving the identical set of prices clears all markets. Different distributions of cash holdings determine different patterns of saving and dissaving, but each corresponds to a specific pattern of transfers. For our purposes this is a sufficiently cogent demonstration that equilibrium can exist in the commodity markets for any likely distribution of the supply of money.

There is one important difference between a system of fixed monetary transfer payments and a pattern of saving and dissaving based on changes in cash balances. The pattern of saving and dissaving cannot persist even though prices do not change. At the given level of prices each economic unit brings actual cash balances into equality with desired balances by saving or dissaving. With prices remaining the same each unit has no further incentive to alter cash balances and equates expenditure to income. Some units reduce expenditure and others increase expenditure, but there is again no reason to expect that the changes will offset each other exactly, leaving excess demand unchanged in all markets. The previous pattern of saving and dissaving altered the distribution of cash balances. For the altered distribution there is a new set of market clearing prices. When equilibrium rests on the equality of desired and actual balances for every unit, it can be destroyed only from outside, by changes in external conditions. When equilibrium rests only on equality in the aggregate, not only can it be destroyed from inside, but it must be.

The Supply of Money and the Level of Prices

Textbooks in economics frequently make the assertion that a doubling of the supply of money will double all prices. The economy is taken to be in general equilibrium initially with desired and actual cash balances everywhere equal. The supply of money is then assumed to double, but nothing is said about the specific way in which the new money enters the system. One possibility is that all individual balances are doubled. A new, unique equilibrium does exist at double the previous level of prices. But a doubling of the supply of money rarely, if ever, takes the form of a doubling of all cash balances. Under such an artificial restriction, the assertion that prices will double has little significance. What must be shown is that, no matter how the increase in money enters the system, ultimately it becomes redistributed in the form of doubled cash balances for every unit. The point at issue, then, is not the existence of equilibrium but its stability.

After the new money enters the system, the economy attains a temporary equilibrium in which all markets are cleared but only the aggregate excess demand for cash is zero. There is established a pattern of saving and dissaving by which some units are augmenting their cash balances and others are reducing them by an equal amount. The equilibrium cannot persist and is succeeded by a new set of market clearing prices and a new pattern of saving and dissaving. The process of redistributing cash among economic units must continue so long as the desired and actual balances are not equal for every unit. If a state is reached in which both prices and individual cash balances have doubled, the process of redistribution must cease. Further, given the uniqueness of general equilibrium, it is the only state at which the redistribution can cease. The case for a doubling of prices following a doubling of the money supply is plausible but not rigorous. We are not sure that the system will converge to the new equilibrium level; economic units might continue indefinitely to reshuffle the cash holdings. Economists have not yet proved the stability of general equilibrium with cash balances included.[4]

[4]For a discussion of the problem and a suggested solution see Paul A. Samuelson, "What Classical and Neoclassical Monetary Theory Really Was," *Canadian Journal of Economics/Revue Canadienne d'Economique*, I, No. 1 (1968), pp. 11–13.

SUMMARY

For a purely competitive model of the economy we have examined the key issues of existence and uniqueness of equilibrium, stability of equilibrium, and determinateness of the absolute price level. There remains the important question of the optimality of the resultant equilibrium, to be examined in Chapter 19. Because of the interrelation of all markets the economic system possesses a broad general property that is independent of its ability to attain equilibrium. If economic units in the aggregate return to the economic system as buyers all receipts they obtain as sellers, the aggregate value of excess demand in all markets must be zero. When economic units can save and add to cash balances or spend more than income by drawing down cash balances, the aggregate value of excess demand is zero only if we include in the equation the excess demand for money. If economic units can acquire other financial or physical assets, these must also enter the equation. For example, in national income analysis we conclude that, if supply equals demand in all commodity and input markets, then saving must equal investment.

A short-run allocative model of the economy rests upon several basic conditions: the aggregate supply of all primary inputs and their distribution over consuming units are fixed, tastes and preferences do not change, the technological conditions governing the conversion of inputs to outputs remain invariant, and no changes occur in either the population of firms or the distribution of the inputs trapped within firms. The existence of equilibrium requires little more than the ability of consumers and firms to optimize at any given set of nonnegative prices. As brought out in earlier chapters, the essential requirements for optimization are the convexity or concavity of the appropriate contours, nonsatiability for consumers, and the absence of increasing returns for firms.

We assumed earlier in the chapter that the inputs trapped within each industry were of uniform quality and optimally distributed among firms. They need not be optimally distributed among industries. The requirement for an optimal distribution is that the marginal revenue productivity or internal prices be the same from industry to industry. But marginal revenue productivities depend on prices. Hence, short-run equilibrium implies an optimal distribution of fixed inputs over all industries only if the marginal revenue productivities are everywhere equal when the market clearing set of prices is established.

When marginal revenue productivities are everywhere equal, there is no incentive to shift any input from one industry to another. If we add also equal internal prices for entrepreneurship, there is no incentive for firms to move to another industry. Such a state is not necessarily long-run general equilibrium for the economy. As pointed out in Chapter 16, we must also show that there is no incentive to increase the amounts of those inputs that are augmentable. Specifically, there must be no incentive for consumers or firms to save and no incentive for firms to invest in additional productive capacity. Under these conditions, long-run equilibrium is the stationary state in which all inputs have constant total supply and are allocated in the same way period after period.

If firms have an incentive to augment productive capacity and if consumers, firms, or both have an incentive to save, the economy cannot remain in a stationary state. General equilibrium for the economy implies a state in which there is no incentive to reallocate existing resources, including the amounts being devoted to new productive capacity. But the previous state of equilibrium cannot persist once the new productive capacity becomes available. The enlargement of productive capacity is but one facet of growth. The labor force also grows, and other primary inputs, such as raw materials, may be augmented by new discoveries or depleted by use. Finally there is research and technological change which feed upon themselves and display true growth trends over time. Long-run growth models must supersede general equilibrium models in the study of the economy, but the mechanism by which existing resources are allocated remains an important component of the models. Growth rates and growth paths depend in part on how effectively current resources are utilized.

EXERCISES

1. *A Graphical Illustration of Walras' Law*

(a) Draw a pair of supply and demand curves. Choose a price above the equilibrium level and draw a rectangle whose area is equal to the value of excess supply (negative excess demand). Choose a price below the equilibrium level and draw a rectangle whose area equals the value of excess demand.

(b) Draw a set of supply and demand curves for two inputs and two outputs similar to those of Figure 17–1. Choose a set of prices such that three markets are not in equilibrium. Use the area of the rectangle representing excess demand and supply to explain precisely where the fourth price must be.

(c) Draw on the same diagram new sets of curves that show how the curves must shift and the areas of the rectangle must change when all prices double.

2. *Transfers of Income Among Consumers*

(a) Consider first a single consumer whose indifference curves are parallel along rays and whose income-consumption curves are rays. From some initial base the consumer's income increases by a specific amount, say $10, and from the same initial base it decreases by the same amount. Show graphically that equal increases and decreases in income from the same base cause changes of the same magnitude in the quantities demanded of each commodity.

Suppose instead that the income-consumption curve is not a ray but bends upward. Show graphically that equal increases and decreases in income from the same base will not cause changes of the same magnitude in the demand for each commodity. Specifically, how do the increases and decreases compare for each commodity?

(b) Assume that there are two consumers with identical preferences and also with indifference curves parallel along rays. Show graphically that a transfer of money income from one consumer to the other leaves unchanged the quantity demanded of each commodity.

Next consider the case where preferences are identical but income-consumption curves bend upward. Draw a graph for each consumer and demonstrate that quantities demanded will not remain the same except in the special case where each consumer after the transfer has the same income as the other consumer before the transfer.

Finally, assume that preferences are not identical but that each consumer's income-consumption curves are rays. Use two diagrams to show that a transfer of income does not leave quantities demanded unchanged.

Make a general statement relating preferences to changes in demand when the budget lines of two consumers shift by equal amounts in opposite directions.

(c) A system of monetary transfers is in existence by which one consumer transfers to the other a constant amount of money per period. All prices and the money incomes of both consumers change proportionately from one period to the next. Write the budget equation for each consumer and compare the amounts by which the budget lines shift.

Use the results of (a) and (b) to state the conditions under which there will or will not be changes in the total quantity demanded of each commodity. What is the more likely outcome?

3. *Transfer Payments, Walras' Law, and Zero Homogeneity*

(a) Draw up simple accounts for a consuming sector and a producing sector when every unit makes or receives a monetary transfer payment. Show the sum of all transfer payments in the accounts, but do not assume that transfers necessarily sum to zero for the sectors or for the economy as a whole. From the accounts for both sectors derive an accounting identity including transfer payments.

(b) Suppose that monetary transfers do not sum to zero. Does Walras' law hold? What are the implications for the existence of equilibrium? Under what circumstances can firms and consumers, on balance, receive monetary supplements to income? Does Walras' law hold if transfers sum to zero?

(c) Let the monetary transfer payment that a consumer makes or receives be a constant fraction of his money income. Show that proportional changes in all prices and money income leave the quantities demanded unchanged. Assuming that only consumers make or receive transfers make a general statement of the conditions under which the aggregate excess demand functions are homogeneous of degree zero.

(d) Each consumer desires cash balances that are a constant fraction of money income. As a simplification firms do not hold cash. Write the expanded version of Walras' law.

At current levels of prices and money income all units desire larger cash balances than they have. Is this condition consistent with Walras' law? What must happen to prices?

Assume that all markets are cleared at the going prices but that consumers are not satisfied with their cash balances. What can we infer about the desired changes in those balances?

Give reasons for challenging or supporting the following statements: Saving and accumulating cash has the same effect on purchases as, in the absence of cash balances, making an equal transfer payment would have. Dissaving has the same effect on purchases as receiving an equal amount in transfers.

4. *Cash Balances, Walras' Law, and Market Equilibrium*

(a) In a two-input, two-output economy take all prices initially to be \$1. Draw up simple accounts for each of two firms and for each of two consumers. All units spend the total value of receipts. Choose figures for each unit's receipts and expenditures that satisfy Walras' law but do not give equilibrium in any market. By combining accounts verify that Walras' law is satisfied. Modify the figures to give equilibrium in every market.

(b) As a simplification assume that firms do not hold cash. Each consumer desires to hold cash balances equal to 10% of money income. Using the figures of (a) that give equilibrium in every market, calculate each consuming unit's demand for cash and supply each unit with an amount equal to the demand.

Double each unit's supply of cash. Give a careful statement of the argument that a doubling of all prices, and only a doubling of prices, will restore equilibrium. Show that the reaction of consumers to the change in the money supply causes prices to change in the right direction.

(c) Return to the original equilibrium in which all consumers have the desired cash balances. Make an arbitrary shift of cash from one consumer to another. Show that the accounts cannot remain in balance unless consumers change expenditures. Can the previously prevailing prices continue to be the equilibrating set of prices? Are they likely to? (For a detailed analysis see Exercise 2.)

Assume that a set of prices is established at which all markets are cleared and both consumers are making the desired changes in cash balances. Give a precise statement of the reasons why that set of prices is not likely to clear all markets in the next period.

5. *A Specific Linear Model of the Economy*

An economic system has two final commodities (x_1, x_2) and two primary inputs (x_3, x_4), formerly labeled (z_1, z_2). The following excess demand equations constitute a simple linear model of the economy:

$$
\begin{aligned}
-4p_1 + p_2 + p_3 + 2p_4 &= x_1^d - x_1^s \\
p_1 - 4p_2 + 2p_3 + p_4 &= x_2^d - x_2^s \\
p_1 + p_2 - 4p_3 + 2p_4 &= x_3^d - x_3^s \\
2p_1 + 2p_2 + p_3 - 5p_4 &= x_4^d - x_4^s.
\end{aligned}
$$

(a) Choose any convenient set of prices and check to see whether Walras' law holds. Are the excess demand equations homogeneous of degree zero?

(b) Check the system for redundancy by attempting to reduce to diagonal form. Verify that a solution exists that is nonnegative and unique up to a positive multiple. Write algebraic expressions for the set of all possible nonnegative solutions.

(c) Suppose that a barred coefficient of p_4 on the right-hand side had turned out to be negative, say $(-\bar{a}_{14}) < 0$. What would this imply about the existence of equilibrium? Convert the excess demand equations to inequalities, add slack variables, and reinterpret the result.

(d) Write in symbolic form, as in the text, the separate linear demand and supply functions for one of the commodities. By successively holding all prices but one constant, write each coefficient as the rate of change of one variable with respect to another.

Which coefficients are the slopes of the commodity's own demand and supply curves? What sign must they have for stability under a tâtonnement process in a purely competitive market? What sign must the excess demand coefficients have? Check the numerical example to determine whether each market by itself is stable.

(e) If two final commodities are gross substitutes, explain how a change in the price of one affects the quantity demanded and quantity supplied of the other. Extend the explanation to the combination of a final commodity and a primary input. If all commodities are gross substitutes, what sign must the appropriate coefficients have in the excess demand equations? Use the rates of change derived in (d). Check the coefficients in the numerical example for gross substitutability.

If all commodities are gross substitutes, what additional conclusions can you draw about the preceding numerical model of the economy?

18

The Leontief Input-Output System

The model of general equilibrium just developed utilizes only very broad assumptions that are essentially qualitative in nature. Indifference curves and isoproduct contours may take on any specific shape whatsoever, so long as they remain convex to the origin. All commodities are gross substitutes, and so on. Unfortunately, we can extract from a logical model only what has been put in originally, although in a different and often more useful form. The conclusions that can be extracted are comparably broad and qualitative in nature. For example, if the supply of an input increases we can infer that its price will be lower relative to other prices after the system settles down to its new equilibrium. Similarly, a shift in preference that increases the demand for a commodity will raise its price.

The preceding chapters have emphasized the general properties common to any competitive economic system. But economists are also interested in the special properties of the specific economic system they are studying. They need to know, as accurately as possible, the size of the response that the economic system and its component parts will make to precisely specified changes in underlying conditions. If increases or decreases in military spending are to be superimposed upon the pattern of private demand, it is important to be able to trace out the impact on all affected industries. Changes in tax or fiscal policies and substantial shifts in the balance of payments also initiate waves of repercussions through the economy that appreciably alter the pattern of allocation. To provide a quantitative prediction of the effects such changes will generate, we must employ a simplified first approximation to the economic system and endow it with specific quantitative data. The only detailed approximation now available is the Leontief input-output model.

The core of the input-output system is the sale of variable inputs by one industry to another. An industry could conceivably be so highly integrated that it used only primary inputs from the consuming sector and sold only final products to the consuming sector. Such a high degree of vertical integration has never been attained, and each industry typically buys some inputs from other industries and sells some of its output to other industries. There are, of course, wide differences among industries. Retail firms sell almost exclusively to the consuming sector, while basic iron and steel manufacturers sell very little. Products like paper, gasoline, and electric power are sold in large amounts both to other firms and to consumers. The interrelationships within the producing sector would be simplified considerably if a hierarchy could be established in which industries higher on the scale only sold to industries lower on the scale but did not buy from them. While such instances do occur, the general pattern is one of circular interdependence. Paper manufacturers purchase sulphur and electric power and also provide the supplying industries with stationery, data processing cards, and cartons. Zero purchases by one industry from another are a welcome simplification, but the model must allow for the possibility that each industry deals with every other industry.

In contrast to the input-output system the general equilibrium model developed previously has focused upon the interrelationships of consumers with producers. The two models are not antithetical but highly complementary. Together they give an expanded and more realistic version of the private economy, which consists of the interrelationships among firms and between the producing and consuming sectors. The private economy is itself embedded in a broader model that includes taxation and the purchase of goods and services by governments. Also, both the Leontief system and the general equilibrium model developed previously focus upon the allocation of variable inputs in the short run when productive capacity is taken to be fixed. The producing sector does not confine itself to providing firms with materials, supplies, and power; it also constructs plants and builds machinery. However, while purchased electric power is used as an input in the period when it is produced, plant and equipment generally are not. Since they do not feed back into the stream of production immediately, the durable capital goods turned out by the producing sector are treated similarly to the purchases by consumers or governments. Paralleling the investment decisions by firms is saving by consumers. Thus, the short-run allocative mechanism of the private economy is embedded in a broader process in which productive capacity is currently being expanded. Finally, many industries make sales outside the country and may also purchase from foreign firms. The domestic economy is but a part of the world economy.

An industry typically sells variable inputs to other industries and makes final sales to the consuming sector. As just noted, the producing sector also sells to governments and to foreign countries, and supplies firms with durable producers' goods. In constructing an input-output model, all such sales are regarded, like consumer goods, as being made to an outside sector distinct from the producing sector itself. In the interest of a simpler exposition, we shall analyze the interindustry system in a setting in which consumers form the only outside or final sector. By so doing, we shall be able to combine the input-output system and the preceding treatment of general equilibrium into a more detailed and realistic model of the private economy in the short run.

THE TRANSACTIONS TABLE

The first step in constructing an input-output model is to group firms together into industries. In practice this is a difficult task that requires much judgment and many compromises. We postpone discussion of the practical problems and continue for a time the simplification that the producing sector consists solely of single-product, purely competitive firms. Firms can then be grouped unambiguously into industries on the basis of output alone. Any one industry disposes of its product in one or more of the following three ways: adds it to inventory, sells it within the producing sector, or sells it as final product to outside sectors. In general equilibrium analysis, changes in inventories are not considered explicitly. A firm cannot continue to produce less than it sells without exhausting inventories. Similarly, a rate of production in excess of sales causes a steady pile-up of inventories. Short-run static equilibrium for the firm requires that inventories be at the desired level. In the transition between equilibrium levels inventories may well change, but general equilibrium analysis deals with states of equilibrium, once attained, and not the path between them. In tying the input-output model to the preceding general equilibrium analysis, we shall omit changes in inventories.

The sales within the producing sector are broken down into amounts sold to each of the industries comprising the sector, including the industry producing the output. Just as agriculture uses seed corn, any industry may utilize some of its own product. If there are only four industries and no change in inventories, a simple balancing equation, like the following, applies to any one industry:

Value of output of industry A
equals
sales to industry A plus sales to industry B
plus sales to industry C plus sales to industry D
plus
final sales to the consuming sector.

Each industry also uses variable inputs, some of which come from other industries and at least one, labor services, from the consuming sector. In general, the total value of output or total revenue exceeds total variable cost, and the excess represents such items as depreciation, interest payments, and the earnings of stockholders or other owners. We shall not stretch the model to include the process by which saving, including retained earnings and depreciation charges, is channeled into capital formation. We merely assume that productive capacity is maintained and that all net earnings on capital are paid out to consumers and spent on consumer goods. Like sales, the purchases of any one industry can be expressed by a simple balancing equation:[1]

Total value of industry A's output
equals
purchases from industries
A, B, C, and D
plus
payments for inputs supplied by the consuming sector.

Both types of balancing equations can be expressed conveniently in the two-way input-output or transactions table shown in Table 18–1. Each row represents the first of the balancing equations and shows the disposition of an industry's output. The left-hand entry in the first row contains the value of net output for industry A, the amount produced less the amount used within the industry. The next three entries record the value of sales to industries B, C, and D. The last entry on the right is the value of the amount sold as a final commodity to the consuming sector. Each column represents the second type of balancing equation and records the purchases from the other industries and the payments to the consuming sector. The essential core of the input-output system is the 4×4, or $n \times n$, table in which every industry appears once in a row as seller to the other industries and once in

TABLE 18–1

A Simplified Transactions Table (Billions of Dollars)

		Purchaser				
		Industry				*Consumers (final demand)*
Supplier		*A*	*B*	*C*	*D*	
Industry	A	90	7	20	3	60
	B	2	80	1	2	75
	C	12	5	65	8	40
	D	5	3	2	45	35
Consumers		71	65	42	32	210

[1]The equation depends on inventories of materials remaining constant. To the extent that inventories of materials are drawn down, the amount used exceeds the amount purchased, and the total value of output is larger than the total of purchases and payments.

the corresponding column as purchaser from the other industries. The entries along the diagonal show the value of each industry's net output.

The figures presented in Table 18–1 are hypothetical, but transactions tables have been constructed for many countries and for regions of countries summarizing actual transactions. The number of industries shown separately depends upon the availability of data, the cost of compilation, and the use to which the table is to be put. In practice, it is not possible to group firms on the basis of a single homogeneous product. Most firms produce more than one distinguishable product, some an almost unbelievable number. In a study of the United States Steel Corporation some years ago, a group of economists were able to identify "at least fifty thousand steel 'products' and a multitude of nonsteel items."[2] It is obviously out of the question to base an input-output table on separate products. We have to group products together and rely on a fairly high degree of stability in the ratio of the components.

When an input-output table is to be used for predictions, another limitation arises. The number of computations increases as the cube of the number of industries.[3] Even with modern electronic computers there are limits to the size of the table that can be handled, although these limits do not appear to have been reached as yet and, with advances in the art, may never be. The original Leontief system of 1936 contained only 9 industries. The official 1958 United States table contains 83 productive sectors, but a more extensive table showing 450 industries was prepared earlier from the 1947 data.[4] There is a projected 500–600 industry table based on 1963 figures, but it has not yet appeared. Even the largest input-output tables require the grouping together of many distinct products and many firms that might on purely theoretical grounds be assigned to separate industries.

Even if no further use could ever be made of it, a transactions table is extremely valuable in revealing the structure of the producing sector. The national income accounts record in detail the composition of final output but they purposely omit intermediate transactions. The transactions table is a valuable supplement to the national income accounts since it shows precisely how productive activity is distributed throughout the sector and how broad industrial groupings are related to each other. But the interindustry accounts are also used to construct a simple, quantitatively specified model of the economy and to predict how the economic system will respond to changes.

[2]Committee on Price Determination, *Cost Behavior and Price Policy* (New York: National Bureau of Economic Research, 1943), p. 93.

[3]R. Dorfman, P. Samuelson, and R. Solow, *op. cit.*, p. 264.

[4]The official 1958 United States table is in U.S. Department of Commerce, *Survey of Current Business*, 45, No. 9 (Sept. 1965). For an excellent summary of interindustry research up to 1959, see H. B. Chenery and P. G. Clark, *Interindustry Economics* (New York: John Wiley and Sons, Inc., 1959), Chapter 7. An excellent elementary discussion of the construction of transactions tables and their relation to the national income accounts appears in W. H. Miernyk, *The Elements of Input-Output Analysis* (New York: Random House, 1965).

THE INPUT-OUTPUT MODEL OF THE PRODUCING SECTOR

For each industry a column in the transactions table records the value of net output and the value of each variable input used in producing the output. A transactions table is converted to a table of input coefficients by the simple operation of dividing the total cost of each input by the total value of net output. Such a procedure can be rigorously justified only by some strong assumptions and drastic simplifications. We must, in effect, assume that the data were generated by a producing sector in which each industry consists of single-product firms using the same linear production process. If p_1x_1 denotes the value of net output for the first industry, c_2z_2 the total cost of the second input, and a_{21} the true but unknown input coefficient, then

$$\frac{c_2z_2}{p_1x_1} = \frac{c_2a_{21}x_1}{p_1x_1} = \frac{c_2}{p_1}a_{21}.$$

If both prices have remained constant over the period or have changed only proportionately, division by the price ratio yields a_{21}. Alternatively, we may follow the procedure of Chapter 7 and temporarily redefine each unit as the amount that can be sold for \$1. The ratio of the value sums equals the technological coefficient in terms of the redefined units. In general, these will not be conventional units but the quantities can always be reconverted after the analysis is completed.

The entries in an actual transactions table represent the total value of distinct products that are grouped together as a necessary simplification. When an entry in a column is divided by the total value of net output, the resultant ratio shows the amount that must be spent on the composite input for each dollar's worth of the composite output. Even though all prices remain constant, the ratios will vary if the composition of the input or of the output changes; the separate components must maintain the same ratio to each other.

This is an all-too-familiar problem in economics. The economic system contains such complexity of detail that it can be understood only after much simplification. To simplify or not to simplify is not the question, but how best to do it. The most prevalent solution is to group distinct quantities together into composites or aggregates. The aggregates must then be treated like single, homogeneous quantities or the advantages of aggregation are lost. Most economic models, and the results derived from them, are rigorously valid only if all quantities can be measured in invariant, homogeneous units. For example, most national income and aggregative growth models are strictly correct only if the nation's total output consists of a single, homogeneous product. The results derived from economic models are then given broader application by allowing the variables to represent aggregates. Such an extension is justified to the extent that the aggregates are so constructed as to behave approximately like single quantities. An extensive literature has developed on the correct principles of aggregation and its effects on inter-industry systems.[5] We shall not go further into the problems of aggregation but shall concentrate on an input-output model in which each industry turns out a single, homogeneous commodity rather than a composite. The results remain approximately correct when applied to an actual system in which there must be a considerable amount of aggregation.

A Linear Programming Version of Input-Output

In the simplest input-output model all firms in each industry use the same linear process to turn out a single, homogeneous product. The producing sector closely resembles the multiproduct firm of earlier chapters and can be successfully analyzed by the method of linear programming once we set up the constraints and the objective function. The producing sector seeks to supply the demands of the consuming sector. In this respect it resembles the version of the firm in Chapter 10 and has quotas to meet or exceed. The difference is that each industry in the sector sells to other industries, so total output cannot merely equal final demand. To meet a specified pattern of final demand, each constraint must have the form

Total output *equals or exceeds* total quantity
used as input *plus* amount of final demand.

The quantity used within the producing sector depends on the input coefficients and the output levels for every industry. Thus, the constraint for the first commodity is

$$x_1 \geqq a_{11}x_1 + a_{12}x_2 + a_{13}x_3 + a_{14}x_4 + q_1,$$

or

$$(1-a_{11})x_1 - a_{12}x_2 - a_{13}x_3 - a_{14}x_4 \geqq q_1.$$

In linear programming format, the input-output model becomes

$$\begin{aligned}
(1-a_{11})x_1 - \quad a_{12}x_2 - \quad a_{13}x_3 - \quad a_{14}x_4 &\geqq q_1 \\
-a_{21}x_1 + (1-a_{22})x_2 - \quad a_{23}x_3 - \quad a_{24}x_4 &\geqq q_2 \\
-a_{31}x_1 - \quad a_{32}x_2 + (1-a_{33})x_3 - \quad a_{34}x_4 &\geqq q_3 \\
-a_{41}x_1 - \quad a_{42}x_2 - \quad a_{43}x_3 + (1-a_{44})x_4 &\geqq q_4 \\
a_{01}x_1 + \quad a_{02}x_2 + \quad a_{03}x_3 + \quad a_{04}x_4 &= z(\text{min}).
\end{aligned}$$

[5]References cited on page 462 give an excellent summary of the topic.

The coefficients in the objective form are the direct labor coefficients, the number of man-hours required per unit of each output. The direct labor coefficients are found by dividing the wage payments in each industry by the total value of output. For analytical purposes, the unit of labor is then temporarily adjusted to the amount that sells for $1.

The presence of the objective function needs some clarification. Originally, an input-output model was regarded simply as a set of equations to be solved rather than as an optimizing problem. After linear programming appeared in the late 1940s, economists immediately recognized the formal similarity of an input-output model to the constraints in a linear programming problem. They also saw that linear programming could be used to eliminate from interindustry models the arbitrary restriction of a single process for each industry. The difficulty lay in attributing optimization to the entire producing sector, so the suggestion of labor minimization was put forward tenatively and hesitantly.[6] Previous chapters have shown that we need not be hesitant about interpreting an input-output model as a linear programming problem. The producing sector is similar to a multiproduct industry. As Chapter 16 established, if all firms of a multiproduct industry use the same prices in their optimizing decisions, the output levels will be produced with minimal use of any one input subject to constant levels for any other inputs. This is all we need at present to justify the inclusion of the objective function. Later, when we add choice of processes to the model, we shall give a more rigorous justification.

Since each output is produced by a single process, quotas are never exceeded and surplus variables never appear in the optimal solution. Elementary operations reduce the problem to the following canonical form:

$$
\begin{aligned}
x_1 \qquad\qquad\quad &= \bar{a}_{11}q_1+\bar{a}_{12}q_2+\bar{a}_{13}q_3+\bar{a}_{14}q_4 \\
x_2 \qquad\quad &= \bar{a}_{21}q_1+\bar{a}_{22}q_2+\bar{a}_{23}q_3+\bar{a}_{24}q_4 \\
x_3 \quad &= \bar{a}_{31}q_1+\bar{a}_{32}q_2+\bar{a}_{33}q_3+\bar{a}_{34}q_4 \\
x_4 &= \bar{a}_{41}q_1+\bar{a}_{42}q_2+\bar{a}_{43}q_3+\bar{a}_{44}q_4 \\
z &= \bar{a}_{01}q_1+\bar{a}_{02}q_2+\bar{a}_{03}q_3+\bar{a}_{04}q_4.
\end{aligned}
$$

The $\bar{a}$ coefficients in the first four rows show how much of each output must be produced to yield one unit of a final commodity. They summarize the totality of the interrelationships within the producing sector. For example, a unit of q_1 does not merely require an output level of one unit. The first commodity must also be supplied to other industries so that they may in turn provide the intermediate commodities needed for a unit of q_1. The first

[6]See, for example, H. Chenery and P. Clark, *Interindustry Economics* (New York: John Wiley and Sons, Inc., 1959), p. 82, or R. Dorfman, P. Samuelson, and R. Solow, *op. cit.*, p. 211.

commodity may also be needed in its own production. When q_1 increases by one unit and the entire producing sector adjusts to the new level, all output levels will in general have increased. The $\bar{a}$ coefficients in the first column show precisely how much each output must rise to sustain a one-unit increase in q_1. Since no substitution of processes can occur, the $\bar{a}$ coefficients remain constant for all levels of the final commodities. Hence, for any specified change in the pattern of final demand we can readily calculate the change in output levels that must accompany it.

As always, reduction to canonical form yields the quantity optimized as a linear function of the quantities in the constraints. The barred coefficients show the total amount of labor, direct and indirect, required for one unit of a final commodity. When q_1 is increased, more labor is required to produce the additional units. But more of x_1 requires more of x_2 and more of x_1 to produce the higher level of x_2. Every change in output levels calls for a change in the employment of labor. When q_1 increases, output levels everywhere in the sector must adjust to the change. After the adjustment is complete and the new output levels are just sufficient to sustain the increase in final demand, the total increase in labor everywhere in the sector can be calculated. It will be $\bar{a}_{01}$ units of labor per unit of q_1. The $\bar{a}$ coefficients in the input function are the marginal labor requirements of the entire producing sector.

GRAPHICAL PRESENTATIONS

For graphical presentation we shall drop the third and fourth products and use the simpler system

$$\begin{aligned}(1-a_{11})x_1 - \quad a_{12}x_2 &\geqq q_1^* \\ -a_{21}x_1 + (1-a_{22})x_2 &\geqq \quad\quad q_2^* \\ a_{01}x_1 + \quad a_{02}x_2 &= 0q_1^* + 0q_2^* + z(\text{min}).\end{aligned}$$

Like any other linear programming problem, such as the multiproduct firm of Chapter 7, there are two graphical interpretations. Figure 18–1 plots the column vectors $\mathbf{a}_1 = [(1-a_{11}), -a_{21}]$ and $\mathbf{a}_2 = [-a_{12}, (1-a_{22})]$ in final commodity or (q_1, q_2) space, as distinct from output or (x_1, x_2) space. When x_1 and x_2 are assigned nonnegative values, the two vectors generate the corresponding rays $x\mathbf{a}_1$, $x_2\mathbf{a}_2$ and form a cone. For the constraints to be satisfied, the point (q_1^*, q_2^*), or some point beyond it, must lie inside the cone. As the rays are drawn in Figure 18–1, the entire nonnegative orthant lies inside the cone of the production processes, so the constraints are satisfied exactly for any pair of nonnegative final quotas. In economic terms, the geometric result means that the producing sector can always hit upon output levels that will take care of internal needs and leave excess output to satisfy any pattern of final demand.

This is a sweeping and important conclusion, so we must determine whether it will always hold.

In plotting $\mathbf{a}_1$ and $\mathbf{a}_2$ we must take $(1-a_{11})$ and $(1-a_{22})$ to be positive. It makes no sense to consider technological processes that cannot satisfy their own requirements. Both $-a_{21}$ and $-a_{12}$ are plotted as negative numbers on the assumption that each product is an input to the other process. It is technologically possible for a process to yield both outputs jointly. When a process yields a commodity as output rather than using it as an input, the corresponding coefficient has its sign reversed. If either vector has positive components, the cone no longer contains the entire nonnegative orthant, and some patterns of final demand are not attainable.

A Leontief input-output model does not allow for joint production. Of course, joint products can and do exist, but we must remember that a transactions table based on actual data groups commodities together. In most cases, joint products belong to the same group, and the relations between them are lost in the construction of aggregates. The simplified theoretical model goes further and omits joint production processes entirely. Hence, each vector has one component that is positive and one that is negative, or possibly zero.

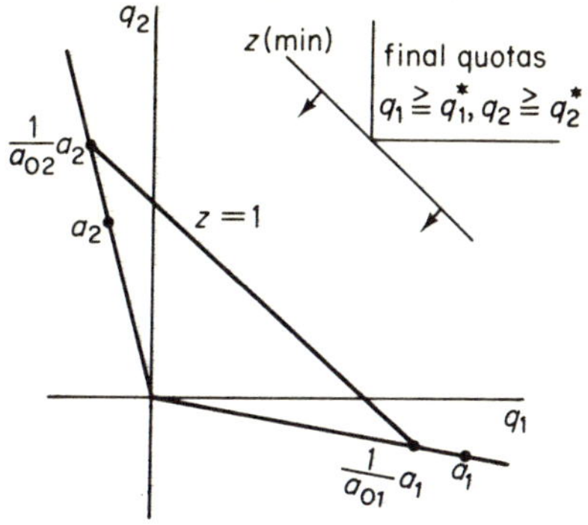

Fig. 18-1 The Input-Output Model in Final Commodity Space

As drawn, the cone of the production processes contains the entire nonnegative orthant. A different choice of points can, however, generate a cone that opens in the opposite direction and has no point except the origin in common with the nonnegative orthant. The producing sector is then incapable of satisfying any set of positive final demands. The following numerical example clarifies the underlying conditions for such a result:

$$(1-\tfrac{1}{4})x_1 - \tfrac{3}{8}x_2 \geqq q_1 = 0$$
$$-\tfrac{1}{4}x_1 + (1-\tfrac{7}{8})x_2 \geqq q_2 = 0.$$

As readers may verify, both vectors lie on the same line through the origin and the cone degenerates to that line. Each unit of x_1 requires one-fourth of a unit of x_2. But the second industry has such heavy internal requirements that it must produce two units of x_2 to provide one-fourth of a unit for the production of one unit of x_1. In producing two units the second industry requires three-fourths of a unit of x_1, which is the total net output. The producing sector is just capable of satisfying its own requirements and has nothing left over to meet the final demand. With higher internal requirements, the producing sector could operate only if q_1 and q_2 were negative and final commodities were being fed in.

Obviously a competitive economy cannot exist unless it is capable of turning out some net output. On economic grounds, then, we are able to rule out the preceding geometric possibilities and decree that the cone of the production processes must contain the nonnegative orthant of final commodity space. The mathematical requirements that insure the desired result for any number of commodities are known as the *Hawkins–Simon conditions.* Any set of coefficients derived from an actual transactions table must satisfy these conditions. We have, then, the important result: If the producing sector is capable of satisfying *any* set of final demands, it is capable of satisfying *all* sets, subject, of course, to the availability of labor and any other required inputs.

To draw the objective function, we need to identify on each ray points that represent the use of equal amounts of labor. As demonstrated in Chapter 7, the correct procedure is to divide the coefficients in each column by the coefficient in the objective function. The line passing through these points shows all combinations of final quotas using the same amount of labor. The parallel line through the point (q_1^*, q_2^*) identifies the optimal solution.

In the alternative graphical presentation of Figure 18–2, the constraints are graphed as inequalities in output, not final commodity, space. In slope-intercept form the inequalities are

$$(1) \qquad x_2 \leqq \frac{1-a_{11}}{a_{12}} x_1 - \frac{1}{a_{12}} q_1^*$$

$$(2) \qquad x_2 \geqq \frac{a_{21}}{1-a_{22}} x_1 + \frac{1}{1-a_{22}} q_2^*.$$

The first inequality is reversed because of division by the negative number, $-a_{12}$. The point of intersection of the two straight lines shows the total amounts of x_1 and x_2 that have to be produced for exact fulfillment of the final requirements. The economic system is capable of satisfying the final demands if and only if x_1 and x_2 are both nonnegative. For this alternative version of the problem, the Hawkins–Simon conditions are the mathematical requirements that the constraints intersect in the nonnegative orthant of output space. In two dimensions, the result clearly depends on the relationship between the slopes and vertical intercepts of the two lines. Readers may derive the conditions and show that they are equivalent to the first version.

Output levels in the crosshatched region satisfy both constraints. Elsewhere one or both of the outputs is too low to yield the prescribed final quotas. The optimal solution is obviously at the point of exact fulfillment and is independent of the labor requirements of the two outputs. Even if one of the labor coefficients is reduced to zero and the objective function becomes either vertical or horizontal, the optimal solution is not affected.

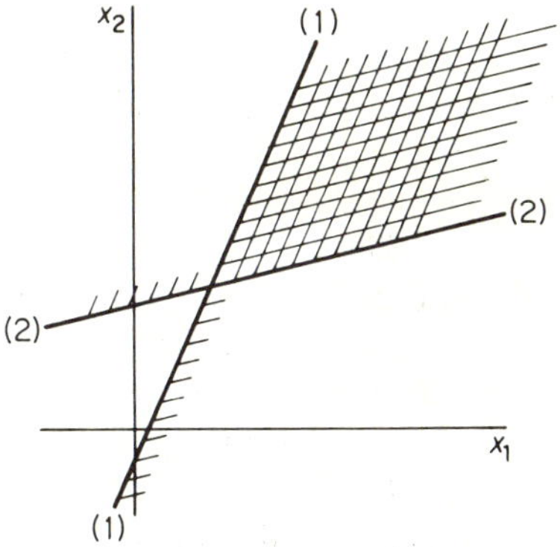

Fig. 18-2 The Input-Output Model in Output Space

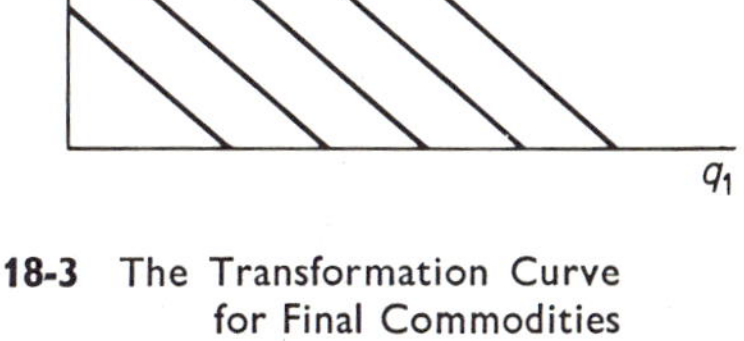

Fig. 18-3 The Transformation Curve for Final Commodities

The derived input function for labor, $z = \bar{a}_{01}q_1 + \bar{a}_{02}q_2$, generates the product transformation curves of Figure 18–3 for the final commodities. For each level of the labor supply there is a straight line of the form

$$q_2 = -\frac{\bar{a}_{01}}{\bar{a}_{02}}q_1 + \frac{z}{\bar{a}_{02}}.$$

The points on a line represent all combinations of final commodities that can be produced with the given labor supply. Changes in the level of employment merely cause proportional parallel shifts in the product transformation curve. When general equilibrium is established at positive levels for both final commodities, the ratio of commodity prices must equal the rate of product transformation:

$$\frac{p_1}{p_2} = \frac{\bar{a}_{01}}{\bar{a}_{02}}$$

But, under the rigid technological conditions, the rate of product transformation cannot vary, and relative prices are fixed. Should the price ratio differ from the rate of product transformation, one of the commodities would not be produced.

Figures 18–1 and 18–2 portray the input-output system as a special case of linear programming. They are not the kind of diagrams generally employed in economic analysis. The product transformation curve of Figure 18–3 is, however, a familiar economic diagram and permits us to visualize the input-output model as a very special version of the economic system. We can go still further in this direction and cast the input-output model into the familiar mold of demand and supply analysis.

As earlier chapters established, the marginal cost or internal price for a product equals the marginal input requirement times the input price. In the present case, marginal cost is simply the wage rate (c_0) times the marginal labor requirement, or $c_0\bar{a}_{01}$ and $c_0\bar{a}_{02}$. With no change in process, the marginal labor requirements remain constant and the marginal cost curves are horizontal lines that shift only when the wage rate changes. Since labor is the only primary input, a constant wage rate determines income and the demand curves for the commodities. So long as the market price is above marginal cost, output expands and equilibrium occurs, as in Figure 18–4,

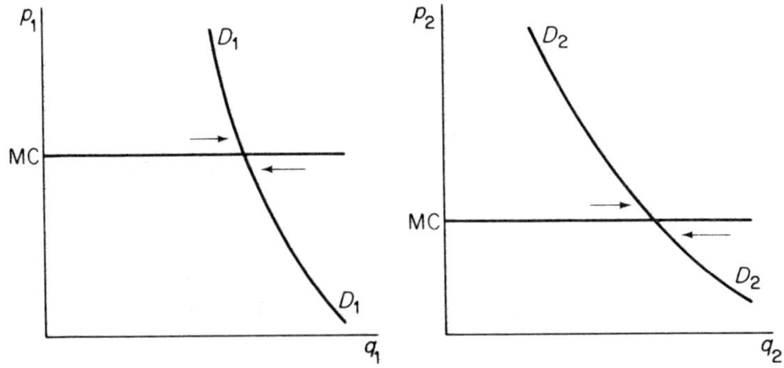

Fig. 18-4 Marginal Cost and Final Demand Curves for the Input-Output Model

at the intersection of the horizontal marginal cost curves with the demand curves for final commodities.[7]

Once the wage rate is set, equilibrium levels are determined for the price and output of each commodity. To produce the outputs requires a specific amount of labor. But, with commodity prices determined, the amount of labor supplied depends solely on the wage rate. To close the circle we must show that supply equals demand at the given wage rate.

The marginal physical productivity of an input is the reciprocal of the marginal input requirement, and multiplication by output price gives marginal revenue productivity. In equilibrium, labor must be so distributed as to have equal marginal revenue productivity in both industries. Hence the marginal revenue productivity of labor is

$$\frac{p_1}{\bar{a}_{01}} = \frac{p_2}{\bar{a}_{02}}.$$

Thus, for constant output prices, the marginal revenue productivity is a horizontal line. The supply curve, shown in Figure 18–5, is assumed to be

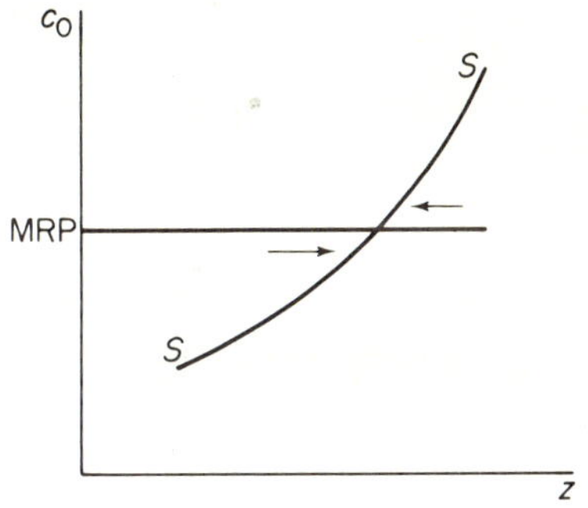

Fig. 18-5 Marginal Revenue Productivity and Supply Curves for Labor

upward sloping. Firms will expand the use of labor so long as the marginal revenue productivity exceeds the wage rate, so equilibrium is established at the intersection of the two curves. Can we be sure that the labor consumers wish to supply is just sufficient to produce the commodities they demand? If a discrepancy exists, it cannot be corrected by price changes. Under the

[7]As usual, horizontal marginal cost curves create some difficulties since they cannot represent true supply curves. The market cannot be brought into equilibrium by a tâtonnement process since supply is zero below the equilibrium price and excess supply is unlimited above it. Instead, equilibrium must come about by a moderate response of output to differences between the market price and the internal price, marginal cost. The second difficulty is that the share of individual firms is not determined. Part of the trouble stems from the oversimplified model and will be eliminated later.

rigid technological conditions and the employment of only one primary input, prices must always change proportionately. By the zero homogeneity property, equiproportional changes in all prices will not affect the quantities demanded and the amount of labor supplied.

Since consumer budgets are balanced, income equals expenditure for the consuming sector:

$$c_0 z^s = p_1 q_1^d + p_2 q_2^d.$$

From the input function for labor, the total amount of labor services required depends on the amounts demanded of the final commodities:

$$z^d = \bar{a}_{01} q_1^d + \bar{a}_{02} q_2^d,$$

or

$$c_0 z^d = c_0 \bar{a}_{01} q_1^d + c_0 \bar{a}_{02} q_2^d.$$

But marginal cost equals price for each commodity:

$$c_0 \bar{a}_{01} = p_1 \qquad c_0 \bar{a}_{02} = p_2.$$

With price replacing marginal cost, the final result is

$$c_0 z^s = p_1 q_1^d + p_2 q_2^d = c_0 z^d.$$

Hence, labor will always be supplied in the right amount to produce the quantities demanded.

The simplest input-output model is a strange special case of an economic system in which nearly everything but the absolute level of prices is determined by technological conditions. Relative prices are technologically fixed, and with given relative prices each consumer supplies a constant amount of labor and demands a constant amount of each commodity. So long as the population and the preferences do not change, there is a fixed pattern of total demand for commodities and total supply of labor.

The simplest version of the interindustry system seemingly overlooks the need for fixed productive capacity. To make the model acceptable we must assume that fixed inputs are used but that output falls short of capacity in every industry. A slack variable appears in every fixed input constraint, and the corresponding imputed value is zero. The entire revenue from all final commodities is allocated to the variable inputs and ultimately to labor alone when all intermediate products are broken down into their labor content. With a single linear process in each industry, only one primary variable input, and operation everywhere short of capacity, the simplest input-output system is logically consistent and can be interpreted as the preceding linear programming problem. Both the assumptions and the consequences, such as a zero return to capital, are objectionable. The restrictive assumptions will be relaxed in stages, beginning with the absence of choice in methods of production.

SUBSTITUTION IN AN INTERINDUSTRY SYSTEM

The model shown below contains three processes for each product. To save space we revert to the use of symbols like e_{11} in place of $1-a_{11}$ to measure the net output of each process:

$$e_{11}v_1+e_{12}v_2+e_{13}v_3-a_{14}v_4-a_{15}v_5-a_{16}v_6 \geqq q_1$$

$$-a_{21}v_1-a_{22}v_2-a_{23}v_3+e_{24}v_4+e_{25}v_5+e_{26}v_6 \geqq q_2$$

$$a_{01}v_1+a_{02}v_2+a_{03}v_3+a_{04}v_4+a_{05}v_5+a_{06}v_6 = z(\min).$$

The first three processes yield the first commodity, and the next three processes yield the second commodity. So long as the final quotas are positive and the processes do not turn out the commodities jointly, the solution must contain one process for each product. There may, of course, be alternative optimal solutions in which either of two processes can be chosen for a product, or any weighted average of those processes. Since nothing essential is omitted, we shall consider only basic solutions in which one process appears for each product.

We assume that every pair of processes, one for each product, is capable of supplying some set of nonnegative final quotas. Otherwise, that pair would never be chosen, and choice is restricted to the remaining pairs. But if the pair of processes can supply one such set of quotas, it can supply all. Thus, the Hawkins–Simon conditions are satisfied for all possible choices of processes.

Suppose, then, that a standard application of the simplex method turns up processes one and four as the unique optimal solution for one particular set of final demands. The processes not chosen must have barred coefficients in the objective form that are positive, indicating that their use would increase rather than decrease the labor services required. When the final demands change, a parametric programming problem emerges. An important theorem in parametric programming states that, when the constants in the constraints are varied, a solution remains optimal so long as it continues to be feasible. The reason is that varying the constants on the right has no effect on the barred coefficients in the objective form, which are the sole criterion of optimality. What causes a solution to become infeasible is the presence of some negative barred coefficients affixed to the constants on the right. As shown on pages 91–96 of Chapter 5, a variable in the solution ultimately goes negative, forcing a change of process.

In the present input-output model, any pair of processes satisfies the Hawkins–Simon conditions, so there are no negative $\bar{a}$ coefficients affixed to the final quotas on the right. The same solution remains feasible and, hence, optimal for all patterns of final demand. The choice of processes turns out to be no choice at all. This result is the well-known Samuelson theorem on substitution, or lack of it, within the interindustry system.

The reason for the result is intuitively clear. So long as production takes place with unused capacity, and so long as labor is the only primary input, the cost of every product depends solely upon the amount of direct and indirect labor per unit. The pattern of final demand cannot alter the basic technological requirements, so firms in an industry always choose the same process on the basis of lower cost. It makes no difference how many processes are available. We can go so far as to let the number of processes increase without limit and endow each industry with a smooth linear and homogeneous output function. All firms would employ the produced inputs and labor in fixed ratios regardless of the output level. No substitution occurs because no change can ever take place in the relative prices of inputs. The prices of produced inputs always change by the same percentage as the wage rate.[8]

LIMITATIONS OF CAPACITY

When capacity is limited, firms can and will choose processes that economize on the use of fixed inputs and require more labor. Chapter 10 analyzed a multiplant firm in which each plant had a fixed input and supplied its output as intermediate input to the other plants. Readers should review pages 243–47. By letting industries take the place of plants, we can convert the multiplant firm into a model for the producing sector. With some minor changes in symbols the firm of Chapter 10 becomes the following input-output model for a producing sector with two industries:

$$\begin{aligned}
e_{11}v_1+e_{12}v_2+e_{13}v_3-a_{14}v_4-a_{15}v_5-a_{16}v_6 &\geqq q_1\\
-a_{21}v_1-a_{22}v_2-a_{23}v_3+e_{24}v_4+e_{25}v_5+e_{26}v_6 &\geqq q_2\\
-a_{31}v_1-a_{32}v_2-a_{33}v_3 &\geqq -b_3\\
-a_{44}v_4-a_{45}v_5-a_{46}v_6 &\geqq -b_4\\
a_{01}v_1+a_{02}v_2+a_{03}v_3+a_{04}v_4+a_{05}v_5+a_{06}v_6 &= z(\min).
\end{aligned}$$

As a linear programming model of a multiplant firm, the problem can be solved directly, and the solution yields internal real or monetary prices

[8]The statement holds only when general equilibrium prevails. In the transition between equilibria, firms may continue to sell materials out of inventory at constant prices even after the wage rate and the replacement cost have risen.

for the quantities under constraint. Alternatively, the firm can simulate a market system and let plant managers make independent optimizing decisions. At the prevailing wage rate and at the current internal price for the second product, the manager of the first plant can calculate minimal total cost for all levels of output. The calculations also determine marginal cost as the familiar step function of earlier chapters. The second plant has a demand curve for x_1, which results from a parametric variation of the internal price, all other conditions being constant. There is also the external demand represented by the final quota. As Chapter 10 demonstrated, the marginal cost and demand curves for x_1 determine both the internal price and the quantity produced. A similar set of curves exists for x_2.

The firm can determine internal prices either by solving the cost minimizing problem or by finding the market clearing set of internal prices. With the minor exception of multiple optima, the results are identical. As we saw in Chapter 4, the primal and the dual must have simultaneous optimal solutions or no optimal solutions. The dual reaches its optimal solution by successively eliminating excess demand. Hence, the set of prices that clears both markets must provide an optimal solution to the primal. For an industry composed of independent firms, the emphasis is reversed. There is no central agency that directly determines optimal output levels for the firms. Rather, the market mechanism eliminates excess demand and solves the dual. From the solution to the dual we infer that the primal also has an optimal solution.

Figure 18–6 displays the marginal cost curve for one industry. Along the initial and lowest step there is excess capacity of the fixed input, and its internal price is zero. As soon as capacity is fully utilized, further increases in x_1 bring in new production processes to keep the solution feasible. The

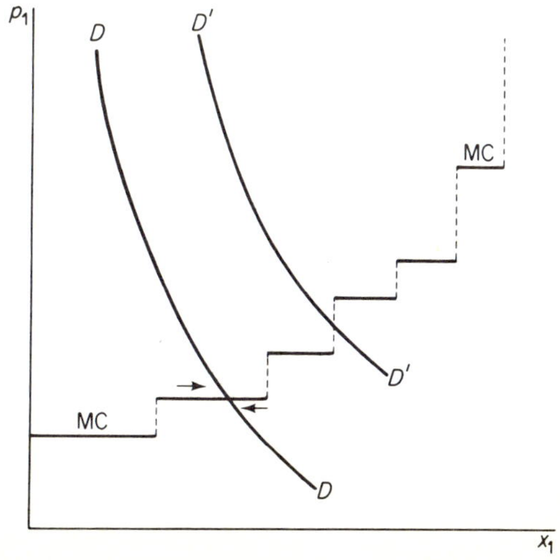

Fig. 18-6 A Rising Step Function for Marginal Cost

purpose of the new processes is to economize in the use of the fixed input by substituting labor for it. They are more costly, so the marginal cost curve jumps upward at each change of process, generating a rising step function. As soon as capacity is fully utilized, the services of the fixed input are no longer a free good, and its marginal revenue productivity or internal price rises with each change of process.

Figure 18–6 shows a smooth demand curve for total output x_1 not q, alone. Readers may make the necessary modifications for a step function. If the demand curve passes through a horizontal segment, output continues to expand so long as the market price is above marginal cost, and equilibrium occurs at the point of intersection. Equilibrium is also possible when the demand curve passes through a vertical gap. Within the gap, shifts in the demand curve do not change output but do affect net revenue. Since the variable inputs are purchased at constant prices, an upward shift of the demand curve within a gap raises the marginal revenue productivity of the fixed input and the return going to the owners, who have supplied the fixed input. There are two important differences from the simplest input-output model. The ratio between p_1 and the wage rate does not remain constant for all levels of output. The ratio does remain constant along each horizontal segment but changes along the vertical segments. Second, the income of the consuming sector does not consist of wages alone but also contains some return to the suppliers of capital.

With capacity limitations in the second industry, p_2 will not always be in the same ratio to the wage rate. Consequently, the cost coefficients for the first industry's processes may change disproportionately, creating a second parametric programming problem. As demand for the product shifts and input prices vary, the firms in each industry have to keep solving a double parametric programming problem to attain the equilibrium solution.

When the markets for both x_1 and x_2 reach equilibrium, the producing sector, like the multiplant firm, has found the solution to the primal optimizing problem. We can then reduce to canonical form to obtain the following input function for the producing sector:

$$z = \bar{a}_{01}q_1 + \bar{a}_{02}q_2 - \bar{s}_3 b_3 - \bar{s}_4 b_4.$$

The coefficients of q_1 and q_2 are again the marginal input requirements, the total amount of direct and direct and indirect labor required per unit. The barred coefficients, $\bar{s}_3$ and $\bar{s}_4$, are the rates of technical substitution or rates of input substitution between the fixed inputs and labor. With labor available at a fixed wage rate, c_0, the input function converts to the cost function:

$$C = c_0 z = w_1 q_1 + w_2 q_2 - y_3 b_3 - y_4 b_4.$$

As shown for the firm, the marginal cost or internal price for the outputs must clear both markets. Hence, we get the familiar conditions:

$$p_1 = w_1 \qquad p_2 = w_2.$$

We pause to reemphasize the economic rationale of input minimization by the entire producing sector. There is no centralized decision to minimize the use of labor; the result follows from the optimizing decisions of individual firms within the market mechanism. In early formulations, the interindustry system emphasized technological relationships almost exclusively and appeared to be independent of the market system. When economists noted the formal similarity to linear programming, they realized immediately that the solution of an input-output model implied a set of dual variables or prices, in terms of which the model could be given a conventional economic interpretation. The order is, of course, reversed. The producing sector does not solve an explicit input minimizing problem and in the process generate shadow prices, which can then be used to rationalize the result. Rather, firms use prices to solve their own problems and the unplanned result of their optimizing decisions within the market mechanism is to minimize the use of labor at all production levels.

For each level of the labor supply the input function for the producing sector generates a transformation curve for final commodities. At one extreme the labor force may be so small that, even if allocated wholly to one industry, it does not permit full utilization of the fixed capacity. Regardless of the allocation of labor, each industry remains on the first and lowest segment of its marginal cost curve. There is no change of process in either industry, the marginal labor requirements are constant, and the transformation curves are a family of parallel line segments, as they were in the earlier input-output model of page 469.

When the labor supply is large enough to permit full utilization of capacity in either industry, a change of process must occur as the bulk of labor supply is allocated to that industry. As graphed in Figure 18–7 the transformation contours become piecewise linear. That the contours must bulge outward from the origin can be inferred readily from the rate of product transformation $\bar{a}_{01}/\bar{a}_{02}$. When most of the labor force is employed by the second industry, firms must adopt a process that economizes on the fixed input and uses more labor. The rise in the marginal labor requirement $\bar{a}_{02}$ means that the transformation contour becomes flatter when q_2 is large relative to q_1. Similarly, the contour becomes steeper at high levels of q_1.

There is a range over which a rising supply of labor permits greater substitution of processes and increases the number of line segments in the transformation contours. The next critical level is reached when the labor supply permits either industry to produce its maximum attainable output. The maximum *final* output must be less than maximum output. Even if q_1 is zero, x_1 must be produced as an intermediate input for x_2, and x_1 also requires x_2

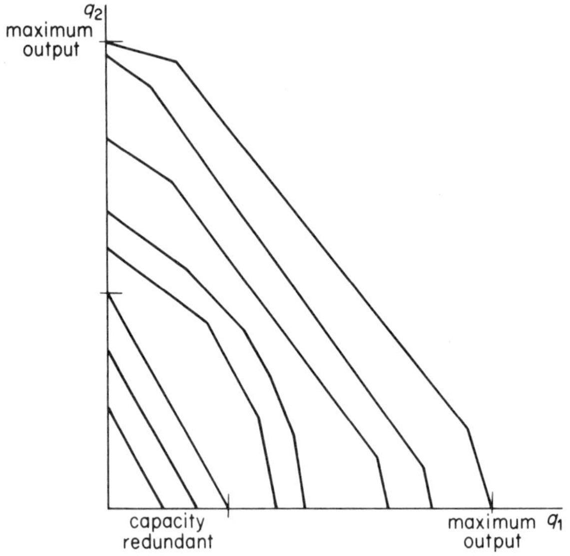

Fig. 18-7 Transformation Curves with Substitution and Capacity Limitations

as an intermediate input. There is an outermost product transformation curve that shows the highest attainable q_2 when q_1 is zero. Further increases in labor have no effect, since the fixed inputs limit further output. The outermost curve slopes downward as increases in q_1 divert greater fractions of the total output of x_2 to use as an intermediate input.

Under more realistic conditions, where choice of process is combined with limitation of capacity, the input-output system loses some of its simple properties. Changes in final demand may induce substitution of processes and cause variations in all barred coefficients. The previously computed coefficients may not give accurate predictions of the new output and employment levels. Since there are no other ways available at present for deriving detailed, specific predictions, we need to know the conditions under which the simplest type of input-output system is a reasonably close approximation to more general economic models. If each combination of processes remains optimal over fairly wide ranges of output and if the vertical steps in the marginal cost curves are small, there is a high probability that equilibrium for each industry will fall within a horizontal segment. Moderate shifts in final demand can then occur without altering the marginal input requirements determined by the existing solution. When Professor Leontief collects data for a transactions table and computes input coefficients, he obtains the coefficients for specific weighted averages of processes. These weighted averages give constant coefficients for a single process and will yield valid predictions over a limited range of variation in the final demand quotas.

A second possibility is that industries have smooth, gently sloping marginal cost curves that do not differ appreciably from horizontal lines over moderately wide ranges of output. Smooth marginal cost curves imply continuous substitution of inputs or, equivalently, a continuum of productive processes. For the marginal cost curves to slope gradually upward, the rates of technical substitution, particularly between labor and the fixed input, must change very gradually from process to process; the input substitution curve must approximate a linear segment. In equilibrium each industry uses only one process, and the Leontief measurements capture the input requirements of that process. So long as there is a fairly wide range over which processes do not differ appreciably in their marginal input requirements, predictions based on constant input requirements are valid approximations. We shall not pass judgment on whether the smooth or the linear technology is the more realistic, since conditions vary from industry to industry. Whatever the explanation, statistical studies reveal that industries can vary output over fairly wide ranges at approximately constant marginal cost, thus buttressing the use of input-output models.

THE PRODUCING SECTOR WITH SMOOTH TECHNOLOGY

To complete the topic and prepare the way for Chapter 19, we must analyze in more detail the adjustment of the producing sector when all firms have smooth output functions. In every industry all firms are assumed to have identical linear and homogeneous output functions, so the various curves for the industry are large-scale versions of those for any one firm. We can, then, dispense with explicit consideration of individual firms and focus upon the industry. As emphasized many times before, smooth technological conditions imply that cones shrink to the limiting case of rays, and straight line segments on the various contours shrink to points. For each firm, and hence for the industry, the optimal choice is always a single process, since the cost line must be tangent to the input substitution curve, except possibly at the axes. The smooth case can be interpreted as a demand curve for a product passing through the industry's marginal cost curve in a horizontal segment that has shrunk to the single point of intersection.

When the producing sector attains equilibrium under smooth technological conditions, each industry is using a single process, just as it is in the simplest input-output model. At the margin, then—which means in the neighborhood of a point—the two models satisfy the same conditions. In equilibrium, profit maximization by firms within the market mechanism guarantees that intermediate products will be selling at prices equal to their marginal costs of production. But these conditions in turn guarantee that any set of final demands will be supplied with the smallest possible use of labor. As the pattern of final demand varies and the sector adjusts to it, the requirements for intermediate products also change, and the producing sector also adjusts internally by equating to marginal cost price for intermediate commodities. The internal adjustment of the producing sector implicitly generates a smooth input function for labor that shows the minimal amount required for specified quantities of the final commodities. Unless specific technological information is fed in, as in the Leontief model, all we know about the input function is what can be inferred from the general assumptions about the nature of the technology and the way firms make their decisions. These assumptions imply that the product transformation curves generated by the input function must be smooth and concave to the origin.

Most economic models of general equilibrium focus upon the relations between consumers and producers and tend to overlook the relationships within sectors. The preceding analysis gives a justification for such a simplification. If the producing sector is in equilibrium internally, the intermediate products wash out and final commodities can be related directly to the labor and other primary inputs supplied by the consuming sector. The central problem of the economy becomes solely the allocation of primary inputs to satisfy final demands of consumers. There are also internal relations within the consuming sector, particularly the supplying of labor services by one consumer to another. Readers may write down the analogous conditions under which these transactions cancel out. The transactions between separate units within the consuming sector are of minor importance and are rarely even mentioned except in the national income accounts. Gross national product contains the value of productive services supplied by one consuming unit to another but not the services supplied by one member of a consuming unit or family to other members.

In Chapter 19 we return to the model in which consumers confront producers, but a second primary input is added. The internal adjustment of the producing sector cannot minimize the amounts of both inputs but only the amounts of one input subject to a constant level of the other. Like the fixed productive capacity, the second primary input must appear explicitly in the input function for labor.

EXERCISES

1. *Transactions Tables and Input-Output Models*

Convert Table 18–1 into a table showing the corresponding input coefficients. Assume that the consuming sector supplies only one primary input, labor services. What assumptions do you have to make in order to derive the input coefficients?

Use the coefficients just derived to write out in full a numerical version of an input-output model in linear programming form.

2. *The Primal and the Dual of the Input-Output Model*

(a) In a four industry input-output model the constraints only have been reduced to canonical form, as in the text. What is the difference between the $\bar{a}$ coefficients and the original a coefficients? Which are likely to be larger? Why?

(b) Specify the elementary operations required to eliminate the output levels from the objective form. Use these operations to derive an explicit formula for an $\bar{a}$ coefficient in the objective form, say $\bar{a}_{01}$. Use the formula to explain the economic meaning of an objective $\bar{a}$ coefficient.

(c) Introduce a constant wage rate and rewrite the objective form as the minimization of cost. Derive an explicit formula for the objective coefficient of a final commodity. Use the formula to explain the economic meaning of the coefficient.

Introduce market prices for the products and assume that equilibrium prevails in all markets. What further conclusions can you draw about the economic meaning of the barred objective coefficients for the final commodities?

(d) Set up the mathematical dual to the cost minimization problem. Give an economic interpretation of the dual variables. Show that the constraints can be rewritten to compare explicitly the internal value of an output with the cost of producing it. What can you conclude when a constraint is satisfied by a strict inequality?

(e) (Optional) Interpret the constant quotas of final commodities as vertical demand curves. Write the expression for the barred objective coefficient of a dual variable in terms of the implicit multipliers (see Chapter 4). Assume that a nonoptimal solution exists and show that the barred objective coefficient for a nonbasic variable measures excess demand. What economic condition does the optimal solution of the dual imply?

3. *Graphs for an Input-Output Model*

A two-process, two-output model of the producing sector has the following coefficients and constants: $a_{11} = 0.1$, $a_{21} = 0.4$, $a_{12} = 0.3$, $a_{22} = 0.2$, $a_{01} = 0.6$, $a_{02} = 0.3$, $q_1^* = 75$, $q_2^* = 100$.

(a) Set up as a linear programming problem. Reduce to canonical form and find all barred coefficients for the final output quotas. Write the input function.

(b) Graph the problem in final commodity space. Identify the constraint set, the objective function, and the optimal solution.

(c) Graph the model in output space, showing the constraint or feasible set, the objective function, and the optimal solution.

(d) Draw transformation curves in final commodity space. What is the value of the rate of product transformation? How do the transformation curves and the objective function in (b) compare with respect to slope? Introduce market prices for the final commodities and show graphically the maximization of revenue for a given supply of labor. Identify the possible solutions and give an economic interpretation of each.

(e) Derive and draw marginal cost curves for each final commodity and a marginal revenue productivity curve for labor. Draw in demand curves for the final commodities and show the process of adjustment in each market.

(f) In (b) we took as given the quantities of the final commodities and the wage rate. In (d) we took as given the prices of the commodities and the quantity of labor. Interpret each case in terms of supply and demand curves.

4. *An Input-Output Model with Capacity Limitations*

The text presented, in symbolic form, a two-output model with choice of processes and fixed capacity limitations within each industry. Introduce a constant monetary wage rate for labor services and convert to a cost minimization problem.

(a) Assume that the problem has been reduced to canonical form for an optimal solution and write cost as a linear function of the four quantities under constraint. Give an economic interpretation of each coefficient. Explain the negative sign that precedes the coefficients of the fixed inputs.

Choose a process and use the internal prices to compute the value of output, the cost of the intermediate input, and the cost of the fixed input. Assuming a unique optimum, write the algebraic conditions a basic and a nonbasic process must satisfy. Give an economic interpretation. What happens to the conditions for optimality if an intermediate input has different internal prices in the two industries?

(b) Split the problem into a separate cost minimizing problem for each output. The output of each industry must provide for both the final quota and the amount used as input by the other industry. Denote by z_1 and z_2 the amounts of the first and second products used as inputs. For the first industry the three quantities on the right are (q_1+z_1), $-z_2$, and $-b_3$. Let the first industry minimize C_1, the second C_2 for constant levels of z_1 and z_2 as well as the other quantities.

Assuming that each industry attains an optimal solution write each industry's labor cost as a linear function of the quantities under constraint. What is the economic meaning of each coefficient? Show specifically that the coefficients of the inputs are the rates of change of *net* revenue with revenue itself constant at the level of zero.

(c) Suppose that the internal value of z_2 within the first industry is greater than the internal value within the second industry. Show that the optimum for the sector has not been attained because one industry is employing too much labor and the other too little.

When z_2 varies parametrically what curve does it generate in the first industry and in the second? Treating q_2 as a vertical demand curve, draw appropriate demand and supply curves for the second product. Ignoring the improbable outcomes, show equilibrium in the market. Demonstrate that there is no further possibility of reducing labor cost by expanded production and use of the second product.

Verify that the equilibrium quantity established by the market is the only quantity at which both industries can have equal internal prices for the second output. Show further that the equilibrium market price is the only level at which the internal prices can be equal. Use the preceding results in combination with (a) to summarize the relationship between market equilibrium and optimality.

We have implicitly simplified the problem by assuming that (q_1+z_1) is constant at the optimal level and that q_1 may change a bit to accommodate the necessary variations in z_1. In a broader treatment both z_1 and z_2 vary simultaneously. There are shifts of demand and supply curves as well as movements along them, but the conditions for final equilibrium and optimality remain the same.

5. *Transformation Curves under Capacity Limitations*

(a) Draw typical marginal cost curves for each of two industries with linear technology, choice of processes, and capacity limitations. Labor is the only primary input. What causes the steps in the marginal cost curves?

(b) Use the pair of marginal cost curves to explain the following features of the product transformation contours: the presence of a single line segment when labor is in short supply; the increase in the number of segments as labor becomes more plentiful; the subsequent decrease in number of segments as the labor supply continues to grow; why the outermost contour does not consist solely of a horizontal and a vertical segment at full capacity.

19

Equilibrium and Optimality for the Economy

Chapter 17 developed general equilibrium for the economy by the use of demand and supply curves for inputs and outputs. Demand and supply curves are especially well adapted to illustrating and explaining how the economic system attains equilibrium. In each individual market the direction and rate of change of the price depend on the horizontal difference between the demand and supply curves. The transmission of effects from market to market takes the form of shifts in the demand and supply curves as other prices change. Stability requires that these effects become generally weaker and more diffused as they pass through the system.

For portraying the final state of equilibrium and, most especially, for appraising it, another type of diagram is more effective: product transformation curves and input substitution contours. These diagrams were first developed for the multiproduct firm, next applied to single-product and multiproduct industries, and in Chapter 18 derived for the entire producing sector under special conditions. We shall now carry the progression to its conclusion and present the various two-dimensional contours for the producing sector under more general conditions than those of Chapter 18.

Chapter 14 developed a similar set of contours for a single consumer supplying more than one input and buying more than one commodity. We immediately extended the results to a consuming unit with more than one member by deriving commodity substitution, or Scitovsky, contours. The present chapter completes the development by generalizing the results from the family to the entire consuming sector. The two sets of diagrams for the separate sectors fit together into a geometric presentation of general equilibrium for the economy. The final stage, which constitutes a branch of the subject known as *welfare economics*, is to appraise the final state of general equilibrium in terms of some generally acceptable standards.

THE PRODUCING SECTOR

In the economy as a whole, industries take the place formerly occupied by firms in an industry and originally occupied by plants in a firm. We can, then, profitably recapitulate at this stage some results from earlier models. For a single-plant, purely competitive firm there are two types of inputs: those purchasable in the market at prices taken to be constant, and those inputs that are fixed in amount for the period over which decisions are being made. An input purchased in the market is employed up to the level at which the horizontal market reaction curve passes through a vertical gap in the marginal revenue productivity curve or intersects it in the smooth version. For the fixed inputs the optimal solution to the primal determines internal prices that are the optimal solution to the dual. Since the successive iterations of the dual raise prices to eliminate positive excess demand, the optimal solution is a set of internal prices that equates the quantity demanded and quantity supplied of each input, except when supply exceeds demand at a zero price.[1]

A multiplant firm adds the possibility of inputs fixed within the firm but transferable among plants. The revenue maximizing solution for the firm establishes a firm-wide internal price for any such input, which equates demand to supply for the firm as a whole. Alternatively, the firm's management may offer to supply the input at a constant internal price. Each plant manager then chooses to employ the input up to the level at which the horizontal price line passes through a vertical gap in the marginal revenue productivity curve for the plant or intersects it. The individual optimizing decisions will result in an optimum for the firm as a whole if each plant manager bases his decision on the internal market clearing price for the firm.[2]

In the cost minimizing version of the firm, outputs replace inputs, and a marginal cost curve takes the place of a marginal revenue productivity curve in determining the optimal amount of an output to supply at a given price. When an output has a fixed quota or fixed total demand, the optimal solution determines an internal price that equates supply to demand for the output. The management of a multiplant firm can set internal prices at which it stands willing to buy outputs from the plants. The resultant solution is optimal for the firm if each plant manager optimizes at the internal market clearing prices for the firm. When some plants turn out products that are used as inputs by other plants, the optimal solution for the firm also

[1]In the linear model, the vertical supply curve passes through a horizontal gap in the demand curve. Supply and demand are equated in the sense that the quantity demanded exceeds quantity supplied at any lower price and falls short of it at any higher price.

[2]If the dual for the firm does not have a unique optimal solution, there will be a whole range of market clearing prices. If the primal for the firm does not have a unique optimum, there will not be a unique allocation of the shared input among plants. In developing a model for the entire producing sector, we shall ignore these qualifications.

yields internal market clearing prices. Optimization by individual plants yields an optimum for the firm as a whole, provided that the plants supplying the product and the plants using it base their decisions on the firm-wide market clearing prices.

Chapter 16, which should be reviewed at this stage, extended the preceding results to both single-product and multiproduct industries. In passing on to the producing sector as a whole we must first note the vast complexity of detail. There are inputs fixed within plants and within firms, inputs specific to a single industry or to groups of industries, inputs produced by some firms for the use of other firms, and primary inputs, such as labor services, that are supplied from outside the sector and used by all firms inside the sector. Within each classification of inputs there may be great diversity and heterogeneity, but it is possible, conceptually, to assume that all requisite data are available and to set up the entire producing sector as a vast linear programming problem. To make the problem specific we shall temporarily take all primary inputs to be in a fixed supply and all output prices to be constant. What emerges is a model similar to the revenue maximizing version of a firm.

Some central planning authority could conceivably solve the problem, thus determining how much to produce of each output and how much of each transferable input to allot to every plant, firm and industry. The optimal solution to the primal would also generate internal prices for all inputs. Further, each input would have the same price within the limits of shiftability. The inputs trapped within plants or firms need not have uniform internal prices within the sector, but diversity in prices reflects inefficiency in the short-run allocation of these inputs. The internal prices generated by the primal are also market clearing prices that bring the quantity demanded into equality with the vertical supply of each input. By offering to supply inputs at these prices, the central authority could rely on individual optimization by firms to attain the revenue maximizing solution for the sector at the given output prices. Or the central authority could dispense with the setting of prices and simply rely on purely competitive markets to generate the equilibrium level of prices. When inputs have upward-sloping but not vertical supply curves, the prices of inputs also determine the quantities available to the sector. Equilibrium in the input markets then implies that whatever amounts of the inputs the producing sector obtains are allocated in such a pattern as to maximize revenue at the given output prices.

The use of constant output prices can be justified only as a convenient expository device since the adjustment of the entire producing sector is bound to have a profound effect on prices. When a firm maximizes revenue at given prices it also obtains one solution to the technological maximizing problem. For a two-product firm the locus of all solutions to the technological maximizing problem is the product transformation curve. At a unique revenue maximizing solution the revenue line either passes through a vertex or is tangent to a smooth curve. If we allow both prices to vary parametrically through the entire nonnegative range, except for simultaneous zeros, the resultant set of all revenue maximizing solutions traces out the entire product transformation contour. For the producing sector as a whole we can draw an important conclusion: Whatever level output prices may take, equilibrium in the input markets implies a solution somewhere on the product transformation curve for the sector. With upward-sloping input supply curves, the product transformation contour has to be the one drawn for the equilibrium quantities of the inputs.

When output levels and input prices are constant, the solution to the cost minimizing problem for the sector generates internal prices for outputs that equate the quantity supplied to the vertical demand. Conversely, equilibrium in the output markets implies that cost is minimized for the sector at the given input prices. When a firm minimizes cost at given input prices, it finds an optimal solution at a vertex or point of tangency on its input substitution contour and thus also solves the technological minimizing problem. The locus of all optimal solutions as input prices vary is the input substitution contour. For the sector as a whole we draw the following important conclusion: Whatever the input prices, equilibrium in the output markets implies a solution somewhere along the input substitution contour for the sector. When output demand curves are downward sloping but not vertical, equilibrium in the output markets also determines the quantities that can be sold. Thus, equilibrium in the output markets selects the appropriate input substitution contour as well as the point of equilibrium along it.

Chapter 18 dealt extensively with intermediate inputs and established important results. The solution to the cost minimizing or technological minimizing problem for the producing sector generates internal monetary or real prices that clear the markets for intermediate inputs. Also, the solution to the technological minimizing problem yields an input function for the sector in which the intermediate inputs do not appear explicitly. When equilibrium prevails in the markets for intermediate inputs, we can omit these inputs and relate final outputs directly to primary inputs.

We can now put all the separate results together. When equilibrium prevails in all markets, the producing sector is maximizing revenue for whatever inputs it is using and is minimizing the cost of primary inputs for whatever outputs it is producing. The sector is, thus, maximizing net revenue at the equilibrium set of prices but only at that set of prices. More fundamentally, the sector has found one solution to both the technological maximizing and technological minimizing problems. We can display equilibrium for the sector as points on product transformation and input substitution contours. Thus, equilibrium for the sector implies a technological optimum in which no output can be increased without reducing at least one other output or increasing at least one input. Similarly, no input can be reduced without increasing at least one other input or reducing at least one output.

Output and Input Functions for the Sector

The upshot of the preceding discussion is that we can treat the producing sector as a giant firm and adapt for its use the functions and diagrams developed previously for the firm. In the discussion that follows the producing sector uses two primary inputs and turns out two final products. At any set of prices the independent optimizing decisions of the firms represent one solution to the technological optimizing problem for the sector. All possible equilibria for the industry at all possible sets of prices must also be solutions to the technological optimizing problem. Thus, there exists for the sector as a whole an output function representing all possible solutions to the technological optimizing problem. As demonstrated in Chapter 11, the output function yields various two-dimensional diagrams, product transformation curves, input substitution contours, total product curves, and input requirement curves. Readers may write input and output functions for the sector, using the coefficients shown below, and draw curves like those on page 261.

To hold the model down to two inputs we shall drop from consideration inputs specific to one industry or to a group of industries. This means that we shall not distinguish separate occupations like glass blowing but shall instead treat all labor as homogeneous. The amounts of the fixed inputs and their distribution among firms affect the specific form of the output function but not its existence; the general conclusions remain valid. Fixed inputs enter into the problem because the owners of fixed inputs receive part of the income of the producing sector. The internal prices of the fixed inputs within firms, together with the amounts, determine what their owners receive.

For the firm Chapter 11 demonstrated that the rate of product transformation, or the negative of the slope along the product transformation curve, must equal the ratio of the marginal requirements for both inputs; or, specifically, that

$$\bar{t}_{34} = \frac{\bar{a}_{23}}{\bar{a}_{24}} = \frac{\bar{a}_{13}}{\bar{a}_{14}}.$$

Readers will note a change of subscript from Chapter 11. For the outputs of the producing sector we are using the symbols x_3 and x_4 instead of x_1 and x_2. The reason is that in the economy as a whole the distinction between inputs and outputs gets somewhat blurred. The outputs of production processes become the inputs of consumption processes. There are four inputs to consumption processes, the amounts of the primary inputs devoted to personal use and the outputs of the producing sector. We denote these in order by x_1, x_2, x_3, and x_4. The amounts of the primary inputs supplied to the producing sector are, as before, z_1 and z_2. Thus, the producing sector uses the first two commodities as inputs and yields the third and fourth commodities as outputs. The consuming sector may use all four commodities as inputs but it buys the third and fourth from producers and supplies the first two to producers.

Being a dual variable, $\bar{a}_{23}$ is the internal real price of x_3 in terms of z_2, and $\bar{a}_{24}$ is the internal real price of x_4 in terms of the same input. Thus, the solution to the technological maximizing problem requires that the ratio of the internal real prices for the products be identical in terms of either input as a standard. Along the transformation curve for the sector, the same ratio must prevail in every plant, firm, and industry. Thus, a point on the product transformation curve for the sector determines a unique ratio of real prices for outputs.[3]

Along the input substitution contour for the sector, the analogous condition is

$$\bar{s}_{12} = \frac{\bar{e}_{41}}{\bar{e}_{42}} = \frac{\bar{e}_{31}}{\bar{e}_{32}}.$$

The inputs must have the same ratio of internal real prices in terms of either output, and the ratio must be identical in every plant, firm, and industry within the sector. With x_3 and z_1 constant, the solution to the technological optimizing problem for the firm generates a total product curve whose slope is $\bar{e}_{42}$, the marginal productivity of the second input with respect to the fourth commodity. At every point on the total product curve for the sector, the marginal productivity of the second input must be the same in every plant, firm, and industry. Otherwise x_4 could be increased by shifting the second input. This is a most important condition. With only the ratios equal, both $\bar{e}_{41}$ and $\bar{e}_{42}$ could be at a higher level in one firm or one industry. Now we can assert that in terms of any one output an input must have the same real price everywhere in the sector.

If all firms within the sector base their optimizing decision on the same set of market prices, they will satisfy the preceding conditions and find a solution to the technological optimizing problem for the sector. Conversely, every solution to the technological optimizing problem provides a unique set of price ratios or relative prices for all pairs of outputs and inputs. If we select one particular technological optimum and chose market prices in the same ratio as the real prices, that technological optimum becomes the equilibrium for the sector. We are back where we started in Chapter 4. Solving the dual pricing problem also provides a solution to the primal optimizing problem, and conversely. For an industry or the sector as a whole, the solution to the dual pricing problem is equilibrium. The primal is the technological optimizing problem. Hence, equilibrium implies an optimum, and an optimum provides a set of relative prices for an equilibrium.

[3]If the curve is piecewise linear, the appropriate qualification has to be made for vertices.

THE CONSUMING SECTOR

In the development of a model for the consuming sector the family bears essentially the same relationship to the entire sector as the multiplant firm does to the producing sector. As prototype for the consuming sector we shall take the simplest model of the family developed in Chapter 14. Each member receives a share of the total income and optimizes independently; the consumption processes of one member have no effect on the utility of any other member. The consuming sector as a whole receives aggregate income that is the sum of the incomes going to individual consuming units. Thus, each unit receives a share of the sector's income and makes independent decisions that have no direct effect on the well being of other consuming units. When concentrating on the sector as a whole, we cannot give attention to what is happening within families. Hence, we assume that every consuming unit either consists of one individual or acts as if it did. Under the foregoing assumptions we can treat the family and the entire consuming sector interchangeably and utilize the results of Chapter 14, which should be reviewed before going on.

Equilibrium and Optimality for the Sector

The consuming sector is in equilibrium with respect to the purchase of final commodities when no consuming unit has an incentive to make any changes. Hence, with a given distribution of income and constant prices, equilibrium for the sector implies that every unit is maximizing utility and making its choice where its budget line is tangent to an indifference curve.[4] The individual rates of commodity substitution, which are ratios of marginal utilities, are equal to the same price ratio and hence equal to each other.

Equilibrium for the sector also implies optimality for the sector. To show this we hold the utility of every consumer constant at the level attained in the equilibrium and then minimize expenditure for the sector. For the specified levels of utility a commodity substitution or Scitovsky contour is the lower boundary of all commodity bundles capable of yielding all consumers at least the prescribed levels of utility. Expenditure is minimized at the point of tangency of the expenditure line with the contour. The negative of the slope along the contour is the rate of commodity substitution for the sector as a whole. With only two commodities and two consuming units, the sector's rate of commodity substitution is

$$\bar{s}_{34} = \frac{\bar{u}_{23}}{\bar{u}_{24}} = \frac{\bar{u}_{13}}{\bar{u}_{14}}.$$

[4]For a simplified general treatment we shall not consider explicitly the piecewise-linear case, but readers may make the appropriate extension of the conditions to cover this case.

Since commodities are inputs to consumption processes, the symbol $\bar{s}$ is retained. Being dual variables, $\bar{u}_{23}$ is the marginal utility or internal price of the third commodity to the second consuming unit and $\bar{u}_{24}$ is the internal price of the fourth commodity to that same unit. The final term is the ratio of internal prices or personal evaluations for the first consumer. Thus, the rate of commodity substitution for the sector as a whole must equal the rate of commodity substitution for each individual consumer. The presence of more than two consumers merely adds more ratios on the right in the expression above.

When the sector is minimizing expenditure for given utility levels the price ratio must equal the sector's rate of commodity substitution, which in turn equals the individual rate of commodity substitution for each unit. The second part of the requirement implies that each unit is optimizing and that the sector is in equilibrium. The conditions for equilibrium and expenditure minimization at given prices are identical, so one implies the other. Hence, the sector, like the family in Figure 14-6 on page 358, is in equilibrium when the aggregate income line is tangent to a Scitovsky contour.

We can also give a slightly different interpretation of optimality for the sector. A Scitovsky contour results from the minimization of one commodity subject to inequality constraints for the remaining commodity and the utility levels of all consumers. The contour is the lower boundary of all commodity bundles capable of yielding every consumer at least the prescribed minimum level of utility. Thus, a Scitovsky contour is the lower boundary of a convex set in commodity space. Commodity bundles within the set are capable of yielding every consumer at least the minimum level of utility. Commodity bundles outside the set cannot satisfy the requirement; no matter how they are distributed among consumers, the utility of at least one consumer must fall below the prescribed minimum. When expenditure is minimized at the point of tangency on the boundary of the convex set, any other bundle in the set costs more. Any commodity bundle that costs the same amount lies outside the set; its purchase must make at least one consumer worse off. Thus, tangency of the expenditure or income line to a Scitovsky contour is Pareto optimal or satisfies the criterion of Pareto optimality, as defined in Chapter 14. At the given level of expenditure it is impossible to make one consumer better off without making at least one other consumer worse off.

As Chapter 14 demonstrated for the family, constant prices and constant aggregate income do not determine a unique equilibrium or optimum for the sector. With aggregate income and prices constant, a change in the distribution of income causes consumers to attain different levels of utility in the equilibrium for the sector. Each combination of utility levels defines a different Scitovsky contour, which is tangent to the sector's income line at a different point. The new equilibrium is also Pareto optimal but we cannot say whether it is better or worse than the original equilibrium unless we bring in some standard of value in the form of a welfare function. All we can say is that each distribution of income determines a unique equilibrium along the sector's income line and that each equilibrium is Pareto optimal.

Equilibrium and Optimality in the Supply of Inputs

There are many similarities between the producing and consuming sectors but there is also one basic difference. The final outputs of the producing sector return to the economic system as inputs to consumption processes. But the final outputs of consumption processes are levels of consumer satisfaction or utility that obviously do not feed back into the system. Leontief and other economists have at times employed closed models of the economy in which the outputs of the consumption processes feed back into the system as the services of primary inputs supplied to the producing sector. Thus, individuals are regarded as consuming in order to stoke themselves for the provision of productive services. Such treatments, however, dispense with the traditional theory of consumer's choice. In Chapter 14 we extended the theory of consumer's choice to include the supply of inputs by a single consumer. We must now make a further extension to the consuming sector. As in the purchase of commodities from given income, the essential difference between one consumer and the entire sector is that Scitovsky contours must replace individual indifference curves.

When every consumer supplies constant amounts of the primary inputs, the level of money income depends solely on input prices and is beyond the consumer's control. The statement also holds when consumer's receive income from either direct or indirect ownership of the fixed inputs of business firms. So long as the pattern of ownership does not change, the return to owners depends on the internal prices established for these inputs. Whether we do or do not include income from an ownership interest in business, the income of each consuming unit is at the mercy of input prices. The levels of input prices determine the aggregate money income for the sector. Also, so long as all consuming units do not have proportional endowments of the primary inputs, changes in the relative prices of inputs alter the distribution of income.

When an individual consumer can vary the supply of inputs, the model expands considerably. We saw in Chapter 14 that a consumer must solve three separate but related problems: how to spend any given level of income optimally; how to earn optimally any given level of income; and how to determine whether the level of income is itself optimal. In supplying inputs to earn a given level of income, the consumer finds the optimal combination of the inputs he can retain for his personal use and still earn the required amount of income. Figure 14–3b shows the optimal solution. With quantities retained measured from the conventional origin, the optimum is the familiar point of tangency of the income line with a convex indifference curve. The rate of substitution between the retained inputs must equal the ratio of input prices. We can also flip over the diagram and measure quantities supplied from the conventional origin. The indifference curve, which is now concave, shows all combinations the consumer can give up and be equally well off. Also, the nearer the curve is to the origin the smaller are the amounts of the inputs given up and the higher is the level of utility. The concave indifference contour tangent to the income line represents the highest attainable level of utility from retained inputs.

When every consumer is supplying inputs optimally to earn a given income, the sector is in equilibrium with respect to the supply of primary inputs for a given level of aggregate income. Does equilibrium for the sector again imply optimality, or can the sector, by supplying a different combination of primary inputs, earn the same aggregate income and permit at least one consumer to attain a higher level of utility? Since retained inputs could have been sold, each unit of an input has an opportunity cost equal to its market price. Optimality for the sector requires that the cost of the retained inputs be minimized at prescribed utility levels for all consumers. A Scitovsky contour in input space is the lower boundary of all retained input combinations that are capable of yielding at least the prescribed utility levels. At the point of tangency cost is minimized, and the input price ratio equals the sector's rate of substitution between retained inputs, which in turn equals that of every consumer. Once again the conditions for optimality and for equilibrium are identical.

To show the inputs supplied we subtract the primary inputs retained from the total amount available. As Chapter 14 demonstrated (Figure 14–3b), a contour that is convex to the conventional origin in terms of x_1 and x_2 becomes concave to the conventional origin in terms of z_1 and z_2. Thus, the Scitovsky contour is flipped over, as drawn in Figure 19–1a. Tangency of the income line to the contour identifies the maximum amount of income the sector can earn subject to the prescribed minimum utility levels from the retained inputs. Since the total amounts of the primary inputs are fixed, maximizing income from the sale of inputs is equivalent to minimizing the opportunity cost of retaining inputs. Tangency of the sector's income line to a Scitovsky contour portrays equilibrium for the sector in the supply of inputs; the input price ratio must equal every consumer's rate of substitution between primary inputs.

When the Scitovsky contour is in its original position and convex to the origin, it is the lower boundary for combinations of primary inputs retained by the sector. Only the combinations of retained inputs lying beyond the contour are capable of yielding higher utility for at least one consumer. When the Scitovsky contour is flipped over, as in Figure 19–1a, only the combinations nearer the origin can yield a higher level of utility for at least one consumer. Only when the sector supplies smaller amounts of the primary inputs can at least one consumer be better off and the others be no worse off with respect to the personal use of primary inputs.

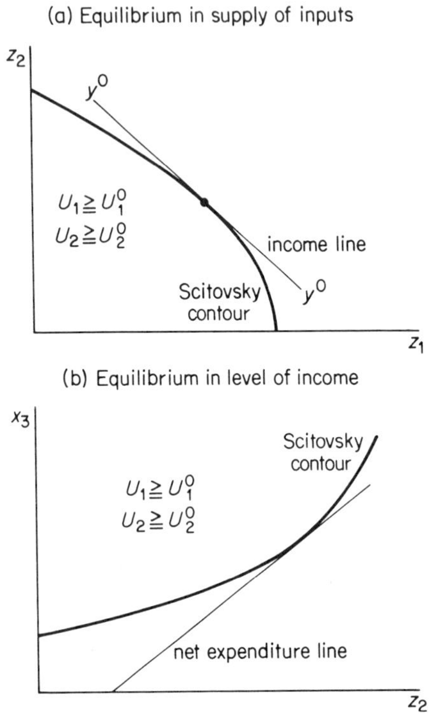

Fig. 19-1 Equilibrium in Supply of Inputs

Equilibrium and Optimality in the Level of Income

The final decision of a consumer, which fixes the level of income, is to determine the optimal balance between the primary inputs retained and the final commodities purchased from the sale of inputs. An individual must decide whether an additional hour of leisure is worth more than the amount of a commodity an hour's work will buy. As Figure 14–3c showed, a net expenditure line must be tangent to an indifference curve between hours worked and one commodity. The remaining commodity x_4 and the remaining input z_1 are constant in amount, as are their prices. The amount earned from supplying z_1 less the amount spent on x_4 is a constant, $c_1 z_1^0 - p_4 x_4^0$, which may be either positive or negative. To keep expenditure equal to income, the individual's supply of labor z_2 and purchases of x_3 must satisfy the constraint

$$p_3 x_3 - c_2 z_2 = (c_1 z_1^0 - p_4 x_4^0).$$

The optimal solution requires that the slope of the net expenditure line equal the slope of the indifference curve, or that $c_2/p_3 = \bar{u}_2/\bar{u}_3$. The rate of substitution between hours worked and commodity purchased must equal the price ratio.[5]

When all consumers make similar, independent optimizing decisions, the sector is in equilibrium and we can portray that equilibrium, as in Figure 19–1b, by tangency of a net expenditure line to a Scitovsky contour. The price ratio equals the sector's rate of substitution between the final commodity and the primary input. The contour shows the minimal amounts of x_3 the sector must receive, together with the maximal amounts of z_2 it can give up, and still attain the prescribed levels of utility. Combinations below the contour or to the right of it necessarily reduce the utility of at least one consumer. Hence, equilibrium for the sector minimizes net expenditure for the sector and satisfies the criterion of Pareto optimality.

When the consuming sector buys two final commodities and sells two primary inputs, three Scitovsky contours display the full equilibrium for the sector. The appropriate market price ratio must equal the sector's rate of substitution between the final commodities, the primary inputs, and between a final commodity and a primary input. For x_3 and z_2 the required condition is

$$\frac{c_2}{p_3} = \bar{s}_{23} = \frac{\bar{u}_{12}}{\bar{u}_{13}} = \frac{\bar{u}_{22}}{\bar{u}_{23}}.$$

The sector's rate of substitution must equal that of each consumer, as is shown on the right for the first two consumers. Readers may write out the equations for two final commodities and two primary inputs. When the equalities hold for three of the possible six pairs, they must hold also for the remaining three pairs. In general, when there are n quantities instead of four, all equalities are satisfied if $n-1$ are.

Scitovsky contours emerge when the amount of one commodity is minimized at constant levels of the remaining commodity and every consumer's utility. One dual variable is the rate of substitution between commodities, which represents an internal real price for one commodity in terms of the other. The internal real price for the sector has to be equal to the ratio of the internal prices or marginal utilities within each consuming unit. Thus, the optimal solution to the commodity minimization problem requires that real prices or relative prices be the same in every consuming unit throughout the sector. There is also a utility maximization problem in which the utility of one consumer is maximized for constant amounts of the commodities and constant levels of utility for the remaining consumers. Except when all consumers are satiated with the same commodity, the solution to one problem implies the solution to the other. When the sector comes into equilibrium

[5]Interpreted strictly, p_3 is a price paid and c_2 is a price received, so they must have different signs. But $\bar{u}_2$ is the internal price of a commodity sold and $\bar{u}_3$ is the internal price of a commodity bought. Their ratio should also be preceded by a negative sign, restoring the equality.

at a given set of external market prices, the ratios of internal prices, being equal to the ratios of market price, are the same everywhere throughout the consuming sector. Hence, equilibrium for the sector solves both the commodity minimizing and the utility maximizing problems.

EQUILIBRIUM FOR THE ECONOMY

What remains is to put together the separate diagrams and display simultaneous equilibrium for both the producing and consuming sectors. For the first pair of diagrams we take the supplies of the primary inputs to be fixed. The producing sector has a unique product transformation curve, as drawn in Figure 19–2a. At the initial prices for outputs the producing sector comes into equilibrium at point *P*. The pair of output levels determines an input substitution contour through the point in input space representing the fixed supplies of the primary inputs. The slope of the contour determines the ratio of input prices, and the condition that all receipts be paid out

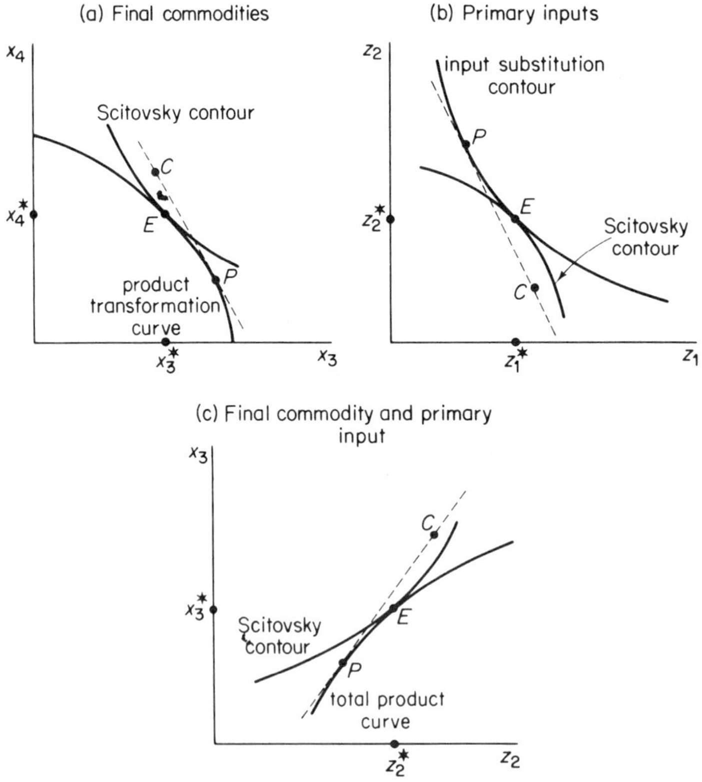

Fig. 19-2 General Equilibrium

determines the level. The internal prices for fixed inputs also have unique values. The total income of the consuming sector equals the total receipts of business, and the distribution of that income depends on the allocation among consumers of primary inputs and of shares in the ownership of fixed inputs.

With all receipts paid out by the producing sector, the dotted price line through P is also the aggregate income of consumers. The consuming sector comes into equilibrium along that line at point C, which depends on the distribution of income. A system of monetary transfer payments of the type introduced in Chapter 17 alters the distribution of income and could bring about equilibrium for both sectors at point P. In the absence of transfer payments, the initial set of prices does not permit both sectors to be in equilibrium simultaneously and cannot persist. A comparison of points P and C shows excess demand for x_4 and excess supply for x_3. The resultant rise in p_4 and fall in p_3 reduces the numerical value of the slope, $-p_3/p_4$. The price line becomes flatter and, if the system is stable, approaches equilibrium at some point such as E on the transformation curve. Whether the system is stable or not, an equilibrium exists somewhere along the transformation curve, and we assume it is at E.

When both sectors are in equilibrium, the product transformation curve is tangent to a Scitovsky contour through the point E. Hence, the rate of product transformation must equal the rate of commodity substitution for all consumers. We can combine the conditions derived independently for each sector in the equation

$$\frac{\bar{a}_{23}}{\bar{a}_{24}} = \frac{\bar{a}_{13}}{\bar{a}_{14}} = \frac{p_3}{p_4} = \frac{\bar{u}_{13}}{\bar{u}_{14}} = \frac{\bar{u}_{23}}{\bar{u}_{24}}.$$

When both sectors are in equilibrium simultaneously, the ratio of internal prices for the two commodities must be the same everywhere in the economy. No consumer can have a ratio of personal valuations that is different from the ratio of real prices in any firm.

Once again equilibrium implies a solution to the primal optimizing problem, now for both sectors simultaneously. The production transformation curve is the outer boundary of commodity combinations producible from the fixed supplies of the inputs. The Scitovsky contour is the lower boundary of commodity combinations for given utility levels. Points beyond the Scitovsky contour are technologically unattainable. Compared with the point of tangency all attainable points cause at least one consumer to be worse off.

To display separately a second requirement for general equilibrium, we fix output levels and let inputs vary along an input substitution contour. The consuming sector must now earn optimally a sufficient amount of income to buy the fixed quantities of the final commodities. At the initial set of input prices, the producing sector comes into equilibrium at point P in Figure 19–2b. The choice of inputs determines the slope of the product transformation curve through the fixed point in output space, and the slope represents the ratio of output prices. The equality of receipts and expenditures determines the actual level. Thus the input price line through P also represents the income the consuming sector must earn to buy the commodities. The payments to owners of fixed inputs represent equal additions to consumer income and value of final commodities. The consuming sector comes into adjustment somewhere along the desired income line, say at point C. At the initial prices consumers do not wish to supply inputs in the quantities demanded. Input prices vary in response to excess demand until both sectors come into equilibrium at E.

Simultaneous equilibrium for both sectors, or tangency of the contours, implies

$$\frac{\bar{e}_{41}}{\bar{e}_{42}} = \frac{\bar{e}_{31}}{\bar{e}_{32}} = \frac{c_1}{c_2} = \frac{\bar{u}_{11}}{\bar{u}_{12}} = \frac{\bar{u}_{21}}{\bar{u}_{22}}.$$

The ratio of internal prices for the inputs must be the same throughout the economy. Ratios are shown for only two consumers, but the equality holds for however many consuming units there may be. As before, equilibrium implies simultaneous solutions to primal optimizing problems for both sectors. The only way for at least one consumer to be better off and no consumers to be worse off is to have the sector supply a smaller combination of inputs inside the Scitovsky contour. But then at least one output must be reduced. A simultaneous solution to both primal optimizing problems also determines an equilibrium price ratio for the inputs.

For full equilibrium of the economy, input and output levels must be adjusted to each other. With final commodity levels fixed, consumers can make an optimal choice among the input combinations capable of turning out those levels. But given freedom of choice, they may prefer to supply smaller amounts of the inputs, buy less of the final commodities, and devote larger amounts of the primary inputs to personal use. Figure 19–2c shows the final requirement for general equilibrium as tangency between a total product curve for the producing sector and a Scitovsky contour for the consuming sector. The slope of the total product curve, which is the marginal productivity of the input everywhere in the sector, must equal the rate of substitution between the commodity and the input for every consumer. For two consumers the condition is

$$\bar{e}_{32} = \frac{c_2}{p_3} = \frac{\bar{u}_{12}}{\bar{u}_{13}} = \frac{\bar{u}_{22}}{\bar{u}_{23}}.$$

Each additional consumer adds another ratio on the right.

Readers may verify that by attaining equilibrium the market mechanism again generates simultaneous solutions to primal optimizing problems for both sectors. The solutions to these problems provide much insight into the nature of equilibrium. The marginal utilities of each consumer are personal valuations or internal prices. Hence, the tangency condition may be expressed as

$$\bar{u}_{13}\bar{e}_{32} = \bar{u}_{12}.$$

Expressed in terms of the first consumer's own prices, the marginal revenue productivity of the second input in producing the third commodity must equal the input price. A consumer has two choices: devote a primary input to personal use, or supply the primary input to the producing sector and receive a final commodity in exchange. At the optimum the two options must yield equal returns in terms of the consumer's own personal set of valuations. The condition must hold simultaneously for all consumers, and it must hold between any primary input and any final commodity. In fact, as readers may show, the first two conditions for general equilibrium guarantee that, if the third condition holds for one pair, it holds for all. As is true for a two-input, two-output firm, three conditions determine a solution.

Fundamentally, then, general equilibrium for the economy is a state in which all consumers are simultaneously in adjustment with respect to their use of the primary inputs they possess. A consumer may use primary inputs directly or supply them to the producing sector and receive produced commodities. The economy is in equilibrium when no consumer has an incentive to change the balance between direct and indirect use. The basic requirements for general equilibrium depend upon the marginal productivities of the inputs and the relative valuations or marginal utilities of all consumers. The marginal productivities are, in turn, the result of technological conditions, the level of fixed inputs, and their distribution throughout the producing sector. The marginal utilities depend upon the tastes and preferences of consumers, the level of primary inputs, and their distribution among consumers.

In the short run, the amounts of the fixed inputs and their distribution among firms affect the shape and position of the producing sector's product transformation and other curves. Similarly, the amounts of the fixed inputs and the distribution of their ownership among consumers influence the distribution of income and, through it, the shape and position of the Scitovsky contours. Over time economic forces may alter the distribution of fixed inputs, and the economic process of saving and investing can change the total amounts. Thus, the substrata of noneconomic conditions upon which economic equilibrium rests consist of technology, consumer preference, and the supplies of primary inputs, including the population.

TAXATION AND PARETO OPTIMALITY

General equilibrium for the economy as a whole requires a set of prices on the basis of which all economic units make mutually consistent decisions.

If ratios of internal prices are everywhere equal for those quantities that are variable, an equilibrium level of market prices also implies a solution that is at the same time technologically optimal and Pareto optimal. No individual can gain except at the expense of others. A market system that functions perfectly and without external interference assures a unique set of prices for all decision makers and guarantees the ubiquitous equality of internal price ratios. But, general equilibrium can exist even though all economic units are not responding to the same prices. In a single market, for example, the quantity demanded and quantity supplied can be equal when buyers are paying a higher price than sellers are receiving. A tax on the commodity has precisely this effect. If the tax is paid by sellers, the net price, on which they base their decisions, is less than the market price, to which buyers are responding. Hence, equilibrium can exist without the universal equality of internal price ratios that is necessary for simultaneous optimal solutions of the primal problems for both sectors.

Imperfections in the functioning of markets are one cause of a non-optimal result; because of ignorance, time lags, or other factors, all buyers and all sellers may not be basing their decisions on identical market prices. A still more important reason is monopoly power, the topic of Chapter 20. Externally imposed restrictions on perfectly functioning markets can also prevent optimal solutions to the primal problems. Examples are taxes, tariffs, quotas, rationing, and the like, but we shall take up only various forms of taxation.

Excise Taxes with Primary Inputs Constant

To develop the analysis in stages, we return to the simple case where all consumers supply fixed amounts of the primary inputs. Income is at the mercy of the market prices and is not a result of decision making by individuals. Taxes on income at most affect the distribution of income among members of the consuming sector. Unless the tax receipts taken from the system return to it, then by Walras' law there cannot be zero excess demand in all markets. To avoid the introduction of purchases by a government sector, we simply assume that tax receipts return to the private economy as transfer payments to individuals. A change in the distribution of income shifts the equilibrium to a new point on the producing sector's product transformation curve. But the new equilibrium is also Pareto optimal so long as all consuming units base their independent optimizing decisions on the same set of commodity prices.

When both commodities are taxed but at the same percentage of their market prices, the only effects arise from the apportionment of the tax receipts. All economic units base their decisions on the same external price *ratios*, so the ratios of internal prices are everywhere the same. Suppose, instead, that only one commodity is taxed and that firms pay the tax. Since the net price governs business decisions, equilibrium for the producing sector lies at a new point on the product transformation curve, say P' in Figure 19–3. If consumers initially base their decisions on the previously existing market prices and all happen to receive transfers that maintain the same incomes, equilibrium for the consuming sector remains at E. But markets are not in equilibrium, so prices must change, and both income and its distribution must adjust in response to the change in market prices and the apportionment of the tax receipts. Ultimately, market clearing prices are reestablished and both sectors come into equilibrium at some intermediate point on the transformation curve, such as E'. But at that point the slope of the transformation curve must be numerically equal to the ratio of the *net* prices received by business, while the slope of the Scitovsky contour must be numerically equal to the ratio of market prices. Hence, the Scitovsky contour cuts through the product transformation curve, and the result is not Pareto optimal. There are attainable output combinations inside the Scitovsky contour, so at least one consumer can benefit without penalizing others.

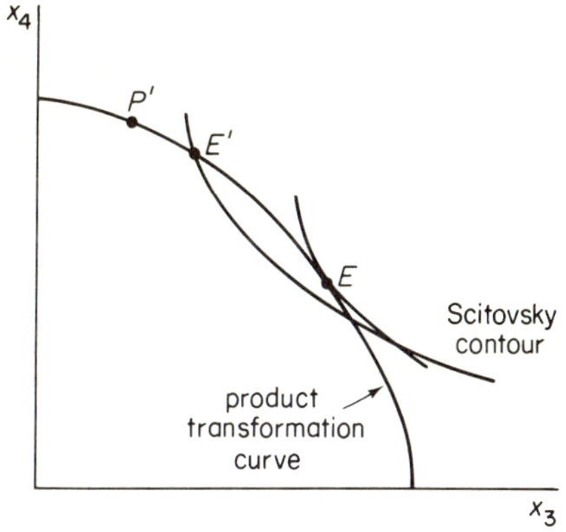

Fig. 19-3 A Tax on a Single Commodity

Taxation with Primary Inputs Variable

Taxes on primary inputs with commodities constant obviously have similar effects, so we pass on to the more general case where both inputs and commodities are variable. The same percentage tax on all commodities now has an effect on equilibrium apart from any distributional consequences. For the producing sector the appropriate diagram is now a total product curve, such as Figure 19–2c, between any final commodity and any primary input. The producing sector comes into equilibrium where the marginal productivity of the input equals the ratio of the input price to the *net* commodity price. But the consuming sector comes into equilibrium where the slope of the Scitovsky contour equals the ratio of market prices for the input and the commodity. Hence, equilibrium for both sectors occurs at a point where the Scitovsky contour intersects the total product curve. Symbolically, the condition for the jth consumer becomes

$$\frac{c_1}{p_3(1-t)} = \bar{e}_{31} \neq \frac{c_1}{p_3} = \frac{\bar{u}_{j_1}}{\bar{u}_{j_3}} \qquad \text{or} \qquad \bar{u}_{j_3}\bar{e}_{31} \neq \bar{u}_{j_1}.$$

In terms of each consumer's personal valuations, the marginal value productivity of the primary input does not equal its value in personal use. The tax prevents a typical consumer from allocating primary inputs optimally between direct personal use and the indirect exchange for final commodities.

Equal percentage taxes on the inputs supplied have a similar effect. A proportional income tax takes a constant fraction of every dollar earned and has the same general consequences as an equal percentage tax on all inputs supplied. A progressive income tax is more complex, but it clearly takes the economy further from the state of equal internal price ratios everywhere.

We can now summarize the consequences of different types of taxation. For the present model the following taxes have the same general effect: an equal percentage tax on all inputs supplied, a proportional income tax, and a general sales tax on all final commodities without any exemptions. All of these taxes prevent tangency of Scitovsky contours with total product curves, but they do not keep Scitovsky contours from becoming tangent to product transformation curves or input substitution contours. A tax on a single commodity or different percentage taxes on all commodities prevent tangency of Scitovsky contours to both the product transformation curve and the total product curves. Thus, an excise tax on a single commodity causes greater distortion per dollar of revenue raised. A similar conclusion holds for a tax on a single input. In a broader model in which individuals also save, a general sales tax and a proportional income tax do not have identical effects. Any tax on final commodities alone, including an excise tax on a single commodity, distorts the decision between consumption and saving. If equilibrium is to be Pareto optimal under a system of taxation, taxes must permit all economic units to adjust to the same price ratios. The only such tax is a lump-sum tax which takes income arbitrarily from economic units and permits them to spend optimally what is left. The amounts taken from each consumer must, however, be unknown and unexpected. If consumers know what the taxes are going to be, or have expectations, tax levels will enter into their decisions.

EXTERNAL EFFECTS AND PARETO OPTIMALITY

So long as all economic units affect each other only through markets and market prices, the equilibrium achieved by perfectly functioning, unfettered markets satisfies Pareto optimality. The conclusion does not hold when there are economic effects that are not transmitted through markets. There are many varieties of external effects, and their importance grows as the economic world shrinks. Chapter 14 took up one type of external effect, the interdependence of consumption processes, which prevents individual optimizing from attaining the optimum for the family. The consuming sector as a whole contains similar interdependencies, with the same general result.

The consumption processes of one consumer may affect the utility levels of other consumers adversely, say by noise or litter, or favorably, as by the beautification of property. With interdependence it is still possible conceptually to minimize one commodity for a constant amount of the other commodity and prescribed levels of utility. The resultant Scitovsky contours will not be the same as those derived by arbitrarily neglecting the interdependence and basing each consumer's utility solely on his own combination of commodities. When each consumer optimizes independently, equilibrium for the sector occurs where the sector's income line is tangent to the contour based on neglect of cross-effects. The sector generally will be buying too much of a commodity with adverse cross-effects and too little of a commodity with favorable cross-effects. The same total income spent differently would benefit at least one consumer without harming any other. Thus, independent optimization at the same set of prices does lead to an equilibrium, but it is not Pareto optimal.

Externalities within the Producing Sector

We shall now consider another type of externality and show how it prevents equilibrium from being Pareto optimal. Of ever increasing importance are the waste products of industry, atomic waste, smoke, used chemicals, and the like. These wastes are essentially joint products that have no market and no market price. Firms wish to dispose of them and, in the absence of any constraint, choose the least costly way, which may be simply letting them escape into the air or dumping them into a river. But when disposed of in these ways, the joint products become unwanted inputs to other producers or to consumers. An unwanted input adds a process of its own that either lowers output or raises the requirements for other inputs.

Suppose, instead, that the processes putting forth the unwanted product and the processes involuntarily using it operate within the same firm, say in different plants. The manager of the plant responsible for the noxious by-product must dispose of it or find his output reduced. If the by-product is valueless and there is a method of costless disposal, the manager chooses it to achieve the optimal solution. But the method of disposal causes the by-product to become unwanted inputs for other plants. The problem is formally similar to the model analyzed in Chapter 10, where the output of one plant becomes an input for other plants. Since the by-product has no value of its own and reduces other outputs, it has a negative marginal revenue productivity to the firm and a negative firm-wide price.

To find the firm-wide price we first set up an optimizing problem for the firm that includes all production processes, output-reducing processes, and disposal processes. The solution will choose optimally from the following courses of action: select different production processes within the offending plant that reduce the deleterious joint product but at the cost of smaller saleable output from the plant; employ disposal or elimination processes that are not costless but do reduce the loss to other plants. With all data available the optimal solution will correctly balance off gains and losses for the firm and will establish a firm-wide negative price for the noxious joint product. A negative price is a charge or a tax that alters the relative cost of all production and disposal processes within the offending plant. The plant manager is induced to make an independent optimizing decision that is optimal for the firm as a whole. There may also be joint products that are valueless within the producing plant but affect favorably the output of other plants. Subsidies are needed to discourage disposal and to favor production processes that yield large amounts of the joint product.

We can now extend the results to the producing sector as a whole. When firms optimize independently, neglecting external effects, the resultant equilibrium for the sector will not be a solution to the true technological optimizing problem. The reason is the intermediate inputs representing the external effects do not have the same internal price throughout the sector. Solving the technological minimizing problem with external effects neglected generates an input function and from it a transformation curve for the sector, but it lies inside the true efficiency frontier. To guide firms to the correct solution the neglected by-products must have positive prices or subsidies, negative prices or taxes. The correct levels come from the optimal solution to the technological minimizing or cost minimizing problem for the sector.

External Effects Between Sectors

There is another possibility. Even though there are no external effects between industries and between consumers, the activities of one sector may have external effects on the other. For the economy as a whole the final commodities of the producing sector play the same role as intermediate inputs within the sector. They are outputs of production processes but inputs to consumption processes. Similarly, the harmful or beneficial by-products of production are intermediate inputs for which markets do not exist. Hence, their internal prices within the producing sector, presumably zero, do not correspond to the negative or positive valuations within the consuming sector. To simplify the analysis of the problem we assume that the primary inputs are in fixed supply, and that there are no external or nonmarket effects within the producing or consuming sectors. It is possible conceptually to set up an optimization problem for both sectors together. With primary inputs constant, the utility of one consumer is maximized at prescribed utility levels for the other consumers.

If the model includes all production and output-reducing processes and all disposal or elimination processes, the solution will determine the optimal way of utilizing primary inputs. Optimality may require a choice of production processes that reduce the deleterious joint products and expand the beneficial; or it may divert primary inputs into the elimination of the undesirable products. In either case the producing sector cannot reach the efficiency frontier that emerges when external effects on consumers are ignored. The cost to society of reducing or eliminating undesirable joint products and expanding the beneficial joint products is lower production of final commodities, or a lower GNP as currently defined.

The optimal solution to the foregoing problem also generates as dual variables relative prices for both primary inputs and final commodities. If all producing and consuming units optimize independently on the basis of these prices the result is Pareto optimal. However, the prices are not those that result from the perfect operation of unfettered markets; prices must be guided into the correct ratios by appropriately chosen taxes and subsidies.

It is not only the producing sector that generates undesirable joint products. Consumers who supply their labor services by driving their own automobiles to work are partly responsible for the smog that adversely affects both production processes and consumption processes. The adverse effect can be reduced by a different choice of supply processes, car pools or public transportation, or by the use of elimination processes. It is again a question of allocating resources optimally and of finding the proper set of monetary incentives and deterrents to guide the economy to the correct solution.

In the absence of external effects individual optimization and unfettered markets establish a general equilibrium that is Pareto optimal. Taxes and subsidies do not prevent the attainment of equilibrium but they do in general keep it from being optimal. When external effects are present, the conclusions are reversed. Some outside interference in the form of taxes and subsidies is needed to insure Pareto optimality.

ECONOMIC WELFARE FUNCTIONS

To analyze the relationship between economic welfare functions and Pareto optimality we revert to the simpler model in which there are no externalities. When individuals optimize within a market system that functions without imperfections and outside interference, a general equilibrium exists that satisfies both technological optimality and Pareto optimality. Since both types of optimality are formally similar, we shall use Pareto optimality to cover both. Proving that general equilibrium satisfies Pareto optimality does not involve any value judgments and belongs within positive economics. Also, showing that various types of taxes do or do not produce Pareto optimal results lies within the realm of positive economics. This is not so when we assert that one tax is better than another *because* it satisfies Pareto optimality. We have then set up Pareto optimality as a standard of value or criterion by which economic situations are to be judged. In so doing we have implicitly introduced an economic welfare function with certain broad properties. Chapter 14 presented welfare functions as a formal method of resolving the indeterminancy in family decision making. Readers should review pages 361–64. We shall briefly extend the results to the consuming sector as a whole.

As an economic norm Pareto optimality avoids the ranking of individuals, or interpersonal comparisons of utility. It is individualistic in that it accepts each individual's ranking of his own economic welfare. An individual's economic welfare can be defined broadly, but the most important component must always be the final commodities and primary inputs available for personal use. Customarily, this most important component is taken to be the sole component. Further, in ranking levels of economic welfare the individual uses the same utility function or preference scale that guides his decisions as a consumer. The final and most important requirement for Pareto optimality is that no individual have a negative or zero weight in measuring the nation's economic welfare. When at least one individual ranks his current situation more highly and no individual records a lower ranking, the nation's economic welfare has risen.

As Chapter 14 demonstrated, Pareto optimality as an economic norm amounts to assuming that economic welfare is an increasing function of individual utility levels. Alternatively, it corresponds to a partial ordering of vectors in utility space. Economic welfare satisfies only the criterion that more is better than less; whenever a ranking of utility vectors exists, the welfare ranking coincides with it. All we can conclude about the isowelfare contours in utility space is that they are downward sloping; a constant level of economic welfare requires that one consumer's utility decreases whenever the other consumer's utility increases. Pareto optimality even permits linear isowelfare contours along which welfare remains constant even though one individual's utility goes to zero.

Since it corresponds to the partial ordering of vectors, a welfare function that satisfies only the conditions of Pareto optimality leaves many economic situations unranked relative to each other. Technological optimality requires only that prices or relative weights be positive, and Pareto optimality requires only that the weights assigned to individual utility levels be positive. To reduce the possibility of unranked situations, we must narrow the ranges of the weights assigned to utility levels. The formally correct and rigorous solution is to make welfare the same type of function of utility combinations that utility itself is of commodity combinations. Such a function partitions utility space into a set of nonintersecting isowelfare contours. The partition carries over into commodity space and provides a set of nonintersecting curves, known as Bergson contours, which show all commodity combinations capable of providing the same level of economic welfare. Like the isorevenue contours in the input space of a multiproduct firm, each Bergson contour is an envelope curve, being tangent at every point to a Scitovsky contour. Final commodity space, for example, is partitioned into a set of nonintersecting, convex Bergson or isowelfare contours, similar to an individual's indifference map. Economic welfare attains its maximum at the unique point of tangency between the efficiency frontier and an isowelfare contour. Hence, a smooth welfare function with the same general properties as a utility function implies the existence of a unique welfare optimum.

Society has obviously not devised welfare functions of the preceding type that rank all possible utility combinations. But policies such as the progressive income tax and proposals for a negative income tax or a floor under incomes imply properties of the welfare function that go beyond the very weak requirements of Pareto optimality. The consensus of society is that economic welfare is raised by reducing wide disparities in income and utility levels. Intermediate combinations of utility rank above extremes, so the isowelfare contours must be convex at least in the vicinity of the axes. Public policy has not yet decreed that welfare rises when any disparity in income or utility levels is reduced. In intermediate ranges the isowelfare contours may possibly be line segments, or they may simply not be defined beyond the requirements for Pareto optimality.

EXERCISES

1. *Equilibrium and Optimality for the Producing Sector*

Consider only the smooth version of a producing sector that uses two primary inputs and turns out two final commodities.

(a) Both primary inputs are in fixed supply to the sector. Demonstrate that equilibrium in the input markets implies maximum revenue at given output prices. Use the results of earlier chapters and the following suggestions on points to cover:

(1) Equilibrium in one input market implies that revenue cannot be increased by shifting the input between firms, industries, or products. It also implies the impossibility of increasing revenue by using more of the input.

(2) Write the full conditions for tangency of the total revenue line to a product transformation curve. Show that tangency implies equality of each input's marginal revenue productivity in the production of both outputs. Show conversely that equilibrium in the input markets implies the conditions for tangency.

(b) Interchange inputs and outputs. Demonstrate in analogous fashion that equilibrium in output markets implies cost minimization at given input prices.

(c) When inputs and outputs are both variable, explain why the maximization of net revenue at given prices requires also that a net revenue line be tangent to one total product curve. Demonstrate that equilibrium in the corresponding input market implies the required tangency.

(d) Give an analogous demonstration that equilibrium in an output market implies tangency of a net cost line to a marginal input requirement curve.

2. *Equilibrium and Optimality for the Consuming Sector*

Consider only the smooth version of a consuming sector that consists of two consumers supplying two primary inputs and buying two final commodities.

(a) The primary inputs are supplied by the consuming sector in fixed total amounts. Specify the optimizing problem that generates a Scitovsky contour in final commodity space. Draw a typical contour. Explain how a contour classifies all commodity bundles in the space with respect to the satisfaction they can yield the consumers.

Show graphically the expenditure minimizing solution for given utility levels. Write out in full the algebraic conditions for a minimum. Also write the conditions for each consumer to be in equilibrium at a given commodity price. Show that one implies the other. If aggregate income equals the minimal expenditure on commodities, what requirement determines the distribution of income between consumers?

(b) With final commodities constant in total amount and in distribution between consumers, specify the optimizing problem that generates a Scitovsky contour in primary input space. Draw a typical contour. Explain how it partitions input space, taking into account the fixed total amounts of the primary inputs. Show graphically the minimization of opportunity cost. Write out in full the algebraic conditions for a minimum. Relate to the conditions for equilibrium of both consumers and of the sector.

Demonstrate the equivalence of minimizing the opportunity cost of primary inputs retained and maximizing the income from inputs supplied. Draw a contour for inputs supplied. Explain how it partitions the space.

(c) Hold constant the amount purchased of one final commodity and the amount supplied of one primary input. Specify the optimizing problem that defines the Scitovsky contour for the remaining final commodity and primary input. Distinguish between points inside and outside the contour. Show graphically the minimization of net expenditure. Write the full algebraic conditions for a minimum and relate to the requirements for equilibrium of the sector.

3. *Equilibrium and Optimality for the Economy*

Consider only a smooth version of an economy with two final commodities and two primary inputs.

(a) The consuming sector chooses to supply fixed amounts of the primary inputs at all levels of prices. Draw a typical product transformation curve. By considering Scitovsky contours that lie beyond the efficiency frontier and others that intersect it, state why equilibrium can occur only at a point of tangency. Explain why equilibrium can occur at almost any point along a product transformation curve, except possibly at the axes. What determines the precise point at which equilibrium occurs?

In what sense is the preceding equilibrium optimal? Distinguish between the effects of each of the following changes on the equilibrium and its optimality: the amounts of the primary inputs supplied are redistributed among firms; the amounts of the primary inputs supplied are redistributed among consumers.

(b) The amounts supplied of the primary inputs are variable. Draw the additional diagrams necessary to portray general equilibrium. Show once again that tangency between pairs of contours is the only configuration consistent with equilibrium. In what way is the equilibrium optimal?

4. *The Optimal Allocation of Primary Inputs*

Explain why general equilibrium requires primary inputs and final commodities to have the same ratio of internal prices everywhere throughout the economy. Deduce from the general requirement the following result: In terms of any one consumer's personal valuations, the marginal revenue or value productivity of a primary input must equal its supply price or opportunity cost. Does a tax on a final commodity force a consumer to have more or less than the optimal amount of leisure?

In an economy with two primary inputs and two final commodities there are four input-output pairs. Both sectors are simultaneously in equilibrium with respect to three of the pairs. Show that the economy must be in general equilibrium.

5. *Taxes and Pareto Optimality*

With two primary inputs and two final commodities there are six pairs for which contours can be drawn. The tax to be imposed is a percentage of the market price. Producers pay the tax whether it is levied on final commodities sold or primary inputs purchased. For each of the following taxes or combinations of taxes, identify all pairs of contours, if any, that will not be tangent in equilibrium:

(1) A tax on one final commodity.

(2) Equal percentage taxes on both final commodities.

(3) Unequal percentage taxes on both final commodities.

(4), (5), (6) Repeat the preceding taxes for primary inputs.

(7) Equal percentage taxes on a final commodity and a primary input.

(8) Equal percentages taxes on all commodities and inputs.

Which of the preceding taxes correspond to a general sales tax and which to a proportional income tax? (Assume no income from ownership of fixed inputs.) How do the effects compare?

20

Monopoly, Monopolistic Competition, and Oligopoly

Economics is advancing on many fronts but not at the same pace and not under any centralized control. For many decades much time and intellectual energy have gone into constructing a model of the entire economy and proving certain general properties of the model. To achieve the objective, economists imposed drastic simplifications on the decision models of firms and consumers. This has led to some misunderstanding. Both in the classroom and in reading, most students of economics feel that they can formulate more realistic models of both firms and consumers. They are undoubtedly correct, but that is not the issue. The crucial question is whether they can formulate more realistic versions of economic units, build them into a model of the whole economic system, and deduce the general properties of the system. As yet no one has done this rigorously.

While work on the purely competitive model proceeded, economists have also been devoting much time to expanded and modified decision models of the firm under more varied and complex conditions. Firms advertise to influence consumer preferences, produce a great variety of products, alter the quality of products, develop new products, and engage in research that points toward new products and new processes in the future. Also, firms in an industry may specialize on slightly different varieties of the product, and each may have some limited power to vary prices on its particular batch of differentiated products. Further, the firms in an industry may be few in number; each may watch closely the policies of the others and respond directly to changes in those policies rather than to the resultant effects on the firm's own sales. Finally, firms do not buy all inputs in purely competitive markets; they may obtain supplies of some inputs only after hard bargaining.

For inclusion in a general equilibrium model the economic theory of the firm has concentrated upon the production decision. As detailed earlier, the traditional smooth version of the firm assumes that the technological optimizing problem has been solved and the technological data summarized in the form of a smooth output or input function. Technological change means that the data underlying the technological optimizing problem have changed, altering the output or input function. Since it does not explicitly solve the technological optimizing problem, the conventional theory of the firm has generally defined and classified technological change in terms of the effects it has on the output or input functions. When a firm engages in research and development it is operating at a more basic level and is in effect employing processes whose output consists of entirely new production processes or modifications of existing processes. Further, these research and development processes use inputs and lay claim to part of the scarce financial resources of the firm.

At given input prices the firm seeks to minimize cost for any combination of output levels. With selling prices fixed, this solution also maximizes net revenue for every combination of outputs. When selling prices are not fixed, there exists a separate problem of marketing the products. The objective of marketing can be defined as seeking maximum net revenue from previously produced combinations of outputs. There are many different marketing processes, and the aim is to find the optimal combination. A firm with many products and some control over prices has a difficult problem in choosing prices, since the level chosen for one product affects the demand for the others. Beyond this, the firm may try to shift demand curves by advertising.

A firm generally cannot purchase all inputs at constant prices, so there is an analogous problem of purchasing optimally. Thus, the production problem, which simplified models of the firm treat almost exclusively, is embedded in a whole complex of related problems. Ideally, the problems should not be solved separately; the firm should not produce a technologically efficient but unsalable automobile and leave it to the marketing department to sell it somehow. However, the great complexity compels suboptimization plus some attempt to fit the separate optimal solutions into an overall optimum for the firm.

A large firm presents a fascinating problem in decision making and has received much attention. But we do not as yet know the precise implications for the economy as a whole of greatly expanding the decision model for the firm. To analyze the effects on the economy as a whole, we need to return to the purely competitive model and introduce changes singly. Space permits us to take up only one modification, where firms possess some degree of control over selling prices, some monopoly power, and do not simply take the market price as given.

MONOPOLY IN OUTPUT MARKETS

For any constant level of prices the independent optimizing decisions of firms in a purely competitive industry succeed in maximizing revenue from given inputs and in minimizing cost for any combination of outputs. At those prices there is no way to widen the spread between total revenue and total cost, but firms acting collectively have the power to influence prices by controlling the level of output or the purchase of inputs. We shall consider first the case where the firms, even though acting collectively, regard their influence on input prices as negligible and ignore it. To isolate the principal issues we shall also restrict the discussion to a single-product industry.

The Optimum for the Firm

When a single firm takes over the productive capacity of a purely competitive industry, the previously independent firms assume the role of plants. At given input prices and at any specified level of output, the firm minimizes cost when the internal price or marginal cost of the product has the same value in every plant. The horizontal summation of the marginal cost curves for the plants, which becomes the marginal cost curve for the firm, displays for each level of output the common internal price and determines the optimal allocation of output quotas among plants. In and by itself, the monopolization of a previously competitive industry does not alter either the total or the marginal cost of any level of output.

What does change is the optimal output level. Net revenue is at its maximum when increases in output cause total cost to rise at a greater rate than total revenue, and when decreases in output cause total cost to fall at a lower rate than total revenue. The marginal cost curve shows the rate of change of total cost at each level of output. We need the marginal revenue curve or rate of change of total revenue. When the selling price is constant, it is also the marginal revenue, since $R = px$ varies linearly with output. A fall in price as quantity increases along a demand curve implies that marginal revenue is less than price. How much less depends on the price elasticity of demand and is expressed by the following equation:

$$\text{marginal revenue} = R_3' = p_3\left(1+\frac{1}{s_3}\right) \qquad s_3 < 0.$$

As the price elasticity of demand s_3 increases numerically, the expression in parentheses increases toward the limit of 1, when marginal revenue equals price. For example, when $s_3 = -2$, $R_3' = \frac{1}{2}p_3$; but when $s_3 = -10$, $R_3' = \frac{9}{10}p_3$. With a demand curve of constant elasticity, marginal revenue has everywhere the same ratio to the market price. Figure 20–1 shows the

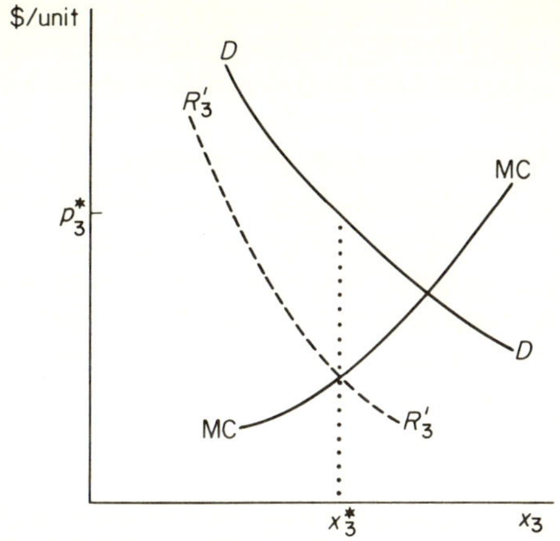

Fig. 20-1 The Optimum for a Monopolist

relationship between the demand and marginal revenue curves. The intersection of the downward-sloping marginal revenue curve and the upward-sloping marginal cost curve identifies the output that maximizes net revenue.

Multifirm Monopoly

When a single firm takes over, it can allocate output quotas at will. In order to reap the benefits of monopoly while retaining ownership of the productive capacity, firms sometimes enter into cartels or other collusive arrangements with each other. Efficiency dictates that output quotas be so assigned as to equalize marginal cost, but it does not determine the division of the profits. As an extreme illustration, a firm may have both large capacity and a marginal cost curve that lies between the marginal revenue and the price in the optimal solution. Unless paid handsomely to shut down, such a firm has a powerful incentive to disrupt the arrangement by producing and selling a shade below the cartel's price. But large rewards for inefficiency may irk the efficient firms and cause them to pull out. It is bargaining power and not efficiency alone that determines a firm's share of the profits.

If antitrust laws prohibit overt agreements, firms sometimes tacitly follow practices that have the effect of establishing quotas based primarily on productive capacity. The share of the profits each firm receives depends on the sale of its own quota. Such arrangements are not likely to minimize cost for the industry as a whole.

Single-Firm Monopoly as a Decision Model

The familiar concept of the supply curve, which is crucial in pure competition, is no longer defined and ceases to exist under monopoly. The supply curve emerges from the conceptual experiment of varying an output price parametrically and observing the output decisions of the firm. Under the economic model of monopoly it is not enough to provide a firm with the market price; our hypothetical central agency must furnish an entire demand curve specifying the quantities buyers will take at all possible prices. For each entire demand curve the monopolist chooses the optimal quantity to supply. The analogous conceptual experiment is to vary or shift the entire demand curve and observe the resultant decisions. Within our simplified model of the economy, the position of a demand curve depends primarily on other prices, income, its distribution, and preferences. We could vary some other price or income and derive the quantity supplied as a function of either of these independent variables, but the monopolistic decision model simply does not yield quantity supplied as a function of its own price.

The monopolistic firm of economic theory neglects any effects its decisions may have on other industries. But the decisions do have effects. As the monopolist adjusts price along his demand curve, all other demand curves tend to shift, and the industries react to the shifts. The consequent changes in other prices feed back into the monopolist's demand curve, causing it to move about and forcing new decisions on the monopolist. Since the monopolist of economic theory simplifies his decision making by incorrectly assuming the demand curve to be independent of his own decisions, a corrective process must take place. But the corrective process is nothing more nor less than the adjustment of the whole producing sector and, even, of the whole economic system. Unfortunately, once purely competitive assumptions are dropped, proving the existence and stability of general equilibrium becomes much more difficult. As one prominent economist has recently written:

> The existence of equilibrium in an economy with imperfect competition is an unsolved problem of great complexity. Most of the traditional models of firms in imperfect competition (including monopoly) are so rooted in partial [equilibrium] concepts that they need to be rebuilt to fit into a general equilibrium framework.[1]

In the following section we shall specify a set of special conditions under which monopolized and purely competitive industries can produce the same outputs. Since general equilibrium exists for pure competition it must also exist for monopoly under these special conditions. This does not, however, prove the existence of equilibrium under more general conditions that include the possibility of increasing returns to scale. Nor does it solve the problem of stability of equilibrium.

[1]Kelvin Lancaster, *Mathematical Economics* (New York: Crowell-Collier and Macmillan, Inc., 1968), p. 140.

Since there are always some repercussions, the economic model of pure monopoly becomes a more plausible hypothesis about economic behavior when there are no close substitutes. Otherwise, if cross elasticities of demand are high with respect to some products, a change in the monopolist's price will cause a sizable shift in the demand curves for these products and a significant response to the shift. The monopolist is likely to perceive that price changes are not having the effects on qunatity sold predicted by the demand curve. The firm has then to decide whether it is better off continuing to ignore these repercussions or trying to estimate them ahead of time and take them into account in the decision making. Once repercussions are taken into account, the industry slips out of monopoly into oligopoly, a topic for later discussion.

Pure Competition and Monopoly Compared

We can most readily compare a purely competitive and a monopolized industry when the following two conditions prevail: the demand curve is elastic, and the monopolized industry produces on the rising portion of its marginal cost curve beyond the minimal average cost of any of its plants. Under these conditions monopolization has essentially the same effect as an *ad valorem* tax imposed on the output of a purely competitive industry. The price after tax, on which firms base their decisions,[2] is $p_3\ (1-t_3)$. If we choose $-t_3 = 1/s_3$, the purely competitive industry will produce the same output as the monopolized industry and sell it at the same price inclusive of tax.

An inelastic demand curve, $-s_3 < 1$, implies that both $(1+1/s_3)$ and R_3' are negative. A monopolist would continue to restrict output until the demand curve became elastic[3] and marginal revenue came into equality with the always-positive marginal cost. If the demand curve is everywhere inelastic above the supply curve of a purely competitive industry, there is no *ad valorem* tax that will induce the industry to operate at the same level as a monopolist. When a purely competitive industry faces an inelastic demand, an *ad valorem* tax has relatively little effect on output, but the same inelasticity causes a monopolist to make a drastic reduction in output.

[2]In Chapter 19 we assumed that producers based their decisions on p_3 and added the tax. Although the specific tax rates differ slightly, readers may show that the two methods are equivalent.

[3]A demand curve that is everywhere inelastic is a mathematical possibility. The simple, unmodified economic theory of monopoly then predicts that the firm will reduce output toward zero and raise the price toward infinity. Demand curves cannot actually be inelastic everywhere since this implies some positive demand even when the price exceeds the money income of the richest consumer. Should a demand curve become elastic only at an excessively high price it is unlikely that any monopolist would dare to exploit such a high degree of inelasticity. The simple profit maximizing model would give incorrect predictions and would have to be modified.

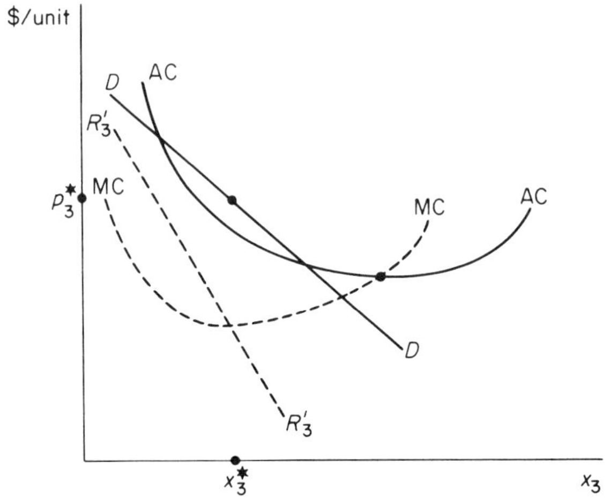

Fig. 20-2 Monopoly under Decreasing Average Cost

A second cause of divergence between monopoly and pure competition is increasing returns to scale. As drawn in Figure 20–2, the demand curve passes through the average cost curve[4] to the left of the minimum point. Production without loss can occur only in the range of declining average cost or increasing returns. Since there is room for only one firm in the industry, the necessary conditions for pure competition do not exist. The monopolist maximizes net revenue at the intersection of marginal revenue with marginal cost, which may be downward sloping. Even if it is not downward sloping, the marginal cost curve must be below the declining average cost curve. If we try to impose purely competitive decision making on the industry by having a central agency set a price, the firm will suffer losses if it produces where marginal cost equals the price. Unless paid a subsidy the firm will exercise the option of shutting down. The important question, to be considered shortly, is whether the firm should be allowed to shut down or whether it should be kept in operation either by a subsidy or by permitting monopolistic pricing.

The partial equilibrium analysis of a monopolized versus a purely competitive industry is a necessary first step but it does not go far enough. When a monopolized industry reduces output it also frees inputs which must seek employment elsewhere. We have to consider the effects on the sector as a whole. In doing this we shall rely primarily on the case where demand is elastic and the monopolist produces along what is the supply curve for the purely competitive industry.

[4]With some modifications that readers can readily make, the analysis can be applied to either the long-run or the short-run average cost curve.

MONOPOLY AND PARETO OPTIMALITY

A monopolist has the same incentive as a purely competitive firm to produce any given output at minimum cost. Further, if all industries are monopolized but all base their cost minimizing decisions on the same input prices, they will solve the cost minimizing problem for any combination of outputs the sector turns out. The tangency of the particular cost line to the input substitution curve also represents one solution to the technological minimizing problem. Further, as Chapter 11 demonstrates, if no inputs go idle and require slack processes, and if no outputs are overproduced and require disposal processes, the solution to the technological minimizing problem implies a solution to the technological maximizing problem. Specifically, we can choose the cost minimizing input combination and the internal prices or marginal costs of the outputs as determined by the optimal solution. The input combination generates a product transformation curve, and a revenue line based on the internal prices is tangent to it at the levels of output the sector is producing.

Under the appropriate set of *ad valorem* taxes, purely competitive industries produce the same quantities as monopolized industries. We know from previous results that a purely competitive sector, taxed or not, solves the technological optimizing problem. This is additional confirmation that a monopolized producing sector also solves the technological optimizing problem and ends up on the product transformation contour. But the actual revenue line, $R = p_3x_3+p_4x_4$, will be tangent to the contour at that point only if the selling prices are all equal to, or bear the same ratio to, the internal prices. Since monopolists equate marginal revenue and marginal cost, the following relations hold for a two-commodity sector:

$$w_3 = R_3' = p_3\left(1+\frac{1}{s_3}\right) \qquad w_4 = R_4' = p_4\left(1+\frac{1}{s_4}\right).$$

Only in the exceptional case where the demand curves have the same elasticity ($s_3 = s_4$) will the selling prices be proportional to the marginal costs. In general, the ratio of selling prices, on which consumers base their decisions, will not equal the ratio of internal prices within the producing sector. At the equilibrium point the Scitovsky contour appropriate to the distribution of income intersects the product transformation contour. Other attainable output combinations would benefit at least one consumer and harm none.

Monopoly pricing also affects the functional distribution of income. The suppliers of primary inputs receive less and the owners of businesses receive more. There need not be an equally great change in the personal distribution of income among consuming units, since many individuals and families receive income from both sources. The net effect, though, is likely to be greater inequality in the personal distribution of income. If society deems greater inequality of income to be undesirable, then monopoly can be condemned even when it produces the same outputs as pure competition. The criterion of Pareto optimality accepts the distribution of income and is neutral with respect to it.

Variable Supplies of Primary Inputs

When primary inputs are not in vertical supply, then even equiproportional taxes or equal price elasticities under monopoly distort the decision to supply inputs. As always, each consumer equates the ratio of market prices to the rate of substitution between a primary input and a final commodity. In minimizing cost a monopolist pays the supplier of an input the value of the marginal product based on the internal price or marginal cost, which is less than the selling price. For the monopolized industry and for the jth consumer the following equations hold:

$$c_1 = w_3 e_{31} = p_3\left(1+\frac{1}{s_3}\right) \qquad \frac{c_1}{p_3} = \frac{\bar{u}_{j1}}{\bar{u}_{j3}}.$$

When $-s_3 > 1$, $w_3 < p_3$, so

$$\bar{e}_{31} = \frac{c_1}{w_3} > \frac{c_1}{p_3} = \frac{\bar{u}_{j1}}{\bar{u}_{j3}} \qquad \text{or} \qquad \bar{u}_{j3}\bar{e}_{31} > \bar{u}_{j1}.$$

The jth consumer has two possibilities: devote the primary input to personal use or exchange it for the final commodity, When monopoly is present, the jth consumer is prevented from equalizing the value of the two options in terms of his own preference scale.

Compared with pure competition a monopolized producing sector forces down input prices relative to final commodity prices. Not only do consumers earn less by supplying inputs, but the opportunity cost or price they must pay for the personal use of an input also declines. The pure substitution effect causes consumers to devote more of a primary input to personal use and to supply less. The income effect may go in either direction. If leisure is an inferior commodity, the consumer will enjoy more leisure as income goes down, and the income effect reinforces the pure substitution effect. Conversely, if leisure is a normal commodity, the two effects counteract and the outcome depends on the relative strengths. Without stronger axioms or additional information, the theory of consumer's choice does not predict whether an individual will work more or less when the wage rate falls.

We can now see clearly the danger in jumping from the results of partial equilibrium analysis to conclusions about the entire economy. With conditions unchanged, the monopolization of a single, previously competitive industry reduces output, but the monopolization of both industries in a two-commodity model simply moves the producing sector to a different point on the transformation contour, reducing one output and increasing the other. In the special case of equal elasticities and constant input supplies, the monopolized sector may turn out the same combination of outputs. With primary inputs variable, the monopolization of both industries and the consequent lowering of input prices could expand the supplies of the inputs and yield greater amounts of both final commodities. The result illustrates one of many fallacies in using gross national product or national income as an indicator of economic welfare. People are producing more but enjoying it less since monopoly pricing prevents them from devoting the optimal amounts of primary inputs to personal use.

Increasing Returns and Pareto Optimality

Several decades ago some economists, impressed by the efficiency of pure competition, used it as a model for decentralized decision making in a planned economy. In so doing, they encountered the problem depicted in Figure 20–2, where a commodity must be produced in the range of decreasing average cost. In general, the revenue line can be tangent to both the product transformation contour and the appropriate Scitovsky contour only if the selling prices equal the internal prices. But a decreasing cost product will then be selling for less than the value of the inputs used in its production. Consumers are willing to buy the product at prices that exceed average cost, but these prices distort the allocation of resources.

We need to answer two key questions. If the decreasing-cost product is produced, at what price should it sell? Should the product be produced at all? The answer to the first question is clear and simple: at a price equal to its marginal cost. If the product sells at its marginal cost the industry must receive a subsidy to cover losses, and the subsidy must be a lump sum to avoid distortion. The subsidy must be paid for by taxes, which we shall assume to be lump-sum taxes on consumers. Each consumer must evaluate his own position in each of the following situations: (1) the decreasing-cost product is not produced and resources are devoted to other products; (2) the product is produced, resources are drawn from other products, and consumers pay lump-sum taxes. If there is a set of lump-sum taxes such that at least one consumer prefers situation 2 and none prefers situation 1, then by the criterion of Pareto optimality the product should be produced, the subsidy paid, and the taxes collected. For discrete changes, such as adding or dropping a commodity, each individual must evaluate his own personal state of economic welfare before the change is made and after the full effects of the change have occurred. If every proposal causes losses as well as gains, a welfare criterion is needed to weigh the gains of some against the losses of others.

MONOPSONY AND MONOPOLY OF INPUTS

Single-firm monopsony exists when one firm is the sole buyer of an input. If the input is supplied competitively and the firm neglects any influence it may have on the output price, we can use the analogy with monopoly to show the optimum for the firm. With a rising supply curve, the firm must offer a higher price for all units in order to secure an additional unit. Hence, as drawn in Figure 20–3, the marginal input cost to the firm exceeds the

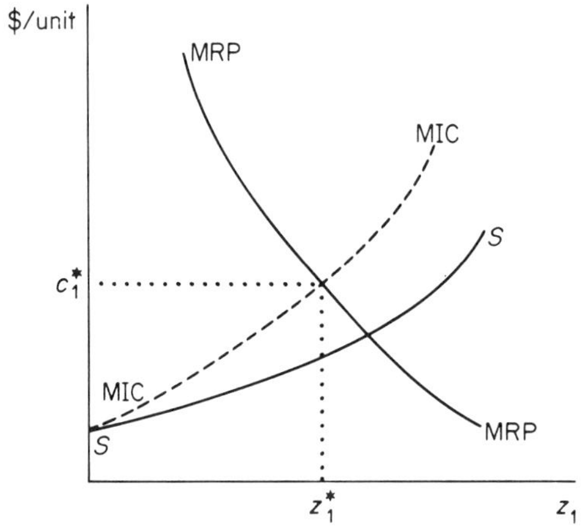

Fig. 20-3 The Optimum for a Monopsonist

price of the input as shown by the supply curve. The optimum for the firm occurs when the marginal input cost curve intersects the marginal revenue productivity curve based on the given output price. If the firm is also a monopolist in the output market, the use of more input causes the output price to fall and marginal revenue must replace price in the determination of marginal revenue productivity.

When a single seller controls the supply of the input, a monopsonist confronts a monopolist in the same market, and the situation is termed *bilateral monopoly*. There is no determinate solution to bilateral monopoly. The problem may be analyzed by use of the Edgeworth box diagram presented in Chapter 14, but this device at best narrows the range of solutions to the contract locus or a portion thereof. A second approach, based on the theory of games, emphasizes the importance of actual or potential threats in determining the outcome of the bargaining. It does not, however, provide a determinate solution unless one makes some additional assumption about the "fairness" of the participants in offering and accepting concessions.

The preceding cases implicitly assume an input specific to an industry for technological reasons. Whatever the outcome of the bargaining, it does not prevent every input from having the same price in every industry, nor does it affect the motivation to minimize cost. Hence, the producing sector continues to solve the technological optimizing problem. Of more significance is collective bargaining between an industry and a union that effectively controls the supply of labor to an industry. Many of the elements of bilateral monopoly are present, but there is the additional factor that the input being supplied is not specific to the industry in a technological sense. The collective bargaining agreements are not likely to give a uniform wage rate throughout the economy. Cost minimizing decisions by firms will not solve the technological optimizing problem for the sector as a whole. This is not a condemnation of collective bargaining, since technological efficiency is but one of many goals for an economic system.

Complete monopolization of a primary input combined with sales to all industries at the same price would permit the producing sector to solve the technological optimizing problem. The results would be essentially the same as a tax on an input under pure competition.

COST-PLUS PRICING

Under pure competition, firms need to know only the current market price, not the demand curve for the product. By contrast, the economic model of monopoly requires that the firm have exact knowledge of the demand curve, a far stronger assumption. Apart from the problem of existence of equilibrium, the economic theory of monopoly has serious defects as a decision model for the firm. Exact knowledge of the demand curve requires much more than exact knowledge of current prices. A firm has to determine the demand curve either by experiment or by statistical study. Walras favored the former method, suggesting a modification of his tâtonnement process whereby the monopolist would test out various prices and progressively narrow the range containing the optimal price. Such a method could lead the firm fairly close to the net revenue maximizing solution, provided that the demand curve did not shift either as a result of the firm's own experiments or because of other changes. With a shifting demand curve, estimation of its properties involves expense and is subject to considerable statistical error. When a monopolist does not have precise knowledge of the demand curve, the theory does not predict whether the firm will spend money to obtain the best estimate or will adopt some other method of determining price that does not require a precise knowledge of the demand curve.

The most widely used method of determining prices is cost-plus pricing or full-cost pricing. In its simplest form a firm simply adds to the average variable cost a percentage markup to cover the cost of the fixed inputs and return some profits. The problem for the firm then becomes the optimal choice of the percentage markup. Under some simplifying assumption the solution can be found. First, we assume that the monopolist operates under linear technology and has a step function for marginal cost of the type derived in Chapter 8. Since marginal cost is constant and equal to average variable cost over ranges of output, it provides a convenient base for affixing the percentage markup. If the elasticity is constant everywhere along the demand curve, or at least in the relevant range, marginal revenue is a constant fraction of the selling price. The reciprocal of that fraction provides the markup that will maximize net revenue. From the earlier net revenue maximizing condition,

$$w_3 = R_3' = p_3\left(1+\frac{1}{s_3}\right).$$

Hence, $p_3 = s/(1+s_3)w_3$, and the term in parentheses determines the optimal markup, which can be expressed as a percentage markup on w_3.

As Figure 20–4 shows, the same base and the same markup can be used, so long as the demand curve shifts without changing elasticity, and output stays within the same horizontal range. Shifts to a new range merely alter the base if the elasticity of demand does not vary. Difficulties arise when output falls in a vertical gap for marginal cost. At the lower price there is excess demand, and at the higher price excess supply. Except at these output levels, the monopolist can attain maximum profits with information on the elasticity of demand only. Many firms use the method even when the elasticity

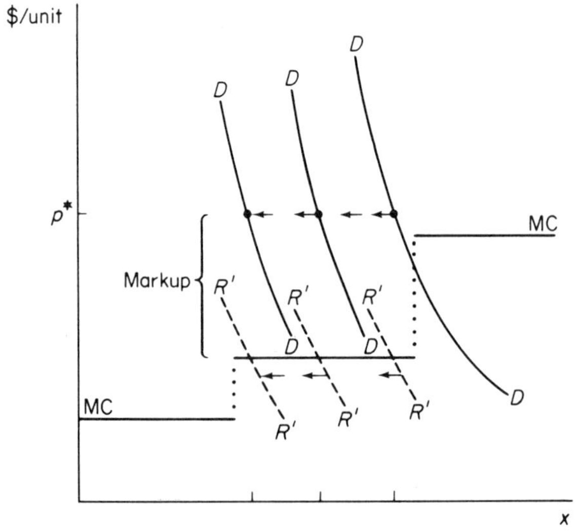

Fig. 20-4 Cost-Plus Pricing

of demand is not known, but there are reasons for believing that percentage markups conform to the probable range of elasticity. The presence of close substitutes cautions a firm to use restraint in choosing the percentage markup, and it also renders the demand curve more elastic.

Cost-plus pricing is a widely used practical method for determining prices even when the elasticity of demand is not constant, or is not known, and when average variable cost varies with output. Markups are not optimal, so the profit maximizing outputs are not produced. The use of markups does keep marginal cost from equaling price, and Pareto optimality is not attained. But cost-plus pricing does not prevent firms from minimizing cost at uniform input prices. Hence, the sector solves the technological optimizing problem but ends up producing a different combination of outputs from either monopoly or pure competition.

THE CLASSIFICATION OF INDUSTRIES

In classifying industries economists rely heavily on the twin criteria of number of firms and the presence or absence of a differentiated product. Monopoly, sometimes called pure monopoly, and pure competition represent polar extremes with respect to number of firms selling a homogeneous or undifferentiated product. The intermediate case is *pure oligopoly*, where the number of firms exceeds one but is not large enough to induce purely competitive decision making.

We must distinguish between mere differences in product and genuine differentiation of product. Nearly all firms are technologically capable of producing a range of different products, at least when we count different grades, qualities, and sizes. There are, for example, many different properties of steel—such as hardness, carbon content, and so on. Manufacturers of steel produce a great variety of steel products to suit different uses. So long as many firms are technologically capable of producing every specification of the product, and so long as buyers are indifferent between the outputs of the different firms, the industry is classified as multiproduct and purely competitive. Most purely competitive industries fall into this classification. Similarly, nearly all pure oligopolies are multiproduct, the outstanding examples being the steel and aluminium industries, which turn out many thousands of products.

It is easier to describe what economists mean by differentiation of the product than to define it rigorously. There is some identifiable commodity, such as toothpaste, with certain generic properties, but there are also variants or brands of the commodity that differ from each other in specific ways. These differences need not be physically identifiable by a battery of scientific tests but may exist only in the image that advertising has created in the minds of buyers. For each variant of the product there are some consumers who believe it is not quite the same as the others. When all variants sell at the same price, buyers express their preferences by choosing one over the others. Further, when the price of one variant rises with all other prices constant, at least some buyers remain loyal and continue to buy, although possibly in reduced amounts. Thus, each variant has a determinate demand curve that can be captured by the conceptual experiment of varying only the one price and observing consumer choices. The demand curve may be highly elastic, reflecting the presence of many close substitutes, but it does exist and is distinct from the horizontal gap that occurs when outputs are perfect substitutes for each other. The crucial condition for differentiation of the product, as distinct from mere differences, is that each producer has a limited degree of monopoly over his own special variant. No other firm can duplicate it exactly, at least in the minds of some buyers. When one, few, or many firms produce a differentiated product, the corresponding industries are classified as *differentiated monopoly*, *differentiated oligopoly*, and *differentiated* or *monopolistic competition.*

MONOPOLISTIC COMPETITION

Monopolistic competition exists when many firms produce a differentiated product. The decision model for each firm is that of single-firm monopoly. Each firm exploits fully its limited degree of monopoly by producing where marginal revenue equals marginal cost. To do this the firm must have exact knowledge of its demand curve. Monopolistic competition is sometimes explained as merely giving a slight downward tilt to the supposedly horizontal demand curve of a purely competitive firm. This is clearly not correct. A purely competitive firm, as we saw earlier, bases its decisions not on a demand curve, which doesn't exist, but on a horizontal approximation to a market reaction curve. All the firm needs to know is the current market price. The monopolistically competitive firm, like a monopolist, needs a true demand curve; it must know how much consumers will buy at each level of price, all other prices remaining constant.

As one firm moves along its demand curve, the demand curves of other firms shift, and these firms must in turn adjust output and price to remain in equilibrium. The theory of monopolistic competition plausibly assumes that any one firm will not take into account these adjustments by other firms and the consequent feedback on its own sales. The firm simply responds to the induced shifts in its own demand curve as it would to shifts that have their origin outside the industry. In some presentations of the theory the additional claim is made that there will in fact be no feedback and that the firm can move along its demand curve without causing the curve to shift. There are so many firms, the argument runs, that the effect on any one firm is minute and will go unnoticed. This is invalid. Suppose that all $n-1$ firms lower their prices consecutively. Each individual cut goes unnoticed by the nth firm, but the cumulative effect is substantial and the nth firm simply does not know where its demand curve is. What holds for the nth firm holds for all firms, so the theory breaks down. In reality firms certainly do fail to perceive small changes, but economists have replaced the firm of reality with a smooth model based on the calculus. Within that model, firms are assumed to be sensitive to the slightest change along the demand curve as well as to the slightest shift of that curve.

As a model of an industry, monopolistic competition is incomplete. Firms base their decisions on simplified, objectively incorrect assumptions, just as they do under pure competition. What is needed is a demonstration that a stable equilibrium exists for the industry even though all firms act on partially false information. Economists have not yet provided such a demonstration. This is one reason why some authors abandon the concept of a monopolistically competitive industry and treat monopolistically competitive firms as small, independent monopolists in a general equilibrium framework. There is a loss in doing this since producers of very close substitutes are linked together in ways that producers of distant substitutes are not. Also, in making fruitful empirical studies it is necessary to concentrate upon subsets of firms without being concerned with repercussions throughout the entire economy.

If we assume the entire producing sector is monopolistically competitive and treat it as a sector of many small monopolists, we can use some of the results derived for monopoly. Monopolistically competitive firms minimize cost at uniform input prices and thus solve the technological optimizing problem. They are not likely to produce along a rising marginal cost curve beyond minimal average cost. The presence of many close substitutes so reduces the demand for any one product that firms produce in the range of falling average cost. In fact, the theory posits that positive profits will attract new firms to produce even closer substitutes for the successful variants of the product. The process of entry terminates with demand curves tangent to downward-sloping average cost curves. Readers may illustrate the process by moving the demand curve to the left in Figure 20–2. Since purely competitive firms end up at the minimum point on the long- and short-run average cost curves, monopolistic competition has been charged with a waste of resources in overly small plants.

There is an apparent contradiction in a monopolistically competitive producing sector solving the technological optimizing problem and still being charged with inefficiency. But technological optimization merely guarantees efficient production of any given set of commodities. It does not assert that the set of products is itself optimal. A purely competitive sector has lower average cost because it produces fewer products. What we need to know is whether the greater variety is worth the greater cost to consumers. Unfortunately, as explained earlier in the chapter, there is no shortcut answer;

each consumer must evaluate his own state of economic well being in the two situations. A particularly thorny difficulty is that the differentiation of the product may be the result of advertising, which has changed the preferences of consumers between the two situations.

When many firms produce close substitutes, the demand curve for any one product is likely to shift about a great deal in reponse to changes in price of the competing products. Realistically, a firm faces an almost impossible task in determining how much it can sell at various prices. Thus, the conventional model of monopolistic competition predicts what a firm would do if it had exact knowledge of the demand curve. In the absence of that knowledge firms are not likely to try to acquire it by experiment or statistical estimation. They are more likely to adopt methods such as cost-plus pricing that do not require explicit knowledge of the demand curve. Reflecting the closeness of substitutes the percentage markup is likely to be much smaller than for a single-firm monopolist, but otherwise the general remarks made earlier apply also in this case.

OLIGOPOLY

Oligopoly has a lower limit of two firms, which is called *duopoly*, but no specific upper limit. The standard economic models of pure competition, monopoly, and monopolistic competition posit that each firm neglects any effects its decisions may have on other firms. The essential characteristic of oligopoly is that firms are keenly aware that their decisions do affect the rival firms. A small number of close rivals makes this awareness more acute, but there is no way of specifying in general how small the number of rivals must be.

In making decisions an oligopolist must ask: "What are my rivals likely to do, and if they react as predicted, will I be better off by making the change than I am now?" Oligopoly falls into the general area of the theory of games, which deals with games of strategy, such as poker, and with bargaining, diplomacy, and war. The theory of games has done much to clarify the issues in the situation of oligopoly, has provided a useful frame of analysis, has furnished needed general terminology, and has provided penetrating insights. But, to date, the solutions emanating from the theory of games have been disappointing. One reason is that rigorous solutions to game problems require that the participants have a high degree of knowledge of the situations they face, even to the point of knowing the opponent's utility function. Since the requirements of knowledge go beyond even those customarily employed in economics, the models become unrealistic. Also, as the number of participants in a game increases, so does the number of possible solutions, and it may not be possible to predict which solution will emerge.

There is no general economic theory of oligopoly, and there may never be, since the choice of strategies and the predicted responses of rivals vary greatly with the particular situation. What economists have done is to devise a number of special solutions, each of which fits some oligopolistic situations but not others. Perhaps the most widely accepted of these special solutions is the kinked demand curve, which applies when a relatively few firms produce a homogeneous or slightly differentiated product.

The Kinked Demand Curve

When all firms raise and lower their prices together, the quantity demanded varies along the demand curve for the industry. Even if the outputs are slightly differentiated, there will be a demand curve under these conditions, since the outputs can be treated as a composite commodity. Each firm makes the reasonable assumption that its demand is a constant percentage of the total demand. Thus, each firm has a share-of-the-industry demand curve, shown as *DD* in Figure 20–5, which is a small-scale replica of the industry's

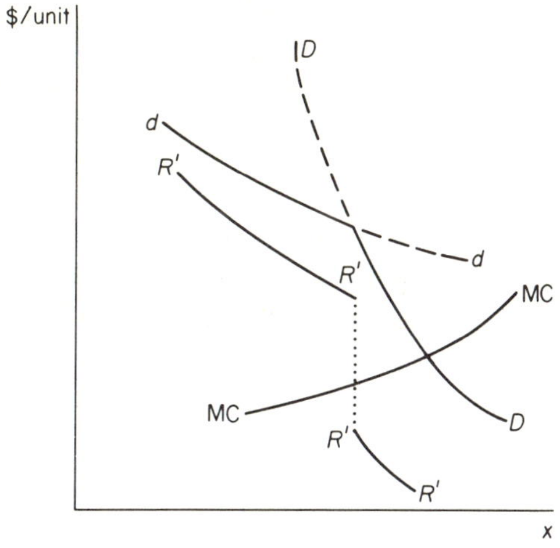

Fig. 20-5 The Kinked Demand Curve of Oligopoly

demand curve. When a single firm changes price but the others do not match the change, it can expect to sell greater amounts at lower prices and smaller amounts at higher prices. Through every point on the curve *DD* there passes a more elastic curve *dd* that shows the results of unilateral action.

A firm is at some point on the share-of-the-industry demand curve and contemplates a price change. It assumes an asymmetric reaction on the part of rivals; they will match a price cut but ignore a price rise. Thus, the effective demand curve for the firm is *dd* above the current price and *DD* below. The sudden change from the highly elastic *dd* curve to the much less elastic *DD* curve means that the marginal revenue curve has a vertical gap. If the marginal cost curve passes through the gap—and it is likely to if the gap is large—the firm has no incentive to alter its price.

The kinked demand curve explains why a price, once established, under oligopoly, may be highly resistant to change. It is not a complete theory since it does not explain how prices are established in the first place or how they vary in response to drastic changes in the underlying economic conditions. One explanation, which fits the cigarette industry between the two world wars, is that one firm is the price leader, taking the initiative in announcing prices, which the other firms match. The followers have demand curves that are kinked at the leader's price, explaining why they do not take independent action. The leader has to look out for the interest of the firms as a group, setting prices high enough to ensure an acceptable level of profits but not so high as to attract an influx of new firms.

The Cournot Solution and Later Refinements

The best known of all solutions is the one that Cournot put forth, well over 100 years ago, to the problem of pure duopoly. Suppose that firm A is initially alone in the market producing the monopoly output. Firm B enters and makes the simplifying assumption that the original firm will go on producing the same output. The new entrant subtracts this constant amount or vertical supply curve from the demand curve for the commodity. The result, shown as Figure 20–6, is a market reaction curve showing how firm B's output affects the market price at which both must sell. Firm B then chooses optimally by producing where marginal cost equals the marginal revenue derived from its market reaction curve. Firm A adopts the same

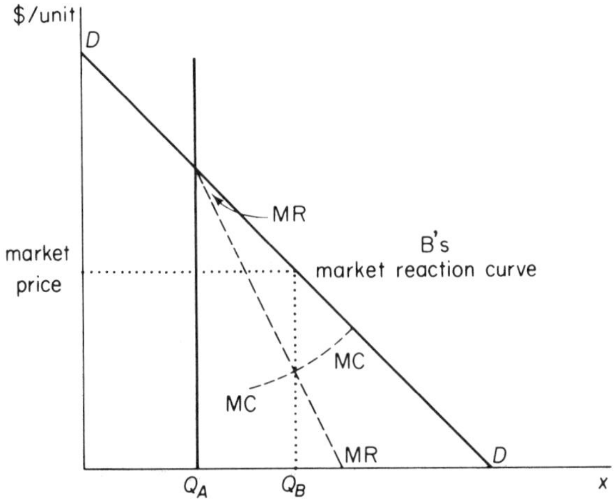

Fig. 20-6 The Cournot Model for Pure Duopoly

strategy, assumes B's output constant, and maximizes along its own market reaction curve. Each firm assumes falsely that output changes do not affect its rival but, in fact, these changes cause the market reaction curve to shift and force a new decision.

As in the purely competitive case, we must ask whether an equilibrium exists and whether it is stable. Each output chosen by one firm determines a unique market reaction curve and a unique optimal output for the other. Equilibrium is a set of mutually consistent optimal outputs. Firm A takes q_B^* as given and produces q_A^*, but q_A^* determines a market reaction curve such that q_B^* is optimal. An equilibrium always exists for the Cournot model of pure duopoly. To prove stability we must show that, regardless of the amounts the firms are producing initially, outputs converge toward their equilibrium levels. The equilibrium is generally stable, but instability may sometimes occur when firms are producing along declining marginal cost curves.

In the simple Cournot model each firm continues to assume, despite mounting evidence to the contrary, that changes in output have no affect on its rival. The next stage occurs when one firm surmises that the rival's strategy is the same as its own. Instead of reacting passively to shifts in its market reaction curve, the firm that first makes the discovery can choose output levels deliberately to affect the resultant position of its own market reaction curve. With complete knowledge of B's cost curves, firm A could predict B's choice for each level of its own output. Since B's output determines A's market reaction curve, firm A can, in effect, choose its own best market reaction curve and its own highest level of profits. In the absence of complete information, firm A can still experiment with different output levels to see how they affect profits.

But two can play the same game. If both adopt the new strategy, then each is again basing its own decisions on an objectively false assumption about the rival's behavior. The expected levels of price and profits will not materialize, and further development of the model requires that we specify how firms react to the divergence between expected and actual results. In the end the simple Cournot model turns out to be the more plausible. Rather than strive for the greatest possible profits, firms may well prefer a stable division of the industry and a satisfactory level of profits. To achieve this each must pursue a live-and-let-live strategy, being willing to accept the rival's share of the market. Assuming the other firm's output constant is a conciliatory strategy that is consistent with a stable division of the market.

A firm in pure duopoly or oligopoly has the same incentive as any other firm to minimize cost, but neither centralized direction nor market forces equate marginal cost between firms. The industry will not be minimizing cost, and the sector as a whole will not end up on the product transformation curve. The same conclusion obviously holds also for the kinked demand curve solution. A single-firm monopolist could take over an oligopolistic industry and solve the cost minimizing problem, but multifirm monopolistic agreements would not necessarily give a better solution.

When the product is sufficiently differentiated each oligopolistic firm can base its decisions on its own separate demand curve rather than on a market reaction curve. But interdependence is still present, and each firm must come to grips with it. At one extreme each firm does not itself respond to price changes by other firms and assumes that rivals in turn will ignore its own adjustments of price. Such a policy is consistent with independent profit maximization if the conditions of Figure 20–2 prevail, a demand curve that shifts without changing elasticity and marginal cost that is constant over a range of output. Small price changes by rivals would tend to be ignored but not large changes. When the exact conditions do not prevail, firms act as if they do, maintaining price and letting output be the buffer. Under these assumptions the concept of an oligopolistic industry is unnecessary, since firms act like monopolists using cost-plus pricing.

At the other extreme, a firm can try to take into account the full effect of its actions. With two firms the results are similar to those in pure duopoly. As a firm varies price, it must calculate in turn: (1) the shift of the rival's demand curve; (2) the consequent change in the rival's output and price; (3) the resultant shift in its own demand curve. Thus, the firm must construct a new demand curve, building into it the effect of the rival's expected reaction. It can then maximize along this new curve. But the result is valid only so long as the rival adjusts passively and does not adopt the same strategy. Since the most elaborate calculations lead only to indeterminacy, we can appreciate the preference of firms for simple inaccurate assumptions.

Nonprice Competition

It is no secret that oligopolists abhor price competition and much prefer to compete in advertising, in product variation, and in research and development activities. One reason is that anyone can match a price cut but not everyone may be able to match a clever advertising campaign, an improvement of product, or new methods of production. To date economists have concentrated on developing expanded decision models for firms to take into account the whole range of possible strategies. Relatively little has been accomplished in working out the effects on the industry and the economy. One reason is that product variation and, particularly, research and development are inescapably dynamic. The concept of static equilibrium that is the essence of allocative models is no longer sufficient. Since nonprice competition generates growth and requires growth models for its analysis and evaluation, this is an appropriate place to end.

SUPPLEMENTARY READINGS FOR PART FOUR

Once again readers are referred to the textbooks on microeconomic theory listed in the Supplementary Readings for Parts Two and Three.

On the behavior of competitive markets the following articles give interesting summaries of experimental simulations:

Chamberlin, Edward H. "An Experimental Imperfect Market," *Journal of Political Economy* (April 1948).

Smith, Vernon L. "An Experimental Study of Competitive Market Behavior," *Journal of Political Economy* (April 1962).

——— "Effect of Market Organization on Competitive Equilibrium," *Quarterly Journal of Economics* (May 1964).

For additional information on the construction and analysis of input-output models, the following books are highly recommended:

Miernyk, William H. *The Elements of Input-Output Analysis.* New York: Random House, Inc., 1965.

Chenery, Hollis B. and Clark, Paul G. *Interindustry Economics.* New York: John Wiley and Sons, Inc., 1959.

Dorfman, Robert, Samuelson, Paul A., and Solow, Robert M. *Linear Programming and Economic Analysis.* New York: McGraw-Hill Book Company, 1958, Chapters 9 and 10.

Chapters 13 and 14 of the preceding reference also provide a definitive statement of the existence and optimality of equilibrium for a linear model of the economy. The following books give excellent treatments of the same topic for a smooth model of the economy, but they do require a knowledge of differential calculus:

Henderson, James M. and Quandt, Richard E. *Microeconomic Theory: A Mathematical Approach.* New York: McGraw-Hill Book Company, 1958.

Quirk, James and Saposnik, Reuben. *Introduction to General Equilibrium Theory and Welfare Economics.* New York: McGraw-Hill Book Company, 1968.

A very enlightening article on welfare economics is:

Bator, Francis M. "The Simple Analytics of Welfare Maximization," *American Economic Review* (March 1957).

Index

Frequently Used Symbols: Explanation and References

General rule: a symbol with a bar above it generally has the same meaning but is the result of reduction to canonical form, 38.

a an input coefficient showing units of input per unit of output, 5-8; the rate of change of an input with respect to an output.

$\bar{a}$ *in objective form,* marginal input requirement, 176, 273, 254-58.
in right-hand side of contraints, a relative input coefficient, 227-28; in input-output model, units of output per unit of final commodity, 465.
exception, as coefficient of nonbasic variable, 41, 43-44, 228-29.

b the amount of a fixed input, 7-8.

$\bar{b}$ *as objective coefficient in dual,* excess demand for input and rate of change of input cost with respect to input price, 65-66.
in right-hand side of constraints, solution values of variables, generally output levels, 39, 42-43.

c the market price of an input, 79, 103-104, or the unit cost of an input-using process, 226.

$\bar{c}$ relative cost coefficient of a nonbasic process, 229.

e an input coefficient showing units of output per unit of an input, 226; the rate of change of an output with respect to an input.

$\bar{e}$ *in right-hand side of constraints,* productivity coefficient, 86-7.
in objective form, marginal productivity, 174, 254-58.
exception, as coefficient of nonbasic variable, 228-29.

p the market price of an output or commodity.

q an output or commodity when fixed in amount, an output quota, 226, 301; also, the amount of a final commodity in input-output model, 464-7.

r a revenue or a net revenue coefficient, 34, 79-80; the rate of change of revenue or net revenue with respect to a process level.

$\bar{r}$ relative revenue or net revenue coefficient of a nonbasic process, 39-40, 45-46, 180.

s elasticity of demand: price, 378-80; cross, 382; income, 383.

$\bar{s}$ (unrelated to s) rate of input or technical substitution for firm, 177, 254-58, and for producing sector, 489; also, rate of commodity (input) substitution for family, 358-59, and consuming sector, 490-91, 494.

t tax rate, 107, 502, and transfer payment, 446-8; also, as subscript, time period.

$\bar{t}$ (unrelated to t) rate of product transformation for firm, 238, 254-58, industry, 418-19, and producing sector, 488; also rate of utility transformation for family, 353-54.

u utility number and objective coefficient, 300-1; the rate of change of utility with respect to a process level.

$\bar{u}$ the marginal utility of a commodity, 301-2, and of income, 311-12.

v the level of a process, 172-3, 236, 252-3, 354, 365.

w the marginal cost of an output, 101, 206, 230, 253.

x the amount of an output or commodity when variable.

y an internal or imputed monetary price for an input, 57-9, 61-3; also marginal revenue productivity, 240, 253, and marginal net revenue productivity, 88-9.
(unrelated meaning determined by economic usage) the money income of a consumer.

z the amount of an input when variable, 5, 79, 85.